HARDPRESS.NET
HOME OF HARD-TO-FIND BOOKS

California Citations
by Robert Desty

Address:
HardPress
8345 NW 66TH ST #2561
MIAMI FL 33166-2626
USA
Email: info@hardpress.net

Spencer.

CALIFORNIA CITATIONS:

AN ALPHABETICAL TABLE

OF ALL THE

CASES CITED IN THE OPINIONS OF THE CALIFORNIA REPORTS,

AND OF THE

CALIFORNIA CASES CITED IN THE REPORTS OF OTHER STATES;

WITH THE POINTS AS TO WHICH THEY ARE CITED, APPROVED, AFFIRMED, CRITICISED, DOUBTED, DENIED, OR OVERRULED.

By ROBERT DESTY,

ATTORNEY-AT-LAW.

SAN FRANCISCO:
SUMNER WHITNEY & CO.
1874.

ENTERED, according to Act of Congress, in the year 1874, by

ROBERT DESTY,

In the Office of the Librarian of Congress, at Washington, D. C.

JOHN WALLACE,
      Law Printer.

PREFACE.

THE character of this work is set forth in the title-page. Its object is to show the value as authority in California of cases both foreign and domestic referred to by our Supreme Court, and the extent to which California cases have been adopted or denied by the Supreme Courts of other States and Territories.

A brief statement of the subjects discussed, and, as far as possible, the point as to which each case has been cited, is given, and the effect of the citation expressed in the words—approved, affirmed, cited, commented on, criticised, distinguished, disapproved, doubted, denied, followed, limited, modified, or overruled.

It is believed the addition of the points discussed will greatly increase the usefulness of a work of this nature, as it will enable the practitioner not only to discover what cases have been doubted, disapproved, or overruled, but also to ascertain the point so doubted or overruled, while the general doctrines sustained by the decision may remain unchanged.

The addenda includes citations from the decisions contained in late volumes of Reports issued from the press during the progress of the present work.

The preparation of this work has involved the necessity of an examination of all cases referred to, and the aim of the author has been to render it as complete and accurate as possible. It is hoped that its usefulness will be found to bear some reasonable proportion to the amount of labor bestowed in its preparation.

ROBERT DESTY.

SAN FRANCISCO, *Dec.* 17, 1873.

CALIFORNIA CITATIONS.

Abadie v. Carillo, 32 Cal. 174. Cited, Appeal, presumptions as to regularity of proceedings, 39 Cal. 586.

Abbe v. Marr, 14 Cal. 210. Cited, Remedies, an illegal or immoral contract cannot be enforced, 15 Cal. 415; neither by action nor in defense, 34 Cal. 90; where no cause of action is shown, a judgment by default will be reversed on appeal, 39 Cal. 502.

Abbey v. Chase, 6 Cush. 54. Cited, Agent, liable on contract, 29 Cal. 571.

Abbott v. American Hard Rubber Co., 33 Barb. 580. Commented on, Corporations, property of, may be transferred, 37 Cal. 595.

Abbott v. Abbott, 7 Taunt. 452. Cited, Statutory Construction, authority given by statute must be strictly pursued, 20 Cal. 687.

Abbott v. Aspinwall, 26 Barb., 202. Cited, Corporations, formation of, 22 Cal. 440.

Abbott v. Douglass, 28 Cal. 295. Cited, Appeal, statement must be filed in time, 30 Cal. 221; affidavit and notice of motion to strike out are not part of judgment roll, 31 Cal. 240; record, how made up, 32 Cal. 323, 33 Cal. 554; minutes of clerk no part of, 33 Cal. 173.

Abbott v. Inhabitants of Third School District, 7 Greenl. 96. Commented on, Contracts, implied promises, 9 Cal. 470.

Abbott v. Merriam, 8 Cush. 588. Cited, Fraud, equitable relief from, 28 Cal. 484.

Abbott v. Mills, 3 Vt. 526. Cited, Dedication to public use, 22 Cal. 489.

Abbott, Adm'r, v. Coburn, 28 Vt. 667. Cited, Jurisdiction of Probate Courts, presumptions in favor of their decisions, 18 Cal. 505.

1*

Abbotts v. Barry, 5 Moore, 98, 102. Cited, Fraud vitiates contract, 12 Cal. 462.

Abel v. Love, 17 Cal. 237. Cited, Mining Stockholders as tenants in common, 35 Cal. 369.

Abell v. Calderwood, 4 Cal. 90. Cited, Deed as a mortgage, parol evidence of, 8 Cal. 433; administrators' sales, 9 Cal. 196; specific performance of verbal contract, 10 Cal. 158.

Abell v. Douglass, 4 Denio, 305. Cited, Judicial Notice, 15 Cal. 254.

Abercrombie v. Allen, 29 Ala. 281. Cited, Evidence, admissions by silence, 22 Cal. 238.

Aberdeen v. Blackmar, 6 Hill, 324. Cited, Pleading, complaint in action on undertaking, 25 Cal. 174.

Able v. Chandler, 12 Tex. 92. Cited, Executor, power to bind estate, 38 Cal. 23.

Abrams v. Ervin, 9 Iowa, 87. Cited, Officers, powers of deputy, 25 Cal. 186.

Acker v. Campbell, 23 Wend. 371. Commented on, Replevin, demand when not necessary, 1 Cal. 161. Cited, 12 Cal. 495; 30 Cal. 191.

Acker v. White, 25 Wend. 614. Commented on, Replevin, subsequent levy, 11 Cal. 273.

Ackley v. Chamberlain, 16 Cal. 181. Cited, Judgment, no lien on homestead, 23 Cal. 400; Homestead, what constitutes, 13 Iowa, 373.

Ackley v. Finch, 7 Cow. 292. Cited, Chattel Mortgage, 27 Cal. 269.

Ackworth v. Kempe, 1 Doug. 40. Cited, Sheriff, liability for trespass of deputy, 14 Cal. 199.

Adams v. Barnes, 17 Mass. 365. Cited, Res Adjudicata, former recovery as a bar, 26 Cal. 498; 36 Cal. 37.

Adams v. City of Oakland, 8 Cal. 510. Cited, New Trial, waiver of motion by failure to file statement, 9 Cal. 247.

Adams v. Cuddy, 13 Pick. 463. Cited, Conveyance of mining claim, 11 Cal. 160; construction of conveyance, 12 Cal. 167.

Adams v. DeCook, 1 McAll. 253. Cited, Probate of Will, 20 Cal. 269.

Adams v. Freeman, 9 John. 118. Cited, Trespass of Sheriff, 34 Cal. 635; dictum overruled, 5 Wend. 506; 13 John. 414; and cited as overruled, 4 Den. 321.

Adams v. Gorham, 6 Cal. 68. Cited, Sale and Delivery, goods mingled with others, 6 Cal. 543; property not segregated, 27 Cal. 463.

Adams v. Hackett, 7 Cal. 187. Affirmed, Insolvency, distribution of assets, 8 Cal. 158; rights of creditors, 8 Cal. 544; 9 Cal. 26. Questioned and restricted, execution, levy, and sale of choses in action, 13 Cal. 22; cited, to same point, 34 Cal. 88; cited, proceedings supplementary, 10 Cal. 28; McAll. 446.

Adams v. Halley, 12 How. Pr. 326. Cited, Pleading, common counts, 10 Cal. 338; "ownership" a conclusion of law, 11 Cal. 168.

Adams v. Haskell, 6 Cal. 113. Commented on, Insolvency, distribution of assets, 6 Cal. 477. Cited, Execution, property in custody of the law not leviable, 7 Cal. 37; explained 8 Cal. 158.

Adams v. Haskell, 6 Cal. 316. Cited, Contempt, commitment for, 6 Cal. 319; 34 Tex. 672.

Adams v. Hastings, 6 Cal. 126. Cited, Per Terry, J., Insolvency, distribution of assets, 7 Cal. 205. Referred to, Attorney and Counsel, negligence, 13 Cal. 210.

Adams v. Howe, 14 Mass. 345. Cited, Statutory Construction, validity of statutes, 25 Cal. 569.

Adams v. Lansing, 17 Cal. 629. Referred to, Title, under will, 18 Cal. 481. Commented on, Contracts, conditions precedent, 22 Cal. 93.

Adams v. McKenzie, 18 Ala. 698. Cited, Foreclosure, rights of mortgagee, 26 Cal. 602.

Adams v. Norris, 23 How. 353. Cited, Probate Law, not retrospective, 33 Cal. 423.

Adams v. Pearson, 7 Pick. 341. Cited, Res Adjudicata, flowage of land, 14 Cal. 229.

Adams v. People, 1 N. Y. 173. Cited, Jurisdiction, offenses commenced without and consummated within the State, 31 Cal. 114.

Adams v. Pugh, 7 Cal. 150. Approved, Contract, action on special contract, 26 Cal. 20.

Adams v. Robinson, 1 Pick. 461. Cited, Amendment, of Sheriff's returns, 23 Cal. 81.

Adams v. Rockwell, 16 Wend. 285. Cited, Boundaries, acquiescence in division line, 25 Cal. 627, 630. Denied, 16 Mo. 282. Commented on, 5 Minn. 263; 19 Wend. 325; 47 Barb. 293. See 14 Mo. 489.

Adams v. Roman, Cal. Sup. Court, Jan. T. 1856 (not reported.) Cited, Execution, property in custody of the law not leviable, 7 Cal. 204.

Adams v. Saratoga & Wash. R.R. Co., 10 N. Y. 328. Cited, Condemnation of Land, proceedings on, 23 Cal. 329.

Adams v. Smith, 5 Cow. 280. Cited, Execution, title under execution sale, 23 Cal. 362. See 4 McLain, 616.

Adams v. Story, 1 Paine's C. C. 79. Cited, State Insolvent Laws, 37 Cal. 210.

Adams v. Terre-Tenants of Savage, 2 Ray. 855. Cited, Judgments, as property, 12 Cal. 190.

Adams v. Turrentine, 8 Ired. 149. Cited, Statutory Construction, 13 Cal. 518.

Adams v. Woods, 8 Cal. 152. Cited, Insolvency, rights of creditors, 8 Cal. 544. Explained, 9 Cal. 13, 29; 14 Cal. 456.

Adams v. Woods, 18 Cal. 30. Distinguished, Insolvency, order distributing funds, 21 Cal. 165.

Adams v. Woods, 21 Cal. 165. Cited, Insolvency, appointment of receiver not a special proceeding, 26 Cal. 454.

Adamson v. Robinson, 1 Pick. 461. Cited, Assignment, rights of assignee, 12 Cal. 98.

Adderly v. Dixon, 1 Sim. & S. 610. Cited, Specific Performance, contracts relating to personal property, 13 Cal. 523; 27 Cal. 463.

Addy v. Grix, 8 Ves. 504. Cited, Deed, validity of execution, 25 Cal. 81.

Adkinson v. Stevens, 7 J. J. Marsh. 237. Cited, Record, amendment of, 9 Cal. 173, 352.

Administrators of Conn. v. Executors of Gano, 1 Ham. 483. Cited, Negotiable Instruments, pleading, averment of demand, 11 Cal. 323.

Agar v. Regents' Canal Co., Coop. 77. Cited, Injunction, when it lies, 13 Cal. 313.

Ah Hee v. Crippen, 19 Cal. 491. Approved, Miners' Licenses, 24 Cal. 566.

Ah Thaie v. Quan Wan, 3 Cal. 216. Cited, Judgment, counsel fees, 13 Cal. 588; cited to same point, 23 Iowa, 342.

Ahl v. Johnson, 20 How. 511. Cited, Specific Performance, time not essence of contract, 40 Cal. 11, 13; equitable title to real estate, 40 Cal. 571.

Aiken v. Quartz Rock G. M. Co., 6 Cal. 186. Approved, Summons, service on corporation, 10 Cal. 344.

Aikin v. Buck, 1 Wend. 466. Cited, Trespass, possession sufficient to maintain action, 12 Cal. 463.

Ainslie v. Mayor of N. Y., 1 Barb. 169. Cited as not authority in California, Ejectment, defense by landlord, 37 Cal. 395.

Ainsworth v. Wamsley, Law Rep. 1 Eq. 523. Cited, Trade Marks, 35 Cal. 76.

Airey v. Merrill, 2 Curt. 11. Cited, Common Carrier, exception in contract construed, 27 Cal. 28, 39.

Albany and Sch. R. R. Co. v. Osborn, 12 Barb. 225. Cited, Taxation, assessment, 32 Cal. 509.

Albany and W. Stockbridge R. R. Co. v. Town of Canaan, 16 Barb. 247. Cited, Taxation, assessment, 32 Cal. 509.

Albany Street, Matter of, 11 Wend. 149. Cited, Taxation, assessment, 27 Cal. 624.

Alcott v. Avery, 1 Barb. Ch. 347. Cited, Bankruptcy, effect of discharge, 14 Cal. 176.

Alden v. Clark, 11 How. Pr. 209. Cited, Scire facias, writ abolished, 21 Cal. 134. Doubted, 53 Barb. 589; 37 How. Pr. 130.

Alden v. Murdock, 13 Mass. 259. Cited, Easement, dedication of street, 22 Cal. 490.

Alderman's Estate, Cal. Sup. Court, April T. 1859 (not reported.) Overruled, Administrator's claim against estate, 16 Cal. 434.

Alderson v. Bell, 9 Cal. 315. Cited, Jurisdiction, no presumptions in favor of Justice's jurisdiction, 23 Cal. 404; 34 Cal. 420, 421; recital in judgment imparts verity, 34 Cal. 428. Approved, 8 Nev. 308; sufficiency of record to support judgment, 34 Cal. 616; separate appearance of wife, 34 Cal. 616.

Alderson, Ex parte, 1 Mad. 53. Cited, Assignment, order for money, 14 Cal. 407.

Aldrich v. Cheshire R. R. Co., 21 N. H. 361. Cited, Street Assessments, appeal to board, 29 Cal. 87.

Aldrich v. Inhabitants of Pelham, 1 Gray, 510. Cited, Evidence, personal injury by defective highway, 36 Cal. 580.

Aldrich v. Palmer, 24 Cal. 513. Cited, Verdict, setting aside, 25 Cal. 474; for excessive damages, 34 Cal. 623; 36 Cal. 484; in personal torts, 36 Cal. 591. Cited as inapplicable, liability of master for injury to servant, 31 Cal. 382.

Aldridge v. Hawkins, 6 Blackf. 125. Reviewed and explained, Jurisdiction, actions on statutory rights and remedies, 33 Cal. 218.

Aldridge v. Lord Wallscourt, 1 Ball & B. 312. Cited, Will, construction of, 31 Cal. 603.

Aldridge v. Williams, 3 How. 24. Cited, Statutory Construction, Congressional Acts construed, 28 Cal. 95.

Alexander v. Alexander, 2 Ves. 642. Cited, Powers, discretionary power cannot be delegated, 39 Cal. 290.

Alexander v. Byron, 2 Johns. Cas. 318. Cited, Continuance, discretion of court, 11 Cal. 22.

Alexander v. Greene, 7 Hill, 547. Cited, Common Carriers, construction of contract, 27 Cal. 32.

Alexander v. Greenup, 1 Munf. 134. Cited, Illegal Patent, 16 Cal. 327.

Alexander v. Kerr, 2 Rawle, 90. Cited, Estoppel, silence cannot be urged as, 10 Cal. 631.

Alexander v. Lively, 5 Monr. 160. Commented on and approved, Deed, parol evidence to explain, 10 Cal. 625.

Alexander v. Pendleton, 8 Cranch, 462. Approved, Title, by adverse possession, 34 Cal. 387. Cited to same point, 36 Cal. 541.

Alger v. Scoville, 1 Gray, 391. Cited, Statute of Frauds, original and collateral promise, 9 Cal. 334.

Alger v. Thacher, 19 Pick. 51. Cited, Contracts, restraint of trade, 36 Cal. 357, 358.

Algier v. Steamer Maria, 14 Cal. 167. Cited, Findings, objections when to be taken, 14 Cal. 418.

Allard v. Mouchon, 1 Johns. Cas. 280. Cited, Referee, setting aside report of, 5 Cal. 93.

Alleghany City v. McClurkan, 14 Penn. 81. Approved, Municipal Corporations, liability on its contracts, 9 Cal. 472; 16 Cal. 268.

Allen v. Anthony, 1 Meriv. 282. Cited, Title, notice by possession, 36 Cal. 272.

Allen v. Bates, 6 Pick. 460. Cited, Deed, description in, 24 Cal. 444.

Allen v. Citizen's St. Nav. Co., 22 Cal. 28. Cited, Corporations, ratification of contracts, 33 Cal. 199; 40 Cal. 238.

Allen v. Cook, 26 Barb. 374. Cited, Judgment, lien of, 16 Cal. 220.

Allen v. Culver, 3 Denio, 285, 291. Cited, Debtor and Creditor, application of payments, 14 Cal. 449.

Allen v. Deschamps, 13 Ves. Jr. 228. Cited, Specific Performance, 10 Cal. 325; time as essence of contract, Id. 330.

Allen v. Dundas, 3 Durn. & E. 131. Cited, Wills, validity of, 20 Cal. 266.

Allen v. Dykers, 3 Hill, 594. Commented on, Bailment, sale of pledge by bailee, 3 Cal. 162. Cited, 42 Cal. 105. See 27 N. Y. 375.

Allen v. Fennon, 27 Cal. 68. Cited, Appeal, review of evidence, 26 Cal. 599, 27 Cal. 475; rule as to conflicting evidence, 29 Cal. 391; review of findings of referee, 30 Cal. 287; of the Court, 35 Cal. 359.

Allen v. Hayward, 7 Q. B. 960. Cited, Respondeat, Superior, liability for injuries, 8 Cal. 496. See 19 N. H. 442.

Allen v. Hopson, 1 Freeman, 276. Cited, Jurisdiction, concurrent jurisdiction, 21 Cal. 442.

Allen v. Mills, 17 Wend. 202. Cited, Statute of Limitations, 8 Cal. 459.

Allen v. Patterson, 3 Seld. 478. Cited, Pleading, facts to be set out in complaint, 10 Cal. 338; 14 Cal. 458; 32 Cal. 174; new matter in answer, 30 Cal. 175.

Allen v. Rivington, 2 Saund. 111, and 6 Taunt. 548. Cited, Ejectment, prior possession, 1 Cal. 309. Denied, 3 Man. & R. 112.

Allen v. Scott et al., 21 Pick. 25.   Cited, Deed, construction of, 15 Cal. 196.

Allen v. Sewall, 2 Wend. 327.   Approved, Corporations, individual liability, 14 Cal. 267.   Reversed, 6 Wend. 335.

Allen v. Smith, 7 Halst. 199.   Cited, Forcible Detainer, who may remove tenant, 29 Cal. 171.

Allen v. Stevens, 29 N. J. Law R. 509.   Cited, Constitutionality of road law, 32 Cal. 255.

Allen v. Trumble, 4 Bibb, 23.   Approved, Deed, execution of sheriff's deed, 8 Cal. 408.

Allen v. Watson, 2 Hill, S. C., 319.   Approved, Judicial Notice, law of foreign State, 15 Cal. 253.

Allender v. Fritz, 24 Cal. 447.   Approved, Non-appealable order, 29 Cal. 362.   Rule since changed by Stat. Code, §§ 939, 963.

Allentown Bank v. Beck, 49 Penn. St. 409.   Cited, Execution Sale, 38 Cal. 657.

Allison v. Bank, 6 Rand. 204.   Cited, Crimes, conviction for felony as a suspension of civil rights, 1 Cal. 435.

Allison v. Matthieu, 3 John. 235.   Cited, Fraud, vitiates sale of goods, 12 Cal. 462.

Almond v. Almond, 4 Rand. 662.   Cited, Alimony, without divorce, 38 Cal. 270.

Almy v. Harris, 5 John. 175.   Cited, Rights and Remedies, 7 Cal. 129; statutory, 16 Cal. 525.

Almy v. State of California, 24 How. 169.   Reviewed and cited as conclusive, Taxation, State has no power to tax commerce, 18 Cal. 268; 33 Cal. 340; 34 Cal. 498, 499.   Cited, police regulations, 20 Cal. 580.

Alton Marine and Fire Ins. Company v. Buckmaster, 13 Ill. 205.   Cited, Cloud on Title, 39 Cal. 21.

Alvarez v. Brannan, 7 Cal. 503.   Cited, Fraud, inferred from facts, 7 Cal. 355; a party is bound to remember his own acts, Id. 378; purchaser to know state of his business, 8 Cal. 215; remedy on fraudulent representations, 22 Cal. 604; Pleading, defect of parties waived by failure to demur, 10 Cal. 170.

Alverson v. Jones, 10 Cal. 9.   Cited, Husband and Wife, conveyance to wife *prima facie* common property, 22 Cal. 288; Execution, sale of wife's property creates a cloud, 25 Cal. 357, and may be restrained, 28 Cal. 527; sole trader act, 29 Cal. 566.

Ambler v. Bradley, 6 Vt. 119. Cited, Contract with broker does not create partnership, 14 Cal. 76.

Ambrose v. Rees, 11 East, 370. Cited, Dedication to public use, 14 Cal. 649.

Amelung v. Seekamp, 9 Gill. & J. 474. Cited, Injunction, what must be shown, 7 Cal. 322; 13 Cal. 190.

American Bank v. Doolittle, 14 Pick. 126. Cited, Release of joint debtor, 11 Cal. 220; 38 Cal. 532, 537.

American Company v. Bradford, 27 Cal. 360. Cited, Jurisdiction, concurrent, 30 Cal. 585.

American Exch. Bank v. Morris Canal & B. Co., 6 Hill, 366. Cited, Attachment Lien, 37 Cal. 150.

American Ins. Co. v. Canter, 1 Pet. 511. Cited, Political, Cession of Territory, effect on law, 1 Cal. 286, 314; by conquest, 15 Cal. 560. Approved, Admission of State, 40 Cal. 342. See Dred Scott v. Sandford, 19 How. 442.

American Ins. Co. v. Oakley, 9 Paige, 496. Cited, Attorney and Counsel, unauthorized appearance by, 30 Cal. 447.

American Leading Cases, 296. Cited, Debtor and Creditor, application of payments, 14 Cal. 449.

American L. & F. Ins. & Tr. Co. v. Ryerson, 2 Halst. Ch. 9. Referred to, Power of court to settle controversy, 15 Cal. 501.

American Print Works v. Lawrence, 1 Zab. 258, 264. Cited, Nuisance, abatement of, by destroying house to stop conflagration, 1 Cal. 356; 3 Cal. 73.

Ames v. Hoy, 12 Cal. 11. Cited, Judgment, action on, 16 Cal. 375; 19 Cal. 170; Evidence, secondary, of contents of record, 22 Cal. 64.

Amesbury Man. Co. v. Amesbury, 17. Mass. 461. Cited, Taxation, *situs* of personal property, 23 Cal. 139.

Amherst v. Inhab. of Hadley, 1 Pick. 38. Cited, Verdict, when not set aside for irregularity, 9 Cal. 537.

Amiable Nancy, The, 3 Wheat. 546. Cited, Damages, for personal injuries, 7 Cal. 120. Cited, 36 N. H. 19.

Ammant v. New Alexandria & Pittsburg Trans. Co., 13 Serg. & R. 210. Commented on, Execution, property exempt, 15 Cal. 590.

Amory v. McGregor, 15 John. 24.   Commented on, Forfeiture, 25 Cal. 241.   Disapproved, 1 Story, 135.

Amoskeag Manufacturing Co. v. Spear, 2 Sand. 599. Cited, Trade Marks, injunction, 35 Cal. 64, 75, 76.

Amsby v. Dickhouse, 4 Cal. 102.   Cited, Verdict, juror cannot impeach, 25 Cal. 475.

Ancaster, Duke of, v. Mayer, 1 Bro. Ch. 462.   Cited, Will, construction of, 31 Cal. 600.

Anderson v. Administrator of Brady, 2 Yerg. 297.   Approved, Evidence, competency of witness, 6 Cal. 195.

Anderson v. Anderson, 8 Ohio, 108.   Cited, Judgment, cannot be collaterally attacked, 30 Cal. 446.

Anderson v. Cameron, Morris, 437.   Cited, Infancy, suit by infant, 32 Cal. 119.

Anderson v. Dunn, 6 Wheat. 204.   Cited, Legislature, power and privileges of, 29 Cal. 405.

Anderson v. Fisk, 36 Cal. 625.   Approved, Conveyances, section of act construed, 38 Cal. 221.

Anderson v. Jackson, 16 John. 382.   Cited, Wills, construction of term "die without issue," Stare decisis, 15 Cal. 603.   Dissenting opinion of Chancellor Kent disapproved 6 R. I. 534; 20 Geo. 824; cited, 2 Cow. 389; explained, Id. 396; and reviewed, 12 Wheat. 162.

Anderson v. Lemon, 4 Sand. 552; S. C. Reversed, 8 N. Y., 4 Seld., 237.   Distinguished, Lease, 9 Cal. 677.

Anderson v. Mannon, 7 B. Monr. 217.   Cited, Surety, discharge of, 10 Cal. 426.

Anderson v. Parker, 6 Cal. 197.   Cited, Instructions, practice, 32 Cal. 289; Evidence, hearsay of death of party, 30 Wis. 178.

Anderson v. Pennie, 31 Cal. 265.   Cited, Mandamus, 41 Cal. 77.

Anderson v. Rhea, 7 Ala. 106.   Cited, Statutory Undertaking, 13 Cal. 508.

Anderson v. Roberts, 18 John. 514.   Cited, Attachment, fraudulently obtained is void as to creditors, 12 Cal. 264; Fraud, relief from, 13 Cal. 69; Probate, validity of administrators' sales, 29 Cal. 35, 40.

Anderson v. Tompkins, 1 Brock. 458.   Cited, Assignment, partners, 13 Cal. 288.

Andover and Medford T. Co. v. Gould, 6 Mass. 42. Commented on, Taxes, enforcement of payment of, 16 Cal. 524. Cited, statutory rights and remedies, 33 Cal. 217.

Andrew v. Bradley, 10 La. Ann. 606. Cited, Husband and Wife, conveyance to wife, 17 Cal. 582; community property, 12 Cal. 253.

Andrew v. Dieterich, 14 Wend. 31. Cited, Fraud, vitiates contract, 12 Cal. 462. Doubted, as to remedy of purchaser of fraudulent instrument, 3 Barb. Ch. 458.

Andrews v. Avory, 14 Gratt. 236. Commented on, Jurisdiction, judgment of Probate Court not subject to collateral attack, 18 Cal. 505.

Andrews v. Estes, 2 Fairf. 267. Cited, Written Instruments, sealed and unsealed, 13 Cal. 235.

Andrews v. Etheridge, 9 Mass. 385. Cited, Parties entitled to appeal, 8 Cal. 315.

Andrews, Ex parte, 18 Cal. 678. Cited, State Government, duty of, 22 Cal. 321; Legislature, power to regulate trade, 33 Cal. 282, 283, 285; 29 Cal. 271.

Andrews v. Foster, 17 Vt. 560. Cited, Contract, implied promises in action for services, 7 Cal. 573.

Andrews, Matter of, 1 Johns. Ch. 99. Cited, Guardians, power of court over, 37 Cal. 664.

Andrews v. Mok. Hill Co., Cal. Sup. Court, Jan. T. 1857 (not reported.) Referred to on rehearing, 7 Cal. 333.

Andrews v. Mok. Hill Co., 7 Cal. 330. Cited, Pleading, defects waived by failure to demur, 10 Cal. 170.

Andrews v. Wolcott, 16 Barb. 21. Cited, Redemption, purchase of equity of, 14 Cal. 34; purchasers at foreclosure sale, 40 Cal. 235.

Andrews v. Woodmansee, 15 Wend. 232. Cited, Libel, pleading, innuendo, 34 Cal. 60.

Andrews' Heirs v. Brown's Heirs, 21 Ala. 437. Cited, Estates of deceased persons, rights of surviving partner, 17 Cal. 268.

Andrus v. Foster, 17 Vt. 556. Cited, Gratuitous services, 22 Cal. 510.

Angier v. Ash, 26 N. H. 99. Referred to, Process, return of, 14 Cal. 143.

Angle v. Miss. & M. R. R. Co., 9 Iowa, 487. Cited, Common Carriers, contract construed, 31 Cal. 53.

Angulo v. Sunol, 14 Cal. 402. Referred to, Contract for services, action on, 13 Cal. 643; implied contract, 14 Cal. 415.

Anonymous, Amb. 209. Cited, Injunction, 23 Cal. 84.

Anonymous, 1 Atk. 19. Cited, Specific Performance, 38 Cal. 200.

Anonymous, 3 Atk. 313. Cited, Redemption, 23 Cal. 34.

Anonymous, 6 Cow. 389. Cited, Place of Trial, change of, 15 Cal. 419.

Anonymous, 6 Geo. II., cited by Selw. Cited, Judgments, as property, 12 Cal. 190.

Anonymous, 1 Hay. N. C., 526. Cited, Bridges and Ferries, 6 Cal. 594.

Anonymous, 1 Hill, 217, 218. Cited, Service by Mail, 30 Cal. 184.

Anonymous, 1 Hill, S. C., 258. Cited, Witness, impeaching, 27 Cal. 636.

Anonymous, Jenk. Cent. 25. Cited, Record, what constitutes, 34 Cal. 423.

Anonymous, Jenk. Cent. 120. Cited, Record, what enrolled on, maxim, 34 Cal. 423.

Anonymous, 4 John. 191. Cited, Attorney and Counsel, practice of law, 22 Cal. 321.

Anonymous, 8 Mod. 244. Cited, Judgments, as property, 12 Cal. 190.

Anonymous, 12 Mod. 256. Cited, Office, holding over, 28 Cal. 52, 54.

Anonymous, 2 Show. 283. Disapproved, Freight, recovery back of freight paid, 6 Cal. 370. See 3 Sum. 66.

Anonymous, 1 Wend. 90. Cited, Computation of Time, publication of notice, 32 Cal. 352. Overruled, 21 N. Y. 153. See 5 Nev. 427.

Anonymous, 25 Wend. 677. Cited, Service, of papers and notices, strict compliance with statute required, 30 Cal. 184.

Antelope, Case of, 10 Wheat. 66. Cited, Appeal, affirmance, 32 Cal. 633.

Anthony v. Dunlap, 8 Cal. 26. Approved, Injunction, Court cannot restrain judgments of coördinate tribunal, 9 Cal. 614; 37 Cal. 269. Cited to same point, 22 Wis. 486.

Anthony v. Leftwich, 3 Rand. 246. Cited, Specific Performance, time as essence of contract, 10 Cal. 326, 328; 19 Cal. 459; averments in complaint essential, 42 Cal. 354.

Anthony v. Nye, 30 Cal. 401. Cited, Pleading, complaints in foreclosure, 39 Cal. 391.

Anthony v. Wessel, 9 Cal. 103. Cited, Title, under Sheriff's sales, 14 Cal. 680.

Apollon, The, 9 Wheat. 374. Cited, Judicial Notice, foreign laws, 39 Cal. 40.

Appleton v. Binks, 5 East. 148. Cited, Agent, when personally liable, 13 Cal. 48.

Apthorp v. North et al., 14 Mass. 166. Cited, Official Bond, 7 Cal. 441.

Arayo v. Currel, 1 La. 531. Cited, Judicial Notice, not taken as to foreign laws, 15 Cal. 254. See 3 Story, 465.

Arberry v. Noland, 2 J. J. Marsh. 422. Cited, Attachment, issuance of writs, priority, 25 Cal. 209.

Archer v. Masse, 2 Vern. 8. Cited, Wills, validity of, 20 Cal. 266.

Archer v. Noble, 3 Greenl. 418. Cited, Trespass, by officer, 14 Cal. 198.

Arfridson v. Ladd, 12 Mass. 173. Cited, Agent, when liable on contract, 13 Cal. 48.

Argenti v. City of San Francisco, 6 Cal. 677. Cited, Deed, inadequacy of consideration, 15 Cal. 608.

Argenti v. City of San Francisco, 16 Cal. 255, followed in 16 Cal. 284. Affirmed, San Francisco City and County warrants not negotiable, 16 Cal. 286; 23 Cal. 126. Commented on and held not authority as to 20 Cal. 108; commented on as to liability of city on its contracts, 28 Cal. 593; cited, 55 Ill. 419; affirmed, duty of city to restore property illegally obtained, 21 Cal. 362; approved, as to power of municipal corporation to bind city by contract, 29 Cal. 186; cited, as to ratification of contract by corporation, 33 Cal. 191, 199; 24 Wis. 42; referred to, modification of judgment on rehearing, 30 Cal. 461; cited, Street contracts, primary liability of city on, 6 Kan. 298; actions against counties, 1 Nev. 378; liability on implied contract, 2 Wall. 457.

Argenti v. The City of San Francisco, 30 Cal. 458. Referred to, Appeal, law of case, 32 Cal. 415; effect of reversal, 39 Cal. 646.

Arglasse v. Muschamp, 1 Vern. 75. Cited, Specific Performance, jurisdiction, 38 Cal. 201. See 6 Cranch, 159.

Arguello v. Edinger, 10 Cal. 160. Explained, Specific Performance, of verbal contract, 13 Cal. 132. Cited, Part performance construed, 19 Cal. 461; 22 Cal. 616; effect of part performance, 24 Cal. 176; Ejectment, equitable defenses, 24 Cal. 141; 35 Cal. 649; must be specifically stated in answer, 25 Cal. 597, with fullness and particularity, 26 Cal. 39; order of trial of legal and equitable defenses, 19 Cal. 273. Affirmed on this point, 19 Cal. 457, 671.

Arguello v. United States, 18 How. 548. Cited, Mexican Grant, 15 Cal. 30; validity of, 26 Cal. 623; title under, 39 Cal. 245. See 24 How. 264; 434.

Armour v. Alexander, 10 Paige, 572. Cited, Trust, implied, 30 Cal. 594.

Armstrong v. Hayward, 6 Cal. 183. Cited, Debt, part payment by co-debtor, 12 Cal. 324; release of joint debtor, 38 Cal. 531; discharges the whole, 38 Cal. 537.

Armstrong v. Jackson, 1 Blackf. 374. Cited, Constitutionality of Settlers' Act, 7 Cal. 23.

Arnold v. Bell, 1 Hayw. 396–7. Cited, Evidence, to impeach title, declarations of grantor, 38 Cal. 282.

Arnold v. Dimon, 4 Sand. 680. Cited, Pleading, inconsistent defenses, 13 Cal. 625.

Arnold v. Foot, 12 Wend. 330. Cited, Water Rights, diversion of water, 8 Cal. 144.

Arnold v. Lyman, 17 Mass. 400. Cited, Action, for money in hands of third party, legal privity, 15 Cal. 347; on agreement with debtor to pay creditor, 37 Cal. 537; cited, 2 Met. 403.

Arnold v. Mayor of Poole, 4 Man. & G. 860. Cited, Corporations, contracts of, 7 Cal. 382.

Arnold v. Rees, 18 N. Y. 57. Cited, Special Cases, 15 Cal. 92; 23 Cal. 147; claims to town lots, 19 Cal. 574.

Arnold v. Skaggs, 35 Cal. 684. Cited, New Trial, affidavit of newly discovered evidence, 38 Cal. 194.

Arnot v. Post, 6 Hill, 67. Reversed, 2 Den. 361. Commented on, Tender, of mortgage debt, 14 Cal. 529.

Arrington v. Liscom, 34 Cal. 365. Cited, Title by adverse possession, 36 Cal. 540; 1 Saw. 620; Statute of Limitations, as a bar and extinguishment of right, 37 Cal. 351; 40 Cal. 54; instanced in action to quiet title, 40 Cal. 565; how pleaded, 36 Cal. 632; Pleading, prayer in complaint, 37 Cal. 304.

Arrington v. Sherry, 5 Cal. 513. Cited, Confession of Judgment, 37 Cal. 336.

Arrington v. Tupper, 10 Cal. 464. Cited, Error, abuse of discretion, 20 Cal. 633.

Artcher v. Zeh, 5 Hill, 205. Cited, Statute of Frauds, delivery, 1 Cal. 402.

Arthur Legat's Case, 10 Coke, 109. Cited, Grant, construction of, 13 Cal. 453.

Arthur v. Bokenham, 11 Mod. 150. Approved, Statutory Construction, 13 Cal. 95.

Arthur v. Weston and Strode, 22 Mo. 378. Approved, Title under Conveyance, 29 Cal. 410.

Arundell, Lady, v. Phipps, 10 Ves. 148. Cited, Specific Performance, of contract for chattel when decreed, 23 Cal. 392; doubted as to contract between husband and wife, 9 Humph. 482.

Ash v. Patton, 3 Serg. & R. 300. Cited, Witness, competency of, interest, 14 Cal. 268.

Ash v. Putnam, 1 Hill, 302. Cited, Fraud, vitiates sale of goods, 8 Cal. 213. Denied, Doctrine of recovery by vendor, 32 Barb. 179.

Ashburner v. Balchen, 7 N. Y., 262. Cited, Measure of Damages, breach of contract, 38 Cal. 666.

Ashby v. James, 11 Mees. & W. 542. Cited, Account, limitation of action, 30 Cal. 130.

Ashley v. Harrison, 1 Esp. 48; Peake, 194. Cited, Measure of Damages in tort, 14 Cal. 557. Doubted, 2 El. & B. 241.

Ashman v. Williams, 8 Pick. 402. Cited, Conveyance, land and structure in severalty, 15 Cal. 197.

Aslin v. Parkin, 2 Burr. 665.   Cited, Res Adjudicata, 20 Cal. 486.

Aspindall v. Brown, 3 D. & E., 265.   Cited, Dedication, public use, 14 Cal. 649.

Astley v. Tankerville, 3 Bro. Ch. 548.   Cited, Wills, devise of mortgaged lands, 31 Cal. 608.

Astor v. Hoyt, 5 Wend. 603.   Commented on and distinguished, Title to mortgaged premises, mortgagee in and out of possession, 15 Cal. 292; 21 Cal. 624.   Commented on, 8 N. Y. 469.

Astor v. Wells, 4 Wheat. 466.   Cited, Notice to agent is notice to principal, 31 Cal. 165.

Astrom v. Hammond, 3 McLean, 108.   Cited, Taxation of preëmption claim, 30 Cal. 648; claim to public land, 31 Cal. 268; 37 Cal. 495.

Atkins v. Boardman, 2 Met. 457.   Cited, Trespass, pleading, justification, 32 Cal. 581.

Atkins v. Kinnan, 20 Wend. 241.   Referred to, Eminent Domain, 19 Cal. 60.   Cited, Statutory Construction, statutes divesting title to be strictly pursued, 16 Cal. 525; conclusiveness of judgment, 18 Cal. 505.

Atkinson v. Lester, 2 Ill. 407.   Cited, Forcible Entry and Detainer defined, 12 Cal. 527; 16 Cal. 109.

Atlantic DeL. Co. v. Tredick, 5 R. I. 179.   Cited, Negotiable Instrument, presumptive dishonor of note, 39 Cal. 352.

Atlantic Fire and Marine Ins. Co. v. Boies, 6 Duer, 583.   Commented on and doubted, Pledge, negotiable instrument, 38 Cal. 352, 356.

Attersoll v. Stevens, 1 Taunt. 201.   Cited, Landlord and Tenant, 8 Cal. 596.

Attorney-General v. Bank of Niagara, 1 Hop. 403.   Cited, Jurisdiction, over corporate bodies, 16 Cal. 150.

Attorney-General v. Burridge, 10 Price, 350.   Cited, Nuisance, 30 Cal. 390.

Attorney-General v. Bouwens, 4 Mees. & W. 171.   Cited, Probate, power of administrator, 12 Cal. 189.

Attorney-General v. Brunst, 3 Wis. 787.   Cited, Office, term of, 22 Cal. 311.   Construed, 13 Wis. 170.

Attorney-General v. Cleaver, 18 Ves. 216. Cited, Nuisance, 30 Cal. 387.

Attorney-General v. College of William and Mary, 1 Ves. Jr. 244. Cited, Actions by relator, parties, 25 Cal. 250.

Attorney-General v. Day, 1 Ves. Sr. 221. Cited, Specific Performance. 10 Cal. 158.

Attorney-General v. Earl of Clarendon, 17 Ves. 491. Cited, Jurisdiction, over corporations, 16 Cal. 148.

Attorney-General v. East India Co., 11 Sim. 380. Cited, Actions by Relator, parties, 25 Cal. 250.

Attorney-General, Ex parte, 1 Cal. 85. Cited, Jurisdiction, of Supreme Court, 1 Cal. 343; 3 Cal. 390; 21 Cal. 169.

Attorney-General v. Johnston, 2 Wils. Ex. 101. Cited, Nuisance, 30 Cal. 389.

Attorney-General v. Lord Eardley, 8 Price, 69. Cited, Grant, construction of, 13 Cal. 453.

Attorney-General v. Lord Weymouth, 1 Amb. 22. Cited, Title of Act, 9 Cal. 522; Field, C. J., to same point, 20 Cal. 582.

Attorney-General v. Middleton, 2 Ves. Sr. 330. Cited, Action by Relator, parties, 25 Cal. 249.

Attorney-General v. Montgomery, 2 Atk. 378. Cited, Verdict, conclusiveness of, 15 Cal. 379.

Attorney-General v. Morgan, 2 Russ. 306. Cited, Cloud on Title, equitable relief, 10 Cal. 576.

Attorney-General v. N. J. R. and Trans. Co., 2 Green Ch. 136. Cited, Nuisance, 30 Cal. 388; abatement of, 36 Cal. 196.

Attorney-General v. Parmeter, 10 Price, 378. Cited, Nuisance, 30 Cal. 390.

Attorney-General v. Purmort, 5 Paige, 620. Cited, Specific Performance, time not the essence of the contract, 40 Cal. 11.

Attorney-General v. Richards, 2 Anst. 603. Cited, Bridges and Ferries, franchise, entitled to protection, 6 Cal. 595; suits by relator, 25 Cal. 248; Nuisance, obstructions to tide waters, 30 Cal. 389. See 2 Johns. Ch. 380.

Attorney-General v. Road Company, 2 Mich. 138. Cited, Statutory Construction, 27 Cal. 402.

Attorney-General v. Smart, 1 Ves. Sr. 72. Cited, Action by Relator, parties, 25 Cal. 249.

2

Attorney-General v. Squires. See People v. Squires.

Attorney-General v. State Board of Judges, 38 Cal. 291. Cited, Government, legislative discretion, 41 Cal. 177.

Attorney-General v. Utica Insurance Co., 2 Johns. Ch. 371. Cited, Jurisdiction over Corporations, 16 Cal. 150; Nuisance, 30 Cal. 387, 390; abatement of, 36 Cal. 196.

Attorney-General v. Vernon, 1 Vern. 277 and 370; 2 Ch. R. 353. Cited, Action to Annul Patent, 14 Cal. 366; parties in action, 25 Cal. 248.

Attorney-General v. White's Executrix, 2 Comyn's R. 433. Cited, Enforcement of Taxes, 16 Cal. 528.

Attorney's License Case, 1 Zab. 345. Cited, Attorney and Counselor, charge against, 22 Cal. 320.

Attorney's Oaths Case, 20 John. 492. Cited, Attorney and Counselor, oaths of, 22 Cal. 312; 24 Cal. 244.

Atwood v. Reliance Transportation Co., 9 Watts, 88. Cited, Common Carriers, construction of contract, 27 Cal. 28, 39.

Attwood v. Clarke, 2 Me. 229. Cited, Reasonable time, 30 Cal. 558.

Attwood v. Fricot, 17 Cal. 37. Cited, Mining Claim, title by possession, 17 Cal. 115. Affirmed, 23 Cal. 576. Cited, constructive possession under deed, 38 Cal. 487.

Attwood v. Munnings, 7 Barn. & C. 279. Cited, Contract based on several interests, 6 Cal. 375.

Aubry v. Fortescue, 10 Mod. 206. Cited, Statute of Limitations, 35 Cal. 639, 640.

Auchmuty v. Ham, 1 Den. 495. Cited, Ferocious Animal, 41 Cal. 141.

Aud v. Magruder, 10 Cal. 282. Cited, Sureties, joint makers of note all principals, 32 Cal. 577; approved, 34 Cal. 281.

Auditor v. Woodruff, 2 Pike, 73. Cited, Official Bond, 7 Cal. 440.

Aulanier v. The Governor, 1 Tex. 653. Cited, Constitutional Construction, taxation, 4 Cal. 51.

Ault v. Gassaway, 18 Cal. 205. Cited, Lis Pendens, actual notice, 22 Cal. 211; 23 Cal. 38.

Aurora, City of, v. West, 9 Ind. 74. Commented on, Constitutional Construction, local taxation for internal improvements, 13 Cal. 184. Cited, Corporations, legislative power to create, 22 Cal. 428.

Austin's Case, 5 Rawle, 204. Cited, Attorney and Counsel, striking from roll, 22 Cal. 320.

Austin v. Imus, 23 Vt. 286. Cited, Interest, computation of, 29 Cal. 392.

Austin v. Lamar, 23 Miss. 189. Cited, Probate, finality of decree, 14 Cal. 130.

Austin v. Manchester, Sheffield, and L. R.R. Co., 70 E. C. L., 453. Cited, Common Carriers, contract construed, 27 Cal. 42.

Austin v. Vandermark, 4 Hill, 262. Cited, Negotiable Instruments, notice of accommodation indorsement, 37 Cal. 120.

Averill v. Lyman, 18 Pick. 346. Cited, Sureties, contract of, 11 Cal. 220.

Averill v. Steamer Hartford, 2 Cal. 308. Explained, Jurisdiction, admiralty and maritime, 5 Cal. 272. Overruled, 4 Wall. 427; and see Id. 555. Adopted, service of process equivalent to actual seizure of vessel, 7 Cal. 408. Cited to the same point, 8 Cal. 422.

Averill v. Wilson, 4 Barb. 180. Cited, Estoppel, by deed, 18 Cal. 476.

Avery v. Bowman, 40 N. Y. 453. Cited, Tax Sale, validity of, 23 Cal. 298; execution, when irregular, 38 Cal. 380.

Avery v. Chappel, 6 Conn. 270. Cited, Writs, cannot be varied by parol evidence, 35 Cal. 340.

Avery v. Inhabitants of Tyringham, 3 Mass. 160, 177. Cited, Office, term of, 6 Cal. 292. See 16 Mass. 510.

Avery v. Pixley, 4 Mass. 460. Cited, Statutory Construction, "month" defined, 21 Cal. 396; 31 Cal. 176.

Aylet v. Dodd, 2 Atk. 238. Cited, Contract, liquidated damages, 9 Cal. 587.

Ayre v. Ayre, Cases in Chan. 33. Cited, Probate, executor *de son tort*, 17 Cal. 192.

Ayres v. Bensley, 32 Cal. 620. Cited, Lands, constructive possession under deed, 38 Cal. 487. Questioned, 38 Cal. 676. Commented on and modified, 39 Cal. 280.

Babb v. Reed, 5 Rawle, 158. Concurred in, Mutual Relief associations, 14 Cal. 536.

Babcock v. Beaman, 11 N. Y. 200. Cited, Negotiable Instruments, indorsement by agent, 7 Cal. 541.

Babcock v. Gill, 10 John. 287. Cited, Conversion, measure of damages, 23 Cal. 311; 17 Wis. 553.

Babcock v. Hubbard, 2 Conn. 536. Cited, Sureties, liability on joint note, 20 Cal. 136.

Babcock v. Lamb, 1 Cow. 239. Cited, Pleading, justification in trespass, 27 Cal. 367.

Bachelor v. Bachelor, 1 Mass. 256. Cited, Summons, publication, computation of time, 32 Cal. 352; 5 Nev. 426.

Backus v. McCoy, 3 Ohio, 211. Cited, Covenants, action for breach of warranty, 5 Cal. 264. See 4 Maule & S. 53.

Bacon v. Cropsey, 7 N. Y. 195. Cited, Execution, issuance of, 28 Cal. 285.

Bacon v. Dyer, 3 Fair. 19. Cited, Negotiable Instruments, demand, place of payment, 11 Cal. 321.

Bacon, Ex parte, 6 Cow. 392. Cited, Mandamus, discretion, 10 Cal. 376.

Bacon v. Robertson, 18 How. 480. Cited, Corporations, acquisition of real property, 38 Cal. 174.

Bacon v. Scannell, 9 Cal. 272. Overruled, Statute of frauds, change of possession, 15 Cal. 507. Cited as overruled, 26 Cal. 323.

Badeau v. Mead, 14 Barb. 328. Cited, Dedication, to public use, 14 Cal. 647; how evinced, Id. 648.

Badger v. Phinney, 15 Mass. 359. Cited, Fraud, fraudulent purchaser acquires no title, 12 Cal. 462; fraud vitiates contract, Id. 463. That replevin will lie for an unlawful detention without an unlawful taking, denied, 1 Mass. 319; 1 Wend. 109; 15 John. 401; 4 Cranch C. C. 66; 5 Dutch. 195. Doubted, 43 N. H. 39.

Badger v. Williams, 1 Chip. 137. Cited, Agreement, against public policy, void, 15 Cal. 404.

Baggett v. Meeux, 1 Phil. 628. Cited, Husband and Wife, alienation of wife's separate estate, 32 Cal. 385.

Baggott v. Boulger, 2 Duer, 160. Cited, Probate, decree against administrator conclusive on sureties, 25 Cal. 222.

Bagley v. Eaton, 10 Cal. 126. Cited, Secondary Evidence, 12 Cal. 105; preliminary evidence, 14 Cal. 575; 17 Cal. 573.

Bagley v. Mayor, etc. of New York, 3 Hill, 531. Cited, Negligence, construction and repairs, 10 Cal. 418.

Bagley v. McMickle, 9 Cal. 430. Affirmed, Evidence, secondary, of destroyed instruments, 10 Cal. 148.

Bagley v. Peddie, 5 Sand. 192. Cited, Contract, stipulated damages in, 6 Cal. 263. Commented on, Penalty, liquidated damages, 19 Cal. 682; 25 Cal. 75. Reversed, 16 N. Y. 469.

Bagnell v. Broderick, 13 Pet. 436. Cited, Title, validity of United States Patent, 29 Cal. 311. Commented on, 33 Cal. 88, 92. Cited, of conflicting patents, 34 Cal. 512; 42 Cal. 615. Questioned, 7 La. An. 663.

Bailey v. Adams, 10 N. H. 162. Cited, Surety, on note, delay when not a discharge of, 10 Cal. 425; 23 Vt. 149.

Bailey v. Bailey, 8 Humph. 230. Cited, Equity, relief from mistake, 19 Cal. 673.

Bailey v. Bryant, 24 Pick. 198. Cited, Confession of Judgment, 27 Cal. 234.

Bailey v. Burton, 8 Wend. 339. Cited, Pleading, prayer in complaint, power of court to grant relief conformable to bill, 2 Cal. 285. Commented on, Mortgage, fraudulent, 35 Cal. 308.

Bailey v. Carleton, 12 N. H. 9. Cited, Lands, constructive possession under deed, 25 Cal. 135.

Bailey v. Clay, 4 Rand. 346. Cited, Pleading, defects cured by verdict, 2 Cal. 462.

Bailey v. Culverwell, 8 Barn. & C. 448. Cited, Presumptions, of authority granted by beneficiary of an act performed, 4 Cal. 169.

Bailey v. Damon, 3 Gray, 92. Cited, Contract, for services, measure of damages, 38 Cal. 666.

Bailey v. Foster, 9 Pick. 139. Cited, Witness, competency of, 23 Cal. 446.

Bailey v. Freeman, 4 John. 280. Cited, Pleading, consideration in specialty, 34 Cal. 147.

Bailey v. Irby, 2 Nott & McC. 343. Cited, Pleading, allegations of actual possession, 19 Cal. 690.

Bailey v. Mayor, etc. of New York, 3 Hill. 531. Affirmed, 2 Denio, 433. Cited, Municipal Corporations, powers of, 7 Cal. 376. Commented on, Liability for injuries from insufficient structure, 8 Cal. 497; contracts of, how construed, 16 Cal. 270. Cited, Counties not liable for acts of officers, 21 Cal. 115. See Mayor of N. Y. v. Bailey.

Bailey v. New World, 2 Cal. 370. Affirmed, Personal Property, possession *prima facie* evidence of ownership, 8 Cal. 617.

Bailey v. Shaw, 4 Fost. 297. Cited, Principal and Agent, when incompetent as witnesses, 7 Cal. 256.

Bailey v. Taaffe, 29 Cal. 422. Cited, Default, affidavit to open, 33 Cal. 325; explained, Id. 326; approved, affidavit of merits essential, 34 Cal. 80, 81. Cited, Discretion of court in setting aside judgment by default, 37 Cal. 249. Adopted, 4 Nev. 453.

Bainbridge v. Clay, 3 Mart. N. S. 262. Commented on, Insolvency, rights of debtor under statute to be strictly pursued, 7 Cal. 430.

Baird v. Bank of Washington, 11 Serg. & R. 411. Cited, Corporations, powers of, 22 Cal. 629.

Baird v. Byrne, 3 Wall. Jr. 1. Cited, Naturalization, when effected, 22 Cal. 85.

Baird v. Walker, 12 Barb. 300. Cited, Factors, liability does not attach till demand made, 8 Cal. 457.

Bakeman v. Pooler, 15 Wend. 637. Cited, Pleading, averment of tender on mutual covenants, 41 Cal. 422.

Baker v. Bailey, 16 Barb. 54. Cited, Pleading, denial of conjunctive allegations, 31 Cal. 195.

Baker v. Baker, 13 Cal. 87. Approved, Evidence, admissions of defendant competent in divorce, 41 Cal. 107. Cited, Divorce, 3 Allen, 611.

Baker v. Bartol, 6 Cal. 483. Referred to, 13 Cal. 302.

Baker v. Bartol, 7 Cal. 551. Reviewed and approved, 13 Cal. 302. Cited, Injunction Bond, who may sue on,

28 Cal. 543; on attachment, bond, 29 Cal. 200; or on promise made to third party, 33 Cal. 127.

Baker v. Bolton, 1 Camp. 493. Cited, Action, for causing death, exclusively statutory, 25 Cal. 435. Cited, 15 Geo. 350; 16 Mich. 190.

Baker v. Briggs, 8 Pick. 121. Cited, Surety, discharged by neglect of creditor, 26 Cal. 542; 29 Cal. 198.

Baker v. Dening, 8 Ad. & E. 94. Cited, Deed, Execution of, 25 Cal. 81.

Baker v. Fales, 16 Mass. 147. Cited, Fraud, contract vitiated by, ownership of goods obtained by fraud, 12 Cal. 462.

Baker v. Hathaway, 5 Allen, 103. Commented on, Husband and Wife, executory contract by wife, 40 Cal. 561.

Baker v. Johnson, 5 Hill, 347. Cited, Eminent Domain, compensation on condemnation of land, 31 Cal. 559.

Baker v. Joseph, 16 Cal. 173. Cited, New trial, on ground of newly discovered evidence, showing required, 22 Cal. 163; 35 Cal. 687. Approved, 3 Or. 43; 3 Nev. 543. Cited, Evidence, hostility of witness, 27 Cal. 68; examination of witness, 16 Mich. 526; Trust, continuing trust, 27 Cal. 279.

Baker v. Lorillard, 4 Coms. 257. Cited, Contract, ratification by implication, 30 Cal. 414.

Baker v. Rosenthal (not reported.) Distinguished, Appeal, from order after final judgment, 8 Cal. 57.

Baker v. Stackpoole, 9 Cow. 420. Cited, Evidence, admissions of partner, 23 Cal. 102.

Baker v. Thrasher, 4 Denio, 493. Cited, Contract, conditional for conveyance of land, construed, 9 Cal. 551.

Baker v. Vining, 30 Maine, 127. Cited, Trust, resulting trust, when it arises, 25 Cal. 326.

Baker v. Walker, 14 Mees. & W. 468. Commented on, Surety, discharge of, by delay of creditor, 10 Cal. 427.

Baker v. Washington, 5 Stewt. & P. 142. Cited, Appeal, presumptions as to regularity of proceedings, 23 Cal. 305.

Baker v. Wheeler, 8 Wend. 505. Cited, Replevin, action lies for timber cut, 16 Cal. 578. Distinguished, 44 Barb. 451. Commented on, Damages, measure of, 23 Cal. 311; 38 Me. 177.

Baldwin v. Bennett, 4 Cal. 392. Cited, Measure of Damages, on breach of contract, 9 Cal. 364; 4 Nev. 307.

Baldwin v. Johnson, Saxt. Ch. 441. Cited, Title, possession as notice of, 21 Cal. 628.

Baldwin v. Kimmel, 16 Abb. Pr. 353. Cited, Execution, for costs against married woman, 26 Cal. 445.

Baldwin v. Kramer, 2 Cal. 582. Construed and affirmed, Jurisdiction, court loses power over judgment or to grant a new trial after expiration of term, 4 Cal. 106; 5 Cal. 407; 19 Cal. 707; 25 Cal. 17; 28 Cal. 337. Cited, Records, not amendable after adjournment of term, 25 Cal. 51.

Baldwin v. Palmer, 10 N. Y. 232. Cited, Action, for money or services, on void contract, 38 Cal. 110.

Baldwin v. Simpson, 12 Cal. 560. Cited, Land, constructive possession under color of title, 23 Cal. 437; 25 Cal. 138. Commented on, and doctrine approved, 38 Cal. 487, 488; 38 Cal. 675; sufficiency of inclosure to prove actual possession, 32 Cal. 22.

Baldwin v. Whiting, 13 Mass. 57. Cited, Tenant in Common, conveyance of specific part of property, 35 Cal. 587.

Ball v. Dunsterville, 4 Term Rep. 313. Cited, Deed, execution of, 22 Cal. 565.

Ballance v. Forsyth, 13 How. 18. Cited as inapplicable, Taxation, assessment of lands, 8 Cal. 387.

Ballance v. Papin, 19 How. 342. Cited, Ejectment, surveys and patents as evidence, 13 Cal. 413.

Ballard v. Burgett, 47 Barb. 646. Cited, Personal Property, possession as evidence of ownership, 42 Cal. 147.

Ballou v. Hudson, 13 Gratt. 672. Commented on, Probate, judgments conclusive, 20 Cal. 270.

Balls v. Westwood, 2 Camp. 11. Reversed, Use and Occupation, defense showing title extinguished, 1 Ell. & B. 630. Commented on, 3 Cal. 204.

Balston v. Bensted, 1 Camp. 463. Cited, Water Rights, title by adverse possession, 25 Cal. 509. Overruled, 7 H. L. Cas. 368. Doubted, 50 Barb. 327.

Baltimore v. State, 15 Md. 376. Cited, Constitutionality of Statute, obnoxious provisions in statute, their effect, 22 Cal. 386.

Bancroft v. Wardwell, 13 John. 489. Cited, Use and Occupation, action for, 3 Cal. 204; 35 Cal. 194.

Bangor v. Lancy, 21 Me. 472. Cited, Street Assessments, time to make, 36 Cal. 413.

Bangs v. Strong, 1 Denio, 619. Cited, Insolvency, effect of discharge, 14 Cal. 178.

Bangs v. Strong, 4 N. Y. 315. Cited, Surety, when discharged by delay of creditor, 10 Cal. 426.

Bank v. Chester, 11 Penn. St. 290. Cited, Foreclosure, of instalment mortgage, 23 Cal. 31. Denied, 37 Ala. 361.

Bank v. Commonwealth, 10 Penn. St. 448. Cited, Statutory construction, concurrent statutes, repeal by implication, 35 Cal. 709.

Bank of Augusta v. Earle, 13 Pet. 519. Cited, Corporations, powers of, how restricted, 1 Cal. 356; law of comity between States as applied to corporation contracts, 9 Cal. 163; 13 Gratt. 774; 5 Bush, 76.

Bank of Chillicothe v. Town of Chillicothe, 7 Ohio, 358. Cited, Municipal Corporations, contracts of, how construed, 16 Cal. 270. Estoppel in pais, 16 Cal. 628.

Bank of Columbia v. Hagner, 1 Pet. 455. Approved, Contracts to Convey Lands, covenants dependent, 35 Cal. 662.

Bank of Columbia v. Newcomb, 6 John. 98. Cited, Constitutionality of Statute, execution against joint debtor not served with process, 39 Cal. 97.

Bank of Columbia v. Okely, 4 Wheat. 235. Cited, Constitutionality of Statute, summary remedies under statute, 2 Cal. 247; 12 Wheat. 342; 10 Wis. 382.

Bank of Columbia v. Patterson, 7 Cranch, 299. Cited, Corporations, liability on implied contracts, 9 Cal. 471; 12 Wheat. 100.

Bank of Commerce v. New York City, 2 Black, 620. Cited, Acts of Congress, as the supreme law and rule of judgment, applied to legal tender notes, 25 Cal. 434; to State taxation of bonds, 29 Cal. 537; and securities, Id. 546.

Bank of England v. Tarleton, 23 Miss. 173. Cited, Mortgage, securing several notes, 23 Cal. 30.

Bank of Genessee v. Patchin Bank, 13 N. Y. 309. Corporation, power of officers to bind by note, 27 Cal. 257.

Bank of Kentucky v. McWilliams, 2 Marsh. J. J. 257. Cited, Land, constructive possession, 25 Cal. 135.

Bank of Kentucky v. Schuylkill Bank, 1 Pars. Sel. Cas. 250. Cited, Corporations, presumptions as to their proceedings, 33 Cal. 191, 193. Distinguished and doubted, 13 N. Y. 641.

Bank of Metropolis v. New England Bank, 1 How. 234. Cited, Corporate Stock, transfer of, 42 Cal. 147; 9 Bosw. 343. Doubted, 15 Mo. 343.

Bank of Missouri v. Wells, 12 Mo. 361. Distinguished, Lien of judgment, 10 Cal. 82.

Bank of Monroe, Ex parte, 7 Hill, 177. Cited, Affidavit, by agent, what must state, 27 Cal. 299.

Bank of Monroe v. Schermerhorn, Clark's Ch. 300. Cited, Injunction, granting or dissolving in discretion of court, 39 Cal. 167.

Bank of Mount Pleasants v. Sprigg, 1 McLean, 183. Cited, Conveyance, when a mortgage, 8 Cal. 430.

Bank of New York v. Stryker, 1 Wheel. Cr. Ca. 330. Cited, Attorney and Counsel, stricken from roll, 22 Cal. 321.

Bank of Niagara, Matter of, 6 Paige, 213. Cited, Receiver, not entitled to counsel fees, 8 Cal. 321.

Bank of North America v. Meredith, 2 Wash. C. C. 47. Cited, Debtor and Creditor, application of payments, 14 Cal. 449.

Bank of Orleans v. Merrill, 2 Hill, 295. Cited, Negotiable Instruments, certificates of deposit, 29 Cal. 506; 35 Cal. 120.

Bank of Peru v. Farnsworth, 18 Ill. 563. Cited, Negotiable Instruments, certificate of deposit, 29 Cal. 506.

Bank of the Republic v. County of Hamilton, 21 Ill. 53. Cited, Taxation, of securities deposited by corporation, 29 Cal. 546.

Bank of Rochester v. Bowen, 7 Wend. 158. Negotiable Instruments, unauthorized indorsement of partner, 37 Cal. 117. Reviewed and applied, notice of accommodation indorsement, 37 Cal. 120.

Bank of Rochester v. James, 4 Denio, 489. Sale and Delivery, by bill of lading, 8 Cal. 614.

Bank of Rome v. Village of Rome, 18 N. Y. 38. Statutory Construction, 25 Cal. 646.

Bank of United States v. Bank of Washington, 6 Pet. 19. Cited, Appeal, effect of reversal, 14 Cal. 680.

Bank of United States v. Covert, 13 Ohio, 240. Cited, Mortgage, securing several notes, priority, 23 Cal. 30.

Bank of United States v. Dandridge, 12 Wheat. 64. Cited, Corporation, estopped from denying authority of its agents or officers, 9 Cal. 473; 16 Cal. 270; 33 Cal. 696; 37 Cal. 588.

Bank of United States v. Daniel, 12 Pet. 55. Cited, Equity, relief from mistake of law, 16 Cal. 565.

Bank of United States v. Davis, 2 Hill, 451. Cited, Principal and Agent, notice to agent is notice to principal, 31 Cal. 165; 3 Md. Ch. Dec. 389.

Bank of United States v. Housman, 6 Paige, 526. Cited, Deed, validity of deed of gift, 30 Cal. 27. Reviewed, 16 Ohio, 444.

Bank of United States v. Lee, 13 Pet. 107. Cited, Husband and Wife, separate property of wife, 13 Cal. 498.

Bank of United States v. Owens, 2 Pet. 527. Cited, Contracts, unlawful, not enforceable, 29 Cal. 271; unlawful consideration renders contract void, 30 Cal. 524. Distinguished, 9 Pet. 403; and cited, 13 Md. 219; 10 Wis. 237; 7 How. Miss. 527.

Bank of United States v. Schultz, 2 Ohio, 471. Cited, Injunction, restraining judicial sale, 9 Cal. 548. Cited, Pleading, facts must be stated, they cannot be supplied by the evidence, 10 Cal. 332.

Bank of United States v. Sill, 5 Conn. 106. Cited, Evidence, secondary evidence of destroyed bill when admissible, 9 Cal. 448; 10 Cal. 148, 149.

Bank of Utica v. Bender, 21 Wend. 643. Approved, Negotiable instruments, notice of dishonor, diligence required, 33 Cal. 181.

Bank of Utica v. Merserau, 3 Barb. 528. Cited, Conveyance, sufficiency of, 25 Cal. 48; 13 Abb. Pr. 71.

Bank of Utica v. Smalley, 2 Cow. 777. Commented on, Corporation, transfer of stock, 5 Cal. 188.

Banks v. American T. Society, 4 Sand. Ch. 438. Cited, Practice, stipulations binding, 35 Cal. 606.

Banks v. Fowler, 3 Litt. 332.   Cited, Jurisdiction, cannot be conferred by consent of parties, 29 Cal. 463.

Banks v. Moreno, 39 Cal. 233.   Commented on, Mexican Grants, title, 13 Wall. 489, 493, 496.

Banks v. Pike, 15 Me. 268.   Cited, Counter-claim, to joint demand, 41 Cal. 59.

Banks v. Poitiaux, 3 Rand. 136.   Cited, Corporations, property necessary for its purposes, 14 Cal. 552; questions of violation of charter subject exclusively to legislative investigation in a direct proceeding, 22 Cal. 630.

Banks v. Walker, 2 Sand. Ch. 344.   Cited, Mortgage, operation upon subsequently acquired title, 14 Cal. 634.

Banton v. Wilson, 4 Tex. 490.   Approved and adopted, Office and Officer, term of office, 11 Cal. 88; 12 Cal. 390.

Barber v. Reynolds, 33 Cal. 498.   Followed, Pleading, amended complaint takes the place of the original, 8 Nev. 60.

Barber v. Rose, 5 Hill, 76.   Approved, Pleading, unskillful performance to be specially pleaded, 1 Cal. 372; so, as to counter-claim for damages set up in answer, 26 Cal. 308.

Barber v. Spencer, 11 Paige, 518.   Cited, Counter-claim, when set-off enforceable in equity, 11 Cal. 102.

Barbet v. Langlois, 5 La. An. 212.   Commented on, Husband and Wife, separate and community property, 14 Cal. 606; 26 Cal. 568.

Barbour v. Mott, Cal. Sup. Ct. Oct. T. 1851 (not reported.) Cited, Office, appointment to fill vacancy, 1 Cal. 536.

Barbour v. Whitlock, 4 B. Monr. 180.   Cited, Lands and Land Titles, actual possession as notice of title, 8 Cal. 467; 36 Cal. 272.

Barclay v. Bailey, 2 Camp. 527.   Cited, Negotiable Instruments, presentation and demand, reasonable hours, 8 Cal. 633.

Barclay v. Howell's Lessee, 6 Pet. 498.   Cited, Dedication, to public use, how evinced, 14 Cal. 649; 22 Cal. 489; ownership of property dedicated, 15 Cal. 548; railroad, an easement, 19 Cal. 596.

Bardwell v. Ames, 22 Pick. 333.   Cited, Water Rights, interest acquired by purchase, 29 Cal. 207.

Bardwell v. Town of Jamaica, 15 Vt. 438. Cited, Bridges, defined, 24 Cal. 488.

Barhyte v. Hughes, 33 Barb. 320. Commented on and approved, Counter-claim cannot be set up in actions of tort, 35 Cal. 281.

Barickman v. Kuykendall, 6 Blackf. 22. Cited, Vendor and Vendee, rescission of contract, 16 Cal. 628; recovery back of money paid by vendee, 33 Cal. 195.

Barker v. Elkins, 1 John. Ch. 465. Commented on, Equity, relief from judgment at law, diligence required, 12 Cal. 447.

Barker v. Gates, 1 How. Pr. 77. Cited, Execution, application of money, several judgment liens, 37 Cal. 136.

Barker v. Hall, 13 N. H. 298. Cited, Mortgage, by insolvent debtor, 10 Cal. 276.

Barker v. Koneman, 13 Cal. 9. Commented on and declared not applicable, Husband and Wife, conveyance to wife, 17 Cal. 581; 31 Cal. 445, 447. Cited, gift from husband to wife, 31 Cal. 653.

Barker, Matter of, 6 Wend. 510. Construed, Corporations, not entitled to vote on stock held by trustees, 37 Cal. 27.

Barker v. People, 3 Cow. 686. Approved, Office and Officer, constitutional restriction on divestiture of office, 2 Cal. 212; 12 Wis. 310.

Barker v. Salmon, 2 Met. 32. Cited, Vendor and Vendee, vendee may deny vendor's title, 18 Cal. 476.

Barkley v. Barkley, 3 McCord, 269. Cited, Deed, parol evidence cannot be admitted to vary terms of, 24 Cal. 417.

Barley v. Carleton, 12 N. H. 9. Commented on, Land and Land Titles, constructive possession under color of title, 25 Cal. 136.

Barlow v. Bishop, 1 East, 432; 3 Esp. 266. Cited, Negotiable Instruments, acceptance by agent, 13 Cal. 48.

Barlow v. Whitlock, 4 Mon. 180. Cited, Vendor and Vendee, equitable title can only be lost by adverse possession, 40 Cal. 571.

Barnard v. Lee, 97 Mass. 92. Cited, Specific Performance, waiver of forfeiture in contract, 40 Cal. 13.

Barnard's Heirs v. Ashley's Heirs, 18 How. 43. Cited, Preemptioner, rights of, 27 Cal. 519; 29 Cal. 320; 37 Cal. 517.

Barnes, Case of, W. Jones, 352. Cited, Executors and Administrators, powers of, under will, 32 Cal. 440.

Barnes v. Hurd, 11 Mass. 59. Cited, Judgment, on defective complaint, 30 Cal. 488.

Barnes v. Perine, 12 N. Y. 18; 15 Barb. 249. Cited, Deed, parol proof of consideration, 26 Cal. 474.

Barnesly v. Powell, 1 Ves. Sr. 284. Overruled, 6 H. L. Cas. 601. Commented on, Probate, decree conclusive, 20 Cal. 267.

Barnet v. Barbour, 1 Litt. 396. Cited, Constitutionality of Statutes, suspension of remedies, 4 Cal. 167.

Barnet v. Barnet, 15 Serg. & R. 72. Cited, Constitutionality of Statutes, validating and curative acts, 30 Cal. 144. Denied, 39 N. H. 387.

Barnewell v. Cawdor, 3 Madd. Ch. 453. Cited, Probate Procedure, marshaling assets to pay mortgage debts, 31 Cal. 608.

Barney, Case of Mrs., 5 Mod. 323. Cited, Bail, admission to, in capital offenses, 19 Cal. 548.

Barney v. Griffin, 2 N. Y. 365. Approved, Insolvency, fraudulent assignment, 2 Cal. 113. Doubted, 15 N. Y. 118.

Barns v. Hatch, 3 N. H. 304. Cited, Deed, delivery a question of fact, 5 Cal. 319.

Barnum v. State, 15 Ohio, 717. Cited, Criminal Procedure, indictment for forgery, 35 Cal. 507.

Barr v. Gratz's Heirs, 4 Wheat. 213. Cited, Land, constructive possession under color of title, 23 Cal. 437; 25 Cal. 133; Ejectment, ouster of co-tenant, 24 Cal. 377.

Barr v. Hatch, 3 Ohio, 529. Approved, Equity, relief from mistake or defective execution of power, 20 Cal. 36. Cited, 41 Cal. 349.

Barr v. Lapsley, 1 Wheat. 151. Cited, Specific Performance, agreements as to personal property, when not enforced, 25 Cal. 571.

Barrere v. Barrere, 4 John. Ch. 187. Commented on, Divorce, cruelty, 14 Cal. 80.

Barrett v. Amerein, 36 Cal. 322. Cited, Taxation, title of purchase at tax sale, 39 Cal. 357.

Barrett v. Graham, 19 Cal. 632. Cited, Appeal, orders in discretion not reviewable, 29 Cal. 424.

Barrett v. Power, 25 Eng. L. & E. 524. Cited, Civil Death, effect, civilly. of conviction for felony, 35 Cal. 398.

Barrett v. Swann, 17 Me. 180. Cited, Partnership, 28 Cal. 577.

Barrett v. Tewkesbury, 9 Cal. 13. Commented on, Married Woman, conveyance by, 23 Cal. 566; 25 Cal. 374; 40 Cal. 562. Explained, 25 Cal. 374; 30 Cal. 142; 30 Cal. 518. Cited, 31 Cal. 645.

Barrett v. Tewkesbury, 15 Cal. 354. Affirmed on rehearing, Appeal, statement must contain the grounds, or appeal stands on the judgment roll, 15 Cal. 358. Approved, Id. 361; 375. Recognized, Id. 396. Cited, 22 Cal. 494; 24 Cal. 372. Commented on, 25 Cal. 485; and approved, Id. 491; 28 Cal. 165.

Barrett v. Warren, 3 Hill, 348. Cited, Lands, possession of servant is possession of master, 1 Cal. 161.

Barretto v. Snowden, 5 Wend. 181. Cited, Witness, competency of, 13 Cal. 87.

Barric v. Dana, 20 John. 307. Cited, Execution, when premature, is void, 9 Cal. 498.

Barringer v. Warden, 12 Cal. 311. Affirmed, Pleading, defense of statute of limitations, how presented, 20 Cal. 217. Commented on, 23 Cal. 353.

Barron v. Frink, 30 Cal. 486. Approved, Executory Contracts, mutual and dependent covenants, allegations in complaint, 35 Cal. 662. Cited, Independent Promises, 38 Cal. 200.

Barron v. Kennedy, 17 Cal. 574. Commented on and approved, Statute of Limitations, part payment, when it avoids, 21 Cal. 149; 22 Cal. 103. Commented on, 5 Nevada, 214.

Barrs v. Jackson, 1 Younge & C. 19 Eng. Ch. 585; 1 Phil. 588. Commented on, Probate, conclusiveness of proceedings, 29 Cal. 523, 525.

Barry v. Gamble, 3 How. 32. Explained, Title, confirmation of foreign land grant, 24 Cal. 667; location of land grant, 27 Cal. 520. Cited, Survey essential, 30 Cal. 508.

Barry v. Gamble, 8 Mo. 88. Cited, Title, patent to land reserved from entry is void, 23 Cal. 443.

Barry v. Merchants' Ex. Co., 1 Sànd. Ch. 280. Approved, Corporation, power to make contracts, 22 Cal. 627.

Barstow v. Newman, 34 Cal. 90. Cited, Parties, change of plaintiffs, 37 Cal. 389.

Bartholomew v. Candee, 14 Peck. 167. Cited, Pleading, matter of estoppel to be specially pleaded, 26 Cal. 38.

Bartholomew v. Hook, 23 Cal. 277. Distinguished, Homestead, filing declaration, 24 Cal. 639.

Bartholomew v. Jackson, 20 Johns. 28. Cited, Work and Labor, services voluntarily performed create no liability, 20 Cal. 107.

Bartle v. Coleman, 4 Pet. 184. Approved, Contracts, no remedy on illegal or immoral, 15 Cal. 404.

Bartlett v. Crozier, 17 John. 440. Commented on, Pleading, cause of action must be shown in complaint as a ground for judgment, 30 Cal. 489.

Bartlett v. Harlow, 12 Mass. 347. Cited, Tenant in Common, conveyance by, 8 Cal. 275; 15 Cal. 369. Dicta denied, 9 Vt. 140; 35 Cal. 187. Cited, Right to partition in grantee, 15 Cal. 370; 35 Cal. 594.

Bartlett v. Hogden, 3 Cal. 55. Cited, New Trial, newly discovered evidence, Id. 114; 22 Cal. 163; and see 3 Cal. 399. Approved, that evidence must not be merely cumulative, 3 Or. 43.

Bartlett v. Judd, 23 Barb. 263. Commented on and applied, Trust and Trustees, statute of limitation does not run in favor of trustee, 40 Cal. 570.

Bartlett v. King, 12 Mass. 536. Cited, Will, construction of, surplus words, 36 Cal. 81.

Bartlett v. Lang, 2 Ala. 401. Cited, Statutory Construction, remedial statutes, 4 Cal. 137.

Bartlett v. Pickersgill, 1 Eden, 515. Approved, Resulting Trust, purchase by agent, 21 Cal. 100. Distinguished, 3 Story, 288.

Barto v. Himrod, 8 N. Y. 483. Distinguished, Statutory Construction, acts to take effect on contingencies are valid, 13 Cal. 357. Commented on, 17 Cal. 34. Cited as inapplicable, 25 Cal. 646. Denied, 3 Mich. 347, note; 13 Gratt. 83. Cited, 23 N. Y. 447; 2 Kan. 487. Criticised, 26 Vt. 362. Commented on, 24 Wis. 154.

Bartol v. Calvert, 21 Ala. 42. Cited, Statutory Construction, "month" defined, 21 Cal. 396; 31 Cal. 176.

Barton v. McLean, 5 Hill, 258. Cited, Contract, term "agreed" defined, 27 Cal. 38.

Barwick v. Thompson, 7 Term Rep. 488. Cited, Title, by adverse possession, 34 Cal. 383.

Basset v. Nosworthy, 2 Lead. Cas. in Eq. pt. 1, p. 35. (Finch, 102.) Cited, Notice, in equity, what sufficient, 36 Cal. 437.

Bassett v. Carleton, 32 Me. 553. Approved, Remedies, statutory remedies not exclusive, 16 Cal. 526.

Bassler v. Niesly, 2 Serg. & R. 355. Cited, Vendor and Vendee, right of possession in vendee, 22 Cal. 617.

Batchelder v. Kelly, 10 N. H. 436. Cited, Statutory Construction, penalty in statute to be strictly construed, 15 Cal. 474.

Bateman v. Bluck, 14 Eng. L. & E. 69. Approved, Dedication to public use, *cul de sac*, 35 Cal. 498.

Bateman v. Willoe, 1 Sch. & L. 201. Reviewed, Injunction, when equity will not interfere with proceedings at law, 12 Cal. 446.

Bates, Case of, 1 Vent. 41. Cited, Government, constitutional power of taxation confided to legislature, 41 Cal. 164.

Bates v. Coe, 10 Conn. 280. Approved, Insolvency, mortgage by insolvent not an assignment, 10 Cal. 276. Cited, 10 Conn. 423.

Bates v. Conkling, 10 Wend. 389. Approved, Witness, competency of, party not served, 6 Cal. 194.

Bates v. Cooper, 5 Ohio, 118. Cited, Eminent Domain, compensation a condition precedent to exercise of right, 31 Cal. 559.

Bates v. State Bank, 2 Ala. 451. Cited, Corporation, power to make contracts, 22 Cal. 629.

3

Battey v. Button, 13 John. 187.   Cited, Res Adjudicata, former recovery when a bar, 38 Cal. 647.

Batty v. Carswell, 2 John. 48.   Cited, Principal and Agent, ratification, by act operating as an estoppel, 30 Cal. 414.

Baughan v. Graham, 1 How. Miss. 220.   Cited, Pleading, averment of demand in action on written instrument not essential, 22 Cal. 278.

Baugher v. Nelson, 9 Gill, 300.   Cited, Constitutionality of Statute, statutes suspending rights and remedies, 22 Cal. 327.

Baum v. Grigsby, 21 Cal. 172.   Approved, Vendor's Lien, not assignable, 21 Cal. 189; 21 Cal. 228.   Cited to same point, 35 Cal. 204; 36 Cal. 321; it is a mere equitable right to be enforced, 23 Cal. 636; 32 Cal. 59. Commented on and principle adopted, 35 Cal. 204, 206.   Cited, waiver of, 25 Cal. 328.   Approved, 4 Bush, 126.

Bax v. Whitbread, 16 Ves. Jr. 26.   Cited, Trust, equity will compel execution of, 32 Cal. 443.

Bay v. Pope, 18 Cal. 694.   Cited, Ejectment, improvements when may be set off, 31 Cal. 495; 35 Cal. 355.

Bayard v. Smith, 17 Wend. 88.   Cited, Statutory Construction, penal statutes defined, 29 Cal. 512.

Bayerque v. San Francisco, 1 McAll. 175.   Cited, San Francisco, warrants drawn on special fund not negotiable, 16 Cal. 287.

Bayles v. Baxter, 22 Cal. 575.   Cited, Statute of Frauds, contract creating resulting trust excepted from, 35 Cal. 487.

Bayless v. Orne, 1 Freem. Ch. 171.   Approved, Corporations, power of, removal of officers, 16 Cal. 149.

Bayley v. Bates, 8 John. 188.   Cited, Execution, trial of rights to property, 10 Cal. 192.

Bayley v. Greenleaf, 7 Wheat. 46.   Distinguished, Vendor's Lien, 6 Cal. 227.   Cited, 25 Ark. 161; 3 Whart. 493; 26 Geo. 318; 6 Nev. 315.

Baylis v. Dineley, 3 Maule & S. 477.   Cited, Infant, affirmance of deed by, 24 Cal. 212.

Bayly v. Schofield, 1 Maule & S. 338.   Approved, Insolvency, defined, 33 Cal. 625.

Baynster v. Trussel, Cro. Eliz. 516. Cited, Felony, effect, civilly, of conviction for, 35 Cal. 398.

Beach v. Farish, 4 Cal. 339. Cited, Lease, covenants in, 39 Cal. 153.

Beach v. Forsyth, 14 Barb. 499. Cited, Probate, money received by administrator, when not assets, 22 Cal. 518.

Beach v. Fulton Bank, 7 Cow. 485. Cited, Municipal Corporations, liability of, restitution of property, 16 Cal. 632.

Beach v. Fulton Bank, 2 Wend. 225. Cited as not in point, Appeal, 1 Cal. 136.

Beach v. Gabriel, 29 Cal. 580. Cited, Statute of Limitations, begins to run only from date of patent, 1 Saw. 560.

Beach v. Raymond, 2 E. D. Smith, 500. Cited, Pleading, assignment, sufficient allegation of, 34 Cal. 149.

Beadleston v. Sprague, 6 John. 101. Cited, Statutory Construction, statutes not retrospective, 4 Cal. 136.

Beaird v. Foreman, 1 Ill. 385. Cited, Execution, notice of motion not sufficient to stay execution, 8 Cal. 134.

Bealey v. Shaw, 6 East, 208. Cited, Water, title to, by adverse possession, 25 Cal. 509; 27 Cal. 366; 2 Conn. 596; 4 Rand. 65.

Beall v. Beck, 3 Harr. & McH. 242. Construed, Official Bonds, sureties not concluded by judgment against principal alone, 14 Cal. 205. Denied, 4 McLean, 579; 12 Wheat. 523; 36 Vt. 384.

Beals v. Allen, 18 John. 363. Cited, Agent, authority of, to bind principal, 24 Cal. 140.

Beals v. Amador Co., 28 Cal. 449. Commented on and explained, Taxation, 35 Cal. 631. Cited, Statutory Construction, interest on county bonds, 39 Cal. 136.

Beals v. Amador County, 35 Cal. 624. Cited, Municipal Corporations, legislative control over, 41 Cal. 530.

Bean v. Atwater, 4 Conn. 3. Cited, Contracts, executory contracts, dependent and independent covenants, when enforceable, 35 Cal. 663; 38 Cal. 200.

Bean v. Parker, 17 Mass. 591. Referred to, Sheriff, return of process conclusive, 14 Cal. 143. Cited, Official Bonds, validity of joint bond, 14 Cal. 423; 21 Cal. 589.

Bean v. Quimby, 5 N. H. 94. Approved, Witness, privileged communications, 5 Cal. 452.

Bean v. Smith, 2 Mason, 274. Approved, Fraudulent Conveyances, title of innocent purchasers, 12 Cal. 497. Criticised, Chancery, power to reach property of debtor, 11 N. H. 326.

Bear River and A. W. and M. Co. v. Boles, 24 Cal. 354. Cited, New Trial, notice of motion to be filed in time, 26 Cal. 284; record must contain evidence of its service, 28 Cal. 154; order allowing time must be in writing, 41 Cal. 518; form of entry of order extending time, 27 Cal. 339. Approved, Notice of motion for new trial must be in writing, 2 Nev. 40.

Bear River and A. W. and M. Co. v. New York Min. Co., 8 Cal. 327. Referred to and principle applied, Water Rights, protection of first appropriator, 8 Cal. 339; 10 Cal. 187. Limited, 11 Cal. 162. Commented on, Injuries to Water Rights, 23 Cal. 488.

Bearce v. Jackson, 4 Mass. 408. Cited, Survey, admissibility and effect in evidence, 11 Cal. 142.

Beard v. Federy, 3 Wallace, 478. Cited, Mexican Grants, confirmation of, 32 Cal. 371; jurisdiction of board of commissioners, 36 Cal. 143; United States patent, 38 Cal. 71.

Beard v. Knox, 5 Cal. 252. Approved, Husband and Wife, common property, wife's interest absolute on death of husband, 7 Cal. 459; 12 Cal. 225; 13 Cal. 469, 470; 18 Cal. 301; 29 Cal. 348; 39 Cal. 164. Cited as decisive, 42 Cal. 213.

Beardsley v. Knight, 10 Vt. 190. Cited, Equity, relief from mistakes, 19 Cal. 673.

Beardsley v. Smith, 16 Conn. 368. Disapproved, Municipal Corporations, individual liability of inhabitants for debts of, 10 Cal. 408; 25 Miss. 441.

Beardsley v. Torrey, 4 Wash. C. C. 286. Cited, Alienage, transfer of cause to Federal Court, application how made, 20 Cal. 169.

Beatty v. Clark, 20 Cal. 11. Cited, Equity, when will aid in execution of a power, 32 Cal. 652; 41 Cal. 349.

Beatty v. Gilmore, 16 Penn. St. 463. Cited, Negligence, burden of proof in action for injuries, 5 Cal. 366; 7 Cal. 255; negligence not presumed, 34 Cal. 164.

Beatty v. Kurtz, 2 Pet. 566. Cited, Dedication, to public uses, 22 Cal. 489; 7 Vt. 285.

Beatty v. Wray, 19 Penn. St. 516. Cited, Probate Proceedings, surviving partner not entitled to pay for winding up affairs, 23 Cal. 430.

Beaty v. Lessee of Knowler, 4 Pet. 152. Cited, Statutory construction, statutes in derogation of common law to be strictly construed, 19 Cal. 60.

Beaubien v. Brinckerhoff, 3 Ill. 273. Cited, Jurisdiction, intendments as to municipal courts, 1 Cal. 344; 13 Ill. 444. Affirmed, of Superior Court of San Francisco, 10 Cal. 295; 36 Cal. 697.

Beaudry v. Valdez, 32 Cal. 269. Commented on, Street Assessments, letting contract, 35 Cal. 696. Remedy, by appeal to board, exclusive, 38 Cal. 75.

Beaumont v. Crane, 14 Mass. 400. Cited, Contract, to work on shares not a lease, 17 Cal. 546.

Beaumont v. Field, 1 Barn. & A. 247. Cited, Conveyance, descriptions in, what passes, 27 Cal. 63.

Beaumont v. Meredith, 3 Ves. & B. 180. Approved, voluntary benevolent societies are mere partnerships, 14 Cal. 536.

Beaumont v. Yeatman, 8 Humph. 542. Cited, Officers, official certificates, power of deputy, 20 Cal. 157.

Beck v. Simmons, 7 Ala. 76. Approved, Specific Performance, when decreed, 11 Cal. 237.

Becker, Ex parte, 4 Hill, 613. Cited, Redemption, payment to sheriff, kind of money, 26 Cal. 663.

Becker v. Lamont, 13 How. Pr. 23. Cited, Practice, relief from stipulation under mistake of fact, 29 Cal. 464.

Beckett v. Selover, 7 Cal. 215. Affirmed, Jurisdiction, of probate court, 17 Cal. 238. Cited, is limited and inferior, 19 Cal. 205; jurisdictional facts to exist, 10 Cal. 118. Commented on, fact of residence, 18 Cal. 507. Questioned, as to right of collateral attack on judgment, 18 Cal. 504. Cited, Property vests in heir, subject to lien of administrator for payment of debts, 10 Cal. 120. Approved, on this point, 20 Cal. 627; and cited, 18 Cal. 459; 31 Cal. 604; 42 Cal. 463; administrator entitled to possession of personal estate, 29 Cal. 510. Commented on, Allowance of Claims, effect of, 23 Cal. 363. Cited, Public Administrator, rights of, 11 Cal. 128; 34 Cal. 468.

Beckford v. Wade, 17 Ves. Jr. 87. Cited, Land and Land Ttitles, title by adverse possession, 34 Cal. 383; statutory construction, 35 Cal. 642; statute of limitations runs in all cases not therein expressly excepted, Id. 640.

Beckman v. McKay, 14 Cal. 250. Commented on, conversion of property of estate, 29 Cal. 512.

Beckman v. Shouse, 5 Rawle, 189. Cited, Common Carriers, contracts construed, 27 Cal. 33.

Beckwith v. Benner, 6 Car. & P. 681. Approved, Witness, privileged communications, rule admitting testimony, 36 Cal. 507, 508.

Bedford v. Shilling, 4 Serg. & R. 401. Cited, Statutory Construction, statutes not retrospective, 4 Cal. 136.

Beebe v. Elliott, 4 Barb. 457. Cited, Pleading, in ejectment, 26 Cal. 505.

Beebe v. Hutton, 47 Barb. 187. Cited, Pleading, defense of omission of revenue stamp, 34 Cal. 175.

Beeby v. Beeby, 1 Hagg. Ecc. 789. Cited, Divorce, adultery, 10 Cal. 255.

Beed v. Blandford, 2 Young & J. 278. Cited, Contract, rescission of, 15 Cal. 458; 34 Cal. 144.

Beekman v. Platner, 15 Barb. 550. Cited, Pleading, complaint, common counts sufficient, 10 Cal. 338.

Beekman v. Saratoga and Schenectady R. R. Co., 3 Paige, 45. Cited, Eminent Domain, 18 Cal. 252; "necessity" defined, Id. 250; Legislature, power to judge of necessity, Id. 252; compensation, how ascertained, 16 Cal. 255; proceedings are special, 24 Cal. 454; railroads concern public interest, 30 Cal. 437. Approved, 31 Cal. 371. Cited, Legislative control of county revenues in aid of railroads, 30 Cal. 439. Disapproved, 1 Chand. Wis. 100; 4 Ohio St. 326. Explained, 3 C. E. Green, 67.

Beekman Street, Matter of, 20 John. 269. Cited, Special Cases, review of, 24 Cal. 454. Commented on, 2 Den. 334; 20 How. Pr. 494.

Beem v. McCusick, 10 Cal. 538. Cited, Deed, as an escrow, 23 Cal. 536.

Beers v. Housatonic R. R. Co., 19 Conn. 566. Commented on, Negligence, liability for injury to cattle, 18 Cal. 356.

Beers v. Squire, 1 Code R. 84. Cited, Pleading, insufficient denials, practice, 1 Cal. 196; 32 Cal. 573.

Beeson v. Hutchinson, 4 Watts, 442. Cited, Evidence, how far parol evidence to explain deed is admissible, 24 Cal. 417.

Began v. O'Reilly, 32 Cal. 11. Cited, Variance, when immaterial, 39 Cal. 175.

Beirne v. Mower, 13 Smedes & M. 427. Cited, Judgment, lien of, statutory limitation, 10 Cal. 80.

Belcher v. Capper, 4 Man. & G. 502. Commented on, Charter Party, lien for freight, 1 Cal. 424.

Belden v. Seymour, 8 Conn. 19. Cited, Deed, descriptions how construed, 12 Cal. 165; questioned as to application of principle, 11 Conn. 335.

Belden v. Seymour, 8 Conn. 311. Approved, Estoppel, deed how far an estoppel, 30 Cal. 25; 36 Cal. 370.

Belding v. Pitkin, 2 Caines, 147. Cited, Contracts, performance of acts prohibited by law not enforceable in equity, 38 Cal. 310; 2 Wall. 79.

Belknap v. Trimble, 3 Paige, 605. Cited, Water Rights, variance in use, 15 Cal. 181.

Bell v. Bedrock T. & M. Co., 36 Cal. 214. Cited, Abandonment, a question of intention, 36 Cal. 340.

Bell v. Brown, 22 Cal. 671. Cited, Pleading, consistent and inconsistent defenses may be set up in answer, 30 Cal. 200; 1 Saw. 72; 7 Nev. 81.

Bell v. Crippen, 28 Cal. 327. Cited, Jurisdiction, when concurrent, 30 Cal. 581.

Bell v. Ellis, 33 Cal. 620. Approved, Sale and Delivery, validity of sale by insolvent, 4 Nev. 300.

Bell v. Ingram, 2 Penn. St. 490. Doubted, Judgment, lien of, not prolonged by execution, 10 Cal. 82.

Bell v. Morrison, 1 Pet. 351. Approved, New Promise, nature of acknowledgment to avoid the statute, 36 Cal. 185. Cited, 12 Me. 14; 2 Tex. 573; 24 Miss. 166.

Bell v. Morse, 6 N. H. 205. Cited, Mortgage, transfer by mortgagee, 9 Cal. 429. Criticised, 16 N. H. 64; evidence, parol evidence not admissible to vary deed, 24 Cal. 417.

Bell v. Moss, 5 Whart. 189. Cited, Common Carrier, stoppage in transitu, notice by vendor, 37 Cal. 632.

Bell v. Phyn, 7 Ves. Jr. 453.   Disapproved, Descent and Distribution, partnership, real estate, 28 Cal. 582. Commented on and doubted, 20 Mo. 180; 1 Sum. 184.

Bell v. Raymond, 18 Conn. 95.   Cited, Res Adjudicata, estoppel by judgment, 36 Cal. 37.

Bell v. Rowland, 1 Hardin, 301.   Cited, New Promise, sufficiency of acknowledgment, 36 Cal. 186.

Bell v. Thompson, 19 Cal. 706.   Commented on and followed, Judgment, motion to set aside, 21 Cal. 273. Cited, Jurisdiction, lost upon adjournment of term, 25 Cal. 52; 28 Cal. 338; power of court to vacate void judgments, 31 Cal. 173; 37 Cal. 529.

Bell v. Twilight, 22 N. H. 518.   Cited, Conveyances, notice of title imparted by possession, 29 Cal. 490.

Bell v. Wood's Adm'r., 1 Bay, 249.   Commented on as mere obiter and not authority, negotiable instruments, 2 Cal. 67.

Bell v. Drummond, 1 Peake, 45.   Distinguished, Services and Labor, presumptions as to extra services, 9 Cal. 202.

Bellasis v. Compton, 2 Vern. 294.   Approved, Trust, resulting trust may be proved by parol, 22 Cal. 580.

Balloo v. Rogers, Cal. Sup. Court (not reported.)   Referred to, 9 Cal. 124.

Belloc v. Rogers, 9 Cal. 123.   Cited, Mortgage, legal title remains in mortgagor, 9 Cal. 411; jurisdiction in foreclosure of mortgages against estates, 10 Cal. 559; jurisdiction in equity, 24 Cal. 499.   Cited as authority only to the extent of its special concurrence, 14 Cal. 642.   Explained, Title under foreclosure sale, 16 Cal. 469.

Bellows v. Hallowell & Augusta Bank, 2 Mason, 31.   Followed, Corporations, powers restricted within the terms of their charter, 2 Cal. 554.

Belmain v. Shore, 9 Ves. Jr. 500.   Disapproved, Descents and Distribution, partnership real estate, 28 Cal. 583.

Belt v. Davis, 1 Cal. 134.   Cited, Judgment, final, defined, 23 Cal. 136; 24 Cal. 338; 39 Cal. 584.   Approved and adopted, 1 Nev. 514; presumptions in favor of verdict or decision, 24 Cal. 378.   Approved, finality of judgment of nonsuit, 1 Nev. 514.

Bemis v. Smith, 10 Met. 194. Cited, Covenant, of warranty, what constitutes an eviction, 39 Cal. 368.

Benedict v. Bunnell, 7 Cal. 245. Cited, Homestead, residence required under original act, 41 Cal. 83; actual residence of family required to impress with the character of a homestead, 16 Iowa, 452; 45 Miss. 178; 46 N. H. 52.

Benedict v. Cozzens, 4 Cal. 381. Overruled, Record, supplying place of lost pleading, 27 Cal. 523.

Benedict v. Danbury and Norwalk R. R., 24 Conn. 320. Cited, Building Contract, no privity between subcontractor and owner, 22 Cal. 571.

Benedict v. Gaylord, 11 Conn. 332. Cited, Deed, description in deed, 12 Cal. 165.

Benedict v. Lynch, 1 Johns. Ch. 370. Approved, Specific Performance, plaintiff must show diligence, 10 Cal. 327; 19 Cal. 459. Denied, 8 Mich. 469; election of remedy on bond for title, 14 Cal. 73.

Benham v. New York Cent. R. R. Co., 13 How. Pr. 198. Cited, Witness, form of notice to party to testify, 22 Cal. 173.

Benham v. Rowe, 2 Cal. 387. Cited, Mortgage, a mere security, 8 Cal. 267. Approved, power of sale in mortgage, 43 Mo. 167.

Benjamin v. Delahay, 3 Ill. 574. Cited, Pleading, complaint on joint contract, 6 Cal. 181.

Bennett v. Bedford Bank, 11 Mass. 421. Cited, Fraudulent Conveyances, 13 Cal. 72.

Bennett v. Boggs, 1 Bald. 74. Approved, Legislature, power to enact laws within constitutional restriction is supreme, 7 Cal. 21; sole remedy for unwise or oppressive legislation, 7 Cal. 21; 9 Cal. 528.

Bennett v. City of Buffalo, 17 N. Y. 383. Cited, Local Improvements, assessment as a charge on property, 31 Cal. 676.

Bennett v. Clemence, 6 Allen, 10. Approved, Ejectment, ouster by tenant in common, 27 Cal. 560.

Bennett v. Hamill, 2 Scho. & L. 575. Commented on, Judgment, infant bound by decree, 31 Cal. 2t 3.

Bennett v. His Creditors, 22 Cal. 38. Overruled and practice suggested, Insolvency, 32 Cal. 410, 413. Cited, Jurisdictional facts, 34 Cal. 24.

Bennett v. Holmes, 1 Dev. & B. 486. Cited, Judgment, how far conclusive, 20 Cal. 486.

Bennett v. Irwin, 3 John. 363. Approved, Release, when void, 24 Cal. 606.

Bennett v. Judson, 21 N. Y. 239. Cited, Fraudulent Representations, as to value of corporate stock, 29 Cal. 592.

Bennett v. Soloman, 6 Cal. 134. Cited, Evidence, parol proof of consideration in written instrument, 10 Cal. 402; 20 Cal. 676; 21 Cal. 51; 30 Cal. 57.

Bennett v. Taylor, 5 Cal. 502. Cited, Mortgage, a mere incident to the debt, 6 Cal. 483. Cited as affirmed on this point, 9 Cal. 410.

Benninger v. Wattles, 28 How. Pr. 206. Cited, Trade Marks, use of words, 35 Cal. 76.

Benny v. Pegram, 18 Mo. 191. Cited, Factor, cannot pledge, 19 Cal. 72.

Benny v. Rhodes, 18 Mo. 147. Cited, Factor, cannot pledge goods of principal, 19 Cal. 72.

Bensley v. Atwill, 12 Cal. 231. Cited, Appeal, error in granting or refusing new trial must affirmatively appear, 33 Cal. 525; Evidence, of execution of deed, 18 Iowa, 250.

Bensley v. Mountain Lake Wat. Co., 13 Cal. 306. Referred to, Condemnation of Land, compensation to precede taking, 14 Cal. 107. Cited to same point, 24 Cal. 435; 29 Cal. 117. Distinguished, 31 Cal. 547. Cited, Statutes divesting title to be strictly construed, 19 Cal. 60. Commented on and approved, same point, 24 Cal. 432; 27 Cal. 172; 46 Miss. 11. Cited, 30 Cal. 537; 39 Cal. 491. Cited, Lis Pendens, actual notice, effect of, 22 Cal. 211.

Benson v. Aitken, 17 Cal. 163. Cited, Homestead, power of husband after death of wife, 23 Cal. 120; original act construed, 41 Cal. 83.

Benson v. Bruce, 4 Desaus. 463. Cited, Executor and Administrator, duty as to surplus funds, 37 Cal. 430.

Benson, Ex parte, 6 Cow. 592. Cited, Appeal, sufficiency of undertaking, 13 Cal. 509.

Benson v. Fash, 1 Code Rep. 50. Cited, Injunction, practice on motion to dissolve, 35 Cal. 59.

Benson v. Mayor of Albany, 24 Barb. 248. Legislature, power of taxation, 13 Cal. 355.

Benson v. Monroe, 7 Cush. 125. Cited, Money paid, voluntary payment under mistake of law not recoverable, 18 Cal. 271.

Benson v. Remington, 2 Mass. 113. Cited, Parent and Child, services of infant due to parent, 8 Cal. 123.

Bent v. Baker, 3 Term Rep. 27. Cited, Principal and Agent, legal and moral obligations, fraudulent collusion, 29 Cal. 146.

Bentley's Heirs v. Deforest, 2 Ohio, 222. Cited, Conveyance, insufficient to pass title to land, 10 Cal. 368.

Bentley v. Jones, 4 How. Pr. 202. Cited, Pleading, "ownership" a legal conclusion, 11 Cal. 168; sham answer, denial of legal conclusions, 32 Cal. 573.

Bentley v. Phelps, 2 Woodb. & M. 426. Cited, not in point, Deed as a Mortgage, 8 Cal. 430.

Benton v. Dale, 1 Cow. 160. Cited, Pleading, demand for treble damages must be stated in complaint, 5 Cal. 240.

Benton v. Jones, 8 Conn. 186. Cited, Conveyance, when fraudulent as to creditors, 13 Cal. 72.

Bequette v. Caulfield, 4 Cal. 278. Cited, Land, possession as evidence of title, 9 Cal. 5. Approved, but held not apposite, 13 Cal. 593. Cited, Title, by prior possession, 21 Cal. 325; ejectment on prior possession, 24 Cal. 348; McAll. 232.

Bergen v. Bennett, 1 Caines Cas. 1. Cited, Agent, termination of authority on death of principal, 15 Cal. 18. Approved, Powers, irrevocable power, interest necessary to create, 32 Cal. 617. Cited, Purchase by mortgagee under power of sale in mortgage, 21 Cal. 330. Approved, regularity of sale inferred from lapse of time, acquiescence, 22 Cal. 590. Questioned as to latter point, 1 Zab. 507.

Berger v. Duff, 4 Johns. Ch. 368. Cited, Powers, discretionary, cannot be delegated by assignment, 39 Cal. 290.

Berghaus v. Calhoun, 6 Watts, 219. Cited, New Promise, sufficiency of acknowledgment, 36 Cal. 185.

Berkeley v. Brymer, 9 Ves. Jr. 355. Cited, Injunction, dissolution on denials of answer, 7 Cal. 323.

Berkeley v. Elderkin, 1 Ell. & B. 806. Cited, Forfeiture and Penalty, statutory remedies to be strictly pursued, 33 Cal. 218.

Berks and Dauphine T. R. Co. v. Myers, 6 Serg. & R. 12. Cited, Corporations, corporate seal affixed to contract, as evidence, 16 Cal. 639; presumptions arising therefrom, 37 Cal. 598.

Berkshire Wool. Co. v. Proctor, 7 Cush. 423. Approved, Innkeeper, liable for property of guest deposited, 33 Cal. 605.

Berley v. Rampacher, 5 Duer, 183. Cited, Statutory Construction, statutes not retrospective, 27 Cal. 159.

Berly v. Taylor, 5 Hill, 582. Cited, Conversion, election of remedy, waiver of tort, 12 Cal. 90.

Bernal v. Gleim, 33 Cal. 668. Cited, Execution, sheriff's deed void, 38 Cal. 438.

Bernal v. Hovious, 17 Cal. 541. Cited, Tenants in Common, raising crops on shares, 19 Cal. 621. Approved, Lease, on shares, 25 Cal. 63. Cited, Statute of Frauds, growing crops not within, 37 Cal. 638.

Bernal v. Lynch, 36 Cal. 135. Cited, Tax Title, title cannot be acquired by party whose duty it is to pay the tax, 36 Cal. 326; 39 Cal. 357; 7 Kan. 123.

Bernard v. Flournoy, 4 J. J. Marsh. 102. Cited, Evidence, oral evidence of declarations and admissions not favored, 26 Cal. 44.

Bernard v. Monnot, 34 Barb. 93. Cited, Agent, commissions for sale of property, 25 Cal. 82.

Bernard v. Shaw, 9 Mart. 79. Cited, Real Actions, under the Civil Law, 1 Cal. 289; sufficiency of possession to maintain, 1 Cal. 289; Id. 320.

Bernett v. Taylor, 9 Ves. Jr. 381. Cited, Will, attestation, 10 Cal. 479.

Berri v. Patch, 12 Cal. 299. Cited, Cloud on Title, void proceeding creates no cloud, 36 Cal. 71.

Berry v. Bates, 2 Blackf. 118. Cited, Covenant, not to sue is no bar to an action, remedy on covenant, 5 Cal. 502.

Berry v. Metzler, 7 Cal. 418. Approved, Continuance, newly discovered evidence a ground for motion, 22 Cal. 163.

Bertie v. Beaumont, 16 East, 33. Cited, Forcible Entry and Detainer, possession of agent is possession of principal, 20 Cal. 48.

Bertie v. Walker, 1 Rob. La. 431. Cited, Husband and Wife, common property, 30 Cal. 35.

Besser v. Hawthorn, 3 Or. 129. Cited, Foreclosure, purchaser at foreclosure sale, 40 Cal. 236.

Bessy v. Pintado, 3 La. 488. Cited, Warranty, eviction necessary to constitute breach, 2 Cal. 570.

Bettle v. Wilson, 14 Ohio, 257. Cited, Husband and Wife, articles of separation through trustee valid, 9 Cal. 493.

Betton v. Cutts, 11 N. H. 179. Cited, Pleading, new promise must be specially pleaded, 19 Cal. 482.

Betts v. Bagley, 12 Pick. 572. Cited, Official Bond, discretion on approval of, 7 Cal. 438.

Betts v. Jackson, 6 Wend. 173. Approved, Nonsuit, compulsory nonsuit, 1 Cal. 114.

Betts v. Lee, 5 John. 348. Cited, Conversion, measure of damages for timber cut, 23 Cal. 311.

Betts v. Starr, 5 Conn. 550. Cited, Res Adjudicata, distinction between fact *in issue* and fact *in controversy*, 26 Cal. 494; 36 Cal. 37.

Betts v. Williamsburgh, 15 Barb. 256. Cited, Eminent Domain, compensation, benefits and advantages to be considered, 31 Cal. 374.

Beverley v. Lincoln, G. L. & C. Co. 6 Ad. & E. 829. Cited, Corporations, authority to convey property, 7 Cal. 381.

Bevins v. Ramsey, 15 How. 179. Cited, Officers, liability for malfeasance or omissions, 36 Cal. 214.

Bibend v. Kreutz, 20 Cal. 109. Cited, Pleading, demurrer waived by plea, 30 Iowa, 222.

Bibend v. Liverpool, etc., Ins. Co., 30 Cal. 78. Cited, Insurance, assignment of policy, 58 Cal. 544; assent of insurer required, Id. 544.

Bickerstaff v. Doub, 19 Cal. 109. Approved, Sheriff, execution as justification for seizure, 19 Cal. 622.

Bickham v. Cruttwell, 3 Mylne & C. 769.   Cited, Will, devise of lands mortgaged; charge on assets, 31 Cal. 608.

Bickford v. Page, 2 Mass. 455.   Cited, Assignment, choses in action not assignable, 37 Cal. 189.

Biddle v. Starr, 9 Penn. St. 466.   Cited, Statutory Construction, 17 Cal. 562.

Bidleman v. Kewen, 2 Cal. 248.   Commented on, Jurisdiction, power of court over judgment, upon adjournment of term, 6 Cal. 22; 28 Cal. 337.   See 3 Cal. 134.

Bierce v. Red Bluff Hotel Co., 31 Cal. 160.   Cited, Principal and Agent, notice to agent is notice to principal, 37 Cal. 633.

Bigelow v. Bush, 6 Paige, 345.   Cited, Foreclosure, mortgagor, when a necessary party, 9 Cal. 125.

Bigelow, Executors of, v. Sacramento Cal. Sup. Ct. (not reported.)   Cited, Statutory Construction, statutes not retrospective, 4 Cal. 136.

Bigelow v. Grannis, 2 Hill, 120.   Approved, Infancy, transfer of note by agent of infant, valid title avoided, 24 Cal. 208.

Bigelow v. Gove, 7 Cal. 133.   Commented on and qualified, Pleading, misjoinder of causes, 10 Cal. 237.   Cited, Prayer in Complaint, construction of, 37 Cal. 304.

Biggs, Heirs of, v. Blue, 5 McLean, 149.   Cited, Records, of court, import absolute verity, 34 Cal. 428.

Bilbie v. Lumley, 2 East, 472.   Cited, Equity, mistake of law, cognizance of law presumed, 18 Cal. 271.   See 1 McLean, 311.

Billingham's Case, 1 Collinson on Lunacy, 636.   Commented on, Pleading, defense of insanity, to be clearly made out, 24 Cal. 236.

Billings v. Billings, 2 Cal. 107.   Construed, Fraud, presumptive evidence of, 2 Cal. 541.   Cited, when not a question for the jury, 6 Cal. 122.

Billings v. Detten, 15 Ill. 218.   Cited, Taxation, levy, when to be made, 34 Cal. 442.

Billings v. Hall, 7 Cal. 1.   Approved, on the principle of *stare decisis*, Constitutional Construction, inalienable rights, 9 Cal. 510; Statute of Limitations, as to real actions, 25 Cal. 596.   Cited, as to limitation under

"Settler's Act," 36 Cal. 633; Statutory Construction, statutes divesting property to be strictly pursued, 13 Cal. 316; 67 Penn. St. 494. See 5 Wall. 133.

Billings v. Harvey, 6 Cal. 381. Affirmed, Statute of Limitations, real actions, when time begins to run, 7 Cal. 3; upon principle of *stare decisis*, 15 Cal. 284; 25 Cal. 596.

Billings v. Morrow, 7 Cal. 171. Cited, Principal and Agent, ratification by principal, 8 Cal. 244; of sale by agent, 10 Cal. 367. Referred to, construction of power of attorney, 16 Cal. 510, 512.

Billington v. Welsh, 5 Bin. 132. Cited, Lands, possession as notice of title, 31 Cal. 184; 1 Penn. St. 475.

Binney, Case of, 2 Bland Ch. 145. Cited, Easement, as real property, 32 Cal. 507.

Birch v. Wright, 1 Term Rep. 378. Cited, Use and Occupation, action for, 3 Cal. 203, 205. Dictum doubted, 4 Cranch, 302.

Birckhead v. Brown, 5 Hill, 635. Approved, Negotiable Instruments, what are, 1 Cal. 79.

Bird v. Bird, Wright, 98. Cited, Divorce, adultery, 10 Cal. 254.

Bird v. Dennison, 7 Cal. 297. Referred to, Separate opinion of Burnett, J., Evidence, objections to admission of deed in, 7 Cal. 416; Lands, possession as notice of equitable title, 8 Cal. 467. Construed, Actual adverse possession, as notice of title, 9 Cal. 6; 10 Cal. 184. Cited, Statutory Construction, exceptions in statute, 9 Cal. 128; presumptions as to effects intended by statute, 10 Cal. 191.

Bird v. Holbrook, 4 Bing. 628; S. C. 1 Moore & P. 609. Cited, Negligence, contributory negligence, 18 Cal. 357.

Bird v. Lisbros, 9 Cal. 1. Cited, Ejectment, on prior possession, outstanding title in third party not in issue, 10 Cal. 30; 21 Cal. 325; 23 Cal. 536; 24 Cal. 348; 29 Cal. 129; 38 Cal. 370; possession as evidence of title, 10 Cal. 183; Abandonment, not presumed from lapse of time, 10 Cal. 183. Approved, as to abandonment, 1 Nev. 202.

Birdsall v. Phillips, 17 Wend. 464.   Cited, Landlord and Tenant, notice to quit conclusive on sub-tenants, 23 Cal. 231.

Birdsall v. Taylor, 1 How. Pr. 89.   Cited, Service, by mail, strict compliance with statute, 30 Cal. 184.

Birks v. Trippet, 1 Saund. 32.   Cited, Demand, failure to make, does not discharge the debt, 11 Cal. 322.

Birmingham Co. v. Lloyd, 18 Ves. Jr. 515.   Cited, Presumptions, acquiescence from lapse of time, 22 Cal. 592; effect on equitable rights and remedies, 23 Cal. 84.

Birney v. Hann, 3 A. K. Marsh. 324.   Cited, Assignment, choses in action not technically assignable, 37 Cal. 189.

Birrell v. Schie, 9 Cal. 104.   Cited, Mortgage, subrogation to rights of prior mortgagees, 13 Cal. 530.

Birt v. Kershaw, 2 East, 458.   Cited, Costs, 22 Cal. 250. Cited as overruled, 3 Conn. 105.

Bishop v. Halsey, 3 Abb. Pr. 400; S. C. 13 How. Pr. 154. Cited, Insolvency, assignment by debtor, 10 Cal. 277; 27 Cal. 315, 316.

Bishop v. Hayward, 4 Term Rep. 470.   Cited, Judgment, must be sustained by complaint, 30 Cal. 489.

Bishop v. Mayor of Macon, 7 Geo. 200.   Commented on, Municipal Corporations, 1 Cal. 358.

Bishop of Winchester v. Beavor, 3 Ves. Jr. 314.   Cited, Foreclosure, necessary parties, 10 Cal. 552; 11 Cal. 315.

Bishop of Winchester v. Paine, 11 Ves. Jr. 194.   Cited, Foreclosure, necessary parties, 10 Cal. 553; decree in action to redeem, 34 Cal. 655.

Bissel v. Drake, 19 John. 66.   Cited, Pledge, negotiable instrument as collateral, 3 Cal. 164.

Bissell v. Briggs, 9 Mass. 468.   Commented on, Judgment, effect of foreign judgment, 8 Cal. 455, 456.   Doubted, 2 McLean, 473.

Bissel v. Hopkins, 3 Cow. 189.   Commented on, Fraudulent Conveyances, 29 Cal. 477.   Cited, 1 Tex. 425.

Bissel v. Payn, 20 John. 3.   Cited, Foreclosure, title of purchaser at execution sale, 9 Cal. 412.   Commented on, 31 Cal. 300, 302.

Bissell v. Michigan S. & N. S. R.R. Co., 22 N. Y. 262. Approved, Stare Decisis, as to matters of practice, 36 Cal. 49. Commented on and approved, Corporations, acts *ultra vires*, 37 Cal. 578, 580, 587; corporation estopped from setting up defense of *ultra vires*, Id. 579.

Bissell v. N. Y. Cent. R.R. Co., 25 N. Y. 442. Disapproved, Common Carriers, restricting clause in contract construed, 27 Cal. 45, 46.

Bissell v. Penrose, 8 How. 317. Approved, Mexican Grants, title in confirmee, 13 Cal. 412; segregation and survey of, Id. 413. Cited, 1 Black, 189.

Bixby v. Franklin Ins. Co., 8 Pick. 86. Cited, Evidence, ship's register as evidence of ownership, 1 Cal. 482.

Black v. Paul, 10 Mo. 103. Cited, Assignment, order when an assignment, 12 Cal. 98.

Black v. Shaw, 20 Cal. 68. Cited, Judgment, entry of *nunc pro tunc* on death of party, 21 Cal. 609.

Black v. Zacharie, 3 How. 511. Cited, Assignment, of chose in action, when creditors cannot attach, 11 Cal. 349.

Blackburn v. Scholes, 2 Camp. 343. Cited, Principal and Agent, payment to agent of undisclosed principal, 18 Cal. 495.

Blackham, Case of, 1 Salk. 290. Distinguished, Probate, judgments conclusive, 29 Cal. 521.

Blackley v. Sheldon, 7 John. 33. Cited, Verdict, polling jury in civil cases, 20 Cal. 71.

Blackman v. Pierce, 23 Cal. 508. Cited, Stoppage *in transitu*, carrier when liable for conversion, 37 Cal. 632.

Blackman v. Simmons, 3 Carr. & P. 138. Cited, Injuries, ferocious animal, 41 Cal. 141.

Blackamore's Case, 4 Coke, 156. Cited, Amendment, power of court over its records and judgments, 25 Cal. 51, 53.

Blackwell v. Atkinson, 14 Cal. 470. Approved, Witness, vendor with warranty, not a competent witness as to title of vendee, 22 Cal. 603.

Blade v. Noland, 12 Wend. 174. Approved, Evidence, secondary, of lost instrument, when admissible, 9 Cal. 448.

4

Blair v. Hamilton, 32 Cal. 49. Cited in dissenting opinion, Certiorari, return of writ, 32 Cal. 585; 34 Cal. 362; evidence of proceedings in justice's court, 34 Cal. 328. Commented on, Appeal, undertaking, 38 Cal. 603.

Blair v. Smith, 16 Mo. 273. Approved, Boundary, line by agreement, binding upon parties, 25 Cal. 630.

Blair v. Wallace, 21 Cal. 317. Distinguished, Arbitration, submission to, 42 Cal. 483.

Blake v. Bunbury, 4 Bro. Ch. Cas. 24. Commented on, Will, election under devise, 29 Cal. 347.

Blake v. Clark, 6 Greenl. 436. Cited, Conveyances, construction of, what passes, 15 Cal. 197.

Blake v. Doherty, 5 Wheat. 359. Cited, Evidence, private survey ineffectual, 11 Cal. 142; Deed, sufficiency of description in, 12 Cal. 166.

Blake v. Ferris, 5 N. Y. 48. Approved and applied, *Respondeat Superior*, rule of, 8 Cal. 489; superior not liable for acts of employés of contractor, Id. 492. Cited, 3 Gray, 364.

Blake v. Howe, 1 Aiken, 306. Approved, New Trial, surprise, what must be shown, 19 Cal. 36; 32 Cal. 212.

Blanc v. Bowman, 22 Cal. 24. Approved, Appeal, rehearing, practice, 24 Cal. 191. Cited, Remittitur, loss of jurisdiction on its transmission, 24 Cal 58.

Blanc v. Klumpke, 29 Cal. 156. Cited, Nuisance, concurrent jurisdiction, 30 Cal. 585; private action, when it lies, 36 Cal. 195; 40 Cal. 406; Pleading, ambiguity and uncertain, waived by failure to demur, 36 Cal. 196.

Blanc v. Lafayette, 11 How. 104. Cited, Mexican Grant, validity of floating grant, 3 Cal. 42.

Blanchard v. Beideman, 18 Cal. 261. Cited, Street Assessments, pleading, what complaint must show, 35 Cal. 448.

Blanchard v. Brooks, 12 Pick. 47. Cited, Conveyances without warranty, construed, 11 Cal. 160; with warranty attached to grantor's present interest, 25 Cal. 452. See 3 Wheat. 449.

Blanchard v. Hill, 2 Atk. 484. Cited, Trade Marks, right to, 29 Cal. 295. Cited, 4 McLean, 517.

Blanchard v. Russell, 13 Mass. 1.   Cited, Conflict of Laws, comity between States, 9 Cal. 166; validity of State laws, 10 Cal. 572; of State insolvent laws, 37 Cal. 210. Commented on, 7 Cush. 33.

Bland v. Ansley, 2 Bosanq. & P. N. R. 331.   Cited, Witness, competency of, vendor of chattel, 23 Cal. 446.

Blandford v. Foote, 1 Cowp. 138.   Approved, Bankruptcy, effect of discharge on prior judgments, 14 Cal. 175.

Blanding v. Burr, 13 Cal. 343.   Cited, Legislature, power over municipal corporations, to regulate local taxes, 16 Cal. 345; 18 Cal. 631; 41 Cal. 530; 42 Cal. 450.   Commented on, 17 Cal. 31; 35 Cal. 632; and to make special appropriations from municipal funds, 17 Cal. 31; 26 Cal. 650; 27 Cal. 209; 28 Cal. 395; 30 Cal. 438; 35 Cal. 632; 41 Cal. 530; 42 Cal. 450; to authorize issuance of bonds, 25 Cal. 646.   Approved as to legislative power over local taxation generally, 2 Neb. 501; 17 Wis. 684; 29 Wis. 674.

Blaney v. Bearce, 2 Greenl. 137.   Distinguished, 6 Greenl. 238.   Cited, Mortgage, rights of mortgagor and mortgagee to possession, 9 Cal. 407.

——— **v. Moor**, 1 Maule & S. 284.   Cited, Libel and Slander, evidence in mitigation, 41 Cal. 384.

Blankman v. Vallejo, 15 Cal. 638.   Cited, Pleading, evasive denials in answer, 22 Cal. 168; 31 Cal. 194; 38 Cal. 290.

Blanton v. King, 2 How. Miss. 856.   Cited, Probate Court, jurisdiction not exclusive, 12 Cal. 435.

Blatchford v. N. Y. & N. H. R. R. Co., 7 Abb. Pr. 322. Cited, Injunction practice, contesting motion to dissolve, 35 Cal. 59.

Bledsoe v. Well, 4 Bibb, 329.   Cited, Void Patent, 16 Cal. 325.   Reviewed, impeachment of void patent, Id. 326. Doubted, 1 Tex. 728.

Bleecker v. Ballou, 3 Wend. 263.   Cited, Street Assessments, personal liability, 31 Cal. 678.

Bleecker v. Smith, 13 Wend. 530.   Cited, Landlord and Tenant, receipt of rent, a waiver of forfeiture, 25 Cal. 394.

Blen v. Bear Riv. and A. W. & M. Co., 20 Cal. 602.   Cited, Corporation, ratification by, burden of proof, 10 Abb. Pr. N. S. 49.

Blessing v. Lessee of House, 3 Gill & J. 290.   Cited, Municipal Corporations, effect of confirmation of void act, 24 Cal. 605.

Blight's Lessee v. Rochester, 7 Wheat. 535.   Cited, Estoppel, landlord and tenant, disputing landlord's title, 2 Cal. 560; vendee may dispute vendor's title, 18 Cal. 476.

Blin v. Pierce, 20 Vt. 25.   Cited, Assignment, rights of assignees, 12 Cal. 98.

Bliss v. Wyman, 7 Cal. 257.   Approved, Malicious Prosecution, defense of action under advice of counsel, 35 Ill. 507.

Blood v. Goodrich, 12 Wend. 525.   Cited, Principal and Agent, ratification by principal, 14 Cal. 400.

Blood v. Light, 31 Cal. 115.   Cited, Pleading, evasive denials, 38 Cal. 290.

Blood v. Light, 38 Cal. 649.   Cited, Execution, not subject to collateral attack, 38 Cal. 382.   Approved, that presumptions are in favor of validity of sale, 13 Wall. 514.

Blood v. Sayre, 17 Vt. 609.   Cited, Taxation, *situs* of personal property, 23 Cal. 139.

Bloodgood v. Bruen, 8 N. Y. 362.   Cited, Probate, partnership property, 26 Cal. 67.

Bloodgood v. Mohawk & H. R. R. Co., 14 Wend. 51.   Commented on, Condemnation of land, 31 Cal. 554.   Cited, Railroads, are public highways, Id. 371.

Bloodgood v. Mohawk & H. R. R. Co., 18 Wend. 9.   Approved, Eminent Domain, exercise of right by agent of legislature, 31 Cal. 372; 41 Cal. 179; compensation to be provided before condemnation, 12 Cal. 529; 13 Cal. 318; 31 Cal. 372.

Bloom v. Burdick, 1 Hill, 130.   Affirmed, 2 N. Y. 461.   Reviewed and approved, Probate proceedings essential to confer jurisdiction on application for sale of real estate, 7 Cal. 235; requisites of petition, 13 Cal. 577; 19 Cal. 208, 409; strict compliance with statute essential, 20 Cal. 312, 314; 31 Cal. 349, 356.   Cited, Jurisdiction, no intendments in favor of courts of inferior jurisdiction, 25 Cal. 309; judgment must show jurisdiction, 31 Cal. 348; facts on which it depends must appear, 31 Cal. 356; 33 Cal. 536.

Bloom v. Richards, 2 Ohio St. 387. Approved, Constitutionality of Statute, Sunday laws, 9 Cal. 525. Cited, 18 Cal. 681; 2 West Va. 395.

Bludworth v. Lake, 33 Cal. 255. Cited, Mortgage, a mere security, 36 Cal. 39; constructive trust, 38 Cal. 92.

Blue v. Kibby, 1 Mon. 195. Cited, Witness, impeachment of, 27 Cal. 636.

Blum v. Robertson, 24 Cal. 127. Cited, Pleading, equitable defenses must be specially pleaded, 25 Cal. 597; 4 Nev. 460; with fulness and particularity, 26 Cal. 39; defendant thereupon becomes actor, 42 Cal. 352; Powers, party bound to know powers of agent, 29 Cal. 188; Specific Performance, when decreed, 39 Cal. 301.

Board, Ex parte, 4 Cow. 420. Cited, Redemption, payment to sheriff, 26 Cal. 663.

Board of Commissioners v. Younger, 29 Cal. 172. Cited, Equity, relief in, when not granted, 29 Cal. 449; rescission of contract for sale of land, 35 Cal. 726.

Board of Education v. Fowler, 19 Cal. 11. Cited, San Francisco, title under Van Ness Ordinance, 28 Cal. 223; pueblo lands held in trust, 42 Cal. 556.

Boardman v. Gore, 15 Mass. 331. Cited, Felony, conviction as a suspension of civil rights, 1 Cal. 435. Criticised, 4 Me. 166. Cited, 1 Gray, 97.

Boardman v. Lessees of Reed, 6 Pet. 328. Cited, Mexican Grant, patent not subject to collateral attack, 29 Cal. 311.

Bode v. State, 7 Gill, 326. Cited, Constitutionality of Statute, Sunday laws, 18 Cal. 681.

Bodley v. Ferguson, 30 Cal. 511. Cited, Husband and Wife, statute concerning, not retrospective, 32 Cal. 383. Commented on, Conveyances, contracts to convey, by married women, Id. 384, 385; 40 Cal. 562; Pleading, equitable defense in ejectment, 32 Cal. 652; in action to quiet title, 40 Cal. 566.

Bodwell v. Osgood, 3 Pick. 379. Approved, New Trial, excessive damages in tort, 24 Cal. 517.

Bodwell v. Webster, 13 Pick. 411. Cited, Mortgage, by deed and defeasance, 33 Cal. 332.

Bogard v. Gardley, 4 Smedes & M. 302. Cited, Fraudulent Conveyances, 13 Cal. 72.

Bogardus v. Clark, 4 Paige, 625. Cited, Probate of will of personalty conclusive, 20 Cal. 270.

Bogert v. Burkhalter, 2 Barb. 525. Cited, Pleading, nuisance, special damages must be particularly stated, 41 Cal. 565.

Boggs v. Fowler & Hargrave, 16 Cal. 559. Cited, Mortgage, not a conveyance, 18 Cal. 488; foreclosure, necessary parties in, 18 Cal. 475; decree in, effect, when grantee of mortgagor not a party, 21 Cal. 92; 25 Cal. 161; when no notice actual or constructive has been given, 24 Cal. 562; foreclosure sale, purchaser not entitled to relief, 21 Cal. 92. Affirmed, as to doctrine of *caveat emptor*, 24 Cal. 608; 2 Nev. 289. Questioned, as to vacation of sale, 36 Cal. 399. Cited, Power of court over its judgments, 37 Cal. 228. Referred to, 23 Cal. 630.

Boggs v. Merced Min. Co., 14 Cal. 279. Cited, Mexican Grants, confirmation of, on whom conclusive, 24 Cal. 669; 26 Cal. 627; United States Patent, not subject to collateral attack, 14 Cal. 469; 22 Cal. 111; 1 Saw. 569; by alleging fraudulent survey, 18 Cal. 435; nature of proceedings to set aside patent, 7 Wall. 228; Mineral Lands, U. S. patent carries title to minerals, 18 Cal. 435; no legal license from Government to extract minerals, 14 Cal. 464. Approved, Mining Claims, possessory right sufficient to maintain action to quiet title, 35 Cal. 34. Commented on and approved, Estoppel, from assertion of title, by party's admissions, 16 Cal. 626; 23 Cal. 15; 23 Cal. 308; 24 Cal. 281. Affirmed on this point, 17 Cal. 402. Construed and adopted, 26 Cal. 40; and cited, 31 Cal. 153, 494; 37 Cal. 50; 38 Cal. 315; 13 Wall. 432.

Bogy v. Shoab, 13 Mo. 365. Cited, Deed, construction of, 30 Cal. 347.

Bohr v. Steamboat Baton Rouge, 7 Smedes & M. 715. Cited, Appeal, errors without injury, 26 Cal. 467.

Boileau v. Rutlin, 2 Ex. R. 665. Cited, New Trial, erroneous admission of evidence, 35 Cal. 361.

Boissier v. Metayer, 5 Mart. O. S. 678. Cited, Grant, conditional grants, 14 Cal. 605.

Boker v. Chapline, 12 Iowa, 205. Cited, Judgment, collateral attack on, 34 Cal. 428.

Bolander v. Stevens, 23 Wend. 103. Overruled, 1 Denio, 14. Commented on, Statutes, impeachment of, pleading, 30 Cal. 263.

Bole v. Horton, Vaughn, 382. Cited, Judicial Opinions, dicta, 4 Cal. 156; 9 Id. 733.

Boles v. Johnson, Cal. Sup. Ct. Jan. T. 1860 (not reported.) Cited, Ejectment, pleading sufficiency of complaint, 16 Cal. 247.

Boles v. Welfenback, 15 Cal. 144. Cited, Ejectment, pleading sufficiency of complaint, 15 Cal. 151.

Bollman and Swartwout, Case of, 4 Cranch, 75. Cited, Supreme Court, power to issue writ of habeas corpus, 1 Cal. 147.

Bolt v. Rogers, 3 Paige, 154. Cited, Fraudulent Conveyance, as to creditors, valid as between grantor and grantee, 27 Cal. 316.

Bolton v. Landers, 27 Cal. 104. Cited, Replevin, pleading, effect of, denial of title in answer, 38 Cal. 512.

Bolton v. Stewart, 29 Cal. 615. Cited, Appeal, review of order granting or refusing new trial, 38 Cal. 506; 5 Kan. 238.

Bonaparte v. Camden & A. R.R. Co., 1 Bald. C. C. 205. Cited, Injunction, restraining injury to land, 13 Cal. 313; constitutionality of Statute, retroactive statutes void, 25 Cal. 311; Eminent Domain, compensation to owner concomitant and inseparable, 31 Cal. 372.

Bond v. Bond, 7 Allen, 1. Cited, Insanity, proof of, 27 Cal. 381.

Bond v. Pacheco, 30 Cal. 530. Cited, Jurisdiction, of judge at chambers, 34 Cal. 332; 35 Cal. 691; Default, acts of clerk ministerial, 32 Cal. 636; 3 Or. 252.

Bond v. The Supervisors, Cal. Sup. Ct. (not reported.) Cited, Municipal Corporations, appropriations by, 17 Cal. 462.

Bond v. Ward, 7 Mass. 123. Cited, Indemnity, sheriff entitled to, before execution of writ, 36 Cal. 459.

Bonds v. Hickman, 29 Cal. 460. Affirmed, Patent, issued to administrator, valid, 32 Cal. 204; appeal, record not amendable in Supreme Court, 36 Cal. 521.

Bonner v. State of Georgia, 7 Geo. 481. Cited, Mandamus, 16 Cal. 45.

Bonsall v. Town of Lebanon, 19 Ohio, 418. Cited, Street Improvements, liability of owner for repairs, 12 Cal. 478; 31 Cal. 684.

Bonsteel v. Vanderbilt, 21 Barb. 26. Cited, Amendments, during trial, 29 Cal. 640.

Boody v. Keating, 4 Greenl. 164. Doubted, Felony, conviction for, as a suspension of civil rights, 1 Cal. 434.

Boody v. McKenney, 23 Me. 517. Disapproved, Infancy, disaffirmance of acts must be within a reasonable time after majority, 24 Cal. 213, 216.

Boomer v. Laine, 10 Wend. 527. Cited, Jurisdiction, evidence *aliunde* the record, when admissible, 34 Cal. 327.

Boon v. Murphy, 6 Blackf. 273. Cited, Vendor's Lien, waived by taking security, 17 Cal. 74.

Boone v. Chiles, 10 Pet. 177. Cited, Trust, when statute of limitations runs in favor of trustee, 36 Cal. 433; of trustee by implication, 40 Cal. 571.

Boos v. Ewing, 17 Ohio, 521. Doubted, Vendor's Lien, waiver of, 12 Cal. 305.

Booth v. Barnum, 9 Conn. 286. Cited, Mortgage, for future advances, valid, 19 Cal. 351.

Booth v. Commonwealth, 7 Met. 286. Cited, Law of the case, previous decision not revisable, 15 Cal. 83.

Booth v. Lord Warrington, 4 Bro. Parl. Cas. 163. Cited, Statute of Limitations, fraudulent concealment stops running of statute, 8 Cal. 458.

Booth v. Town of Woodbury, 32 Conn. 128. Commented on, Legislature, power over taxation and appropriation conclusive, 41 Cal. 172. Commented on, 1 Bush, 593.

Bootle v. Blundell, 1 Mer. 230. Cited, Will, devise of lands mortgaged, charge on general assets, 31 Cal. 600.

Borden v. Fitch, 15 John. 140. Cited, Judgment, rendered against absentee defendant, 8 Cal. 457.

Borden v. Manchester, 4 Mason, 112. Cited, Dedication, to public use, how evinced, 14 Cal. 649.

Borel v. Rollins, 30 Cal. 408. Cited, Land Title by possession, actual and adverse, 41 Cal. 582.

Boren v. Chisholm, 3 Ala. 513. Cited, Injunction, legal remedy after dissolution, 15 Cal. 111.

Borkheim v. N. B. and M. Ins. Co., 38 Cal. 623. Distinguished, Practice, verbal stipulations, when binding, 40 Cal. 126.

Borland v. Mayo, 8 Ala. 112. Cited, Witness, competency of, vendor of chattels, 8 Cal. 327; 23 Cal. 447.

Borland v. O'Neal, 22 Cal. 504. Affirmed, Execution, selection of exempt property, when waived, 23 Cal. 82.

Borland v. Thornton, 12 Cal. 440. Approved, Injunction, enjoining enforcement of judgment, 20 Cal. 449. Cited, Power of County Judge to grant injunction is auxiliary to jurisdiction, 27 Cal. 152. Commented on, Order granting, made *ex parte*, may be vacated without notice, 33 Cal. 390. Cited, Notice defined, 24 Cal. 365; 2 Nev. 40; Equity, relief not granted where there is a remedy by motion, 37 Cal. 228.

Borland v. Walker, 7 Ala. 280. Cited, Fraudulent Conveyance, *ab initio*, is void, 18 Cal. 170.

Borst v. Beecker, 6 John. 332. Cited, Alienage, 30 Cal. 189.

Bosanquet v. Wray, 6 Taunt. 597. Cited, Debtor and Creditor, application of payments, 14 Cal. 449.

Boston v. Binney, 11 Pick. 1. Cited, Use and Occupation, action founded on contract, 3 Cal. 202; denial of title a termination of tenancy, 3 Cal. 204.

Boston v. Haynes, 31 Cal. 107. Cited, Appeal, notice when to be filed, 33 Cal. 317; record not amendable in Supreme Court, 36 Cal. 521. Approved, that filing must precede or be contemporaneous with service of notice, 8 Nev. 178.

Boston v. Haynes, 33 Cal. 31. Cited, Foreclosure, Parties, subsequent incumbrancers proper but not necessary parties, 40 Cal. 235.

Boston and Sandwich G. Co. v. Boston, 4 Met. 189. Cited, Money paid, under mistake of law, not recoverable, cognizance of law presumed, 18 Cal. 271.

Boston Wat. Pow. Co. v. Boston & W. R. R., 23 Pick. 395. Cited, Eminent Domain, exclusive power in legislature, 18 Cal. 252.

Bostwick v. Leach, 3 Day, 476. Cited, Statute of Frauds, sale of growing crops not within, 23 Cal. 69.

Bostwick v. Lewis, 1 Day, 250.   Cited, False Representations, on sale of land, 9 Cal. 227.

Bostwick v. McCorkle, 22 Cal. 669.   Overruled, Exceptions, as to acquiescence in decision on demurrer.

Boswell v. Laird, 8 Cal. 469.   Cited, Negligence, liability for injuries, *respondeat superior*, 29 Cal. 249; 38 Cal. 634; 40 Ill. 436.   Commented on and approved, Id. 692; County not liable for negligence of sub-employés, 2 Neb. 342.

Bosworth v. Danzien, 25 Cal. 296.   Cited, Error, when immaterial, 33 Cal. 513.

Botsford v. Burr, 2 Johns. Ch. 404.   Cited, Trust, resulting trust, proportional interest on part payment of consideration, 21 Cal. 99; 38 Cal. 193; resulting trust, when it arises, 40 Cal. 637.

Bottomly v. Grace Church, 2 Cal. 90.   Approved, Mechanic's Lien, by material man, showing required, 5 Cal. 240.   Cited, Statutory Construction, lien laws to be strictly construed, 16 Cal. 127; 29 Cal. 286; 13 Gray, 132; 1 McAll. 515.

Bottorf v. Conner, 1 Blackf. 287.   Disapproved, Vendor's Lien, enforcement of, 15 Cal. 193.

Bouchaud v. Dias, 3 Denio, 238.   Cited, Surety, release of one is a discharge of all, 11 Cal. 220.

Boucher v. Wiseman, 1 Croke, 440.   Cited, Execution, title of purchaser at sheriff's sale, 38 Cal. 656.

Bouchier v. Taylor, 4 Bro. Cas. in P. 708.   Reviewed, Probate, judgments conclusive, 29 Cal. 523.

Boulton v. Bull, 2 H. Blacks. 463.   Cited, Legislative Grants, construed, 13 Cal. 456.

Boulware v. Craddock, 30 Cal. 190.   Cited, Claim and Delivery, demand when not necessary, 38 Cal. 584.

Bourke v. Booquet, 1 Desaus. 142.   Cited, Specific Performance, waiver of demand and tender, 25 Cal. 281.

Bourland v. Hildreth, 26 Cal. 161.   Cited, Constitutional Construction, 29 Cal. 482; powers of Government, State and Federal, 41 Cal. 162.   Approved, Statutory Construction, constitutionality of general laws, 31 Cal. 263.   Cited, 32 Cal. 527; 33 Cal. 281; 35 Cal. 199; 37 Cal. 375; 38 Cal. 710.

Bourne v. Gatliffe, 3 Man. & G. 643. Cited, Written Instruments, extrinsic evidence to explain terms, 34 Cal. 629.

Bours v. Webster, 6 Cal. 660. Affirmed, Statute of Frauds, sale of growing crops, 17 Cal. 545. Cited, 37 Cal. 638.

Bouteflour v. Coates, 1 Cowp. 25. Cited, Bankruptcy, effect of discharge, 14 Cal. 175.

Bouton v. Neilson, 3 John. 475. Cited, Street Assessments, acquiescence by neglect to appeal, 29 Cal. 87.

Bovill v. Wood, 2 Man. & S. 23. Cited, Judgment, several judgment on joint demand, 1 Cal. 169.

Bowdell v. Parsons, 10 East, 364. Cited, Default, irregularities and omissions cured by, 6 Cal. 174.

Bowen v. Aubrey, 22 Cal. 566. Cited, Pleading, complaint, 23 Cal. 112; Mechanic's Lien, sub-contractors have no lien, 27 Cal. 594; extent of their lien under act of 1862, 36 Cal. 298.

Bowen v. Bell, 20 John. 338. Cited, Deed, parol proof of consideration, 36 Cal. 370.

Bowen, Estate of, 34 Cal. 682. Cited, Jurisdiction, trial of issues in probate court, 35 Cal. 510.

Bowen v. Lease, 5 Hill, 221. Approved, Statutory Construction, repeal by implication not favored, 18 Cal. 442; 26 Cal. 382; 35 Cal. 709.

Bowerbank v. Morris, Wall. C. C. 118. Cited, Office, removal from, 10 Cal. 117.

Bower v. Higbee, 9 Mo. 256. Cited, Public Lands, inchoate rights of settlers upon, 30 Cal. 650. Approved, 37 Cal. 493; title vests only on payment, Id. 502.

Bowes v. Howe, 5 Taunt. 30. Commented on and declared not authority; Negotiable Instruments, demand at time and place of payment, 11 Cal. 319, 325.

Bowie v. Duvall, 1 Gill & J. 181. Cited, Negotiable Instruments, demand, place of payment, in note, 11 Cal. 324.

Bowker v. Hoyt, 18 Pick. 555. Cited, Pleading, recoupment, damages to be specially alleged in answer, 1 Cal. 54.

Bowler v. Lane, 3 Met. Ky. 313. Cited, Death by Wrongful Act, measure of damages, 42 Cal. 218.

Bowman v. Cudworth, 31 Cal. 148. Cited, Estoppel, in pais, 31 Cal. 440; 38 Cal. 316; Title, surrender or destruction of deed does not revest title, 33 Cal. 693; 34 Cal. 38; 37 Cal. 207.

Bowman v. Ely, 2 Wend. 250. Cited, Place of Trial, grounds for change of venue, 21 Cal. 265.

Bowman v. Middleton, 1 Bay, 252. Cited, Constitutionality of Statute, retrospective statutes, 25 Cal. 311.

Bowman v. Norton, 16 Cal. 213. Cited, Homestead, 23 Cal. 74; reviewed, mortgage on, 23 Cal. 121; judgment no lien on, 23 Cal. 400. Affirmed, Homestead Right, under statute prior to act of 1860, 31 Cal. 531.

Bowman v. Wood, 15 Mass. 534. Cited, Pledge, of negotiable instrument, 37 Cal. 25.

Bowman's Devisees v. Wathen, 2 McLean, 376. Cited, Ferry Rights, when regarded as realty, 32 Cal. 507, 508. Disapproved, 1 Or. 36.

Bowyer v. Bampton, 2 Str. 1155. Disapproved, Negotiable Instruments, validity of gaming notes in hands of innocent holder, 2 Cal. 66.

Boyce v. Anderson, 2 Pet. 150. Questioned, Common Carriers, liability of owners of stage coaches for injuries, 13 Cal. 603.

Boyce v. California Stage Co., 25 Cal. 460. Cited, Negligence, damages for personal injuries, burden of proof, 27 Cal. 430; *prima facie* evidence of negligence, 28 Cal. 628; Verdict, affidavits of jurors when not admissible to impeach, 29 Cal. 262; Instructions, court may modify or refuse instructions presented, 30 Cal. 450; 32 Cal. 288.

Boyce v. Holmes, 2 Ala. 54. Cited, Statutory Construction, statutes not to be construed to give a retrospective effect, 4 Cal. 135, 137.

Boyce v. Russell, 2 Cow. 444. Cited, Supervisors, powers of, 16 Cal. 212.

Boyd v. Anderson, 1 Overton, 438. Approved, Money paid, on invalid warrant may be recovered back, 22 Cal. 463.

Boyd v. Blankman, 29 Cal. 19. Cited, Statute of Limitations, begins to run only from discovery of fraud, 34 Cal. 258.

Boyd, Estate of, 25 Cal. 511. Cited, Practice, new trial, and appeal, 27 Cal. 112; statement on questions of law, 34 Cal. 605.

Boyd v. Hoyt, 5 Paige, 78. Cited, Parties, to be brought in, in equity, 31 Cal. 429.

Boyd v. Martin, 10 Ala. 700. Cited, Undertaking, action on bond securing several obligees creates several liability, 10 Cal. 351.

Boyd v. McLean, 1 Johns. Ch. 582. Cited, Resulting Trust, parol evidence admissible to prove, 13 Cal. 131; evidence necessary to establish, 27 Cal. 140, 144. Distinguished, 40 Cal. 637.

Boyd v. Plumb, 7 Wend. 309. Cited, Partnership, authority of partner to bind firm, 37 Cal. 117.

Boyd v. Siffkin, 2 Camp. 326. Cited, Contract, sale of goods to arrive, construed, 1 Cal. 447.

Boydell v. Drummond, 11 East, 157. Cited, Evidence, parol evidence of written contract, 37 Cal. 65.

Boyden v. Boyden, 9 Met. 519. Approved, Infancy, ratification of purchase by infant, 24 Cal. 216.

Boyd's Lessee v. Graves, 4 Wheat. 513. Approved, Lands, acquiescence in division line, 25 Cal. 627.

Boyreau v. Campbell, 1 McAll. 119. Referred to, 17 Cal. 621; ejectment, 19 Cal. 387; execution for costs of suit, 23 Cal. 99; satisfaction of, 32 Cal. 135, 136.

Brace v. Duchess of Marlborough, 2 P. Wm. 491. Cited, Judgment, lien of, 37 Cal. 133.

Brace v. Shaw, 16 B. Mon. 82. Cited, Execution, writ when voidable, 38 Cal. 380.

Bracken v. Miller, 4 Watts & S. 102. Cited, Principal and Agent, notice to agent is notice to principal, 31 Cal. 165.

Bracket v. McNair, 14 John. 170. Counter-claim, loss of profits on contract, 26 Cal. 307.

Brackett v. Wait, 6 Vt. 426. Cited, Deed, consideration may be explained by parol evidence, 6 Cal. 137.

Bradbury v. Dougherty, 7 Blackf. 467. Cited, Witness, competency of, vendor of chattel, 23 Cal. 446.

Braddee v. Brownfield, 2 Watts & S. 271. Commented on, Legislature, powers restricted only by constitutional limits, 7 Cal. 21; legislative supremacy, 17 Cal. 562.

Bradfield v. Tupper, 7 Eng. L. & E. 541. Cited, New Promise, by part payment, 17 Cal. 577.

Bradford v. Bradford, 5 Conn. 132. Cited, Judgment, in ejectment, conclusive, 26 Cal. 503.

Bradford v. Bryan, 1 Willes, 270. Commented on, Arbitration, submission to, 12 Cal. 342.

Bradford v. Haynes, 20 Me. 108. Approved, Will, specific bequest defined, 31 Cal. 601.

Bradford v. Manly, 13 Mass. 144. Cited, Warranty, in sale of chattels implied, 4 Cal. 21.

Bradish v. Schenck, 8 John. 151. Cited, Agreements, renting on shares, 23 Cal. 521.

Bradley v. Amidon, 10 Paige, 239. Approved, Parties, action by infant to be in his name, but by his guardian, 32 Cal. 117.

Bradley v. Bardsley, 14 Mees. & W. 878. Cited, Pleading, defense of omission of revenue stamp, 34 Cal. 175.

Bradley v. Baxter, 15 Barb. 122. Cited, Constitutionality of Statutes, conditional legislation, 17 Cal. 32; 13 Gratt. 97.

Bradley v. Bosley, 1 Barb. Ch. 152. Approved, Vendor's Lien, enforcement of, 15 Cal. 193.

Bradley v. Bradley, 24 Mo. 311. Cited, Wills, cannot be varied by parol evidence, 35 Cal. 340.

Bradley v. Harkness, 26 Cal. 69. Cited, Mining Partnerships, what constitute, 28 Cal. 587; 42 Cal. 642; stockholders, in the nature of tenants in common, 35 Cal. 369.

Bradley v. McCrabb, Dallam, 504. Approved, Office, term of, 11 Cal. 88.

Bradley v. McDaniel, 3 Jones N. C. 128. Cited, Ejectment, who bound by judgment, 22 Cal. 207.

Bradley v. N. Y. & N. H. R. R. Co., 21 Conn. 294. Cited, Eminent Domain, exercise of right through agents of Government or directly through medium of corporations, 31 Cal. 372.

Bradley v. Root, 5 Paige, 632. Cited, Assignment, legal effect of order, 8 Cal. 105; order as an equitable assignment, 14 Cal. 407.

Bradshaw v. Callaghan, 8 John. 563. Cited, Partition, proper parties in action, 35 Cal. 593.

Bradshaw v. Rodgers, 20 John. 103. Cited, Eminent Domain, compensation concomitant and inseparable from right, 31 Cal. 373.

Bradshaw v. Treat, 6 Cal. 172. Cited, Public Lands, rights of settlers on, 23 Cal. 537.

Bradstreet, Ex parte, 7 Pet. 634. Cited, Mandamus, jurisdiction of Supreme Court, 1 Cal. 147.

Bradstreet v. Huntington, 5 Pet. 402. Cited, Ejectment, disseisin by tenant in common, 24 Cal. 377. Approved, Title by adverse possession, 34 Cal. 382; 36 Cal. 541. See 5 Wall. 213.

Bradstreet v. Supervisors of Oneida Co., 13 Wend. 546. Cited, Alien, power to hold real property under common law, 5 Cal. 378; under civil law, 26 Cal. 477.

Brady v. Mayor, etc., of Brooklyn, 1 Barb. 584. Distinguished, Street Improvements, liability of city under charter, 7 Cal. 474; 9 Cal. 472.

Brady v. Mayor, etc., of New York, 2 Bosw. 173; S. C. 16 How. Pr. 432. Approved, Municipal Corporations, ratification of contract, 20 Cal. 103; power of officers to bind by contract, 29 Cal. 188.

Brady v. McCosker, 1 N. Y. 214. Cited, Practice, dismissal of suit on disclaimer, 17 Cal. 270.

Brady v. Reynolds, 13 Cal. 31. Cited, Guarantor, on note, 34 Cal. 675.

Brady v. Spurck, 27 Ill. 478. Cited, Covenants, breach of warranty, what constitutes eviction, 39 Cal. 367.

Brady v. Supervisors of N. Y., 2 Sand. 460. Distinguished, Actions against counties, 6 Cal. 256.

Brady v. Waldron, 2 John. Ch. 147. Cited, Mortgage, right of mortgagee to restrain waste by mortgagor in possession, 14 Cal. 633; 27 Cal. 436.

Bradyll v. Ball, 1 Bro. Ch. 427. Cited, Attachment, possession obtained by replevin does not divest lien of, 11 Cal. 272; 1 N. Y. 166.

Brainard v. Bushnell, 11 Conn. 17. Cited, Time, point of time, of performance of act, when to be proved, 1 Cal. 408.

Brainard v. Cooper, 10 N. Y. 356. Cited, Foreclosure, parties, 40 Cal. 238.

Braly v. Seaman, 30 Cal. 610. Overruled, Judgment Roll, what constitutes, 34 Cal. 404, 421.

Braman v. Hess, 13 John. 52. Cited, Negotiable Instruments, measure of recovery by indorsee, 16 Cal. 160.

Bramwell v. Lucas, 2 Barn. & C. 745. Cited, Witness, privileged communications, 23 Cal. 334.

Branch Bank at Decatur v. Kinsey, 5 Ala. 12. Cited, Evidence, recitals in deed as, 26 Cal. 87.

Brandt v. Ogden, 1 John. 156. Cited, Deed, calls in, 25 Cal. 298. Approved, Adverse Possession, successive possessions, 37 Cal. 354.

Branger v. Chevalier, 9 Cal. 172. Cited, Jurisdiction, to set aside judgment, lost on adjournment of term, 28 Cal. 338.

Branger v. Manciet, 30 Cal. 624. Cited, Landlord and Tenant, lessor not bound to make repairs, without express covenant, 33 Cal. 347.

Branham v. Mayor, etc., of San Jose, 24 Cal. 585. Cited, Municipal Corporations, contracts of, 29 Cal. 188; San Francisco, tenure of pueblo lands of a judiciary nature, 42 Cal. 556.

Brannan v. Mesick, 10 Cal. 95. Cited, Deed, construction of, 12 Cal. 25; 26 Cal. 112.

Brannin v. Johnson, 19 Me. 361. Approved, Trespass, measure of damages, 11 Cal. 25; 14 Cal. 557.

Brashier v. Gratz, 6 Wheat. 528. Cited, Specific Performance, time as essence of contract, 10 Cal. 329; 40 Cal. 11, 13.

Brass Crosby, Case of, 3 Wils. 188. Cited, Legislature, jurisdiction in, contempts, 29 Cal. 400.

Bratton v. Clawson, 2 Strob. 478. Cited, Fixtures, 10 Cal. 264.

Bray v. Redman, 6 Cal. 287. Cited, Appeal, from justice's court, fees of justice, 9 Cal. 573.

Brazier, Case of, 1 Leach, 199. Cited, Witnesses, competency of infant, 10 Cal. 67.

Brazier v. Clap, 5 Mass. 10. Cited, Appeal, errors without injury, 26 Cal. 467.

Brazill v. Isham, 12 N. Y. 17. Cited, Ejectment, special pleas, 10 Cal. 27, 30.

Breckbill v. Turnpike Co., 3 Dall. 496. Cited, Corporations, contracts of, at common law, 7 Cal. 381. Disapproved, 4 Serg. & R. 16.

Breckinridges v. Todd, 3 Mon. 54. Cited, Deed, presumption as to delivery, 30 Cal. 72.

Bree v. Holbech, Doug. 655. Commented on, Statute of Limitations, fraud to take case out of, 8 Cal. 458. Cited, 3 Yeates, 534.

Breed v. Cunningham, 2 Cal. 368. Cited, Dedication, of street, 22 Cal. 490.

Breeze v. Doyle, 19 Cal. 101. Cited, Findings, by the court, sufficiency of, 28 Cal. 596; 35 Cal. 35; Verdict, special verdicts, how found, 30 Cal. 286.

Brennan v. Swasey, 16 Cal. 140. Cited, Mechanic's Lien, sufficiency of notice, 17 Cal. 131; 29 Cal. 287. Approved, 8 Nev. 237.

Brennan v. Wallace, 25 Cal. 108. Cited, Homestead, 31 Cal. 531.

Brett v. Levett, 13 East, 213. Cited, Negotiable Instruments, waiver of notice and protest, 7 Cal. 575. Commented on, 5 Leigh, 533.

Brewer v. Boston & Worcester Railroad, 5 Met. 461. Approved, Equitable estoppel, 14 Cal. 370. Cited, 26 Cal. 41. Disapproved, 49 Mo. 101.

Brewer v. Bowman, 9 Geo. 37. Cited, Roads and Highways, constitutionality of statutes, 32 Cal. 255.

Brewer v. Harris, 5 Gratt. 285. Adopted, Statutory Construction, "month" defined, 21 Cal. 396; 31 Cal. 176.

Brewer v. Isiah, 12 How. Pr. 481. Cited, Exceptions, practice, 34 Cal. 686.

Brewer v. Temple, 15 How. Pr. 286. Cited, Pleading, joinder of causes of action, 17 Cal. 498. Overruled, 53 Barb. 244.

5

Brewer v. Thorp, 3 Ind. 262. Cited, Statutory Construction, specific contract act, 26 Cal. 49.

Brewster v. City of Syracuse, 19 N. Y. 116. Cited, Street Assessments, legislative power to direct, 28 Cal. 352; a personal liability, 31 Cal. 677; expense of opening streets a matter for legislative control, 41 Cal. 532.

Brewster v. Ludekins, 19 Cal. 162. Approved, Insolvency, jurisdiction, how obtained, 22 Cal. 42. Cited, 34 Cal. 24; petition, how addressed, 32 Cal. 408; verification, 32 Cal. 409.

Brewster v. Silence, 8 N. Y. 207. Overruled, Statute of Frauds, promise of guarantor when not within, 38 Cal. 136.

Brice v. Smith, Willes, 1. Cited, Will, attestation, intendment from lapse of time, 10 Cal. 479.

Bridenbecker v. Lowell, 32 Barb. 17. Cited, Mining Stock, owner of, bound by acts of trustee, 42 Cal. 147.

Bridge v. Eggleston, 14 Mass. 245. Approved, Evidence, of fraud on sale of goods admissible, 7 Cal. 392. Cited, Declarations of vendor, 12 Cal. 496.

Bridge v. Ford, 4 Mass. 641. Cited, Recognizance, a matter of record, averments in complaint in action on, 30 Cal. 630.

Bridge v. Grand Junction Railway Co., 3 Mees. & W. 244. Cited, Negligence, action for injury to cattle, when it lies, 37 Cal. 423. Criticised, 22 Vt. 223.

Bridge v. Payson, 5 Sand. 210. Cited, Pleading, several defenses in answer, 22 Cal. 679.

Bridgeport v. Housatonic R. R. Co., 15 Conn. 475. Cited, Constitutionality of Statute, statutes granting county aid to railroads, 13 Cal. 188. Approved, 41 Cal. 193. Cited, Legislature, power of taxation, 13 Cal. 355.

Bridges v. Armour, 5 How. 91. Cited, Witness, competency of, party to record, 6 Cal. 195.

Bridges v. Paige, 13 Cal. 640. Approved, Pleading, new matter, what is, 14 Cal. 415.

Brig Sarah Ann, 2 Sum. 211. Cited, Assignment, right of action for wrongful taking assignable, 22 Cal. 142.

Briggs v. Hosford, 22 Pick. 289. Cited, Will, construction of bequest, 31 Cal. 603.

Briggs v. Hill, 6 How. Miss. 362. Cited, Vendor's Lien, not assignable, 21 Cal. 177.

Briggs v. McCullough, 36 Cal. 542. Cited, Execution, exemption of insurance policy, 41 Cal. 304.

Briggs v. Williams et als., 2 Vt. 283, 286. Dicta cited, Debtor and Creditor, application of payments, 14 Cal. 449.

Bright v. Hutton, 12 Eng. L. & Eq. 1. Cited, Judicial Decisions, dicta, 15 Cal. 601.

Bright v. Wagle, 3 Dana, 252. Cited, Mortgage, as distinguished from conditional sale, 10 Cal. 207.

Bright v. Supervisors of Chenango Co., 18 John. 243. Cited, Counties, liability for beneficial services, 30 Cal. 239.

Brinckerhoff v. Brown, 7 Johns. Ch. 217. Cited, Equity, verity of pleadings in Chancery practice, 1 Cal. 142.

Brinckerhoff v. Lansing, 4 Johns. Ch. 65. Cited, Pleading, estoppel in pais to be specially pleaded, 26 Cal. 39.

Brinckerhoff v. Thallhimer, 2 Johns. Ch. 486. Cited, Foreclosure of mortgage payable by instalments, 23 Cal. 31.

Brinkerhoff v. Marvin, 5 Johns. Ch. 320. Cited, Mortgage, securing future advances, valid, 35 Cal. 309.

Brinley v. Mann, 2 Cush. 337. Approved, Deed, by corporation must bear corporate seal, 22 Cal. 157.

Brinley v. Tibbets, 7 Greenl. 70. Commented on, Covenants, when dependent, what must be shown in action on, 1 Cal. 341.

Brintnall v. Foster, 7 Wend. 105. Cited, Evidence, *aliunde* the record, of jurisdictional facts, 34 Cal. 327.

Brisbane v. Dacres, 5 Taunt. 143. Cited, Judicial decisions, dictum, 9 Cal. 832, 733; Equity, will not relieve from mistake of law, cognizance of law presumed, 18 Cal. 271.

Briscoe v. Bank of Commonwealth of Kentucky, 11 Pet. 257. Cited, Municipal Corporations, issuance of negotiable securities, 7 Cal. 477.

Bristol v. Burt, 7 John. 254. Cited, Conspiracy, agreement to convert property, 25 Cal. 559.

Bristol v. Sprague, 8 Wend. 424. Cited as inapplicable, Pledge, notes pledged as collateral, 3 Cal. 164.

Bristol v. Wilsmore, 1 Barn. & C. 514. Approved, Fraud, vitiates contract of sale, 12 Cal. 462.

British Com. Life Ins. Co. v. Com. of Taxes, 18 Abb. Pr. 130. Approved and followed, Taxation, bonds deposited by foreign insurance company liable to taxation, 29 Cal. 545.

Brittain v. Kinnaird, 4 Moore, 50. Cited, Official discretion, 7 Cal. 438.

Broadus v. Nelson, 16 Cal. 79. Cited, New trial, insufficient grounds, 23 Cal. 337.

Brook v. Bruce, 5 Cal. 279. Cited, Jurisdiction, of county court, 9 Cal. 146; confined to special cases, 23 Cal. 147, 149. Doctrine not conceded, as to enforcement of mechanic's lien, 8 Nev. 231.

Brockett v. Brockett, 2 How. 238. Approved, Appeal, time within which to appeal, 32 Cal. 260.

Brockway v. Allen, 17 Wend. 41. Cited, Negotiable Instruments, note indorsed by agent, 7 Cal. 541.

Broderick v. McGraw, cited in 8 Wall. 639, note. See Magraw v. McGlynn.

Brodhead v. Milwaukee, 19 Wis. 652. Cited, Taxation, validity of assessment, 41 Cal. 173.

Brodie v. Campbell, 17 Cal. 11. Cited, Office, legislative power over right to, 22 Cal. 319.

Brodie v. Weller. See People v. Weller.

Bromage v. Prosser, 4 Barn. & C. 247. Approved and adopted, Malice, defined, 34 Cal. 53.

Bronson v. Kinzie, 1 How. 311. Affirmed, 2 How. 608; that right and remedy are equally parts of the contract, 3 How. 717. Approved, Constitutionality of Statute, that legislature may vary nature and extent of remedy, or prescribe time and mode, but a statute changing the right, suspending, impairing, or altering the remedy is unconstitutional, as impairing the obligation of contracts, 2 Cal. 548, 552; 4 Cal. 139, 155; 9 Cal. 517; 10 Cal. 308; 16 Cal. 31; 22 Cal. 328; that the law is part of the contract, 7 Cal. 496; 15 Cal. 528; remedy part of contract, 9 Cal. 517; applied to right of redemption under mortgage with power of sale, 15 Cal. 528, 529.

Bronson v. Rodes, 7 Wall. 229. Cited, **Legal** Tender, specific contract, 38 Cal. 254. Commented on, 32 Tex. 458.

Brooke v. Mitchell, 6 Mees. & W. 473. Cited, Award, alteration not to vitiate, 23 Cal. 368.

Brooke v. White, 1 Bosanq. & P. N. R. 330. Cited, Action, for goods sold and delivered, on special contract, 26 Cal. 22.

Brooklyn White Lead Co. v. Masury, 25 Barb. 416. Cited, Trade Marks, 35 Cal. 75. Commented on, 13 Wall. 325.

Brookman v. Rothschild, 3 Sim. 153. Distinguished, Bailment, sale of stock by bailee, 42 Cal. 102.

Brooks v. Calderwood, 19 Cal. 124. Cited, Transfer of cause to Federal Court, in discretion, 20 Cal. 169. Approved, Appeal, no appeal lies from order refusing transfer of cause to Federal Court, 4 Nev. 446.

Brooks v. Calderwood, 34 Cal. 563. Approved, Action to determine adverse claim, possession essential, 37 Cal. 307. Referred to on second appeal, 42 Cal. 112.

Brooks v. Chaplin, 3 Vt. 281. Cited, Acknowledgment, sufficiency of certificate, 20 Cal. 159.

Brooks v. Douglass, 32 Cal. 208. Referred to, 38 Cal. 671. Cited, Presumption, as to regularity of proceedings on trial of issues, 39 Cal. 586.

Brooks v. Harrison, 2 Ala. 209. Cited, Equity, when relief from judgment at law will be granted, 14 Cal. 143.

Brooks v. Hyde, 37 Cal. 366. Cited, Constitutional Construction, uniform operation of statutes defined, 37 Cal. 691; 38 Cal. 710.

Brooks v. Lyon, 3 Cal. 113. Cited, New Trial, surprise, showing required, 22 Cal. 163; 3 Or. 43.

Brooks v. Maltbie, 4 Stewt. & P. 96. Cited, Mortgage, to secure debt where there is no written contract, limitation of action on, 22 Cal. 626.

Brooks' and Joseph's Appeal, 32 Cal. 558. Cited, Special Cases, appeal entertained by Supreme Court, 42 Cal. 68.

Broom v. Broom, 3 Myl. & K. 443. Cited, Partnership, all property considered as personalty, 28 Cal. 582.

Bross v. Nicholson, 1 How. Pr. 158. Cited, Service, by mail, strict compliance with statute required, 30 Cal. 184.

Brotherton v. Hart, 11 Cal. 405. Cited, Appeal, orders entered by consent not reviewable, 37 Cal. 158; 42 Cal. 518.

Broussard v. Her Husband, 11 Rob. La. 446. Cited, Husband and Wife, property sold to wife, common property, 30 Cal. 35.

Brower v. Peabody, 13 N. Y. 126. Cited, Personal Property, title passes by delivery of warehouse receipts, 8 Cal. 614.

Brown v. Anderson, 4 Mart. N. S. 416. Cited, Execution, right in note may be sold, 34 Cal. 88.

Brown v. Artcher, 1 Hill, 266. Cited, Pleading, new matter in answer, 21 Cal. 436.

Brown v. Austin, 1 Mass. 208. Cited, Officers, when not personally liable, 1 Cal. 392.

Brown v. Barkham, 1 Strange, 35. Cited, Judicial Opinions, dicta, 9 Cal. 732.

Brown v. Bement, 8 John. 96. Instanced, Chattel mortgage and pledge distinguished, 8 Cal. 150; 35 Cal. 414. Cited, Chattel Mortgage, legal effect and operation, 27 Cal. 269. Cited and applied, title vests in mortgagee on failure to redeem, 35 Cal. 412.

Brown v. Branch Bank at Montgomery, 20 Ala. 420. Cited, Bankruptcy, effect of discharge on judgment debt, 14 Cal. 176.

Brown v. Brown, 14 Me. 317. Cited, Pleading, libel, innuendo cannot supply place of colloquium, 41 Cal. 481.

Brown v. Butcher's and Drover's Bank, 6 Hill, 443. Cited, Written Instruments, execution in wrong name, error when immaterial, 25 Cal. 81.

Brown v. Cobb, 10 La. 180. Reviewed, Husband and Wife, common and separate property under Spanish law, 30 Cal. 29, 32.

Brown v. Commonwealth, 2 Leigh, 769. Cited, Juror and Jury, ground of challenge in criminal case, 1 Cal. 385.

Brown v. Commonwealth, 4 Rawle, 259. Commented on, Judgments, in criminal case, 22 Cal. 137.

Brown v. Commonwealth, 4 Met. Ky. 221. Cited, Crockett, J., Civil Rights Bill, unconstitutionality of, 36 Cal. 687.

Brown v. County Commissioners, 21 Penn. St. 43. Cited, Statutory Construction, repeal by implication, 18 Cal. 442.

Brown v. Covillaud, 6 Cal. 566. Affirmed, Deed, construction of covenants in, 10 Cal. 322. Cited, Specific Performance, time not the essence of contract, 40 Cal. 11, 13. Distinguished, 11 Cal. 237; 19 Cal. 460.

Brown v. Dewey, 1 Sand. Ch. 56. Cited, Mortgage, what constitutes a mortgage on homestead, 8 Cal. 275; deed as a mortgage, 9 Cal. 550; what necessary to constitute, 10 Cal. 211.

Brown v. Dickerson, 12 Penn. St. 372. Cited, Covenant of Warranty, what constitutes an eviction, 39 Cal. 368.

Brown v. Doe, 7 How. Miss. 181. Cited, Statute of Frauds, contract creating trust not within, 35 Cal. 487.

Brown v. Dysinger, 1 Rawle, 408. Cited, Landlord and Tenant, when tenant may impeach landlord's title, 33 Cal. 253; 35 Cal. 571.

Brown, Ex parte, 1 How. Miss. 303. Cited, Attorney and Counsel, name stricken from roll, 22 Cal. 320.

Brown, Ex parte, 7 Cow. 468. Cited, Appeal, bonds on, statute to be strictly complied with, 13 Cal. 509.

Brown v. Frost, 10 Paige, 243. Cited, Judicial Sales, relief of purchaser, 16 Cal. 470; Id. 564, 565; where to be sought, 37 Cal. 228.

Brown v. Gibson, 1 Nott & McC. 326. Cited, Probate, proceedings not subject to collateral attack, 18 Cal. 505.

Brown v. Gilman, 4 Wheat. 255. Cited, Vendor's Lien, lost by taking other security, 12 Cal. 305.

Brown v. Graves, 2 Cal. 118. Followed, Appeal, facts will not be reviewed without a motion for new trial, 2 Cal. 121; otherwise as to errors of law, 7 Cal. 399. Approved and adopted, as to review of facts, 3 Nev. 303.

Brown v. Haff, 5 Paige, 235. Reviewed, Fraudulent representations, 7 Cal. 509.

Brown v. Hodgson, 4 Taunt. 189. Cited, Practice, bill of particulars, 32 Cal. 638.

Brown v. Howard, 14 John. 119. Cited, Witness, incompetency of party to record, 6 Cal. 194. Distinguished, Forfeiture, 25 Cal. 241.

Brown v. Howard, 2 Brod. & B. 73. Reviewed, Statute of Limitations, effect of fraudulent concealment, 8 Cal. 459.

Brown v. Hutchinson, 11 Vt. 569. Cited, Taxation, validity of tax deed, 25 Cal. 48.

Brown v. Johnson, 10 Mees. & W. 331. Cited, Charter Party, lay days, 1 Cal. 483.

Brown v. Lester, 13 Smedes & M. 392. Cited, Writs, duty of clerk on issuance, 36 Cal. 214.

Brown v. Lipscomb, 9 Port. Ala. 475. Cited, Chattel Mortgage, right to possession under, 27 Cal. 269.

Brown v. Lusk, 4 Yerg. 210. Cited, Negotiable Instruments, days of grace, 4 Cal. 37.

Brown v. Manning, 6 Ohio, 303. Cited, Dedication, to public use, by conveyance, 22 Cal. 489.

Brown v. Marsh, 7 Vt. 320. Cited, Surety, release of one as discharge of all, 11 Cal. 220.

Brown v. Marsh, 8 Vt. 309. Cited, Evidence, party as witness, 17 Cal. 604.

Brown v. Martin, 25 Cal. 82. Approved, Pleading, demurrer, on ground of statute of limitations, objection how stated, 28 Cal. 107; 29 Cal. 72; 30 Cal. 672; objection to be taken by demurrer or answer, 31 Cal. 46.

Brown v. Maxwell, 6 Hill, 592. Cited, Negligence, mutual, when no action lies for injuries, 37 Cal. 422. Disapproved, 35 N. H. 277.

Brown v. McCune, 5 Sand. 224. Reviewed and approved, Estoppel, doctrine of, has no reference to infants, 25 Cal. 153.

Brown v. McDonald, 1 Hill Ch. 302. Cited, Pleading, in equity, prayer in complaint, 2 Cal. 284.

Brown v. Mott, 7 John. 360. Cited, Negotiable Instruments, action by indorsee against indorsers, measure of relief, 16 Cal. 160.

Brown v. O'Connor, 1 Cal. 419. Cited, Ejectment, on prior possession, 1 McAll. 231.

Brown v. Orr, 29 Cal. 120. Cited, Husband and Wife, separate estate of wife not chargeable on contract of wife ratified by husband, 38 Cal. 233.

Brown v. Parish, 2 Dana, 6. Cited, Deed, description in, construed, 12 Cal. 165.

Brown v. Payson, 6 N. H. 448. Cited, Witness, privileged communications, 36 Cal. 507, 508.

Brown v. Ryckman, 12 How. Pr. 313. Cited, Pleading, defenses in answer, 22 Cal. 680.

Brown v. San Francisco, 16 Cal. 451. Affirmed, San Francisco, tenure of pueblo lands, 30 Cal. 506. Cited, 42 Cal. 556; Mexican Grants, 1 Black, 345.

Brown v. Saul, 4 Mart. N. S. 434. Cited, Intervention, interest to sustain right of, 13 Cal. 70.

Brown v. Sax, 7 Cow. 95. Cited, Timber cut, election of remedy, 16 Cal. 578; measure of damages for conversion of, 23 Cal. 311; 38 Me. 177.

Brown v. Scott, 25 Cal. 189. Cited, Pleading, sham answer, 31 Cal. 195; 32 Cal. 458; answer on information and belief, when sufficient, 32 Cal. 607.

Brown v. Smith, 10 Cal. 508. Cited, Water Rights, diversion of water, 37 Cal. 313.

Brown v. State, 32 Miss. 450. Cited, Evidence, in criminal cases, extra-judicial confessions of prisoner, 31 Cal. 568.

Brown v. State of Maryland, 12 Wheat. 419. Cited, State Sovereignty, power of taxation, 1 Cal. 236. Doubted, as to license tax for sale of imported goods, 4 Cal. 56; 13 Wall. 32; 11 Pet. 134. Reviewed and approved, State cannot levy tax on or regulate commerce, 20 Cal. 571, 580; 33 Cal. 340; 34 Cal. 498, 499; 13 Wall. 32, and cases cited.

Brown v. Stead, 5 Sim. 535. Cited, Foreclosure, necessary parties, vendee of mortgagor, 23 Cal. 35.

Brown v. Tolles, 7 Cal. 398. Cited, Appeal, review on, 25 Cal. 61; Id. 159; where there is no motion for new trial, verdict is conclusive, 27 Cal. 69; 3 Nev. 303; review of errors of law, 7 Nev. 121.

Brown v. Union Bank of Florida, 4 How. 465. Cited, Writ of Error, to U. S. Supreme Court, practice, 20 Cal. 172.

Brown v. Ward, 3 Duer, 660. Commented on and doubted, Pledge, of negotiable instrument, 38 Cal. 352.

Brown v. Williams, 4 Wend. 368. Cited, Practice, bill of particulars, 32 Cal. 638.

Browne v. Meverell, Dyer, 216 *b*. Cited, Award, omissions in, 12 Cal. 341.

Browne v. Strode, 5 Cranch, 303. Cited, Transfer of Cause, to federal court, 28 Cal. 99; 13 Wall. 67. .

Brown's Lessee v. Clements, 3 How. 666. Cited, Public Lands, preëmption rights, 37 Cal. 515.

Brownell v. Flagler, 5 Hill, 282. Cited, Negligence, contributory, 37 Cal. 422; mutual negligence, when action will not lie, 1 Cal. 367.

Browner v. Davis, 15 Cal. 9. Referred to, 13 Cal. 591. Cited, Action on Undertaking, conditions precedent, 38 Cal. 604.

Browning v. State of Mississippi, 33 Miss. 47. Cited, Legislature, power of special legislation, 17 Cal. 561.

Bruce v. Delaware & H. Canal Co., 8 How. Pr. 440. Cited, Injunction, modification, without notice, 9 Cal. 19; 12 Cal. 449; injunction, when granted, 23 Cal. 85, 467.

Bruce v. Ruler, 17 Eng. C. L. 700; 2 Man. & R. 3. Cited, Fraudulent Contract, concealment of facts, when fraudulent, 8 Cal. 215.

Bruce v. Tilson, 25 N. Y. 197. Approved, Action, distinction between action for specific performance and action for breach of contract, demand before suit only affects costs, 25 Cal. 282.

Bruck v. Tucker, 32 Cal. 425. Referred to in S. C. 42 Cal. 349.

Bruen v. Hone, 2 Barb. 596. Cited, Res Adjudicata, former recovery as a bar, 38 Cal. 647.

Brumagim v. Bradshaw, 39 Cal. 24. Cited, New Trial, statement on motion, 40 Cal. 83.

Brumagim v. Tillinghast, 18 Cal. 265. Followed, 18 Cal. 404; Id. 408; Involuntary Payment, what constitutes compulsion or coercion, 18 Cal. 407; State cannot tax or regulate commerce, 33 Cal. 340, 34 Cal. 498.

Brummagim v. Tallant, 29 Cal. 503. Cited, Negotiable Instruments, certificate of deposit, a promissory note, 35 Cal. 120.

Brumfield v. Reynolds, 4 Bibb, 388. Cited, Forcible Entry, what constitutes, 5 Cal. 159; possession of agent is possession of principal, 16 Cal. 109.

Brummel v. Prothero, 3 Ves. Jr. 114. Cited, Will, construction of devise, 31 Cal. 603.

Brumskill v. James, 11 N. Y. 294. Cited, Judgment, practice, several recovery on joint liability, 18 Cal. 404.

Bruner v. Manlove, 4 Ill. 341. Cited, Public Lands, Preëmptioner, rights of, 37 Cal. 498, 517.

Brunn v. Murphy, 29 Cal. 326. Cited, Tax Deed, recitals in, sufficiency of description, 32 Cal. 107.

Brush v. Ware, 15 Pet. 93. Cited, Title, patentee as trustee of real parties in interest, 30 Cal. 307. Approved, Notice of Trust, 31 Cal. 435.

Brusie v. Griffith, 34 Cal. 302. Cited, Execution, exemption, act construed, 38 Cal. 384.

Bryan v. Berry, 6 Cal. 394. Approved, Negotiable Instruments, agent signing as surety, 7 Cal. 538. Distinguished, 9 Cal. 23. Overruled, Liability of joint maker as surety, 10 Cal. 289. Dictum disapproved, Judicial decisions, as authority, 9 Cal. 526.

Bryan v. Berry, 8 Cal. 130. Affirmed, Appeal, what transcript must show, 8 Cal. 340; 28 Cal. 59; steps to be taken in perfecting appeal, 10 Cal. 31; amendment of undertaking, 8 Cal. 33. Cited, Execution, setting aside sale, 21 Cal. 59.

Bryan v. Forsyth, 19 How. 334. Cited, Ejectment, patent controlled by subsequent survey, 13 Cal. 413. See 1 Black, 150; 2 Black, 563, 568.

Bryan v. Maume, 28 Cal. 238. Approved, Findings, should be specific, 30 Cal. 229; 4 Nev. 337. Approved, Appeal, practice on, 3 Or. 565.

Bryan v. Ramirez, 8 Cal. 461. Cited, Acknowledgment, facts to be stated in certificate to deed, 8 Cal. 584; Title, possession as notice of conveyance, 17 Cal. 304. Affirmed, Estoppel, by fraudulent concealment, 23 Cal. 37; 13 Mich. 377.

Bryan v. Spruill, 4 Jones Eq. 27. Cited, Pleading, fraud, sufficiency of statement of, 30 Cal. 674.

Bryant v. Craig, 12 Ala. 354. Cited, Trust, statute of limitations not to run in favor of trustee, 16 Cal. 176.

Bryant v. Mead, 1 Cal. 441. Doubted, Gaming, contracts void, 2 Cal. 66. Approved, that money won at play cannot be recovered, 2 Cal. 81; 3 Cal. 329. Cited, Money staked on wagers, 37 Cal. 675. Followed, 7 Nev. 422.

Bryant v. Watriss, 13 Cal. 85. Cited, Witness, competency of, 19 Cal. 485. Approved, indorser of note, 25 Cal. 189.

Buchan v. Sumner, 2 Barb. Ch. 165. Cited, Partnership, accounting, 28 Cal. 579; real estate of, Id. 580. Commented on, Id. 581, 583.

Buchanan's Estate, Matter of, 8 Cal. 507. Cited, Husband and Wife, rights of wife in common property, 12 Cal. 225. Commented on, 13 Cal. 470. Construed, Homestead, a joint tenancy, 22 Cal. 638; 25 Cal. 114.

Buck v. Hardy, 6 Greenl. 162. Cited, Amendment, of Sheriff's returns, 23 Cal. 81.

Buck v. Holloway's Devisees, 2 J. J. Marsh. 180. Cited, Lands, notice imparted by continued adverse possession, 36 Cal. 272.

Buckelew v. Estell, 5 Cal. 108. Cited, Injunction, to restrain injury to freehold, 22 Cal. 491.

Buckeridge v. Ingram, 2 Ves. Jr. 633. Reviewed and adopted, Grant to use of street for railroad an easement, and the estate is property, 32 Cal. 506.

Buckholder v. Byers, 10 Cal. 481. Affirmed, Appeal, filing of notice must precede filing of undertaking, 19 Cal. 81.

Buckingham v. Smith, 10 Ohio, 288. Approved, Estoppel, equitable estoppel, in court of law, 8 Cal. 467; 37 Ala. 361.

Buckingham v. Waters, 14 Cal. 146. Cited, Pleading, complaint insufficiency of several causes, how pleaded, 41 Cal. 19.

Buckinghamshire, Lord, v. Drury, Wilmot's Opin. 177, sec. 194. Commented on, Statutory Construction, statute of limitations, exceptions in, 35 Cal. 640, 642.

Buckley v. Buckley, 11 Barb. 74. Cited, Partnership, tenure of real estate property, 28 Cal. 580.

Buckley v. Carlisle, 2 Cal. 420. Approved, Partnership, partner cannot sue associate, 39 N. H. 53.

Buckley v. Carter, cited in 17 Ves. Jr. 11. Cited, Partnership, dissolution of friendly society, 14 Cal. 538.

Buckley v. Leonard, 4 Denio, 500. Cited, Ferocious Animal, liability of owner for injuries, 41 Cal. 141.

Buckley v. Packard, 20 John. 421. Cited, Factor, cannot pledge, 19 Cal. 72.

Buckman v. Whitney, 24 Cal. 267; S. C. 28 Cal. 555; S. C. Cal. Sup. Ct. Oct. T. 1863 (not reported.) Referred to in same case, 28 Cal. 557. Approved, Forcible Entry and Detainer, definition of unlawful entry, under statute, 28 Cal. 532; 38 Cal. 422. Reviewed and approved, as to remedy on erroneous execution of writ of assistance, 29 Cal. 220. Cited, Appeal, transcript, Supreme court has no control over record of inferior court, 29 Cal. 464; 36 Cal. 522.

Buckmaster v. Grundy, 2 Ill. 310. Cited, Vendor and Vendee, demand and tender of deed, 25 Cal. 279.

Buckout v. Swift, 27 Cal. 433. Cited, Injunction, when not granted to restrain removal of building, 34 Cal. 18.

Buddington v. Davis, 6 How. Pr. 402. Cited, Pleading, frivolous denials, striking out, 32 Cal. 573.

Buel v. Street, 9 John. 443. Cited, Appeal, interlocutory orders appealable only in special cases, 10 Cal. 528.

Buel v. Trustees of Lockport, 3 N. Y. 197. Cited, Statutory Rights, may be waived, 22 Cal. 571.

Buel v. Van Ness, 8 Wheat. 312. Construed, Appeal to U. S. Supreme Court, writ of error, when it lies, 11 Cal. 180; 20 Cal. 171. Cited, 25 Cal. 608.

Buffalo Steam Eng. Works v. Sun Mut. Ins. Co., 17 N. Y. 401. Cited, Insurance, construction of contract, 38 Cal. 543.

Buffandeau v. Edmondson, 17 Cal. 436. Cited, Action, against sheriff for violation of duty, 28 Cal. 286.

Buffendeau v. Edmondson, 24 Cal. 94. Cited, Appeal, practice, dismissal for want of undertaking, 24 Cal. 609. Approved, Filing of Notice, indispensable to perfecting appeal, 29 Cal. 463; filing must precede or be contemporaneous with service on adverse party, 34 Cal. 518; 8 Nev. 178; service of notice to be proved by record, 30 Cal. 184; 30 Cal. 529.

Buffington v. Curtis, 15 Mass. 528. Cited, Statute of Frauds, delivery, sufficiency of, 37 Cal. 638.

Buffington v. Gerrish, 15 Mass. 156. Cited, Fraud, vitiates contract, ownership not changed when goods procured by fraud, 12 Cal. 462; 23 Cal. 361.

Bufford v. Holliman, 10 Tex. 564. Cited, Estates of Deceased Persons, rights of heirs to, 18 Cal. 459.

Buffum v. Chadwick, 8 Mass. 103. Cited, Principal and Agent, contract of agent construed, 13 Cal. 48.

Buford v. Gaines, 6 J. J. Marsh. 34. Ejectment, parties, landlord admitted to defend, 22 Cal. 205.

Bugbee v. Surrogate of Yates Co., 2 Cow. 471. Approved, Probate, jurisdiction, fact of residence, 24 Cal. 189.

Buhler v. Wentworth, 17 Barb. 649. Cited, Pleading, several defenses in answer, 22 Cal. 680.

Buhols v. Boudousquie, 6 Mart. N. S. 153. Approved, Powers, regularity in its exercise presumed from lapse of time, 22 Cal. 592.

Bulger v. Roche, 11 Pick. 37. Cited, Statute of Limitations, does not destroy the debt, it only takes away the remedy, 42 Cal. 499.

Bulkeley v. Keteltas, 6 N. Y. 384; S. C. 2 Duer, 261. Approved, Malicious Prosecution, want of probable cause a mixed question of law and fact, 29 Cal. 649, 651; where probable cause affirmatively appears, defendants entitled to verdict, 29 Cal. 656. Cited, Actual Malice must be proved, 39 Cal. 488.

Bulkley v. Derby Fishing Co., 2 Conn. 252. Cited, Municipal Corporations, doctrine of estoppel not to apply to acts *ultra vires,* 16 Cal. 628.

Bull v. Allen, 19 Conn. 106. Cited, Sureties, rights and remedies of, 24 Cal. 165.

Bullard v. Bell, 1 Mason, 283. Reviewed and approved, Statutory Construction, action for debt lies on obligation created by statute, 16 Cal. 526.

Bullard v. Briggs, 7 Pick. 533. Cited, Deed, consideration clause may be explained by parol, 6 Cal. 137; 21 Cal. 51; 30 Cal. 57.

Bulling v. Frost, 1 Esp. 235. Cited, Gaming, money won at play not recoverable, 1 Cal. 443.

Bullock v. Boyd, 1 Hoff. Ch. 294. Approved, Interest, statutes changing rate, construed prospectively, 42 Cal. 284.

Bullock v. Burdett, Dyer, 281 *a*. Cited, Election of Remedy, election how manifested, 13 Cal. 144.

Bullock v. Wilson, 2 Port. Ala. 436. Cited, Ejectment, right of entry and possession sufficient to sustain action, 38 Cal. 43.

Bullock v. Wilson, 5 Port. Ala. 338. Cited, Public Lands, validity of preemption cannot be questioned by party not in privity with source of paramount title, 33 Cal. 458.

Bumpus v. Platner, 1 Johns. Ch. 213. Cited, Contract, sale of land with warranty, for notes of grantee, creates independent covenants, 5 Cal. 264.

Bunce v. Reed, 16 Barb. 347. Cited, Publication, of summons and notices, computation of time, 32 Cal. 352; sufficiency of affidavit of publication, 33 Cal. 513; 29 Barb. 301.

Bunn v. Guy, 4 East, 190. Approved, Restraint of Trade, agreements in partial restraint valid, 36 Cal. 358.

Bunn v. Morris, 3 Caines, 54. Cited, Action, separate action lies for expenses incurred by agents on joint services, 12 Cal. 128.

Bunn v. Riker, 4 John. 426. Approved, Wagers, upon elections are void, 37 Cal. 672.

Bunten v. Orient Mut. Ins. Co., 4 Bosw. 262. Cited, Jury and Juror, province of jury, 40 Cal. 546.

Burdett v. Abbott, 14 East, 293. Cited, Legislature, powers of investigation by testimony of witnesses, 29 Cal. 405.

Burdett v. Colman, 15 East, 163. Cited, Legislature, powers of, investigation by testimony of witnesses, 29 Cal. 405.

Burdett v. Silsbee, 15 Tex. 615. Approved, Probate, judgments not subject to collateral attack, 18 Cal. 506.

Burdge v. Smith, 14 Cal. 380. Approved, Public Lands, right of entry on mineral lands, 15 Cal. 105; 23 Cal. 456.

Burdge v. Underwood, 6 Cal. 45. Approved and adopted, Statutory Construction, statute legalizing entry of miners on public lands, not to be extended by implication, 11 Cal. 112. Cited, 22 Cal. 453.

Burdick v. McVanner, 2 Denio, 171. Cited, Chattel Mortgage, legal effect and operation, 27 Cal. 269. Commented on, 35 Cal. 411.

Burford, Ex parte, 3 Cranch, 448. Cited, Habeas Corpus, jurisdiction of Supreme Court, 1 Cal. 147.

Burgess v. Burgess, 3 Am. Law Rev. 189; 3 D. M. & G. 896. Cited, Trade Marks, appropriation of words, 35 Cal. 76.

Burgess v. Clements, 4 Maule & S. 306. Disapproved, innkeepers, liability of, 1 Cal. 227.

Burgess v. Commonwealth, 2 Va. Cas. 483. Cited, Murder, of first degree, defined, 17 Cal. 398.

Burgess v. Gray, 1 Com. B. 50 Eng. C. L. 578. Reviewed, Negligence, superior not liable for acts of employés of contractor, 8 Cal. 490.

Burgh v. Legge, 5 Mees. & W. 418. Cited, Negotiable Instruments, notice of dishonor, how waived, 7 Cal. 575.

Burgoyne v. San Francisco, 5 Cal. 9. Cited, Government, distribution of powers, legislature cannot confer ministerial powers upon the judiciary, 5 Cal. 114; Id. 344; 6 Cal. 89; Id. 144; Id. 442, 540; 10 Cal. 403; 12 Cal. 54; 20 Cal. 42; 30 Cal. 167. Upon this point the above cases were reviewed and overruled, 34 Cal. 525. Cited, Jurisdiction, Supreme Court in criminal cases, 5 Cal. 295. Referred to, 18 Cal. 59.

Burhans v. Van Zandt, 7 N. Y. 523. Reversing S. C. 7 Barb. 91. Cited, Trusts, implied trust created by contract, 30 Cal. 594; Vendor and Vendee, vendor remaining in possession as tenant of vendee, 37 Cal. 374.

Burk v. Baxter, 3 Mo. 207. Cited, Fixtures, 14 Cal. 68.

Burk v. State, 2 Harr. & J. 426. Cited, Indictment, distinct offenses, 27 Cal. 401.

Burk v. Carruthers, 31 Cal. 467. Approved, Judgment, interest on, a statutory provision, 34 Cal. 247; 38 Cal. 549.

Burke v. Cruger, 8 Tex. 66. Cited, Surety, when discharged by delay of creditor, 10 Cal. 426.

Burke v. Elliott, 4 Ired. 355. Cited, Municipal officers, legal presumptions in favor of their authority, 3 Cal. 453.

Burke v. Miller, 7 Cush. 547. Cited, Witness, practice on cross-examination, 36 Cal. 228.

Burke v. Smyth, 3 Jon. & L. 193. Cited, Equitable title to real estate, 40 Cal. 571.

Burke v. Table Mt. Wat. Co., 12 Cal. 403. Cited, Pleading, insufficient denials in answer, 26 Cal. 292; 26 Cal. 418; 28 Cal. 567; Ejectment, to be brought against occupant, Id. 536.

Burkle v. Luce, 1 N. Y. 239. Cited, Appeal, jurisdiction lost on sending remittitur, 1 Cal. 195; Replevin, loss of lien of writ by filing undertaking, 11 Cal. 273.

Burlingame v. Burlingame, 7 Cow. 92. Cited, Infant, emancipation to be inferred from circumstances, 8 Cal. 123; doctrine of, 25 Cal. 152; services, recovery of value, on a *quantum meruit,* 33 Cal. 195.

Burn v. Carvalho, 4 Mylne & C. 690. Cited, Debtor and Creditor, equitable rights of creditors to property appropriated by debtor, 13 Cal. 122.

Burne v. Richardson, 4 Taunt. 720. Cited, Landlord and Tenant, liability of sub-tenant for rent, 1 Cal. 473.

Burnet v. Bisco, 4 John. 235. Cited, Pleading, consideration in simple contract, 34 Cal. 147.

Burnett v. Madden, Cal. Sup. Ct. (not reported.) Approved, Forcible Entry and Detainer, city recorder has no jurisdiction, 4 Cal. 122.

Burnett v. Mayor of Sacramento, 12 Cal. 76. Cited, Street Assessments, what property assessable, 28 Cal. 352. Commented on to same point, Id. 361. Approved, 40 Cal. 514; legislature may authorize a general or a local assessment, 5 Bush, 229; 2 Or. 158. Cited, 104 Mass. 482; as to constitutionality of act levying a special assessment, denied, 34 Ill. 214, 238, 281.

Burnett v. Pacheco, 27 Cal. 408. Cited, New Trial, statement, 36 Cal. 120.

Burnett v. Phalon, 9 Bosw. 192. Cited, Trade Marks, 35 Cal. 75, 82.

Burnett v. Stearns, 33 Cal. 468. Cited, Findings, to be confined to issues, 41 Cal. 284.

6

Burnett v. Whitesides, 13 Cal. 156.   Cited, Injunction,
practice on dissolution, 23 Cal. 84; importance of question of insolvency of defendant, 23 Cal. 85; 24 Cal.
473.

Burnham v. Aiken, 6 N. H. 307.   Cited, Execution, immaterial errors in sale not to invalidate, 23 Cal. 298.

Burnham v. De Bevorse, 8 How. Pr. 160.   Cited, Pleading,
waiver of objection by failure to demur, 10 Cal. 560.

Burnham v. Hays, 3 Cal. 115.   Cited, Statutory Construction, in general, 22 Cal. 98; of amendments, extending
remedies, 22 Cal. 126.

Burnham v. Morrissey, 14 Gray, 226.   Approved, Legislature, power of inquest into official conduct, 29 Cal.
402; to summon and examine witnesses, 29 Cal. 405.

Burnley v. Duke, 2 Rob. Va. 102.   Cited, Probate, judgments conclusive, 18 Cal. 505.

Burns v. Morse, 6 Paige, 108.   Cited, Judgments, fraudulent
and void, 7 Cal. 356.

Burnside v. Merrick, 4 Met. 541.   Cited, Partnership, estate
in real property, 28 Cal. 580.

Burpee v. Bunn, 22 Cal. 194.   Cited, Insolvency, preference
of partnership creditors, 23 Cal. 501.

Burr v. Hunt, 18 Cal. 303.   Cited, Cloud on Title, void proceeding creates no cloud, as applied to tax deeds, 36
Cal. 71.

Burr v. Ross, 19 Ark. 250.   Reviewed, Statute, impeachment
of enrolled statute, 30 Cal. 269.

Burr v. Sim, 4 Whart. 150.   Approved, Presumption, of
death from lapse of time, 8 Cal. 65.

Burr's Case, 1 Wheel. Cr. Cas. 503.   Cited, Attorney and
Counsel, stricken from roll, 22 Cal. 320.

Burridge v. Manners, 3 Camp. 193.   Approved, Negotiable
Instruments, presentment and demand, and notice of
dishonor, 8 Cal. 633.

Burrill, Ex parte, 24 Cal. 350.   Cited, Costs, 29 Cal. 282.

Burrill v. Nahant Bank, 2 Met. 163.   Cited, Title, corporate
deed as evidence of, 16 Cal. 639; 37 Cal. 597; Corporations, concluded by acts of directors, 34 Cal. 54.

Burritt v. Gibson, 3 Cal. 396.   Cited, New Trial, ground of
newly discovered evidence, statements essential, 22
Cal. 163.

Burrough v. Moss, 10 Barn. & C. 558. Cited, Pleading, defense on note, 41 Cal. 59; 11 Ired. 506.

Burrowes v. Lock, 10 Ves. Jr. 475. Reviewed, False Representations, evidence of fraudulent intent, 7 Cal. 508.

Bursley v. Hamilton, 15 Pick. 40. Qualified, Estoppel, of owner of property attached for another's debt, 10 Cal. 176. Cited, 4 Met. 383; 15 Mo. 77; 21 Mo. 111. Doubted, 11 N. H. 563.

Burt v. Cassety, 12 Ala. 734. Cited, Cloud on Title, equity will remove, 2 Cal. 589.

Burson v. Cowles, 25 Cal. 535. Construed, Appeal, from justice's court, 33 Cal. 219.

Burt v. Scrantom, 1 Cal. 416. Approved and followed, Judgment, by default, irregularly taken, appeal the proper remedy, 3 Nev. 385.

Burt v. Wilson, 28 Cal. 632. Cited, Trusts, 7 Kan. 207.

Burton v. Lies, 21 Cal. 87. Cited, Foreclosure, necessary parties, grantee of mortgagor, 25 Cal. 161; Husband and Wife, control of common property in husband, 26 Cal. 420.

Burton v. Reeds, 20 Ind. 87. Cited, Pleading, validity of defense in action on foreign judgment, 39 Cal. 539.

Burton v. Stewart, 3 Wend. 239. Approved, Pleading, fraudulent representations as a defense in action on note, 29 Cal. 592.

Busenius v. Coffee, 14 Cal. 91. Cited, Pleading, insufficient denials, legal conclusions insufficient, 19 Cal. 639; 22 Cal. 168; 26 Cal. 418; 29 Cal. 532; 31 Cal. 195.

Bush v. Bradley, 4 Day, 298. Cited, Ejectment, tenant in common may maintain, 20 Cal. 162; 1 Conn. 87.

Bush v. Marshall, 6 How. 284. Cited, Public Lands, title to, 30 Cal. 657; 31 Cal. 457.

Bush v. Peru Bridge Co., 3 Ind. 21. Cited, Bridge and Ferry Franchises, 21 Cal. 252; 25 Cal. 288.

Bush v. Steinman, 1 Bosanq. & P. 404. Overruled, 4 Ex. 254. Cited, Respondeat Superior, doctrine not to apply in building contracts as to owners and sub-contractors, 8 Cal. 494, 496.

Bush v. Western, Finch, Pre. Ch. 530. Cited, Adverse Possession, title by, 34 Cal. 388.

Buslok v. State, 19 Ohio, 198. Cited, New Trial, ground for, 9 Cal. 311.

Bussard v. Levering, 6 Wheat. 102. Cited, Negotiable Instruments, presentment and demand, 8 Cal. 634.

Butler v. Butler, 1 Pars. Cas. 329. Reviewed and approved, Divorce, cruelty, 22 Cal. 361.

Butler v. Butler, 4 Litt. Ky. 202. Approved, Alimony, without divorce, 38 Cal. 268, 270.

Butler v. Collins, 12 Cal. 457. Referred to, Fraud, ownership of goods procured by fraud, 18 Cal. 35.

Butler v. Durham, 2 Kelly, Geo. 422. Reviewed, Equity, when relief will not be granted, 10 Cal. 577.

Butler v. Kent, 19 John. 228. Cited, Pleading, special damages to be particularly stated, 41 Cal. 565.

Butler v. Lewis, 10 Wend. 544. Cited, Records of Court, validity of, 9 Cal. 498.

Butler v. Mayor, etc., of New York, 1 Hill, 489. Cited, Award, validity of, 9 Cal. 146; intendments in favor of, 17 Ill. 481.

Butler v. Miller, 1 N. Y. 500. Cited, Chattel Mortgage, legal effect and operation, 27 Cal. 269.

Butler v. Palmer, 1 Hill, 324. Cited, Statutory Construction, inherent rights as affected by repeal of statute, 4 Cal. 165; 15 Cal. 523; 22 Cal. 318.

Butler v. Pennsylvania, 10 How. 402. Cited, Fees of office, control of Legislature, 22 Cal. 319.

Butler v. Stevens, 26 Me. 484. Cited, Lands, possession as notice of title, 31 Cal. 185.

Butler v. Wentworth, 9 How. Pr. 282; S. C. 17 Barb. 649. Cited, Pleading, several defenses, 22 Cal. 680.

Butler v. Wigge, 1 Saund. 65. Approved, Appeal Bond, construction of, 8 Cal. 551.

Butler and Baker's Case, 3 Coke, 34. Cited, Statutory Construction, 40 Cal. 523.

Butte Canal & D. Co. v. Vaughn, 11 Cal. 143. Approved, Water Rights, rights of first appropriator, 2 Nev. 277.

Butterfield v. Forrester, 11 East, 60. Cited, Negligence, railroads when liable for injury to cattle, 18 Cal. 356. Rule modified, 22 Vt. 221; 6 Iowa, 452; 37 Mo. 553;

Evidence, burden of proof as to contributory negligence, 34 Cal. 163; 11 Wis. 169.

Butterfield v. Kinzie, 2 Ill. 445. Cited, Negotiable Instruments, demand, place of payment, 11 Cal. 323.

Button v. Hudson Riv. R. R. Co., 18 N. Y. 248. Cited, Negligence, when action lies for injury by, 34 Cal. 164; burden of proof, 11 Wis. 171.

Buxton v. Lister, 3 Atk. 383. Cited, Specific performance of contract for chattels, 13 Cal. 523; when will be decreed, 23 Cal. 393; Sale and Delivery, title to goods mingled with others, 27 Cal. 464.

Buyck v. United States, 15 Pet. 215. Cited, Land Grants, validity of conditional grants, 3 Cal. 42; description of land in conveyance, 6 Cal. 312.

Byers v. Aiken, 5 Ark. 419. Cited, Vendor and Vendee, tender of deed, 25 Cal. 278. Commented on, 7 Ark. 208.

Byrne v. Crowninshield, 1 Pick. 262. Cited, Statute of Limitations, construction of "return," 16 Cal. 96.

Byrne v. Stewart, 3 Dessau. 466. Cited, Attorney and Counsel, attorneys as officers, 22 Cal. 315.

Bynton's Case, cited in 2 Salk. 420. Cited, Statute of Limitations, construed, 35 Cal. 639.

Byron v. Byron, Cro. Eliz. 472. Cited, Personal Property, judgments, *situs* of, 12 Cal. 190.

Cady v. Norton, 14 Pick. 236. Cited, Elections, safeguards, effect of informalities, 12 Cal. 361.

Cahill v. Benn, 6 Binney, 99. Cited, Appeal, decision on division of court, 32 Cal. 633.

Cahoon v. Levy, 4 Cal. 243; S. C. 6 Cal. 295. Cited on third appeal, reviewed and construed, 10 Cal. 216. Followed, 10 Cal. 435; McAll. 516; 42 N. H. 81. Cited, Mechanic's Lien, notice operates as an attachment, 29 Cal. 286.

Cahoon v. Marshall, 25 Cal. 197. Cited, Evidence, declarations of vendor made before sale, 36 Cal. 207; made after sale, 38 Cal. 282, 284; Instructions, jury the exclusive judges of the facts, 38 Cal. 370.

Cahoon v. Robinson, 6 Cal. 225. Cited, Vendor's Lien, 28 Cal. 638.

Caisergues v. Dujarreau, 1 Mart. 5. Cited, Interest, usury, 2 Cal. 570.

Calder v. Bull, 3 Dall. 386. Cited, Legislature, powers of, 1 Cal. 235; 7 Cal. 23; Statutory Construction, statutes not to be construed retrospectively, 4 Cal. 135; 39 N. H. 304; statutory rights and privileges subject to control of legislature, 22 Cal. 319. Reviewed, 4 Mich. 248.

Calderwood v. Brooks, 28 Cal. 151. Cited, Judgment, in ejectment construed, 32 Cal. 194; Ejectment, defense by landlord, conduct of, action, 37 Cal. 394; Summons, presumptions as to service of, 41 Cal. 317.

Calderwood v. Pyser, 31 Cal. 333. Cited, Ejectment, parties not affected by the judgment, 37 Cal. 348; Practice, review of former action is on motion for new trial, 38 Cal. 531; alteration of judgment on review, 42 Cal. 507. Referred to on second appeal, 42 Cal. 112.

Calderwood v. Tevis, 23 Cal. 335. Commented on, Homestead, title necessary, 37 Cal. 373.

Caldwell v. Cassidy, 8 Cow. 271. Reviewed, Negotiable Instruments, effect of failure of presentment at place fixed, 11 Cal. 320. Cited, 13 Geo. 294.

Caldwell v. Hennen, 5 Rob. La. 20. Cited, Estoppel, 14 Cal. 598.

Caldwell v. Taggart, 4 Pet. 190. Cited, Parties, in equity, 31 Cal. 427.

California N. R.R. Co. v. Gould, 21 Cal. 254. Cited, Public Lands, rights of settlers upon, 24 Cal. 258.

California Steam N. Co. v. Wright, 6 Cal. 258. Referred to on second appeal, 8 Cal. 589. Cited, Contracts, liquidated damages in, 9 Cal. 587; 10 Cal. 517.

Calkins v. Calkins, 3 Barb. 305. Cited, Mortgage, possession of mortgage does not extend lien, 24 Cal. 409; statute of limitations, right to foreclose and right to redeem reciprocal, 24 Cal. 410; 34 Cal. 369, 372, 373. Reviewed, Id. 377, 378; and distinguished, Id. 379.

Calkins v. Isbell, 20 N. Y. 147. Cited, Redemption, limitation of right of action, 34 Cal. 369. Commented on, Id. 372, 373. Distinguished, Id. 378.

Calkins v. Packer, 21 Barb. 275. Cited, Pleading, new matter must be specially pleaded, 10 Cal. 30.

Call v. Hastings, 3 Cal. 179. Affirmed, Conveyances, registration act, to be rigidly construed, 7 Cal. 294, 309; intent of act, 7 Cal. 304; 20 Cal. 223; prior deed must be first recorded, 36 Cal. 634; 7 Cal. 487. Commented on and distinguished, 7 Cal. 498.

Callagan v. Hallett, 1 Caines, 104. Cited, Appeal, substantial defects, objections in appellate court, 10 Cal. 561.

Callaghan v. Aylett, 3 Taunt. 397. Reviewed, Negotiable Instruments, effect of non-presentation at place fixed, 11 Cal. 324.

Callahan v. Patterson, 4 Tex. 61. Cited, Husband and Wife, execution of conveyance by wife, 7 Cal. 274; 31 Cal. 646.

Callender v. Marsh, 1 Pick. 418. Cited, Street Improvements, estimate of benefits, 32 Cal. 541; right to change grade of street, immunity from liability for damage, 42 Cal. 438.

Callis v. Ridout, 7 Gill & J. 1. Cited, Injunction, to restrain waste of funds in hands of trustees, 10 Cal. 588.

Callis v. Waddy, 2 Munf. 511. Disapproved, Statute of Limitations, begins to run from discovery of the fraud, 8 Cal. 460.

Calloway v. McElroy, 3 Ala. 406. Cited, as to qualification of rule of equitable relief from fraud, 17 Cal. 385.

Calvin's Case, 7 Coke, 1. Cited, Alien, inheritance, 5 Cal. 376.

Calye's Case, 8 Coke, 32. Commented on and approved, Innkeeper, liability as insurer, 1 Cal. 226; 33 Cal. 600, 601. Construed, 23 Vt. 177.

Camberford v. Hall, 3 McCord, 345. Cited, Attachment, when irregularities will not vitiate, 18 Cal. 155.

Camden v. Mullen, 29 Cal. 564. Cited, Pleading, effect of insufficient denials, 38 Cal. 290.

Camden v. Vail, 23 Cal. 633. Affirmed, Mortgage, of married woman, assignee of, 24 Cal. 396. Cited, Vendor's Lien, waived by taking other security, 3 Or. 417.

Camden City v. Allen, 2 Dutch. 398. Cited, Tax, not a debt, 20 Cal. 350.

Cameron v. Ward, 8 Geo. 245.   Cited, Resulting Trust, when it arises, 27 Cal. 140, 144.

Cameron v. Young, 6 How. Pr. 372.   Cited, Judgment, *scire facias,* abolished, 21 Cal. 134.

Cammack v. Johnson, 1 Green Ch. 169.   Cited, Partnership, priority of debts of, 6 Cal. 353.

Cammeyer v. United German Lu. Churches, 2 Sand. Ch. 208.   Reviewed and approved, Corporations, exercise of corporate powers, 33 Cal. 22.

Camp v. Camp, 2 Ala. 632.   Cited, Fraud, relief from fraudulent representations of title, 17 Cal. 385.

Camp v. Camp, 5 Conn. 291.   Cited, Principal and Agent, authority presumed by benefit derived, 4 Cal. 169.

Camp v. Clark, 14 Vt. 390.   Cited, Negotiable Instruments, presumptive dishonor, 39 Cal. 352.

Camp v. Gifford, 7 Hill, 169.   Cited, Judgment, several, on joint liability, 1 Cal. 169.

Camp v. Homesley, 11 Ired. 212.   Cited, Tenant in Common, may recover damages for an ouster by his cotenant, 29 Cal. 333.

Camp v. Root, 18 John. 22.   Cited, Arbitration, effect of submission, 1 Cal. 47; 4 Wis. 184.

Camp v. Smith, 2 Minn. 155.   Cited, Public Lands, in California, relation of U. S. Government, 30 Cal. 658. Explained, 7 Minn. 455; Mortgage, of claim, not defeated by subsequent title under Federal Homestead Act, 31 Cal. 457.

Campbell v. Baldwin, 2 Humph. 248.   Cited, Vendor's Lien, waived by taking other security, 17 Cal. 74.

Campbell v. Bear Riv. & Aub. W. & M. Co., 35 Cal. 679. Cited, Negligence, liability for injury by dam, 1 Saw. 442.

Campbell v. Fleming, 1 Ad. & E. 40.   Cited, Fraud, conditions precedent to relief from, 29 Cal. 593.

Campbell v. Galbreath, 5 Watts, 423.   Cited, Witness, competency of, party to record, 14 Cal. 268.

Campbell v. Hall, 1 Cowp. 204. Cited, Territorial Law, effect of conquest, 15 Cal. 560; 8 Wheat. 594.

Campbell v. Macomb, 4 Johns. Ch. 534. Cited, Foreclosure, by holder of several mortgages, 15 Cal. 501; of instalment mortgage, 23 Cal. 31.

Campbell v. Mackay, 1 Myl. & C. 603. Commented on, Pleading, in equity, multifariousness, 31 Cal. 429.

Campbell v. Mesier, 4 Johns. Ch. 334. Cited, Judgment, death of appellant, entry *nunc pro tunc,* 20 Cal. 69; Sureties, contribution between, 20 Cal. 135; on joint debt, Id. 185. Approved as to contribution on joint liability, 15 N. Y. 607.

Campbell v. Miller, 3 Mart. N. S. 149. Cited, Judicial Notice, not taken as to foreign laws, 15 Cal. 254.

Campbell v. Mississippi Union Bank, 6 How. Miss. 625. Cited, Constitutionality of Statute, obnoxious provision not to invalidate, 22 Cal. 386.

Campbell v. Parker, 9 Bosw. 326. Approved, Pledge, assignment of *chose in action,* 34 Cal. 132; sale of a conversion, Id.

Campbell v. Phelps, 17 Mass. 246. Cited, Officer, acts of deputy, allegation in trespass, 39 Cal. 318.

Campbell v. Stakes, 2 Wend. 145. Commented on, Jurisdiction, on appeal, 1 Cal. 35.

Campbell v. State, 9 Yerg. 333. Cited, Criminal Procedure, pleading former acquittal or conviction, 4 Cal. 379; discharge of jury when equivalent to an acquittal, 38 Cal. 478; 6 Humph. 415.

Campbell v. Twemlow, 1 Price, 81. Cited, Marriage, proof of, where marriage is not the foundation of the claim to be enforced, 26 Cal. 133.

Campbell v. Young, 3 How. Miss. 303. Cited, Probate, allowed claims have force and effect of judgments, 6 Cal. 669.

Canal Appraisers v. People, 17 Wend. 570. Cited, Territorial Law, effect of conquest and cession, 2 Cal. 48.

Canal Bank v. Bank of Albany, 1 Hill, 287. Approved, Negotiable Instruments, certificates of deposit on footing of promissory notes and bills, 22 Cal. 248.

Canal Bank v. Mayor, etc., of Albany, 9 Wend. 244. Cited, Local Improvements, assessment and benefits, 27 Cal. 624.

Canal Street, Matter of, 11 Wend. 154. Cited, Special Proceedings, review of, 24 Cal. 454; Street Improvements, assessments and benefits, 27 Cal. 624.

Canal and Walker Streets, Matter of, 12 N. Y. 406. Cited, Street Improvements, construction of statute as to appeals in cases of, 42 Cal. 56.

Canal Trustees v. Chicago, 12 Ill. 405. Reviewed, Local Improvements, assessment as a tax, 28 Cal. 359.

Candor's Appeal, 5 Watts & S. 515. Reviewed, Parent and Child, conveyance to child when fraudulent as to creditors, 8 Cal. 125.

Caney v. Silverthorne, 9 Cal. 67. Cited, New Trial, failure to give notice is a waiver of motion, 41 Cal. 518.

Canfield v. Monger, 12 John. 346. Cited, Assignment, of future interests, 30 Cal. 90. Approved, Former Recovery, when not a bar, 38 Cal. 647.

Canfield v. Tobias, 21 Cal. 349. Cited, Pleading, evidence not an issuable fact, 33 Cal. 128.

Canfield v. Westcott, 5 Cow. 270. Cited, Forfeiture, waiver of, 38 Cal. 251.

Cannon v. Folsom, 2 Iowa, 101. Cited, Damages, in conversion, 39 Cal. 424.

Cannon v. Stockmon, 36 Cal. 535. Cited, Statute of Limitations, effect of, on title, 37 Cal. 352; 1 Saw. 621.

Cannon v. Union Lumber Co., 38 Cal. 672. Modified, Lands, constructive possession under deed, 39 Cal. 280.

Canovar v. Cooper, 3 Barb. 115. Cited, Infant, effect of emancipation of minor, 25 Cal. 152.

Capen v. Foster, 12 Pick. 485. Cited, Constitutionality of Statute, election laws, 26 Cal. 209.

Caperton v. Schmidt, 26 Cal. 479. Referred to, Id. 514. Cited, Former Recovery, in actions to recover real estate, when and when not a bar, 27 Cal. 359; 29 Cal. 521. Approved, 32 Cal. 189, 199; 36 Cal. 38, 514. Construed, limitation of bar, 32 Cal. 197, 200; 33 Cal. 459; 3 Nev. 26. Same principles, see 2 Wall. 35; 3 Wall. 245; 4 Wall. 174.

Cappe v. Brizzolara, 19 Cal. 607. Approved, New Trial, discretion of court in setting aside orders, 5 Kan. 133.

Carden v. Tuck, Cro. Eliz. 89. Cited, Deed, what passes by, 15 Cal. 196.

Carder v. Baxter, 28 Cal. 99.   Cited, Ejectment, evidence of title, patent not subject to collateral attack, 29 Cal. 312; patent conclusive, 38 Cal. 83.   Distinguished, 32 Cal. 365; New Trial, practice laches, 39 Cal. 435.

Carey v. Berkshire R. R. Co., 1 Cush. 475.   Cited, Action, for damages caused by death, statutory, 25 Cal. 435.

Carey v. Giles, 9 Geo. 253.   Referred to, Legislature, special legislation, 17 Cal. 562.

Carey v. McDougald, 7 Geo. 84.   Cited, Negotiable Instruments, certificates of deposit, 29 Cal. 506.

Carey v. Philadelphia and C. Petroleum Co., 33 Cal. 694. Cited, Former recovery when not a bar, account stated, effect of, 42 Cal. 372.

Carey v. Tice, 6 Cal. 629.   Cited, Homestead, foreclosure of mortgage upon, 13 Cal. 649.

Cariaga v. Dryden, 29 Cal. 307.   Cited, Mandate and Prohibition, grounds for writ of prohibition, when writ will not lie, 30 Cal. 246; of mandate, 35 Cal. 214; 39 Cal. 411.

Carleton v. Townsend, 28 Cal. 219.   Cited, Evidence, identity of name, presumptions from, 28 Cal. 218; 29 Cal. 520; New Trial, statements on, evidence contained, 36 Cal. 120; particulars as to insufficiency to be stated, 38 Cal. 280; San Francisco, tenure of pueblo lands, 42 Cal. 557.

Carley v. Vance, 17 Mass. 389.   Cited, Negotiable Instruments, place of payment need not be averred, 11 Cal. 321, 322.

Carlile v. Carlile, 7 J. J. Marsh. 625.   Cited, Appeal, restitution on reversal, 14 Cal. 678.

Carlisle v. Rich, 8 N. H. 44.   Cited, Fraudulent Conveyance, construed, 13 Cal. 72.

Carll v. Brown, 2 Mich. 401.   Cited, Negotiable Instruments, presumptive dishonor, 39 Cal. 352.

Carlton v. Bailey, 27 N. H. 234.   Cited, Negotiable Instruments, presumptive dishonor, 39 Cal. 352.

Carmack v. Commonwealth, 5 Bin. 184.   Cited, Officer, liability on bond for trespass or misfeasance, 14 Cal. 199; sureties, how bound, 14 Cal. 206.   Doubted, 4 Hill, 572; 4 Dutch, 236.

Carmichael v. Browder, 3 How. Miss. 252.   Cited, Probate Court, jurisdiction, 12 Cal. 435.

Carmichael v. Governor, 3 How. Miss. 236.   Approved, Official Bond, when judgment against principal not conclusive on sureties, 14 Cal. 207.

Carneal v. Banks, 10 Wheat. 189.   Cited, Treaty Stipulations, 5 Cal. 382; rights of property under, Id. 386.

Carnegie v. Morrison, 2 Met. 381.   Cited, Sureties, rights of, when discharged, 11 Cal. 220.

Carpenter v. Brown, 6 Barb. 147.   Cited, Vendor and Vendee, demand of deed by vendee a condition precedent to right of action, 25 Cal. 279.

Carpenter's Case, 2 Pars. Cas. 537.   Cited, Election contests, 12 Cal. 361.

Carpenter v. Nixon, 5 Hill, 260.   Cited, Witness, party on own behalf, privilege of, 39 Cal. 450.

Carpenter v. Providence W. Ins. Co., 4 How. 185.   Cited, Pleading, sham answer, 32 Cal. 573.

Carpenter v. Wall, 11 Ad. & E. 803.   Cited, Witness, impeachment of, 16 Cal. 179.

Carpenter v. Whitman, 15 John. 208.   Cited, Pleading, general denial equivalent to general issue, 11 Cal. 70.

Carpentier v. Atherton, 25 Cal. 564.   Approved, Specific Contract Act not in conflict with Congressional Acts, and is constitutional, 26 Cal. 48; 28 Cal. 292; 4 Nev. 465; overruling 1 Nev. 603; Pleading, allegations that contract was payable in specific kind of money are material, 27 Cal. 499; Judicial Notice, cannot be taken of different values of money, 31 Cal. 80; Judgment, 35 Cal. 357.

Carpentier v. Gardiner, 29 Cal. 160.   Cited, Instructions, to be supported by evidence, 32 Cal. 235; New Trial, findings contrary to evidence, 35 Cal. 359; 38 Cal. 531; Ejectment, sufficient proof of ouster, 41 Cal. 610; as to power of court to vacate findings and render different judgment, 42 Cal. 507.

Carpentier v. Hart, 5 Cal. 406.   Affirmed, Jurisdiction, after adjournment of term court loses power over its judgments, unless served by motion, 8 Cal. 521; 25 Cal. 51; 28 Cal. 337.

Carpentier v. Mendenhall, 28 Cal. 484. Approved and followed, Ejectment, by co-tenant, 29 Cal. 162, 333; damages on ouster by co-tenant, Id. 334; 32 Cal. 580; effect of purchase by trespasser, *pendente lite*, 35 Cal. 356.

Carpentier v. Mitchell, 29 Cal. 330. Followed, 29 Cal. 162. Approved, Limitations, as to damages in ejectment, 31 Cal. 496.

Carpentier v. Oakland, 30 Cal. 439. Approved, Records, of superior courts, presumptions as to, 34 Cal. 402; not subject to impeachment, Id. Cited, Pleading, equitable rights, when may be pleaded, 36 Cal. 55.

Carpentier v. Small, 35 Cal. 346. Commented on, Pleadings, admissions in, 37 Cal. 165. Cited, Variance, 39 Cal. 175; Findings operating as a surprise, 40 Cal. 267; Appeal, findings to support judgment will be presumed, 38 Cal. 421.

Carpentier v. Thirston, 24 Cal. 268. Cited, Equitable Estoppel, doctrine of, 26 Cal. 41; Mexican Grant, constructive possession under, 33 Cal. 108.

Carpentier v. Webster, 27 Cal. 524; S. C. Cal. Sup. Ct. July T. 1863 (not reported.) Cited, Ejectment, ouster by co-tenant, 23 Cal. 242; 28 Cal. 485, 487. Followed, 29 Cal. 162; Id. 333. Commented on, Occupation of lands by tenants in common, 38 Cal. 239.

Carpentier v. Williamson, 25 Cal. 154. Cited, Appeal, injury presumed from error, 30 Cal. 400; 39 Cal. 612; Practice on review of questions of law, 7 Nev. 121. Cited, Foreclosure, necessary parties, grantee of mortgagor, 33 Cal. 264; Ejectment, quitclaim deed passes sufficient title to maintain ejectment, 37 Cal. 521.

Carpue v. London & B. R. Co., 5 Q. B. 747. Cited, Damages for personal injury, liability for, 28 Cal. 628.

Carr v. Caldwell, 10 Cal. 380. Cited, Mortgage, new mortgage, subrogation, 13 Cal. 530. Limited, when payment on mortgage operates as a discharge, 16 Cal. 199. Distinguished, Mortgage on Homestead, 16 Iowa, 154.

Carr v. Lancashire and Yorkville R. Co., 14 Eng. L. & E. 340. Reviewed, Common Carriers, construction of restriction in contract, 27 Cal. 42.

Carr v. LeFevre, 27 Penn. St. 413. Cited, Corporations, issuance of certificates of stock, 37 Cal. 30.

Carr v. Wallace, 7 Watts, 400. Cited, Equitable Estoppel, 10 Cal. 631.

Carradine v. O'Connor, 21 Ala. 573. Cited, Foreclosure, power of sale in mortgage does not affect right, 22 Cal. 125.

Carrier v. Brannan, 3 Cal. 328. Approved, Gaming, money won at, not recoverable, 7 Nev. 422.

Carroll v. Board of Police, 28 Miss. 38. Reviewed and approved, Mandamus, the proper remedy to enforce the duty of supervisors, 21 Cal. 702.

Carroll v. Boston M. Ins. Co., 8 Mass. 515; S. C. 2 Am. Lead. Cas. 5th ed. 863, notes. Cited, Insurance, assignment of policy, 38 Cal. 543.

Carroll v. Perry, 4 McLean, 25. Cited, Public Lands, preëmption claim taxable, 30 Cal. 648; proprietary interest by location of land warrant, 31 Cal. 268; lands reserved from right of preëmption, 37 Cal. 495.

Carroll v. Safford, 3 How. 441. Cited, Taxation, preëmption claims when taxable, 30 Cal. 648; Public Lands, effect of location of warrant, 31 Cal. 268; withdrawal of land from preëmption, 37 Cal. 495.

Carson v. Murray, 3 Paige, 483. Cited, Husband and Wife, deeds of separation, when valid, 9 Cal. 493.

Carson v. Pearl, 4 J. J. Marsh, 93. Cited, Judgments of court of record not subject to collateral attack, 34 Cal. 428.

Carter v. Champion, 8 Conn. 549. Cited, Attachment, lien of, 29 Cal. 375; 37 Cal. 143. Disapproved, 32 Vt. 108.

Carter v. Toussaint, 5 Barn. & Ald. 855. Cited, Statute of Frauds, constructive delivery, how shown, 22 Cal. 105.

Carter v. Walker, 2 Rich. 40. Cited, Contract, rescission of, conditions precedent, 29 Cal. 594.

Carter's Lessee v. Parrot, 1 Overton, 237. Cited, Ejectment, Evidence, deed executed after commencement of action, 22 Cal. 516.

Caruthers v. Humphrey, 12 Mich. 270. Cited, Mortgage, tender after law day, 32 Cal. 171; 37 Cal. 226.

Carver v. Jackson, 4 Pet. 1. Reviewed and approved, Evidence, conclusiveness of recitals in written instruments, 15 Cal. 367; 24 Cal. 418; 5 Wall. 806.

Cary v. Hotailing, 1 Hill, 311. Cited, Fraud, ownership of property not changed by contract based on, 12 Cal. 461; election of remedy against fraudulent vendee, 18 Cal. 534. Criticised, 3 Sand. 712.

Cary v. Randall, Cal. Sup. Ct. April T. 1856 (not reported.) Referred to, Redemption, 9 Cal. 405; costs on appeal, when not part of original judgment, 14 Cal. 241.

Cary v. Stephenson, 2 Salk. 421; S. C. Skin. 555; Statute of Limitations, construed, 35 Cal. 638.

Cary v. Tice, 6 Cal. 625. Approved, Homestead, actual occupancy necessary, 7 Cal. 246; 41 Cal. 83; 16 Iowa, 452. Cited, on mortgaged premises, 7 Cal. 91.

Caryl v. McElrath, 3 Sand. 176. Cited, Corporations, formation of, not subject to collateral attack, 22 Cal. 441.

Case v. Boughton, 11 Wend. 109. Cited, Chattel Mortgage, legal effect and operation of, 27 Cal. 269.

Case v. Case, 17 Cal. 598. Cited, Marriage, proof of, where marriage is not the foundation of the claim to be enforced, 26 Cal. 133.

Case v. Codding, 38 Cal. 191. Cited, Resulting Trust, when it arises, how proved, 40 Cal. 637.

Case v. Hall, 24 Wend. 102. Approved, Warranty, of chattels, no breach till possession disturbed, 41 Cal. 116.

Casement v. Ringgold, 28 Cal. 337. Cited, Judgment, entry of, merely ministerial, 32 Cal. 160.

Casgrave v. Howland, 24 Cal. 457. Cited, Election Contests, are special proceedings, 34 Cal. 640.

Cass v. Dillon, 2 Ohio St. 607. Cited, Legislature, power over local taxation, county aid to railroads, 13 Cal. 188; Id. 355.

Cass v. N. Y. & N. H. R. R. Co., 1 E. D. Smith, 522. Cited, Assignment of Personal Property, action by assignee, 22 Cal. 142.

Cassamajor v. Strode, 1 Sim. & S. 381. Cited, Equity, when relief from mistake will not be granted, 16 Cal. 565.

Cassiday v. McKenzie, 4 Watts & S. 282. Denied, Principal and Agent, authority of agent on death of principal, 15 Cal. 17, 18; 13 Ohio St. 594. See 26 Mo. 313.

Castellanos v. Jones, 5 N. Y. 164.   Cited, Publication of Summons, when order erroneous, but not void, 31 Cal. 350.

Castle v. Noyes, 14 N. Y. 330.   Cited, Former Recovery, when a bar, 36 Cal. 37.

Castleman v. Belt, 2 B. Mon. 157.   Cited, Mortgage, estate of tenant of mortgagor, 16 Cal. 590.

Castro v. Castro, 6 Cal. 158.   Cited, Will, probate of unknown, prior to organization of State, 6 Cal. 625; proof of execution under Mexican law, 10 Cal. 477; 23 How. 363; Customs, as law, 10 Cal. 477; 31 Cal. 522.

Castro v. Gill, 5 Cal. 40.   Cited, Lands, possession as evidence of title, 7 Cal. 319; description of, may be rendered certain by extrinsic evidence, 12 Cal. 166; sufficiency of description, 23 Cal. 163. Approved, Verdict, cannot be impeached by affidavit of juror, 25 Cal. 475; Ejectment, pleadings and practice, 3 Wall. 494.

Castro v. Hendricks, 23 How. 438.   Construed, Mexican Grants, conclusiveness of patents, 19 Cal. 274; Supervision of Land Office Commissioner over surveys, 20 Cal. 229; 33 Cal. 457; title held in trust, under patent, 30 Cal. 307; 31 Cal. 439.

Castro v. Richardson, 18 Cal. 478.   Approved, Probate, proceedings conclusive, 20 Cal. 273.

Castro v. Richardson, 25 Cal. 49.   Cited, Amendment of Records, jurisdiction lost on adjournment of term, 25 Cal. 171.

Castro v. United States, 3 Wall. 46.   Construed, Mexican Grant, decree of confirmation, 32 Cal. 461, 464. Cited, Appeal to Supreme Court of U. S., citation required, 5 Wall. 824.   Explained, 6 Wall. 358, 359.

Castro v. Wetmore, 16 Cal. 379.   Cited, Pleading, insufficient denials, 17 Cal. 571; 26 Cal. 418; 38 Cal. 290.

Castro's Executors v. Armesti, 14 Cal. 38.   Cited, Exceptions, practice, 3 Nev. 530.

Caswell v. Districh, 15 Wend. 379.   Cited, Contract, letting on shares, tenancy in common of crops, 17 Cal. 545; 23 Cal. 522. Commented on, Construction of the contract, 25 Cal. 63, 64.

Cathcart v. Robinson, 5 Pet. 264. Cited, Specific Performance, when delay will defeat enforcement of, 10 Cal. 330. Commented on, 36 Miss. 65.

Catlin v. Gunter, 1 Duer, 253. Commented on, Pleading, denial of legal conclusions, insufficient, 32 Cal. 572.

Catlin v. Hull, 21 Vt. 156. Commented on, Taxation, bonds deposited by foreign corporation, 29 Cal. 540.

Catlin v. Jackson, 8 John. 520. Cited, Statute, equitable relief from statute procured by fraud, 2 Cal. 546. Approved, Lien, of judgment, 37 Cal. 132.

Catlin v. Lyman, 16 Vt. 46. Cited, Interest, on interest past due, 29 Cal. 392.

Catlin v. Munger, 1 Tex. 598. Cited, Statutory Construction, 4 Cal. 161.

Catskill Bank v. Stall, 15 Wend. 364. Cited, Negotiable Instruments, protest, duty of notary, 33 Cal. 183.

Caufman v. Congregation of Cedar Spring, 6 Bin. 59. Approved, Evidence, declarations of deceased as to boundaries admissible, 15 Cal. 280.

Caufman v. Sayre, 2 B. Mon. 206. Cited, Mortgage, foreclosure and redemption, rights reciprocal, 24 Cal. 410.

Caulfield v. Hudson, 3 Cal. 389. Affirmed, Jurisdiction, district courts have no appellate power, 3 Cal. 379; 4 Cal. 342; 5 Cal. 52; 9 Cal. 86; distribution of judicial powers, 5 Cal. 230; appellate jurisdiction in special cases, 5 Cal. 43; of supreme court, 5 Cal. 295; powers of district courts to issue writs, 6 Cal. 681.

Caulfield v. Sanders, 17 Cal. 569. Cited, Instructions, as to matters of fact erroneous, error without injury will not justify reversal, 18 Cal. 378; Pleading, denial of legal conclusion insufficient, 22 Cal. 168; 31 Cal. 195; averment of legal conclusions insufficient, 31 Cal. 393. Cited, Action, "commencement" defined, 35 Cal. 126.

Caulfield v. Stevens, 28 Cal. 118. Cited, Jurisdiction, of county courts, in forcible entry and detainer, 29 Cal. 662; 42 Cal. 324. Affirmed, 37 Cal. 162. Approved, Construction of term, "forcible entry and detainer," 38 Cal. 157. Commented on and disapproved, Concurrent jurisdiction, 30 Cal. 577, 582, 584. See 26 Cal. 372.

7

Cavis v. Robertson, 9 N. H. 524.   Cited, Election, validity of, 11 Cal. 66.

Caykendoll, Ex parte, 6 Cow. 53.   Cited, Verdict, cannot be impeached by affidavit of juror, 25 Cal. 400.

Cayuga Co. Bank v. Hunt, 2 Hill, 635.   Reviewed, Negotiable Instruments, sufficiency of protest, 8 Cal. 636.

Cayuga Co. Bank v. Warden, 1 N. Y. 413.   Cited, Negotiable Instruments, notice of protest, 24 Cal. 383. Commented on, 9 Abb. Pr. 425.   .

Central Pacific R. R. Co. v. Pearson, 35 Cal. 247.   Approved, Eminent Domain, review of report of commissioners assessing damages on condemnation, 5 Nev. 368; report cannot be confirmed unless strict compliance with statute be shown, 8 Nev. 104.   Cited, Evidence, opinions of witnesses, 35 Cal. 544; evidence in chief, how confined, 36 Cal. 580; Special Cases, proceedings on new trial not applicable, 35 Cal. 622; appeal in, 42 Cal. 68.

Certain Logs of Mahogany, 2 Sum. 589.   Cited, Pleading, when another action pending is a bar, 29 Cal. 314; 32 Cal. 630.

Chace v. Brooks, 5 Cush. 43.   Cited, Surety, when discharged by delay of creditor, 10 Cal. 425.

Chace v. Westmore, 13 East, 357.   Cited, Award, validity, how tested, 2 Cal. 78.

Chadwick v. Moore, 8 Watts & S. 49.   Questioned, Constitutionality of statute, statutes suspending remedies, 4 Cal. 160; 10 Iowa, 486.

Chaffee v. Thomas, 7 Cow. 358.   Cited, Statute of Frauds, consideration to written instrument, 12 Cal. 289.

Chaffin v. Doub, 14 Cal. 384.   Approved, Statute of Frauds, what constitutes delivery under, 25 Cal. 553.

Chalmers v. Lanion, 1 Camp. 383.   Cited, Negotiable Instruments, transfer before maturity, effect of, 39 Cal. 351.

Chamberlain v. Bagley, 11 N. H. 234.   Cited, Contract, liquidated damages in, 6 Cal. 263.

Chamberlain v. Barnes, 26 Barb. 160.   Cited, Fraudulent Conveyance, validity as between vendor and vendee, 27 Cal. 317.

Chamberlain v. Beller, 18 N. Y. 115. Commented on and applied, Conveyances, registration of deed as notice, 31 Cal. 320. Cited, Sheriff, may demand indemnity before executing writ, 36 Cal. 459.

Chamberlain v. Blue, 6 Blackf. 491. Cited, Specific Performance, when will be decreed, 13 Cal. 523; 23 Cal. 277.

Chamberlain v. Dempsey, 13 Abb. Pr. 422. Cited, Publication of Notices, computation of time, 32 Cal. 352.

Chamberlain v. Inhab. of Dover, 13 Me. 466. Cited, Principal and Agent, ratification, 16 Cal. 624.

Chamberlain v. Lyell, 3 Mich. 448. Cited, Homestead, not subject to lien of judgment, 16 Cal. 220.

Chamberlain v. Sibley, 4 Minn. 312. Cited, Mandamus, may issue to Governor, 39 Cal. 210.

Chamberlin v. Reed, 16 Cal. 207. Approved, Appeal Bond, dismissal of appeal operates as discharge of sureties, 29 Cal. 139; 1 Colorado, 190.

Chambers v. Chambers, 1 Hagg. Const. 439. Cited, Divorce, adultery, 10 Cal. 255.

Chambers v. Goldwin, 9 Ves. Jr. 264. Cited, Accounts stated, when may be opened, 9 Cal. 361.

Chambers v. McKee, 1 Hill, S. C. 229. Cited, Attachment, irregularities in procurement of, not to vitiate, 18 Cal. 155.

Chambers v. Satterlee, 40 Cal. 497. Cited, Assessments for street work, 40 Cal. 531.

Chambers v. Waters, 7 Cal. 390. Cited, Replevin Bond, sureties on, 21 Cal. 279.

Champion v. Bostwick, 18 Wend. 181. Cited, Partnership, intention, participation in profits and losses, 38 Cal. 213.

Champion v. Brown, 6 Johns. Ch. 398. Cited, Specific Performance, when action lies, 13 Cal. 523.

Champlain and St. Lawrence R. R. Co. v. Valentine, 19 Barb. 484. Cited, Parties, in equitable actions, may be brought in, 9 Cal. 270. Approved, Ejectment, interest sufficient to maintain action, 38 Cal. 571.

Champlin v. Butler, 18 John. 169. Cited, Deed as a Mortgage, parol evidence admissible, 36 Cal. 44

Champlin v. Parish, 11 Paige, 405.   Cited, Pleading, statute of frauds, 29 Cal. 599.

Chancellor v. Wiggins, 4 B. Mon. 201.   Cited, Warranty, when statute of limitations begins to run, 41 Cal. 115.

Chandler v: Belden, 18 John. 157.   Approved, Lien, for freight, detention of goods grows out of usage of trade, 1 Cal. 424.   Reviewed, 17 How. 61.

Chandler v. Spear, 22 Vt. 388.   Cited, Tax Deed, sufficiency of, 25 Cal. 48.

Chandler v. Thurston, 10 Pick. 205.   Cited, Lease on Shares, construed, 25 Cal. 65.

Chapel v. Congdon, 18 Pick. 257.   Cited, Undertaking, validity of, 13 Cal. 558.

Chapin v. Bourne, 8 Cal. 294.   See Grant of lands to city, 6 Wall. 429.

Chapin v. Broder, 16 Cal. 403.   Cited as inapplicable under statutory amendments in foreclosure, Judgment, personal judgment as a lien, 22 Cal. 125; 23 Cal. 623; 4 Nev. 389.   Commented on, when lien attaches, 25 Cal. 349, 352; 28 Cal. 524; insertion of costs, 23 Cal. 222; 2 Nev. 135.

Chapin v. Thompson, 20 Cal. 681.   Cited, Judgment, entry by clerk, 30 Cal. 534.   Distinguished, Confession of judgment, 37 Cal. 337.

Chaplin v. Chaplin, 3 P. Wm. 368.   Commented on, Infancy, actions against, 31 Cal. 280.

Chaplin v. Rogers, 1 East, 192.   Cited, Statute of Frauds, constructive delivery, 23 Cal. 69.   Commented on and approved, 19 Wis. 346.   •

Chapman v. Albany & S. R. R. Co., 10 Barb. 362.   Cited, Street Railroad, not a nuisance, 35 Cal. 333.

Chapman v. Allen, 15 Tex. 278.   Cited, Husband and Wife, presumption that property acquired is community property, 12 Cal. 224, 252; 17 Cal. 581.   Commented on, Deed, parol evidence of consideration, 30 Cal. 39.

Chapman v. Armistead, 4 Munf. 380.   Cited, Ejectment, *lis pendens* does not apply, effect of judgment in, 29 Cal. 135.

Chapman v. Doe ex dem Bennett, 2 Leigh, 329.   Commented on, Evidence, to explain deed, 10 Cal. 626.

Chapman v. Chapman, 13 Ind. 397.　Cited, Husband and Wife, alimony, 38 Cal. 277.

Chapman v. Chunn, 5 Ala. 397.　Cited, Vendor's Lien, 4 Cal. 111.

Chapman v. Gray, 8 Geo. 341.　Cited, Husband and Wife, agreement for separation, valid, 9 Cal. 494.

Chapman v. Holmes, 5 Halst. 20.　Cited, Assignment, choses in action not assignable, 37 Cal. 189.

Chapman v. Searle, 3 Pick. 38.　Cited, Warehousement, receipts of, as an estoppel, 6 Cal. 71.

Chappedelaine v. Dechenaux, 4 Cranch, 308.　Cited, Accounts stated, when may be opened up, 9 Cal. 361. Citizenship, as affecting jurisdiction of the person, 28 Cal. 99; 13 Wall. 67.

Chappel v. Brockway, 21 Wend. 157.　Cited, Contracts, in restraint of trade, when valid, 6 Cal. 261; 36 Cal. 358; when void, Id. 359.

Chappel v. Chappel, 12 N. Y. 215.　Cited, Confession of Judgment, when fraudulent, 13 Cal. 442; 11 Iowa, 563. See 18 Cal. 581.

Chard v. Stone, 7 Cal. 117.　Cited, Bridges and Ferries, franchises, protection of, 22 Cal. 423.

Charles, Matter of, 14 East, 198.　Cited, Assignment, claim for malicious prosecution not assignable till after judgment, 22 Cal. 178.

Charles Riv. Bridge v. Warren Bridge, 11 Pet. 420.　Commented on, Franchise, construction of grants, 13 Cal. 452, 454, 455, 457.　Approved, that exclusive privileges are not granted, 13 Cal. 519; 21 Cal. 252.　Construed, 25 Cal. 287.　Cited, 3 Wall. 75.　See Id. 213.

Charter v. Stevens, 3 Denio, 33.　Cited, Chattel Mortgage, remedies of mortgagee, 27 Cal. 270.　Explained, 35 Cal. 415.

Chase v. Blackstone Canal Co., 10 Pick. 244.　Approved, Mandamus, when it will not issue, 24 Cal. 83; 28 Cal. 169.　Reviewed and criticised, 18 Pick. 446.

Chase v. Dwinal, 7 Greenl. 134.　Cited, Money Paid, under protest, cognizance of law presumed, 9 Cal. 417; 18 Cal. 271.

Chase v. Merrimack Bank, 19 Pick. 568. Disapproved, Municipal Corporations, individual liability of inhabitants for debts of, 10 Cal. 403.

Chase v. Miller, 41 Penn. St. 418. Commented on, Constitutionality of Statute, elections, 26 Cal. 207, 222, 223.

Chase v. Smith, 5 Vt. 556. Cited, Infancy, emancipation of minor, 25 Cal. 152.

Chase v. Steel, 9 Cal. 64. Approved, Debtor and Creditor, priority of partnership debts, 22 Cal. 199; 23 Cal. 501.

Chase v. Walker, 26 Me. 558. Cited, Res Adjudicata, former recovery as a bar, 36 Cal. 37.

Chase v. Westmore, 5 Maule & S. 185. Cited, Judicial Decisions, dicta, 9 Cal. 733.

Chase, Case of Hannah K., 1 Bland. Ch. 213. Cited, Insolvency, appointment of receiver, 7 Cal. 199.

Chater v. Beckett, 7 Term Rep. 201. Cited, Statute of Frauds, contract partly within, 38 Cal. 109.

Chater v. San Francisco, Sug. Ref. 19 Cal. 219. Qualified, Corporations, as special partnerships, 22 Cal. 388. Cited, Specific Performance, contract for delivery of stock, 23 Cal. 392.

Chautauque County Bank v. Davis, 21 Wend. 584. Cited, Negotiable Instruments, indorsement without consideration, 14 Cal. 454; Corporations, contracts when presumed to be valid, 22 Cal. 628.

Cheetham v. Ward, 1 Bosanq. & P. 633. Cited, Release, of one joint obligor is a release of all, 38 Cal. 532, 537.

Chemical Bank v. Mayor of N. Y., 1 Abb. Pr. 79. Approved, Tax, no cloud on title, 12 Cal. 299.

Chemung Canal Bank v. Judson, 4 Seld. 254. Cited, Judgment, not subject to collateral attack, 23 Cal. 404; 30 Cal. 448.

Chenery v. Palmer, 5 Cal. 131; S. C. 6 Cal. 119. Approved, Evidence, practice on cross-examination, 7 Cal. 567; 17 Minn. 248. Referred to, Statute of Frauds, sale of chattel, 23 Cal. 584.

Chenyworth v. Daily, 7 Ind. 284. Cited, Chattel Mortgage, statute to be strictly pursued, 23 Cal. 301.

Cheriot v. Barker, 2 John. 346. Cited, Charter party, recovery back of freight paid, 6 Cal. 32.

Chesapeake & Ohio Canal Company v. Baltimore and Ohio Railroad Co., 4 Gill & J. 1. Cited, Corporations, power of self-dissolution of private corporations, 38 Cal. 172; Statutory Construction, repeal by implication not favored, 35 Cal. 709.

Chesnut v. Shane's Lessees, 16 Ohio, 599. Cited, Constitutionality of Statute, validating and confirming statutes, 30 Cal. 144.

Chester, Ex parte, 5 Hill, 555. Cited, Sheriff, liability on official bond, for misfeasance, 14 Cal. 198.

Chester v. Painter, 2 P. Wms. 336. Cited, Will, construction of devise, 31 Cal. 603.

Chester Glass Co. v. Dewey, 16 Mass. 94. Cited, Corporations, estopped from denial of indebtedness under contract *ultra vires*, 16 Cal. 265; power of corporation to make contracts, 22 Cal. 630; violation of charter cannot be collaterally inquired into, Id.

Chesterman v. Gardner, 5 Johns. Ch. 29.• Approved, Lands, possession as notice of equitable title, 8 Cal. 467; 14 Cal. 678; 36 Cal. 272.

Chettle v. Pound, 1 Ray. 746. Reviewed, Landlord and Tenant, estoppel of tenant, 35 Cal. 571.

Chever v. Hays, 3 Cal. 471. Explained, Insolvency, assignment to conform to statute, 5 Cal. 210; 10 Cal. 277; 14 Cal. 456. Cited, 6 Cal. 139; requisites of statute to be fully complied with, 7 Cal. 430; 9 Cal. 478.

Chew v. Barnet, 11 Serg. & R. 389. Cited, Equitable Title, purchaser takes subject to equities, 10 Cal. 368; *caveat emptor*, 11 Cal. 160. Disapproved, 41 Penn. St. 265.

Chew v. Calvit, 1 Walk. Miss. 60. Cited, Grant of Land, consideration, 14 Cal. 600.

Child v. Chappel, 9 N. Y. 246. Cited, Easement, ejectment will not lie to try right to enjoyment of, 24 Cal. 488; acceptance of land dedicated to public use, 42 Cal. 554.

Child v. Wells, 13 Pick. 121. Cited, Deed, parol evidence to explain, 24 Cal. 417.

Childress v. Black, 9 Yerg. 317. Cited, Forcible Entry, what constitutes, 5 Cal. 159; 12 Cal. 527.

Chiles v. Jones, 4 Dana, 479. Cited, Title, by adverse possession, 34 Cal. 383; 36 Cal. 541.

Chiles v. Stephens, 1 A. K. Marsh. 333. Cited, Forcible Entry and Detainer, actual possession under statute, 16 Cal. 109. Commented on, Action, as a remedy, 29 Cal. 216.

Chilson v. Philips, 1 Vt. 41. Cited, Parent and Child, emancipation of minor, 25 Cal. 152.

Chipman v. Bowman, 14 Cal. 157. Cited, Judgment, when equity will not relieve from, 16 Cal. 202; remedy on void judgment, 19 Cal. 708; 31 Cal. 172; 37 Cal. 529.

Chipman v. Emeric, 3 Cal. 273. Cited, Landlord and Tenant, demand necessary to work forfeiture of lease, 25 Cal. 397; 40 Cal. 385.

Chipman v. Hibbard, 8 Cal. 268. Cited as inapplicable, Injunction, restraining execution of judgment, 15 Cal. 134; judgment of coördinate court cannot be enjoined, 37 Cal. 269; 39 Cal. 162.

Chipman v. Morrill, 20 Cal. 130. Cited, Sureties, right of contribution, 42 Cal. 506; limitation of action on claim of, 31 Iowa, 168.

Chirac v. Chirac, 2 Wheat. 259. Cited, Alien, right of inheritance under treaty, 5 Cal. 382; rights under treaty, Id. 386.

Chirac v. Reinicker, 11 Wheat. 280; S. C. 2 Pet. 613. Cited, Ejectment, conclusiveness of judgment, 14 Cal. 468; Witness, competency of, attorney and counsel, 36 Cal. 507; rule of examination, 36 Cal. 508.

Chitty v. Glenn, 3 Mon. 424. Cited, Constitutionality of Statute, waiver of right to impeach statute, 4 Cal. 168.

Chotard v. Pope, 12 Wheat. 586. Approved, Public Lands, entry under congressional act, 37 Cal. 485. Distinguished, Id. 489.

Choteau v. Jones, 11 Ill. 322. Cited, Tax Titles, purchaser whose duty it is to pay tax, acquires no title, 25 Cal. 45.

Christ's Hospital v. Budgin, 2 Vern. 683. Cited, Husband and Wife, property acquired during marriage belongs to community, 12 Cal. 255.

Christy v. Cummins, 3 McLean, 386. Cited, Contract, conditions precedent to rescission of, 29 Cal. 594.

Christy v. Dana, 42 Cal. 174. Cited, Mortgage, enforcement of mortgage after death of mortgagor, 42 Cal. 505.

Christy v. Sacramento Co., 39 Cal. 3.   Cited, Office, legislative power to extend term of, 46 N. Y. 62.

Chryalin, 4 Cow. 80.   Cited, Appeal Bonds, statute to be strictly complied with, 13 Cal. 509.

Church v. Brown, 21 N. Y. 315.   Cited, Guaranty, sufficiency of, 27 Cal. 84.

Church v. Bull, 2 Denio, 430; S. C. 5 Hill, 207.   Cited, Will, acceptance of devise by wife, effect of, 29 Cal. 348.

Church v. Crocker, 3 Mass. 18.   Cited, Will, construction of, failure to name children, 18 Cal. 302; 23 Ark. 574.

Church v. Gilman, 15 Wend. 656.   Cited, Presumptions, of act, or adoption of act, arise from benefit derived, 4 Cal. 169; 15 Iowa, 112.

Churchill v. Hunt, 3 Denio, 321.   Cited, Indemnity, construction of contract, 13 Cal. 524; evidence to sustain damage, 25 Cal. 172.

Churchill v. Gardner, 7 Term Rep. 597.   Cited, Pleading, allegation of execution of note construed, 36 Cal. 302.

Churchill v. Merchant's Bank, 19 Pick. 532.   Cited, Statutory Construction, definition of "month," 31 Cal. 176.

Churchwardens, Case of the, 10 Coke, 67.   Cited, Grant, construction of, 13 Cal. 453.

Chusan, Case of Barque, 2 Story, 455.   Construed, Vessels, enforcement of lien on, 9 Cal. 731.

Cincinnati, City of, v. Rice, 15 Ohio, 225.   Cited, Constitutionality of statute, Sunday laws constitutional, 18 Cal. 681.

Cincinnati, City of, v. White's Lessee, 6 Pet. 431.   Cited, Easement, dedication to public use, assent how manifested, 14 Cal. 649; 2 Wis. 179; otherwise than by conveyance, 22 Cal. 489; by selling lots on plat, 35 Cal. 501; legal title after dedication, 15 Cal. 548; acceptance, how manifested, 42 Cal. 554. See 6 Pet. 498.

Cincinnati H. & D. R. R. Co. v. Waterson, 4 Ohio St. 424. Cited, Railroads, liability for injury by negligence, 18 Cal. 358.

Cincinnati I. & C. R. R. v. Clarkson, 7 Ind. 595.   Cited, Corporation, issuance of stock by, 37 Cal. 30.

Cincinnati W. and Z. R. R. Co. v. Clinton Co., 1 Ohio St. 77. Cited, Legislature, may authorize local aid to railroads, 13 Cal. 188; power of legislature to confer authority or discretion to be exercised in pursuance of law, 13 Cal. 359; 17 Cal. 33, 34; validity of remedial statutes, 41 Cal. 77.

City Council v. Benjamin, 2 Strob. 508. Disapproved, Constitutionality of Statute, Sunday laws, 9 Cal. 525; 18 Cal. 681.

Claflin v. Butterly, 5 Duer, 327. Commented on, Judgment, several on joint liability, 18 Cal. 404.

Claiborne v. Tanner, 18 Tex. 68. Cited, Husband and Wife, presumptions that property acquired belongs to community, 12 Cal. 224; Id. 253; Conveyance to wife, 17 Cal. 581; parol testimony of consideration for, 30 Cal. 41.

Clapham v. Moyle, 1 Lev. 155. Cited, Contracts, construction of, 15 Cal. 635.

Clapp v. Bromagham, 9 Cow. 530. Cited, Ejectment, possession of co-tenants, 24 Cal. 377; 5 Pet. 444.

Clark v. Baker, 5 Met. 452. Cited, Estoppel, parol declarations, 26 Cal. 41.

Clark v. Baker, 14 Cal. 612. Cited, Mortgage, a mere security, 16 Cal. 468; 21 Cal. 621; effect of on, after acquired title, 14 Cal. 635; 18 Cal. 474; 25 Cal. 500; 31 Cal. 457; Id. 593; 34 Cal. 554; 42 Cal. 179; Foreclosure, estate affected by, 18 Cal. 474. Construed and distinguished, as to after acquired title, 18 Cal. 476. Cited, 40 Cal. 299.

Clark v. Bazadone, 1 Cranch, 77. Cited, per Burnett, J. Jurisdiction, in admiralty cases, 9 Cal. 736.

Clark v. Beach, 6 Conn. 142. Commented on, Evidence, of title under mortgage deed, 21 Cal. 624; estoppel by judgment, 26 Cal. 503.

Clark v. Boyreau, 14 Cal. 634. Referred to, Modification of judgment, 14 Cal. 420. Cited, Practice, on rehearing, 30 Cal. 461.

Clark v. Brown, 18 Wend. 213. Cited, Measure of Damages, a question of law, 14 Cal. 557; Statute Remedies, election, where statute gives new remedy, 16 Cal. 525.

Clark v. City of Washington, 12 Wheat. 40. Approved, Corporations, liability on implied contracts, 9 Cal. 472. Commented on, 5 Pet. 391.

Clark v. Clark, 25 Barb. 77. Cited, Trade Marks, law of, 35 Cal. 75.

Clark v. Cock, 4 East, 57. Cited, Negotiable Instruments, acceptance of bill of exchange, 29 Cal. 601.

Clark v. Cort, 1 Craig & P. 154. Cited, Set-off, when enforceable in equity, 7 Cal. 547; 11 Cal. 102.

Clark v. Downing, 1 E. D. Smith, 406. Cited, Assignment, pleading consideration, 34 Cal. 149.

Clark v. Duval, 15 Cal. 85. Cited, Mines and Mining, grant to right to mine, what it includes, 22 Cal. 454.

Clark v. Ellis, 2 Blackf. 8. Cited, Constitutionality of Statute, where some of the provisions are obnoxious, 22 Cal. 386, 393.

Clark v. Ely, 2 Sand. Ch. 166. Cited, Debtor and Creditor, rights of creditors, 35 Cal. 145.

Clark v. Farrington, 11 Wis. 325. Cited, Corporations, issuance of stock by railroad corporations, 37 Cal. 30.

Clark v. Fitch, 2 Wend. 463. Approved, Parent and Child, emancipation of minor, 8 Cal. 124.

Clark v. Flint, 22 Pick. 231. Cited, Specific Performance, lies to enforce contract for chattels, 23 Cal. 392.

Clark v. Hall, 7 Paige, 385. Commented on, Vendor's Lien, enforcement of, 15 Cal. 194.

Clark v. Henry, 2 Cow. 324. Cited as not in point, Deed as a mortgage, 8 Cal. 429; form of mortgage, Id. 434. Cited, Conditional Sale, when a mortgage, 33 Cal. 333; Mortgage, contract cannot be changed to convey absolute ownership, 26 Cal. 602.

Clark v. Huber, 20 Cal. 196. Cited, Appeal, modification of judgment, 25 Cal. 145; Id. 187.

Clark v. Jones, 1 Denio, 519. Cited, Lease, forfeiture, 38 Cal. 251.

Clark v. Kirwan, 4 E. D. Smith, 21. Cited, Negligence, action for injuries from, when it lies, 34 Cal. 164.

Clark v. Lockwood, 21 Cal. 220. Cited, Title, Mexican Grants, legal title vests in confirmee, 26 Cal. 124; 32 Cal. 463; patentee as trustee of confirmee, 30 Cal. 307;

holder of legal title proper party in ejectment, 32 Cal. 462; title under Sheriff's deed, on what it depends, 38 Cal. 438; Id. 654.

Clark v. Marsiglia, 1 Denio, 317. Cited, Contract, for services, damages on breach of, 24 Cal. 178; 35 Cal. 241; 38 Cal. 666; 50 Barb. 333. Denied, that when contract is terminated one party shall have damages measured by his actual loss, while the other damages are measured by larger rule, 38 Cal. 666; 12 Ohio St. 370.

Clark v. Mauran, 3 Paige, 373. Cited, Assignment, equitable assignments, 13 Cal. 122; by order, 14 Cal. 407.

Clark v. Mayor, etc., of New York, 4 N. Y. 338. Cited, Breach of contract, entire contract, action lies immediately on breach, for entire damages resulting, 35 Cal. 242. Approved, Measure of Damages, 35 Cal. 245. Commented on, 12 Ohio St. 369.

Clark v. McElvy, 11 Cal. 161. Cited, Appeal, instructions contradictory a ground of reversal, 39 Cal. 577.

Clark v. Mundal, 1 Salk. 124. Cited, Debtor and Creditor, effect of payment by note, 12 Cal. 322.

Clark v. Newsam, 1 Ex. 130. Commented on, Trespass, evidence in aggravation of damages, 18 Cal. 326.

Clark v. Norwood, 12 La. An. 598. Cited, Husband and Wife, purchase by wife, *prima facie* community property, 30 Cal. 37.

Clark v. O'Margey, 2 Brev. 134. Cited, Conveyance, conveying equitable title only, 10 Cal. 368.

Clark v. People, 26 Wend. 606. Quoted, Constitutionality of Statute, 26 Cal. 227.

Clark v. Pinney, 7 Cow. 681. Cited, Conversion, measure of damages, 33 Cal. 120. Commented on and qualified, 39 Cal. 422.

Clark v. Reese, 35 Cal. 89. Explained, Witness, privilege of party as witness, 39 Cal. 449.

Clark v. Richards, 3 E. D. Smith, 89. Cited, Principal and Agent, death of principal terminates agency, 15 Cal. 18.

Clark v. Rowling, 3 N. Y. 216. Cited, Bankruptcy, effect of discharge on judgment debt, 14 Cal. 176.

Clark v. Rush, 19 Cal. 393. Cited, Sale and Delivery, delivery of goods mingled with others, 22 Cal. 541.

Clark v. Swift, 3 Met. 390. Cited, Assignment, choses in action not technically assignable, 37 Cal. 189.

Clark v. Troy, 20 Cal. 219. Cited, Conveyances, prior deed to be first recorded, 36 Cal. 634, 636. Cited, Acknowledgment competent proof of execution, 4 Nev. 420.

Clark v. Viles, 32 Me. 32. Cited, Husband and Wife, purchase by wife during coverture, burden of proof as to being her separate estate, 30 Cal. 43.

Clark v. Willett, 35 Cal. 534. Cited, Evidence, of side issues, should be rejected, 36 Cal. 265; Id. 580. Approved, Attorney's license as *prima facie* evidence, 39 Cal. 684.

Clark v. Young, 1 Cranch, 181. Cited, Debtor and Creditor, payment by note, effect of, 12 Cal. 322.

Clarke v. Baird, 7 Barb. 65. Cited, Ejectment, what constitutes legal notice of action, when party not bound by judgment, 9 Cal. 226; conveyance without covenants, effect of, 9 Cal. 229.

Clarke v. Bell, 8 Humph. 26. Cited, Official Bond, sureties when bound by judgment against principal, 14 Cal. 206.

Clarke v. Cummings, 5 Barb. 359. Cited, Landlord and Tenant, when receipt of rent waives forfeiture, 25 Cal. 394.

Clarke v. Dutcher, 9 Cow. 674. Cited, Money paid by mistake of law cannot be recovered back, 18 Cal. 271. Doubted, 19 Conn. 559.

Clarke v. Huber, 25 Cal. 593. Cited, Pleading, equitable estoppel, how pleaded, 26 Cal. 39.

Clarke v. Imperial Gaslight Co., 4 Barn. & Ad. 326. Cited, Corporation, validity of deed of, presumption as to execution, 37 Cal. 598.

Clarke v. Matthewson, 2 Sum. 264. Cited, Statutory Construction, powers, execution of, by boards of officers, 6 Cal. 125.

Clarke v. Perry, 5 Cal. 58. Cited, Jurisdiction, of probate court, limited and special, 9 Cal. 129; 12 Cal. 436; 19 Cal. 205; District Courts not divested of their chancery jurisdiction over estates, 12 Cal. 436; 23 Cal. 429. Commented on, Accounting by administrators, 37 Cal. 426.

Clarke v. Rochester, City of, 5 Abb. Pr. 124. Cited, Railroads, concern public interest, 30 Cal. 437.

Clarke v. Rochester, City of, 24 Barb. 447; reversing S. C. 13 How. Pr. 204. Referred to, Legislature, power to authorize local subscription to stock for railroads, etc., 13 Cal. 188; power of taxation and appropriation, 13 Cal. 355; may confer on municipal corporations power of taxation, and the creation of debts, Id. 356; 17 Cal. 33; and discretion in the exercise of such powers pursuant to law, Id. 359; Statutory Construction, validity of statutes dependent on conditions, 17 Cal. 36; 25 Cal. 646.

Clarke v. Rochester and S. R. R. Co., 14 N. Y. 574. Cited, Common Carrier, liability for injuries, 27 Cal. 429.

Clarke v. Sanderson, 3 Bin. 194. Cited, Evidence, handwriting, when may be proved, 26 Cal. 410, 411.

Clarke v. State, 8 Ohio St. 630. Cited, Criminal Procedure, indictment for forgery, 35 Cal. 507.

Clarke v. Wilson, 15 Ves. Jr. 317. Cited, Vendor and Vendee, lien of vendor, 2 Cal. 287.

Clarke v. Wright, 5 Mart. N. S. 122. Cited, Insolvency, promissory note on schedule, 7 Cal. 430.

Clarke's Lessee v. Courtney, 5 Pet. 319. Cited, Lands, constructive possession under deed, 25 Cal. 133.

Clark's Exrs. v. Van Reimsdyk, 9 Cranch, 155. Cited, Principal and Agent, contract made by agent, 13 Cal. 48.

Clarkson and Vanderslice v. Hanks, 3 Cal. 47. S. C. Id. 27. Distinguished as to forfeiture of conditional grants, 5 Cal. 307. Commented on, Pueblo Lands, 8 Cal. 198. Approved, Conditional grant subject to be defeated till approved by supreme government, 10 Cal. 616; McAll. 164. Overruled, Grantee entitled to possession, till so defeated, 3 Cal. 621. Cited, Effect of decision as a rule of property, 15 Cal. 598. Reviewed, upon the principles of *stare decisis*, 15 Cal. 606. See 6 Cal. 269, 270, and cases cited.

Clary v. Hoagland, 5 Cal. 476. Distinguished, Certiorari, 7 Cal. 245. Cited, Appeal, law of the case conclusive, 13 Cal. 211; 15 Cal. 82. Affirmed, on principle of *stare decisis*, 20 Cal. 417.

Clason v. Shotwell, 12 John. 31. Commented on, Appeal, jurisdiction, distinction between judgment and order, 1 Cal. 136, 137.

Clavering v. Clavering, 2 P. Wms. 388. Cited, Injunction, when will be granted, 23 Cal. 84.

Clay v. Dennis, 3 Ala. 375. Cited, Covenant, action on, defense of payment of incumbrance, 5 Cal. 264.

Clay v. Harrison, 10 Barn. & C. 106. Cited, Mortgage, rent of mortgaged premises, 8 Cal. 598.

Clay v. Scott, 7 B. Mon. 554. Cited, Attachments, priority in issuance of, 25 Cal. 209.

Clay v. Walton, 9 Cal. 328. Approved, New Promise, consideration for, 12 Cal. 553.

Clayborn v. Hill, 1 Wash. Va. 177. Cited, Chattel Mortgages, statute to be strictly construed, 23 Cal. 301.

Clayton v. Gregson, 4 Nev. & M. 602. Cited, Contract, parol evidence to explain, 11 Cal. 198.

Clayton v. Wardwell, 4 N. Y. 230. Cited, Divorce, adultery, actual marriage must be proved, 17 Cal. 601.

Clayton v. West, 2 Cal. 381. Cited, Appeal, judgment will not be disturbed for errors without injury, 5 Cal. 410.

Clayton's Case, 1 Mer. 606. Cited, Debtor and Creditor, application of payments, 14 Cal. 449.

Cledirbone v. Pedistone, Year Book, 18 Ed. II. 594. Cited, Will, construction of devise, 27 Cal. 443.

Clemens v. Loggins, 1 Ala. 622. Cited, Vendor and Vendee, payment of purchase money cannot be resisted where vendee acquires possession, 5 Cal. 265.

Clemens v. Mayor of Baltimore, 16 Md. 208. Commented on, Street Assessments, who liable for, 31 Cal. 682.

Clement v. Bixler, 3 Watts, 248. Cited, Witness, competency of, parties to record, 14 Cal. 268.

Clement v. Jones, 12 Mass. 60. Cited, Principal and Agent, effect of ratification, 14 Cal. 400.

Clements v. Benjamin, 12 John. 299. Approved, Nonsuit, power of compulsory nonsuit, 1 Cal. 114.

Clements v. Village of West Troy, 10 How. Pr. 199; S. C. 16 Barb. 253. Cited and statutory provisions distinguished, Dedication, of streets, acceptance, 35 Cal. 497; opening and laying out streets, proceedings, Id. 500.

Clerk v. Withers, 6 Mod. 290; S. C. 1 Salk. 322. Commented on and followed, Execution, ex-sheriff to complete execution of process, 8 Cal. 407; doctrine denied, 14 Ark. 575.

Cleavland v. Burton, 11 Vt. 139. Cited, Evidence, parol evidence of declarations and admissions, not favored, 26 Cal. 44.

Cleevland v. Burrill, 25 Barb. 532. Cited, Specific Performance decreed when subject matter is within jurisdiction, 38 Cal. 201.

Cleveland v. Chamberlain, 1 Black, 419. Cited, Appeal, questions not presented in good faith will not be considered, 30 Cal. 225.

Cleveland v. Cleveland, 12 Wend. 172. Cited, Dedication, to public use, assent how manifested, 14 Cal. 649.

Cleveland v. Rogers, 6 Wend. 438. Cited, Pleading, jurisdictional facts in collateral action, 33 Cal. 536.

Cleveland C. and C. R. R. Co. v. Elliott, 4 Ohio St. 474. Cited, Railroads, liability for injury to cattle, 37 Cal. 423.

Cleveland P. and A. R. R. Co. v. Erie, 27 Penn. St. 380. Cited, Corporations, special powers conferred on, by statute, 22 Cal. 428.

Clift v. White, 15 Barb. 70; S. C. reversed, 12 N. Y. 519. Cited, Assignment, of judgment, merges the lien of attachment, 9 Cal. 81.

Clifton v. Bogardus, 2 Ill. 33. Cited, Witness, competency of, vendor of chattel, 23 Cal. 446.

Clifton v. Burt, 1 P. Wms. 679. Cited, Will, construction of devise of land, 31 Cal. 603; a specific legacy, Id. 610.

Clinan v. Cooke, 1 Sch. & L. 22. Cited, Specific Performance, of verbal contract, part performed, 10 Cal. 159; 19 Cal. 461.

Clinton v. Phillips' Admr. 7 Mon. 119. Cited, Appeal Bond, interpretation of, 13 Cal. 509.

Clinton v. Strong, 9 John. 370. Cited, Money Paid, under mistake of law, when cannot be recovered back, 9 Cal. 417.

Clinton v. York, 26 Me. 167. Cited, Parent and Child, emancipation of minor, 25 Cal. 152.

Clopper's Admr. v. Union Bank of Maryland, 7 Har. & J. 92; Covenant, remedy on breach of covenant not to sue, 5 Cal. 502. Cited, 2 Mich. 414.

Clopton v. Martin, 11 Ala. 187. Cited, Equity, relieves from mistakes, 19 Cal. 673.

Clossman v. Lacoste, 28 Eng. L. & E. 141. Cited, Contract, action for breach of, 35 Cal. 242.

Cloud v. El Dorada Co., 12 Cal. 128. Cited, Title, under sheriff's deed, on what it depends, 21 Cal. 224; 38 Cal. 438; Id. 654; recitals in deed as evidence of sale, 30 Cal. 288; Judgment, by confession, not subject to collateral attack, 37 Cal. 336.

Cloyes v. Thayer, 3 Hill, 564. Commented on, Witness, examination of party as, 35 Cal. 95.

Cluggage, Lessee of, v. Swan, 4 Bin. 150. Cited, Verdict, testimony of juror not admissible to impeach, 1 Cal. 405.

Clum v. Smith, 5 Hill, 560. Cited, Verdict, testimony of juror not admitted to impeach, 1 Cal. 405.

Clute v. Robison, 2 John. 595. Cited, Specific Performance, defense of failure of title, 6 Cal. 573.

Clute v. Wiggins, 14 John. 175. Cited, Innkeeper, liability of, 33 Cal. 602.

Clymer v. Willis, 3 Cal. 363. Cited, Attachment, money in legal custody, in hands of sheriff, not attachable, 14 Wis. 293; 33 Ill. 516.

Coates v. Coates, 1 Duer, 664. Cited, Injunction Bond, when action lies on, 18 Cal. 628.

Coates v. Mayor, etc., of New York, 7 Cow. 585. Commented on, Constitutionality of Statute, 33 Cal. 285.

Coates v. Stevens, 1 Younge & C. 66. Cited, Husband and Wife, gift to wife, 12 Cal. 255.

Coats v. Holbrook, 2 Sand. Ch. 586, 603. Cited, Trade Marks, 35 Cal. 75; measure of damages, 40 Cal. 599.

8.

Coble v. Wellborn, 2 Dev. 390. Cited, Covenant, what sufficient eviction to constitute a breach, 39 Cal. 365.

Coburn, Ex parte, 1 Cow. 570. Cited, Right of way, may be assigned, 32 Cal. 506.

Cochran v. Collins, 29 Cal. 129. Cited, Street Improvements, resolutions of intention, validity of, 31 Cal. 244; Id. 473; contracts for, may be assigned, 31 Cal. 248.

Cochran v. Van Surlay, 20 Wend, 365. Commented on, Constitutionality of statute, rule of judicial decision, 7 Cal. 22; 22 Cal. 322; 4 Mich. 249.

Cockburn v. Thompson, 16 Ves. Jr. '321. Cited, Equity, may decree the dissolution of voluntary benevolent societies, 14 Cal. 538; Parties, when too numerous, need not be joined, 14 Cal. 539.

Cocke's Adm. v. Gilpin, 1 Rob. Va. 20. Cited, Appeal, decree when not final, 9 Cal. 635.

Cooker v. The Franklin Manf. Co., 3 Sum. 532. Commented on, Contract, reasonable time of performance when a question of law, 30 Cal. 559.

Cookerell v. Cholmeley, 3 Eng. Ch., 1 Russ. & M. 418. Commented on, Estoppel, confirmation of act, what necessary to effect, 7 Cal. 386.

Codd v. Codd, 2 Johns. Ch. 224. Cited, Divorce, adultery, evidence of, 10 Cal. 254; 3 Tex. 183.

Coddington v. Bay, 20 John. 637. Commented on and distinguished, Negotiable Instruments, securities held in trust, sale of, 3 Cal. 164; no title passes on fraudulent receipt of chattel, 23 Cal. 361. Criticised, 42 Ill. 31. Commented on, 16 Pet. 17.

Coddington v. Davis, 3 Denio, 16. Cited, Negotiable Instruments, "protest" construed, 8 Cal. 636. Disapproved, 6 La. An. 470; Contra, 20 La. An. 539.

Codman v. Freeman, 3 Cush. 314. Cited, Trespass by sheriff, demand before action not necessary, 30 Cal. 191.

Codman v. Jenkins, 14 Mass. 96. Cited, Use and Occupation, action will not lie to try title to land, 3 Cal. 202.

Codrington v. Johnstone, 1 Beav. 520. Approved, Mortgagor, right to sell property severed from realty, 27 Cal. 438.

Coffeen v. Brunton, 4 McLean, 516. Reviewed, Trade Marks, alterations only colorable, 35 Cal. 75, 81.

Coffin v. Coffin, 4 Mass. 35. Cited, Legislature, power of investigation and examination of witnesses, 29 Cal. 405.

Coffin v. Tracy, 3 Caines, 129. Cited, Appeal, consent may waive error but will not confer jurisdiction, 29 Cal. 463.

Coffinberry v. Horrill, 5 Cal. 493. Followed, Judgment, rendition of, in vacation, is void, 7 Cal. 53.

Coggs v. Bernard, 2 Ld. Ray. 909; 1 Smith Lead. Cas. 346. Cited, Principal and Agent, paid and unpaid agents, 29 Cal. 146; as applied to liabilities of innkeepers, 33 Cal. 596. Criticised, Gilp. 585.

Coghill v. Marks, 29 Cal. 673. Cited, New Trial, review of order granting or refusing, discretion of court, 38 Cal. 506; 5 Kan. 238.

Cogswell v. Bull, 39 Cal. 390. Cited and distinguished, Corporation, demand in action by stockholders against trustees, 40 Cal. 622.

Cogswell v. Dolliver, 2 Mass. 221. Cited, Evidence, admission of entry in books as, 14 Cal. 576. Doubted, 23 N. H. 224.

Cohas v. Raisin, 3 Cal. 443. Cited, Territorial Law, Mexican laws in force in California after conquest, 5 Cal. 307; 15 Cal. 569; 1 Black, 562; 9 Wall. 602. Cited, San Francisco, title to pueblo lands, 5 Cal. 402; Id. 307; 9 Wall. 602. Commented on and construed, 8 Cal. 187, 199; 15 Cal. 589, 617. Approved, 7 Cal. 348. Referred to, Alcaldes, power to grant pueblo lands, 15 Cal. 498. Cited, 27 Cal. 285; validity of grant, 15 Cal. 558. Approved, 21 Cal. 40. See 12 Wall. 319.

Cohen v. Barrett, 5 Cal. 196. Approved, Insolvency, proceedings construed, 8 Cal. 47; 29 Cal. 418. Cited, Power of court when jurisdiction attaches, 37 Cal. 613.

Cohen v. Davis, 20 Cal. 187. Followed, Homestead, mortgage when a valid incumbrance, 23 Cal. 314. Cited, what operates as an abandonment, 25 Cal. 116.

Cohen, Ex parte, 6 Cal. 318. Cited, Process, issuance of, when void, 9 Cal. 552; 34 Tex. 671.

Cohen v. Hoff, 3 Brev. 500. Approved, Constitutional Construction, office, tenure of, 2 Cal. 213.

Cohen v. Hume, 1 McCord, 440. Cited, Ferrymen, liable as common carriers, 5 Cal. 364.

Cohen v. Morgan, 6 Dowl. & R. 8.   Cited, Malicious Prosecution, question of malice, 8 Cal. 225.

Cohen & Jones, Matter of, 5 Cal. 494.   Approved, Contempt, judgments and orders on, conclusive, 40 Ala. 168.

Cohen v. Wright, 22 Cal. 293.   Approved, Constitutionality of Statute, statutes relating to attorneys-at-law, 22 Cal. 421; 24 Cal. 243; 4 Wall. 356.   Cited, 2 West. Va. 180; Attorneys not public officers, 35 Geo. 288.

Cohens v. Virginia, 6 Wheat. 264.   Approved, Judicial Decisions, interpretation of general expressions, 9 Cal. 615; 15 Cal. 598; Jurisdiction of Supreme Court of U. S., general government supreme within constitutional limits, 9 Cal. 714, 718; 25 Cal. 431; Appellate Power, under judiciary act, 9 Cal. 722, 723.

Cohn v. Mulford, 15 Cal. 50.   Approved, Evidence, statements made by vendor after sale not admissible, 36 Cal. 207.

Coit v. Haven, 30 Conn. 190.   Cited, Judgment, record of court of general jurisdiction imports verity, 30 Cal. 446; jurisdiction presumed, 34 Cal. 403, 415; of federal courts, 34 Cal. 413; records of courts of inferior jurisdiction do not import absolute verity, Id. 417.

Coit v. Sheldon, 1 Tyler, 300.   Cited, Judgment, of courts of record conclusive, 30 Cal. 447; remedy for unauthorized appearance of attorney, Id. 447.

Coit v. Tracy, 8 Conn. 268.   Cited, Judgment, conclusiveness of decree, 20 Cal. 483, 486.

Colburn v. Downes, 10 Mass. 21.   Cited, Bail Bond, validity of, 13 Cal. 558.

Colby v. Kenniston, 4 N. H. 266.   Cited, Lands, possession as notice of title, 36 Cal. 272.

Colden v. Eldred, 15 John. 220.   Cited, Statutory Construction, election between remedies given by statute, 16 Cal. 525.

Cole v. McGlathry, 9 Greenl. 131.   Cited, Statute of Limitations, fraudulent concealment to avoid, 8 Cal. 460. Contra, reply to plea of, 28 Miss. 736.

Cole v. Ross, 9 B. Mon. 393.   Reviewed, Action, on specific contract, sufficiency of tender, 26 Cal. 49.

Cole v. Swanston, 1 Cal. 51.   Cited, Pleading, special damages must be specially pleaded, 41 Cal. 565.

Colegrave v. Santos, 3 Dowl. & R. 255. Cited, Fixtures, as part of the demise, 14 Cal. 72.

Coleman v. Carpenter, 9 Penn. St. 178. Cited, Negotiable Instruments, notice of dishonor, when may be given, 8 Cal. 634.

Coleman v. Doe, 3 Ill. 251. Cited, Ejectment, judgment on failure of defendant to answer, 10 Cal. 378.

Coleman v. Riches, 16 Com. B. 104. Cited, Master and Servant, when master not liable for acts of servant, 38 Cal. 634.

Coleman v. Woodworth, 28 Cal. 567. Cited, Pleading, objection that claim was not presented to administrator must be taken in court below, 33 Cal. 278; 42 Cal. 134.

Coleman v. Wolcott, 1 Conn. 285. Cited, Adverse Possession, under color of title, 25 Cal. 133.

Coles v. Bowne, 10 Paige, 526. Cited, Pleading, statute of frauds, 29 Cal. 599.

Coles v. Coles, 15 John. 319. Commented on, Partition, proper parties in, 35 Cal. 594. Cited, Mortgage, a mere lien, 36 Cal. 58; interest of mortgagee, Id. 41:

Coles v. Soulsby, 21 Cal. 47. Commented on, Estoppel, recitals in deed how far conclusive, 30 Cal. 24, 56. Cited, how far conclusive, 23 Wis. 523; Evidence, parol evidence admissible of consideration, 31 Cal. 476; what may be shown by, 36 Cal. 369, 370. Approved, Pleading, new matter must be specially pleaded, 30 Cal. 472.

Collier v. Corbett, 15 Cal. 183. Cited, Probate, presumptions arising from lapse of time, 22 Cal. 68.

Collins v. America, 9 B. Mon. 569. Cited, National Comity, right of transit, 9 Cal. 163.

Collins v. Blantern, 2 Wils. 341. Contract, no remedy on illegal contract, 37 Cal. 175.

Collins v. Bristol & Exeter Railroad, 36 Eng. L. & E. 482. Cited, Common Carriers, contract construed, connecting routes, 31 Cal. 53.

Collins v. Butler, 14 Cal. 223. Referred to and followed, Fraud, 18 Cal. 35.

Collins v. Gibbs, 2 Burr. 900. Cited, Default, effect of, proceedings to set aside, 6 Cal. 174.

Collins v. Inhab. of Dorchester, 6 Cush. 396. Cited, Evidence, as to collateral issues not admissible, 36 Cal. 580.

Collins v. Montgomery, 16 Cal. 398. Cited, Corporation, action against, must be brought by use of corporate name, 26 Cal. 635.

Collins v. Ongly, cited 5 Maule & S. 185. Cited, Judicial Decisions, dictum, 9 Cal. 733.

Collins v. Torry, 7 John. 277. Cited, Mortgage, a mere lien, estate of mortgagor, 36 Cal. 58.

Collins Co. v. Brown, 3 Kay & J. 423. Cited, Trade Marks, protection of, 29 Cal. 296.

Colman v. Clements, 23 Cal. 245. Cited, Mining Claim, forfeiture, regulations to be strictly construed, 6 Nev. 222.

Colman v. Eastern Counties Railway Co., 10 Beav. 1. Cited, Railroads, limitation of powers of corporation, 40 Cal. 88.

Colman v. Packard, 16 Mass. 39. Denied, Mortgage, title of mortgagee, 9 Cal. 407.

Colman v. Sarrel, 1 Ves. Jr. 51. Cited, Contract, no remedy on illegal contract, 15 Cal. 405.

Colson v. Thompson, 2 Wheat. 336. Cited, Specific Performance, parol sale of lands, what must be shown, 24 Cal. 142; 33 Cal. 133; 39 Cal. 302.

Colt v. Nettervill, 2 P. Wms. 304. Cited, Specific Performance of contract for chattels, 23 Cal. 392.

Colton v. Rossi, 9 Cal. 595. Cited, Eminent Domain, compensation to be first provided, 31 Cal. 547.

Colton v. Seavey, 22 Cal. 496. Cited, Deed, description in, landmarks to govern lines, 22 Cal. 491; conclusiveness of recitals in deed, 26 Cal. 87; Subsequent Purchaser, seeking to avoid deed, what must be shown, 34 Cal. 38; execution of deed by portion of grantors construed, 23 Cal. 239.

Colton v. Wilson, 3 P. Wms. 190. Cited, Specific Performance, time not of essence of contract, 11 Cal. 238.

Columbine v. Chichester, 2 Phill. Ch. 27. Cited, Pleading, capacity to contract must be shown, 37 Cal. 257.

Colvin v. Burnet, 17 Wend. 564. Cited, Water Rights, title by adverse possession, 25 Cal. 509.

Colwell v. Woods, 3 Watts, 188. Approved, Deed and Defeasance, when a mortgage, 10 Cal. 209.

Coman v. State, 4 Blackf. 241. Cited, Surety, when discharged by delay of creditor, 10 Cal. 426.

Combes' Case, 9 Coke, 75. Approved, Agent, deeds executed by, to be in name of principal, 32 Cal. 651. Cited, 8 Wheat. 202.

Comeau v. Fontenot, 19 La. 406. Cited, Husband and Wife, property acquired during marriage belongs to the community, 12 Cal. 253; 30 Cal. 32.

Comegys v. Vasse, 1 Pet. 193. Cited, Assignment, things not *in esse* are not assignable, 22 Cal. 177.

Comerford v. Dupuy, 17 Cal. 308. Cited, Injuries by Cattle breaking close, statutory remedy exclusive, 38 Cal. 581.

Commercial Bank v. Canal Commissioners, 10 Wend. 26. Cited, Mandamus, rules of pleading, 27 Cal. 672, 684.

Commercial Bank v. Cunningham, 24 Pick. 274. Cited, Mortgage, to secure future advances, valid, 35 Cal. 309.

Commercial Bank v. Kortright, 22 Wend. 348. Approved, Conversion, measure of damages where value fluctuates, 33 Cal. 120; Personal Property, possession as evidence of ownership, rule applied to corporate stock, 42 Cal. 147.

Commercial Bank v. Norton, 1 Hill, 501. Approved, Agent, cannot delegate powers, 7 Cal. 542.

Commissioners of Funded Debt of San Jose v. Younger, 29 Cal. 147. Cited as not in conflict, Attorney and Counsel, signature of attorney to pleading, 30 Cal. 200. Distinguished, authority of, to act, 35 Cal. 538.

Commissioners of Knox Co. v. Aspinwall, 21 How. 539. Cited, Corporations, presumptions as to official acts of officers, 37 Cal. 588.

Commissioners of the Poor v. Lynch, 2 McCord, 170. Cited, Public Officers, official discretion not subject to review, 4 Cal. 179.

Commonwealth v. Addicks, 5 Bin. 520. Commented on, Divorce, custody of child, 14 Cal. 517.

Commonwealth v. Alburger, 1 Whart. 469. Cited, Dedication, by deed, when inoperative, 42 Cal. 553.

Commonwealth v. Alger, 7 Cush. 53. Cited, Statutory Construction, 27 Cal. 402.

Commonwealth v. Aves, 18 Pick. 217. Cited, National Comity, right of transit with slaves, 9 Cal. 163; effect of local law, Id.; 1 Dill. 226; 19 How. 591.

Commonwealth v. Bacon, 6 Serg. & R. 322. Cited, Legislature, power over salaries of office, 22 Cal. 319; 10 How. 418.

Commonwealth v. Bigelow, 3 Pick. 31. Commented on, Forcible Entry, when action will not lie against sheriff, 29 Cal. 219.

Commonwealth v. Binns, 17 Serg. & R. 220. Cited, Office, eligibility to, 13 Cal. 155.

Commonwealth v. Breed, 4 Pick. 460. Cited, Eminent Domain, legislature exclusive judges of necessity for condemnation, 18 Cal. 252.

Commonwealth v. Buzzel, 16 Pick. 153. Cited as inapplicable, juror and jury, examination of juror, 2 Cal. 259; Elections, irregularities which will not invalidate, 12 Cal. 361.

Commonwealth v. Chambre, 4 Dall. 143. Cited, Statutory Construction, "month" defined, 21 Cal. 396; 31 Cal. 176.

Commonwealth v. Chapman, 11 Cush. 422. Cited, Murder, sufficiency of indictment, 21 Cal. 403; 102 Mass. 159.

Commonwealth v. Chase, 6 Cush. 248. Cited, Municipal Corporations, validity of ordinance, 23 Cal. 372.

Commonwealth v. Chevalier, 7 Dane's Abr. 134. Cited, Burglary, what constitutes, 19 Cal. 578.

Commonwealth v. Child, 10 Pick. 252. Cited, Instructions to Jury, common law rule as to weight of evidence changed, 17 Cal. 170; 27 Cal. 513.

Commonwealth v. Clue, 3 Rawle, 498. Cited, Criminal Procedure, former acquittal, when jeopardy attaches, 41 Cal. 216.

Commonwealth v. Commissioners of Allegheny Co., 32 Penn. St. 218. Cited, Municipal Corporations, payment of debts, 21 Cal. 698. Reviewed and approved, Id. 701.

Commonwealth v. Cook, 6 Serg. & R. 577. Cited, Criminal Procedure, when discharge of jury operates as an acquittal, 38 Cal. 478. Commented on as to constitutional rights of prisoner, Id. 479; when not an acquittal, 41 Cal. 216.

Commonwealth v. Coombs, 2 Mass. 489. Cited, Eminent Domain, rule of compensation, 32 Cal. 541.

Commonwealth v. Cummings, 3 Cush. 212. Cited, Criminal Procedure, discharge of jury when an acquittal, 38 Cal. 478.

Commonwealth v. Dow, 10 Met. 382. Cited, Municipal Corporations, validity of ordinance, 23 Cal. 372.

Commonwealth v. Downing, 4 Gray, 29. Cited, Evidence, of feigned accomplice requires no corroboration, 30 Cal. 317.

Commonwealth v. Duane, 1 Bin. 601. Cited, Statutory Construction, 27 Cal. 402.

Commonwealth v. Eaton, 15 Pick. 274. Cited, Indictment, distinct acts may be coupled in one count, 27 Cal. 401.

Commonwealth v. Fowler, 10 Mass. 293. Cited, Parties, Attorney-General, informations by, 25 Cal. 247.

Commonwealth v. Green, 1 Ashm. 296. Commented on, Murder, degrees defined, 17 Cal. 395. Approved, 25 Cal. 365.

Commonwealth v. Green, 17 Mass. 515. Cited, New Trial, power of court to grant in criminal case, 28 Cal. 464.

Commonwealth v. Grey, 2 Gray, 501. Approved, Criminal Procedure, indictment, insufficiency of disjunctive statement, 35 Cal. 509.

Commonwealth v. Grimes, 10 Gray, 470. Cited, Indictment, larceny, description of goods, 36 Cal. 247.

Commonwealth v. Hanley, 9 Penn. St. 513. Disapproved, Offices, vacancy, 6 Cal. 290 Cited, 37 Cal. 621; Id. 641; term of office, 10 Cal. 44.

Commonwealth v. Hardy, 2 Mass. 317. Cited, Evidence, of character, in criminal cases, 5 Cal. 130.

Commonwealth v. Harrison, 2 Va. Cas. 202. Cited, Former Acquittal, what operates as an acquittal, 38 Cal. 478.

Commonwealth v. Hayden, 4 Gray, 18. Commented on, Juror and Jury, excusing juror, 32 Cal. 46.

Commonwealth v. Hope, 22 Pick. 1. Cited, Indictment, distinct acts in one count, 27 Cal. 401.

Commonwealth v. Hultz, 6 Penn. St. 470. Cited, Mandamus, 28 Cal. 641.

Commonwealth v. Hutchinson, 10 Mass. 225. Cited, Witness, competency of, infant, examination, 10 Cal. 67.

Commonwealth v. Jones, 1 Leigh, 598. Commented on, Murder, degrees of, 17 Cal. 396; statutory construction, 27 Cal. 586.

Commonwealth v. Judges of Court of Common Pleas, 3 Bin. 273; 1 Serg. & R. 187. Cited, Mandamus, 28 Cal. 640, 641.

Commonwealth v. Justices, etc., of Middlesex, 9 Mass. 388. Cited, Jury, province of, 32 Cal. 541; Eminent Domain, estimation of damages, 31 Cal. 374; 32 Cal. 541.

Commonwealth v. Keeper of the Prison, 2 Ashm. 231. Cited, Murder, degree of guilt, 17 Cal. 396.

Commonwealth v. Kimball, 21 Pick. 376. Cited, Statutory Construction, repeal by implication, 10 Cal. 316.

Commonwealth v. Lancaster Co., 6 Bin. 5. Commented on, Jurisdiction, mandamus, 1 Cal. 343.

Commonwealth v. Leath, 1 Va. Cas. 151. Cited, Criminal Procedure, judgments to take effect at completion of term of imprisonment, 22 Cal. 137.

Commonwealth v. McCaul, 1 Va. Cas. 305. Commented on, Verdict, vitiated by separation of jury, 21 Cal. 340.

Commonwealth v. McCloskey, 2 Rawle, 381. Cited, Quo Warranto, jurisdiction in actions by, 1 Cal. 344.

Commonwealth v. McKisson, 13 Serg. & R. 144. Doubted, Judgment, lien of, 10 Cal. 82. Cited, 37 Cal. 143.

Commonwealth v. McPike, 3 Cush. 181. Cited, Evidence, declarations as part of the *res gestæ*, 35 Cal. 51; 8 Wall. 406. Criticised, 2 Allen, 140.

Commonwealth v. McWilliams, 11 Penn. St. 61. Cited, Legislature, power to confer authority for local aid to railroads, etc., 13 Cal. 188; 41 Cal. 160.

Commonwealth v. Merrifield, 4 Met. 468. Cited, Indictment, what must state, 19 Cal. 601.

Commonwealth v. Miller's Admrs., 8 Serg. & R. 452. Cited, Surety, discharged by negligence of creditor, 26 Cal. 542; 29 Cal. 198.

Commonwealth v. Milton, 12 B. Mon. 212. Approved, Taxation, action lies for taxes, 16 Cal. 529.

Commonwealth v. Moltz, 10 Penn. St. 531. Commented on, Equitable Estoppel, doctrine when applied, 14 Cal. 368. Cited, 26 Cal. 40.

Commonwealth v. Murray, 2 Ashm. 43. Cited, Murder, degree of guilt, 17 Cal. 396.

Commonwealth v. Olds, 5 Litt. 139. Cited, Criminal Procedure, defense of former acquittal, 28 Cal. 463.

Commonwealth v. Phillips, 16 Mass. 423. Cited, Criminal Procedure, accessories, 10 Cal. 70.

Commonwealth v. Pittsburg, 34 Penn. St. 496. Cited, Municipal Corporations, payment of debts, powers conferred by legislature, 21 Cal. 698; remedy by mandamus, Id. 701.

Commonwealth v. Purchase, 2 Pick. 520. Cited, Criminal Procedure, retrial on discharge of jury, 27 Cal. 399; 41 Cal. 216.

Commonwealth v. Ray, 3 Gray, 441. Cited, Criminal Procedure, sufficiency of indictment for forgery, 35 Cal. 507.

Commonwealth v. Roby, 12 Pick. 496. Cited, Criminal Procedure, separation of jury a ground for setting aside verdict, 5 Cal. 276; polling jury, practice, 20 Cal. 72; retrial on discharge of jury, 27 Cal. 399.

Commonwealth v. Rogers, 7 Met. 500; 1 Am. Lead. Cas. 111. Disapproved, Criminal Procedure, sanity presumed, burden of proof of insanity, 20 Cal. 520.

Commonwealth v. Sawtelle, 11 Cush. 142. Cited, Larceny, sufficiency of description of property in indictment, 36 Cal. 247.

Commonwealth v. Scannel, 11 Cush. 548. Cited, Rape, sufficiency of indictment, 29 Cal. 576.

Commonwealth v. Searle, 2 Bin. 332. Cited, Forgery, sufficiency of indictment, 35 Cal. 509.

Commonwealth v. Sessions of Norfolk, 5 Mass. 435. Cited, Verdict, setting aside for disqualification of juror, 9 Cal. 537.

Commonwealth v. Shortridge, 3 J. J. Marsh. 638. Cited, Statutory Construction, "month" defined, 31 Cal. 176.

Commonwealth v. Small, 26 Penn. St. 35. Cited, Quo Warranto, when it lies, 14 Cal. 46.

Commonwealth v. Stearns, 10 Met. 256. Cited, Criminal Procedure, evidence admissible to prove forgery, 28 Cal. 515.

Commonwealth v. Stockton, 5 Mon. 192. Cited, Sheriff, liability on official bond, in case of trespass, 14 Cal. 199. Questioned, 4 Hill, 572.

Commonwealth v. Sugland, 4 Gray, 7. Cited, Rape, sufficiency of indictment for, 29 Cal. 576.

Commonwealth v. Sullivan, 6 Gray, 477. Cited, Rape, sufficiency of indictment, 29 Cal. 576.

Commonwealth v. Thompson, 13 B. Mon. 161. Cited, Public Officers, when injunction lies to restrain from receipt of trust funds, 10 Cal. 588.

Commonwealth v. Townsend, 5 Allen, 216. Cited, Criminal Procedure, retrial on discharge of jury, 27 Cal. 399.

Commonwealth v. Trimmer, 1 Mass. 476. Cited, Criminal Procedure, allegation of ownership of stolen property of firm in indictment, 19 Cal. 599; 36 Cal. 248.

Commonwealth v. Tuck, 20 Pick. 360. Cited, Indictment, charging distinct offenses, 27 Cal. 401.

Commonwealth v. Wade, 17 Pick. 395. Cited, Criminal Procedure, discharge of jury, when an acquittal, 38 Cal. 478.

Commonwealth v. Webster, 5 Cush. 295. Cited, Homicide, sufficient allegation in indictment, 34 Cal. 201; Id. 210; Instructions, practice, 28 Cal. 426; 32 Cal. 283. Approved, Reasonable Doubt, 30 Cal. 155. Cited, 39 Cal. 333. Commented on, 19 Ohio St. 268.

Commonwealth v. Westchester R. R. Co., 3 Grant, Pa. 200. Disapproved, Railroad, issuance of corporate stock, 42 Cal. 209.

Commonwealth v. Wilkinson, 16 Pick. 176. Approved, Roads and Highways, turnpike road a public highway, 24 Cal. 490.

Commonwealth v. Willard, 22 Pick. 476. Cited, Criminal Procedure, evidence of feigned accomplice does not require corroboration, 30 Cal. 317.

Commonwealth v. Williams, 2 Cush. 582. Cited, Criminal Procedure, assistant counsel in criminal cases, 27 Cal. 67.

Commonwealth v. Wright, 3 Amer. Jur. 185. Cited, Wharf and Wharfage, 1 Cal. 469.

Commonwealth v. York, 9 Met. 93. Cited, Criminal Procedure, degree of proof necessary, 5 Cal. 130.

Comstock v. Clemens, 19 Cal. 77. Cited, Jurisdiction, power of court to control its judgment, 37 Cal. 228; Certiorari, review on, 8 Nev. 362.

Comstock v. Smith, 13 Pick. 116. Cited, Conveyance, not under seal, construed, 11 Cal. 160; without warranty, does not convey after-acquired title, 14 Cal. 628; so with covenant confined to estate conveyed, 25 Cal. 452.

Comstock v. Smith, 23 Me. 210. Cited, Appeal, judgment not reversed where error was without injury, 26 Cal. 467.

Conant v. Conant, 10 Cal. 249. Approved, Jurisdiction of Supreme Court, 13 Cal. 30; 26 Cal. 386; 30 Cal. 579; 31 Cal. 84, 86, 89; appeals in special cases, 29 Cal. 418. Commented on, 42 Cal. 64. Approved, 42 Cal. 68.

Conger v. Johnston, 2 Denio, 96. Cited, Pleading, affirmative allegations, when not new matter, 21 Cal. 436.

Conger v. Weaver, 6 Cal. 548. Cited, Mining Claims, vested rights, 7 Cal. 327; appropriation of water, 8 Cal. 338; 10 Cal. 238; notice as evidence of possession, 8 Cal. 280.

Congregational Society v. Sperry, 10 Conn. 200. Commented on, Officers, term of office, right to hold over, 28 Cal. 53, 57.

Coniff v. Hastings, 36 Cal. 292. Approved, Street Assessment, personal judgment cannot be rendered against lot owner, 36 Cal. 105.

Conklin v. Dutcher, 5 How. Pr. 388. Cited, Undertaking, validity of, 29 Cal. 199.

Conlin v. Seaman, 22 Cal. 546. Affirmed, Street Improvement, power of superintendent, 22 Cal. 552; review of assessments, appeal to board, 29 Cal. 87. Distinguished, as to statutory enactments, 30 Cal. 538; 32 Cal. 487. See 31 Cal. 240; 32 Cal. 269; 38 Cal. 72; 34 Cal. 310; 35 Cal. 512.

Connah v. Hale, 23 Wend. 462. Cited, Demand, objections when to be taken, 16 Cal. 77.

Conn v. Penn, 5 Wheat. 424; S. C. 1 Pet. C. C. 511. Commented on, Land Titles, survey as evidence, 10 Cal. 627. Cited, Parties, in equity, 31 Cal. 427.

Connecticut v. Jackson, 1 Johns. Ch. 13. Cited, Interest, computation on partial payments, 3 Cal. 233.

Conner v. Henderson, 15 Mass. 321. Commented on, Contract, rescission of, for fraud, 29 Cal. 593, 594.

Conner v. New York City, 5 N. Y. 285. Cited, Fees of office, power of legislature over, 22 Cal. 319.

Conner v. Paxson, 1 Blackf. 168. Cited, Franchise, validity of license cannot be collaterally impeached, 6 Cal. 599.

Connolly v. Goodwin, 5 Cal. 220. Cited, Seal, sufficiency of, 5 Cal. 318.

Connolly v. Taylor, 2 Pet. 556. Cited, Jurisdiction, removal of action to Federal Court, 28 Cal. 99; 7 Pet. 261.

Connor v. Morris, 23 Cal. 447. Commented on, Appeal, practice on, 28 Cal. 595.

Conovar v. Cooper, 3 Barb. 115. Cited, Parent and Child, emancipation of minor, 8 Cal. 123.

Conover v. Warren, 1 Gilm. Ill. 498. Cited, Vendor's Lien, waived by taking security, 17 Cal. 74.

Conrad v. Lindley, 2 Cal. 173. Cited, Instructions, may be modified, 5 Cal. 491; 25 Cal. 470; Findings, when conclusive, 24 Cal. 176; Specific Performance, what must be shown by party seeking to enforce, 38 N. H. 407.

Conrad v. Shomo, 44 Penn. St. 193. Cited, Husband and Wife, conveyance to wife during coverture, presumed common property, 30 Cal. 43.

Conro v. Port Henry Iron Co., 12 Barb. 27. Commented on, Corporations, management of affairs, by whom conducted, 33 Cal. 20; proceedings to set aside transfers, 37 Cal. 596.

Conroy v. Woods, 13 Cal. 626. Referred to, 22 Cal. 187. Approved and followed, Partnership, lien of attachment of firm creditors preferred, 22 Cal. 199; 23 Cal. 501; 25 Cal. 106, 107.

Consequa v. Fanning, 3 Johns. Ch. 587. Cited, Account Stated, conclusiveness of, 9 Cal. 361.

Considerant v. Brisbane, 22 N. Y. 389. Cited, Parties, Trustee of an express trust, proper party-plaintiff, 34 Cal. 138.

Contra Costa Co. v. Alameda County. See People *v.* Alameda County.

Contra Costa C. M. R.R. Co. v. Moss, 23 Cal. 323. Cited, Eminent Domain, lands appropriated by one company cannot be taken from it by another, 31 Cal. 217; exercise of judicial powers, in condemnation to railroad purposes, 36 Cal. 645; Appeal, jurisdiction of Supreme Court in special cases, 42 Cal. 68.

Conway v. Alexander, 7 Cranch, 237. Commented on, Deed, as a mortgage, 9 Cal. 549; 7 Tex. 150; defeasable contract of sale, 33 Cal. 333; 41 Cal. 27. Cited, 19 How. 299.

Conwell v. Evill, 4 Blackf. 67. Cited, Deed as a mortgage, parol evidence admissible to prove, 13 Cal. 130.

Cook v. Allen, 2 Mass. 464. Commented on, Partition, conclusiveness of judgment, 35 Cal. 594.

Cook v. Arnham, 3 P. Wms. 283. Cited, Redemption, equity may be barred by lapse of time, 23 Cal. 34; 10 Wheat. 170.

Cook v. Bonnet, 4 Cal. 397. Cited, Statutory Construction, 1 McAll. 223.

Cook v. Cockrill, 1 Stewt. 475. Cited, Negotiable Instruments, action by indorsee against indorser, measure of recovery, 16 Cal. 160.

Cook v. Cox, 3 Maule & S. 113. Commented on, Libel and Slander, construction of allegation in action for, 8 Cal. 624.

Cook v. Darling, 18 Pick. 393. Cited, Judgment, presumptions in favor of regularity of proceedings, 9 Cal. 321; judgment not subject to collateral attack, 30 Cal. 446.

Cook v. De La Guerra, 24 Cal. 237. Cited, Appeal, findings presumed in support of judgment, 29 Cal. 142. Approved, 4 Nev. 336.

Cook v. Dickerson, 1 Duer, 686. Cited, Judgment Roll, papers mingled not falling within statutory definition, no part of judgment roll, 33 Cal. 513.

Cook, Estate of Martin E., 14 Cal. 129.   Approved, Probate, decree conclusive, 18 Cal. 505.   Cited, 26 Cal. 431.

Cook v. Farren, 34 Barb. 95.   Cited, Jurisdiction, proof of facts necessary to confer jurisdiction of the person, 31 Cal. 349.

Cook v. Hoyt, 13 Ill. 144.   Cited, Appeal, remedy exclusive, 8 Cal. 300.

Cook v. Klink, 8 Cal. 347.   Approved, Homestead, wife a necessary party in action of foreclosure of mortgage on, 13 Iowa, 584.

Cook v. Manotus, 4 Johns. Ch. 166.   Cited, Judgment, on the pleadings, 1 Cal. 143.

Cook v. Manotus, 5 Johns. Ch. 94.   Commented on, Foreclosure, necessary parties, 10 Cal. 552.

Cook v. McChristian, 4 Cal. 23.   Cited, Homestead Act, character of homestead title impressed by residence previous to passage of act, 10 Cal. 297; Homestead, how constituted, selection and dedication commented on, 6 Cal. 235; 7 Mich. 504.   Distinguished, 4 Cal. 272.   Commented on and followed, Occupancy of Family, test of dedication, 6 Cal. 167; 7 Mich. 510.
. Approved, Occupancy presumptive evidence of dedication, 15 Cal. 204; 25 Cal. 111.   Cited, Notice imparted by possession and residence, 7 Cal. 345.   Explained, 7 Cal. 490.   Approved, general policy of statute, 45 Miss. 181.   Cited, what property exempt under, 47 N. H. 270; character of estate, a joint tenancy with right of survivorship, 22 Cal. 638; valid sale of, how made, 6 Cal. 73; wife not bound by mortgage of husband, 31 Cal. 530; judgment no lien on, 23 Cal. 400.

Cook v. Moseley, 13 Wend. 277.   Cited, Pleading, counter claim, 26 Cal. 306.

Cooke v. Gibbs, 3 Mass. 193.   Cited, Execution, enforcement of attachment lien, 29 Cal. 383.

Cooke v. Graham's Admrs., 3 Cranch, 235.   Approved, Undertaking, construction of, intention of parties to govern, 8 Cal. 551.

Cooke v. Smith, 7 Hill, 186.   Approved, Set-off, judgments how set-off, 11 Cal. 103.

Cooke v. Spears, 2 Cal. 409.   Cited, Powers, execution of, may be enforced, 30 Cal. 437.

Cook's Lessee v. Carroll, 6 Md. 112. Cited, Title, conclusiveness of patent, 14 Cal. 469.

Cooley v. Betts, 24 Wend. 203. Approved, Factors, demand necessary to fix liability, 8 Cal. 457.

Cooley v. Board of Wardens, 12 How. 299. Approved, Commerce, relative powers of Federal and State legislation over, 42 Cal. 589; constitutional construction, 19 How. 616.

Cooley v. Rose, 3 Mass. 221. Cited, Interest, on interest after due, 29 Cal. 392.

Coolidge v. Payson, 2 Wheat. 66. Cited, Negotiable Instruments, liability of drawee, on promise to accept, 29 Cal. 601.

Coolidge v. Williams, 4 Mass. 140. Cited, Statutory Construction, implications in statute, 13 Cal. 457.

Coope v. Lowerre, 1 Barb. Ch. 45. Commented on, Probate, order of administration, test of incompetency, 23 Cal. 480.

Cooper v. Bakeman, 33 Me. 376. Cited, Replevin, damages may be recorded in subsequent action, 10 Cal. 521.

Cooper v. Bigalow, 1 Cow. 206. Cited, Assignment, assignee of judgment takes subject to equities, 22 Cal. 433.

Cooper v. Martin, 1 Dana, 25. Cited, Foreclosure, necessary parties, 10 Cal. 552.

Cooper, Matter of, 22 N. Y. 81. Cited, Attorney and Counsel, admission of attorneys-at-law, 22 Cal. 315; Government, distribution of official powers, 34 Cal. 541.

Cooper v. Pena, 21 Cal. 403. Cited, Specific Performance, contract for sale of land, payment in services, 24 Cal. 178; when equity will not enforce, 40 Cal. 68.

Cooper v. Roberts, 18 How. 176. Reviewed, Title, validity of State Patent, 16 Cal. 328; conclusiveness of, in actions of ejectment, 13 Cal. 413.

Cooper v. Schultz, 32 How. Pr. 107. Cited, Statutes, validity of, legislative power to determine facts, 33 Cal. 286.

Cooper v. Sunderland, 3 Iowa, 114. Cited, Judgment, of court of record, not subject to collateral attack, 34 Cal. 428.

Cooper v. Whitney, 3 Hill, 101. Commented on, Assignment, in trust, 36 Cal. 430.

9

Cooper's Lessee v. Galbraith, 3 Wash. C. C. 550. Approved, Execution, title of purchaser at sale, 38 Cal. 658.

Coovert v. O'Conner, 8 Watts, 470. Cited, Easement, no distinctions between land covered or not covered with water, 31 Cal. 590.

Cope v. Williams, 4 Ala. 362. Cited, Money Paid, recovery back of money paid under void contract, conditions, precedent, 16 Cal. 638.

Copeland v. Copeland, 28 Me. 539. Commented on, Equitable Estoppel, 14 Cal. 369. Cited, 26 Cal. 40.

Copper Hill Min. Co. v. Spencer, 25 Cal. 11. Cited, New Trial, motion, not a stay of execution, 28 Cal. 71.

Copper Hill Min. Co. v. Spencer, 25 Cal. 18. Cited, Mining Claims, conveyance by verbal sale, 30 Cal. 363.

Coppin v. Gunner, 2 Ld. Ray. 1572. Cited, Civil Death, effect, civilly, of conviction for felony, 35 Cal. 398.

Coppinger v. Rice, 33 Cal. 408. Cited, Tax Title, purchase by agent of one in possession does not pass the title, 36 Cal. 146; party in possession cannot acquire title at sale, 36 Cal. 326; 38 Cal. 223; 39 Cal. 357. Explained, Probate, unknown under Mexican system, 37 Cal. 89. Doubted, Id. 90. Affirmed on principle of *stare decisis,* Rhodes, J. Id. 91.

Corbett v. Eno, 13 Abb. Pr. 65. Cited, Pleading, sham answer, 32 Cal. 574.

Corbin v. Jackson, 14 Wend. 619. Cited, Deed, grantee of land not segregated, as tenant in common with grantor, 24 Cal. 111; 37 Cal. 521.

Corcoran v. Doll, 32 Cal. 82. Cited, Negotiable Instruments, parties, holder of note may recover, 32 Cal. 574; Pleading, demand for relief, 37 Cal. 324.

Cordier v. Schloss, 12 Cal. 143. Reviewed on second appeal and principle affirmed, 18 Cal. 580. Cited, Confession of Judgment, when fraudulent, 27 Cal. 235; 37 Cal. 336; 1 Saw. 76; 2 Or. 182; Pleading, answer not evidence, 16 Cal. 73.

Corey v. Mann, 14 How. Pr. 163. Commented on, Landlord and Tenant, lessor when under obligations to repair, 33 Cal. 346.

Cormerais v. Genella, 22 Cal. 116. Cited, Foreclosure, personal judgment in, 23 Cal. 623; 4 Nev. 390.

Cornell v. Moulton, 3 Denio, 12. Cited, Negotiable Instruments, days of grace, computation of time, 38 Cal. 410.

Corning v. Greene, 23 Barb. 50. Cited, Statutory Construction, statutes, conditional on votes of citizens, 25 Cal. 646.

Corning v. Slosson, 16 N. Y. 294. Cited, Judgment, irregularities not to vitiate, 22 Cal. 26.

Corning v. Smith, 6 N. Y. 82. Approved, Foreclosure, adverse titles not proper subjects for determination, 18 Cal. 474. See 2 Black. 509.

Corning v. Troy Iron Co., 6 How. Pr. 89. Cited, Issues, facts conceded need not be tried, 8 Cal. 397.

Cornish v. Searell, 8 Barn. & C. 471; 15 Eng. C. L. 234. Cited, Landlord and Tenant, disputing landlord's title, 8 Cal. 596; 33 Cal. 245, 254. Reviewed, 35 Cal. 573.

Cornish v. Young, 1 Ashm. 153. Cited, Municipal Officers, legal presumptions in favor of acts of, 3 Cal. 453.

Cornwall v. Culver, 16 Cal. 423. Affirmed, Ejectment, lies directly on Mexican grant, 18 Cal. 199; 19 Cal. 97; 21 Cal. 577; 24 Cal. 580; 31 Cal. 493; 33 Cal. 108. Cited, Confirmation of Grant, 21 Cal. 579; segregation of land in grant, 1 Saw. 682.

Cornwall v. Haight, 8 Barb. 329. Cited, Pleading, evidence must correspond with contract as set out, 36 Cal. 179.

Corp v. McComb, 1 Johns. Cas. 329. Cited, Negotiable Instruments, presentation and demand, when may be made, 8 Cal. 632.

Corporations, Case of The, 4 Coke, 78. Cited, Corporations, exercise of corporate powers, 33 Cal. 22.

Corporation of New York v. Dawson, 2 Johns. Cas. 335. Cited, Use and Occupation, action for, when it lies, 3 Cal. 204.

Correas v. San Francisco, 1 Cal. 452. Cited, Corporations, powers how restricted, 22 Cal. 628.

Corser v. Craig, 1 Wash. C. C. 424. Cited, Wager, stakeholder as garnishee, duty of, 11 Cal. 350; Assignment, equity protects rights of assignee, 12 Cal. 98.

Cortelyou v. Lansing, 2 Caines Cas. in E. 200. Approved, Conversion, measure of damages where value fluctuates, 9 Cal. 563. Qualified, 33 Cal. 119; 39 Cal. 421; Pledge, distinction between pledge and chattel mortgage, 35 Cal. 411.

Corwin v. Daly, 7 Bosw. 222.   Cited, Trade Marks, law applicable to, 35 Cal. 75; ordinary words not subject of property, Id. 76.

Corwin v. Freeland, 6 How. Pr. 241.   Cited, Fraud, when arrest of party is authorized, 10 Cal. 412; 6 N. Y. 562. Distinguished, 30 N. Y. 581.

Corwin v. Merritt, 3 Barb. 341.   Cited, Jurisdiction, of probate courts, limited and special, 19 Cal. 209; compliance with statute essential to confer, 20 Cal. 312, 314.

Corwin v. N. Y. & Erie R. R. Co., 13 N. Y. 42.   Cited, Railroads, liability for injury to cattle, 18 Cal. 355.   Commented on and statute distinguished, 21 Ohio St. 594.

Cory v. Cory, 3 Stock. 400.   Cited, Alimony, wife entitled to, on separation, 38 Cal. 277.

Coryell v. Cain, 16 Cal. 567.   Referred to, 32 Cal. 201; Mining Claims, 17 Cal. 119.   Commented on, Ejectment, on title by prior possession, 21 Cal. 324.   Cited, 4 Nev. 67, 69; possession must be actual, 30 Cal. 355; 32 Cal. 20; 39 Cal. 44; defendant may show outstanding title, rule qualified as to public lands, 22 Cal. 516. Distinguished, 23 Cal. 536.   Cited, Pleading, evidence must not be set forth, 30 Cal. 200; Id. 565; 32 Cal. 456; 36 Cal. 233; 3 Or. 455; Appeal, orders and judgments entered by consent not reviewable, 37 Cal. 158; 42 Cal. 518.

Cosgrove v. Johnson, 30 Cal. 509.   Cited, New Trial, authentication of statement, 7 Nev. 323.   Construed and distinguished, Appeal, dismissal of, 2 Or. 254.

Coslake v. Till, 1 Russ. 376.   `Cited, Contract, when time is of essence, 10 Cal. 327.

Cossitt v. Biscoe, 7 Eng. 95.   Cited, Probate, conclusiveness of decree, 14 Cal. 130.

Costigan v. Mohawk & H. R. R., 2 Denio, 609.   Cited, Contract, measure of damages on breach of contract for services, 38 Cal. 666.

Cotes v. Carroll, 28 How. Pr. 436.   Cited, Appeal, adverse party defined, 38 Cal. 641.

Cotes v. Davis, 1 Camp. 485.   Cited, Negotiable Instruments, execution or acceptance of bill by agent, 13 Cal. 48.

Cotten v. Ellis, 7 Jones, N. C. 545.   Cited, Mandamus, may issue to executive officer, 39 Cal. 211.

Cotton v. Thurland, 5 Term Rep. 405. Cited, Wagers, money in hands of stakeholders, when recoverable, 37 Cal. 673.

Cotton v. United States, 11 How. 229. Cited, Public Lands, trespass upon, by cutting timber, may be maintained by United States, 22 Cal. 455.

Cottrill v. Myrick, 12 Me. 222. Cited, Eminent Domain, province of legislature to judge of necessity, etc., 31 Cal. 372.

Couch v. Jeffries, 4 Burr. 2460. Cited, Statutory Construction, statutes not to be construed retrospectively, 4 Cal. 133.

Couch v. Terry's Admrs. 12 Ala. 228. Cited, Sureties, contribution between, 20 Cal. 135.

Couch v. Ulster & Orange Branch T. Co., 4 Johns. Ch. 26. Cited, Injunction, practice on dissolution, 35 Cal. 60.

Coulson v. Walton, 9 Pet. 62. Commented on, Equitable Titles, how divested, 40 Cal. 571.

Coulter v. Stark, 7 Cal. 244. Cited, Certiorari, what reviewable under writ, 8 Nev. 362.

Coulter's Case, 5 Coke, 30. Commented on, Ejectment, recoupment of damages, 7 Cal. 7; 8 Wheat. 81.

Countess of Rutland's Case, 5 Coke, 25. Commented on, Contracts, computation of time, 8 Cal. 417.

Countryman v. Boyer, 3 How. Pr. 386. Explained, Assignment, verdicts in actions of tort, 22 Cal. 178; of Judgment, rights of assignee, 33 Cal. 528.

County Court of Warren v. Daniel, 2 Bibb, 573. Cited, Mandamus, when will not issue to inferior tribunal, 24 Cal. 84.

Courtwright v. B. R. & A. W. & M. Co., 30 Cal. 573. Approved, Jurisdiction, of district courts to prevent or abate nuisance, 36 Cal. 195; of county court, for recovery of possession of premises held over by tenants, 42 Cal. 325.

Coutant v. People, 11 Wend. 512. Approved, Office and Officer, term of office, 11 Cal. 88.

Coveney v. Tannahill, 1 Hill, 33. Cited, Witness, privileged communications, 23 Cal. 334.

Covanhoven v. Hart, 21 Penn. St. 495. Cited, Insolvency, preference of creditors, 10 Cal. 277; Id. 494; 19 Cal. 46.

Covill v. Hill, 4 Denio, 323.   Cited, Personal Property, possession as evidence of ownership, 19 Cal. 76; 42 Cal. 147.

Covillaud v. Tanner, 7 Cal. 38.   Followed, Exceptions, to relevancy and sufficiency of evidence, must be taken at the trial, 7 Cal. 423; 3 Nev. 520; point must be specifically stated, 10 Cal. 268; 12 Cal. 245; 16 Cal. 248.

Covington, City of, v. McNickle's Heirs, 18 B. Mon. 286. Cited, Statutory Construction, general words may be restrained by special expressions, 24 Cal. 558.

Cowell v. Buckelew, 14 Cal. 640.   Cited, Probate, statutory provisions as to sales of property construed, 21 Cal. 31; 29 Cal. 373.   Cited as inapplicable, Mandamus, 28 Cal. 71.

Cowell v. Doub, 12 Cal. 273.   Approved, Taxation, power of government to enforce payment of tax, 16 Cal. 344; avoiding tax by failure of Board of Equalization to meet, what must be shown, 18 Cal. 632; 23 Cal. 115; presumptions in favor of regularity of Board, Id. 117; provisions in tax law directory, 43 Ala. 639.

Cowing v. Rogers, 34 Cal. 648.   Cited, Specific Performance, decree may prescribe terms, 34 Cal. 517.   Cited, Practice, remedy on defective findings, 38 Cal. 531; on motion for new trial, Id. 536.

Cowles v. Whitman, 10 Conn. 121.   Cited, Specific Performance, relief will be granted on contracts relating to chattels, 23 Cal. 393.

Cowperthwaite v. Jones, 2 Dall. 55.   Cited, Verdict, validity of, 25 Cal. 401.

Cox v. Davis, 17 Ala. 716.   Cited, *Stare decisis*, 15 Cal. 622; Evidence, of handwriting, when admissible, 26 Cal. 412.

Cox v. Hall, 18 Vt. 191.   Cited, Witness, vendor of chattel, competency of, 23 Cal. 446.

Cox v. Jagger, 2 Cow. 638.   Cited, Award, good in part, 9 Cal. 146; when submission to arbitration may be made, 21 Cal. 321.

Cox v. Mayor, etc., 18 Geo. 735.   Cited, Injunction, granting and continuance, in discretion of court, 39 Cal. 167.

Cox v. Robinson, 2 Stewt. & P. 91.   Cited, Principal and Agent, authority of agent to bind principal, 24 Cal. 140.

Cox v. Thomas, 9 Gratt. 323.   Cited, Probate, proceedings and orders not subject to collateral attack, 18 Cal. 505.

Cox v. Wheeler, 7 Paige, 248. Cited, Mortgage, equity of redemption, 14 Cal. 34; power of sale in, does not affect remedy by foreclosure, 22 Cal. 125; purchaser at foreclosure sale, title acquired by, 40 Cal. 235.

Coye v. Palmer, 16 Cal. 158. Cited, Negotiable Instruments, certificate of deposit, a promissory note, 22 Cal. 249; 35 Cal. 120.

Cozine v. Graham, 2 Paige, 177. Cited, Specific Performance, verbal contract for sale of lands, 10 Cal. 160; Pleading, sufficient allegation under statute of frauds, 29 Cal. 599.

Crafts v. Dexter, 8 Ala. 769. Cited, Injunction, when equity will relieve from judgment at law, 14 Cal. 143.

Craig v. Hawkins' Heirs, 1 Bibb. 54. Commented on, Deed, calls in, meanders of river to be reduced to straight line, 25 Cal. 142; 11 Wheat. 219.

Craig v. Leslie, 3 Wheat. 563. Cited, Alien, may hold real estate until office found, 5 Cal. 378; or denouncement in civil law, 26 Cal. 477; 12 How. 107.

Craig v. Radford, 3 Wheat. 594. Cited, Public Officers, presumption as to regularity of their proceedings, 3 Cal. 448.

Craig v. State of Missouri, 4 Pet. 410. Cited, Bills of Credit, defined, 7 Cal. 477. Distinguished, 18 Geo. 434.

Craig v. Tappin, 2 Sand. Ch. 78. Cited, Mortgage, to secure future advances, valid, 35 Cal. 309. Approved, 35 Ill. 294.

Craig v. Wells, 11 N. Y. 322. Commented on, Deed, restrictions in *habendum*, clause construed, 17 Cal. 52.

Crampton v. Admin. of Ballard, 10 Vt. 251. Cited, Interest, indebtedness as a consideration for payment of, 6 Cal. 130.

Crandall v. Amador Co., 20 Cal. 72. Approved, Mandamus, what must appear to authorize issuance of, to Board of Supervisors, demand and refusal essential, 37 Cal. 363; 23 Wis. 429.

Crandall v. Blen, 13 Cal. 15. Cited, Execution, levy and sale of chose in action, 34 Cal. 89.

Crandall v. State of Nevada, 6 Wall. 35. Commented on, Commerce, powers of State to regulate, 42 Cal. 588; 34 Md. 368, *et seq.*

Crandall v. Woods, 8 Cal. 136.   Affirmed, Water Rights, possession of land gives right to flowing water, 8 Cal. 323; 10 Cal. 183; 7 Nev. 267, 289; abandonment not presumed from lapse of time, 10 Cal. 183.   Cited, Injunction, power of county judge to issue, 23 Cal. 468; Acts, auxiliary to jurisdiction of district court, 27 Cal. 172.

Crane v. Brannan, 3 Cal. 192.   Cited, Judgments and decrees cannot be collaterally attacked, presumptions, 9 Cal. 321; 11 Cal. 317.

Crane v. Roberts, 5 Greenl. 419.   Cited, Sureties, contract of, construed, discharge of, 11 Cal. 220.

Crane v. Deming, 7 Conn. 388.   Cited, Mortgage, description of debt in, 19 Cal. 351.

Crane, Ex parte, 5 Pet. 190.   Commented on, Jurisdiction, issuance of mandamus, etc., by supreme court, 1 Cal. 147.

Crans v. Hunter, 28 N. Y. 395.   Cited, Pleadings, objections to insufficient allegations of fraud must be taken at trial, 34 Cal. 106.

Crary v. Campbell, 24 Cal. 634.   Cited, Evidence of lost instrument, preliminary evidence, 30 Cal. 365.

Crary v. Goodman, 12 N. Y. 266.   Cited, Pleading, legal and equitable defenses, 36 Cal. 46; trial of issues on, 10 Cal. 160; 19 Cal. 457.

Cravens v. Dewey, 13 Cal. 40.   Cited, Nonsuit, review of order, 31 Cal. 650; 33 Cal. 114.

Crawford v. Mead, 7 Ala. 157.   Approved, Attachment, insufficient defense of garnishee, 7 Cal. 563.

Crawford v. Morrell, 8 John. 253.   Cited, Fraudulent Contract, action not maintainable on, 38 Cal. 110; Contract void in part is void in toto, Id. 40 Cal. 348.

Crawford v. Slade, 9 Ala. 887.   Approved, Attachment, liability of garnishee, 18 Cal. 164.

Crawshay v. Maule, 1 Swanst. 523.   Cited, Mines and Mining, lands held in partnership, 28 Cal. 584.   Doctrine disapproved, 1 Whart. 387.

Craythorne v. Swinburne, 14 Ves. Jr. 164.   Cited, Sureties, right of contribution between, 20 Cal. 135; 3 Denio, 132.

Crayton v. Clark, 11 Ala. 787. Cited, Assignment, to be set up on notice to assignee of pending action, 12 Cal. 98.

Crayton v. Munger, 9 Tex. 292. Cited, Estates of deceased person, not liable for injuries caused by neglect of administrator, 38 Cal. 23.

Creanor v. Nelson, 23 Cal. 464. Cited, Injunction, when not granted, 46 Miss. 12.

Crease v. Babcock, 10 Met. 531. Cited, Parties, in equity, 31 Cal. 427.

Crease v. Barrett, 1 C. M. & R. 932. Cited, Appeal, errors without injury no ground for reversal, 26 Cal. 467.

Creery v. Holly, 14 Wend. 30. Cited, Contract of Sale, construction of, 24 Cal. 465.

Creighton v. Lawrence, Cal. Sup. Ct. Jul. T. 1866 (not reported.) Approved, Street Improvements, resolutions to be signed by President of Board, 30 Cal. 180.

Creighton v. Manson, 27 Cal. 613. Modified, Street Improvements, assessments for, 28 Cal. 348. Construed, Personal Liability, 29 Cal. 124. Approved, Resolution of Intention, 30 Cal. 179, 180. Overruled, 31 Cal. 243. Referred to, 42 Cal. 448.

Creighton v. Pragg, 21 Cal. 115. Cited, Statutory Construction, acts not construed retrospectively, 22 Cal. 554.

Creighton v. San Francisco, 42 Cal. 446. Approved, Legislature, power over municipal funds, appropriation of, 29 Wis. 674.

Creighton v. Scott, 14 Ohio St. 438. Cited, Street Improvements, right of corporation to make, 31 Cal. 684.

Cresinger v. Lessee of Welch, 15 Ohio, 193. Cited, Infant, acquiescence, from lapse of time, 24 Cal. 214.

Cresson v. Stout, 17 John. 116. Cited, Fixtures, when severed, become personal property, 10 Cal. 265.

Crest v. Jack, 3 Watts, 239. Cited, Equitable Estoppel, 10 Cal. 631; 14 Cal. 368.

Crippen v. Hudson, 13 N. Y. 161. Cited, Fraudulent Conveyance, 27 Cal. 315, 316.

Crisp, Ex parte, 1 Atk. 134. Cited, Specific Performance, when will be decreed, 42 Cal. 354.

Crocker v. Crocker, 31 N. Y. 507.   Cited, Corporate Stock, possession as *indicia* of ownership, 42 Cal. 147.

Crocker v. Radcliffe, 3 Brev. 23; S. C. 1 Const. S. C. Rep. 83.   Cited, Attachment, construction of statute, 29 Cal. 367.   Statutes distinguished, Id. 378.   Commented on, 2 Spear, 639.

Crofoot v. Bennett, 2 N. Y. 258.   Cited, Sale and Delivery, chattels mingled with others, 27 Cal. 463.

Croft v. Pawlet, 2 Strange, 1109.   Cited, Will, attestation to, sufficiency of evidence, 10 Cal. 479.

Crofton v. Ormsby, 2 Sch. & L. 603.   Cited, Title, equitable titles, how lost, 40 Cal. 571.

Crommelin v. Minter, 9 Ala. 594.   Approved, Patent, validity cannot be impeached by stranger, 16 Cal. 328.

· **Cromwell v. March**, 1 Ill. 295.   Cited, Arbitration, proceedings on, 42 Cal. 129.

Crop v. Norton, 9 Mod. 233.   Disapproved, Resulting Trust, enforcement of, 21 Cal. 99.   Cited as to same principle, 3 Sum. 466.

Cropsey v. Sweeney, 27 Barb. 310.   Cited, Services, no action lies for gratuitous services, 22 Cal. 510.

Crosby v. Chase, 17 Me. 371.   Cited, Mortgage, effect of tender, 14 Cal. 529.   Distinguished, 30 Me. 396.

Crosby v. Watkins, 12 Cal. 85.   Cited, Award, in action on, tender need not be averred, 23 Cal. 369.

Cross v. Harrison, 16 How. 164.   Cited, Territorial Laws, not affected by conquest or cession, 15 Cal. 559.   Approved, 19 How. 523.

Cross v. Peters, 1 Greenl. 376.   Commented on, Goods and Chattels, what constitutes fraudulent sale of, 8 Cal. 213. Distinguished, 1 Wis. 149.

Cross v. Pinckneyville Mill Co., 17 Ill. 54.   Cited, Corporation, proceedings not invalidated by minor defects in formation of, 22 Cal. 440, 441.

Crosswell v. Byrnes, 9 John. 290.   Cited, Records, import verity, 34 Cal. 423.

Croswell v. Crane, 7 Barb. 191.   Cited, Statutory Construction, conveyances, 11 Cal. 294.

Crouch v. Gridley, 6 Hill, 250. Cited, Assignment, claim founded on tort cannot be assigned before judgment, 22 Cal. 178.

Crouch v. Hall, 15 Ill. 265. Cited, Judicial Notice, not taken of foreign laws, 15 Cal. 254.

Crouch v. London & N. W. Railway Co., 25 Eng. L. and E. 287. Commented on, Railroads, construction of contracts, through tickets, 31 Cal. 53, 55, 57, 61.

Crow v. State of Missouri, 14 Mo. 237. Disapproved, Taxation, of stock of foreign corporation, 4 Cal. 53. Referred to and statutory provision distinguished, 34 Cal. 450.

Crowell v. Bebee, 10 Vt. 33. Cited, Land, entry under deed, 25 Cal. 135.

Crowell v. Gilmore, 13 Cal. 54. Affirmed, S. C. 195. Referred to, Mechanic's Lien, 18 Cal. 371. Cited, 23 Cal. 525.

Crowley v. Commonwealth, 11 Met. 575. Commented on, Criminal Procedure, indictment charging two offenses, presumptions on appeal, 27 Cal. 403.

Crowther v. Rowlandson, 27 Cal. 376. Cited, New Trial, after reference, when motion to be made, 41 Cal. 406.

Crozier v. Hodge, 3 La. 357. Cited, Judicial Notice, not taken of foreign laws, 15 Cal. 254.

Cruger v. Douglass, 2 N. Y. 571. Cited, Probate, interlocutory decree affecting partnership relations of deceased, 9 Cal. 635.

Cruger v. Hudson Riv. R. R Co., 12 N. Y. 190. Cited, Notice, essential in special proceedings, 24 Cal. 433.

Cruyt v. Phillips, 7 Abb. Pr. 209. Cited, Attachment, when to issue, 28 Cal. 286.

Cruz Cervantes v. United States, 16 How. 619. Cited, Condition Grant, estate of grantee, 10 Cal. 616.

Cudlipp v. Whipple, 1 Abb. Pr. 107. Cited, Pleading, complaints under common counts sufficient, 10 Cal. 338; Landlord and Tenant, title in action for unlawful holding over, 23 Cal. 520.

Culling v. Tuffhall, Bullers N. P. 34. Cited, Fixtures, what constitute, 14 Cal. 65.

Cullum v. Bank of Alabama, 4 Ala. 21. Cited, Warranty, equitable relief of vendee on breach of covenant, 5 Cal. 265; 17 Cal. 385; 22 How. 327.

Cullum v. Erwin, 4 Ala. 452. Doubted, Foreclosure of mortgage securing several notes, rule of priority, 23 Cal. 30.

Culver v. Avery, 7 Wend. 380. Cited as dictum, False Representations, on sale of lands, 9 Cal. 227.

Culver v. Parish, 21 Conn. 408. Cited, Negotiable Instruments, when presumptively dishonored, 39 Cal. 352.

Culver v. Rogers, 28 Cal. 520. Approved, Foreclosure, when judgment becomes a lien, 4 Nev. 390.

Cumber v. Wane, 1 Strange, 426. Cited, Debtor and Creditor, discharge of judgment for less amount, void, 27 Cal. 613.

Cumming v. Mayor of Brooklyn, 11 Paige, 596. Cited, Street Assessment as a personal charge on owner, 31 Cal. 675.

Cummings v. Chevrier, 10 Cal. 519. Followed, Common Property, descent and distribution, 10 Cal. 520.

Cummings v. Nichols, 13 N. H. 421. Cited, Evidence, entries in books, admissibility of, 14 Cal. 576.

Cummings v. Noyes, 10 Mass. 433. Cited, Appeal, restoration on reversal, 14 Cal. 679. Commented on, Rights of tenant to recover mesne profits, 15 Cal. 469

Cummings v. Wyman, 10 Mass. 468. Cited, Ejectment, ouster by co-tenant, inference from facts a question for the jury, 27 Cal. 558; 28 Cal. 487.

Cummins v. Scott, 20 Cal. 83. Referred to on second appeal, 23 Cal. 527.

Cunningham v. Goelet, 4 Denio, 71. Cited, Affidavit, sufficiency of, 27 Cal. 299.

Cunningham v. Cassidy, 17 N. Y. 276. Cited, Execution, sale in mass, when will be set aside, 21 Cal. 59.

Cunningham v. Dorsey, 6 Cal. 19. Cited, Contract, measure of damages in action for breach of contract for services, 12 Ind. 125.

Cunningham v. Harris, 5 Cal. 81. Cited, Judgment, on part of entire demand, a bar to subsequent action, 23 Cal. 387.

Cunningham v. Hawkins, 24 Cal. 403. Cited, Mortgage, mortgagee in possession does not extend lien, 24 Cal. 473; rights of mortgagee, 27 Cal. 146; action to redeem, when barred, 34 Cal. 369; right to redeem and right to foreclose reciprocal, Id. 372. Commented on, 36 Cal. 434.

Cunningham v. Hawkins, 27 Cal. 603. Cited, Deed, as a mortgage, parol evidence admissible to prove, 29 Cal. 19; 30 Cal. 28; 33 Cal. 332; Id. 690; 37 Cal. 454. Approved, 36 Cal. 48. Commented on and explained, 36 Cal. 63; mortgage does not pass title to grantee, 36 Cal. 49.

Curiac v. Abadie, 25 Cal. 502. Approved, Legal Tender Act, constitutional, 38 Cal. 254. Cited, Tender, evidence of, 29 Cal. 196.

Curiac v. Packard, 29 Cal. 194. Cited, Exceptions, objections to admission of testimony to be made at the trial, 29 Cal. 223; Replevin Bond, sheriff has no interest in, 6 Nev. 135.

Curle v. Barrel, 2 Sneed, 63. Cited, State Grant, when void, 23 Cal. 443.

Curran v. Shattuck, 24 Cal. 427. Cited, Statutory Construction, statutes divesting titles to be strictly pursued, 27 Cal. 174; 27 Cal. 628; 30 Cal. 537; 39 Cal. 491. Referred to, Defect in Statute, 32 Cal. 256. Cited, Injunction, against railroad company for failure strictly to pursue statute, 46 Miss. 10.

Currey v. Allen, 34 Cal. 254. Approved, Resulting Trust, what must be shown on enforcement of, 38 Cal. 193. Referred to on second appeal, 41 Cal. 320.

Currie v. Stewart, 27 Miss. 55. Cited, Probate, authority of court to order sale is statutory, 20 Cal. 312.

Currier v. Earl, 13 Me. 216. Cited, Vendor and Vendee, effect of continued possession of vendor, 37 Cal. 374.

Curtin v. Patton, 11 Serg. & R. 311. Commented on, Infant, ratification of contract by, 24 Cal. 213.

Curtis v. Groat, 6 John. 168. Cited, Conversion, measure of damages, 23 Cal. 311.

Curtis v. Mills, 5 Carr. & P. 489. Cited, Ferocious Animal, liability for injury by, 41 Cal. 141.

Curtis v. Patterson, 8 Cow. 67. Cited, Indemnity, to sheriff, practice under statute, 36 Cal. 459.

Curtis v. Richards, 9 Cal. 33. Approved, Undertaking on Appeal, validity of, 9 Cal. 285; 14 Cal. 423; 38 Cal. 604. Cited, Pleading, denial to verified complaint must be specific, 9 Cal. 473; 10 Cal. 232; 13 Cal. 371; 25 Cal. 196.

Curtis v. Slosson, 6 Penn. St. 265. Cited, Bankruptcy, effect of discharge on judgment debt, 14 Cal. 176.

Curtis v. Sutter, 15 Cal. 259. Referred to, Action to quiet title, 13 Cal. 116. Cited, When action lies, 17 Cal. 461; 34 Cal. 389; 1 Saw. 649; 6 Wall. 409; title by possession sufficient to maintain action, 28 Cal. 202; 35 Cal. 34; possession in plaintiff essential, 37 Cal. 307. Commented on, effect on decree of adverse possession shown in a third party, 39 Cal. 19, 21. Doubted, that restriction was universal before the passage of the Practice Act, 3 Or. 409. Cited, Averment of possession in complaint material, 34 Cal. 559; Parties, administrator proper party, 18 Cal. 20; injunction, dissolved till validity of title is established, 23 Cal. 84.

Curtis v. Treat, 21 Me. 525. Approved, Use and Occupation, when action will not lie, 35 Cal. 194.

Curtis v. Tyler, 9 Paige, 432. Cited, Debtor and Creditor, rights of creditor as against surety, 35 Cal. 145.

Cushing v. Gore, 15 Mass. 73. Commented on, Consideration, on express promise, 13 Cal. 333.

Cushing v. Longfellow, 26 Me. 306. Cited, Conversion, measure of damages for chattel severed from realty, 23 Cal. 311.

Cushman v. Haynes, 20 Pick. 132. Distinguished, Negotiable Instruments, acceptance, 8 Cal. 106.

Cushman v. Smith, 34 Me. 247. Cited, Eminent Domain, what constitutes appropriation by railroad, 29 Cal. 117; Compensation to be made to owners, 31 Cal. 373, 559, 562; Damages, how ascertained, 31 Cal. 553.

Cutler v. Coxeter, 2 Vern. 302. Cited, Will, construction of, 31 Cal. 603.

Cutler v. Dickinson, 8 Pick. 386. Cited, Deed, parol defeasance insufficient, 36 Cal. 60.

Cutler v. Powell, 6 Term Rep. 320. Cited, Contracts to convey real estate, dependent and independent covenants, 35 Cal. 663; 38 Cal. 200; 20 N. Y. 200.

Cutter v. Whittemore, 10 Mass. 442. Cited, Undertaking, validity of joint bond, 14 Cal. 423.

Cutts v. Haskins, 9 Mass. 543. Approved, Probate Proceedings, 7 Cal. 236. Distinguished, 39 Ill. 563. Disapproved, 10 Gratt. 378.

Cutts v. Salmon, 12 Eng. L. & E. 316. Cited, Attorney and Client, transactions between, 33 Cal. 440.

Dabovich v. Emeric, 12 Cal. 178; S. C. Cal. Sup. Ct. Jan. T. 1858 (not reported.) Cited, Damages, on breach of contract, 17 Cal. 416.

Daggett v. Rankin, 31 Cal. 321. Approved, Mortgage, how created in equity, 32 Cal. 389; Id. 653.

Daily Post Co. v. McArthur, 7 Am. Law Reg. N. S. 462. Cited, Libel, corporations liable for, 34 Cal. 56.

Dakin v. Hudson, 6 Cow. 221. Cited, Pleading, jurisdictional facts in special proceedings to be set forth, 33 Cal. 536.

Dakin v. Williams, 17 Wend. 451. Cited, Written Instruments, construction of, 35 Cal. 44.

Dale v. The Governor, 3 Stewt. 387. Cited as inapplicable, Statutory Construction, when act takes effect, 4 Cal. 136; power of repeal, Id. 165; 22 Cal. 320.

Dale v. The State, 10 Yerg. 551. Cited, Murder, degrees of, construction of terms in statute, 27 Cal. 581.

Dally v. King, 1 H. Black. 1. Cited, Ejectment, allegations in complaint essential, 5 Cal. 512.

Daly's Lessee v. James, 8 Wheat. 495. Cited, Will, power of sale, construed, 32 Cal. 444.

Damon v. Bryant, 2 Pick. 412. Commented on, Trespass, justification by officer, 7 Cal. 562; 34 Cal. 350.

Dana v. San Francisco, 19 Cal. 486. Approved, County Warrants, drawn on special fund, not negotiable instruments, 22 Cal. 462; 23 Cal. 126.

Dana v. Sawyer, 22 Me. 244. Approved, Negotiable Instruments, presentment and demand to be made within reasonable hours, 8 Cal. 633.

Dana v. Stanfords, 10 Cal. 269. Approved, Insolvency, conveyance giving preference to creditor not fraudulent, 10 Cal. 494; 13 Cal. 332; 19 Cal. 46; 23 Cal. 550; 41 Cal. 569, 570.

Dana v. Tucker, 4 John. 487. Approved, Verdict, cannot be impeached by testimony of juror, 1 Cal. 405; 5 Cal. 46; 25 Cal. 400; Chance Verdicts, 5 Cal. 46; 25 Cal. 400.

Dando v. Tremper, 2 John. 87. Cited, Judgment, effect of when taken against party not served, 39 Cal. 97; 11 How. 173.

Dane v. Corduan, 24 Cal. 157. Cited, Surety, rights of, 26 Cal. 543; surety on joint note, 34 Cal. 281; remedy of, 42 Cal. 507; when not discharged, 32 Cal. 577; 42 Cal. 500.

Dane v. Zignego, Cal. Sup. Ct. Oct. T. 1863 (not reported.) Cited, Sheriff's Sale, rights of purchaser, to remove cloud on title, 29 Cal. 57.

Danforth v. Schoharie Turnpike Co., 12 John. 227. Approved, Corporations, liability on implied contract, 9 Cal. 471.

Danglada v. De La Guerra, 10 Cal. 386. Cited, Estates of Deceased Persons, statute of limitations, 19 Cal. 86.

Daniel v. Daniel, 2 J. J. Marsh. 52. Cited, New Trial, newly discovered evidence, practice, 3 Cal. 57; Id. 117.

Daniel v. Mitchell, 1 Story C. C. 190. Cited, Equity, relief from mistake, 7 Cal. 510.

Daniels v. Davison, 16 Ves. Jr. 249. Cited, Title, adverse possession as notice, 36 Cal. 272.

Daniels v. Hallenbeck, 19 Wend. 410. Cited, Pleading, insufficient defense on note, 36 Cal. 301.

Dannebroge G. Q. Min. Co. v. Allment, 26 Cal. 286. Cited, Corporation, incorporation cannot be collaterally inquired into, 28 Cal. 519; as to irregularities in formation, 37 Cal. 361; Id. 541.

Danzey v. Swinney, 7 Tex. 629. Cited, Probate, procedure, 7 Cal. 239.

Darlington v. Pritchard, 4 Man. & G. 783. Denied, Estoppel in pais, common law rule, 26 Cal. 38.

Darrington v. Bank of Alabama, 13 How. 12. Cited, Constitutionality of Statute, power of legislature to pass special acts, 17 Cal. 562.

Dart v. Dart, 7 Conn. 250. Cited, Deeds, estate conveyed by quit claim deeds, 14 Cal. 628.

Dartmouth College v. Woodward, 4 Wheat. 518. Cited, Treaty, rights of property under, not subject to legislative interference, 15 Cal. 612; legislature cannot pass statute impairing obligation of contracts, 16 Cal. 30; cannot interfere with vested rights, 18 Cal. 613; revolution cannot affect private rights, 8 Wheat. 481. Affirmed, Power of legislature over corporations, 10 How. 536. Cited, 51 Ill. 281; powers of State government under treaty, 12 Wheat. 298; 5 Pet. 47; 22 How. 377.

Darvin v. Hatfield, 4 Sand. 468. Cited, Equity, relief against decrees when granted, 16 Cal. 470; Id. 564.

Dash v. Van Kleeck, 7 John. 497. Cited, Equity, doctrine of election, when applicable, 13 Cal. 142; Statutory Construction, prospective operation presumed, 27 Cal. 159; Probate act retroactive, 28 Cal. 506.

Daubenspeck v. Grear, 18 Cal. 443. Cited, Injunction, to restrain waste, 25 Cal. 519.

Daubigny v. Duval, 5 Term. Rep. 604. Cited, Factor, cannot pledge, 19 Cal. 72; 11 How. 224.

Daumiel v. Gorham, 6 Cal. 43. Approved, Attachment, officer entitled to notice of claim of third person, 6 Cal. 514. Cited, 12 Cal. 476; Id. 495; demand when not necessary, 30 Cal. 191; 3 Nev. 563; 8 Min. 79.

Dauphin Turnpike Road v. Meyers, 6 Serg. & R. 12. Cited, Corporations, omissions of words in formation of corporation not to vitiate grant to, or act done by corporation, 39 Cal. 515.

Davan v. Walker, Cal. Sup. Ct. April T. 1857 (not reported.) Cited, Instructions, equivalent instructions, practice, 8 Cal. 392.

Davenport v. Tilton, 10 Met. 320. Cited, Attachment, statutory construction, 29 Cal. 367, 381–3; Lean of attachment, 29 Cal. 375, 378; enforcement of, Id. 372.

Davey v. Turner, 1 Dall. 11. Cited, Deed, acknowledgment by wife, 1 Cal. 499; 1 Bin. 477; 2 Bin. 345.

David v. Ellice, 5 B. & C. 196. Cited, Account Stated, partnership accounts, 33 Cal. 697.

Davidson v. Dallas, 8 Cal. 227. Commented on and doubted on second appeal, Indemnity Bond, construction of, 15 Cal. 78. Cited, Principal and Agent, liability on un-

10

authorized contract made by agent, 29 Cal. 571. Distinguished, Trespass, liability of joint trespassers under legal process, 34 Cal. 633.

Davidson v. Dallas, 15 Cal. 75. Approved, Law of the Case, previous decision of supreme court to govern, 20 Cal. 417, 45, 311; 28 Cal. 594. Distinguished, Trespass, liability of joint trespassers under legal process, 34 Cal. 633.

Davidson v. Gorham, 6 Cal. 343. Referred to, 15 Cal. 79.

Davidson v. Phillips, 9 Yerg. 93. Cited, Forcible Entry and Detainer, actual possession construed, 16 Cal. 109.

Davidson v. Powell, 16 How. Pr. 467. Cited, Pleading, sham answers, 31 Cal. 195.

Davidson v. Rankin, 34 Cal. 503. Cited, Corporation, liability of stockholders, 39 Cal. 654.

Davidson v. Remington, 12 How. Pr. 311. Cited, Counterclaim, 26 Cal. 306.

Davidson v. Root, 11 Ohio, 98. Commented on, Judgment, lien of, 17 Cal. 475.

Davidson v. Stuart, 10 La. 146. Cited, Husband and Wife, presumptions that property acquired during marriage is common property, 12 Cal. 253; 17 Cal. 581; 30 Cal. 31.

Davies v. Mann, 10 Mees. & W. 546. Cited, Railroads, liable for injuries resulting from negligence, 37 Cal. 423; 22 Vt. 223.

Daviess v. Fairbairn, 3 How. 636. Cited, Statutory Construction, repeal by implication, 10 Cal. 316.

Davis v. Cain's Exr., 1 Ired. Eq. 309. Cited, Will, construction of devise, 31 Cal. 603.

Davis v. Crow, 7 Blackf. 129. Commented on, Judgment, counsel fees as part of damages, 3 Cal. 217.

Davis v. Davis, 26 Cal. 23. Cited, Equitable Estoppel, doctrine of, 31 Cal. 153; Id. 439, 440; Id. 494; 37 Cal. 50; 38 Cal. 316; 1 Saw. 563; Mexican Grants, statute of limitations runs from date of patent, 33 Cal. 479; 1 Saw. 559, 560. Affirmed, Estates of Deceased Persons, term "representatives" defined, 33 Cal. 446; when incompetent as a witness, 36 Cal. 512.

Davis v. Duffie, 8 Bosw. 617. Cited, Crimes, effect of civil death, 35 Cal. 398.

Davis v. Easley, 13 Ill. 192. Cited, Trespass, for timber cut, election of remedy, 16 Cal. 578.

Davis v. Ehrman, 8 Harris, 256. Cited, Judgment, lien of, not extended by execution, 10 Cal. 82.

Davis v. Eppinger, 18 Cal. 378. Cited, Intervention, creditors may intervene to set aside attachment, 21 Cal. 287; Negotiable Instruments, days of grace, 38 Cal. 410.

Davis v. Ham, 3 Mass. 33. Cited, Statutory Construction, revenue, what constitute debts, 37 Cal. 526.

Davis v. Hemmingway, 29 Vt. 438. Cited, Mortgage, with power of sale construed, 22 Cal. 125.

Davis v. Hone, 2 Sch. & L. 341. Cited, Specific Performance, when will be decreed, 25 Cal. 281.

Davis v. Lee, 2 B. Mon. 300. Cited, Forcible Entry, actual possession construed, 16 Cal. 109.

Davis v. Livingston, 29 Cal. 290. Cited, Mechanic's Liens, rights of sub-contractors, 36 Cal. 298.

Davis v. Marshall, 14 Barb. 96. Cited, Attachment, void unless issued in conformity with statute, 34 Cal. 640.

Davis v. Mayor, etc., of New York, 14 N. Y. 522. Cited, Street Railroads, authority conferred by law may be exercised in building road, 35 Cal. 333; 12 Iowa, 256.

Davis v. Mitchell, 34 Cal. 81. Cited, Execution, partnership notes liable to seizure and sale, 38 Cal. 352; Id. 614.

Davis v. People, 6 Ill. 409. Cited, Surety, discharge of one is a discharge of all, 11 Cal. 220.

Davis v. Perley, 30 Cal. 630. Cited, Statute of Limitations, adverse possession of pueblo lands, 31 Cal. 229; what sufficient to constitute adverse possession, 32 Cal. 18; constructive possession under deed, 38 Cal. 487; under Van Ness ordinance, 40 Cal. 309.

Davis v. Rainsford, 17 Mass. 207. Cited, Deed, description of land in, reference to map, 10 Cal. 623, 628; 15 Cal. 306; 24 Cal. 444, 446; 2 Black, 504; rule of construction, 26 Cal. 632.

Davis v. Robinson, 10 Cal. 411. Cited, Arrest and Bail, what must be shown to authorize arrest for fraud, 36 Cal. 166. Commented on and approved, Practice, 36 Cal. 167.

Davis v. Russell, 47 Me. 445. Cited, Eminent Domain, compensation as a condition precedent, 31 Cal. 559.

Davis v. Simms, 4 Bibb. 465. Cited, Street Improvements, sufficiency of publication of notice, 34 Cal. 284.

Davis v. Stratton, Cal. Sup. Ct. Jan. T. 1856 (not reported.) Cited, Appeal, Stipulations not embodied in a statement or bill of exceptions form no part of judgment roll, 11 Cal. 214; so as to agreements inserted among the papers, Id. 361.

Davis v. Tallcot, 12 N. Y. 187. Cited, Estoppel, *res adjudicata*, 36 Cal. 37.

Davis v. Williams, 13 East, 232. Distinguished, Probate Procedure, proof of official character of administrator, 34 Cal. 469.

Davison v. Gill, 1 East, 64. Cited, Statutory Construction, statutes divesting titles to be strictly pursued, 24 Cal. 432.

Davoue v. Fanning, 2 Johns. Ch. 252. Cited, Foreclosure, power of sale in, purchase by mortgagee not void but voidable, 21 Cal. 330; so as to purchase by administrator at his own sale, 29 Cal. 34, 38. Approved, as applied to trustees generally, 4 How. 556.

Davy v. Burnsall, 6 Term Rep. 30. Cited, Will, construction of devise, 27 Cal. 448.

Dawes v. Cope, 4 Bin. 258. Approved, Statute of Frauds, construed, as to possession of vendor of chattel, 15 Cal. 506; 11 Wheat. 102, note *a*.

Dawley v. Hovious, 23 Cal. 103. Overruled, Appeal, presumption that statement embodies evidence on point of exception, 28 Cal. 311.

Dawson v. Chamney, 5 Adol. & E. N. R. 164. Disapproved, Innkeepers, liability of, 1 Cal. 227, 228.

Dawson v. Coles, 16 John. 51. Approved, Assignment, instrument under seal may be assigned by writing without seal, 34 Cal. 148.

Dawson v. Danbury Bank, 15 Mich. 489. Commented on, Title, notice imparted by adverse possession, 36 Cal. 275.

Dawson v. Real Estate Bank, 5 Ark. 283. Cited, Surety, not discharged by mere delay of creditor, 10 Cal. 425.

Dawson v. Shepherd, 4 Dev. 497. Cited, Execution, unlawful issuance of, 38 Cal. 378.

Day v. Alverson, 9 Wend. 223. Cited, Ejectment, prior possession sufficient to maintain, 4 Cal. 79; 21 Cal. 305.

Day v. Graham, 1 Gilm. 435. Approved, Execution, notice of appeal does not operate as a stay, 8 Cal. 135. Distinguished, 21 Cal. 59.

Day v. Jones, 31 Cal. 261. Cited, Appeal, jurisdiction, in special cases, 42 Cal. 64.

Day v. Perkins, 2 Sand. Ch. 364. Cited, Fixtures, right to remove, 10 Cal. 264; 14 Cal. 72.

Day v. Stetson, 8 Greenl. 365. Cited, Election, notice of special election, 11 Cal. 66.

Dayton, City of, v. Pease, 4 Ohio St. 80. Commented on, Municipal Corporations, liability for injury through negligence of agents, 16 Cal. 267.

Dean v. De Lezardi, 24 Miss. 424. Cited, Mortgage, securing contingent debts, description sufficient, 19 Cal. 351.

Dean v. Duffield, 8 Tex. 235. Approved, Administrators, act of one or more of joint administrators is the act of all, 24 Cal. 500.

Dean v. McKinstry, 2 Smedes & M. 213. Cited, Appearance, recitals in record not conclusive, 13 Cal. 561.

Deane v. Clayton, 7 Taunt. 489. Cited, Negligence, right of action for injuries from, 18 Cal. 357.

Dearborn v. Cross, 7 Cow. 48. Cited, Pleading, parol agreement as a defense in specialty, 4 Cal. 316; performance as to time may be waived by parol, 39 Cal. 175.

Dearborn v. Parks, 5 Me. 81. Cited, Debtor and Creditor, action by creditor on agreement of third party to pay debts of debtor, 37 Cal. 537.

Deathridge v. State, 1 Sneed, 75. Cited, Evidence, confessions, presumptions as to, 41 Cal. 455.

DeBarry v. Lambert, 10 Cal. 503. Cited, Appeal, non-appealable orders, 10 Cal. 528; 31 Cal. 367; remedy in such cases, 24 Cal. 84; Striking out Statements, practice, 32 Cal. 326.

DeBoom v. Priestly, 1 Cal. 206. Cited, Action, on special contract, 26 Cal. 20.

DeBow v. People, 1 Denio, 9. Approved, Statute, impeachment of, due passage of act a question of law, 30 Cal. 259, 268; engrossed bill and enrolled act, 30 Cal. 261; printed statute as evidence, Id. 263.

Decamp v. Feay, 5 Serg. & R. 323. Cited, Contract, construction of, time not of essence of, 30 Cal. 407.

DeCastro v. Richardson, 25 Cal. 49. Cited, Jurisdiction, power of court over judgment lost on adjournment of term, 28 Cal. 338. Construed, Loss of Jurisdiction, 30 Cal. 198. Cited, New Trial, statement, practice, 32 Cal. 312. Overruled, as to proceedings for new trial not being subject to amendment, 34 Cal. 481. Referred to, 29 Cal. 13.

Decatur v. Paulding, 14 Pet. 497. Commented on, Mandamus, to ministerial officer, 7 Cal. 71; 16 Cal. 42. Cited, 6 How. 101; 7 How. 56; 11 How. 290; 17 How. 304.

Deckard v. Case, 5 Watts, 23. Cited, Insolvency, assignment, in trust by partner of firm property, 13 Cal. 288.

Deck's Estate v. Gherke, 6 Cal. 666. Cited, Probate, allowance of claim, effect of, 23 Cal. 363; 26 Cal. 430. Approved, Claim for expenditures, allowance when conclusive, 38 Cal. 88.

De Costa v. Massachusetts Flat W. & M. Co., 17 Cal. 613. Cited, Appeal, modification of judgment on, 25 Cal. 187.

De Forest v. Hunt, 8 Conn. 185. Cited, New Promise, acknowledgment required, 36 Cal. 185.

De France v. Austin, 9 Penn. St. 309. Cited, Services, gratuitous services, proof of, to defeat action, 7 Cal. 513; 22 Cal. 510.

De Gaillon v. L'Aigle, 1 Bosanq. & P. 368. Cited, Agent, when personally liable on contract, 13 Cal. 48.

De Grave v. Corporation of Monmouth, 4 Car. & P. 111; 19 Eng. C. L. 109. Denied, Municipal Corporations, powers of, 33 Cal. 145; liability on implied contracts, 16 Cal. 269.

DeGroot v. Van Duzer, 20 Wend. 390. Cited, Contract, unlawful contracts not enforceable, 29 Cal. 271; 30 Cal. 524. Approved, Contracts void in part, 29 Cal. 272.

Deidesheimer v. Brown, 8 Cal. 339. Cited, Appearance, what rights not waived by, 8 Cal. 569.

Dejarnet v. Dejarnet, 5 Dana, 499. Cited, Divorce, decree in, 10 Cal. 256.

De Johnson v. Sepulbeda, 5 Cal. 149. Cited, Tenants in Common, interest in estate defined, as parties to real actions, 5 Cal. 401; 8 Cal. 79; Bill of Exceptions, matter of record need not be embodied in, 2 Nev. 138; Statement, instructions how certified, 6 Cal. 205; practice, 23 Cal. 337; 2 Or. 252.

Delafield v. State of Illinois, 2 Hill, 177; S. C. 26 Wend. 192, affirming 8 Paige, 527. Commented on, Jurisdiction, not in its nature exclusive, 9 Cal. 734; 30 Cal. 580. Cited, State Bonds, negotiability of, 15 Cal. 341; 21 How. 577. Cited generally, 16 Cal. 270.

De La Guerra v. Burton, 23 Cal. 592. Approved, Disqualification from consanguinity, rule of computation, 24 Cal. 77.

De La Guerra v. Packard, 17 Cal. 182. Commented on, Probate, Mexican system, 28 Cal. 505; 33 Cal. 423. Cited, 37 Cal. 89; Id. 91.

Delaire v. Keenan, 3 Desaus. 74. Commented on, Mortgage, agreement for, as a lien, 31 Cal. 326.

Delaney, Estate of, 37 Cal. 176. Cited, Homestead, setting off, to surviving wife, 41 Cal. 36.

Delano v. Blake, 11 Wend. 85. Commented on, Infant, ratification of contract by lapse of time, 24 Cal. 208, 211, 215.

Delaplaine v. Bergen, 7 Hill, 591. Approved, Appeal, loss of jurisdiction on filing remittitur, 1 Cal. 195. Cited, 24 Cal. 59.

Delaplaine v. Hitchcock, 6 Hill, 16. Commented on, Estoppel in pais, 14 Cal. 369.

Delassus v. United States, 9 Pet. 117. Cited, Territorial Law, not affected by conquest or cession, 1 Cal. 286; Id. 314; Id. 326; titles not affected, protection by treaty stipulations, 15 Cal. 553; 16 Cal. 23; 18 Cal. 24; 24 Cal. 660; 37 Cal. 497; 2 Black, 233; 8 How. 304; 20 How. 63; 22 How. 459.

Delaunay v. Burnett, 4 Gilm. 492. Cited, Public Lands, improvements on, are property, 30 Cal. 657.

Delhi, Trustees of, v. Youmans, 50 Barb. 316. Approved, Water Rights, rule of law as to subterranean streams, 42 Cal. 311.

Delmonico v. Guillaume, 2 Sand. Ch. 367.   Cited, Estates of deceased persons, rights of surviving partner, 17 Cal. 268.

Deloach v. Myrick, 6 Geo. 413.   Cited, Attachment, trial of rights of property, 10 Cal. 192.

Delovio v. Boit, 2 Gall. 398.   Cited, Jurisdiction, admiralty jurisdiction as to contracts, 34 Cal. 679; 5 How. 473; 6 How. 420.   Commented on, 12 Wheat. 638.

Demarest v. Wynkoop, 3 Johns. Ch. 146.   Commented on, Statute of Limitations, exceptions in, disabilities, 35 Cal. 640.   Cited, 1 How. 53.

Demick v. Chapman, 11 John. 131.   Cited, Pleading, justification for trespass by seizure, to be specially pleaded, 10 Cal. 304; 27 Cal. 367.

DeMott v. Hagerman, 8 Cow. 220.   Cited, Contracts, lease on shares construed, 23 Cal. 521.

Demyer v. Souzer, 6 Wend. 436.   Cited, Nonsuit, power of court to order, 1 Cal. 222; 26 Cal. 525.

Den v. Den, 6 Cal. 81.   Cited, Officer, presumptions as to official acts, 17 Wis. 541.

Den v. Vancleve, 2 Southard, 589.   Cited, Witness, competency of infant, 10 Cal. 67.

Den v. Webster, 10 Yerg. 513.   Cited, Ejectment, demand for possession when necessary, 24 Cal. 145.

Den v. Winans, 2 Green, N. J. 6.   Cited, Execution, purchaser's title, on what depends, 38 Cal. 659.

Denison v. Hyde, 6 Conn. 516.   Cited, Judgment, conclusiveness of, 26 Cal. 510.

Denn v. Allen, 1 Penning, 43.   Cited, Will, competent witness to execution of, 1 Cal. 506.

Denn v. Cornell, 3 Johns. Cas. 174.   Commented on, Estoppel, by recitals in bond, 17 Cal. 639; 4 Pet. 87.   Cited, 11 How. 323.

Denn v. Morrell, 1 Hall, 424.   Cited, New Trial, evidence to be fully set forth in affidavit, 1 Cal. 433.

Dennen v. Haskell, 45 Me. 430.   Cited, Negotiable Instruments, presumptive dishonor, 39 Cal. 352.

Dennett v. Wymans, 13 Vt. 489.   Cited, Negotiable Instruments, presumptive dishonor, 39 Cal. 352.

Denning v. Smith, 3 Johns. Ch. 332. Cited, Deed, executed under a power, validity, on what depends, 22 Cal. 590.

Dennis v. Burritt, 6 Cal. 670. Commented on, Conveyances, actual notice of unrecorded instrument, 7 Cal. 306; 20 Cal. 516.

Dennis v. People, 1 Parker, 469. Cited, Counterfeiting, proof of existence of corporation, 41 Cal. 654.

Dennison v. Smith, 1 Cal. 437. Cited, Bill of Particulars, practice, 32 Cal. 637.

Denny v. Cabot, 6 Met. 89. Cited, Partnership, actual intention necessary to constitute, 38 Cal. 213.

Denny and the Manhattan Co., Matter of, 2 Hill, 223. Cited, Debtor and Creditor, "claim" and "debt" defined, 9 Cal. 636.

Dent v. State Bank, 12 Ala. 275. Disapproved, Debtor and Creditor, application of payments, 14 Cal. 449.

Dent v. Summerlin, 12 Geo. 5. Cited, Injunction, order for continuance of, will not be disturbed on appeal except for abuse of discretion, 39 Cal. 167.

Dentzel v. Waldie, 30 Cal. 138. Cited, Married Woman, execution of conveyance by, 31 Cal. 645, 654. Commented on and questioned, constitutionality of statute respecting disabilities of, 31 Cal. 645; 7 Nev. 229.

Denver v. Burton, 28 Cal. 550. Cited, Pleading, allegation by way of recital, insufficient, 30 Cal. 321.

Deputy v. Stapleford, 19 Cal. 302. Cited, Appeal, testimony can only be reviewed upon motion for new trial, 27 Cal. 475.

Depuy v. Swart, 3 Wend. 139. Cited, New Promise, must be pleaded, 39 Cal. 436.

Depuy v. Williams, 26 Cal. 309. Cited, Pleading, allegation of possession of land sufficiency of, 32 Cal. 110.

Derby v. Johnson, 21 Vt. 21. Cited, Employment Contract, damages on breach of, 24 Cal. 178; 35 Cal. 241; when action lies on, 35 Cal. 242, 247.

De Rothschild v. Royal M. S. Packet Co., 7 Ex. 734. Cited, Common Carriers, restrictive clauses in contract construed, 27 Cal. 33, 39.

DeRutte v. Muldrow, 16 Cal. 505. Cited, Lease, with privilege to lessee to purchase, specific enforcement of, 40 Cal. 68.

DeSilvale v. Kendal, 4 Maule & S. 37. Commented on, Money Paid, for freight, may be recovered back, on loss of ship or non-performance of voyage, 6 Cal. 370.

Deslonde v. Darrington's Heirs, 29 Ala. 95. Approved, Probate, of will, conclusive, 20 Cal. 270.

Desmond v. Norris, 10 Allen, 250. Cited, Revenue Stamp, statements in pleading to defeat recovery on unstamped note, 34 Cal. 175.

Despard v. Walbridge, 15 N. Y. 374. Cited, Deed as Mortgage, parol evidence admissible to prove, 30 Cal. 28; 36 Cal. 45, 65; Vendor and Vendee, vendee how far estopped by deed, 38 Cal. 124.

Despatch Line of Packets v. Bellamy Manf. Co., 12 N. H. 232. Commented on, Municipal Corporation, ratification of contract by, 16 Cal. 623. Cited, Fixtures, rights of vendee, 10 Cal. 264; 14 Cal. 68.

Despau v. Swindler, 3 Mart. N. S. 705. Cited, Judicial Notice, signatures of officers, 32 Cal. 108.

De Uprey v. De Uprey, 27 Cal. 329. Approved, Partition, what may be tried in action for, 32 Cal. 294; 33 Cal. 465; 35 Cal. 597; order of trial of issues, 33 Cal. 468; necessary parties, 36 Cal. 116.

Devlin v. Platt, 20 How. Pr. 167. Cited, Certiorari, review under writ, 40 Cal. 480.

Devonsher v. Newenham, 2 Sch. & L. 208. Cited, Quieting Title, action for, when it lies, 15 Cal. 263.

Devor v. McClintock, 9 Watts & S. 80. Approved, Taxation, lien of assessment not affected by change in county boundaries, 35 Cal. 47.

Devore v. Pitman, 3 Mo. 187. Cited, Guardians, must bring suit in name of infant, 32 Cal. 117.

Dew v. Judges of Sweet Springs, 3 Hen. & M. 1. Cited, Mandamus, when will issue, 3 Cal. 172.

Dewey v. Bowman, 8 Cal. 145, overruling S. C. decided at the April Term, 1857, (not reported,) that facts will not be reviewed where there was no motion for new trial. The unreported case cited on this point, 8 Cal. 108. Cited, Assignment, of note not due, as collateral security, 8 Cal. 267; Chattel Mortgage and Pledge distinguished, legal effect of, as to title, 14 Cal. 246; 27 Cal. 271; 34 Cal. 132; 35 Cal. 414; 37 Cal. 25; 3 Nev. 316; Pleading, insufficient denials, 8 Cal. 280.

Commented on, Appeal, review of findings, 15 Cal. 381. Overruled, Exception as to equity cases, 18 Cal. 396; Id. 449.

Dewey v. Field, 4 Met. 381. Cited, Attachment, proof of ownership, on claim of third party, 10 Cal. 176.

Dewey v. Gray, 2 Cal. 374. Cited, Law of the Case, prior judgment on appeal, even if erroneous, controls, 7 Cal. 592; 20 Cal. 417. Commented on and affirmed on principle of *stare decisis,* 15 Cal. 82.

Dewey v. Lambier, 7 Cal. 347. Referred to as affirming, 3 Cal. 443; San Francisco, tenure of pueblo lands, 8 Cal. 201. Cited, Alcalde Grants, validity of, 21 Cal. 41; Legislature, want of power in, to alter or destroy nature of estates, 20 Cal. 195.

Dewey v. Latson, 6 Cal. 130. Commented on and explained, Appeal, as a suspension of judgment lien, 16 Cal. 420; 12 Iowa, 445. Followed on the principle of *stare decisis,* legislative interposition suggested, 25 Cal. 351. Doubted, 29 Cal. 237. Distinguished, 31 Cal. 397.

Dewey v. Osborn, 4 Cow. 329. Cited, Ejectment, conclusiveness of judgment, 14 Cal. 468.

Dewitt v. Hays, 2 Cal. 463. Cited, Injunction, not granted where there is a remedy at law, 6 Cal. 275; 25 Cal. 120; 29 Cal. 55; 36 Cal. 71; 43 Miss. 759. Commented on, Effect of tax deed as evidence, 8 Cal. 388.

DeWitt v. Potter, 13 Cal. 171. Cited, Pleading, allegations under common counts sufficient, 32 Cal. 175.

Dexter v. Harris, 2 Mason, 531. Cited, Personal Property, title in innocent vendee of property fraudulently obtained, 12 Cal. 498.

Dexter v. Taber, 12 John. 239. Cited, Libel and Slander, essential averments in complaint, 34 Cal. 60.

Dexter and Limerick Plank Road v. Allen, 16 Barb. 18. Cited, Statutory Construction, repeal by implication, 10 Cal. 316.

Deyo v. Bleakely, 24 Barb. 9. Commented on, Lease, construction of *habendum* clause, 25 Cal. 390.

Dey v. Dunham, 2 Johns. Ch. 182. Cited, Conveyances, possession under unrecorded deed as notice, 29 Cal. 488; effect of record of deed as notice, 36 Cal. 66.

Dey v. Walton, 2 Hill, 405. Cited, Appeal, remedy on frivolous appeal, 23 Cal. 649.

Dezell v. Odell, 3 Hill, 215.   Cited, Equitable Estoppel, 14 Cal. 370; 26 Cal. 40; 31 Cal. 153.   Commented on, 10 Cal. 177.   Questioned, 38 Cal. 314; 5 Minn. 265.

Dibble v. Rogers, 13 Wend. 536.   Cited, Land, acquiescence in division line by lapse of time, 25 Cal. 627.

Dick v. Leverich, 11 La. 576.   Cited, Negotiable Instruments, indorsement an implied warranty, 22 Cal. 249.

Dickenson v. Gilliland, 1 Cow. 481.   Cited, Judgment Lien, not extended by issue of execution, 10 Cal. 80; Execution, sheriff as special agent on redemption, 26 Cal. 663.

Dickerson v. Valpy, 10 Barn. & C. 128.   Commented on, Mining Partnership, authority to bind, not implied on part of member or agent, 23 Cal. 204.   Cited, 28 Cal. 579; 22 How. 267.

Dickey v. Hurlburt, 5 Cal. 343.   Cited, Legislature, cannot confer ministerial powers on judicial officers, 6 Cal. 144; 30 Cal. 167.   Overruled, 34 Cal. 526, 531.

Dickinson v. Fenn, 6 Halst. 185.   Cited, Ejectment, Landlord may defend, 22 Cal. 205.

Dickinson v. Maguire, 9 Cal. 46.   Doubted, Forcible Entry and Detainer, issue of title in action, 23 Cal. 520.   Cited, what constitutes an unlawful entry, 28 Cal. 532; 38 Cal. 422.

Dickinson v. VanHorn, 9 Cal. 207.   Cited, Appeal, presumptions that evidence warranted the judgment, 24 Cal. 378; New Trial, when objections to statement, not being filed in time, do not lie, 27 Cal. 138.   Overruled, Contested Elections, power of county court to grant new trial on, 24 Cal. 455, 456.

Dickinson's Lessee v. Collins, 1 Swan, Tenn. 516.   Cited, Judgment and Lien, not extended by issue of execution, 10 Cal. 80.

Dickson v. Cunningham, Mart. & Yerg. 221.   Cited, Money Had and Received, action lies for money in hands of third party, 15 Cal. 347.

Diehl v. Page, 2 Green Ch. 143.   Cited, Title, possession as notice of, 21 Cal. 628.

Dike v. Lewis, 4 Denio, 238.   Cited, Tax Deed, sufficiency of recitals in, 21 Cal. 303.

Dillon v. Byrne, 5 Cal. 455.   Cited, Mortgage, mortgage to secure moneys paid in discharge of prior lien, rights under, 9 Cal 107; 10 Cal. 385; 13 Cal. 530. Approved, 16 Cal. 199; 23 Cal. 120. Cited, 16 Iowa, 156.

Dillon v. Dillon, 3 Curt. Ecc. 86. Cited, Divorce, adultery, 10 Cal. 255.

Dimick v. Campbell, 31 Cal. 238. Cited, Judgment Roll, motions and orders to strike out are no part of, 36 Cal. 114.

Dimick v. Deringer, 32 Cal. 488. Cited, Ejectment, defense by landlord, conduct of action, 37 Cal. 394; action lies only against person in possession, 41 Cal. 53.

Dimmock v. Bixby, 20 Pick. 368. Cited, Pleading, multifariousness, 31 Cal. 429.

Dinehart v. Wilson, 15 Barb. 595. Cited, Contract, lease on shares construed, 17 Cal. 546; 25 Cal. 63.

Dinsdale v. Eames, 2 Bro. & B. 8. Cited, Bankruptcy, effect of discharge on judgment debt, 14 Cal. 175.

District Township of Dubuque v. County Judge, 13 Iowa, 250. Cited, State School Funds, 37 Cal. 245.

Ditch v. Edwards, 2 Ill. 127. Cited, Summons, insufficiency of, return of service, 11 Cal. 379. Criticised as to signature of deputy, 27 Ill. 497.

Divine v. Harvie, 7 Mon. 440. Reviewed and approved, Parties, State as a party, 7 Cal. 71. Commented on, Mandamus to ministerial officers, 16 Cal. 61.

Divine v. Mitchum, 4 B. Mon. 488. Cited, Partnership, real estate, how held, 28 Cal. 580.

Divver v. McLaughlin, 2 Wend. 596. Cited, Chattel Mortgage, statute to be strictly construed, 23 Cal. 301; mortgage given to secure future advances, when fraudulent, 35 Cal. 308.

Dix v. Van Wyck, 2 Hill, 522. Cited, Conveyances, when voidable and when void, 29 Cal. 36.

Dixey v. Pollock, 8 Cal. 570. Cited, Attachment, junior attaching creditors cannot take advantage of irregularities in prior attachment, 18 Cal. 155; intervention by judgment creditors, 18 Cal. 381; by subsequent attaching creditors, 21 Cal. 287; duty of sheriff as to proceeds, 28 Cal. 287.

Doane v. Broad Street Asso., 6 Mass. 333. Cited, Conveyances, construction of, 15 Cal. 197.

Doane v. Scannell, 7 Cal. 393. Cited, Office, approval of bonds, 7 Cal. 442.

Dob v. Halsey, 16 John. 40. Cited, Partnership, what necessary to constitute, 28 Cal. 577.

Dobbins v. Dollarhide, 15 Cal. 374. Cited, Appeal, statement, grounds to be specifically set forth, 25 Cal. 489.

Dobbins v. State, 14 Ohio St. 493. Cited, Criminal Procedure, discharge of jury, when it operates as an acquittal, 41 Cal. 216.

Dobbins v. Supervisors of Yuba Co., 5 Cal. 414. Cited, Statutory Construction, conflicting statutes, 32 Cal. 144.

Dobell v. Stevens, 3 Barn. & C. 623. Commented on, False Representations, when merged in conveyance, 9 Cal. 227.

Dobson, Ex parte, 31 Cal. 497. Cited, Criminal Procedure, commitment to State prison, what should state, 31 Cal. 622.

Dobson v. Pearce, 12 N. Y. 156. Cited, Pleading, defenses legal and equitable allowed, 36 Cal. 46.

Docker v. Somes, 2 Mylne & K. 655. Approved, Trust and Trustee, character of trustee not changed to that of debtor by mixture of trust funds, 9 Cal. 661; 3 How. 431.

Dodge v. Potter, 18 Barb. 201. Cited, Evidence, parol evidence, to explain written instrument, admissible, 13 Cal. 556.

Dodge v. Strong, 2 Johns. Ch. 231. Cited, Judgment, relief from judgment at law, how obtained, 12 Cal. 448.

Dodge v. Walley, 22 Cal. 224. Cited, Execution, sheriff's deed, construed, 38 Cal. 658.

Dodge v. Woolsey, 18 How. 341. Cited, Equity, jurisdiction, to control corporations, 40 Cal. 27. Commented on, 32 Ill. 108; 43 Miss. 746.

Dodson's Appeal, 25 Penn. St. 232. Cited, Execution, waiver of debtor's right of selection, 22 Cal. 506.

Doe v. Bancks, 4 Barn. & A. 409. Cited, Landlord and Tenant, tenant estopped from setting up his own forfeiture, 38 Cal. 251.

Doe v. Campbell, 10 John. 475. Cited, Title, when successive possessions cannot be added, 37 Cal. 354.

Doe v. Harlow, 12 Adol. & E. 40; S. C. 40 Eng. C. L. 17. Reviewed, Landlord and Tenant, liability of sub-tenant for rent, 1 Cal. 473.

Doe v. Herbert, Breese, 354. Cited, Ejectment, the better title to prevail, 4 Cal. 79.

Doe v. Thomas, 14 East, 323. Cited, Evidence, hearsay, when admissible, 3 Cal. 45.

Doe v. Vallejo, 29 Cal. 385. Cited, Appeal, rule of decision where evidence is conflicting, 32 Cal. 537; 35 Cal. 37.

Dolittle v. Eddy, 7 Barb. 78. Cited, Vendor and Vendee, vendee in possession, 24 Cal. 145.

Doll v. Feller, 16 Cal. 432. Cited, Appeal, modification of judgment, 25 Cal. 187. Approved, Ejectment, sufficiency of description of premises in complaint, 3 Wall. 494.

Doll v. Meador, 16 Cal. 295. Approved, Public Lands, donation by government to State vested a present interest in lands, with right of selection out of any of the public lands, 21 Cal. 335; 25 Cal. 255; 33 Cal. 262; 1 Saw. 632; right of selection, when to be exercised, 21 Cal. 336; 24 Cal. 624; State patent, conclusive as to title and to regularity of proceedings, and not subject to collateral attack, 21 Cal. 423; 22 Cal. 111; 23 Cal. 442; 24 Cal. 568; 38 Cal. 83. Distinguished as to swamp and overflowed lands subsequently granted, 23 Cal. 437; void patent may be assailed in all cases, 21 Cal. 423; 24 Cal. 629; 32 Cal. 362; status of party impeaching patent, privity with paramount source of title essential, 25 Cal. 251; 29 Cal. 312; 3 Or. 114. Cited, Ejectment, to entitle to a recovery, right of entry must be shown at commencement of action, 32 Cal. 338; evidence of title from public lands, 28 Cal. 101.

Doll v. Smith, 32 Cal. 475. Cited, Appeal, affidavit of service of notice, what must be shown, 35 Cal. 187.

Dollfus v. Frosch, 1 Denio, 367. Cited, Negotiable Instruments, special indorsements on bill, 14 Cal. 454.

Doloret v. Rothschild, 1 Sim. & S. 590. Cited, Specific Performance, time when essence of contract, 10 Cal. 327; enforcement of parol contract for delivery of chattels, 23 Cal. 392.

Domingues v. Domingues, 4 Cal. 186. Cited, Adjournment, must be to a term pursuant to statute, 40 Cal. 185.

Dominguez v. Dominguez, 7 Cal. 424. Cited, State Demands, equity will refuse relief on, 23 Cal. 34.

Dominguez v. Lee, 17 La. 295. Cited, Husband and Wife, property acquired during marriage presumed to belong to the community, 12 Cal. 224; Id. 253. Commented on, 30 Cal. 30, 32.

Dominick v. Eaoker, 3 Barb. 17. Cited, Pleading, defense in action on false return, 28 Cal. 286.

Donahue v. McNulty, 24 Cal. 411. Cited, Execution, constable's deed, validity of, 25 Cal. 236; recitals in sheriff's deed as evidence, 30 Cal. 288; 38 Cal. 658; 40 Cal. 611; 2 Nev. 288.

Donahy v. Clapp, 12 Cush. 440. Distinguished, Statutory Rights, lien of mechanics, 23 Cal. 525.

Donellan v. Read, 3 Barn. & A. 899. Cited, Statute of Frauds, action on contract made by agent, 33 Cal. 195. Commented on, 28 Vt. 34; 46 N. H. 152; 10 Wis. 68; 35 Ill. 39.

Donley v. Hays, 17 Serg. & R. 400. Cited, Assignment, of part of debt carries *pro rata* portion of security, 6 Cal. 483. Doubted, Foreclosure, necessary parties, 14 Cal. 218; mortgage securing several notes, 23 Cal. 30.

Donnell v. Jones, 13 Ala. 490. Cited, Breach of Contract, when action of tort lies on, 18 Cal. 534.

Donner v. Palmer, 23 Cal. 40. Referred to, Chance Verdict, 25 Cal. 477. Opinion of Pratt, J. in original action, 1 Pacific Law Mag. 291. Approved, Writ of Error, who may sign citation and take undertaking thereon, 32 Cal. 241.

Donner v. Palmer, 31 Cal. 500. Commented on, Alcaldes' Grants, power vested in alcalde, 37 Cal. 442. Questioned as to power of American alcaldes after the cession, 1 Saw. 661. Cited, Alcalde Records, 37 Cal. 447. Distinguished, 38 Cal. 226; acceptance of grant to infant, 39 Cal. 123.

Dooling v. Moore, 19 Cal. 81; S. C. 20 Cal. 141. Cited, Appeal, not taken in time, practice, dismissal, 25 Cal. 158; 5 Kan. 279.

Dooly v. Norton, 41 Cal. 439. Cited, Appeal, review of special orders after final judgment, 42 Cal. 118.

Doran v. Dinsmore, 20 How. Pr. 503. Cited, Pleading, several defenses, 22 Cal. 679, 680.

Dore v. Covey, 13 Cal. 502. Cited as inapplicable, Judgment lien, 16 Cal. 420. Commented on, Undertaking on appeal, validity of, 38 Cal. 602. Approved, 2 Or. 319.

Dore v. Sellers, 27 Cal. 588. Commented on, Mechanic's Lien, 29 Cal. 290; for materials furnished contractor, 31 Cal. 238; lien of sub-contractors, 36 Cal. 298.

Doremus v. O'Harra, 1 Ohio St. 45. Commented on, Insolvency, assignment in trust, 10 Cal. 276.

Doremus v. Selden, 19 John. 213. Cited, Action, separate action lies, by agents for expenses incurred on joint service, 12 Cal. 128.

Dorente v. Sullivan, 7 Cal. 279. Cited, Jurisdiction, no presumptions in favor of inferior courts, 23 Cal. 404; as to jurisdiction of courts of general jurisdiction, 33 Cal. 512. Approved, Judgment, not subject to collateral attack for mere irregularity of service of summons, 33 Cal. 685. Cited, Setting aside default, 3 Nev. 384.

Dormady v. State Bank of Illinois, 3 Ill. 236. Cited, Evidence, of lost instrument, practice, 10 Cal. 147.

Dorman v. Bigelow, 1 Flor. 281. Cited, Surety, when not discharged by delay of creditor, 10 Cal. 425.

Dormenon's Case, 1 Mart. 129. Approved, Attorney-at-Law, practice of law a privilege, under control of legislature, 22 Cal. 321.

Dorr v. Munsell, 13 John. 430. Cited, Written Instruments, seal imports consideration, 10 Cal. 463.

Dorr v. New Jersey St. Nav. Co., 11 N. Y. 485. Cited, Common Carriers, liability of, for loss of property, 27 Cal. 38.

Dorsey v. Barry, 24 Cal. 449. Approved, Election Contest, proceedings special and summary, 34 Cal. 640; and followed, court cannot grant new trial, 24 Cal. 458. Construed and distinguished, Special Cases, 29 Cal. 115; as inapplicable to cases in insolvency, 29 Cal. 416. Cited, Special Cases, 31 Cal. 169; Appeal, in special cases, 42 Cal. 68.

Dorsey v. Manlove, 14 Cal. 553. Approved, Officers, liable in exemplary damages for torts, 18 Cal. 325. Cited, 40 Miss. 365.

11

Dorsey, Matter of, 7 Port. 395.   Cited, Attorney-at-Law, practice of law a privilege under control of legislature, 22 Cal. 321; not a constitutional officer, Id. 315.

Dorsey v. McFarland, 7 Cal. 342.   Approved, Homestead, mortgage on, when invalid, 8 Cal. 76; 13 Iowa, 581. Cited, Alienation of, how effected, 10 Cal. 172; Judgment, no lien on, 16 Iowa, 457.

Dorsey v. Smyth. See People v. Smyth.

Doss v. Waggoner, 3 Tex. 515.   Cited, Trial, must be in term, 9 Cal. 175.

Doswell v. Buchanan's Exrs., 3 Leigh, 365.   Cited, Conveyance, without warranty, does not pass after-acquired title, 14 Cal. 628.

Doty v. Brown, 4 N. Y. 71.   Cited, Pleading, Estoppel, by judgment, 36 Cal. 37; how pleaded, 26 Cal. 505; jurisdictional facts, when may be proved by parol, 34 Cal. 327.

Doubleday v. Heath, 16 N. Y. 80.   Cited, Town Lots, special cases, jurisdiction in settlement of claims to, 19 Cal. 574; special cases defined, 23 Cal. 148.

Dougherty v. Dorsey, 4 Bibb, 207.   Cited, Witness, competency of co-defendant, trespass, 6 Cal. 194.

Dougherty v. Foley, 32 Cal. 402.   Cited, Street Improvements, re-advertising for bids, 34 Cal. 247; power of Board to re-let contract, 40 Cal. 519.

Dougherty v. Hitchcock, 35 Cal. 512.   Approved, Street Assessment, must be officially attested, 36 Cal. 412. Commented on, Appeal to Board, 40 Cal. 524.   Distinguished, Contract, when divisible, 40 Cal. 530.

Dougherty v. Linthicum, 8 Dana, 200.   Cited, Execution, when sale of land in gross is valid, 6 Cal. 52.

Dougherty v. McColgan, 6 Gill & J. 275.   Cited, Mortgage, rights of mortgagee, 26 Cal. 602.

Doughty v. Devlin, 1 E. D. Smith, 625.   Cited, Building Contract, owner not liable upon contracts made by contractor with sub-contractor, 22 Cal. 571.

Doughty v. Hope, 3 Denio, 253.   Commented on, Street Assessments, personal liability, 31 Cal. 676.

Doughty v. Somerville & E. R. R. Co., 3 Halst. Ch. 629. Cited, Injunction, granting and continuance in discretion of court, 39 Cal. 167.

Douglass v. Howland, 24 Wend. 35. Approved, Surety, judgment against principal when not evidence against surety, 14 Cal. 205.

Douglass v. Kraft, 9 Cal. 562. Approved and followed, Conversion, measure of damages, 33 Cal. 119; 39 Cal. 420, 421. Cited to same point, 34 Cal. 132. Appeal, Objections to form of verdict, when to be taken, 41 Cal. 519

Douglass v. Placerville, 18 Cal. 643. Approved, Corporations, Grants of power to be strictly construed, Dillon on Corp. 104, note, 684.

Douglass v. State, 3 Wis. 820. Cited, Verdict, in criminal case, when a nullity, 28 Cal. 331.

Douglass v. Tousey, 2 Wend. 352. Cited, Criminal Procedure, evidence of good character, when admissible, 7 Cal. 130. Approved, 4 Denio, 510. Cited, 12 How. 555.

Dovaston v. Payne, 2 Smith's Lead. Cas. 6th Am. Ed. 218. Cited, Dedication to public use, acceptance, how shown, 42 Cal. 554.

Dow v. Gould and Curry S. M. Co., 31 Cal. 629. Cited, Husband and Wife, gift from husband to wife, 42 Cal. 361.

Dow v. Norris, 4 N. H. 19. Cited, Statutory Construction, statutes not to be construed retrospectively, 4 Cal. 136.

Dow v. Sayward, 12 N. H. 275. Cited, Partnership, individual liability on contract may be waived, 22 Cal. 389.

Dowling v. Polack, 18 Cal. 625. Approved, Judgment, dismissal of action a final judgment, 21 Cal. 164; and liability thereupon attaches on injunction bond, 46 N. H. 434.

Downer v. Lent, 6 Cal. 94. Cited, Supervisors, powers of, when not discretionary, 10 Cal. 345.

Downer v. Norton. See People v. Norton.

Downer v. Rowell, 26 Vt. 397. Cited, Insolvency, effect of discharge on judgment debt, 14 Cal. 176.

Downer v. Smith, 24 Cal. 114. Cited, Ejectment, equitable defenses may be interposed to title, 24 Cal. 141; 25 Cal. 597; 42 Cal. 352; 4 Nev. 460; equitable estoppel to be specially pleaded, 26 Cal. 39; title under quit claim deed sufficient to maintain action, 25 Cal. 168; 37 Cal.

521. Commented on, Evidence, alcalde's records, 31 Cal. 510, 523; as evidence of delivery of grant, 31 Cal. 513. Approved, Estates of Deceased Persons, descents and distributions under Mexican system prevailed till adoption of probate act, 28 Cal. 505; 33 Cal. 423; 37 Cal. 89, 91; 1 Saw. 199.

Downes v. Phœnix Bank, 6 Hill, 299. Approved, Demand, bringing of action sufficient on debt payable on demand, 29 Cal. 507.

Doyle v. Doyle, 26 Mo. 549. Cited, Alimony, not granted without divorce, dissenting opinion of Sprague, J., 38 Cal. 277.

Doyle v. White, 26 Me. 341. Commented on, Guaranty, when independent promise of is within statute of frauds, 9 Cal. 335.

Drake v. Cockroft, 10 How. Pr. 379. Cited, Pleading, new matter in answer, in avoidance, 30 Cal. 175.

Drake v. Eakin, 10 Cal. 312. Approved and followed, Witness, practice on examination of party as, 10 Cal. 396.

Drake v. Hudson Riv. R. R., 7 Barb. 508. Cited, Street Railroad, right to lay down track, 35 Cal. 331.

Drake v. Palmer, 2 Cal. 177. Approved, New Trial, granting or refusing in discretion, 2 Cal. 353; 10 Cal. 341.

Drake's Lessee v. Ramsay, 5 Ohio, 251. Cited, Infancy, acquiescence in contract, by lapse of time, 24 Cal. 214.

Drayton v. Marshall, 1 Rice, Eq. 373. Cited, Title, acquired by adverse possession, 34 Cal. 381, 382; 36 Cal. 541.

Dred Scott v. Sandford, 19 How. 393. Cited, Appeal, review on, 8 Cal. 109; Constitutional Construction, right to property in slaves, 9 Cal. 162; negroes not citizens, 36 Cal. 663; State Rights, admiralty jurisdiction, 11 Cal. 183; regulations of commerce, 13 Cal. 282.

Dresser v. Brooks, 3 Barb. 429. Approved, Insolvency, discharge of debt discharges judgment thereon, 14 Cal. 176.

Dreux v. Domec, 18 Cal. 83. Cited, Exceptions, objections to admission of testimony must be specific, 24 Cal. 177; Id. 403; 3 Nev. 557; 7 Nev. 415.

Drew v. Davis, 10 Vt. 506. Cited, Taxation, tax sale, when invalid, 10 Cal. 404; 36 Cal. 73.

Driggs' Admr. v. Abbott, 27 Vt. 581. Affirmed on principle of *stare decisis*, Judgments, of courts of limited jurisdiction conclusive, 18 Cal. 505.

Drinkwater v. Tebbetts, 17 Me. 16. Approved, Negotiable Instruments, waiver of notice and demand how proved, 19 Cal. 161.

Drum v. Whiting, 9 Cal. 422. Cited, Judgment, by default, on striking out answer, 28 Cal. 297.

Dublin, Inhabitants of, v. Chadbourn, 16 Mass. 433. Approved, Probate, of will, conclusive, 18 Cal. 480.

Dubois v. Dubois, 6 Cow. 494. Cited, Surety, when not released, 24 Cal. 166.

Dubois v. Hepburn, 10 Pet. 1. Cited, Redemption, right of, 4 Cal. 149; 15 Wend. 248.

Dubois v. Kelly, 10 Barb. 496. Cited, Evidence, parol agreements not admissible to contradict written instrument, 19 Cal. 364.

Dubuque County v. Dubuque & P. R. R. Co., 4 Greene, 1. Cited, Taxation, for county aid to railroads, 41 Cal. 185. Denied, that county may levy the tax, 13 Iowa, 395.

Duchess of Kingston's Case, 20 State Tri. 355; S. C. 11 How. St. Tri. 262; 2 Smith's Lead. Cas. 511. Cited, Estoppel, doctrine, generally, 9 Cal. 207; applied to corporate acts, 16 Cal. 628; estoppel by deed, 25 Cal. 452; 11 How. 323; by verdict, 28 Cal. 516; 36 Cal. 37; 6 How. 599; by judgment or decree, 26 Cal. 494; 27 Cal. 169; 29 Cal. 523; 32 Cal. 198; to be specially pleaded, 23 Cal. 358; 26 Cal. 505; when admissible in evidence, 36 Cal. 38; 37 Cal. 396.

Ducoign v. Schreppel, 1 Yeates, 347. Cited, Evidence, entries in book as, 14 Cal. 576.

Dudley v. Beck, 3 Wis. 285. Cited, Witness, privileged communications, 29 Cal. 71.

Dudley v. Mayhew, 3 N. Y. 9. Approved, Statutory Construction, statute creating a right and providing a remedy for its infringement, to be strictly construed, 33 Cal. 217.

Duff v. Fisher, 15 Cal. 375. Commented on and approved, Appeal, findings will not be reviewed unless there has been a motion for new trial, 18 Cal. 396; 27 Cal. 69; 30 Cal. 287; 3 Nev. 303; rule of determination where evidence is conflicting, 29 Cal. 391; objections to form of verdict or to excessive damages can only be made available on motion for new trial, 41 Cal. 519; Specific Performance, when will be decreed, on contract for chattels, 25 Cal. 571; 38 Cal. 453.

Duff v. Hobbs, 19 Cal. 646. Cited, Set-off, equitable rights cannot be set-off in action at law, 23 Cal. 626, 629; Judgment, when not an estoppel, 23 Cal. 628.

Duffin v. Smith, Peake, 108. Commented on, Witness, privileged communications, 29 Cal. 70.

Duffy v. Hobson, 40 Cal. 240. Cited, Evidence, State legislature possesses supreme power to regulate the rules of evidence in State courts, 40 Cal. 211. Approved, Revenue Stamp, the want of, cannot be set up as a defense on a written instrument, 42 Cal. 417.

Dufour v. Camfranc, 11 Mart. 675. Cited, Sheriff's Deed, as evidence of sale, 30 Cal. 288.

Dugan v. United States, 3 Wheat. 172. Cited, Negotiable Instruments, when holder of indorsed paper may recover, 14 Cal. 454.

Duggan v. England, Harper, 217. Cited, Pleading, conditions precedent, 7 Cal. 572.

Duke of Beaufort v. Berty, 1 P. Wm. 702. Commented on, Guardian and Ward, testamentary guardians, 37 Cal. 663, 665.

Duke of Norfolk, Case of, Dyer, 93ᵃ. Cited, Evidence, printed statutes as, 30 Cal. 264.

Duke of Norfolk v. Worthy, 1 Camp. 337. Cited, Bailee, duty and liabilities of, 11 Cal. 350.

Dukes v. State, 11 Ind. 557. Cited, Criminal Procedure, threats as evidence, rule of admission, 37 Cal. 687, 702.

Dumas, Ex parte, 1 Atk. 233. Cited, Principal and Agent, agent when held as trustee of principal, 13 Cal. 141.

Dummer v. Pitcher, 5 Sim. 35. Cited, Husband and Wife, gift to wife, 12 Cal. 255.

Dumphy v. Guindon, 13 Cal. 28. Cited, Jurisdiction, costs not part of matter in dispute, 20 Cal. 174; 27 Cal. 107. Commented on and distinguished, 23 Cal. 286.

Dunbar v. San Francisco, 1 Cal. 355. Approved, Municipal Corporation, not liable for destruction of building, to stop conflagration. 1 Cal. 452; general powers, how restricted, 22 Cal. 627.

Duncan v. Lyon, 3 John. Ch. 351. Cited, Injunction, averments necessary in action to enjoin judgment, 18 Cal. 47.

Duncan v. Scott, 1 Camp. 100. Cited, Negotiable Instruments, when burden of proving consideration falls on holder, 10 Cal. 526.

Duncan v. Sylvester, 24 Me. 482. Cited, Conveyance, by tenant in common, 35 Cal. 588.

Dunckel v. Wiles, 11 N. Y. 420. Cited, Judgment, as a bar, when extrinsic evidence is admissible to avoid the bar, 25 Cal. 273.

Duncombe v. Prindle, 12 Iowa, 11. Cited, Statute, passage of act, 30 Cal. 276.

Duncuft v. Albrecht, 12 Sim. 189. Cited, Specific Performance, on contract for stock, 23 Cal. 392.

Dundalk W. R. Co. v. Tapster, 1 Q. B. 667. Cited, Statutory Construction, statutes creating rights and a remedy for their violation must be strictly construed, 33 Cal. 218.

Dunham v. Dodge, 10 Barb. 566. Cited, New Promise, tenants in common not bound by act of single co-tenant, 6 Cal. 621; acknowledgment sufficient to bar statute of limitations, 9 Cal. 91.

Dunham v. Drake, Coxe, N. J. 315. Cited, Civil Death, effect, civilly, of conviction for felony, 35 Cal. 398.

Dunham v. Jackson, 6 Wend. 22. Cited, Tender, what constitutes a valid tender, 41 Cal. 422.

Dunham v. Mann, 8 N. Y. 512. Approved, Pleading, complaint on executory contract, what must be shown, 30 Cal. 488.

Dunlop v. Gregory, 10 N. Y. 244. Cited, Contracts, in total restraint of trade are void, 36 Cal. 359.

Dunn v. Tozer, 10 Cal. 167. Cited, Homestead, judgment no lien on, injunction lies to restrain sale under execution, 28 Cal. 527; 47 N. H. 271.

Dunn v. White, 1 Ala. 645. Cited, Vendor and Vendee, covenant of warranty and promise to pay are independent covenants, 5 Cal. 264. Disapproved, 12 Ark. 710.

Dunning v. New Albany & S. R. R. Co., 2 Ind. 437.   Cited, Corporations, presumptions in favor of due organization and formation, 22 Cal. 441.

Dupleix v. De Roven, 2 Vern. 540.   Cited, Statute of Limitations, when it runs, 35 Cal. 640.

Dupont v. Wertheman, 10 Cal. 354.   Cited, Conveyances, bill of sale of real property not under seal, passes only on equity, 11 Cal. 160.   Referred to, Deed of Attorney, 13 Cal. 234.   Cited, 16 Cal. 557; 28 Wis. 693.

Duppa v. Mayo, 1 Saund. 287.   Commented on, Landlord and Tenant, demand for rent, how made, 25 Cal. 392, 397.

Du Pratt v. Lick, 38 Cal. 691.   Cited, Master and Servant, master when liable for acts of servant, 38 Cal. 634.

Dupuy v. Leavenworth, 17 Cal. 262.   Cited, Debtor and Creditor, preference of partnership creditors over creditor of individual partner, 22 Cal. 199; 23 Cal. 501.

Dupuy v. Roebuck, 7 Ala. 488.   Cited, Covenant, of warranty, what constitutes eviction under, 39 Cal. 368.

Dupuy v. Shear, 29 Cal. 238.   Cited, Action, how commenced, 35 Cal. 125.   Distinguished, Time of issuance of summons, 35 Cal. 301, 302.   Cited, Dismissal, for want of prosecution, 39 Cal. 451.

Durell v. Haley, 1 Paige, 492.   Cited, Fraud, purchaser at execution sale against fraudulent vendee acquires no title, 23 Cal. 361.

Durell v. Mosher, 8 John. 445.   Cited, Juror and Jury, ground of challenge in criminal action, 1 Cal. 385.

Durfee v. Plaisted, 38 Cal. 80.   Compared, Patent to purchasers of Suscol Rancho, statute construed, 39 Cal. 452.   Approved, Id. 455.

Durousseau v. United States, 6 Cranch, 307.   Cited, Jurisdiction, appellate jurisdiction of U. S. Supreme Court, 9 Cal. 736; 5 Pet. 203; 14 How. 120.

Duryea v. Burt, 28 Cal. 569.   Cited, Findings, of court, a part of the record, 30 Cal. 229; Mining Partnership, in the nature of a tenancy in common, 30 Cal. 300; 35 Cal. 369; purchaser of interest of partner holds subject to lien of firm debts, 42 Cal. 194; Id. 642.

Dutch Flat Wat. Co. v. Mooney, 12 Cal. 534.   Referred to, Ejectment from mining claim, 23 Cal. 249.

Dutil v. Pacheco, 21 Cal. 438. Cited, Notice, of pendency of action, when necessary, 22 Cal. 208; Equity, when will relieve from judgment at law, 51 N. H. 245.

Dutton v. Solomonson, 3 Bosanq. & P. 582. Cited, Pleading, action on special contract for building, necessary averments, 26 Cal. 22.

Dutton v. Strong, 1 Black, 23. Cited, Riparian Rights, 31 Cal. 121.

Dutton v. Warschauer, 21 Cal. 609. Approved, Mortgage, a mere lien which does not convey the title either before or after condition broken, 35 Cal. 413; 39 Cal. 255, 256. Cited, Foreclosure, grantee of mortgagor not bound by judgment unless made a party to action, 25 Cal. 161; Ejectment, action to be brought against party in possession, 28 Cal. 536; landlord may defend and conduct action, 37 Cal. 394. Construed, Title, possession as notice of, 29 Cal. 490. Cited, 36 Cal. 272. Commented on, Landlord and Tenant, termination of tenancy by eviction, 34 Cal. 268.

Duvall v. Myers, 2 Md. Ch. 401. Approved, Specific Performance, mutuality essential, 21 Cal. 411.

Duval's Heirs v. McLoskey, 1 Ala. 728. Cited, Foreclosure, decree void as to grantee of mortgagor, not made party to action, 16 Cal. 564.

Dwinelle v. Henriquez, 1 Cal. 387. Cited, Administrator, personal liability on contract, 38 Cal. 88.

D'Wolf v. Babbett, 4 Mason, 289. Cited, Fraud, vitiates sale of goods, 8 Cal. 213.

Dye v. Dye, 11 Cal. 163. Doubted, Pleading, rights under statute relating to husband and wife, 22 Cal. 637. Cited, Conditions prescribed by statute must be specially pleaded, 35 Cal. 448; 4 Nev. 472.

Dye v. Kerr, 15 Barb. 444. Cited, Parent and Child, no contract for services implied, 7 Cal. 513.

Dyer v. Clark, 5 Met. 562; S. C. 1 Am. Lead. Cas. 605. Cited, Mortgage, of interest of one of several partners, 25 Cal. 105. Commented on, tenure of real estate by partners, as tenants in common, 28 Cal. 580. Cited, Equitable Mortgage, 32 Cal. 652.

Dyer v. Rich, 1 Met. 180. Cited, Demand, not necessary in action for money payable on demand, 22 Cal. 278.

Dyer v. Tuskaloosa Bridge Co., 2 Port. 296. Cited, Franchises, ferry and road franchises not exclusive grants, 13 Cal. 520; Eminent Domain, exercise of right through agents of government, 31 Cal. 372; 6 How. 539.

Dyett v. North American Coal Co., 20 Wend. 572. Approved, Married Woman, may change her separate estate by herself or her husband as attorney, 32 Cal. 385.

Dygert v. Coppernoll, 13 John. 210. Cited, Evidence, of jurisdictional facts to sustain jurisdiction of inferior court, when admissible, 34 Cal. 327.

Dynen v. Leach, 40 Eng. L. & E. 491. Commented on, Master and Servant, liability for injury to servant, 31 Cal. 381.

Dyson v. Bradshaw, 23 Cal. 528. Cited, Abandonment, intent necessary to constitute, 1 Nev. 202.

Dyson v. State, 26 Miss. 362. Cited, Judgment in criminal action, validity of, 31 Cal. 627.

Dyson v. Wood, 3 Barn. & C. 451. Cited, Evidence of jurisdictional facts *aliunde* the record, 34 Cal. 327.

Eagle Bank of New Haven v. Smith, 5 Conn. 71. Cited, Money Received, action lies for money received by third party, 15 Cal. 347.

Eagle Fire Co. v. Lent, 6 Paige, 637. Cited, Foreclosure, adverse title not subject of determination, 18 Cal. 474.

Eames, Ex parte, 2 Story, 326. Commented on and approved, Bankrupt Act, suspends operation of State insolvent laws, 37 Cal. 210, 222.

Eames v. New England Worsted Co., 11 Met. 570. Cited, Damages, measure of, when a question of law, 14 Cal. 557.

Eames v. Prentice, 8 Cush. 337. Cited, Trespass, on lands, gist of action, 32 Cal. 580.

Earl v. Bull, 15 Cal. 425. Cited, Counter-claim, former action, when not a bar, 26 Cal. 305.

Earl v. Spooner, 3 Denio, 246. Cited, Attachment, action on undertaking, damages, 1 Cal. 411.

Earl v. Shaw, 1 Johns. Cas. 314. Cited, Assignment, of insurance policy, assent of insurer necessary, 38 Cal. 545.

Earl of Falmouth v. Alderson, 1 Mees. & W. 210. Cited, Ejectment, when it lies, 38 Cal. 572.

Earl of Leicester v. Walter, 2 Camp. 251. Disapproved, Libel and Slander, admissibility of evidence, 41 Cal. 384.

Early v. Doe, 16 How. 610. Commented on, Publication of Notices, computation of time, 32 Cal. 351, 352; 5 Nev. 435.

East Anglian Railways Co. v. Eastern Co. R. Co., 7 Eng. L. & E. 505. Commented on, Pleading, defense of *ultra vires*, 37 Cal. 580.

East Hartford v. Hartford Bridge Co., 10 How. 511. Cited, Municipal Corporation, tenure of real property, 15 Cal. 612.

Eastabrooks, Ex parte, 5 Cow. 27. Cited, Appeal Bonds, sufficiency of, 13 Cal. 509.

Easterby v. Larco, 24 Cal. 179. Cited, New Trial, time within which to file motion, 27 Cal. 338; waiver of motion by failure to file statement, 41 Cal. 518.

Easterly v. Bassignano, 20 Cal. 489. Cited, Pleading, "discovery under oath" not permitted in pleading, 22 Cal. 570; Witness, when party not competent as witness for co-defendant, 22 Cal. 575.

Eastern Counties Railway Co. v. Hawkes, 35 Eng. L. & E. 8. Commented on, Corporations, contracts *ultra vires*, 37 Cal. 583, 584, 585, 586.

Eastman v. Cooper, 15 Pick. 276. Commented on, Estoppel, by judgment, 15 Cal. 148; 53 Me. 261.

Eastman v. Fifield, 3 N. H. 333. Cited, Negotiable Instruments, presentment at place of payment not essential, 11 Cal. 322.

Eastman v. McAlpin, 1 Geo. 157. Cited, Insolvency, assignment in trust, rights of creditors, 10 Cal. 277.

Eastman v. Moulton, 3 N. H. 157. Cited, Evidence, entries in book as, 14 Cal. 576.

Eastman v. Wright, 6 Pick. 323. Cited, Release, obtained by fraud, is void, 23 Cal. 351.

Easton v. Calendar, 11 Wend. 95. Cited, Officers, official discretion, 7 Cal. 438.

East Pennsylvania R.R. v. Hiester, 40 Penn. St. 53. Cited, Evidence, opinions of witnesses, 35 Cal. 262.

Eaton v. Aspinwall, 19 N. Y. 119. Cited, Corporations, strict compliance under general law not required in formation of, 22 Cal. 440; irregularities not subject to collateral investigation, 22 Cal. 441; but substantial compliance required, 42 Cal. 209.

Eaton v. Green, 22 Pick. 526. Cited, Mortgage, conveyance when an equitable mortgage, 10 Cal. 209; parol defeasance, effect of, 36 Cal. 61.

Eaton v. Palmer. See Gray *v.* Gray.

Echols v. Chenery, 28 Cal. 157. Cited, Deed, by attorney, must be in name of constituent, 32 Cal. 651.

Eckstein v. Calderwood, 27 Cal. 413. Cited, New Trial, dismissal of motion for failure to prosecute with diligence, 32 Cal. 327.

Eddy v. Simpson, 3 Cal. 249. Approved, Water Rights, how acquired, 37 Cal. 310; Appropriation, priority, 6 Cal. 108. Commented on, 11 Cal. 151. Cited, interest acquired by appropriation, 29 Cal. 206; 37 Cal. 310; by diversion of water, 7 Cal. 49.

Ede v. Johnson, 15 Cal. 53. Cited, Taxation, sworn statement of railroad property, requisites of, 5 Nev. 320.

Edgar v. Fowler, 3 East, 225. Commented on, Wagers, recovery of money staked, 37 Cal. 673.

Edgell v. Francis, 1 Man. & G. 222. Approved, New Trial, on ground of excessive damages, 24 Cal. 517.

Edgerton v. Peckham, 11 Paige, 352. Cited, Specific Performance, waiver of forfeiture as a defense, 40 Cal. 13.

Edick v. Crim, 10 Barb. 445. Cited, Pleadings, complaint, substantial allegations in, 24 Cal. 462.

Edmonds v. Lowe, 8 Barn. & C. 407. Cited, Costs, in former action on negotiable instrument, when recoverable, 22 Cal. 250.

Edmondson v. Alameda County, 24 Cal. 349. Cited, Appeal, affirmance for failure to file briefs, 25 Cal. 488; 28 Cal. 489.

Edmondson v. Hart, 9 Tex. 554. Cited, Probate, *caveat emptor* the rule at probate sale, 9 Cal. 197.

Edmondson v. Mason, 16 Cal. 386. Cited as inapplicable, Fees, prepayment of, 25 Cal. 212.

Edmonson v. Ferguson, 11 Mo. 344. Cited, Statutes, validity of laws suspending rights, 22 Cal. 328.

Edrington v. Mayfield, 5 Tex. 363. Compared, Husband and Wife, separate property, statutory rights, 7 Cal. 271. Approved, capacity of wife in relation to her separate property, 31 Cal. 646; 16 Tex. 286, 292.

Edson v. Dillaye, 8 How. Pr. 273. Approved, Pleading, sham answer, denial of legal conclusions, 32 Cal. 573; allegations of " owner and holder," surplusage, 36 Cal. 302.

Edwards v. Bodine, 11 Paige, 223. Concurred in, Counsel fees, recoverable on injunction bond, 3 Cal. 218. Referred to on this point, 25 Cal. 174.

Edwards v. Coleman, 2 Bibb, 204. Cited, Conveyance, when fraudulent, 13 Cal. 72.

Edwards v. Farmer's F. Ins. and L. Co., 21 Wend. 490. Disapproved, Mortgage, effect of tender, as a discharge, 14 Cal. 529; legal effect of mortgage, 36 Cal. 56.

Edwards v. Grand Junction Railway Co., 1 Myl. & C. 674. Cited, Corporation, contracts *ultra vires,* 37 Cal. 585.

Edwards v. Harben, 2 Term Rep. 587. Cited, Statute of Frauds, possession must accompany sale of goods, 15 Cal. 505. Commented on, 29 Cal. 475.

Edwards v. Hasbrook, 2 Tex. 578. Cited, Negotiable Instruments, presentment and demand at place designated not essential, 11 Cal. 324.

Edwards v. Toomer, 14 Smedes & M. 76. Cited, Appearance, recital in record not conclusive, 13 Cal. 561.

Edwards v. Varick, 5 Denio, 665. Cited, Conveyance, without warranty, does not convey after-acquired title, 14 Cal. 628.

Egberts v. Wood, 3 Paige, 521. Commented on, Insolvency, dissolution of partnership, rights of partners, 7 Cal. 199.

Egerton v. Third Municipality of New Orleans, 1 La. An. 435. Approved, Municipal Corporations, property of, not liable to levy and sale on execution, 15 Cal. 590, 595.

Egery v. Buchanan, 5 Cal. 53. Approved, Sheriff, statute penalties, when recoverable, 6 Cal. 196. Cited, 2 Nev. 378; relief from judgment on ground of false return, 14 Cal. 143.

Egery v. Wells, Cal. Sup. Ct. (not reported.) Cited, Notice of dissolution of partnership, 4 Cal. 263.

Egyptian Levee Co. v. Hardin, 27 Mo. 495. Commented on, Assessments, for local improvements, how regulated, 28 Cal. 370; burden of tax, how distributed, Id. 373; applied to public streets, 31 Cal. 685; 34 Ill. 281.

Eld v. Gorham, 20 Conn. 12. Cited, Statute, impeachment of, 30 Cal. 275.

Elden v. Keddell, 8 East, 187. Distinguished, Administrator, official character, how proved, 34 Cal. 469.

El Dorado County v. Elstner, 18 Cal. 144. Distinguished, County, allowance of claim against, 20 Cal. 595.

Eldred v. Hawes, 4 Conn. 465. Cited, Negotiable Instruments, presentment and demand at place designated not essential, 11 Cal. 322.

Eldridge v. Cowell, 4 Cal. 80. Cited, State Sovereignty, 4 Cal. 368. Commented on, San Francisco, validity of water lot act, McAll. 223.

Eldridge v. Knott, Cowp. 215. Cited, Presumptions, doctrine of, 6 Cal. 556.

Eldridge v. Preble, 34 Me. 148. Cited, Married Woman, rights to property under statute, 30 Cal. 43.

Eldridge v. See Yup Co., 17 Cal. 44. Cited, Deed, equitable relief from mistake, parol evidence of written contract admissible, 23 Cal. 124. Approved, Grantee cannot control use, after sale, 8 Nev. 78.

Elford v. Teed, 1 Maule & S. 28. Cited, Negotiable Instruments, presentation and demand, 8 Cal. 632.

Elias v. Verdugo, 27 Cal. 418. Cited, Homestead, cannot be carved out of lands held in common, 32 Cal. 483. Approved, 26 Wis. 581.

Elizabethport Manf. Co. v. Campbell, 13 Abb. Pr. 86. Cited, Pleading, sham answer, practice, striking out, 32 Cal. 574; 7 Rob. N. Y. 634.

Elkins v. Edwards, 8 Geo. 326. Statutes distinguished, Mortgage, limitations as to mortgage and debt secured thereby, 18 Cal. 488; 42 Cal. 501.

Ellicott v. Pearl, 10 Pet. 412. Commented on and approved, Lands, constructive possession under deed or grant, 6 Cal. 272; 7 Cal. 310; 23 Cal. 437; 30 Cal. 639; adverse possession, what sufficient to constitute, 1 Cal. 289; Id. 320, 321; 19 Cal. 314; 25 Cal. 132, 133, 138, 139.

Elliot v. Cronk's Admr. 13 Wend. 35. Cited, Place of Trial, actions against public officers, 9 Cal. 421.

Elliott v. Armstrong, 4 Blackf. 424. Cited, Landlord and Tenant, liability for rent on eviction, 7 Cal. 24.

Elliott v. Chapman, 15 Cal. 383. Followed, Appeal, undertaking, when to be filed, 15 Cal. 386. Approved, Dismissal for failure to file within five days after notice, 19 Cal. 82; 3 Or. 520.

Elliott v. Horn, 10 Ala. 348. Cited, Fraudulent Conveyance, when not void, 13 Cal. 72.

Elliott v. Knott, 14 Md. 121. Cited, Execution, not subject to collateral attack, 38 Cal. 382.

Elliott v. Piersol, 1 Pet. 328. Approved, Acknowledgment, construction and intendments of certificate, 11 Cal. 295; validity of, on conveyance by married woman, 13 Cal. 498. Cited, Jurisdiction, when it attaches, proceedings thereunder are conclusive, 22 Cal. 64; 2 Pet. 168; 2 How. 343; 8 How. 541.

Elliott v. Shaw, 16 Cal. 377. Cited, Judgment, by default, facts essential in affidavit to open up, 23 Cal. 129.

Elliott v. Swartwout, 10 Pet. 137. Cited, Money paid by mistake of law cannot be recovered back, cognizance of law presumed, 18 Cal. 272; 4 How. 332.

Ellis v. Hamlen, 3 Taunt. 52. Cited, Gratuitous Services, no liability arises from, 21 Cal. 108.

Ellis v. Hull, 23 Cal. 160. Approved, Appeal, dismissal, when sureties are liable on undertaking, 29 Cal. 139. Referred to, 36 Cal. 457.

Ellis v. Janes. See Ellis v. Jeans.

Ellis v. Jeans, 7 Cal. 409; S. C. 10 Cal. 456; 26 Cal. 272. Cited, Ejectment, vendee when estopped from denying vendor's title, 8 Cal. 402; 9 Cal. 590; joint judgment for damages, 26 Cal. 276; Appeal, rule of decision on conflicting testimony, 32 Cal. 537; 35 Cal. 37; Vendor's Lien, 32 Cal. 59.

Ellis v. Polhemus, 27 Cal. 350. Cited, Probate, what "claim" includes, 2 Nev. 337.

Ellis v. Portsmouth & R. R. Co., 2 Ired. 140. Commented on, Railroads, liability for damages done by, 14 Cal. 388. Reviewed, 10 Ired. 402.

Ellis v. Prevost, 19 La. 253. Cited, Real Actions, under civil law, 1 Cal. 289.

Ellis v. Thompson, 3 Mees. & W. 445. Cited, Contract, reasonable time for performance, a question of law, 30 Cal. 559.

Ellis v. White, 25 Ala. 540. Cited, Judicial notice not taken of foreign laws, 15 Cal. 254.

Ellis and Medwin v. Sandham, 1 Term Rep. 705. Cited, Contract, construction of, 30 Cal. 559.

Ellissen v. Halleck, 6 Cal. 386. Distinguished, Probate, allowance of claim, effect of, 6 Cal. 412. Cited, 2 Nev. 337. Overruled, as to mortgage claims, 21 Cal. 29. Cited and this latter case doubted, 27 Cal. 354; mortgage debt against estate, 24 Cal. 498, 499; Pleading, requisites of complaint on claims, 7 Cal. 124; Demurrer, efficiency of, 9 Cal. 501; 10 Cal. 558; 10 Cal. 562; *Stare Decisis*, rules of practice, 10 Cal. 30; 25 Cal. 92.

Ellison v. Bignold, 2 Jac. & W. 511. Cited, Voluntary Benevolent Societies, equitable jurisdiction, 14 Cal. 537.

Ellison v. Daniels, 11 N. H. 274. Commented on, Mortgage, inseparable from debt secured, transfer by mortgagee, 9 Cal. 428; 21 Cal. 622.

Ellison v. Jackson Wat. Co., 12 Cal. 542. Commented on, Mechanic's Lien, construction of statutes, 28 Cal. 203.

Ellmaker v. Buckley, 16 Serg. & R. 72. Cited, Witness, cross-examination, 36 Cal. 228.

Elmendorf v. Mayor, etc., of New York, 25 Wend. 693. Cited, Supervisors, proceedings, how far reviewable on certiorari, 16 Cal. 209.

Elmendorf v. Taylor, 10 Wheat. 152. Cited, *Stare Decisis*, doctrine of, 15 Cal. 603; 4 How. 54; Id. 379; 7 How. 58; 8 How. 410.

Elmore v. Stone, 1 Taunt. 458. Reviewed, Statute of Frauds, sufficiency of delivery, 22 Cal. 104.

Elting v. Scott, 2 John. 156. Cited, Evidence, declarations and admissions, when not admissible, 22 Cal. 237, 238.

Elting v. Vanderlyn, 4 John. 237. Cited, Pleading, under statute of frauds, 29 Cal. 599.

Elwell v. Shaw, 1 Greenl. 339. Cited, Tax Title, validity of tax sale, 10 Cal. 404; 36 Cal. 73.

Elwell v. Shaw, 16 Mass. 42. Cited, Agent or Attorney, act must be in name of principal, 29 Cal. 352.

Elwes v. Maw, 3 East, 38. Commented on, Fixtures, right to, 10 Cal. 264; 2 Pet. 144. Cited, as to landlord and tenant, 14 Cal. 70. Questioned, right of removal, 1 Ohio St. 532.

Elwood v. Klock, 13 Barb. 50. Reviewed, Conveyance, by married woman, acknowledgment, authority of notary, 11 Cal. 293.

Elwood v. Deifendorf, 5 Barb. 398. Cited, Debtor and Creditor, effect of payment by note, 12 Cal. 323.

Ely v. City of Rochester, 26 Barb. 133. Cited, Eminent Domain, public interests superior to private rights and interests, 23 Cal. 467.

Ely v. Ehle, 3 N. Y. 506. Cited, Pleading, justification in trespass must be specially pleaded, 10 Cal. 304.

Ely v. Frisbie, 17 Cal. 250. Cited, Mexican Grants, patent takes effect by relation, 18 Cal. 26; 20 Cal. 160; operation and effect of, Id. 571.

Embrey v. Owen, 4 Eng. L. & E. 466. Cited, Water Rights, appropriation of water, 11 Cal. 153.

Embury v. Conner, 3 N. Y. 511. Cited, Constitutional Construction, inherent rights, 22 Cal. 318.

Emeric v. Gilman, 10 Cal. 404. Cited, County, private property not liable for debts of, 15 Cal. 586; power of mandamus the proper remedy to test power of supervisors on allowance, rejection of claim, 28 Cal. 431; effect of judgment against county, 34 Cal. 291; payment of county warrants, 39 Cal. 275.

Emeric v. Penniman, 26 Cal. 119. Cited, Patent, when patentee holds in trust, 30 Cal. 307; 31 Cal. 439; Ejectment, must be brought by party holding the legal title, 32 Cal. 462, 464.

Emeric v. Tams, 6 Cal. 155. Approved, Judgment, interest on note part of, 9 Cal. 247; Id. 297; 32 Cal. 88.

Emerson v. Crocker, 5 N. H. 162. Cited, Negotiable Instruments, presumptive dishonor, 39 Cal. 352.

Emerson v. Knower, 8 Pick. 66. Cited, Release, by partner, 10 Cal. 125.

12

Emery v. Bradford, 29 Cal. 75. Cited, Street Improvement, constitutional power of legislature to provide for, 31 Cal. 250; 40 Cal. 514; delegation of powers, 34 Cal. 541; Liability, money sued for is a city tax, 32 Cal. 279; personal liability under statute, 29 Cal. 124; Contract, validity of proceedings, 31 Cal. 474; property holder not party to contract, 32 Cal. 485; 36 Cal. 244; 39 Cal. 392; 40 Cal. 526. Affirmed, Contracts, when void, 35 Cal. 526. Cited, Assessment, party not named in, is unaffected thereby, 34 Cal. 319; Work, acceptance of, by superintendent, conclusive, 31 Cal. 248. Approved, Remedy by appeal to board, exclusive, where work not done according to contract, 29 Cal. 131; 40 Cal. 520. Cited, for irregularities in the assessment, 31 Cal. 256; 32 Cal. 278; 34 Cal. 320; 38 Cal. 75.

Emery v. Fell, 2 Term Rep. 28. Cited, Pleading, sufficiency of complaint for goods sold, 32 Cal. 175.

Emery v. Neighbor, 2 Halst. 145. Cited, Contract, mutual covenants, construction of, 21 Cal. 69.

Emery v. San Francisco, 28 Cal. 345. Commented on and approved, Street Improvements, power of legislature to provide for, 31 Cal. 250, 255; Id. 474; Id. 667, 690; 40 Cal. 514. Cited, Liability, assessment, a city tax, 32 Cal. 279; property benefited, 32 Cal. 557; constitutionality of statute, 29 Cal. 82, 83, 95. Approved, personal liability under statute, 29 Cal. 123. Commented on, Contract, validity, on what depends, 31 Cal. 246. Cited, separate works included in, 32 Cal. 276, 279; property owners not parties to contract, 32 Cal. 485; 36 Cal. 244; 39 Cal. 392.

Emmal v. Webb, 36 Cal. 197. Cited, Appeal, findings presumed, 41 Cal. 99.

Enfield v. Day, 11 N. H. 520. Cited, Title, grant as evidence of, 31 Cal. 514.

Enfield v. Permit, 8 N. H. 512. Cited, Title, grant as evidence of, 31 Cal. 514.

Enfield Toll Bridge Co. v. Connecticut R. Co., 7 Conn. 29. Cited, Corporation, power of self-dissolution, 38 Cal. 172.

Engels v. Lubeck, 4 Cal. 31. Commented on, Injunction, will not lie to restrain judgment of coördinate courts, 9 Cal. 615.

England v. Davidson, 11 Adol. & E. 856. Cited, Rewards, liability on offer of, 14 Cal. 137.

Engles v. Marshall, 19 Cal. 320. Cited, Witness, examination, competent testimony, 23 Cal. 334.

English v. Harvey, 2 Rawle, 305. Cited, Administrator, duties of, 37 Cal. 430.

English v. Johnson, 17 Cal. 107. Approved, Mines and Mining, extent of claim may be limited by mining rules, 18 Cal. 48; Title, what sufficient evidence of possession to mining ground, 20 Cal. 209; 23 Cal. 576; 30 Cal. 355; 31 Cal. 390; 7 Nev. 219. Cited, Constructive possession under deed, 38 Cal. 487; Appeal, technical exceptions will not be sustained, 41 Cal. 317.

Englund v. Lewis, 25 Cal. 337. Cited, Judgment, lien of, 28 Cal. 524. Doubted, 29 Cal. 237; 31 Cal. 397; 4 Nev. 389, 391. Approved, Injunction, grantee may enjoin sheriff's sale on execution against grantor, 13 Flor. 301.

Eno v. Woodworth, 4 N. Y. 249. Cited, Pleading, denial of "ownership" insufficient, 32 Cal. 573.

Enos v. Tuttle, 3 Conn. 250. Cited, Evidence, declarations as part of the *res gestæ*, 15 Cal. 74.

Enright v. San Francisco and S. J. R. R. Co., 33 Cal. 230. Cited, Appeal, error without injury disregarded, 33 Cal. 292.

Ensign v. Sherman, 14 How. Pr. 439. Commented on, Ejectment, sufficiency of complaint, 16 Cal. 245.

Ensign v. Wands, 1 Johns. Cas. 171. Cited, Corporations, individual liability may be waived, 22 Cal. 389.

Ensworth v. Lambert, 4 Johns. Ch. 605. Cited, Foreclosure, subsequent incumbrancers, as parties, 11 Cal. 316; when junior mortgagees not affected by decree, 40 Cal. 238.

Episcopal Church of St. Peter v. Varian, 28 Barb. 645. Cited, Undertaking, on discharge from attachment, sufficiency of, 29 Cal. 199.

Eppes v. Randolph, 2 Call, 125. Cited, Deed, parol evidence of consideration admissible, 6 Cal. 137.

Eppinger v. Kirby, 23 Ill. 523. Compared, Taxation, proceedings in action for taxes, 31 Cal. 135.

Erie and North East Railroad v. Casey, 26 Penn. St. 287. Cited, Public Highways, 24 Cal. 490.

Ernst v. Kunkle, 5 Ohio St. 521. Commented on, Street Assessment, liability for, 31 Cal. 684.

Ervine's Appeal, 16 Penn. St. 263. Cited, Constitutional Construction, inherent rights, 22 Cal. 318.

Eschbach v. Pitts, 6 Md. 71. Commented on, Street Assessment, lien of, 31 Cal. 682.

Eskridge v. Jones, 1 Smedes & M. 595. Cited, Summons, sufficiency of service of, 11 Cal. 379.

Esmon v. State, 1 Swan. 14. Cited, Criminal Procedure, when discharge of jury operates as an acquittal, 38 Cal. 478.

Esmond v. Chew, 15 Cal. 137. Cited as not in conflict, Mining Claims, rights of miners in working claims, 19 Cal. 626.

Essex Turnpike Co. v. Collins, 8 Mass. 299. Cited, Corporation, validity of contract by, 4 Cal. 147.

Estrada v. Murphy, 19 Cal. 248. Cited, Mexican Grants, title under, before confirmation, 31 Cal. 437; 42 Cal. 603; claims to be presented for confirmation, 21 Cal. 51; 23 Cal. 37; 35 Cal. 431, 434. Explained, 24 Cal. 669; as to pueblo lands, 36 Cal. 145; Confirmation, conclusive of legal title, 21 Cal. 221; 26 Cal. 124; 32 Cal. 463; 39 Cal. 246; it may be shown that patentee is trustee, 30 Cal. 307. Approved, 31 Cal. 438. Approved, 1 Saw. 205, 208; equity may control legal title, 32 Cal. 462; 13 Wall. 103, 496. Cited, Ejectment, equitable defenses may be set up in action, 24 Cal. 141; 4 Nev. 460. Affirmed on principle of *stare decisis*, 42 Cal. 352; order of trial of issues, 19 Cal. 671.

Etting v. Bank of United States, 11 Wheat. 59. Cited, Appeal, where judges are equally divided, judgment will be affirmed, 32 Cal. 633; 3 How. 424.

Evans v. Ellis, 5 Denio, 640. Cited, Attorney and Client, transactions between, 33 Cal. 440, 442.

Evans v. Evans, 1 Hagg. Const. 35. Cited, Divorce, cruelty, 14 Cal. 80.

Evans v. Gordon, 8 Port. 142. Cited, Negotiable Instruments, place of payment not essence of contract, 11 Cal. 324.

Evans v. Gray, 1 Mart. N. S. 709. Cited, Witness, competency of, how tested, 26 Cal. 132.

Evans v. King, 7 Mo. 411. Commented on, Attachment, lien of, 11 Cal. 275.

Evans v. Llewellyn, 2 Bro. Ch. 150. Cited, Married Woman, power over separate estate, 23 Cal. 566.

Evans v. Merriweather, 4 Ill. 492. Cited, Water Rights, diversion of water, 8 Cal. 144.

Evans v. Montgomery, 4 Watts & S. 220. Commented on, Statutory Construction, statutes altering remedies, 4 Cal. 140, 161, 168.

Evans v. Phillips, 4 Wheat. 73. Approved, Appeal, does not lie from a judgment of nonsuit, 6 Cal. 666.

Evans v. State, 8 Ohio St. 196. Cited, Forgery, sufficiency of indictment, 28 Cal. 211.

Evans v. Tatem, 9 Serg. & R. 252. Cited, Foreign Judgment, on publication summons, effect of, 8 Cal. 457.

Evans v. Wells, 22 Wend. 324. Commented on, Principal and Agent, liability on contract by agent, 7 Cal. 540, 541; 13 Cal. 235.

Everett v. Coffin, 6 Wend. 608. Cited, Warehouseman, waiver of lien by, 23 Cal. 511.

Everett v. Saltus, 15 Wend. 474. Cited, Warehouseman, waiver of lien by, 23 Cal. 511.

Everson v. Carpenter, 17 Wend. 419. Cited, Infant, contracts by, indorsement of note, 24 Cal. 208.

Evertson v. Thomas, 5 How. Pr. 45. Cited, Summons, strict construction of statutes as to publication of, 20 Cal. 82.

Evill v. Conwell, 2 Blackf. 133. Cited, Forcible Entry and Detainer, possession sufficient to maintain action, 16 Cal. 109, 110; 20 Cal. 50.

Evoy v. Tewkesbury, 5 Cal. 285. Commented on, Statute of Frauds, indorsement on contract, by third party, an original promise, not within statute, 27 Cal. 83; 34 Cal. 675; 38 Cal. 135.

Ewart v. Street, 2 Bailey, 157. Cited, Damages, by the elements, acts of God, defined, 35 Cal. 423.

Ewer v. Hobbs, 5 Met. 1. Commented on, Mortgage, a security or lien, 18 Cal. 487; assignment of mortgage without debt, a nullity, 21 Cal. 623.

Ewing v. Burnet, 11 Pet. 41. Commented on, Adverse Possession, what necessary to constitute, 1 Cal. 289, 321; 39 Cal. 45; 1 Gratt. 193.

Ewing v. Cargill, 13 Smedes & M. 79. Cited, Witness, competency of, vendor of chattel, 23 Cal. 446.

Ewing v. Peck, 26 Ala. 413. Cited, Bankruptcy, effect of discharge on judgment debt, 14 Cal. 176.

Ewing v. Smith, 3 Desau. 417. Cited, Married Woman, powers over separate estate, 7 Cal. 270.

Exchange Bank v. Hines, 3 Ohio St. 1. Approved, Constitutionality of Statute, 22 Cal. 393.

Exline v. Smith, 5 Cal. 112. Overruled, Legislature, authority to confer ministerial powers on judicial officers, 34 Cal. 526, 531.

Facey v. Hurdom, 3 Barn. & C. 213. Cited, Contract, reasonable time for performance, when a question of fact, 30 Cal. 559.

Fackler v. Ford, 24 How. 323. Cited, Estoppel, of mortgagor, 31 Cal. 457.

Fagg v. Clements, 16 Cal. 389. Commented on, Jurisdiction, of inferior court, must be affirmatively shown, 34 Cal. 328.

Fair v. McIver, 16 East, 130. Cited, Set-off, trust claim cannot be set-off against legal claim, 23 Cal. 629.

Fair v. Stevenot, 29 Cal. 486. Cited, Conveyance, possession as notice of title, 31 Cal. 184; 36 Cal. 272; Appeal, separate appeals, practice, 35 Cal. 291; new trial will be ordered where court does not adhere to its record, 35 Cal. 359.

Fairbanks v. Dawson, 9 Cal. 89. Affirmed, Statute of Limitations, effect of part payment, 17 Cal. 578; 21 Cal. 149; 22 Cal. 102. Cited, 5 Nev. 215; McAll. 491, 492, 497.

Fairbanks v. Dow, 6 N. H. 266. Cited, Deed, preparation and delivery of, 25 Cal. 279. Commented on, 34 N. H. 81.

Fairburn v. Eastwood, 6 Mees. & W. 679. Cited, Fixtures, right of removal of, by tenant, 14 Cal. 71.

Fairchild v. California Stage Co., 13 Cal. 599. Cited, Negligence, of common carriers, measure of damages for personal injuries, 6 Nev. 233; 48 N. H. 316.

Fairchild v. Holly, 10 Conn. 176. Dicta cited, Debtor and Creditor, application of payments, 14 Cal. 449, 450.

Fairchild v. Slocum, 19 Wend. 329. Cited, Common Carriers, contracts construed, through tickets over several routes, 31 Cal. 54; Pleading, variance, 36 Cal. 178.

Fairfield v. Baldwin, 12 Pick. 388. Cited, Contract, void in part is void *in toto*, 7 Cal. 355; rule applied to judgments, 13 Cal. 441.

Fairis v. Walker, 1 Bailey, 540. Cited, Fixtures, passing with land, what are, 14 Cal. 68.

Fake v. Eddy's Exr. 15 Wend. 80. Cited, Interest, what allowed as damages, 42 Cal. 284.

Fales v. Hicks, 12 How. Pr. 154. Cited, Pleading, insufficient denials, 25 Cal. 196.

Falkinburg v. Lucy, 35 Cal. 52. Approved, Trade Marks, appropriation of words, not protected, 39 Cal. 504.

Falkner v. Folsom's Exrs., 6 Cal. 412. Commented on and disapproved, Estates of Deceased Persons, jurisdiction of probate court exclusive, 21 Cal. 29; 24 Cal. 499. The latter cases, so far as they limit the meaning of the word "claim" to be presented, doubted, 27 Cal. 354.

Falkner v. Hunt, 16 Cal. 167. Cited, Money Paid, under protest, when may be recovered back, 23 Cal. 113; Taxation, the debt and not the security, liable to taxation, 23 Cal. 140; 25 Cal. 604; 2 Or. 330. Commented on, Double Taxation, assessment, valuation, how entered on, 34 Cal. 439, 440; 38 Cal. 467. Cited, Sales of Estates, 2 Nev. 332, 338.

Falkner v. Leith, 15 Ala. 9. Cited, Deed, recitals in, conclusive on grantor, 26 Cal. 87.

Fall v. Paine, 23 Cal. 302. Cited, Certiorari, review of right of supervisors to grant ferry franchise, 23 Cal. 495.

Fall v. Sutter Co., 21 Cal. 237. Commented on, Franchise, grant of bridge or ferry franchise not exclusive, 25 Cal. 288.

Fallon v. Butler, 21 Cal. 24. Cited, Jurisdiction, of district court, in foreclosure, 21 Cal. 76; 24 Cal. 499; 29 Cal. 104, 122. Doubted, Probate, presentation of mortgage claims against estate, 24 Cal. 498; 27 Cal. 354, 356; 2 Nev. 338. Commented on, 42 Cal. 505. Cited, Judicial sales of estates of decedents, 2 Nev. 332, 333.

Falon v. Keese, 8 How. Pr. 341. Cited, Witness, examination, notice to party to testify, 22 Cal. 173.

Falvey and Kilbourn v. Massing, 7 Wis. 630. Commented on, Legislature, inquisitorial powers, examination of witnesses, 29 Cal. 399, 400, 405.

Fanjoy v. Seales, 29 Cal. 243. Cited, Respondeat Superior, liability for injuries from negligence of employé, 38 Cal. 634; 38 Cal. 692.

Farish v. Reigle, 11 Grat. 711. Commented on, Common Carriers, liability for negligence, 13 Cal. 603.

Farley v. Cleveland, 4 Cow. 432. Commented on, Debtor and Creditor, liability of third party on agreement to pay, 22 Cal. 190.

Farley v. Vaughn, 11 Cal. 227. Cited, Specific Performance, right to, may be defeated by delay, 23 Cal. 37; delay as a waiver of forfeiture, 40 Cal. 13.

Farmer v. Arundel, 2 W. Black, 825. Cited, Judicial Decisions, obiter dictum, 9 Cal. 733.

Farmers v. Gross, Cal. Sup. Ct. July T. 1870 (not reported.) Commented on, Conveyance and agreement for reconveyance, when not a mortgage, 42 Cal. 83.

Farmers' and Mechanics' Bank v. Champlain Trans. Co., 23 Vt. 186. Cited, Carrier's Contract, transportation through, 31 Cal. 53.

Farmers' and Mechanics' Bank v. Smith, 3 Serg. & R. 63; S. C. reversed, 6 Wheat. 131. Commented on, Statutory Construction, validity of State law, 26 Cal. 288; 12 Wheat. 333; 5 How. 316; 6 How. 328, 330.

Farmers' and Mechanics' Bank v. Troy City Bank, 1 Doug. 457. Cited, Principal and Agent, instrument made by agent, when principal bound, 13 Cal. 235.

Farmers' and Merchants' Bank v. Chester, 6 Humph. 458. Cited, Officers, presumptions in favor of authority to act, 3 Cal. 453.

Farmers' Bank v. Raynolds, 13 Ohio, 84. Cited, Surety, on note, discharge of, 10 Cal. 426.

Farmers' Bank of Md. v. Duvall, 7 Gill & J. 79. Cited, Negotiable Instruments, presentation and demand, 8 Cal. 634.

Farmers' Loan and T. Co. v. Clowes, 4 Edw. Ch. 575. Cited, Corporations, powers of, loaning money, 22 Cal. 629.

Farmers' Loan and Trust Co. v. Carroll, 5 Barb. 613. Commented on, Corporation, authority restricted by charter, 7 Cal. 375; 16 Cal. 619; 20 Cal. 102; 24 Cal. 550.

Farmers' Loan and Trust Co. v. Perry, 3 Sand. Ch. 339. Cited, Corporation, power to loan money, 22 Cal. 629.

Farmington Academy v. Allen, 14 Mass. 172. Cited, Services, recovery in action on implied promise, 14 Cal. 136.

Farnham v. Hildreth, 32 Barb. 278. Cited, Writ of Possession, execution of, against strangers to record, erroneous, 37 Cal. 348.

Farr v. Newman, 4 Term Rep. 621. Cited, Executor and Administrator, tenure of property of estate in trust, 26 Cal. 429; contra, 3 Mass. 319.

Farrant v. Thompson, 5 Barn. & Ald. 826. Cited, Fixtures, severance of, action lies, 10 Cal. 265.

Farrar v. Stackpole, 6 Greenl. 154. Commented on, Fixtures, 14 Cal. 66, 68. Cited, 1 Ohio St. 536.

Farrar v. United States, 5 Pet. 373. Cited, Powers, delegated authority cannot be delegated, 7 Cal. 542.

Farrell v. Enright, 12 Cal. 450. Cited, Aliens, constitutional rights of, 13 Cal. 165; 18 Cal. 219.

Farrington v. Payne, 15 John. 432. Cited, Pleading, splitting demands, judgment as a bar, 23 Cal. 387.

Farve's Heirs v. Graves, 4 Smedes & M. 707. Cited, Jurisdiction, of probate court, 12 Cal. 436.

Farwell v. Boston & Worcester R. R. Co., 4 Met. 55. Cited, Master and Servant, liability for injury to servant, 6 Cal. 210.

Fash v. Ross, 2 Hill, S. C. 294. Disapproved, Principal and Agent, contract made by, liability on, 13 Cal. 235.

Fatheree v. Long, 5 How. Miss. 664. Cited, Summons, sufficiency of service of, 11 Cal. 379.

Fatman v. Lobach, 1 Duer, 354. Cited, Corporate Stock, is personal property, right of transfer by party in possession, 42 Cal. 147.

Faulkner, Matter of, 4 Hill, 601. Cited, Jurisdiction, evidence to sustain jurisdiction of person, 31 Cal. 350.

Faw v. Marsteller, 2 Cranch, 10. Commented on, Legal Tender Currency, obligations to pay money may be discharged in currency, 27 Cal. 161.

Faw v. Roberdeau's Exr., 3 Cranch, 174. Commented on, Statute of Limitations, when it runs, absence from State, 16 Cal. 96.

Faxon v. Hollis, 13 Mass. 427. Cited, Evidence, book entries as, 14 Cal. 576.

Fay, Petitioner, 15 Pick. 254. Commented on, Municipal Corporations, powers conferred on, are trusts, applied to grant of ferry franchise, 13 Cal. 548.

Featherstonhaugh v. Bradshaw, 1 Wend. 134. Cited, Use and Occupation, when action lies, 3 Cal. 204; 35 Cal. 194.

Feillett v. Engler, 8 Cal. 76. Commented on and approved, Jurisdiction, governed by amount in controversy, 22 Cal. 171.

Fell v. Price, 8 Ill. 189. Cited, Execution, title acquired by purchaser at sale under, 31 Cal. 306.

Fellows's Case, 5 Greenl. 333. Cited, Trial, polling jury, practice, 20 Cal. 72.

Fellows v. Fellows, 4 Cow. 682. Commented on and approved, Specific Performance, joint action by assignees of equitable title, 24 Cal. 177; Equitable Relief, joint action to annul patent, 26 Cal. 360.

Fells v. Read, 3 Ves. Jr. 70. Cited, Specific Performance, when action lies on chattel contract, 25 Cal. 571.

Felter v. Mulliner, 2 John. 181. Commented on, Justices' Courts, proceedings, how construed, 41 Cal. 233.

Felton v. Dickinson, 10 Mass. 287. Cited, Debtor and Creditor, right of action by creditor against third party under agreement to pay debt, 37 Cal. 537; 2 Met. 386.

Felton v. Simpson, 11 Ired. 84. Cited, Nuisance, action for, when it lies, 40 Cal. 406.

Felton v. Wadsworth, 7 Cush. 587. Commented on, Attachment, when fraudulent as to creditors, 13 Cal. 441.

Fenn v. Rills, 9 La. 99. Cited, Vendor and Vendee, subsequently acquired title inures to benefit of vendee, under civil law, 8 Cal. 197.

Fennerstein's Champagne, 3 Wall. 149. Cited, Evidence, paper writings as, 41 Cal. 306.

Fenton v. Goundry, 13 East, 459. Cited, Negotiable Instruments, place of payment on note, demand and notice, 11 Cal. 324.

Fereday v. Wightwick, 1 Russ. & M. 45. Cited, Mining Partnership, conveyance of single interest, 23 Cal. 203; 28 Cal. 578; relation of property to partnership debts, Id. 582. Approved, Interests acquired in lands, Id. 584. Commented on, Purchaser of partner's interest charged with notice of lien of debts of copartnership, Id. 585.

Ferguson v. Carrington, 17 Eng. C. L. 59. Cited, Fraud, vitiates contract, applied to fraudulent purchase of goods, 8 Cal. 213.

Ferguson, Matter of, 9 John. 239. Commented on, Habeas Corpus, allowance of writ by supreme court in discretion, 11 Cal. 226.

Ferguson v. Miller, 6 Cal. 402. Cited, Mortgage, lien of, on fixtures, 22 Cal. 631; 23 Cal. 217.

Ferreira v. Depew, 4 Abb. Pr. 131. Cited, Set-off, when may be pleaded as equitable defense, 19 Cal. 658.

Ferrell v. Underwood, 2 Dev. Law R. 114. Cited, Justice's Court, evidence *aliunde* the record as to jurisdictional facts, 34 Cal. 327.

Ferriday v. Selser, 4 How. Miss. 506. Cited, Evidence, declarations of grantor, when not admissible to impeach title of grantee, 38 Cal. 282.

Ferris v. Coover, 10 Cal. 589. Approved and followed, Ejectment, 11 Cal. 92. Referred to, Mexican Grant, petition and grant to Sutter, 21 Cal. 542. Compared, Estate conveyed by grant, title, and right to possession to exterior boundaries, 13 Cal. 410. Cited to this point, 15 Cal. 277; 16 Cal. 425; 19 Cal. 97; 27 Cal. 564. Approved, 31 Cal. 493; 33 Cal. 108. Cited, Interpretation of grant, description by reference to map, 15 Cal. 306; clause reserving surplus after survey and

measurement, 21 Cal. 577; parol evidence admissible
to explain grant, 16 Cal. 426; ouster by tenant in common, 27 Cal. 564; Estoppel in pais, 26 Cal. 42; Tax
Title, steps prescribed by statute, to be strictly pursued to validate, 13 Cal. 619.   Approved, 14 Cal. 133;
property to be duly assessed, or tax invalid, 29 Cal.
452; no intendments in favor of official jurisdiction,
affirmative showing in proceedings required, 28 Cal.
112.

Ferris v. Coover, 11 Cal. 175.   Approved, Supreme Court
of United States, writ of error, citation, how and when
issued, 20 Cal. 171.   Commented on, Appellate power,
25 Cal. 610, 612, 614; 11 Wis. 525.

Ferris v. Crawford, 2 Den. 598.   Cited, Mortgage, purchaser of equity of redemption, 14 Cal. 34.   Commented on, 29 Barb. 531.

Ferris v. Paris, 10 John. 285.   Cited, Factors and Agents,
liability does not attach till demand made, 8 Cal. 457.

Fetherly v. Waggoner, 11 Wend. 599.   Cited, Will, attestation to, presumptions from lapse of time, 10 Cal. 479.

Fetridge · v. Wells, 4 Abb. Pr. 144.   Cited, Trade Marks,
protection of, 35 Cal. 64; law applicable to, Id. 75.

Ficken v. Jones, 28 Cal. 618.   Commented on and denied,
Ferocious Animal, liability of owner for injuries by,
41 Cal. 141.

Field v. Beaumont, 1 Swanst. 203.   Cited, Injunction, when
will be granted, 23 Cal. 84.

Field, Ex parte, 1 Cal. 187.   Approved, Contempt, what
order must show, 25 Ala. 86.

Field v. Gibbs, 1 Pet. C. C. 157.   Commented on, Record,
imports verity, judgment record how far conclusive, 8
Cal. 245; as to foreign judgments, 4 Zab. 248.

Field v. Holbrook, 14 How. Pr. 103.   Commented on, Equity,
discretionary powers, 10 Cal. 576.

Field v. Holland, 6 Cranch, 8; S. C. 1 Am. Lead. Cas. 268.
Cited, Debtor and Creditor, application of payments,
33 Cal. 657; 3 Wheat. 155, note c.

Field v. Mayor, etc., of New York, 6 N. Y. 186.   Cited,
Assignment, equity upholds, 13 Cal. 123; 30 Cal. 86;
35 Cal. 388; 38 Cal. 521; Id. 545.

Field v. Nickerson, 13 Mass. 137.   Commented on, Negotiable Instruments, indorsement before dishonor, 40 Cal. 116.

Field v. People, 3 Ill. 79.   Commented on and doubted, Office, tenure of, 6 Cal. 293; 22 Cal. 320.

Field v. Ross, 1 Mon. 133.   Cited, Decree, on partnership accounting, finality of, 9 Cal. 635.

Field v. Seabury, 19 How. 323.   Commented on, Patent, to land grant, not subject to collateral attack, 14 Cal. 366; precedence of prior grant, 28 Cal. 151.

Figg v. Mayo, 39 Cal. 262.   Approved, Appeal, presumptions of findings in support of judgment, 29 Wis. 169.

Finch v. Earl of Winchelsea, 1 P. Wms. 279.   Distinguished, Judgment, legal effect of, 37 Cal. 143.

Finch v. Tehama Co., 29 Cal. 453.   Cited, Supervisors, jurisdiction must appear on record of proceedings, 5 Nev. 319; 6 Nev. 97.

Findlay v. Smith, 6 Munf. 142.   Cited, Equity, verity of pleadings, practice, 1 Cal. 142.

Finlay v. King's Lessee, 3 Pet. 346.   Cited, Will, construction of, 36 Cal. 81; 14 How. 501.

Finley v. Carothers, 9 Tex. 518.   Cited, Probate, allowance of claim against estate, 7 Cal. 239; 26 Cal. 430.

Finley v. Finley, 9 Dana, 52.   Cited, Divorce, cruelty, 14 Cal. 80.

Finley v. Philadelphia, 32 Penn. St. 381.   Commented on, Taxation, capital stock of corporations, 29 Cal. 539.

Fireman's Insurance Co., Ex parte, 6 Hill, 243.   Cited, Mandamus, when it will not lie, 16 Cal. 212.

First Baptist Church v. Utica & Schenectady R. R. Co., 6 Barb. 315.   Cited, Street Railroads, not a nuisance, 35 Cal. 333; 25 Vermont, 62.

First Massachusetts T. Co. v. Field, 3 Mass. 201.   Cited, Statute of Limitations, fraudulent concealment to avoid, 8 Cal. 460.

First Parish in Sutton v. Cole, 3 Pick. 232.   Cited, Corporation, omission of part of name at organization not to invalidate grant or acts under grant, 39 Cal. 575.

First Presbyterian Cong. of Salem v. Williams.   Cited in 8 Wend. 483.   Commented on, Estoppel, by declarations as to title, 9 Cal. 206.

Fish v. Chapman, 2 Geo. 349. Cited, Injury by the Elements, acts of God, 35 Cal. 423.

Fish v. Folley, 6 Hill, 55. Cited, Contract, when action lies on breach of entire contract, 35 Cal. 242. Commented on, 2 Barb. 124.

Fish v. Howland, 1 Paige, 20. Cited, Vendor's Lien, waived by taking other security, 12 Cal. 305.

Fish v. Redington, 31 Cal. 185. Cited, Pleading, admissions by denial of allegations conjunctively stated, 31 Cal. 469; insufficient denials, 32 Cal. 110.

Fish v. Weatherwax, 2 Johns. Cas. 217. Cited, Mandamus, when it will not issue, 3 Cal. 171, 175; 4 Cal. 179; 28 Cal. 641.

Fishar v. Prosser, 1 Cowp. 217. Cited, Ejectment, what constitutes ouster by tenant in common, 24 Cal. 376, 377; 27 Cal. 561.

Fisher v. Bartlett, 8 Greenl. 122. Cited, Attachment, claim of third party, when may be asserted, 10 Cal. 176.

Fisher v. Bassett, 9 Leigh, 119. Commented on, Probate proceedings not open to collateral attack, 18 Cal. 505, 506.

Fisher v. Clisbee, 12 Ill. 344. Cited, Ferrymen liable as common carriers, 5 Cal. 364.

Fisher v. Cockerill, 5 Mon. 129. Commented on and approved, Legislature, cannot pass a law divesting vested rights, 7 Cal. 14.

Fisher v. Dennis, 6 Cal. 577. Cited, Negotiable Instruments, filling in blank in note with rate of interest not an alteration, 8 Cal. 112; 22 Mich. 430.

Fisher v. Gordy, 2 La. An. 762. Cited, Husband and Wife, presumption that property acquired belongs to the community, 12 Cal. 224; title in name of wife, no presumption of separate estate, Id. 253; effect of sale to wife, 17 Cal. 581.

Fisher v. McGirr, 1 Gray, 1. Cited, Constitutionality of Statute, legislative intent as to particular provisions, 19 Cal. 530; rule of judicial determination, 41 Cal. 160.

Fisher v. Prince, 3 Burr. 1363. Cited, Conversion, measure of damages on property of fluctuating value, 33 Cal. 120.

Fisher v. Salmon, 1 Cal. 413. Distinguished, Vendor and Vendee, rights of vendee under deed made by agent, 2 Cal. 143.

Fishkill, Town of, v. Fishkill, 22 Barb. 634. Cited, Constitutionality of Statute, 22 Cal. 386.

Fischli v. Fischli, 1 Blackf. 365. Cited, Sprague, J. dissenting, Alimony, inseparable from divorce, 38 Cal. 277.

Fisk v. His Creditors, 12 Cal. 281. Approved, Insolvency, jurisdiction of supreme court on appeal, 28 Cal. 117; 29 Cal. 418.

Fisk v. Norvell, 9 Tex. 13. Cited, Probate, statutory construction, petition for letters, 7 Cal. 223; Proceedings, special statute to be strictly pursued, 7 Cal. 237.

Fiske v. Anderson, 33 Barb. 74. Cited, Jurisdiction of Person, sufficiency of affidavit of publication, 31 Cal. 349.

Fiske v. Witt, 22 Pick. 83. Cited, Negotiable Instrument, authority of holder to fill blank, 8 Cal. 105. Distinguished, Id. 106.

Fister v. La Rue, 15 Barb. 323. Commented on, Corporation, ratification of contract for services, implied, 33 Cal. 196.

Fitch v. Brockmon, 2 Cal. 575. Cited, Notice, the giving of notice to authorize the execution of a power of sale must be proved, it will not be inferred from the deed, 22 Cal. 592.

Fitch v. Bunch, 30 Cal. 213. Cited, Deed, an escrow, 30 Wis. 652.

Fitch v. Peckham, 16 Vt. 150. Cited, Parent and Child, no recovery for gratuitous services, 22 Cal. 510.

Fitch v. Sutton, 5 East, 230. Cited, Debtor and Creditor, liquidated indebtedness cannot be discharged by a sum less than its amount, 27 Cal. 613.

Fitchburg and Worcester R. R. Co. v. Hanna, 6 Gray, 539. Cited, Common Carriers, contract for transportation through, construed, 31 Cal. 53; liability of railroads, Id. 54.

Fitzgerald v. Gorham, 4 Cal. 289. Commented on and approved, Statute of Frauds, actual and continued change of possession essential, 8 Cal. 83; 9 Cal. 273; possession by vendor as agent or attorney fraudulent, 8 Cal.

561. Cited as substantially overruled on this latter point in Stevens v. Irwin, 15 Cal. 503; where the true rule is declared, 26 Cal. 323.

Fitzgerald v. Urton, 5 Cal. 308. Commented on, Mines and Mining, right of entry of miners on public lands under possessory act, 5 Cal. 398; 6 Cal. 46; 14 Cal. 377. Cited, 22 Cal. 453; 23 Cal. 456.

Fitzherbert v. Shaw, 1 H. Black, 258. Cited, Fixtures, right of removal by tenant, 14 Cal. 65, 68; on removal of lease, 14 Cal. 71.

Fitzhugh v. Anderson, 2 Hen. & M. 302. Cited, Statute of Frauds, qualified possession in vendor, 15 Cal. 506.

Fitzsimmons v. Joslin, 21 Vt. 130. Commented on, Fraud, vitiates sale of goods, concealment of insolvency, 8 Cal. 214. Reviewed and distinguished, 33 Cal. 627.

Flagg v. Mann, 14 Pick. 467; S. C. 2 Sum. 486. Cited, Mortgage, when deed and defeasance constitute, 9 Cal. 549. Commented on, 550, 551; effect of parol defeasance, 36 Cal. 60; 12 How. 147, 152; Title, possession of tenant as notice of landlord's title, 21 Cal. 628; doctrine of constructive notice, 13 Cal. 511. Cited, Implied Trusts, purchase by party for common benefit, 30 Cal. 594; 33 Cal. 43.

Flagg v. Tyler, 3 Mass. 303. Cited, Pleading, insufficient defense in action on replevin bond, 4 Cal. 114.

Flagley v. Hubbard, 22 Cal. 35. Cited, Mandamus, when directed to judicial officer, 28 Cal. 641; 37 Cal. 534.

Flanders v. Barstow, 18 Me. 357. Cited, Chattel Mortgage, legal effect and operation, 27 Cal. 269.

Flandreau v. Downey, 23 Cal. 354. Cited, Estoppel, judgments on whom conclusive, 23 Cal. 375; special plea of estoppel, how waived, 36 Cal. 38.

Flandreau v. White, 18 Cal. 639. Cited, Statute of Limitations, bar of, prevented by institution of action, 19 Cal. 577. Approved as to mechanics' liens, 23 Cal. 456. Referred to, Id. 236.

Flatbush Avenue, Matter of, 1 Barb. 286. Cited, Street Improvements, assessment not to exceed value of benefit conferred, 27 Cal. 624.

Flateau v. Lubeck, 24 Cal. 364. Cited, New Trial, right to move, waived by failure to file notice in time, 26 Cal.

284; by failure to serve notice, 28 Cal. 154; statement ineffectual without legal notice, 32 Cal. 312.

Fleckner v. United States Bank, 8 Wheat. 338. Cited, Corporations, validity of act of, not subject to collateral attack, 22 Cal. 630. Commented on, authority to contract, 22 Cal. 630; 12 Wheat. 102; 6 How. 322; 19 How. 323; 21 How. 363. Commented on, 1 Har. & G. 423.

Fleet v. Youngs, 11 Wend. 522. Cited, Deed, identity of grantor in separate deeds, 28 Cal. 222. Commented on, Writ of Error, within what time to issue, 28 Cal. 421.

Fleetwood v. New York, 2 Sand. 476. Commented on, Payment under protest, legal effect, 9 Cal. 417. Cited, 18 Cal. 275.

Fleming v. Alter, 7 Serg. & R. 294. Cited, Debtor and Creditor, action lies on agreement of third party to pay creditor's claim, 37 Cal. 537.

Fleming v. Gilbert, 3 John. 528. Cited, Contract, performance as to time may be waived by parol, 39 Cal. 175. Commented on, Pleading, parol agreement as a defense in action on specialty, 4 Cal. 316.

Fleming v. Hector, 2 Gale, 180. Cited, Contracts, made by agents, 13 Cal. 48.

Fleming v. Page, 9 How. 603. Cited, Territorial Law, conquest or cession does not affect vested rights, 15 Cal. 559.

Flemming v. Marine Ins. Co., 4 Whart. 59. Cited, Trial, province of jury under instructions, 40 Cal. 546.

Fletcher v. Austin, 11 Vt. 447. Cited, Official Bonds, validity of joint bond, 14 Cal. 423, 424; 21 Cal. 589.

Fletcher v. Daingerfield, 20 Cal. 427. Cited, Attorney and Counsel, officers of the court, tenure of office, 4 Wall. 378.

Fletcher v. Dyche, 2 Term. Rep. 32. Cited, Contract, liquidated damages in, 9 Cal. 587; 7 Wheat. 18.

Fletcher v. Dysart, 9 B. Mon. 415. Cited, Municipal Corporation, ratification of acts by, 7 Cal. 386; 16 Cal. 626.

Fletcher v. Grover, 11 N. H. 369. Cited, Sureties, legal right of contribution between, 20 Cal. 135.

13

Fletcher v. Peck, 6 Cranch, 87. Cited, Constitutionality of Statutes, rule of judicial determination, 4 Cal. 158; 9 Cal. 515; 22 Cal. 308; 25 Cal. 420; 25 Cal. 572; 26 Cal. 228; 12 Wheat. 294; 8 Pet. 110; reasonable intendments in support of their validity, 25 Cal. 569; impairing validity of contracts, statutes repealing acts making grants are unconstitutional, 16 Cal. 30, 194; 18 Cal. 613; or statute annulling conveyances, 18 Cal. 612; 12 Wheat. 125. Commented on, Contracts, executed or executory either between individuals, or State and individuals, 16 Cal. 30; 4 Wheat. 656; Id. 682; 11 Pet. 573. Doubted as to contracts between State and individuals, 9 Cal. 349. Commented on, Title in innocent purchasers, 12 Cal. 497.

Fletcher v. Wilson, Smedes & M. Ch. 376. Cited, Contract, waiver of fraud, to prevent the right to a rescission, 17 Cal. 384.

Fleury v. Brown, 9 How. Pr. 217. Cited, Pleading, sham answer defined, 10 Cal. 29.

Fleury v. Roger, 9 How. Pr. 215. Cited, Pleading, sham answer defined, 10 Cal. 29.

Fleury v. Roget, 5 Sand. 646. Cited, Pleading, evidence an insufficient answer properly rejected, 32 Cal. 573.

Flinn v. Chase, 4 Den. 85. Doubted, Administrator, appointment and resignation of, 10 Cal. 116, 119.

Flint v. Clinton Company and Trustee, 12 N. H. 433. Cited, Corporate Deed, seal imports authority, 37 Cal. 598.

Flint v. Haight, Cal. Sup. Ct. Jan. T. 1856 (not reported.) Cited, Appeal, error cannot be assigned on instrument not embodied in statement, 11 Cal. 361.

Flint v. Lyon, 4 Cal. 17. Commented on, Sale and Delivery, implied warranty, 5 Cal. 474; McAll. 55, 57.

Flint v. Sheldon, 13 Mass. 443. Cited, Conveyance, effect of parol defeasance, 36 Cal. 61.

Flint River Steamboat Co. v. Foster, 5 Geo. 194. Cited, Constitutionality of Statutes, rule of judicial decision, presumptions, 9 Cal. 512.

Florentine v. Barton, 2 Wall. 210. Reviewed, Estates of Deceased Persons, constitutionality of special statute authorizing private sale of estate, 39 Cal. 186.

Fluker v. Bullard, 2 La. An. 338. Denied, Execution, promissory note subject to levy and sale, 34 Cal. 88.

Flynn v. Abbott. See People *v.* Abbott.

Flynt v. Arnold, 2 Met. 619. Cited, Conveyances, priority of record of, constructive notice, 41 Cal. 50.

Foden v. Sharp, 4 John. 183. Cited, Negotiable Instrument, demand at place of payment not essential, 11 Cal. 318.

Fogarty v. Sawyer, 17 Cal. 589. Cited, Mortgage, under statute, a mere security, 18 Cal. 488; 21 Cal. 623; 22 Cal. 262; 26 Cal. 144; 35 Cal. 413; 36 Cal. 39. Construed, Statutory provisions in relation to mortgages, 36 Cal. 52, 59; power of sale in mortgage, 23 Cal. 573; 27 Cal. 272; 36 Cal. 60; foreclosure and decree of sale essential to change right of possession, 27 Cal. 270. Cited, Parties, grantee of mortgaged premises a necessary party in foreclosure, 25 Cal. 161.

Fogarty v. Sparks, 22 Cal. 142. Approved, Ejectment, who bound by judgment in, and subject to removal under writ of possession, 22 Cal. 207; Occupant, not bound by judgment unless made defendant, 28 Cal. 536. Doubted, Burden of proof as to who were occupants at the institution of the action, 29 Cal. 666.

Fogg v. Middlesex M. F. Ins. Co., 10 Cush. 346. Cited, Insurance, against loss by fire, contract construed, 38 Cal. 543.

Foley v. Harrison, 15 How. 433. Commented on, State Lands, donation by Congress to State, 16 Cal. 314; 21 Cal. 335; interest attached *in presenti* on admission of State, 25 Cal. 255. Commented on, 27 Cal. 89; 20 La. An. 437.

Follain v. Lefevre, 3 Rob. La. 13. Cited, Judicial Notice, public officers and their signatures, 32 Cal. 108.

Folsom v. Bartlett, 2 Cal. 163. Cited, Contract, to convey real estate, payment by instalments, independent covenants, 35 Cal. 662; 38 Cal. 200.

Folsom v. Root, 1 Cal. 374. Affirmed on principle of *stare decisis,* Appeal, presumption that evidence sustained the judgment, 1 Cal. 453.

Folsom's Exrs. v. Scott, 6 Cal. 460. Approved and followed, Evidence, secondary evidence of lost paper when admissible, 6 Cal. 581; 17 Cal. 573.

Fontaine v. Phoenix Ins. Co., 11 John. 299. Commented on and distinguished, Forfeiture, 25 Cal. 241. Doubted, 19 N. Y. 187. Denied, 1 Story, 134.

Foote v. Colvin, 3 John. 216. Cited, Contract, letting on shares, joint tenancy on crop, 23 Cal. 521.

Foot v. Prowse, 1 Strange, 625. Commented on, Officer, right to hold over office, 28 Cal. 52.

Foot v. Sabin, 19 John. 155. Cited, Partnership, partner as surety on note, burden of proof as to partnership liability, 37 Cal. 117.

Foot v. Stevens, 17 Wend. 483. Cited, Pleading, jurisdiction when presumed, 33 Cal. 536; 34 Cal. 427.

Foote v. West, 1 Den. 544. Cited, Demand, in suit on bond for deed essential, 17 Cal. 276.

Forbes v. Appleton, 5 Cush. 117. Cited, Money, paid under mistake of law not recoverable, cognizance of law presumed, 18 Cal. 271. Commented on, Id. 272.

Forbes v. Cochrane, 2 Barn. & C. 471. Cited, Constitutional Construction, right of transit with property through States secured by, 9 Cal. 163.

Forbes v. Forbes, 11 La. An. 326. Cited, Husband and Wife, presumption that property acquired during marriage belongs to the community, 12 Cal. 253; 30 Cal. 37, 44, 55.

Forbes v. Hyde, 31 Cal. 342. Cited, Jurisdiction, of person by publication of summons, 30 Cal. 621; of superior courts presumed, 34 Cal. 402. Overruled as to affidavit for publication being part of judgment roll, 34 Cal. 404. Commented on, 34 Cal. 421; validity of judgment till reversed, 31 Cal. 286.

Forbush v. Lombard, 13 Met. 109. Cited, Conveyance, construction of, what passes, 15 Cal. 197.

Ford, Ex parte, 2 Root, 232. Cited, Witness, competency of, 1 Cal. 506.

Ford v. Harrington, 16 N. Y. 288. Commented on, Attorney and Client, transactions between, 33 Cal. 442.

Ford v. Ford, 1 La. 201. Cited, Husband and Wife, presumptions as to property acquired during marriage, burden of proof, 12 Cal. 224; burden of proof as to wife's separate property, Id. 253; conveyance to wife, 17 Cal. 581.

Ford v. Harrington, 16 N. Y. 288. Cited, Attorney and Client, transactions between, 33 Cal. 440.

Ford v. Hendricks, 34 Cal. 673. Commented on, Guarantor of note, promise of, when not within statute of frauds, 38 Cal. 135.

Ford v. Holton, 5 Cal. 321. Cited, Appeal, Presumptions in favor of decision and judgment, 24 Cal. 378.

Ford v. Hopkins, 1 Salk, 283. Commented on, Bailment, liability on sale of property by bailee, 42 Cal. 103.

Ford v. Hurd, 4 Smedes & M. 683. Statutes distinguished, Undertaking, remedy for defective undertaking, 15 Cal. 32.

Ford v. Rigby, 10 Cal. 449. Distinguished, Injunction, when it lies, 25 Cal. 519.

Ford v. Stuart, 19 John. 342. Cited, Assignment, of judgment, need not be under seal, 25 Cal. 544.

Fore v. Manlove, 18 Cal. 436. Cited, Assignment, purchaser of judgment takes as assignee only, 23 Cal. 255.

Forney v. Hallacher, 8 Serg. & R. 159. Cited, Marriage, proof of, in cases other than divorce, bigamy, etc., 26 Cal. 133.

Forrest v. Forrest, 10 Barb. 46. Cited, Statutory Construction, rule of determination, 28 Cal. 95.

Forrester v. Lord Leigh, 1 Amb. 173. Cited, Will, construction of devises, 31 Cal. 610.

Forrestier v. Bordman, 1 Story, 43. Cited, Estoppel, waiver of irregularities in execution of a power of sale, 22 Cal. 594.

Forster v. Fuller, 6 Mass. 58. Cited, Principal and Agent, contract made by agent, liability of agent, 13 Cal. 48.

Forsyth v. Palmer, 14 Penn. St. 96. Cited, Witness, competency of, vendor of chattel, 23 Cal. 446.

Forsythe v. Ellis, 4 J. J. Marsh, 298. Cited, Trespass, when action lies against officer on official bond for wrongful levy, 14 Cal. 199.

Fort v. Collins, 21 Wend. 109. Cited, Appeal, rule of determination on insufficiency of evidence, 26 Cal. 525.

Fortitude, The, 3 Sum. 228. Cited, Vessel, pledge or sale of by master for necessaries, 8 Cal. 534.

Forward v. Pittard, 1 Term Rep. 27. Cited, Common Carriers, liability for loss of property, presumptions against carrier, 27 Cal. 431; injuries by the elements, acts of God, 35 Cal. 422.

Fosgate v. Herkimer Nav. and Hyd. Co., 12 N. Y. 582. Cited, Pleading, misjoinder of parties, waived, 29 Cal. 641.

Foss v. Crisp, 20 Pick. 121. Cited, Deed, description in, reference to other deed, 24 Cal. 444.

Foster v. Allanson, 2 Term Rep. 479. Cited, Account Stated, effect of, 33 Cal. 697.

Foster v. Browning, 4 R. I. 51. Cited, Easement, as property, 32 Cal. 506.

Foster, Case of Dr., 11 Coke, 56. Cited, Statutory Construction, cotemporaneous acts, 35 Cal. 709.

Foster v. Davenport, 22 How. 244. Cited, Constitutional Construction, congressional power to regulate commerce exclusive, 34 Cal. 498.

Foster v. Essex Bank, 16 Mass. 245. Cited, Constitutionality of Statute, presumption in favor of, 26 Cal. 228.

Foster v. Hall, 12 Pick. 90. Cited, Witness, privileged communications, 5 Cal. 451; 36 Cal. 508; Evidence, tending to show fraud, when admissible, 7 Cal. 393.

Foster v. Jones, 1 McCord, 116. Cited, Attachment, who may not impeach for irregularities, 18 Cal. 155.

Foster v. Neilson, 2 Pet. 253. Cited, National Law, government of ceded territory, 18 Cal. 23; treaties as law, 24 Cal. 661; 5 Pet. 46; 6 Pet. 710; 12 Pet. 519, 746; 14 Pet. 407; 2 How. 602; 3 How. 228; 7 How. 56; 19 How. 372.

Foster v. Morris, 3 A. K. Marsh. 609. Cited, Estoppel, when tenant not estopped, 21 Cal. 316.

Foster v. Pierson, 4 Term Rep. 617. Cited, Covenant, breach of, sufficiency of eviction, 39 Cal. 365.

Foster v. Poillon, 2 E. D. Smith, 556. Cited, Mechanic's Lien, want of privity between owner and sub-contractor, 22 Cal. 571.

Foster v. Tucker, 3 Greenl. 458. Cited, Felony, conviction of, as a suspension of rights, 1 Cal. 434.

Foster v. White, 9 Port. 221. Cited, Assignment, effect, acceptance of order as, 12 Cal. 98.

Fotheree v. Lawrence, 30 Miss. 416.   Cited, Evidence, will as, preliminary showing of probate required, 18 Cal. 481.

Fourth Avenue, Matter of, 3 Wend. 452.   Cited, Street Improvements, assessment for benefits not to exceed benefit conferred, 27 Cal. 624.

Fowle v. Common Council of Alexandria, 3 Pet. 398. Cited, County, not liable for acts of its officers, 21 Cal. 115.

Fowler v. Armour, 24 Ala. 194.   Denied, Contract, damages on breach of, 35 Cal. 247.

Fowler v. Burns, 7 Bosw. 637.   Commented on, Injunction, practice on motion to dissolve, 35 Cal. 60.

Fowler v. Harbin, 23 Cal. 630.   Cited, Foreclosure, relief of purchaser at sheriff's sale, 36 Cal. 399.

Fowler v. Hunt, 10 John. 463.   Commented on, Statute of Limitations, construction of "return" of debtor, 16 Cal. 97.

Fowler v. Lee, 10 Gill & J. 358.   Approved, Equity, interferes with judgments and proceedings at law only in peculiar cases, 14 Cal. 142, 143.

Fowler v. Padget, 7 Term Rep. 514.   Approved, Crimes and Punishments, it is the intent which constitutes criminality, 27 Cal. 576.

Fowler v. Pierce, 2 Cal. 165.   Cited, Mandamus, when may issue to executive officers, 7 Cal. 80.   Approved, 16 Cal. 46, 63.   Cited, when to inferior tribunal, 41 Cal. 77.   Overruled, Statute, testing validity of, parol evidence not admissible to impeach enrolled statute, 30 Cal. 276, 279.   Cited, Enrolled Act, *prima facie* valid, 35 Ill. 139; 6 Wall. 510; Courts may go behind record evidence to test constitutionality, 43 Ala. 723; 8 Ind. 160; Motives of legislators not subject to inquiry, 39 Cal. 202.

Fowler v. Poling, 6 Barb. 165.   Commented on, Covenant of Warranty, what constitutes eviction under, 39 Cal. 366.

Fowler v. Smith, 2 Cal. 39; S. C. 2 Cal. 568.   Cited, Conveyance of Land, covenants of seizin, not implied, 22 Cal. 598; Territorial Law, laws of ceded territory in force till abrogated, 37 Cal. 92; Covenants, in lease, what constitutes eviction, 39 Cal. 364.

Fowler v. St. Joseph, 37 Mo. 228. Cited, Street Assessments, liability of owners, 31 Cal. 685, 686.

Fox v. Fox, 25 Cal. 587. Construed, Divorce, residence a jurisdictional fact, which must be proved, 28 Cal. 601.

Fox v. Hinton, 4 Bibb. 559. Commented on, Lands, constructive possession under patent, 25 Cal. 134.

Fox v. Mackreth, 2 Bro. Ch. Cas. 400. Cited, Trustee, duties and liabilities as to trust property, 36 Cal. 432; 4 How. 554.

Fox v. Mensch, 3 Watts & S. 446. Cited, Probate Sales, *caveat emptor* the rule, 9 Cal. 197.

Fox v. Minor, 32 Cal. 111. Approved, Judgment, coin judgment in action on official bond, when erroneous, 32 Cal. 149. Commented on, in dissenting opinion, Sanderson, J. 150, 153. Cited, Parties, infant may sue by guardian, 36 Cal. 451.

Fox v. Ohio, 5 How. 410. Cited, Counterfeiting, concurrent powers of legislation as to, 1 Cal. 241; 34 Cal. 186; 18 Gratt. 940; 5 How. 556; 9 How. 568; 14 How. 20. Distinguished, Exclusive jurisdiction of federal courts over crimes against federal law, 38 Cal. 150.

Foxcroft v. Lester, Colles C. P. 108; 1 Am. Lead. Cas. Eq. 510. Cited, Specific Performance, of verbal contract, part performed, 10 Cal. 158; Equitable Mortgage, 31 Cal. 327; 32 Cal. 389.

Foxcroft v. Mallett, 4 How. 353. Commented on, Stare Decisis, as applied to decisions of local tribunals, 15 Cal. 603; 12 How. 148; 19 How. 603.

Foxwist v. Tremaine, 2 Saund. 210. Cited, Pleading, dilatory pleas, technical exactness required, 14 Cal. 42.

Foy v. Domec, 33 Cal. 317. Cited, Appeal, filing motion of appeal must precede or be contemporaneous with service of copy, 8 Nev. 178.

Fraley v. Bispam, 10 Penn. St. 320. Cited, Sale and Delivery, warranty, when not implied, 5 Cal. 474.

Francis v. Welch, 11 Ired. 215. Cited, Executor, *de son tort*, rights and liabilities of, 17 Cal. 192.

Francisco v. Manhattan Life Ins. Co., 36 Cal. 283. Cited, Appeal, for error, in refusing to transfer action, appeal lies, 4 Nev. 447.

Frank v. Brady, 8 Cal. 47. Cited, Criminal Procedure, continuance, practice, 28 Cal. 590.

Frank v. Doane, 15 Cal. 302. Approved and followed, New Trial, abandonment of motion by failure to prosecute, 15 Cal. 304.

Frank v. San Francisco. See People *v.* San Francisco.

Franklin v. Board of Examiners, 23 Cal. 173. Cited, State Debt, in the event of war, 27 Cal. 222.

Franklin v. Dorland, 28 Cal. 178. Cited, Deed, evidence explanatory of, 36 Cal. 505.

Franklin v. Osgood, 14 John. 553; S. C. 2 Johns. Cas. 1. Commented on, Will, construction of power of sale in, 32 Cal. 440. Cited, 4 Wheat. 699, note *a.*

Franklin v. Reiner, 8 Cal. 340. Cited, Appeal, what transcript must show, 9 Cal. 641; 10 Cal. 31; 10 Cal. 491; 28 Cal. 59; 30 Cal. 184; 1 Nev. 98.

Franklin v. Roberts, 2 Ired. Eq. 564. Cited, Deed as Mortgage, parol evidence admissible to prove, 13 Cal. 130.

Franklin v. Talmage, 5 John. 84. Cited, Indictment, middle name not material, 6 Cal. 206.

Franklin Ins. Co. v. Culver, 6 Ind. 137. Cited, Evidence, what constitutes documentary, in insurance cases, 36 Cal. 177.

Franklyn v. Miller, 4 Adol. & E. 599. Vendor and Vendee, rights under contract of sale with conditions, 34 Cal. 144.

Fraser v. Goode, 3 Rich. 199. Cited, Surety, right to contribution, 20 Cal. 136.

Fraylor v. Sonora Min. Co., 17 Cal. 594. Cited, Corporations, action on implied contract for services, 22 Cal. 561; ratification of contract by receipt of benefits, 33 Cal. 199.

Freake v. Cranefeldt, 3 Mylne & C. 499. Cited, Statute of Limitations, rule as to debts of decedent, 35 Cal. 638.

Frear v. Everstone, 20 John. 142. Cited, Witness, incompetency of party to record, 6 Cal. 195.

Free v. Hawkins, 8 Taunt. 92. Cited, Contract, evidence not admissible to vary written contract, 23 Cal. 257.

Freeborn v. Glazer, 10 Cal. 338. Cited, Notice of Motion, practice, insufficiency of notice to strike out, 18 Cal.

204. Pleading, complaints under common counts sufficient, 32 Cal. 175.

Freeman v. City of Boston, 5 Met. 56. Commented on, Reward, liability on offer of, when it attaches, 14 Cal. 136.

Freeman v. Howe, 24 How. 450. Cited, Judgments, conclusiveness of, 27 Cal. 170. Commented on, 7 Minn. 116.

Freeman v. McGaw, 15 Pick. 82. Denied, Mortgage, assignment of, 5 Cal. 336.

Freeman v. People, 4 Denio, 9. Approved, Juror and Jury, ground of challenge must be distinctly stated, 16 Cal. 130.

Freeman v. Thayer, 33 Me. 76. Cited, Presumptions, as to regularity of proceedings from acquiescence and lapse of time, 22 Cal. 591.

Freeman's Bank v. Rollins, 13 Me. 202. Cited, Surety, on note, when delay not a discharge of, 10 Cal. 425; 23 Vt. 149.

Fremont v. Boling, 11 Cal. 580. Cited, Injunction, when it lies to restrain tax sale, 2 Neb. 438.

Fremont v. Crippen, 10 Cal. 211. Commented on and approved, Mandamus, to compel execution of writ of restitution, 22 Cal. 150; 28 Cal. 71; who liable to be dispossessed under writ, 22 Cal. 207; mandamus will not lie where there is a legal remedy, 30 Tex. 726, 727.

Fremont v. United States, 17 How. 542. Cited, International Rights, public rights passed from Mexico to United States under treaty, 14 Cal. 311; so as to title to mineral contained in land, 14 Cal. 358; Mexican Grants, title and interest in, vested personal rights, 8 Cal. 389; 13 Cal. 413; 16 Cal. 320; 27 Cal. 564; 33 Cal. 154; 42 Cal. 603; notwithstanding conditions, imposed, 14 Cal. 605. Commented on, what claims to be presented to board of land commission for confirmation, 19 Cal. 269; 24 Cal. 670; 31 Cal. 437. Cited, Evidence, customs and usages as evidence of grant, 31 Cal. 522; 20 How. 64; location and segregation essential to perfect the title, 13 Cal. 410, 417; 18 Cal. 575; 19 Cal. 270; 24 Cal. 579; 36 Cal. 145; 38 Cal. 66, 67. Doubted, title under inchoate grant sufficient to maintain ejectment, 6 Cal. 269; 10 Cal. 616. Commented on, Validity of grant, 14 Cal. 306; 17 Cal. 211; discovery of mineral not to affect the title, 2 Black, 232. Cited, Alien's right to hold property, 5 Cal. 379.

French v. Carcart, 1 N. Y. 96. Cited, Grant, to lands, construction of, 26 Cal. 108.

French v. Chichester, 2 Vern. 568. Cited, Will, construction of bequest, liability for debts, 31 Cal. 602, 603.

French v. French, 3 N. H. 234. Cited, Conveyance, covenants in, construed, 6 Cal. 314.

French v. Garner, 7 Port. 549. Cited, Equity, enjoining judgment at law on ground of newly discovered facts, 18 Cal. 47.

French v. Shotwell, 5 John. Ch. 555. Cited, Judgment, entry of, on warrant of attorney, 13 Cal. 200.

French v. Teschemaker, 24 Cal. 518. Commented on and judgment construed, Constitutionality of Statute, granting county aid to railroads, 25 Cal. 648; 7 Kan. 506. Explained and adopted, general laws to have a uniform operation, 26 Cal. 256; 29 Cal. 271; 32 Cal. 527; 37 Cal. 375; 38 Cal. 710; 7 Kan. 506; 3 Or. 284; applied to statute liability of stockholders, 35 Cal. 166; 3 Or. 284; to taxation of costs in actions, in certain locality, 35 Cal. 199; to taxation, by dockage and wharf charges, 35 Cal. 616. Cited, Statutory Construction, when statute is mandatory, 36 Cal. 604; 30 Tex. 726, 727; appointment to vacancy in office, 37 Cal. 627. Referred to, Contract of Corporation, 33 Cal. 188, 192, 193.

Frey v. Leeper, 2 Dall. 131. Cited, Replevin, continuance of attachment lien, 11 Cal. 273.

Fridenberg v. Pierson, 18 Cal. 152. Cited, Attachment, junior attachment creditor cannot impeach for irregularities, 28 Cal. 287.

Friedman v. Macy, 17 Cal. 226. Distinguished, Lease, construction of, 19 Cal. 363.

Frier v. Jackson, 8 John. 495. Cited, Exceptions, objections must be specific, 10 Cal. 268; 12 Cal. 245; must be taken on fact not denied, 34 Cal. 686.

Frink v. Green, 5 Barb. 455. Cited, Deed, consideration may be proved by parol, 26 Cal. 474.

Frique v. Hopkins, 4 Mart. N. S. 212. Approved, Husband and Wife, grant of land constitutes common property,

13 Cal. 474; 14 Cal. 602, 604, 611; 21 Cal. 541. Cited, Adverse possession under Spanish law, 21 Cal. 490.

Frisbie v. Price, 27 Cal. 253. Cited, Vendor and Vendee, ejectment of vendee by vendor, 7 Nev. 48.

Frisbie v. Larned, 21 Wend. 451. Cited, Debtor and Creditor, effect of payment by note, 10 Cal. 427.

Frisbie v. Whitney, 9 Wall. 187, reversing S. C. on appeal from supreme court of the District of Columbia. Approved, and the decision in the latter court disapproved, as to occupation of public lands by preëmptioner conferring vested rights, 37 Cal. 490, 493, 496, 500. Cited, Time allowed to preëmptioner to make proofs and pay, Id. 517; provisional rights of preëmptioner, 40 Cal. 298; power of congress to withdraw lands before final payment by preëmptioner, 41 Cal. 493; 41 Cal. 626, 638.

Frisch v. Caler, 21 Cal. 71. Approved, Pleading, affirmative allegations in answer, when not new matter, 21 Cal. 436; 22 Cal. 168; Id. 575.

Frische v. Kramer's Lessee, 16 Ohio, 125. Cited, Foreclosure, execution of decree not stayed by death of mortgagor, 9 Cal. 429. Commented on, 12 Wis. 583.

Frohock v. Pattee, 38 Me. 103. Cited, Statutory Construction, penal statutes, 29 Cal. 512.

Fromont v. Coupland, 9 Eng. C. L. R. 531. Commented on, Partnership, accounting, 9 Cal. 296.

Frontin v. Small, 1 Strange, 705. Cited, Principal and Agent, contract by agent, 13 Cal. 49.

Frost v. Beekman, 1 John. Ch. 288. Commented on, Conveyances, effect of mistake in record of, 7 Cal. 294. Cited, 31 Cal. 321; 12 Iowa, 19.

Frost v. Deering, 21 Me. 156. Cited, Married Woman, execution of deed by, 22 Cal. 565.

Frost v. Harford, 40 Cal. 165. Cited, Pleading, frivolous defenses, 40 Cal. 444.

Frost v. Raymond, 2 Caines, 192. Cited, Deed, covenants in, construed, 9 Cal. 226.

Frost v. Spaulding, 19 Pick. 445. Cited, Deed, construction of description in, 26 Cal. 632.

Frothingham v. Everton, 12 N. H. 239. Cited, Counterclaim, damages by way of recoupment, 26 Cal. 306.

Frothingham v. Haley, 3 Mass. 68. Cited, Debt, when matured under contract, 37 Cal. 526.

Fry v. Hill, 7 Taunt. 397. Cited, Contract, performance, reasonable time for a legal inference, what is a reasonable time a question of fact, 30 Cal. 559.

Frye v. Bank of Illinois, 11 Ill. 367. Cited, Tax Title, party in possession, buying at tax sale, holds title as trustee, 14 Cal. 34; Mortgage, for future advances, valid, 35 Cal. 309.

Fryeburg P. Fund v. Osgood, 21 Me. 179. Cited, Statute of Limitations, part payment to avoid, 17 Cal. 577.

Fullam v. Downe, 6 Esp. 26. Cited, Money Paid, under mistake of law, when not recoverable, knowledge of law presumed, 18 Cal. 271; 1 Ohio St. 274; 11 Ohio St. 538.

Fulton, Ex parte, 7 Cow. 484. Cited, Appeal, sufficiency of undertaking on, 13 Cal. 508.

Fuller v. Acker, 1 Hill, 473. Cited, Chattel mortgage and pledge distinguished, 35 Cal. 411; legal effect and operation of chattel mortgage, 27 Cal. 269; 36 Cal. 429.

Fuller v. Bennett, 2 Hare, 402. Cited, Notice to agent is notice to principal, 31 Cal. 165.

Fuller v. Dame, 18 Pick. 472. Commented on, Contract, void, as being against public interests, 22 Cal. 341.

Fuller v. Ferguson, 26 Cal. 546. Cited, Husband and Wife, grant to lot in pueblo to husband, becomes his separate property, 33 Cal. 703.

Fuller v. Hubbard, 6 Cow. 13. Cited, Vendor and Vendee, demand in action on bond for deed essential, 17 Cal. 276; 25 Cal. 279.

Fuller v. Hutchings, 10 Cal. 523. Cited, New Trial, surprise, what insufficient to constitute, 22 Cal. 163.

Fuller v. Milford, 2 McLean, 74. Cited, Surety on Note, discharge of, by delay of creditor, 10 Cal. 425.

Fuller v. Williams, 7 Cow. 53. Cited as modified, Vendor and Vendee, demand and tender of deed. 25 Cal. 279.

Fuller v. Yates, 8 Paige, 328. Cited, Will, election of surviving wife under, 29 Cal. 348; testamentary provision construed, Id. 349.

Fulton v. Hanlow, 20 Cal. 450. Approved, Res Adjudicata, estoppel by matter of record, 23 Cal. 358, 375; 26 Cal.

494. Cited, San Francisco, interest in pueblo lands not subject to levy and sale under execution, 42 Cal. 556; 5 Wall. 337.

Fulton Bank v. Benedict, 1 Hall, 529. Commented on, Witness, impeachment of, 27 Cal. 635.

Fulwood v. Graham, 1 Rich. 491. Commented on, Deed, description in, how construed, 10 Cal. 629.

Funes y Carillo v. Bank of United States, 10 Rob. La. 533. Cited, Negotiable Instruments, presentment and demand at place specified, 11 Cal. 324.

Funk v. Creswell, 5 Clark, Iowa, 62. Cited, Covenant, breach of, what sufficient to constitute an eviction, 39 Cal. 367.

Funkenstein v. Elgutter, 11 Cal. 328. Cited, Jurisdiction, county court, what issues on appeal may be tried, 1 Nev. 96.

Furman v. Walter, 13 How. Pr. 348. Cited, Attachment, practice on preparation of papers, 38 Cal. 216; 14 Abb. Pr. 67.

Furman Street, Matter of, 17 Wend. 649. Cited, Eminent Domain, compensation for condemnation of lands, 31 Cal. 374; Appeal, review on, as to question of damages, 32 Cal. 541.

Furniss v. Brown, 8 How. Pr. 59. Cited, Amendment, may be made to complaint without prejudice to the injunction, 33 Cal. 502.

Furse v. Sharwood, 2 Q. B. 388. Cited, Negotiable Instruments, notice of dishonor, 8 Cal. 636.

Gadsden v. Brown, Speer Ch. 37. Cited, Debtor and Creditor, subrogation to rights of creditor, 24 Cal. 608.

Gaffield v. Hapgood, 17 Pick. 192. Cited, Fixtures, right of removal by tenant, 14 Cal. 68.

Gage v. Bates, 40 Cal. 384. Approved, Lease, demand for rent necessary to work forfeiture, 41 Cal. 434.

Gage v. Johnson, 1 McCord, 492. Cited, Executors and Administrators, joint administrators, 24 Cal. 501.

Gage v. Rogers, 20 Cal. 91. Cited, Judgment by Default, for amount exceeding prayer in complaint is erroneous, 27 Cal. 102; 29 Cal. 168; 30 Cal. 535; 1 Nev. 317.

Gagliardo v. Hoberlin, 18 Cal. 394. Approved, Appeal, findings will not be reviewed except on motion for new

trial, 27 Cal. 69; Id. 411; Id. 475; 29 Cal. 391; 30 Cal.
287; 3 Nev. 303.

Gahan v. Neville, 2 Cal. 81.   Cited, Gaming, money staked
on wager, 37 Cal. 675.

Gahn v. Niemcewicz, 11 Wend. 318.   Cited, Husband and
Wife, separate property of wife, 20 Cal. 674, 675.

Gaines v. Betts, 2 Doug. Mich. 99.   Approved, Justices'
Courts, proceedings, entry of judgment, 41 Cal. 233.

Gaines v. Chew, 2 How. 645.   Commented on, Wills, equitable jurisdiction on, 20 Cal. 268.

Gaines v. Nicholson, 9 How. 356.   Commented on, Patent,
annulment of, 14 Cal. 364; 14 How. 280.

Galatian v. Gardner, 7 John. 106.   Cited, Dedication, of
highway, assent how shown, 14 Cal. 649.

Gale v. Davis, 7 Mo. 544.   Cited, Preëmption, persons not
in priority with paramount title cannot question rights
of preëmptioner, 33 Cal. 458.   Commented on, rights
of preëmptioner, 19 Mo. 458.

Gale v. Gale, 19 Barb. 249.   Cited, Fraudulent Conveyance,
action to set aside, 27 Cal. 317.

Gale v. Parrott, 1 N. H. 28.   Cited, Parent and Child, emancipation of minor, 25 Cal. 152.

Gallagher v. Delaney, 10 Cal. 410.   Limited and explained,
Amendment after demurrer sustained, 12 Cal. 440; 14
Cal. 202; 30 Cal. 78.

Galland v. Galland, 38 Cal. 265.   Commented on, Husband
and Wife, rights of wife in community property after
separation, 39 Cal. 164.

Galland v. Jackman, 26 Cal. 79.   Cited, Fraudulent Conveyance, validity of, as to subsequent purchasers, 34 Cal.
38.

Galland v. Lewis, 26 Cal. 46.   Approved, Statutory Construction, specific contract act retroactive, 27 Cal. 82.
Denied, 1 Nev. 580; probate act retroactive, 28 Cal.
506.

Gallop v. Newman, 7 Pick. 282.   Cited, Broker, contract
of, construed, 14 Cal. 76.

Galloway v. Hamilton's Heirs, 1 Dana, 576.   Cited, Vendor's Lien, enforcement of, 15 Cal. 193.

Gallup v. Reynolds, 8 Watts, 424. Practice distinguished, Statute of Limitations, when it runs against judgments, 7 Cal. 249.

Galton v. Hancock, 2 Atk. 437. Cited, Will, construction of devise of lands subject to mortgage lien, 31 Cal. 608.

Gamber v. Gamber, 18 Penn. St. 363. Cited, Husband and Wife, separate estate of wife, what constitutes, 12 Cal. 254; presumption that property acquired belongs to community, 30 Cal: 43. Commented on, 29 Penn. St. 47.

Gammon v. Schomoll, 5 Taunt. 344. Denied, Negotiable Instruments, effect of failure to allege demand at place of acceptance designated in bill, 11 Cal. 325.

Gansevoort v. Williams, 14 Wend. 133. Cited, Negotiable Instruments, notice of accommodation indorsement, 37 Cal. 120.

Garber v. Commonwealth, 7 Penn. St. 265. Cited, Judgment, decree in probate against administrator, conclusive on sureties, 25 Cal. 222.

Garcia v. Satrustegui, 4 Cal. 244. Cited, Pleading, omissions in complaint, waived by failure to demur, 22 Cal. 235.

Garcie v. Sheldon, 3 Barb. 232. Commented on, Practice, order of reference, 2 Cal. 248.

Gardenier v. Tubbs, 21 Wend. 169. Cited, Witness, competency of, vendor not competent to impeach sale made by him, 23 Cal. 446; Fraudulent Conveyance, valid as between vendor and vendee, 27 Cal. 307.

Gardner v. Buckbee, 3 Cow. 120. Cited, Judgment, former judgment, when a bar to subsequent action, 14 Cal. 229; 15 Cal. 182; 26 Cal. 494; 36 Cal. 37; Pleading, what may be shown in pleading estoppel by record, 26 Cal. 505; 34 Cal. 327.

Gardner v. Howland, 2 Pick. 599. Approved, Sale and Delivery, effect of delivery by bill of lading, 1 Cal. 83.

Gardner v. Clark, 21 N. Y. 399. Cited, Pleading, several defenses may be set up in answer, 22 Cal. 679, 681.

Gardner v. Gardner, 5 Cush. 483. Cited, Deed, signed by third person, validity of execution, 22 Cal. 565.

Gardner v. Gardner, 22 Wend. 526. Cited, Married Woman, intent necessary in charging separate estate, 23 Cal. 565.

Gardner v. Heartt, 3 Denio, 232. Commented on, Mortgage, lien of, a mere security, 9 Cal. 409; damages may be recovered by mortgagee for injury to estate mortgaged, 24 Cal. 473.

Gardner v. Keteltas, 3 Hill, 330. Cited, Contract to Convey Land, rights of vendee under, 1 Cal. 130.

Gardner v. Newburgh, 2 Johns. Ch. 162. Approved, Eminent Domain, compensation to owner a condition precedent to exercise of power of condemnation, 12 Cal. 529; Forfeiture, how to be asserted, 9 Ind. 442, note.

Gardner v. Perkins, 9 Cal. 553. Cited, Injunction, practice, dissolution of, on denial in answer of entire equities of bill, 13 Cal. 158; 23 Cal. 84; 4 Nev. 415.

Gardner v. Watson, 13 Ill. 347. Cited, Surety on Specialty, when not discharged by delay of creditor, 10 Cal. 426.

Garey v. People, 9 Cow. 640, affirming S. C. 6 Cow. 642. Approved and adopted, Constitutional Construction, term of office, 11 Cal. 88. Construed, 12 Cal. 388.

Garfield v. Williams, 2 Vt. 327. Cited, Assignment, choses in action, not technically assignable, 37 Cal. 189.

Garland v. Rowan, 2 Smedes & M. 617. Commented on, Stare Decisis, rule of, 15 Cal. 602.

Garland v. Wynn, 20 How. 6. Commented on, Jurisdiction, in actions on conflicting claims to property, 20 Cal. 425; 2 Black, 558; 22 How. 339. Cited, Rights under preemption, 29 Cal. 321; on patent fraudulently obtained, 42 Cal. 615; 22 How. 203; 6 Wall. 418; 13 Wall. 85.

Garlick v. James, 12 John. 145. Commented on, Pledge, promissory note as a pledge, 8 Cal. 152.

Garlock v. Geortner, 7 Wend. 199. Commented on, Evidence, secondary evidence of missing instrument, weight of, 9 Cal. 450.

Garner v. Marshall, 9 Cal. 268. Cited, Ejectment, action must be brought against parties in actual possession, 21 Cal. 619; 28 Cal. 98; Id. 536; 37 Cal. 393; judgment conclusive only on such parties, 12 Cal. 409; 14 Cal. 609; Pleading, defects in, cured by verdict or default, 10 Cal. 559; 23 Cal. 130; 3 Or. 43.

Garons v. Knight, 5 Barn. & C. 673. Approved, Deed, delivery of, a question of fact, 5 Cal. 318.

14

Garret v. State, 6 Mo. 1. Cited, Witness, competency of accomplice on separate trial, 5 Cal. 185; 20 Cal. 440.

Garrett v. Logan, 19 Ala. 344. Commented on, Injunction Bond, action on, necessary averments, 25 Cal. 173; 18 Ark. 353.

Garrett v. Noble, 6 Sim. 516. Cited, Trust and Trustees, liability for negligence, 9 Cal. 695.

Garrett v. St. Louis, 25 Mo. 508. Cited, Street Assessments, legislative power to direct, 28 Cal. 352. Commented on, Id. 371.

Garrett v. Stuart, 1 McCord, 514. Approved, Damages, measure of, on breach of contract coupled with fraud, 17 Cal. 496. Cited, Deed, parol evidence of consideration in, how far restricted, 21 Cal. 51; 30 Cal. 57.

Garris v. Portsmouth and Roanoke R. R. Co., 2 Ired. 324. Cited, Railroads, liability for injuries by negligence, 18 Cal. 358.

Garrison v. Sampson, 15 Cal. 93. Cited, Public Lands, possessory action, showing sufficient, 16 Cal. 573; actual possession, what constitutes, 32 Cal. 20, 22; 4 Nev. 69.

Garrison v. Sandford, 7 Halst. 261. Cited, Assignment, choses in action not technically assignable, 37 Cal. 189.

Garrow v. Carpenter, 4 Stewt. & P. 336. Cited, Injunction, effect of appeal from order dissolving, 15 Cal. 111.

Garson v. Green, 1 Johns. Ch. 309. Cited, Equity, relief from fraudulent concealment, 2 Cal. 286.

Garstin v. Asplin, 1 Mad. Ch. 150. Commented on, Injunction, when will issue to restrain a trespass, 7 Cal. 329.

Garvey v. Fowler, 4 Sand. 665. Commented on, Pleading, general averments abolished by the code, 14 Cal. 458.

Garwood v. Eldridge, 1 Green Ch. 145. Commented on, Mortgage, discharge of, 16 Cal. 199.

Garwood v. Garwood, 29 Cal. 514. Cited, Res Adjudicata, former judgment as a bar, 32 Cal. 189; 36 Cal. 38; applied to records in divorce cases, 26 Wis. 162.

Garwood v. Simpson, 8 Cal. 101. Cited, Appeal, findings will not be reviewed except on motion for new trial, 27 Cal. 69; 3 Nev. 303; Written Instrument, when negotiable, McAll. 492.

Gary v. Eastabrook, 6 Cal. 457. Explained, Homestead, appraisement before sale of surplus on execution, 23 Cal. 400.

Gas Company v. San Francisco, 9 Cal. 453. Cited, Pleading, rules of, are general, 11 Cal. 258; Denials, from want of knowledge of facts in verified complaint, insufficient, 13 Cal. 372; 17 Cal. 127; 25 Cal. 196. Approved, Municipal Corporation, liability on implied contracts, 16 Cal. 266; 33 Cal. 696; 3 Nev. 70; Ratification, implied by acceptance of benefits, 33 Cal. 199. Distinguished, mandamus against officers of, 20 Cal. 75; Id. 108. Cited, 28 Cal. 432.

Gashwiler v. Willis, 33 Cal. 11. Approved, Corporation, deed of trustees, when void for want of authority, 37 Cal. 596, 597. Cited, Assignment by officer of, when void, 38 Cal. 594.

Gaskill v. Dudley, 6 Met. 552. Denied, Execution, that property of citizen may be taken in satisfaction of judgment against county, 10 Cal. 408; 15 Cal. 586.

Gaskill v. Trainer, 3 Cal. 334. Cited, Lease, demand for rent necessary to establish forfeiture under, 3 Cal. 283; 25 Cal. 397; 40 Cal. 385; 3 Or. 43.

Gasquet v. Johnson, 1 La. 431. Cited, Intervention, right to intervene, 13 Cal. 70.

Gass v. Stinson, 3 Sum. 114. Cited, Statute of Limitations, mutual accounts, 30 Cal. 130.

Gates v. Buckingham, 4 Cal. 286. Cited, Appeal, papers not embodied in statement or bill of exceptions no part of record, 11 Cal. 214; Id. 361.

Gates v. Kieff, 7 Cal. 124. Cited, Pleading, complaint when demurrable, 10 Cal. 237; objections waived by failure to demur, 10 Cal. 224. Construed, Joinder of legal and equitable causes of action, 32 Cal. 595, 596.

Gates v. McDaniel, 2 Stewt. 211. Commented on, Ferry Franchise, protection of, 6 Cal. 596.

Gates v. Nash, 6 Cal. 192. Cited, Witness, competency of party as, 8 Cal. 579.

Gates v. Salmon, 28 Cal. 320. Cited, Appeal, right of, from interlocutory order in partition, 30 Cal. 21; 31 Cal. 209. Explained, 39 Cal. 314.

Gates v. Salmon, 35 Cal. 576. Cited, Partition, necessary parties to action, 36 Cal. 116; 69 Penn. St. 238; 2 Neb. 310.

Gates v. Teague, Cal. Sup. Ct. Oct. T. 1856 (not reported.) Commented on, Injunction, to restrain trespass on mining claim, 7 Cal. 322; showing required, Id. 330.

Gatewood v. McLaughlin, 23 Cal. 178. Cited, Mining Claim, validity of parol sale of, 23 Cal. 576; 30 Cal. 363; 33 Cal. 381.

Gatliff's Admr. v. Rose, 8 B. Mon. 633. Cited, State Sovereignty, right of transit with slave property, 9 Cal. 166.

Gault v. Saffin, 44 Penn. St. 307. Cited, Husband and Wife, common property, burden of proof, 30 Cal. 43.

Gautier v. English, 29 Cal. 165. Cited, Judgment by default erroneous, but not void, 30 Cal. 535; 34 Cal. 81.

Gautier v. Franklin, 1 Tex. 732. Disapproved, Statute of Limitations, construction of, 7 Cal. 4.

Gaven v. Dopman, 5 Cal. 342. Cited, New Trial, newly discovered evidence must not be merely cumulative, 3 Or. 43.

Gaven v. Hagen, 15 Cal. 208. Doubted, Vendor and Vendee, right of possession in vendee, 615. Distinguished, Id. 618.

Gavin v. Annan, 2 Cal. 494. Commented on and overruled, Pleading, general denial, evidence of accord and satisfaction under, 10 Cal. 30; 21 Cal. 50.

Gaw v. Wolcott, 10 Penn. St. 43. Denied, Pleading, general issue, evidence of unskillful performance admissible under, 1 Cal. 372.

Gay v. Gay, 10 Paige, 376. Approved, Set-off, equity will compel an equitable set-off, 11 Cal. 102. Questioned, rendition of judgment, 28 Cal. 423.

Gay v. Hamilton, 33 Cal. 686. Cited, Mortgage, conveyance absolute on its face when a mortgage, 33 Cal. 43; parol evidence admissible to prove, Id. 49; 37 Cal. 454.

Gay v. Winter, 34 Cal. 153. Cited, Negligence, contributory negligence to defeat action for injuries, 37 Cal. 419; Pleading, sham answers, 35 Cal. 646; Special damages must be particularly stated, 41 Cal. 565.

Gayoso v. Wikoff, 7 Mart. N. S. 486. Cited, Real Actions, under civil law, 1 Cal. 287.

Gayoso de Lemos v. Garcia, 1 Mart. N. S. 324. Commented on, Husband and Wife, common property, 13 Cal. 473; 14 Cal. 601.

Gazley v. Price, 16 John. 267. Cited, Specific Performance, contracts for conveyance of land, covenants dependent, 35 Cal. 663; construction of terms ''good and sufficient deed,'' 6 Cal. 573. Cited as overruled, 62 Barb. 591.

Gebhart v. Shindle, 15 Serg. & R. 235. Cited, Witness, competency of party in interest, 14 Cal. 268.

Gee v. Lane, 15 East, 592. Cited, Confession of Judgment, statute to be strictly pursued, 20 Cal. 687.

Gee v. Moore, 14 Cal. 472. Cited, Homestead, may be established on common property, or on separate property of husband, 22 Cal. 638; as to separate property of wife not determined, 23 Cal. 74; Dedication, a question of fact, case not apposite, 16 Cal. 81. Reviewed and approved, nature of homestead estate, 16 Cal. 216; 25 Cal. 114; 31 Cal. 531. Commented on, Mortgage of, 16 Cal. 218; Alienation of, right of possession in grantee in abeyance, 23 Cal. 121. Cited, 31 Cal. 534; 37 Cal. 374; recovery of, necessary parties, 14 Cal. 508. Cited, Deed, construction of covenants, quit claim deed not an estoppel as to after-acquired title, 25 Cal. 452; 30 Cal. 348; 33 Cal. 289; Herman on Est. 306.

Gee v. Pearse, 2 De G. & S. 325. Commented on, Specific Performance, 10 Cal. 327.

Geiger v. Brown, 4 McCord, 418. Cited, Statute of Limitations, operation, when suspended by death of creditor, 35 Cal. 638.

Geiger v. Clark, 13 Cal. 579. Cited, Guarantor on Note, entitled to notice, 16 Cal. 153; who a guarantor on note, 34 Cal. 675.

Gelpcke v. City of Dubuque, 1 Wall. 175. Cited, Corporations, authority of, presumed from acts, 37 Cal. 588; Legislature, may authorize county aid to railroads, 41 Cal. 183.

Gelston v. Hoyt, 3 Wheat. 246. Reviewed, Jurisdiction, in admiralty cases, 9 Cal. 731; 6 How. 390.

Gelston v. Whitesides, 3 Cal. 309. Overruled, Injunction, dismissal of suit conclusive of liability on the bond, 18 Cal. 627, 629.

Genella v. Relvea, 32 Cal. 159. Cited, Appeal, orders not appealable, 32 Cal. 305; time within which to appeal, 36 Cal. 252. Explained, Rendition of Judgment, entry of, ministerial, 3 Or. 412.

Gennings v. Lake, Cro. Car. 169. Cited, Conveyance, what passes under grant, 13 Cal. 454.

George v. Bank of England, 7 Price, 646. Cited as inapplicable, Husband and Wife, gift to wife, 12 Cal. 255.

George v. Law, 1 Cal. 363. Cited, New Trial, remitting excess of damages found, will defeat motion, 11 Wis. 416.

George v. Ransom, 15 Cal. 322. Cited, Husband and Wife, wife's separate estate, 20 Cal. 674; 24 Cal. 101.

George v. Surrey, 1 Mood. & M. 516. Cited, Negotiable Instruments, evidence of execution of note, 22 Cal. 484.

Georgia v. Towns, 8 Geo. 360. Cited, Government, departments of, presumptions as to acts, 39 Cal. 223.

Gerald v. Bunkley, 17 Ala. 176. Cited, Writs, issuance of, duty and liability of officers, 36 Cal. 214.

Gerard v. People, 4 Ill. 363. Cited, Criminal Procedure, former acquittal, when not available, 28 Cal. 465.

Geraud v. Stagg, 10 How. Pr. 369. Cited, Appeal, restitution on reversal, 26 Cal. 155.

Gerke v. California St. Nav. Co., 9 Cal. 251. Cited, Principal and Agent, when admissions of agent bind principal, 14 Cal. 37. Commented on, Negligence, of steamers, Id. 171.

Germain v. Steam Tug Indiana, 11 Ill. 535. Commented on, Vessels and Boats, lien of attachment on, 8 Cal. 423.

German v. Machin, 6 Paige, 288. Cited, Conveyance of Land, what necessary to validity of parol agreement, 24 Cal. 142.

Germond v. People, 1 Hill, 343. Cited, Jurisdiction, cannot be created by consent, 34 Cal. 333.

Ghirardelli v. McDermott, 22 Cal. 539. Cited, Pleading, denials to verified complaint, when insufficient, 26 Cal. 418.

Gibbons v. Berhard, 3 Bosw. 635. Cited, Undertakings, justification no part of contract, 38 Cal. 603.

Gibbons v. Ogden, 9 Wheat. 1. Commented on, Sovereignty, national and state, relative powers generally, 1 Cal. 236; 2 Cal. 432; 25 Cal. 421; 40 Cal. 218; relative powers in regulation of commerce, 8 Cal. 371, 372, 373, 374; 11 Cal. 86; 20 Cal. 566; Id. 585; 1 Nev. 309; 12 Wheat. 446; 10 Pet. 120; 11 Pet. 134; 3 How. 229; 5 How. 581; 7 How. 394, 405, 540, 558; 12 How. 321; 21 How. 246; 22 How. 239. Cited, 10 Cal. 507; 33 Cal. 340; 34 Cal. 498; 5 How. 625; 7 How. 549, 553, 555, 556; 13 How. 584; 14 How. 575; 19 How. 594, 622.

Gibbons v. Scott, 15 Cal. 284. Cited, Judgment by default, remedy, setting aside, 16 Cal. 202; 23 Cal. 129.

Gibbes v. Mitchell, 2 Bay, 128. Commented on, Execution, by whom to be completed, 8 Cal. 408.

Gibbs v. Bartlett, 2 Watts & S. 29. Cited, Replevin Bond, insufficient defense in action, 4 Cal. 114.

Gibbs v. Champion, 3 Ohio, 336. Cited, Contract, of sale, time not the essence of, 30 Cal. 407. Construed, 8 Ohio, 202.

Gibbs v. Chisolm, 2 Nott & McC. 38. Cited, Interest on Interest, when not allowed, 29 Cal. 392.

Gibbs v. Dewey, 5 Cow. 503. Cited, Judgment, or verdict, must be sustained by the complaint, 30 Cal. 488.

Gibbs v. Nash, 4 Barb. 449. Cited, Pleading, under statute of frauds, 29 Cal. 599.

Gibbs v. Southam, 5 Barn. & A. 911. Cited, Demand, action on agreement to pay on demand, no demand necessary, 22 Cal. 278.

Gibbs v. Swift, 12 Cush. 393. Cited, Title, by quit-claim deed sufficient to maintain ejectment, 37 Cal. 520.

Gibbs v. Thayer, 6 Cush. 30. Cited, Deed, covenant of non-claim in deed construed, 14 Cal. 473.

Giblin v. Jordan, 6 Cal. 416. Commented on, Jurisdiction of Person, statutes providing for substituted service of process to be strictly pursued, 12 Cal. 102. Cited, Homestead, cannot be established on property held in tenancy in common, 23 Cal. 517; 27 Cal. 425; 32 Cal. 483; 26 Wis. 581; 37 Ark. 660.

Gibson v. Armstrong, 7 B. Mon. 481. Cited, Pleading, want of capacity to be specially pleaded, 8 Cal. 590.

Gibson v. Brockway, 8 N. H. 465. Commented on, Conveyance, what passes by, 15 Cal. 196.

Gibson v. Colt, 7 John. 390. Cited, Principal and Agent, principal when bound by act of agent, 8 Cal. 249. Doubted as to fraudulent representations of agent, 6 Hill, 338.

Gibson, Ex parte, 31 Cal. 619. Cited, Habeas Corpus, as a remedy, 35 Cal. 101; judgment in criminal proceedings, 35 Cal. 118.

Gibson v. Jenney, 15 Mass. 205. Cited, Vessels and Boats, proceedings by attachment, 1 Cal. 163.

Gibson v. Jeyes, 6 Ves. Jr. 277. Cited, Attorney and Client, transactions between, 33 Cal. 440. Commented on, Id. 441.

Gibson v. Puchta, 33 Cal. 310. Cited, Water Rights, ditch property how regarded, 35 Cal. 549.

Gibson v. Williams, 4 Wend. 320. Cited, Libel and Slander, evidence of facts not averred inadmissible, 34 Cal. 60; 52 Ill. 240.

Giddings v. Smith, 15 Vt. 344. Cited, Judgments of court of general jurisdiction not subject to collateral attack, 18 Cal. 505.

Giesy v. Cincinnati, W. & Z. R. R., 4 Ohio St. 308. Cited, Railroad, an easement, 19 Cal. 596; Eminent Domain, compensation for condemnation, 31 Cal. 373.

Gifford v. Livingston, 2 Den. 389. Cited, Statute, verity of enrolled statute cannot be impeached, 30 Cal. 259.

Gifford v. New Jersey R. R. Co., 2 Stoct. Ch. 171. Cited, Corporations, additional powers may be conferred by legislature, 22 Cal. 428.

Gifford v. Thorn, 1 Stoct. Ch. 722. Cited, Attorney and Counsel, appearance in, and conduct of action, 13 Cal. 200.

Gilbeaux's Heirs v. Cormier, 8 Mart. N. S. 228. Cited, Husband and Wife, rights of wife to control her separate estate, 30 Cal. 31.

Gilbert v. Columbia Turnpike Co., 3 Johns. Cas. 107. Cited, Eminent Domain, compensation on condemnation, 19 Cal. 59; averments essential in proceedings to condemn, 23 Cal. 329; Notice, must be in writing, 24 Cal. 365.

Gilbert v. Cram, 12 How. Pr. 455. Cited, Ejectment, defenses, new matter must be specially pleaded, 10 Cal. 27; 21 Cal. 436.

Gilbert v. Havemeyer, 2 Sand. 506. Commented on, Street Assessment, liability for, 31 Cal. 673.

Gilbert v. Manchester Iron Manf. Co., 11 Wend. 628. Cited, Assignment, title which passes by, 33 Cal. 323.

Gilbert v. Thompson, 9 Cush. 348. Commented on and approved, Res Adjudicata, judgment, when conclusive in subsequent action, 15 Cal. 148; 20 Cal. 486; 7 Wall. 103.

Gilbert v. Wiman, 1 N. Y. 550. Commented on, Injunction Bond, liability on, when it attaches, 25 Cal. 174.

Gilchrist v. Cunningham, 8 Wend. 641. Cited, Deed as Mortgage, parol evidence admissible to prove, 36 Cal. 44.

Giles v. Brig Cynthia, 1 Pet. Ad. 203. Approved, Freight, may be recovered back on failure to transport, 6 Cal. 32.

Giles v. Hartis, 1 Ld. Ray. 254. Commented on, Tender, what it bars, 11 Cal. 319.

Gillam v. Sigman, 29 Cal. 637. Cited, Pleading, misjoinder of parties waived by failure to demur or answer, 36 Cal. 126.

Gillan v. Hutchinson, 16 Cal. 153. Cited, Mines and Mining, rights of miners, how restricted, 22 Cal. 453, 454; Constitutionality of Statute, statutes taking property without providing compensation invalid, 67 Penn. St. 487.

Gillan v. Simpkin, 4 Camp. 241. Cited, Freight, may be recovered back for failure of transportation, 6 Cal. 32.

Gillespie v. Benson, 18 Cal. 409. Cited, Appeal, jurisdiction, what constitutes amount in dispute, 20 Cal. 91; 23 Cal. 202.

Gillespie v. Broas, 23 Barb. 370. Commented on, Supervisors, powers of, when reviewable on certiorari, 16 Cal. 209, 210.

Gillespie v. Moon, 2 Johns. Ch. 585. Cited, Equity, will relieve from fraud or mistake in written instrument, 12 Cal. 212; 19 Cal. 673; mistake in description of deed, Id. 674.

Gillet v. Maynard, 5 John. 87. Cited, Contract, of sale of land, time not the essence of, 30 Cal. 407.

Gilliam v. Reddick, 4 Ired. 368. Cited, Municipal Corporations, validity of acts of *de facto* officers, 3 Cal. 453.

Gilliam's Adm. v. Perkinson's Adm. 4 Rand. 325. Cited, Evidence, written instruments, proof of handwriting, when required, 26 Cal. 411.

Gilliard v. Chesney, 13 Tex. 337. Cited, Husband and Wife, common property, 12 Cal. 224.

Gillmore v. Lewis, 12 Ohio, 281. Cited, Rewards, liability on offer of reward, 14 Cal. 137.

Gilman v. Brown, 1 Mason, 191. Cited, Vendor's Lien, lost by taking other security, 12 Cal. 305; not assignable, 21 Cal. 177; not such a lien as to bar an attachment, 35 Cal. 206.

Gilman v. Cosgrove, 22 Cal. 357. Approved, Pleading, amended complaint supersedes the original, 28 Cal. 246; 8 Nev. 60.

Gilman v. Contra Costa Co., 5 Cal. 426; S. C. 6 Cal. 676; 8 Cal. 52. Cited, Counties, liability of, 21 Iowa, 418; counties may maintain actions, 8 Cal. 305. Followed, 10 Cal. 508; or may be sued, 1 Nev. 376; satisfaction of judgment against, how made, 10 Cal. 410.

Gilman v. Cutts, 3 Fost. N. H. 376. Cited, Statute of Limitations, not retrospective, 7 Cal. 5.

Gilman v. Lowell, 1 Am. Lead. Cas. 200. Approved, Libel and Slander, what proofs in mitigation not admissible, 41 Cal. 384.

Gilman v. Moore, 14 Vt. 457. Cited, Mortgage, change of note secured by mortgage, 31 Cal. 80.

Gilman v. Philadelphia, 3 Wall. 713. Approved, Sovereignty, Federal and State, relative powers to regulate commerce, 42 Cal. 589.

Gilman v. Stetson, 18 Me. 428. Cited, Amendment, to officers' returns, 23 Cal. 81.

Gilman v. Van Slyck, 7 Cow. 469. Cited, Assignment, of judgment, validity of consideration, 23 Cal. 625.

Gilmer v. Lime Point, 18 Cal. 229; S. C. 19 Cal. 47. Cited, Eminent Domain, condemnation, "public use" a question for the legislature, 23 Cal. 327; proceedings preliminary under general railroad law, 23 Cal. 325, 329;

conditions precedent to exercise of right, 28 Cal. 667; 31 Cal. 548. Commented on, 106 Mass. 363. Cited, Appeal, lies in special cases, 42 Cal. 68.

Gilmore v. Holt, 4 Pick. 257. Cited, Election, notice of special election, 11 Cal. 66.

Gilpin v. Howell, 5 Penn. St. 42. Cited, Bailment, sale of stock by bailee, 42 Cal. 105.

Gimmy v. Culverson, U. S. C. C. Cal. Cited, Preemption, right of, how proved, 33 Cal. 90.

Gimmy v. Doane, 22 Cal. 635. Cited, Divorce, disposition of common property in, 4 Nev. 472.

Gimmy v. Donnelly, Cal. Sup. Ct. (not reported.) Cited, Negotiable Instruments, liability of surety and indorser, 6 Cal. 396.

Gimmy v. Gimmy, 22 Cal. 633. Referred to, 22 Cal. 639. Cited, Divorce, disposition of common property in, 4 Nev. 472.

Ginaca v. Atwood, 8 Cal. 446. Commented on, Replevin Bond, liability of sureties on, 21 Cal. 280; 24 Cal. 150.

Gingell v. Horne, 9 Sim. 539. Cited, Wills, jurisdiction on probate of, 20 Cal. 266. Approved, Conclusiveness of probate, Id. 267; 2 How. 645.

Girard v. Taggart, 5 Serg. & R. 19, 543. Commented on, Contract, measure of damages on breach of, 35 Cal. 246, 247.

Gird v. Ray, 17 Cal. 352. Cited, Possessory Action, actual residence alone gives right of action, 39 Cal. 279.

Gittings' Lessee v. Hall, 1 Harr. & J. 14. Cited, Deed, parol evidence admissible to explain, 24 Cal. 417.

Gladwin v. Stebbins, 2 Cal. 103, erroneously reported as Godwin v. Stebbins. Overruled, Ejectment, materiality of allegation in complaint, 5 Cal. 312; 16 Cal. 245.

Glaister v. Hewer, 8 Ves. Jr. 195. Cited, Husband and Wife, common property, presumptions; 12 Cal. 255; 8 Wheat. 248.

Glazer v. Clift, 10 Cal. 303. Cited, Pleading, new matter must be specially pleaded in the answer, 21 Cal. 50; 30 Cal. 472.

Gleason v. Clark, 9 Cow. 57. Cited, Evidence, admissions of partner, when incompetent, 23 Cal. 102.

Gleason v. Moen, 2 Duer, 639.   Cited, Judgment, relief granted on counter-claim, 26 Cal. 309.

Gleason v. Tuttle, 46 Me. 289.   Cited, Nuisance, prescriptive right to overflow lands, 40 Cal. 406.

Gleim v. Rise, 6 Watts, 44.   Cited, Estoppel, when lessee not estopped, 33 Cal. 245.   Commented on, Id. 251.

Glen v. Gibson, 9 Barb. 634.   Cited, Estoppel, of tenant, 33 Cal. 245; released on restoring possession, 30 Cal. 201.

Glenn v. Grover, 3 Md. 212.   Cited, Insolvency, assignment by insolvent valid, 10 Cal. 277.

Glenn v. United States, 13 How. 250.   Cited, Conditional Grant, when invalid, 6 Cal. 270; Evidence, private survey incompetent to prove title, 13 Cal. 416; 14 Cal. 359.

Glentworth v. Luther, 21 Barb. 145.   Cited, Broker, entitled to commissions for services, 25 Cal. 82.

Glidden v. Lucas, 7 Cal. 26.   Overruled, Factor, cannot pledge, limitation as to technical factor, 19 Cal. 73.

Glidden v. Packard, 28 Cal. 649.   Cited, Default, entry of, ministerial, 30 Cal. 198; 32 Cal. 636; 3 Or. 252; Judgment by default, when void, 30 Cal. 534.

Glover v. Glover, 16 Ala. 446.   Cited, Alimony, without divorce, 38 Cal. 270.

Glover v. Payn, 19 Wend. 518.   Cited, Title, conditional sale of land, legal effect, 9 Cal. 551.

Gluckauf v. Reed, 22 Cal. 468.   Cited, Public Lands, rights lost by abandonment, 23 Cal. 536.

Godchaux v. Mulford, 26 Cal. 316.   Approved, Statute of Frauds, what constitutes sufficient change of possession on sale of goods, 29 Cal. 472.   Commented on, Chattel Mortgage, 1 Saw. 12.

Goddard v. Bulow, 1 Nott & McC., 45.   Cited, Written Instrument, parol evidence to explain, 11 Cal. 198.

Goddard v. Chase, 7 Mass. 432.   Cited, Fixtures, what constitute, 10 Cal. 264; 14 Cal. 68.

Goddard v. Coffin, Davies, 381.   Cited, Appeal, rehearing, equal division of court operates as a denial, 32 Cal. 633.

Goddard's Heirs v. Urquhart, 6 La. 659.   Commented on, Statute of Limitations, computation of time on repeal or change in statute, 7 Cal. 4.

Goddin v. Crump, 8 Leigh, 120. Cited, Constitutionality of Statute, authorizing county aid to railroads, 13 Cal. 188.

Godeffroy v. Caldwell, 2 Cal. 489. Cited, Mortgage, a mere security, 8 Cal. 267; 9 Cal. 409. Cited, Statute of Frauds, parol contract to pay for improvements on land not within statute, 26 Tex. 615; Money advanced to pay for materials, not within mechanic's lien law, 39 Ala. 183; Estoppel, silently permitting sale of land operates as an estoppel, Herman on Est. 417.

Godey v. Godey, 39 Cal. 157. Cited, Injunction, when not dissolved on denial in answer, 42 Cal. 462.

Godfrey v. Chadwell, 2 Vern. 601. Cited, Foreclosure, subsequent incumbrancers, necessary parties, 10 Cal. 552.

Godwin v. Stebbins. See Gladwin *v.* Stebbins.

Gold v. Phillips, 10 John. 412. Cited, Statute of Frauds, agreement to pay debt of third person, when not within, 22 Cal. 190.

Gold v. Strode, Carth. 148. Cited, Judgments, as property, *situs* of, 12 Cal. 190.

Goldschmidt v. Hamlet, 6 Man. & G. 187. Commented on, Execution, levy under separate writs, 8 Cal. 252.

Goldsmith v. Osborne, 1 Edw. Ch. 560. Cited, Redemption, pleading, demand of relief, 22 Cal. 335.

Goller v. Fett, 30 Cal. 481. Cited, Mining Claims, verbal sale no evidence of title, 33 Cal. 321; 35 Cal. 652.

Gonor v. Gonor, 11 Rob. 526. Commented on, Husband and Wife, presumption that property acquired by purchase belongs to the community, 30 Cal. 35, 47, 50.

Gonzales v. Huntley, 1 Cal. 32. Affirmed, Appeal, presumptions in favor of regularity of proceedings and of sufficiency of evidence to sustain judgment, 1 Cal. 42; Id. 116. Commented on and qualified, Id. 140.

Good v. Zercher, 12 Ohio, 364. Cited as overruled in 16 Ohio, 599; Constitutionality of Statute, curative acts, 30 Cal. 144.

Goodale v. West, 5 Cal. 339. Cited, Demand necessary in action on bond for deed, 17 Cal. 276; 25 Cal. 279.

Goodall v. Wentworth, 20 Me. 322. Cited, Surety, right of contribution between sureties, 20 Cal. 136.

Goode v. Smith, 13 Cal. 81. Cited, Acknowledgment, sufficiency of, 7 Cal. 318.

Goodell v. Field, 15 Vt. 448. Cited, Equity, relief from mistake, 19 Cal. 673.

Goodenow v. Ewer, 16 Cal. 461. Cited, Mortgage a mere security, operating solely as a lien or incumbrance, 18 Cal. 488; 21 Cal. 621; 33 Cal. 96; 36 Cal. 39. Commented on and approved, Foreclosure, grantee of mortgagor a necessary party, 16 Cal. 563. Cited, 18 Cal. 475; 21 Cal. 91; 24 Cal. 512; Id. 562; 25 Cal. 161. Approved, Equity will not relieve from mistake of law where no special circumstances are shown, 16 Cal. 565; 20 Cal. 641. Commented on, Relief of purchaser from sale made under decree, 23 Cal. 108; construed, "reasonable time," Id. Approved, Tenants in Common, may recover rents and profits from co-tenants, as incident to partition, 17 Cal. 237.

Goodlet v. Smithson, 5 Port. 246. Cited, Preëmption, right cannot be questioned by party not in privity with source of paramount title, 33 Cal. 458; title and rights of preëmptioner after payment, 37 Cal. 495; 38 Cal. 44.

Goodloe v. Cincinnati, 4 Ohio, 500. Cited, Municipal Corporation, liability on its contracts, 16 Cal. 270.

Goodman v. Grierson, 2 Ball. & B. 279. Commented on, Deed as a mortgage, 9 Cal. 550.

Goodman v. Harvey, 4 Adol. & E. 870. Cited, Negotiable Instruments, presumptive dishonor reasonable time, 40 Cal. 116.

Goodman v. Simonds, 20 How. 343. Cited, Negotiable Instruments, *bona fide* holder by transfer before dishonor, 40 Cal. 114; 20 How. 108.

Goodnow v. Smith, 18 Pick. 414. Cited, Sureties, rights of, contribution between, 10 Cal. 220; release of one is a release of all, 38 Cal. 532, 537.

Goodrich v. James, 1 Wend. 289. Commented on, Bill of Particulars, practice, 32 Cal. 638.

Goodrich v. Woolcott, 3 Cow. 239. Cited, Libel and Slander, pleading meaning of libelous words, 34 Cal. 60.

Goodright v. Wright, 1 P. Wms. 399. Cited, Stare Decisis adherence to rules of property, 15 Cal. 621.

Goodsell v. Myers, 3 Wend. 479. Cited, Infancy, contract made by infant, 24 Cal. 208; ratification of, Id. 213.

Goodspeed v. East Haddam Bank, 22 Conn. 542. Commented on, Corporations, liability for torts, 34 Cal. 53, 55.

Goodtitle v. Baldwin, 11 East, 488. Cited, Presumptions, from lapse of time, 6 Cal. 556.

Goodtitle v. Kibbe, 9 How. 471. Commented on, Sovereignty, validity of congressional grants of land made after treaty and cession of territory, 18 Cal. 28. Affirmed, 13 How. 26; effect of admission of State on power of eminent domain, 18 Cal. 252; State Lands, swamp and overflowed lands, 26 Cal. 353; defense in action of ejectment brought under State patent, 25 Cal. 250.

Goodtitle v. Saville, 16 East, 87. Cited, Lease, construction of covenant, of purchase by lessee, 9 Cal. 676.

Goodtitle v. Tombs, 3 Wils. 118. Cited, Tenant in Common, may recover rents and profits in ejectment against co-tenant, 29 Cal. 333.

Goodtitle v. Welford, 1 Doug. 139. Commented on, Will, competency of witness to establish validity of, 1 Cal. 506.

Goodwin v. Appleton, 22 Me. 453. Cited, Judicial Notice, of political subdivisions, 16 Cal. 231.

Goodwin v. Bowden, 54 Me. 425. Cited, Trust, created by assignment of insolvent, 39 Cal. 287.

Goodwin v. Glazer, 10 Cal. 333. Referred to, Mandamus, will not lie to compel payment of money in custody of the law, 11 Cal. 261; or for refusal to issue execution, 40 Cal. 281; 30 Tex. 726.

Goodwin v. Hammond, 13 Cal. 168. Cited, Fraudulent Conveyance, affords no protection, 23 Cal. 236.

Goodwin v. Holbrook, 4 Wend. 377. Cited, Demand, when not requisite on special contract, 23 Cal. 69.

Goodyear v. Rumbaugh, 13 Penn. St. 480. Commented on, Parties, joinder of husband and wife, 26 Cal. 446.

Gookin v. Whittier, 4 Greenl. 16. Cited, Lands, constructive possession under deed, 25 Cal. 135.

Gordon v. Bulkeley, 14 Serg. & R. 331. Cited, Principal and Agent, ratification by principal, 14 Cal. 400.

Gordon v. Johnson, 4 Cal. 368.   Commented on, Judicial Powers, relatively, Federal and State, 5 Cal. 273.

Gordon v. Ogden, 3 Pet. 33.   Commented on, Jurisdiction, amount in controversy, 2 Cal. 157; 15 How. 208; 4 Wall. 164.

Gordon v. Ross, 2 Cal. 156.   Overruled, Jurisdiction, costs form no part of matter in dispute, 13 Cal. 30.

Gordon v. Searing, 8 Cal. 49.   Cited, Evidence, secondary evidence of destroyed instrument, practice on admission, 10 Cal. 148.

Gore v. Harris, 8 Eng. L. & E. 149.   Cited, Witness, privileged communications, practice, 29 Cal. 72.

Gorham v. Campbell, 2 Cal. 135.   Cited, Powers, time of exercise not of essence of authority, 15 Cal. 223.

Gorham v. Gilson, 28 Cal. 479.   Cited, Corporations, relief to stockholders from act of corporation procured by fraud, 33 Cal. 19.

Gorham v. Springfield, 21 Me. 58.   Cited, Statutory Construction, statute incorporating city, a public act, 35 Cal. 112.

Gorham v. Toomey, 9 Cal. 77.   Explained, Injunction, will not issue to restrain judgment on proceedings of coordinate tribunal, 9 Cal. 615.   Cited as not applicable, 15 Cal. 134.   Approved, 37 Cal. 269.   Cited, 39 Cal. 162; 22 Wis. 486.

Gorman v. Russell, 14 Cal. 531.   Referred to on second appeal, Voluntary Association, 18 Cal. 688.

Gorton v. De Angelis, 6 Wend. 420.   Cited, Malicious Prosecution, what must be shown in action, 29 Cal. 657.

Gossett v. Kent, 19 Ark. 607.   Cited, Deed, designation of grantee in, 29 Cal. 412.

Gostorfs v. Taaffe, 18 Cal. 385.   Cited, Pleading, sham answer, practice on striking out, 32 Cal. 574.

Goszler v. Georgetown, 6 Wheat. 593.   Cited, Street Improvements, authority of city to grade streets, 42 Cal. 438.   Commented on, 10 How. 535.

Goubeau v. N. O. and N. R. R. Co., 6 Rob. 345.   Cited and distinguished, Execution, seizure and sale of promissory note, 34 Cal. 88.

Gough v. Davies, 4 Price, 200.   Cited, Account Stated, equivalent to new promise, 33 Cal. 697.

Gough v. Staats, 13 Wend. 549.   Cited, Negotiable Instrument, presumptive dishonor, reasonable time, 40 Cal. 115.

Gould v. Glass, 19 Barb. 179.   Commented on, Pleading, waiver of defects by failure to demur, 10 Cal. 560.

Gould v. Hudson Riv. R. R. Co., 6 N. Y. 522.   Cited, Eminent Domain, proceedings on assessment of damages, 35 Cal. 263.

Gouldin v. Buckelew, 4 Cal. 107.   Commented on, Vendor's Lien, on executory sale, 7 Cal. 415.

Gouldin v. Buckelew, 4 Cal. 111.   Cited, Vendor's Lien, as a bar to right of attachment, 32 Cal. 59.

Goulet v. Asseler, 22 N. Y. 225.   Cited, Conversion, measure of damages for property of a fixed value, 33 Cal. 120.

Gouverneur v. Lynch, 2 Paige, 300.   Cited, Lands, possession as notice of title, 36 Cal. 272; 10 How. 375.

Gouverneur v. Mayor, etc., of New York, 2 Paige, 434. Cited, Taxation, personal liability for assessment, 31 Cal. 676.

Governor v. Gibson, 14 Ala. 326.   Cited, Attachment, validity of sale under, 7 Cal. 566.

Governor, etc., v. Meredith, 4 Term Rep. 794.   Cited, Street Improvements, authority of city to grade streets, 42 Cal. 438; 6 How. 534.

Governor, etc., v. Ridgway, 12 Ill. 14.   Cited, Officers, duty of, in issuance of writs, 36 Cal. 214.

Governor, etc., v. Wiley, 14 Ala. 172.   Cited, Officers, duty of, in issuance of writs, 36 Cal. 214.

Gower v. Emery, 18 Me. 82.   Commented on, Witness, privileged communications, 29 Cal. 64.   Cited, 36 Cal. 507, 508.

Grace v. Smith, 2 W. Black, 998.   Cited, Partnership, what necessary to constitute, 28 Cal. 577.

Grady v. Early, 18 Cal. 108.   Cited, Witness, competency of, interest, 18 Cal. 618, note; Ejectment, prior possession sufficient to maintain, 38 Cal. 43.

Grady v. State, 11 Geo. 253.   Cited, Criminal Procedure, practice, 31 Cal. 627.

15

Graff v. Kipp, 1 Edw. Ch. 619.   Cited, Judgment Lien, not affected by issuance of execution, 37 Cal. 133, 134.

Graham v. Cammann, 2 Caines, 168.   Cited, Exceptions, practice, 34 Cal. 686.

Graham v. McCampbell, 1 Meigs' Tenn. Rep. 56.   Cited, Vendor's Lien, enforcement of, 15 Cal. 195.

Graham v. Pierson, 6 Hill, 247.   Commented on and approved, Insolvency, effect of discharge on judgment debt, 14 Cal. 177.

Graham v. Strader.   See Strader v. Graham.

Grand Gulf Bank v. Archer, 8 Smedes & M. 151.   Cited, Corporations, contracts *ultra vires* not subject to be collaterally questioned, 22 Cal. 630.

Grand Gulf R. & B. Co. v. Bryan, 8 Smedes & M. 234. Commented on, Executors and Administrators, as legal representatives, 26 Cal. 37.   Cited, Preëmption, rights defined, 30 Cal. 650.

Granger v. Clark, 22 Me. 128.   Cited, Judgment, validity of, how impeached, 30 Cal. 446.

Grant v. Button, 14 John. 377.   Cited, Pleading, former judgment when a bar, 38 Cal. 647.

Grant v. Courter, 24 Barb. 233.   Commented on, Constitutionality of Statute, imposing local taxation for internal improvement, 13 Cal. 187; Id. 355, 356, 359; statutes granting powers dependent on vote of electors, 17 Cal. 32; 25 Cal. 646.

Grant v. Moore, 29 Cal. 644.   Approved, Appeal, order granting or refusing new trial, reasons of order not reviewable, 38 Cal. 506; 5 Kan. 238.

Grant v. Quick, 5 Sand. 612.   Commented on, Injunction, courts cannot restrain proceedings or judgment of co-ordinate tribunals, 8 Cal. 35; 9 Cal. 614.   Cited, 37 Cal. 269; 4 Abb. Pr. 442.

Grant v. White, 6 Cal. 55.   Cited, Appeal, notice to be served on attorney of party, 39 Cal. 151.

Grass Valley Q. M. Co. v. Stackhouse, 6 Cal. 413.   Cited, Evidence, testimony, how given, practice, 10 Cal. 148.

Gratitudine, The, 3 Rob. Adm. 240.   Cited, Vessel, pledge by master, 8 Cal. 534.

Grattan v. Wiggins, 23 Cal. 16.   Cited, Title, by adverse possession, 22 Cal. 595; Mortgage, when debt is barred, mortgage is barred, 23 Cal. 143; 34 Cal. 370. Commented on, rights of foreclosure and redemption reciprocal, 34 Cal. 369, 372, 381; right of entry of mortgagor, 29 Cal. 255.

Gravenor v. Woodhouse, 1 Bing. 38. Cited, Estoppel, tenant when not estopped, 8 Cal. 596. Commented on, 33 Cal. 253, 254; 35 Cal. 573, 574.

Graves v. Woodbury, 4 Hill, 559. Cited, Assignment, assignee of judgment, 22 Cal. 433.

Gray v. Dougherty, 25 Cal. 266. Cited, Negotiable Instruments, action on lost note, indemnity, 28 Cal. 566; Probate Procedure, evidence in contesting administrator's account, 29 Cal. 521; Ejectment, judgment, how far conclusive, 30 Cal. 311; 32 Cal. 189; Id. 296; 36 Cal. 38; 38 Cal. 647; immaterial averments, 36 Cal. 233; Actions, joinder of legal and equitable causes, 32 Cal. 596; Costs, in equity, 28 Cal. 566; 39 Cal. 85; Specific Performance, demand for deed, 4 Nev. 460; Estoppel, judgment in ejectment how far an estoppel, 33 Cal. 459.

Gray v. Eaton, 5 Cal. 448. Commented on, New Trial, in equity, granting or refusing, in discretion, 8 Cal. 286. Overruled, 15 Cal. 380.

Gray v. Gardner, 3 Mass. 399. Commented on, Presumptions, acquiescence from lapse of time, 22 Cal. 591.

Gray v. Gray and Eaton v. Palmer, 11 Cal. 341. Cited, Costs, on appeal, 24 Cal. 352; 29 Cal. 282.

Gray v. Jenks, 3 Mason, 521. Cited, Mortgage, effect and operation of, 9 Cal. 408.

Gray v. Kettell, 12 Mass. 161. Statute distinguished, Taxation, *situs* of intangible property, 23 Cal. 140.

Gray v. Nellis, 6 How. Pr. 290. Cited, Libel and Slander, proof of malice, 39 Cal. 74.

Gray v. Palmer and Eaton v. Palmer, 9 Cal. 616. Approved, Partnership, 9 Cal. 678. Cited, Appeal, interlocutory order, not appealable, 22 Cal. 637. Commented on, Jurisdiction of person, substituted service upon minor, insufficiency of, 1 Saw. 320; 1 Wall. 631.

Gray v. Palmer, 28 Cal. 416. Approved, Appeal, when judgment becomes final, computation of time, 31 Cal. 209; 32 Cal. 159; 36 Cal. 252; 41 Cal. 407; 3 Or. 412. Cited, 1 Saw. 336.

Gray v. Schupp, 4 Cal. 185.   Cited, Appeal, lies from void judgment, 2 Nev. 97.

Gray v. Thompson, 1 Johns. Ch. 82.   Cited, Debtor and Creditor, several action on agreement to pay debts, 37 Cal. 537.

Gray's Exrs. v. Brown, 22 Ala. 263.   Cited, Surety, when discharged by agreement for delay, 10 Cal. 426.

Grayson v. Atkinson, 2 Ves. Sr. 454.   Cited, Will, attestation to, 10 Cal. 479.   Explained, 1 Rand. 472.

Great Falls Co. v. Worster, 15 N. H. 412.   Approved, Evidence, declarations of deceased as to boundaries, admissible, 15 Cal. 280.

Greele v. Parker, 5 Wend. 414; S. C. 2 Wend. 545.   Cited, Negotiable Instruments, liability on promise to accept, 29 Cal. 601.

Greely v. Dow, 2 Met. 176.   Cited, Surety, release of, on agreement to extend time, 10 Cal. 425.

Greely v. Townsend, 25 Cal. 604.   Cited, Instructions, 28 Cal. 224; San Francisco, tenure to pueblo lands, 42 Cal. 556; jurisdiction of U. S. supreme court, transfer of cause to federal court, 25 Wis. 151.

Green v. Armstrong, 1 Den. 550.   Cited, Statute of Frauds, sales of growing crops not within, 23 Cal. 69.

Green v. Biddle, 8 Wheat. 1.   Cited, Constitutionality of Statute, statutes impairing remedies, invalid, 4 Cal. 142; 40 Miss. 33.   Commented on, 7 Cal. 7, 8, 10; 16 Cal. 30; 1 How. 316, note; 6 How. 327, 332; 13 How. 566; 15 How. 319; 14 Tex. 237.

Green v. Borough of Reading, 9 Watts, 382.   Cited, Street Improvement, right of city to grade streets, 42 Cal. 438.

Green v. Butler, 26 Cal. 595.   Cited, Appeal, rule of determination, where evidence is conflicting, 29 Cal. 391.

Green v. Covillaud, 10 Cal. 317.   Approved, Specific Performance, rule of determination in enforcement of executory contracts, 19 Cal. 458, 459, 460.   Cited, Time not of essence of contract, 40 Cal. 11.   Commented on, When lapse of time will defeat rights, 13 Cal. 316. Cited, 23 Cal. 34.   Distinguished, 11 Cal. 237; 19 Cal. 237.   Cited, Equity must be shown by bill, 14 Cal. 143; *allegata* and *probata* must agree, 36 Cal. 179;

pleadings strictly construed against pleader, 29 Cal. 16. Referred to, Former adjudication, 22 Cal. 204.

Green v. Craft, 28 Miss. 70. Commented on, Taxation, validity of assessment, 13 Cal. 617; 16 Cal. 344.

Green v. Demoss, 10 Humph. 374. Cited, Vendor's Lien, not assignable, 21 Cal. 177.

Green v. Doane. See Frank *v.* Doane.

Green v. Fowler, 11 Gill. & J. 104. Cited, Vendor's Lien, enforcement of, 15 Cal. 195.

Green v. Goings, 7 Barb. 653. Commented on, Negotiable Instruments, liability of acceptor, 11 Cal. 320.

Green v. Graves, 1 Doug. Mich. 351. Commented on, Statute, testing validity of, 30 Cal. 275.

Green v. Hudson Riv. R. R. Co., 28 Barb. 9. Cited, Action, who may maintain, for death of person, 25 Cal. 435.

Green v. Jackson Wat. Co., 10 Cal. 374. Cited, Mechanic's Lien, within what time action must be commenced, 23 Cal. 458.

Green v. Kemp, 13 Mass. 515. Commented on, Mortgage, when void, 14 Cal. 475; 29 Cal. 36.

Green v. Liter, 8 Cranch, 229. Cited, Lands, constructive entry under deed, 25 Cal. 135. Explained, 7 Wheat. 29. Cited, 2 Pet. 212; 3 How. 690.

Green v. Palmer, 15 Cal. 411. Approved, Pleading, facts and not the evidence of such facts to be set forth in, 18 Cal. 88; 19 Cal. 483; 22 Cal. 569; 23 Cal. 169; 26 Cal. 21; 28 Cal. 547; 30 Cal. 200; Id. 364; Id. 565; 32 Cal. 456; 36 Cal. 233; 37 Cal. 255; 42 Cal. 351; 3 Or. 359; 3 Nev. 565; 7 Nev. 172.

Green v. Patchen, 13 Wend. 293. Cited, Arbitration, effect of submission to, 1 Cal. 47.

Green v. Price, 13 Mees. & W. 695. Cited, Contract, penalty and liquidated damages, 9 Cal. 587.

Green v. Putnam, 1 Barb. 500. Cited, Deed, as an escrow, 30 Cal. 212.

Green v. Slayter, 4 Johns. Ch. 38. Cited, Equity, what constitutes sufficient notice in, 36 Cal. 437.

Green v. Winter, 1 Johns. Ch. 36. Cited, Trustee, can gain no advantage to detriment of *cestui que trust*, 36 Cal. 432.

Green v. Wells, 2 Cal. 584. Cited, Estoppel, advantage cannot be taken of non-performance occasioned by party's own act, 4 Cal. 317.

Greene v. Jones, 1 Saund. 298. Cited, Trespass, by officer, justification must be specially pleaded, 10 Cal. 304.

Greenfield, Estate of, 14 Penn. St. 490. Cited, Attorney and Client, rule as to proceedings between, 33 Cal. 440.

Greenfield v. Steamer Gunnell, 6 Cal. 67. Cited, Pleading, objection to want of verification cured by failure to demur or answer, 6 Cal. 231.

Greenleaf v. Kellogg, 2 Mass. 568. Cited, Interest, on interest after due, legality of, 29 Cal. 392.

Greenleaf v. Low, 4 Den. 168. Cited, Election, irregularities which do not invalidate, 12 Cal. 361.

Greenby v. Wilcocks, 2 John. 1. Cited, Covenant, personal covenants in deed, 37 Cal. 189.

Greeno v. Munson, 9 Vt. 37. Cited, Estoppel, of tenant, 33 Cal. 244.

Greenough v. Gaskill, 1 Mylne & K. 109. Commented on, Witness, confidential communications, practice, 29 Cal. 71, 72.

Greenup v. Brown, Breese, 193. Cited, Appeal, notice of motion to set aside execution, will not operate to stay proceedings, 8 Cal. 134.

Greenvault v. Davis, 4 Hill, 643. Cited, Covenant, what sufficient eviction to establish breach of, 33 Cal. 306. Approved, 39 Cal. 365.

Greenville and Col. Railway v. Partlow, 5 Rich. 428. Cited, Eminent Domain, compensation on condemnation, how estimated, 31 Cal. 374.

Greenwade v. Greenwade, 3 Dana, 495. Cited, Judicial Notice, not taken of foreign laws, 15 Cal. 254.

Greenway v. Fisher, 1 Car. & P. 190. Commented on, Conversion, bailee when liable for, 2 Cal. 573.

Greenwood v. Brodhead, 8 Barb. 593. Approved, Debtor and Creditor, rights of priority of partnership creditors, 13 Cal. 632.

Greer v. Mezes, 24 How. Cited, Mexican Grants, validity of inchoate grant, 26 Cal. 628.

Gregg v. Bostwick, 33 Cal. 220. Approved, Homestead, actual occupation necessary to constitute, 35 Cal. 319; 37 Cal. 179; 41 Cal. 83.

Gregory v. Doidge, 3 Bing. 475. Cited, Estoppel, tenant when not estopped, 33 Cal. 254.

Gregory v. Ford, 14 Cal. 138. Cited, Equity, relief from judgment by default, and from legal proceedings granted only·in peculiar cases, showing required, 15 Cal. 286; 16 Cal. 202; 23 Cal. 129; 37 Cal. 228.

Gregory v. Haworth, 25 Cal. 653. Cited, Fraud, cannot be made the foundation of a defense by guilty party, 34 Cal. 90.

Gregory v. Haynes, 13 Cal. 591; S. C. 21 Cal. 446. Overruled, Ejectment, that ownership and right of possession are not facts, but conclusions of law, 16 Cal. 246. Approved, Res Adjudicata, conclusiveness of decree, 23 Cal. 410.

Gregory v. McPherson, 13 Cal. 562. Cited as not authority, Probate Procedure, 16 Cal. 501. Approved, Requisites of petition for sale of real estate, 19 Cal. 208; Id. 408, 410. Cited, Mexican Grants, record evidence of, 31 Cal. 510.

Gregory v. Taber, 19 Cal. 397. Cited, Probate, requisites of petition for sale of real estate of decedent, 20 Cal. 314; invalid sale, cannot be confirmed by probate court, 33 Cal. 54.

Gretton v. Haward, 1 Swanst. 420. Cited, Will, effect ·of acceptance under, 29 Cal. 351.

Grewell v. Henderson, 7 Cal. 290. Referred to, Written Instrument, construction of, 8 Cal. 584.

Grey v. Cooper, 3 Doug. 65. Cited, Negotiable Instruments, validity of indorsement by infant, 24 Cal. 209.

Griffen v. House, 18·John. 397. Commented on, Discretion of inferior tribunal not subject to collateral revision, 7 Cal. 437.

Griffin v. Polhemus, 20 Cal. 180. Cited, Continuance, granting or refusing, in discretion, 28 Cal. 590.

Griffin v. Sheffield, 38 Miss. 359. Cited, Conveyance, record of seal, 36 Cal. 203.

Griffin v. Wall, 32 Ala. 149. Approved, Election Contest, practice, list of illegal votes to be furnished, 30 Cal. 399.

Griffith v. Bogardus, 14 Cal. 410. Cited, Replevin, lies for money sealed up in a bag, 29 Cal. 622.

Griffith v. Cochran, 5 Bin. 87. Commented on and restricted to particular case, Mandamus, when it lies, 7 Cal. 71. Cited, 24 Cal. 84.

Griffith v. Frazier, 8 Cranch, 8. Commented on, Administrator, resignation and appointment of, 10 Cal. 119.

Griffith v. Grogan, 12 Cal. 317. Approved, Debtor and Creditor, effect of payment by note, 18 Cal. 333; 23 Cal. 322; 25 Cal. 542.

Griffith v. Ingledew, 6 Serg. & R. 429. Denied, Principal and Agent, consignees and indorsees of bill of lading, 1 Cal. 82, 83.

Griffiths v. Gidlow, 3 Hurl. & N. 648. Cited, Master and Servant, when master not liable for injury to servant, 31 Cal. 381.

Grigg v. Cooks, 4 Sim. 438. Cited, Principal and Agent, when agent held as trustee of principal, 13 Cal. 141.

Griggs v. Austin, 3 Pick. 20. Approved, Freight, may be recovered back on failure of transportation, 6 Cal. 31; 6 Cal. 370, 371.

Grignon's Lessee v. Astor, 2 How. 319. Cited, Probate, jurisdiction how acquired, 7 Cal. 234; 19 Cal. 171; 3 Iowa, 132. Commented on, 13 Wis. 302; residence a jurisdictional fact, 18 Cal. 507; proceedings and judgment conclusive, 34 Cal. 428; presumptions, 13 Wis. 318; 7 How. 181; 12 How. 385; 22 How. 14; 24 How. 203; Mexican law of descents, 37 Cal. 92; Mexican Grant, effect of confirmation, 8 Cal. 198; 9 How. 446; Administrator's Sales, judicial, 9 Cal. 196.

Grigsby v. Napa County, 36 Cal. 585. Cited, Action, dismissal for want of prosecution, in discretion, 39 Cal. 451.

Grimes v. Fall, 15 Cal. 63. Cited, Appeal, injury presumed from erroneous admission of evidence, 28 Cal. 544.

Grimes's Est. v. Norris, 6 Cal. 621. Approved, Probate, statute not retroactive, law regulating descents and distributions of estates of parties who died previous to passage of statute, 10 Cal. 477; 12 Cal. 579; 24 Cal. 123; 33 Cal. 422, 423; 37 Cal. 89, 91; 10 How. 375; 23 How. 363; 1 Saw. 199.

Grimstone v. Carter, 3 Paige, 420. Cited, Conveyances, occupation of land as notice of, title, 36 Cal. 272. Reviewed, Id. 274; notices, actual and constructive, 29 Cal. 488. Commented on, 15 N. Y. 358.

Grinnell v. Cook, 3 Hill, 485. Commented on and approved, Innkepers, liability of, 1 Cal. 229; 33 Cal. 600. Cited, Lien of, for charges, 23 Cal. 364.

Grinnell v. Phillips, 1 Mass. 541. Cited, Verdict, validity of, 25 Cal. 400.

Griswold v. Chandler, 5 N. H. 492. Cited, Administrator, duty of, as to surplus funds, 37 Cal. 429.

Griswold v. Johnson, 5 Conn. 363. Cited, Tenant in Common, cannot convey so as to prejudice co-tenants, 35 Cal. 588.

Griswold v. Sharpe, 2 Cal. 17. Approved, Appeal, lies after judgment from an order refusing to dissolve an attachment, 7 Cal. 518; 1 Nev. 537. Overruled, 24 Cal. 448.

Groat v. Gillespie, 25 Wend. 383. Cited, Damages, counsel fees, not recoverable in action on attachment bond, 1 Cal. 411.

Grogan v. Knight, 27 Cal. 515. Reviewed and approved, State Lands, selections of lien lands before survey confers no title on State, 30 Cal. 604; 34 Cal. 512; 38 Cal. 31, 33; 40 Cal. 363, 370. Commented on, 38 Cal. 43.

Grogan v. Mayor, etc., of N. Y., 2 E. D. Smith, 695. Cited, Building Contracts, owner not liable to sub-contractor for want of privity, 22 Cal. 571.

Grogan v. Ruckle, 1 Cal. 158; S. C. 193. Approved, Appeal, control of action retained till filing of remittitur, 1 Cal. 231; 22 Cal. 25; 24 Cal. 58. Approved, Pleading, genuineness of indorsement need not be denied under oath, 4 Cal. 202. Cited, New matter must be specially set up, 10 Cal. 30.

Grogan v. San Francisco, 18 Cal. 590. Cited, San Francisco, sales of city property to be made at public auction, 21 Cal. 363; invalidity of sale, 21 Cal. 366; validity of ordinance, on what depends, 23 Cal. 318; 22 Ind. 95. Cited, Tenure of lands in trust and mode of alienation, 42 Cal. 556. Referred to and approved, 27 Cal. 416; 33 Cal. 140.

Gronfier v. Minturn, 5 Cal. 492. Distinguished, Foreclosure, costs in action, 5 Cal. 435.

Gronfier v. Puymirol, 19 Cal. 629. Cited, Guardian and Ward, general guardian may appear for and defend action, 20 Cal. 676; 32 Cal. 119; 42 Cal. 486. Commented on, Id. 491.

Groschen v. Page, 6 Cal. 138. Distinguished, Insolvency, conveyance giving preference, 10 Cal. 278. .

Gross v. Fowler, 21 Cal. 392. Cited, Sheriff's Deed, made before expiration of period of redemption, is void, 33 Cal. 675; 38 Cal. 438; "month" defined as calendar month, 2 Wall. 190.

Grout v. Townsend, 2 Hill, 557. Cited, Estoppel, by deed, recital of consideration, 30 Cal. 25.

Groves v. Slaughter, 15 Pet. 449. Cited, Constitutional Construction, relative powers of Federal and State Governments, 1 Cal. 236, 243; 7 How. 555; clause prohibiting slavery, 2 Cal. 455; 9 Cal. 169. Approved, 5 How. 138.

Grow v. His Creditors, 31 Cal. 328. Referred to, 29 Cal. 416. Disapproved and proper practice indicated, Insolvency, proceedings where schedule is defective, 32 Cal. 410.

Grubb's Admrs. v. Cayton's Exr., 2 Hayw. 575. Cited, Statute of Limitations, when running is stopped by death of creditor, 35 Cal. 638.

Guest v. Homfray, 5 Ves. Jr. 818. Commented on, Specific Performance, when delay will defeat right of enforcement, 10 Cal. 329.

Guice v. Lawrence, 2 La. An. 226. Cited, Husband and Wife, interest of wife in common property, 15 Cal. 311. Commented on, 17 Cal. 538.

Guild v. Guild, 15 Pick. 129. Cited, Parent and Child, services gratuitous, no action lies for, 22 Cal. 510.

Guilford, Town of, v. Chenango County, 18 Barb. 615; S. C. 13 N. Y. 143; 4 Abb. Pr. 220. Commented on, Taxation, legislature may authorize local taxation for payment of equitable claims against municipality, 13 Cal. 351, 353, 355; 26 Cal. 649; 27 Cal. 209; 35 Cal. 633; 42 Cal. 450. Cited, Undertaking, form of statutory undertaking, 29 Cal. 199.

Guinard v. Heysinger, 15 Ill. 288. Cited, Judgment by default, against party by wrong name, when not void, 30 Cal. 206.

Guiod v. Guiod, 14 Cal. 506. Cited, Homestead, 16 Cal. 81; mortgage of, by husband, effect of, 16 Cal. 218. Commented on, Rights of wife to, on what dependent, 25 Cal. 114. Cited, Temporary absence not an abandonment, 18 Iowa, 8.

Gullck v. Ward, 5 Halst. 87. Approved, Contracts, agreements respecting government contracts, when void, 20 Cal. 185.

Gullett v. Hoy, 15 Mo. 399. Cited, Counter-claim, defense of, in action on note, 41 Cal. 59.

Gunn v. Bates, 6 Cal. 263. Cited, Mexican Grant, validity of inchoate grant, title under, 10 Cal. 621. Commented on, 25 Cal. 137. Cited, Constructive possession under, 38 Cal. 487.

Gunter v. Geary, 1 Cal. 462. Approved, Appeal, statement or bill of exceptions essential, practice, 1 Cal. 470; 14 Cal. 39; 1 Nev. 530. Cited, Eminent Domain, payment or tender of damages awarded a condition precedent to entry on land condemned, 7 Cal. 579; 29 Cal. 117; Nuisance, what constitutes, a question of fact, 29 Cal. 159; 30 Cal. 384.

Gunter v. Halsey, Amb. 586. Cited, Specific Performance, on verbal contract, 10 Cal. 158.

Gunter v. Janes, 9 Cal. 643. Cited, Trust and Trustee, enforcement of trust against executor, 31 Cal. 23.

Gunter v. Laffan, 7 Cal. 588. Cited, Appeal, law of case, conclusive as to future proceedings, 14 Cal. 249; 15 Cal. 82; 20 Cal. 417; Tenants in Common, right to acquire interest of co-tenant, 19 Cal. 123.

Guttman v. Scannell, 7 Cal. 455. Cited, Married Woman, rights and liabilities under sole trader act, 29 Cal. 566.

Guy v. Franklin, 5 Cal. 416. Approved, Judgment, interest to be computed on note, and included in, 6 Cal. 156; 9 Cal. 247; Id. 297; 32 Cal. 88; error in computation of, to be corrected by motion, 2 Nev. 133; 7 Nev. 222.

Guy v. Hermance, 5 Cal. 73. Cited, Supervisors, purely judicial powers cannot be conferred by statute, 24 Cal. 127; Cloud on Title, right of protection from sale which may create, 25 Cal. 357; McAll. 117; 47 N. H. 271.

Guy v. Ide, 6 Cal. 99. Cited, Mortgage under statute, a mere security, 8 Cal. 267; remedy of mortgagee confined to foreclosure, 9 Cal. 410; remedy barred when debt is barred, 24 Cal. 498.

Guy v. Middleton, 5 Cal. 392. Cited, Redemption, lands sold under decree of foreclosure subject to, 6 Cal. 174; 22 Cal. 650; right of possession not in purchaser till full time of redemption elapsed, 7 Cal. 46.

Gwynne v. Niswanger, 15 Ohio, 367. Approved, Taxation, preëmption claims subject to, 30 Cal. 648; Public Lands, title under location of land warrant, 31 Cal. 268; title of preëmptioner on final payment to government, 37 Cal. 495.

Hackett v. Connett, 2 Edw. Ch. 73. Cited, Res Adjudicata, judgment when not an estoppel, 23 Cal. 628.

Hackett v. Huson, 3 Wend. 249. Cited, Demand, essential to action on bond for deed, 7 Cal. 276; Tender, 25 Cal. 279.

Hackett v. Manlove, 14 Cal. 85. Cited, Chattel Mortgage, legal title in mortgagee, 26 Cal. 526.

Hackley v. Ogmun, 10 How. Pr. 44. Cited, Pleading, several defenses may be set up, 22 Cal. 680.

Hackley v. Sprague, 10 Wend. 113. Approved, Statutory Construction, statutes to be construed prospectively, 27 Cal. 159.

Haddrick v. Heslop, 12 Q. B. 268. Cited, Witness, competency of, joint tort feasor, 17 Cal. 604.

Haffley v. Maier, 13 Cal. 13. Cited, Mortgage, a mere security or lien, 16 Cal. 468; 21 Cal. 621; 36 Cal. 39; remedy barred when debt secured is barred, 24 Cal. 498; Estoppel, of mortgagor, 31 Cal. 457.

Hagedorn v. Oliverson, 2 Maule & S. 485. Cited, Principal and Agent, presumptions of authority of agent by adoption of act by principal, 4 Cal. 171.

Hagan v. Lucas, 10 Pet. 400. Approved, Execution, lien of first execution continues after replevy, 11 Cal. 275, 279.

Hagan v. Providence & Worcester R. R. Co., 3 R. I. 88. Cited, Damages, punitive damages for invasion of personal rights, showing required, 34 Cal. 600.

Hagar v. Lucas, 29 Cal. 309. Cited, Patent to Land, conclusive evidence, 38 Cal. 83.

Hager v. Shindler, 29 Cal. 47. Cited, Cloud on Title, when action lies to prevent or remove, 34 Cal. 389. Approved, Possession not necessary to maintain action, 29 Cal. 190; 28 Cal. 649. Commented on, Limitation of action, 32 Cal. 263. Cited, Judgment, how far an estoppel, 32 Cal. 199.

Hagey v. Detweiler, 35 Penn. St. 409. Cited, Boundary Lines, acquiescence in, 25 Cal. 631.

Haggerty v. Palmer, 6 Johns. Ch. R. 437. Doubted, Vendor and Vendee, rights of second vendee of personal property, 36 Cal. 158.

Haggin v. Clark, 28 Cal. 162. Approved, Appeal, from order after final judgment, statement to contain grounds, 29 Cal. 193; 33 Cal. 554. Referred to, 30 Cal. 232.

Hahn v. Kelly, 34 Cal. 391. Approved and followed, Jurisdiction of Person, how acquired, 33 Cal. 515; Judgments, when void for want of jurisdiction, 39 Cal. 142, 143; collateral attack on, intendments in favor of jurisdiction of courts of record, presumptions as to, 33 Cal. 537; 34 Cal. 616; 37 Cal. 89; Id. 462, 463, 464; 39 Cal. 440; 41 Cal. 51; 42 Cal. 492; 8 Nev. 308. Distinguished as to direct attack, 42 Cal. 577. Approved, Record imports verity, recitals in, conclusive, 35 Cal. 534; 36 Cal. 696; 38 Cal. 437; 39 Cal. 356; 1 Saw. 320, 321, 324, 325, 330.

Haight v. Gay, 8 Cal. 297. Followed, Appeal, jurisdiction, remedy exclusive, 9 Cal. 52. Cited, to be taken within one year, 21 Cal. 169; issuance of writs in aid of jurisdiction, 24 Cal. 336.

Haight v. Green, 19 Cal. 113. Approved, Appeal, order refusing to set aside judgment by default, in discretion, not reviewable, 19 Cal. 606; 29 Cal. 424.

Haight v. Joyce, 2 Cal. 64. Approved, Negotiable Instruments, notes given for gaming consideration, valid, in hands of *bona fide* holder, 4 Cal. 323.

Haile v. State, 11 Humph. 154. Cited, Criminal Procedure, evidence of intoxication, purpose of its admission, 29 Cal. 683.

Haines v. Beach, 3 Johns. Ch. 459. Cited, Foreclosure, subsequent incumbrancers proper, but not necessary parties, 11 Cal. 316; effect of decree on failure to make them parties, 40 Cal. 238. Approved, Prior alienees and incumbrancers, necessary parties, 10 Cal. 552, 553.

Haire v. Baker, 5 N. Y. 359. Cited, Pleading, complaint on bond for release of attachment, what should state, 9 Cal. 501; sufficiency of statement on demurrer for want of facts to sustain action, 25 Cal. 92.

Hale v. Chandler, 3 Gibbs, 531. Approved, Attachment, on debt not due, is void as to creditors, 18 Cal. 382.

Hale v. Gaines, 22 How. 144. Approved, Preëmption statute conferring right, simply permissive and directory, land may be reserved from sale, 37 Cal. 493, 502.

Hale v. Gerrish, 8 N. H. 374. Cited, Infant, ratification of contract by, what constitutes, 24 Cal. 213.

Hale v. Trout, 35 Cal. 229. Commented on, Contract, damages on breach of contract for services, 38 Cal. 664; when action lies on breach of entire contract, 1 Saw. 223.

Haley v. Bennett, 5 Port. 452. Cited, Vendor's Lien, on bond given for conveyance, 4 Cal. 111; election of remedy on part of vendor, 14 Cal. 73; Decree, in action by vendor, 15 Cal. 195.

Hall v. Auburn Turnpike Co., 27 Cal. 255. Cited, Corporation, note of, when void in hands of payee, 29 Cal. 570, 572.

Hall v. Bark Emily, 33 Cal. 522. Cited, Appeal, motions for new trial for insufficiency of evidence addressed to discretion of court, when not reviewable, 39 Cal. 410.

Hall v. Benner, 1 Penn. 402. Cited, Estoppel, tenant when not estopped, 35 Cal. 571.

Hall v. Butler, 10 Adol. & E. 205. Commented on, Estoppel, tenant when not estopped, 33 Cal. 250, 251; 35 Cal. 570.

Hall v. Curzon, 17 Eng. C. L. 290. Cited, Fraud, intent presumed from acts, 8 Cal. 213.

Hall v. Cushing, 8 Mass. 521. Cited, Statutory Construction, beneficial construction intended by legislature, 13 Cal. 456.

Hall v. Doe, 19 Ala. 378. Cited, Mexican Grants, validity dependent on confirmation, 19 Cal. 270; 24 Cal. 663; 26 Cal. 123.

Hall v. Dowling, 18 Cal. 619. Commented on and approved, Taxation, public domain not taxable, 22 Cal. 80; 30 Cal. 655, 657.

Hall v. Farmer, 5 Den. 484. Commented on and distinguished, Guaranty, consideration, sufficiency of, 7 Cal. 34; notice requisite, to fix liability, 16 Cal. 153.

Hall v. Fisher, 9 Barb. 17. Cited, Redemption, sheriff as agent, kind of money receivable, 26 Cal. 663.

Hall v. Hale, 8 Conn. 337. Cited, Witness, indorser a competent witness, 13 Cal. 87.

Hall v. Hall, 2 McCord Ch. 302. Cited, Debtor and Creditor, priority of lien of partnership creditors, 13 Cal. 632.

Hall v. Luther, 13 Wend. 491. Cited, Officer, eligibility to office cannot be collaterally questioned, 23 Cal. 320.

Hall v. Marston, 17 Mass. 574. Commented on, Money had and received, action lies even when privity does not exist, 15 Cal. 346.

Hall v. Phelps, 2 John. 451. Cited, Evidence, sufficiency of admissions of signer to prove execution of note, 22 Cal. 484.

Hall v. Robinson, 2 N. Y. 293. Cited, Assignment, of property wrongfully detained, is valid, 15 Cal. 218; 22 Cal. 142.

Hall v. Snowhill, 2 Green, 9. Commented on, Chattel Mortgage, legal effect and operation, 27 Cal. 269.

Hall v. State, 3 Kelly, 18. Cited, Sunday Laws, constitutional, 18 Cal. 681.

Hall v. Suydam, 6 Barb. 83. Commented on, Malicious Prosecution, probable cause, what is, 8 Cal. 221; a question of fact, 8 Cal. 225.

Hall v. Williams, 6 Pick. 232. Commented on, Foreign Judgment, on publication of summons, not binding *in personam*, 8 Cal. 453.

Hall v. Wybourn, 2 Salk. 420. Commented on, Statute of Limitations, exceptions in, to be strictly construed, 35 Cal. 639, 640.

Halleck v. Mixer, 16 Cal. 574. Approved, Timber, replevin lies for timber cut and severed from realty, 23 Cal. 170; Id. 387; 31 Cal. 157, 159. Explained, 37 Cal. 107, 108, 109; 15 Wis. 228. Cited, Title cannot be tried in action, 28 Cal. 610. Qualified, 39 Cal. 417, 418; averment of facts, insufficient statement, 28 Cal. 550.

Halleck v. Moss, 17 Cal. 339. Referred to on second appeal, Executor's Sale, validity of, 22 Cal. 274.

Hallett v. Beebe, 13 How. 25. Cited, State Sovereignty, right of eminent domain on admission of State, 18 Cal. 252; swamp and overflowed lands, 26 Cal. 354.

Hallett v. Holmes, 18 John. 28. Cited, Sureties, on executor's bond, liability of, 29 Cal. 100.

Hallett v. Righters, 13 How. Pr. 43. Cited, Service of Notices, statute authorizing constructive service to be strictly pursued, 24 Cal. 434.

Hallock v. Jaudin, 34 Cal. 167. Cited, Revenue Stamp, no part of written instrument, 35 Cal. 507; 1 Colorado, 201; 26 Ark. 401; 26 Wis. 166; 33 Tex. 817; 101 Mass. 246; 44 Miss. 445. Overruled, that want of stamp will defeat a recovery, 40 Cal. 243, 244; 42 Cal. 417. Pleading, sufficiency of complaint on written instrument, 38 Cal. 603; Id. 682; 21 Gratt. 79.

Hallower v. Henley, 6 Cal. 209. Commented on, Employer and Employé, liability for injury to employé, 31 Cal. 382; 12 Ohio St. 491.

Halstead v. Mayor, etc., of New York, 3 N. Y. 430. Cited, not in point, 16 Cal. 271.

Hambleton v. Dempsey, 20 Ohio, 172. Doubted, Taxation, proceedings of board of equalization, requisites to validity, 13 Cal. 329.

Hamblin v. Dinneford, 2 Edw. Ch. 529. Cited, Legal Tender and Demand, rights reciprocal, 25 Cal. 576.

Hamer v. Hathaway, 33 Cal. 117. Cited, Replevin, measure of damages, 34 Cal. 645. Commented on, 39 Cal. 420, 421.

Hames v. Castro, 5 Cal. 111. Cited, Husband and Wife, rights of surviving wife in community property, 8 Cal. 510; 13 Cal. 470.

Hamilton v. Commonwealth, 4 Harris, Pa. 129. Cited, Criminal Procedure, validity of judgment, 31 Cal. 627.

Hamilton v. Cummings, 1 John. Ch. 517. Cited, Equity, when jurisdiction will be exercised to grant relief, 10 Cal. 576; 23 Ark. 761; Dictum as to distinction between void instruments denied, 2 Black, 445; 1 McLean, 14; 36 Barb. 48; Deady, 491. Construed, 28 Vt. 482.

Hamilton v. Cutts, 4 Mass. 349. Cited, Covenant, in lease, what constitutes eviction under, 39 Cal. 367.

Hamilton's Lessee v. Marsden, 6 Bin. 45. Cited, Evidence, of conveyance, proof of handwriting, when required, 26 Cal. 411. Commented on, Estoppel, tenant when not estopped, 33 Cal. 252, 253; 35 Cal. 571.

Hamilton v. McDonald, 18 Cal. 128. Referred to, Counterclaim, jurisdiction of justice's court, 23 Cal. 63.

Hamilton v. Russell, 1 Cranch, 309. Commented on, Statute of Frauds, sale of chattels without change of possession, fraudulent, 15 Cal. 506; 29 Cal. 476; 4 Gratt. 434; 3 Yerg. 476; 1 Tex. 423; 11 Wheat. 82.

Hamilton v. Wilson, 4 John. 72. Cited, Covenant, in deed, when personal, 37 Cal. 189.

Hamilton v. Wright, 4 Hawks. 283. Cited, Jurisdiction, of justices' courts, evidence *aliunde* the record, to sustain, 34 Cal. 327.

Hamm v. Arnold, 23 Cal. 373. Cited, Estoppel, when judgment in ejectment operates as, 32 Cal. 199.

Hammond v. People, 32 Ill. 446. Cited, Pleading, matter in abatement must be specially pleaded, party sued by wrong name, 30 Cal. 206.

Hammond v. Ridgely, 5 Har. & J. 245. Commented on, Law of the Case, 20 Cal. 419.

Hammond v. Zehner, 23 Barb. 473. Cited, Water Rights, title by adverse possession, 25 Cal. 509, 511.

Hammond's Lessee v. Inloes, 4 Md. 138. Commented on, Law of the Case, 20 Cal. 419.

Hampshire v. Franklin, 16 Mass. 76. Cited, Corporation, power of dissolution, 38 Cal. 172.

Hampshire Manf. Bank v. Billings, 17 Pick. 87. Commented on, Sureties, on undertaking, discharge of, by tender of debt, 26 Cal. 544.

Hampton v. Hodges, 8 Ves. Jr. 105. Cited, Mortgage, mortgagor in possession, rights of, 27 Cal. 436.

Hance v. Rumming, 2 E. D. Smith, 48. Cited, Pleading, sham answer, insufficient denials, 25 Cal. 196; 32 Cal. 574.

16

Hancock v. Day, 1 McMullen Eq. 69. Disapproved, Tenants in Common, liability of co-tenant for rent, 12 Cal. 423.

Hancock Ditch Co. v. Bradford, 13 Cal. 637. Criticised, Nonsuit, right of, not absolute, 18 Cal. 77.

Hands v. James, Comyn, 531. Commented on, Will, presumptions as to execution of, 10 Cal. 479.

Hankins v. Ingols, 4 Blackf. 35. Cited, Witness, competency of, when vendor competent witness for vendee, 23 Cal. 446.

Hankins v. Lawrence, 8 Blackf. 266. Cited, Constitutional Construction, compensation for condemnation of land, 31 Cal. 554, 559.

Hanford v. McNair, 9 Wend. 54. Cited, Powers, authority of attorney to execute conveyance must be given in writing, 21 Cal. 392.

Hanford v. McNair, 2 Wend. 286. Cited, Default, when counter affidavits not admissible on application to open default, 33 Cal. 326.

Hanly v. Levin, 5 Ohio, 228. Cited, Infant, to appear by guardian, 32 Cal. 117.

Hanly v. Morse, 32 Me. 287. Cited, Land, possession as notice of title to, 21 Cal. 628.

Hanna v. Mills, 21 Wend. 90. Cited, Pleading, action on special contract for services, 26 Cal. 22.

Hannah v. Swarner, 8 Watts, 9. Cited, Trial, delivery of deed a question of fact, 5 Cal. 318.

Hannan v. Osborn, 4 Paige, 336. Commented on, Pleading, sufficiency of complaint in action for accounting by tenant in common, 12 Cal. 423.

Hansard v. Robinson, 7 Barn. & C. 90. Commented on and practice distinguished, Action on lost Note, 28 Cal. 565; 4 How. 274.

Hanscom v. Tower, 17 Cal. 518. Approved, Appeal, from order refusing new trial, brings up the whole record, 23 Cal. 549; 42 Cal. 31.

Hansford v. Barbour, 3 A. K. Marsh, 515. Cited, Constitunality of Statute, right to test validity of statute, 4 Cal. 168.

Hansford v. Elliott, 9 Leigh, 79. Commented on and distinguished, Limitation of Actions, suspension of statute on death of creditor, 35 Cal. 638; 11 Grat. 71.

Hanson v. Armstrong, 22 Ill. 443. Cited, Estoppel, former judgment in ejectment, when admissible in evidence, 37 Cal. 396; judgment on whom conclusive, 22 Cal. 207.

Hanson v. Barnes's Lessee, 3 Gill. & J. 359. Cited, Sheriff's Sale, validity on, what depends, 22 Cal. 590.

Hanson v. Barnhisel, 11 Cal. 340. Cited, Appeal, order granting new trial will not be reversed unless for abuse of discretion, 5 Kan. 133.

Hanson v. Gardiner, 7 Ves. Jr. 305. Cited, Injunction, to restrain waste, 15 Cal. 116; 24 Cal. 473; practice on dissolution, 7 Cal. 323.

Hanson v. Webb, 3 Cal. 236. Cited, Ferries and Toll Bridges, protection of exclusive privileges, 22 Cal. 423.

Harbert v. Dumont, 3 Ind. 346. Cited, Exceptions, objections to admission of evidence to be taken at trial, 23 Cal. 60; Surety, discharged by contract of creditor not to sue, 26 Cal. 542.

Hardenbergh v. Bacon, 33 Cal. 356. Cited, Trust and Trustee, how relation is established, 33 Cal. 352; Mining Stock, equivalent values of similar stock, 42 Cal. 100.

Hardenburgh v. Kidd, 10 Cal. 402. Cited, Powers of Government, legislature cannot invest judiciary with other than judicial powers, 20 Cal. 44; Injunction, will not issue to restrain a void proceeding, 36 Cal. 71; Tax Deed, what essential to validity of, Id. 73.

Harding v. Goodlett, 3 Yerg. 41. Cited, Eminent Domain, necessity, time and mode of its exercise exclusively legislative questions, 31 Cal. 372; 41 Cal. 171.

Harding v. Jasper, 14 Cal. 642. Approved, Dedication to public use, how made, 22 Cal. 490; 29 Iowa, 80. Cited, Acceptance, how established, 31 Cal. 589; 42 Cal. 554; created by prescription, 23 Wis. 555.

Harding v. Watts, 15 East, 556. Cited, Arbitration, selection of umpire, practice, 23 Cal. 367; 8 Pet. 178.

Hardman v. Chamberlin, Morris, Iowa Rep. 104. Cited, Pleading, indorsement need not be denied under oath, 1 Cal. 160.

Hardman v. Willoock, 9 Bing. 382. Cited, Bailment, when bailee not estopped from showing title in third party, 9 Cal. 574.

Hardy v. DeLeon, 5 Tex. 211. Criticised, Trust and Trustee, trustee cannot acquire title by purchase at his own sale, as applied to administrators, 29 Cal. 38.

Hardy v. Gholson, 26 Miss. 72. Cited, Judgment of court of record not subject to collateral attack, 34 Cal. 428.

Hardy v. Harbin, U. S. Circuit Ct. Cited, Trust Title, patentee as trustee, 30 Cal. 307.

Hardy v. Hunt, 11 Cal. 343. Cited, Attachment, garnishment does not secure precedence over assignees of fund assigned before service of process, 15 Cal. 40. Cited on general question, Wagers on elections, 37 Cal. 675.

Hardy v. Johnson, 1 Wall. 371. Commented on, Pleading, subsequently acquired title in ejectment must be set up in supplemental answer, 30 Cal. 472; Judgment in ejectment, upon whom conclusive, 32 Cal. 193, 194.

Hardy v. Thomas, 23 Miss. 544. Commented on, Executor de son tort, liability for assets in his possession, 17 Cal. 192.

Hardy v. Waters, 38 Me. 450. Cited, Negotiable Instrument, note made or indorsed by infant not void, but voidable, 24 Cal. 208.

Hare v. Fury, 3 Yeates, 13. Cited, Tenant in Common, when may recover for mesne profits against co-tenant in ejectment, 29 Cal. 333.

Harger v. McCullough, 2 Denio, 119. Commented on, Corporations, nature of individual liability of stockholders, 14 Cal. 267.

Harker v. Anderson, 21 Wend. 372. Cited, Negotiable Instruments, checks on same footing as bills of exchange, 4 Cal. 37. Denied, 2 Story, 518; 30 Mo. 188; 2 Hill, 430.

Harker v. Conrad, 12 Serg. & R. 301. Dicta denied, Debtor and Creditor, application of payment to be made within reasonable time, 14 Cal. 449. Distinguished, 6 Watts & S. 15. Cited, Mechanic's Lien, sufficiency of description in notice, 2 Cal. 63.

Harker v. Mayor, etc., of New York, 17 Wend. 199. Cited, Judicial Notice, not taken of ordinances and by-laws of corporations, 7 Cal. 474.

Harlan v. Harlan, 15 Penn. St. 507. Cited, Replevin, lies for property severed from realty, 16 Cal. 579; 28 Cal. 610; 39 Cal. 418.

Harlan v. Smith, 6 Cal. 173. Cited, Foreclosure, judgment in, subject to redemption, 9 Cal. 412; 22 Cal. 650.

Harley v. Young, 4 Cal. 284. Cited not in point, New Trial, statement on, 9 Cal. 210.

Harlow v. Humiston, 6 Cow. 189. Cited, Master and Servant, master when chargeable with acts of servant, 38 Cal. 634.

Harmer v. Priestley, 21 Eng. L. & E. 497. Commented on, Mortgage, tender and refusal after law day not a discharge of lien, 14 Cal. 530.

Harmon v. James, 7 Smedes & M. 118. Approved, Married Woman, deed to married woman *prima facie* valid, 13 Cal. 500.

Harnett v. Yielding, 2 Scho. & L. 549. Cited, Specific Performance, time not of essence of contract, 10 Cal. 326; indefinite contracts will not be enforced, 33 Cal. 133; contracts may be enforced in part, 8 How. 161.

Harnsbarger's Adm. v. Kinney, 6 Grat. 287. Cited, Instructions, misapprehension of jury, 11 Cal. 142.

Harper v. Forbes, 15 Cal. 202. Cited, Homestead, recovery of, 16 Cal. 81; occupancy, presumptive evidence of appropriation, 20 Cal. 194; 25 Cal. 111.

Harper v. Freelon, 6 Cal. 76. Cited, Insolvency, proceedings in, are "special cases," 23 Cal. 148.

Harper v. Little, 2 Greenl. 14. Approved, Principal and Agent, authority of agent revoked by death of principal, 15 Cal. 18.

Harper v. Minor, 27 Cal. 107. Commented on and practice criticised, Appeal, order striking out statement on motion for new trial not appealable, 32 Cal. 305. Commented on but not decided, order dismissing motion, Id. 327. Cited, Motions and orders to strike out part of pleadings, no part of judgment roll, 36 Cal. 114; motions and orders made part of record by being embodied in statement, 28 Cal. 299; 32 Cal. 315, 316, 322; 33 Cal. 515; Id. 554; 34 Cal. 605; 35 Cal. 290; 7 Nev. 121; failure to make statement in time waives right thereto, 28 Cal. 262. Commented on, Striking out statement on appeal, 32 Cal. 325. Approved, Irrelevant matter not to be inserted in transcript, 28 Cal. 174; 33 Cal. 173.

Harper v. Richardson, 22 Cal. 251. Cited, Public Highways, when owner cannot recover damages on opening of road, 23 Cal. 467; 28 Cal. 667.

Harrell v. Ellsworth, 17 Ala. 576. Cited, Ferries and Toll Bridges, protection of franchise, 6 Cal. 598, 599; 13 Cal. 13.

Harrell v. Whitman, 19 Ala. 138. Cited, Attachment, equitable demand not liable to garnishment, 35 Cal. 386.

Harrington v. People, 6 Barb. 607. Cited, Officers, jurisdiction and authority cannot be acquired by mere assertion, authority must be shown, 29 Cal. 188; 30 Cal. 607.

Harris v. Allnutt, 12 La. 465. Cited, Assignment, of property in trusts vests in assignee according to the *lex loci*, 13 Cal. 278; Judicial Notice, not taken of foreign laws, 15 Cal. 254.

Harris v. Bell, 10 Serg. & R. 39. Cited, Vendor and Vendee, ejectment by vendee, 22 Cal. 617.

Harris v. Bradley, 7 Yerg. 310. Cited, Negotiable Instruments, effect of indorsement, 22 Cal. 249.

Harris v. Brown, 1 Cal. 98. Cited, Contract, verbal, for sale of land is void, 1 Cal. 121.

Harris v. Burley, 8 N. H. 256. Cited, Libel and Slander, pleading, innuendo cannot supply the place of a colloquium, 41 Cal. 481.

Harris v. Hanson, 11 Me. 241. Cited, Trespass by Officer, liability on official bond, 14 Cal. 199.

Harris v. Harris, 2 Hagg. Eccl. Rep. 409. Commented on, Divorce, confessions as evidence, 13 Cal. 94.

Harris v. King, 16 Ark. 122. Commented on, Vendor and Vendee, statute of limitations when does not run, 40 Cal. 570.

Harris v. Knickerbocker, 5 Wend. 638. Cited, Specific Performance, of verbal contract part performed, 10 Cal. 160.

Harris v. McGregor, 29 Cal. 124. Cited, Statutory Construction, scope of corporation act prohibiting inquiry into right to exercise corporate powers, 37 Cal. 542.

Harris v. Paynes, 5 Litt. 109. Cited, Injunction, equitable relief from judgment, 14 Cal. 143.

Harris v. Rand, 4 N. H. 259.   Cited, Freight, may be recovered back for failure of transportation, 6 Cal. 32.

Harris v. Reynolds, 13 Cal. 514.   Referred to, 18 Cal. 289. Approved, Foreclosure, purchaser at sale entitled to rents and profits pending time for redemption, 17 Cal. 597.   Cited, 22 Cal. 194; 37 Cal. 432; 38 Cal. 425; tenant in possession, 18 Cal. 115.

Harris v. San Francisco Sugar Ref., 41 Cal. 393.   Cited, Reference, report of referee on special fact submitted, 42 Cal. 196.

Harris v. Smith, 2 Dana, 10.   Cited, Cloud on Title, when action lies to remove, 39 Cal. 22.

Harris v. Taylor, 15 Cal. 348.   Cited, Pleading, general averments of fraud insufficient, 19 Cal. 289.   Distinguished, 29 Cal. 60.

Harris v. Yeoman, 1 Hoff. Ch. 178.   Cited, Practice, in actions against heirs, 31 Cal. 280.

Harrison v. Bank of Kentucky, 3 J. J. Marsh. 375.   Cited, Appeal, affirmance of judgment, what constitutes, 15 Cal. 327.

Harrison v. Brown, 16 Cal. 287. Approved, Married Woman, separate property of, how bound by mortgage, 8 Nev. 262.

Harrison v. Handley, 1 Bibb, 443.   Cited, New Promise, what sufficient acknowledgment, 36 Cal. 186; 8 Conn. 184.

Harrison v. Harrison, 4 Moore, P. C. 96.   Commented on, Divorce, confessions as evidence, 13 Cal. 98.

Harrison v. Harrison, 8 Ves. Jr. 185.   Cited, Deed, sufficiency of execution, signature of grantor, 25 Cal. 81; 4 Wheat. 95, note *a*.

Harrison v. McMahon, 1 Bradf. 283.   Cited, Probate Procedure, order of administration, rights under statute, 23 Cal. 481.

Harrison v. Renfro, 13 Mo. 446. Cited, Attachment, construction of statute relating to, 29 Cal. 367.   Commented on and approved, Lien of, lost by death of defendant, Id. 379.

Harrison v. Sterry, 5 Cranch, 289.   Cited, Insolvency, assignment in trust by partner of firm, a foreign resident, validity of, 13 Cal. 288; 11 Wheat. 102, note *a;* 12 Wheat. 361.

Harrison v. Taylor, 33 Mo. 211. Construed as inapplicable, Ejectment, ouster of co-tenant inferred from demand and refusal, 28 Cal. 488.

Harrison, The, 1 Wheat. 298. Cited, Constitutional Construction, appellate jurisdiction of U. S. supreme court, 11 Cal. 182.

Harrison v. Trustees of Phillip's Academy, 12 Mass. 455. Cited, Mortgage, by deed and defeasance, 33 Cal. 332.

Harrison v. Walker, 1 Kelly, 32. Cited, Statutory Construction, effect of repeal, 10 Cal. 316.

Harrison's Devisees v. Baker, 5 Litt. 250. Cited, Evidence, admissions of counsel in prior suit not to affect rights in second action, 22 Cal. 238.

Harrison Justices v. Holland, 3 Gratt. 247. Cited, Constitutionality of Statute, power of legislature to provide county aid to local improvements, 13 Cal. 188.

Harrower v. Heath, 19 Barb. 331. Cited, Contract, cropping contract, tenancy in common of crops, 17 Cal. 546. Approved, 25 Cal. 63, 64.

Hart v. Bulkley, 2 Edw. Ch. 70. Commented on, Trust and Trustees, mixture of funds in hands of trustee, 9 Cal. 660.

Hart v. Burnett, 15 Cal. 530. Cited, Mexican Law, pueblos, right and tenure to lands, 35 Cal. 432; 5 Wall. 337; title vests without special grant, 35 Cal. 433; 5 Wall. 540; boundaries, 16 Cal. 230. Affirmed, Mission Lands, 16 Cal. 457; secularization of, Id. 461. Approved, Conquest and cession of territory does not affect local laws, 16 Cal. 228; legislative control of pueblo lands, 18 Cal. 573, 614. Affirmed on principle of *stare decisis*, 42 Cal. 559. Approved, Mexican Grant, within pueblo to be presented for confirmation, 30 Cal. 506. Reviewed and approved, Alcaldes' Grants, valid, 16 Cal. 225; 1 Black, 345; 9 Wall. 602. Approved, San Francisco as successor to pueblo, tenure of lands, 16 Cal. 226, 240; 20 Cal. 480; 21 Cal. 42; 25 Cal. 615, 616; 42 Cal. 556, 559. Cited, Limitation of power to lease, 27 Cal. 285. Approved, no power to mortgage, 24 Cal. 602; lands not subject to sale on execution against the city, 16 Cal. 291. Cited to this point, 17 Cal. 484; 20 Cal. 482, 485; 21 Cal. 41; 28 Cal. 222. Referred to, Van Ness Ordinance, 19 Cal. 20; as a rule of property, 33 Cal. 445. Cited, 9 Wall. 324, 602. Affirmed on this point on the principle of *stare decisis*, 28 Cal. 223. Cited, Title by possession under Van Ness Ordinance, 17 Cal. 461. Distinguished as to tenure of beach and water lots, 15 Cal. 635.

Hart v. Burnett, 20 Cal. 169. Approved, Legislature, cannot confer jurisdiction on federal courts, 25 Cal. 610, 614.

Hart v. Gaven, 12 Cal. 476. Cited, Street Assessments, power of legislature to direct, 28 Cal. 352, 362; 2 Or. 158.

Hart v. Green, 8 Vt. 191. Cited, Negotiable Instruments, demand at place designated not of essence of contract, 11 Cal. 322.

Hart v. Mayor, etc., of Albany, 3 Paige, 381. Commented on, Appeal, from order dissolving an injunction, effect of, 15 Cal. 111.

Hart v. Mayor, etc., of Albany, 9 Wend. 571. Cited, Nuisance, abatement under common law not abrogated by statute, 1 Cal. 466; 5 Cal. 122.

Hart v. Moon, 6 Cal. 161. Cited, Justices' Courts, limit of jurisdiction, 7 Cal. 105; pleadings in, 23 Cal. 378.

Hart v. Plum, 14 Cal. 148. Cited, Taxation, assessment roll, validity of, 23 Cal. 116; 19 Wis. 516.

Hart v. Rensselaer and Saratoga R. R. Co., 8 N. Y. 37. Cited, Common Carriers, construction of contract for transportation through, 31 Cal. 53.

Hart v. Robertson, 21 Cal. 346. Cited, Married Woman, when deed to is a deed of gift, 30 Cal. 55.

Hart v. Seixas, 21 Wend. 40. Practice distinguished, Jurisdiction, of court of record in insolvency cases presumed, 33 Cal. 536; 34 Cal. 428.

Hart v. Ten Eyck, 2 Johns. Ch. 62. Commented on, Trust and Trustee, mixture of goods, rights of *cestui que trust*, 9 Cal. 660, 661. Cited, Mortgage, legal effect and operation of title does not pass till foreclosure and sale, 27 Cal. 270.

Hart v. Wright, 17 Wend. 267. Cited, Warranty, implied on sale of goods to arrive, 5 Cal. 473.

Hartley v. Cummings, 5 Com. B. 247. Cited, Contracts, in partial restraint of trade, valid, 36 Cal. 358.

Hartley v. Hooker, Cowp. 524. Cited, Certiorari, when writ lies, 1 Cal. 156.

Hartman v. Burlingame, 9 Cal. 557. Cited, Surety, when not discharged by failure to sue, 24 Cal. 165; right of surety to pay and proceed against debtor, 26 Cal. 543.

Hartness v. Thompson, 5 John. 160. Commented on, Judgment, several judgment on joint obligation, 1 Cal. 169.

Hartwell v. Kingsley, 2 Code Rep. 101; S. C. 2 Sand. 674. Cited, Injunction, practice on motion to dissolve, 35 Cal. 59.

Hartwright v. Badham, 11 Price, 383. Cited, New Trial, for surprise, what must be shown, 29 Cal. 607.

Harvey v. Alexander, 1 Rand. 219. Cited, Consideration, in written instrument may be explained by parol, 6 Cal. 137.

Harvey v. Clayton, 2 Swanst. 221, note *a*. Commented on, Witness, privileged communications, 29 Cal. 62, 66.

Harvey v. East India Co., 2 Vern. 395. Commented on, Corporation, actions against, 15 Cal. 585.

Harvey v. Jacob, 1 Barn. & Ald. 159. Cited, Felony, disabilities arising under conviction, 35 Cal. 398.

Harvey v. Rickett, 15 John. 87. Cited, Verdict, validity of chance verdicts, 25 Cal. 400.

Harvey v. Thomas, 10 Watts, 63. Commented on, Constitutionality of Statute, power of legislature to exercise right of eminent domain, 7 Cal. 22. Cited, 32 Cal. 255; 34 Ala. 329; 4 Mich. 250. Doubted, 25 Iowa, 549.

Harwood v. Kirby, 1 Paige, 469. Commented on, Partition, proper parties in action, 35 Cal. 593. Cited, 38 N. H. 134.

Hasbrook v. Paddock, 1 Barb. 635. Cited, Contract, extrinsic evidence to explain, 12 Cal. 162.

Hasoall v. Madison University, 1 Code Rep. N. S. 170. Cited, Injunction, practice on motion for dissolution, 35 Cal. 60.

Haseltine v. Guild, 11 N. H. 390. Cited, Consideration, sufficiency of, for express promise, 13 Cal. 334.

Haskell v. Bartlett, 34 Cal. 281. Approved, Street Assessments, do not draw interest, 34 Cal. 247.

Haskell v. Cornish, 13 Cal. 45. Approved, Principal and Agent, note signed by agent binding on principal, 21 Cal. 47. Cited, 29 Cal. 571; 32 Cal. 654; 2 Nev. 223. Approved, Pleading, immaterial variance, 28 Cal. 265.

Haskell v. Manlove, 14 Cal. 54. Cited as inapplicable, Redemption, 18 Iowa, 544.

Haskins v. People, 16 N. Y. 344. Cited, Indictment, sufficiency of, in larceny, 40 Cal. 654.

Haslewood v. Pope, 3 P. Wms. 324. Cited, Will, construction of devise, 31 Cal. 603.

Hassie v. G. I. W. U. Congregation, 35 Cal. 378. Cited, Attachment, equitable demands not subject to garnishment, 38 Cal. 520.

Hastelow v. Jackson, 8 Barn. & C. 221. Cited, Wagers, money in hands of stakeholder, when recoverable, 37 Cal. 673.

Hastings v. Halleck, 10 Cal. 31. Cited, Appeal, dismissal for neglect to file undertaking in time, 19 Cal. 82; service of notice to be made after or at time of filing, 24 Cal. 229; 26 Cal. 263; 29 Cal. 463.

Hastings v. Halleck, 13 Cal. 203. Cited, Separate Appeals, practice, 25 Cal. 168.

Hastings v. Lovering, 2 Pick. 214. Cited, Warranty, defense of breach of, in action on contract, 4 Cal. 21. Reviewed, 13 Ind. 190.

Hastings v. McGoogin, 27 Cal. 84. Approved, Preëmption, right of, on Suscol Rancho, 27 Cal. 487; 28 Cal. 609; 30 Cal. 650; 37 Cal. 490, 491, 502. Affirmed on principle of *stare decisis,* Id. 503.

Hatch v. Cobb, 4 Johns. Ch. 559. Cited, Fixtures, deed of mortgage or bargain and sale passes fixtures, 14 Cal. 73.

Hatch v. Straight, 3 Conn. 31. Cited, Married Woman, conveyance to, when a gift, 30 Cal. 64.

Hatch v. Vermont Cent. R.R. Co., 25 Vt. 49. Cited, Eminent Domain, measure of compensation for condemnation, 31 Cal. 373.

Hatcher v. Rocheleau, 18 N. Y. 86. Commented on, Name, identity of name as evidence of identity of person, 28 Cal. 222.

Hathaway v. Davis, 33 Cal. 161. Cited, Attachment, when may issue, 38 Cal. 215; Judgment, conclusive upon sureties on attachment bond, 38 Cal. 601.

Hathaway v. De Soto, 21 Cal. 192. Cited, Partition, necessary parties to action, 36 Cal. 116.

Hathaway v. Power, 6 Hill, 453. Commented on, Deed, construction of description in, 12 Cal. 165.

Hatton v. Robinson, 14 Pick. 416. Cited, Witness, privileged communications, practice, 23 Cal. 334.

Haven v. Foley, 18 Mo. 136. Cited, Debtor and Creditor, rights of creditor to property in hands of sureties, 35 Cal. 145.

Haven v. Foster, 14 Pick. 534. Cited, Will, codicil, effect of, 18 Cal. 302.

Haven v. N. H. Insane Asylum, 13 N. H. 532. Cited, Municipal Corporations, ordinances as part of contract, 7 Cal. 474.

Haven v. Snow, 14 Pick. 28. Cited, Amendment of officers' returns, 23 Cal. 81.

Havens v. Dale, 18 Cal. 359. Cited, Mexican Grants, conveyance of, 11 Wall. 576. Commented on, validity of, 26 Cal. 470.

Havens v. Dale, 30 Cal. 547. Approved, Costs, in ejectment, follow the judgment even though but for part of premises, 37 Cal. 207.

Haviland v. Bloom, 6 Johns. Ch. 178. Cited, Alimony, without divorce, 38 Cal. 278. Commented on, 9 Humph. 149.

Haviland v. Chace, 39 Barb. 283. Approved, Railroad Companies, payment of percentage on stock subscription essential to validate act of incorporation, 42 Cal. 209.

Haviland v. Myers, 6 Johns. Ch. 25. Cited, Alimony, without divorce, 38 Cal. 278.

Hawk v. Senseman, 6 Serg. & R. 21. Cited, Adverse Possession, what necessary to constitute, 32 Cal. 21.

Hawken v. Bourne, 8 Mees. & W. 703. Cited, Mining Partnership, liability on contract made by agent, 23 Cal. 205.

Hawkins v. Borland, 14 Cal. 413. Cited, Pleading, what may be shown on denial of indebtedness, 7 Nev. 390.

Hawkins v. Colclough, 1 Burr. 277. S. C. 1 Bac. Abr. 141. Cited, Arbitration, effect of omissions in award, 12 Cal. 342.

Hawkins v. Governor, 1 Ark. 570. Cited, Government, departments of, independent of each other, 39 Cal. 223.

Hawkins v. Hoffman, 6 Hill, 586. Cited and distinguished as to Innkeepers, Bailment, liability of bailee, 33 Cal. 604.

Hawkins v. Reichert, 28 Cal. 534. Approved, Ejectment, to be brought only against the party in possession, 32 Cal. 491; 41 Cal. 53; Appeal, error in granting or refusing a new trial must affirmatively appear, 33 Cal. 525.

Hawkins' Devisees v. Arthur, 2 Bay, 195. Cited, Grants, validity of, ownership and use of property may be distinct, 15 Cal. 548.

Hawley v. Bader, 15 Cal. 44. Approved, Evidence, receipt as, may be explained or contradicted by parol, 23 Cal. 274.

Hawley v. Brown, 1 Root, 494. Cited, Will, competency of witness to, 1 Cal. 506.

Hawley v. Brumagim, 33 Cal. 394. Cited, Corporate Stock, identity of value of shares of stock, 42 Cal. 100.

Hawley v. Cramer, 4 Cow. 717. Cited, Equity, what sufficient notice in equity, 36 Cal. 437; purchaser when chargeable with notice, Id. 2 Black, 390.

Hawley v. Foote, 19 Wend. 516. Cited, Pleading, insufficient defense in action on note, 36 Cal. 301

Hawley v. James, 16 Wend. 161. Cited, Fraud, in part of a contract, vitiates the whole, 8 Cal. 129.

Hawley v. James, 5 Paige, 318. Cited, Powers, discretionary, cannot be delegated by assignment to a stranger, 39 Cal. 290.

Hawtayne v. Bourne, 7 Mees. & W. 595. Commented on, Mining Partnerships, bound by contract of agent, 23 Cal. 205.

Hay v. Cohoes Co., 3 Barb. 42. Cited, Respondeat Superior, what must be shown in case of act or omission of servant, 38 Cal. 634.

Hayden v. Dunlap, 3 Bibb, 216. Cited, Execution, provisions of statute as to levy and notice of sale, directory, remedy for neglect, 6 Cal. 50; 22 Cal. 590; 38 Cal. 654.

Hayden v. Middlesex T. Co., 10 Mass. 397. Cited, Corporations, liability on implied contracts, 9 Cal. 471.

Hayden v. Smithville Manf. Co., 29 Conn. 548. Cited, Employer and Employé, liability of employer for injury to employé, 31 Cal. 380.

Hayden v. Westcott, 11 Conn. 129. Cited, Acknowledgment, act of notary in taking, defined, 11 Cal. 298.

Haydon v. Williams, 7 Bing. 163. Commented on, New Promise, to avoid statute of limitations, 9 Cal. 91.

Hayes v. Bona, 7 Cal. 153. Approved, Contracts, for sale of land, under civil law, must be in writing, 10 Cal. 17; sufficiency of, to pass title, 12 Cal. 166. Commented on, 26 Cal. 469, 470; 11 Wall. 576.

Hayes v. Josephi, 26 Cal. 535. Approved, Sureties, discharge of, by tender of debt, and refusal to accept, 29 Cal. 198; 34 Cal. 36. Cited as to tender of mortgage debt after law day, but question not decided, 32 Cal. 171; 37 Cal. 226.

Hayes v. Ward, 4 Johns. Ch. 123. Cited, Surety, discharge of, by neglect of creditor, 26 Cal. 542; 29 Cal. 198. Distinguished, 1 Watts, 288.

Hayne v. Maltby, 3 Term Rep. 441. Cited, Estoppel, tenant when not estopped, 33 Cal. 245.

Haynes v. Calderwood, 23 Cal. 409. Cited, Lis Pendens, effect of filing on subsequent purchasers, 34 Cal. 615.

Haynes v. Covington, 9 Smedes & M. 470. Cited, Surety, when discharged by agreement for delay, 10 Cal. 426.

Haynes v. Meeks, 10 Cal. 110; S. C. 20 Cal. 288. Commented on, on second appeal, 20 Cal. 311; law of case conclusive, Id. 310. Cited, Probate Court, jurisdiction previous to act of 1858; limited and inferior, 19 Cal. 205; Probate Procedure, appointment of new administrator cannot be made while former is in office, 34 Cal. 468; executor's sale of personal property of estate on insufficient note is invalid, 17 Cal. 344; court cannot confirm invalid sale, 33 Cal. 54. Commented on and distinguished, Sale of property of decedent, 20 Cal. 623. Cited, Order of Sale, on sufficient notice, conclusive, 22 Cal. 276.

Hays v. Bickerstaffe, 2 Mod. 35; S. C. Vaughan, 118. Commented on, Covenant in Case, construction of, 30 Cal. 627.

Hays v. Hogan, 5 Cal. 241. Cited, Taxes, paid under protest and not justly due, may be recovered back, 16 Cal. 170; 23 Cal. 113. Commented on, Compulsory Payments, Deady, 232.

Hays v. May's Heirs, 1 J. J. Marsh, 498. Cited, Decree, in action for partnership accounting, 9 Cal. 635.

Hays v. P. M. S. S. Co., 17 How. 596. Cited, Constitutional Construction, power to regulate commercial intercourse, 34 Cal. 498.

Hays v. People, 1 Hill, 351. Cited, Assault, what constitutes, 8 Cal. 548. Commented on, 12 Ohio St. 471.

Hays v. Riddle, 1 Sand. 249. Commented on and distinguished, Securities, pledged for debt, may be specifically recovered, 3 Cal. 165.

Hays v. Risher, 32 Penn. St. 169. Cited, Constitutionality of Statute, for opening roads, 32 Cal. 255.

Hays v. Stone, 7 Hill, 128. Cited, Debt, effect of payment by note, 12 Cal. 323.

Hayward v. Dimsdale, 17 Ves. Jr. 111. Cited, Cloud on Title, when equity will remove, 10 Cal. 576.

Hayward v. Young, 2 Chit. 407. Cited, Contracts in partial restraint of trade, 36 Cal. 358.

Hazard v. Hazard, 1 Story, 371. Cited, Partnership, what necessary to constitute, 38 Cal. 213.

Hazard v. Martin, 2 Vt. 77. Commented on, Estates of Deceased Persons, validity of administration sales, 22 Cal. 70; 26 Vt. 590, 591.

Hazeltine v. Larco, 7 Cal. 32. Cited, Guaranty, by indorsement at time of execution of instrument valid, 16 Cal. 153; 27 Cal. 83; 34 Cal. 675; 38 Cal. 135. Commented on and approved, Id. 136.

Hazelton v. Allen, 3 Allen, 114. Cited, Insolvency, of trader, when it ensues, 33 Cal. 625.

Head v. Fordyce, 17 Cal. 149. Cited, Lis Pendens, statute not to affect doctrine of actual notice, 22 Cal. 211. Approved, Quieting Title, when action lies, 28 Cal. 204; 31 Cal. 287. Cited, 34 Cal. 389; as to mining claim, 35 Cal. 34.

Head v. Providence Ins. Co., 2 Cranch, 127. Approved, Municipal Corporations, power to make contracts restricted by terms of charter, 1 Cal. 356; 7 Cal. 375; 16 Cal. 619; 20 Cal. 102; 24 Cal. 550; 12 Wheat. 68; Id. 98; 13 Pet. 519; 6 How. 337; 9 How. 172; Id. 184; 21 How. 444.

Headley v. Reed, 2 Cal. 322. Commented on, Reference, review of report of referee, practice, 4 Cal. 125; 9 Cal. 225; 30 Cal. 287. Cited, Debt, receipt for money as evidence, 24 Cal. 327.

Heald v. Cooper, 8 Greenl. 32. Cited, Written Instrument, parol evidence admissible to explain, 11 Cal. 198.

Heard v. Lodge, 20 Pick. 53. Cited, Probate Proceedings, conclusive on sureties on administrator's bond, 25 Cal. 222.

Heath & Roome, Ex parte, 3 Hill, 42. Cited, Statutory Construction, time of performance of official act, directory, 3 Cal. 126; 30 Cal. 527. Commented on, Office, bond and oath of, 7 Cal. 439.

Heath v. Lent, 1 Cal. 410. Overruled, Damages, that counsel fees constitute no part of damages on wrongful suing out of an attachment, 3 Cal. 217, 219.

Heaton v. Angier, 7 N. H. 397. Cited, Statute of Frauds, when agreement to become liable for debt of another not within statute, 22 Cal. 190.

Heaton v. Ferris, 1 John. 146. Cited, Easement, as property, 32 Cal. 506.

Heckscher v. McCrea, 24 Wend. 304. Cited, Contract for Services, measure of damages on breach of, 38 Cal. 666.

Heebner v. Townsend, 8 Abb. Pr. 234. Commented on, Undertaking, on appeal, when action lies on, 38 Cal. 604.

Heffernan v. Addams, 7 Watts, 116. Commented on, Agency, power of attorney construed, 14 Cal. 399.

Hegeler v. Henckell, 27 Cal. 491. Cited, New Trial, right to move waived by failure to file statement in time, 41 Cal. 518.

Heilbron v. Bissell, 1 Bail. Eq. 430. Cited, Debtor and Creditor, application of payments, 14 Cal. 449.

Heinlin v. Castro, 22 Cal. 100. Cited, New Promise, what necessary to avoid statute of limitations, 5 Nev. 215.

Hellen v. Noe, 3 Ired. 493. Cited, Municipal Corporation, validity of city ordinance, 23 Cal. 372.

Helm v. Boone, 6 J. J. Marsh. 351. Cited, Appeal, effect of, 28 Cal. 91.

Helms v. Franciscus, 2 Bland Ch. 544. Cited, Alimony, without divorce, 38 Cal. 278.

Hemming v. Zimmerschitte, 4 Tex. 159. Cited, Vendor and Vendee, statute of limitations does not run against vendee in possession, 40 Cal. 572.

Hemmingway v. Mathews, 10 Tex. 207. Cited, Husband and Wife, property acquired pending marriage belongs to community, 12 Cal. 253; 17 Cal. 581.

Hemp v. Garland, 3 Gale & D. 402; S. C. 45 Eng. C. L; 4 Q. B. 519. Doubted, Debtor and Creditor, waiver of forfeiture by acceptance of interest after default, 38 Cal. 252, 253.

Henderson v. Brown, 1 Caines, 92. Commented on, Supervisors, powers of, in declaring and appointing to fill vacancy in office, 7 Cal. 438.

Henderson v. Eason, 9 Eng. L. & E. 337. Approved, Tenant in Common, right of possession and use of lands, 12 Cal. 420; contra, that he may be sued for an accounting of rents and profits, 16 Gratt. 44.

Henderson v. Grewell, 8 Cal. 581. Cited, Acknowledgment, of deed, sufficiency of, 8 Nev. 318.

Henderson v. Herrod, 10 Smedes & M. 631. Cited, Mortgage, securing several notes, *pro rata* share upon foreclosure, 23 Cal. 30.

Henderson v. Poindexter, 12 Wheat. 530. Cited, Mexican Grants, titles to depend on confirmation, 24 Cal. 663; 26 Cal. 123. Commented on, 24 Cal. 665, 671; 2 Black, 366; 3 How. 761; titles already perfect not contemplated in congressional act, Id. 667.

Hendrick v. Crowley, 31 Cal. 471. Cited, Street Assessments, on coin basis, 32 Cal. 279; a tax on lot owner, 36 Cal. 244, 245; Written Instruments, parol evidence of consideration, 36 Cal. 369.

Hendricks v. Robinson, 2 Johns. Ch. 301. Cited, Insolvency, preference of creditor, payment by debtor of
17

mortgage debt, not fraudulent, 10 Cal. 494; 11 Wheat. 100, note *a*.

Henfree v. Bromley, 6 East, 309.   Cited, Arbitration, effect of alteration in award, 23 Cal. 368.

Henkle v. Royal Exchange Assurance Co., 1 Ves. Sr. 319. Cited, Equity, relieves from mistakes, 19 Cal. 673; 13 How. 64.

Henly v. Hastings, 3 Cal. 341.   Construed, Appeal, from order refusing to set aside former order, 8 Cal. 57.

Hennessy v. Western Bank, 6 Watts & S. 310.   Cited, Partnership, one partner may transfer whole of partnership effects, 13 Cal. 289.

Henriques v. Dutch W. I. Co., 2 Ld. Ray. 1535.   Commented on and distinguished, Arson, proof as to *de facto* corporation, sufficient, 29 Cal. 261.

Henriques v. Hone, 2 Edw. Ch. 120.   Cited, Fraudulent Conveyance, valid between the parties, 13 Cal. 69.

Henry v. Clark, 4 Bibb, 426.   Cited, Forcible Entry, what constitutes, 5 Cal. 159; 16 Cal. 109.

Henry v. Davis, 7 Johns. Ch. 40.   Cited, Mortgage, once a mortgage always a mortgage, 26 Cal. 602.

Henry v. Dubuque & P. R. R. Co., 10 Iowa, 540.   Cited, Constitutional Construction, compensation a condition precedent to, right of condemnation of land, 31 Cal. 560.

Henry v. Everts, 29 Cal. 610; S. C. 30 Cal. 425.   Cited, Appeal, findings to support judgment, implied, 34 Cal. 252; 35 Cal. 87; 38 Cal. 421; 41 Cal. 99; Redemption, right of purchaser to rents and profits pending time for redemption, 38 Cal. 425.

Henry v. Thorpe, 14 Ala. 103.   Cited, Stare Decisis, 15 Cal. 622.

Henshaw v. Sumner, 23 Pick. 446.   Cited, Insolvency, assignment in trust, rights of creditors, 10 Cal. 277.

Hensley v. Tarpey, 7 Cal. 288.   Cited, Evidence, rule as to preliminary evidence of lost or missing instrument, 10 Cal. 147; 12 Cal. 105; 19 Cal. 94.

Hensley v. Tartar, 14 Cal. 508.   Cited, Pleading, sham answer, conjunctive denials, 31 Cal. 195.

Hentsch v. Porter, 10 Cal. 555.   Cited, Pleading, defects cured by default or verdict, 23 Cal. 130.   Approved,

Objections cannot be taken for the first time on appeal, 28 Cal. 568; 42 Cal. 134. Cited, Jurisdiction, of district court, over mortgage claims against estates, 24 Cal. 499.

Hentz v. Long Island R. R. Co., 13 Barb. 647. Cited, Injunction, when not to issue to restrain proceedings to open roads, 23 Cal. 467.

Henwood v. Cheeseman, 3 Serg. & R. 500. Cited, Use and Occupation, action for, when it lies, 35 Cal. 194; 1 How. 159.

Hepburn v. Auld, 5 Cranch, 262. Cited, Specific Performance, when delay will defeat enforcement of contract, 10 Cal. 328; general rule, time not of essence of contract, 40 Cal. 11.

Hepburn v. Dubois, 12 Pet. 345. Cited, Married Woman, conveyance by, when valid, 13 Cal. 498.

Herman v. Sprigg, 3 Mart. N. S. 190; 3 Cons. La. 58. Cited, Contract, usurious contract under civil law, 2 Cal. 570.

Herold v. Smith, 34 Cal. 122. Cited, Pleading, counterclaim in answer need not be denied, 38 Cal. 585.

Herrick v. Borst, 4 Hill, 650. Cited, Surety, on note, not discharged by mere neglect to sue principal, 5 Cal. 176; 9 Cal. 562; 24 Cal. 164. Criticised, 25 N. Y. 556.

Herrick v. Whitney, 15 John. 240. Cited, Certificates of deposit, indorsement, effect of, as a warranty, 22 Cal. 249.

Herries v. Jamieson, 5 Term Rep. 557. Cited, Pleading, pleas in abatement not favored, 14 Cal. 42.

Herrin v. Libbey, 36 Me. 350. Commented on, Fraud, right to rescission of contract fraudulently obtained, 29 Cal. 592.

Herring v. Levy, 4 Mart. N. S. 383. Cited, Insolvency, when discharge not a bar to promissory note, 7 Cal. 430.

Herring v. Sanger, 3 Johns. Cas. 71, 533. Cited, Debt, effect of payment by note, 12 Cal. 322.

Herring v. Wilmington & R. R. R. Co., 10 Ired. 402. Commented on, Railroads, liability for injuries caused by negligence, 14 Cal. 389.

Herriter v. Porter, 23 Cal. 385. Cited, Assignment, of part of entire demand, when void, 38 Cal. 519.

Hersey v. Veazie, 24 Me. 9. Cited, Fraud, equitable relief from, 28 Cal. 484.

Hervey v. Hervey, 2 W. Black. 877. Cited, Marriage, proof of, 26 Cal. 133; 31 Miss. 418.

Heslep v. Sacramento, 2 Cal. 580. Cited, Bounty, not a binding contract, 24 Wis. 208.

Heslep v. San Francisco, 4 Cal. 1. Overruled, Arbitration, entry of judgment on award, 14 Cal. 395.

Hess v. Werts, 4 Serg. & R. 356. Cited, Benevolent Association, a partnership, 14 Cal. 536.

Hess v. Winder, 30 Cal. 349. Referred to, S. C., Mining Claims, 34 Cal. 272.

Hess v. Winder, 30 Cal. 349. Cited, Mining Claim, enclosure of, not necessary, 7 Nev. 220.

Heston v. Martin, 11 Cal. 41. Cited, Mechanic's Lien, sufficiency of description in notice, 29 Cal. 287.

Hestres v. Brannan, 21 Cal. 423. Cited, Land, proof of actual possession, sufficiency of inclosure, 32 Cal. 20, 22.

Hestres v. Clements, 21 Cal. 425. Distinguished, Trial, order of trial of issues, 23 Cal. 336.

Hewes v. Reis, 40 Cal. 255. Approved, Street Assessment, certificate of superintendent as to "unknown" owner conclusive, 40 Cal. 518; right of appeal, not a remedy for illegal acts of supervisors, 40 Cal. 526.

Hewes v. Wiswell, 8 Greenl. 98. Cited, Conveyance, what possession is notice of unrecorded deed, 31 Cal. 185. Reviewed, 51 Me. 531, 532.

Hewins v. Smith, 11 Met. 241. Cited, Dedication of public highway, what constitutes, 14 Cal. 647.

Hewlett v. Chamberlayne, 1 Wash. Va. 367. Commented on, Undertaking, validity of, 13 Cal. 557.

Hewlett v. Cruchley, 5 Taunt. 277. Commented on, Malicious Prosecution, 8 Cal. 225.

Hewson v. Deygert, 8 John. 333. Doubted, Foreclosure, lien of purchaser at sheriff's sale, 9 Cal. 414. Overruled, 1 Hill, 643.

Heyde v. Heyde, 4 Sand. 692. Cited, Divorce, essential averments in complaint on ground of adultery, 10 Cal. 254.

Heydon's Case, 3 Coke, 7.　Cited, Conversion, damages in, 34 Cal. 606.

Heydenfeldt v. Hitchcock, 15 Cal. 514.　Commented on, San Francisco, validity of deed of Commissioners of Sinking Fund, 19 Cal. 21.　Approved, Commissioners of Sinking Fund had no power to sell city property, 31 Cal. 39; 32 Cal. 449.

Heyer v. Burger, Hoff. Ch. 1.　Cited, Husband and Wife, deed of separation, reconciliation to avoid, 9 Cal. 498.

Heyfron, Ex parte, 7 How. Miss. 127.　Cited, Attorney and Counsel, attorney entitled to notice of charges preferred, 1 Cal. 150.

Heyman v. Landers, 12 Cal. 107.　Approved, Damages, legal interest the extent of damages for detaining money under process, 28 Cal. 543.

Heyneman v. Blake.　See People v. Blake.

Heyneman v. Dannenberg, 6 Cal. 376.　Approved, Insolvency, may be proved without issuance of execution and return of *nulla bona*, 8 Cal. 403; lien of attachment sufficient to file creditor's bill without judgment and execution, 13 Cal. 78.　Referred to, Id. 634; material allegations in bill to restrain proceedings on execution against insolvent, 21 Cal. 287; 23 Cal. 78.

Heywood v. Perrin, 10 Pick. 228.　Commented on, Written Instrument, parol evidence admissible to explain, 23 Cal. 343.

Hibberd v. Smith, 39 Cal. 145.　Cited, Appeal, review of order sustaining demurrer, 1 Saw. 559, 560.

Hickley v. Farmers' and Mechanics' Bank, 5 Gill & J. 377.　Statutes distinguished, Insolvency, assignment of debtor, 3 Cal. 472.　Reviewed, 7 Gill & J. 175.

Hickman v. Alpaugh, 21 Cal. 225.　Cited, Presumption, as to foreign laws, 32 Cal. 60.

Hickman v. Dale, 7 Yerg. 149.　Cited, Ejectment, judgment conclusive on tenants coming in pending suit, 22 Cal. 206; 9 How. 49.

Hickman v. O'Neal, 10 Cal. 292.　Approved, Constitutionality of Statute, creating superior court of San Francisco, affirmed on principle of *stare decisis*, 14 Cal. 158; 30 Cal. 579; 36 Cal. 696; 39 Cal. 519; Injunction, will issue to restrain sale under execution of property for debt of another party, 15 Cal. 133. Referred to, 20 Cal. 640.

Hickox v. Lowe, 10 Cal. 197. Distinguished, Mortgage, deed and contract for re-conveyance, when not a mortgage, 14 Cal. 436. Cited, When the bar of the statute to the debt does not affect remedy of foreclosure, 22 Cal. 626; Resulting Trust, how created, 27 Cal. 142.

Hicks v. Bell, 3 Cal. 219. Explained, State Sovereignty, proprietorship in mines of gold and silver, 5 Cal. 39; 7 Cal. 324; 14 Cal. 305; Id. 373, 376. Overruled, 17 Cal. 217; 24 Cal. 257. Approved, Mines and Mining, right of entry on mine, 5 Cal. 145; 6 Cal. 557.

Hicks v. Coleman, 25 Cal. 122. Cited, Lands, constructive possession under deed, 28 Cal. 191; 30 Cal. 358; 38 Cal. 428; 40 Cal. 308. Commented on, 30 Cal. 639. Doctrine explained, 38 Cal. 487. Rule limited, 38 Cal. 676. Modified, 39 Cal. 280. Approved, Prior possession under color of title, 32 Cal. 631, 632. Instanced, Deed, description in, 30 Cal. 542. Cited, by reference to other instrument, 36 Cal. 651. Distinguished, Calls in deed, 32 Cal. 226. Cited, Evidence, secondary, of lost deed, practice, 26 Cal. 413; 38 Cal. 449; Referred to, Nonsuit, when improperly granted, 31 Cal. 420.

Hicks v. Compton, 18 Cal. 206. Followed, Injunction, trespass upon lands, 18 Cal. 210. Cited, Question of insolvency important, 23 Cal. 85.

Hicks v. Davis, 4 Cal. 67. Approved, Title, possession, *prima facie* evidence of, 23 Cal. 537. Commented on, McAll. 232.

Hicks v. Herring, 17 Cal. 566. Approved, Forcible Entry and Detainer, damages for waste may be recovered in a separate action, 38 Cal. 622.

Hicks v. Hinde, 9 Barb. 528. Reviewed and approved, Negotiable Instruments, indorsement on, by party as agent, etc., 7 Cal. 541.

Hicks v. Michael, 15 Cal. 107. Cited, Injunction, to restrain waste, when may issue, 32 Cal. 594; discretion of court in granting or dissolving, 39 Cal. 167.

Hicks v. Whitesides, 18 Cal. 700; S. C. 23 Cal. 404; 35 Cal. 152. Referred to on third appeal, Ejectment, 35 Cal. 152. Approved, Possessory Action, strict compliance with statute requisite, 42 Cal. 656.

Hicks v. Whitmore, 12 Wend. 548. Approved, Statute of Frauds, requisites of memorandum to bind vendor, 1 Cal. 416.

Hidden v. Jordan, 21 Cal. 92; S. C. 28 Cal. 301; 32 Cal. 397. Approved, Findings, manner of finding facts, 28 Cal. 588; 30 Cal. 229; 38 Cal. 577; supplying defects and omissions, 30 Cal. 408; 38 Cal. 531; proceedings to correct findings, 38 Cal. 536; findings necessary to sustain judgment presumed, 31 Cal. 213; 42 Cal. 617; Trust and Trustee, resulting trust, when it arises, 22 Cal. 578; Id. 593; 38 Cal. 193; parol evidence admissible to establish, 22 Cal. 579; enforcement of parol trust, 42 Cal. 568; 8 Nev. 97. Cited, Statute of Frauds, will not afford protection to fraud, 35 Cal. 488, 489; Appeal, presumption that record contains all the evidence pertinent, 34 Cal. 511; 35 Cal. 403.

Hiern v. Mill, 13 Ves. Jr. 118. Cited, Conveyance, possession as notice of title, 36 Cal. 272; 10 How. 375.

Higbee v. Rice, 5 Mass. 344. Cited, Deed, effect of entry under recorded deed, 25 Cal. 135.

Higdon's Heirs v. Higdon's Devisees, 6 J. J. Marsh. 52. Cited, Witness, competency of, interest, 6 Cal. 195.

Higginbotham v. Higginbotham, 10 B. Mon. 371. Cited, Principal and Agent, possession of agent is possession of principal, 20 Cal. 48.

Higgins v. Bear Riv. and Auburn W. & M. Co., 27 Cal. 153. Cited, Constitutionality of Statute, legal tender act constitutional, 38 Cal. 254. Doubted, Distinction made as to contracts before passage of legal tender act, Id. 255.

Higgins v. Butcher, Yelv. 89. Cited, Action, civil action for death of person, exclusively statutory, 25 Cal. 435.

Higgins v. Houghton, 25 Cal. 252. Cited, Taxation, lands held under floating grant are taxable, 33 Cal. 154.

Higgins v. Johnson, 20 Tex. 389. Commented on, Husband and Wife, deed of gift to wife, 30 Cal. 50. Cited, 31 Cal. 447.

Higgins v. Rockwell, 2 Duer, 650. Cited, Pleading, defective allegations, cured by verdict, 10 Cal. 560.

Higgins v. Senior, 8 Mees. & W. 834. Cited, Principal and Agent, interest of principal may be shown by extrinsic evidence, 1 Cal. 482. Dictum denied, 2 Nev. 218.

Higgins v. Wortell, 18 Cal. 330.   Cited, Pleadings, common counts sufficient, 32 Cal. 175; insufficient denial equivalent to an admission, 21 Cal. 218; 22 Cal. 168; 38 Cal. 290.

High v. Batte, 10 Yerg. 186.   Cited, Vendor's Lien, enforcement of, 15 Cal. 193.

High v. Shoemaker, 22 Cal. 363.   Overruled, Taxation, statutes exempting private property unconstitutional, 34 Cal. 449, 458.

Hight v. United States, 1 Morris, 410.   Approved, Indictment, no presumption of guilt, 19 Cal. 543.

Hihn v. Peck, 30 Cal. 280.   Cited, Appeal, findings of referee will not be reviewed except on order denying new trial, 30 Cal. 21; Execution Sale, proof of order of sale, recitals in sheriff's deed as evidence, 30 Cal. 370; purchaser must produce judgment, 31 Cal. 221; 4 Nev. 152; Sheriff's Deed, conclusive on parties to execution, 38 Cal. 658; Evidence, parol evidence of written instrument when not admissible, 31 Cal. 476.   Approved, Objections to deed as evidence, when to be taken, 30 Cal. 64.   Cited, 35 Cal. 598.

Hildebrand v. Fogle, 20 Ohio, 147.   Cited, Written Instrument, extrinsic evidence to explain, admissible, 12 Cal. 162.

Hildreth v. Sands, 2 Johns. Ch. 35.   Cited, Sheriff's Sale, purchaser at, rights of, 29 Cal. 57.

Hildreth's Heirs v. McIntire's Devisee, 1 J. J. Marsh. 206. Cited, Office, title to, cannot be collaterally attacked, 29 Cal. 485.

Hill v. Bellows, 15 Vt. 727.   Cited as to local statute of limitations, 6 Cal. 433.

Hill v. Bostick, 10 Yerg. 410.   Criticised, Surety on Note, discharge of, 10 Cal. 427.

Hill v. Covell, 1 N. Y. 522.   Cited, Findings, special verdict, facts to be found distinct from legal conclusions, 19 Cal. 105.

Hill v. Draper, 10 Barb. 454.   Cited, Ejectment, sufficiency of title to maintain, 21 Cal. 305; presumption of title from possession, 28 Cal. 333.

Hill v. Grigsby, 32 Cal. 55.   Denied, Attachment, vendor's lien not a bar to remedy by attachment, 35 Cal. 202, 208.

Hill v. Grigsby, 35 Cal. 656. Cited, Contract, for sale of land, payment by instalments, independent promises, 38 Cal. 200.

Hill v. Higdon, 5 Ohio St. 243. Cited, Street Assessments, power of legislature to direct, 28 Cal. 352. Approved, Validity of statutes, 28 Cal. 365, 369; 31 Cal. 684.

Hill v. Hobart, 16 Me. 164. Cited, Vendor and Vendee, preparation and tender of deed, 25 Cal. 279. Commented on, Trial, reasonable time for performance of contract when a question of law, 30 Cal. 558.

Hill v. Keyes, 10 Allen, 258. Cited, Insolvency, when assignment takes effect, 39 Cal. 144.

Hill v. King, 8 Cal. 336. Qualified on rehearing, Water Rights, rights of first appropriator, Id. 339. Cited, 23 Cal. 488.

Hill v. Manchester and S. W. W. Co., 5 Barn. & A. 874. Cited, Corporation, validity of written instrument of, 37 Cal. 598.

Hill v. Packard, 5 Wend. 375. Cited, Judicial Notice, taken of political subdivisions, 16 Cal. 231.

Hill v. Payson, 3 Mass. 559. Cited, Mortgage, tender and refusal after law day not a discharge, 14 Cal. 529.

Hill v. Smith, 27 Cal. 476. Cited, Nuisance, concurrent jurisdiction of district and county courts, 30 Cal. 585.

Hill v. Southerland's Exrs., 1 Wash. 128. Cited, Debtor and Creditor, application of payments, 14 Cal. 449.

Hill v. Warren, 2 Stark. 377. Cited, Negligence, action for injuries from, when maintainable, 37 Cal. 422.

Hill v. White, 2 Cal. 306. Construed, Appeal, errors of law will be reviewed without a motion for new trial, 7 Cal. 399. Cited, Order denying new trial when no statement is on file is erroneous, 10 Cal. 66.

Hillary v. Waller, 12 Ves. Jr. 239. Cited, Title, rule of determination as to validity of, 25 Cal. 80.

Hilliard v. Cox, 1 Salk. 37; S. C. 1 Ld. Ray. 562. Cited, Contracts, *situs* of, 12 Cal. 190.

Hilliard v. Connelly, 7 Geo. 172. Cited, Ejectment, complaint in, 26 Cal. 507.

Hills v. Bannister, 8 Cow. 32. Cited, Principal and Agent, note signed by agent when binding on principal, 7 Cal. 541; contra, 20 Vt. 49; 19 N. Y. 316.

Hilton v. Burley, 2 N. H. 193. Cited, Debtor and Creditor, application of payments, 14 Cal. 449. Disapproved so far as relates to illegal charges, 14 N. H. 449.

Hilton v. Granville, 1 Craig & P. 283. Cited, Injunction, when will be granted, 23 Cal. 84; 9 How. 29.

Himely v. Rose, 5 Cranch, 313. Cited, Appeal, law of the case, not revisable, 15 Cal. 83; 3 How. 424.

Himmelmann v. Cofran, 36 Cal. 411. Cited, Street Assessment, duty of superintendent to authenticate record, 38 Cal. 75.

Himmelmann v. Danos, 35 Cal. 441. Commented on, Street Assessments, superintendent to authenticate record, 35 Cal. 521, 522.

Himmelmann v. Oliver, 34 Cal. 246. Cited, Judgment, for street assessment, bears interest from its rendition, 38 Cal. 549.

Himmelmann v. Reay, No. 1666, Cal. Sup. Ct. July T. 1869 (not reported.) Referred to, S. C. 38 Cal. 164.

Himmelmann v. Steiner, 38 Cal. 175. Cited, Street Assessment, validity as to "unknown" owner, 40 Cal. 261; owners not parties to the contract, 39 Cal. 392. Referred to and followed, Judgment upon stipulation, practice, 40 Cal. 126.

Himmelmann v. Sullivan, 40 Cal. 125. Followed, Street Assessment, judgment upon stipulation, practice, Himmelmann v. Goetjen, No. 2377; Himmelman v. King, No. 2378; Himmelman v. Johnson, No. 2379, Cal. Sup. Ct. Oct. T. 1870 (not reported.)

Hinde v. Gray, 1 Man. & G. 195. Cited, Contracts, in total restraint of trade, void, 36 Cal. 358.

Hinde's Lessee v. Longworth, 11 Wheat. 199. Cited, Deed, extrinsic evidence of consideration in, 6 Cal. 137.

Hine, The, v. Trevor, 4 Wall. 555. Cited, Admiralty jurisdiction, when it attaches, 34 Cal. 680. Approved, Grant of jurisdiction to federal courts exclusive, 42 Cal. 473; 46 Ill. 514. Construed, 22 Wis. 531.

Hinkle v. Commonwealth, 4 Dana, 518. Cited, Indictment, several distinct offenses constituting one crime, 27 Cal. 401.

Hinman v. Borden, 10 Wend. 367. Cited, Sheriff, held to reasonable diligence in execution of process, 13 Cal. 339.

Hipwell v. Knight, 1 Younge & C. 415. Cited, Contract, time when not of essence of, 10 Cal. 329.

Hitchcock v. Harrington, 6 John. 290. Cited, Mortgage, mortgagee holds but a chattel interest, 36 Cal. 41; mortgage a mere lien, Id. 58.

Hitchcock v. Sawyer, 39 Vt. 412. Cited, Revenue Stamp, no part of instrument, 34 Cal. 175.

Hitchcock v. Way, 6 Adol. & E. 943. Cited, Statutory Construction, statutes not to be construed retrospectively, 4 Cal. 135.

Hitchin v. Campbell, 2 W. Black, 827. Cited, Pleading, averment of matter in estoppel, 26 Cal. 505.

Hit-tuk-ho-mi v. Watts, 7 Smedes & M. 363. Cited, Patent, to land reserved from sale is void, 23 Cal. 443.

Hoag v. Pierce, 28 Cal. 187. Cited, Forcible Entry and Detainer, title deeds as evidence in action, 28 Cal. 532; constructive possession under deed, 38 Cal. 487.

Hoagland v. Culvert, 1 Spenc. 387. Cited, Municipal Officers, legal presumptions favor their authority, 3 Cal. 453.

Hoare v. Graham, 3 Camp. 57. Cited, Contract, parol evidence not admissible to vary terms of promissory note, 23 Cal. 257; 6 Pet. 57.

Hoare v. Peck, 6 Sim. 51. Cited, Pleading, exception to statute of limitations to be specially set out in complaint, 9 Cal. 425.

Hobart v. Abbot, 2 P. Wms. 643. Cited, Foreclosure, necessary parties in action, 10 Cal. 552.

Hobart v. Butte County, 17 Cal. 23. Approved, Constitutionality of Statute, legislative power to enact, no farther controlled than by the restrictions of the constitution, 22 Cal. 308; 26 Cal. 229; 41 Cal. 160; Id. 186. Cited, it may make local law depend for its effect upon the vote of electors, 22 Cal. 387; 392; 7 Nev. 30; 7 Kan. 506.

Hobbit v. London & N. W. Railway Co., 4 Exc. 254. Commented on, Respondeat Superior, doctrine does not apply as to owner and sub-contractor, 8 Cal. 491.

Hobbs v. Lowell, 19 Pick. 406. Cited, Dedication, to public use, assent how proved, 14 Cal. 649.

Hobbs v. Middleton, 1 J. J. Marsh. 177.　Cited, Surety on Administration Bond, concluded by judgment against principal, 25 Cal. 223.

Hookstacker v. Levy, 11 Cal. 76, following Uhlfelder *v.* Levy, 9 Cal. 607.　Cited, Injunction, court cannot enjoin proceedings of other court of coördinate jurisdiction, 37 Cal. 269.

Hodges v. Buffalo, 2 Den. 110.　Cited, Corporations, powers of, limited by charter, 1 Cal. 356.　Doubted, liability of, on contract *ultra vires,* 16 Cal. 270.

Hodges v. New England Screw Co., 1 R. I. 312.　Commented on, Corporation, may sell its property, 37 Cal. 593.

Hodges v. Tennessee M. & F. Ins. Co., 8 N. Y. 416.　Approved, Deed as a Mortgage, parol evidence admissible to prove, 8 Cal. 430, 435; 13 Cal. 129; 36 Cal. 44, 46; 32 Ill. 105.

Hodges v. King, 7 Met. 583.　Cited, Contract, stipulated damages in, 6 Cal. 263.

Hodgkins v. Jordan, 29 Cal. 577.　Cited, Nonsuit, when may be ordered, 38 Cal. 697.

Hodgman v. Western R. R., 7 How. Pr. 492.　Cited, Assignment, cause of action for tort, not assignable, 22 Cal. 177.

Hodgson v. Ambrose, 1 Doug. 341.　Commented on, Stare Decisis, as a rule of property, 15 Cal. 621; Will, construction of, intent of testator, 27 Cal. 445.

Hodgson v. Bowerbank, 5 Cranch, 303.　Cited, Jurisdiction, when founded on citizenship, in federal courts, 22 Cal. 85.

Hodgson v. Dexter, 1 Cranch, 345.　Cited, Lease, construction of covenants in, 15 Cal. 457; Officers, official liability on contracts, 1 Cal. 392.

Hoen v. Simmons, 1 Cal. 119.　Approved, Contract, for sale of land, when not in writing is invalid, 1 Cal. 210; but reviewed and distinguished, when accompanied with delivery of possession, under Mexican law, Id. 211; 7 Cal. 158; 7 Cal. 490.　Cited, Transfer of land under Mexican law, 14 Cal. 608; Estoppel, by entry under another in subordination, 7 Cal. 416; 8 Cal. 402.

Hoffman v. Brown, 1 Halst. 429.　Cited, Covenant, not to sue, no bar to action, 5 Cal. 502.

Hoffman v. Carow, 22 Wend. 285. Cited, Auctioneer, liable in conversion, for sale of stolen property, 1 Cal. 434. Denied, 2 Cal. 572; presumptions as to foreign laws, 21 Cal. 227.

Hoffman v. Coombs, 9 Gill, 284. Cited, Surety on note, when discharged by agreement for delay, 10 Cal. 426.

Hoffman v. Livingston, 1 Johns. Ch. 211. Cited, Injunction, dissolved on denial of all equities, 9 Cal. 553; practice on motion to dissolve on bill and answer alone, 35 Cal. 60.

Hoffman v. Noble, 6 Met. 68. Cited, Factor cannot pledge, pledgee held to knowledge of factor's powers, 19 Cal. 72.

Hoffman v. State, 20 Md. 425. Cited, Criminal Procedure, when discharge of jury operates as an acquittal, 41 Cal. 216.

Hoffman v. Stone, 7 Cal. 46. Commented on, Water Rights, action for diversion of water appropriated, 7 Cal. 325; 11 Cal. 150; separate rights, 37 Cal. 315.

Hoffman v. Tuolumne Wat. Co., 10 Cal. 413. Cited, Negligence, liability for injuries from breakage of water-dam, 10 Cal. 544; 17 Cal. 98; 23 Cal. 225; 37 Cal. 683; 1 Saw. 442; 15 Wall. 538.

Hoffmire v. Hoffmire, 3 Edw. Ch. 173. Cited, Attorney and Counsel, unauthorized appearance, remedy, 30 Cal. 446.

Hogan v. Ross, 11 How. 294. Cited, Writ of Error, authority to issue citation and approve security, 32 Cal. 240; 12 How. 389.

Hogan v. Weyer, 5 Hill, 389. Cited, Equity, relief from fraud, 17 Cal. 385.

Hogg v. State, 3 Blackf. 326. Cited, Indictment, sufficient statement, in case of larceny, of partnership property, 19 Cal. 599; rule at common law, 36 Cal. 248.

Hoke v. Henderson, 4 Dev. 1. Cited, Statutory Construction, statutes divesting rights to be strictly construed, 22 Cal. 318.

Holbrook v. Burt, 22 Pick. 546. Cited, Equity, relief from fraud, 17 Cal. 385.

Holbrook v. Finney, 4 Mass. 567. Cited, Title, conveyance and simultaneous defeasance vests no title, 8 Cal. 275.

Holbrook v. Holbrook, 1 Pick. 248.   Cited, Statutory Construction, presumptions as to beneficial intent, 13 Cal. 546.

Holcomb v. Holcomb, 2 Barb. 23.   Cited, Foreclosure, prior alienees or incumbrancers not necessary parties, 18 Cal. 474.

Holdane v. Trustees of Cold Spring, 23 Barb. 103.   Cited, Dedication, to public use, streets, 35 Cal. 497. Doubted as to *cul de sacs,* 35 Cal. 498; 7 Mich. 450.

Holden v. Pinney, 6 Cal. 234.   Cited, Homestead, estate in nature of joint tenancy, 25 Cal. 114; actual residence essential to establish dedication, 37 Cal. 372; 45 Miss. 178; 16 Iowa, 452.

Holdforth's Case, 1 Cal. 438.   Cited, Arrest and Bail, constitutional provisions, 6 Cal. 240.

Holdridge v. Gillespie, 2 Johns. Ch. 30.   Cited, Trust and Trustee, acquisition of interests in trustee inure to benefit of *cestui que trust,* 14 Cal. 634; 36 Cal. 432.

Holford v. Adams, 2 Duer, 480.   Cited, Common Carriers, receipt as a contract, 27 Cal. 38.

Holladay v. Frisbie, 15 Cal. 630.   Referred to, San Francisco, Van Ness ordinance, 15 Cal. 623; as a rule of property, 28 Cal. 223; tenure of beach and water lot property, 16 Cal. 125; tenure to lands generally, 42 Cal. 557.

Holladay v. Littlepage, 2 Munf. 316.   Cited, Evidence, admissibility of statements and admissions, 41 Cal. 306.

Holland v. Reed, 11 Mo. 605.   Cited, Landlord and Tenant, removal of tenant, 29 Cal. 171.

Holland v. San Francisco, 7 Cal. 361.   Referred to and followed, 7 Cal. 468.   Referred to, 27 Cal. 416.   Cited, Appeal, directing entry of judgment on reversal, 9 Cal. 421; Municipal Corporations, exercise of powers as distinguished from corporations generally, 9 Cal. 466. Commented on, 16 Cal. 273.   Overruled, Validity of sale of city slip property, 16 Cal. 621; 21 Cal. 362. Cited, Validity of city ordinance, on what depends, 23 Cal. 318; liability on implied contracts, 16 Cal. 270.

Hollenbeck v. Berkshire R. R. Co., 9 Cush. 478.   Cited, Action, civil action for death of person exclusively statutory, 25 Cal. 435.

Hollenbeck v. Clow, 9 How. Pr. 289. Cited, Pleading, defenses under the code, 22 Cal. 680.

Holliman, Heirs of, v. Peebles, 1 Tex. 673. Cited, Alienage, inheritance, 5 Cal. 377.

Hollingsworth v. Napier, 3 Caines, 182. Cited, Sale and Delivery, delivery by order on warehouseman, 8 Cal. 607; New Trial, surprise, what must be shown on motion, 1 Cal. 433.

Hollins v. Mallard, 10 How. Pr. 540. Cited, Injunction, motion to dissolve, practice, 35 Cal. 60.

Hollis v. Francois, 5 Tex. 195. Cited, Married Woman, execution of powers of attorney by, 31 Cal. 646.

Holman v. Criswell, 15 Tex. 394. Cited, Specific Performance, statute does not run against vendee in possession, 40 Cal. 572.

Holman v. Johnson, 1 Cowp. 343. Cited, Contract, no remedy on illegal or immoral contract, 15 Cal. 404; 3 Met. 207. Commented on, 4 Dana, 381. Construed, 21 Vt. 189; 1 Curt. 247.

Holman v. Taylor, 31 Cal. 338. Criticised, Constitutional Construction, jurisdiction of justices' courts, 38 Cal. 684, 685.

Holme v. Karsper, 5 Bin. 469. Cited, Negotiable Instruments, impeachment of consideration, 10 Cal. 526.

Holmes v. Beal, 9 Cush. 223. Cited, Probate Act, construction of limitation to action for recovery of estate sold, 33 Cal. 521.

Holmes v. Bell, 3 Cush. 323. Commented on, Chattel Mortgage, legal effect and operation.

Holmes v. Blogg, 8 Taunt. 35. Commented on, Infancy, contracts of infant how avoided, 24 Cal. 215, 216.

Holmes v. Broughton, 10 Wend. 75. Cited, Judicial Notice, not taken of foreign laws, 15 Cal. 254.

Holmes v. D'Camp, 1 John. 36. Cited, Account states, in nature, a new promise, 33 Cal. 697.

Holmes, Ex parte, 5 Cow. 426. Approved, Corporations, stock held by company not entitled to vote, 37 Cal. 27. Construed, 6 Wend. 510.

Holmes v. Grant, 8 Paige, 243.   Cited, Mortgage, evidence essential where obligations are not mutual, 9 Cal. 551; Conditional Sale, when construed as a mortgage, 33 Cal. 333.

Holmes v. Horber, 21 Cal. 55.   Cited, Jurisdiction, of justices' courts in torts, 1 Nev. 141.

Holmes v. Jennison, 14 Pet. 540.   Commented on, Constitutional Construction, relative powers of Federal and State government, 1 Cal. 236, 243.   Cited, 34 Cal. 498; 5 How. 381, 625, 628; 7 How. 555, 564.

Holmes v. Laffan, Cal. Sup. Ct. (not reported.)   Cited, Injunction will not issue to enjoin judgment by default on ground of false return of sheriff, 14 Cal. 143.

Holmes v. Patterson, 5 Mart. 693.   Cited, Mexican Law, execution of deed under, 26 Cal. 469; donation to wife, 26 Cal. 575.

Holmes v. Rogers, 13 Cal. 191.   Cited, Attorney and Counsel, remedy on judgment procured by unauthorized act of, 22 Cal. 210.

Holmes v. Tremper, 20 John. 29.   Commented on, Fixtures, removal by tenant, 14 Cal. 68; 2 Pet. 148.

Holmes v. Trout, 7 Pet. 171.   Cited, Grant of Land, construction of grant containing surplus, 3 Cal. 43.

Holt v. Robertson, 1 McMull. Eq. 475.   Commented on, Tenant in Common, liability of co-tenant for rents and profits, 12 Cal. 423.

Holt's Case, 9 Coke, 131.   Cited, Grant, construction of, 13 Cal. 453.

Holton v. Bangor, 23 Me. 264.   Cited, Taxation, *situs* of personal property, 23 Cal. 139.

Holton v. Smith, 7 N. H. 446.   Cited, Factor, cannot pledge, pledgee held to knowledge of factor's powers, 19 Cal. 72.

Homan v. Brinckerhoff, 1 Den. 184.   Cited, Attachment, void unless in conformity with statute, 34 Cal. 646. Construed, 3 Denio, 186.

Homer v. Ashford, 3 Bing. 323.   Cited, Contract, in total restraint of trade, void, 36 Cal. 358, 359.

Homer v. Wallis, 11 Mass. 309.   Cited, Evidence, proof of handwriting, 26 Cal. 412.   Commented on, 3 Blackf. 455.

Homes v. Crane, 2 Pick. 607. Cited, Pledge, title to property pledged, 35 Cal. 411.

Hood v. Mathis, 21 Mo. 308. Cited, Attachment Bond, construction of, 17 Cal. 436.

Hood v. New York & N. H. R., 22 Conn. 502. Disapproved, Common Carriers, contracts for transportation through, construed, 31 Cal. 52.

Hooker v. Utica and Minden T. Co., 12 Wend. 371. Cited, Railroads, estate in lands, an easement, 19 Cal. 596.

Hooper v. Wells, 27 Cal. 11. Cited, Common Carriers, liability for loss of property, 100 Mass. 506; 11 Minn. 291.

Hope v. Jones, 24 Cal. 89. Cited, Executor and Administrator, rights of co-executor, 33 Cal. 667; apportionment of commissions between, 38 Cal. 88.

Hope v. Stone, 10 Minn. 141. Cited, Estoppel, of mortgagor, 31 Cal. 457.

Hopkins v. Albertson, 2 Bay, 484. Cited, Will, evidence of execution, proof of signatures, 10 Cal. 479.

Hopkins v. Cheeseman, 28 Cal. 180. Cited as not in point, Jurisdiction, 35 Cal. 273.

Hopkins v. Conrad, 2 Rawle, 316. Cited, Debtor and Creditor, application of payments, 14 Cal. 449.

Hopkins v. Delaney, 8 Cal. 85. Cited, Acknowledgment of Deeds, construction of certificate, 7 Nev. 318.

Hopkins v. Everett, 6 How. Pr. 159. Cited, Pleading, conjunctive denials insufficient, 31 Cal. 195.

Hopkins v. Garrard, 7 B. Mon. 312. Cited, Conveyance, adverse possession as notice of title, 36 Cal. 272. Commented on, 36 Cal. 275.

Hopkins v. Haywood, 13 Wend. 265. Cited, Place of Trial, in actions against officers, 9 Cal. 421.

Hopkins v. Lee, 6 Wheat. 109. Cited, Decree in Chancery, when final is conclusive, 15 Cal. 83; when conclusive, 26 Cal. 494; 1 How. 149; 7 How. 217.

Hopkins v. Mayor of Swansea, 4 Mees. & W. 621. Cited, Municipal Corporations, renewal of charter, 2 Cal. 554.

Hopkins v. Mollinieux, 4 Wend. 465. Cited, Principal and Agent, effect of ratification by principal, 14 Cal. 400.

18

Hoppe v. Robb, 1 Cal. 373. Approved, Appeal, facts will not be reviewed where there is a conflict of evidence, 2 Cal. 23.

Hopper v. Jones, 29 Cal. 18. Cited, Deed, a mortgage, parol evidence to prove, 33 Cal. 332; Id. 690; 36 Cal. 49; 37 Cal. 454.

Hopper v. Kalkman, 17 Cal. 517. Cited, Appeal, order refusing to transfer cause to federal court renewable only on appeal from judgment, 4 Nev. 446.

Hopping v. Burnam, 2 Greene, Iowa, 39. Construed, Conveyances, effect of failure to record deed, 7 Cal. 498. Commented on, 10 Iowa, 356.

Horn v. Baker, 2 Smith's Lead. Cas. 296. Commented on, Fixture, what constitutes, 14 Cal. 64.

Horn v. Jones, 28 Cal. 194. Cited, Lis Pendens, effect of filing in foreclosure, 34 Cal. 615.

Horn v. Volcano Wat. Co., 13 Cal. 62. Cited, Writ of Assistance, purchaser at foreclosure sale entitled to, 21 Cal. 107. Approved, Intervention, when parties may intervene, 21 Cal. 287; 29 Cal. 154; 38 Cal. 611.

Hornbeck v. Westbrook, 9 John. 73. Cited, Deed, limitations and restrictions in, when void, 17 Cal. 52; designation of grantee in, 29 Cal. 412.

Hornblower v. Boulton, 8 Term Rep. 95. Cited, Statutory Construction, presumptions as to intent, 13 Cal. 456.

Hornblower v. Duden, 35 Cal. 664. Approved, County, liability of, for fees of counsel employed by board of supervisors, 7 Nev. 293; 8 Nev. 188.

Horner v. Doe, 1 Ind. 131. Cited, Judgment, of court of record, not subject to collateral attack, 34 Cal. 428.

Horr v. Barker, 6 Cal. 489; S. C. 8 Cal. 603; 11 Cal. 393. Cited, Sale and Delivery, sufficiency of delivery by warehouse receipts, 22 Cal. 541; delivery of property not segregated, 27 Cal. 463. Overruled, Factor, cannot pledge, that rule is limited to technical factor, 19 Cal. 73.

Horsefield v. Adams, 10 Ala. 9. Construed, Forcible Entry and Detainer, does not lie in case of eviction by process of law, 29 Cal. 216.

Horton v. Morgan, 6 Duer, 56. Affirmed, 19 N. Y. 172. Cited, Bailment, liability of bailee on sale of corporate stock, 42 Cal. 105.

Hortsman v. Henshaw, 11 How. 177. Cited, Negotiable Instrument, effect of indorsement on certificate of deposit, 22 Cal. 249.

Hosack v. Rogers, 9 Paige, 461. Cited, Interest, computation of, on partial payments, 35 Cal. 694.

Hosack v. Rogers, 25 Wend. 313. Cited, Law of the Case, established by previous decision, not revisable, 15 Cal. 83.

Hoskins v. Duperoy, 9 East, 498. Cited, Pleading, action on special contract, 26 Cal. 22.

Hostler v. Hays, 3 Cal. 302. Commented on, Estoppel, when estoppel by deed or matter of record may be pleaded or offered in evidence, 23 Cal. 357.

Hotaling v. Cronise, 2 Cal. 60. Cited, Mechanic's Lien, statutory construction, 25 Ark. 494; sufficiency of description in notice, 23 Cal. 213; effect of transfer of property, 37 Ind. 192.

Hotchkiss v. Nichols, 3 Day. 138. Cited, Foreclosure, conclusiveness of decree, 20 Cal. 483, 486.

Houell v. Barnes, Cro. Car. 382. Cited, Executors, powers of, under will, 32 Cal. 440.

Houghton v. Blake, 5 Cal. 240. Construed, Mechanic's Lien, for materials, McAll. 514.

Houghton v. Butler, 4 Term Rep. 364. Cited, Nuisance, abatement of, 1 Cal. 466.

Housatonic Railroad Co. v. Waterbury, 23 Conn. 101. Commented on, Railroads, negligence, and contributory negligence, 18 Cal. 356.

House v. Keiser, 8 Cal. 499. Cited, Forcible Entry and Detainer, possession in statute construed, 9 Cal. 48; 20 Cal. 84; 28 Cal. 191; 32 Cal. 344.

Houser v. Reynolds, 1 Hayw. 143. Commented on, Infancy, ratification of contract by infant, 24 Cal. 213.

Houston v. Moore, 3 Wheat. 433. Cited, Writ of Error, what is not a final judgment under the judiciary act, 20 Cal. 172; practice, dismissal, 11 How. 32.

Houston v. Moore, 5 Wheat. 1. Commented on, State Sovereignty, constitutional construction, 1 Cal. 235; 18 Gratt. 933; concurrent legislative powers of Federal and State government, 1 Cal. 241; 5 How. 585; Id. 625; 7 How. 555.

Houston v. Royston, 7 How. Miss. 548. Cited, Constitutionality of Statute, act creating superior court of San Francisco constitutional, 10 Cal. 295; 36 Cal. 697.

Hovenden v. Lord Annesley, 2 Scho. & L. 607. Approved, Trust and Trustee, possession of trustee is possession of *cestui que trust* and bars running of statute, 40 Cal. 569; 3 Pet. 51.

Hovey v. Hovey, 9 Mass. 216. Cited, Evidence, admissions in prior action not an estoppel in subsequent action, 22 Cal. 237.

Hovey v. Newton, 7 Pick. 29. Cited, Written Instruments, parol evidence to explain, admissible, 24 Cal. 417.

Howard v. Albany Ins. Co., 3 Den. 303. Cited, Assignment, interest required by assignee of insurance policy to entitle to a recovery, 30 Cal. 89.

Howard v. Doolittle, 3 Duer, 464. Cited, Lease, construction of covenant in, 30 Cal. 626. Approved, Landlord not bound to repair, 33 Cal. 345, 346, 347.

Howard v. Gage, 6 Mass. 462. Cited, Attorney and Counsel, mandamus may issue to reinstate in office, 1 Cal. 191.

Howard v. Harman, 5 Cal. 78. Cited, Appeal, from justice's court, when new undertaking may be filed, 7 Cal. 245.

Howard v. Henriques, 3 Sand. 725. Cited, Trade Marks, protection to name of hotel, 21 Cal. 451.

Howard v. Howard, 15 Mass. 196. Cited, Action, of debt, lies upon a decree in equity for a specific sum, 12 Cal. 20; 23 Cal. 354.

Howard v. Kennedy, 4 Ala. 592. Cited, Ejectment, judgment conclusive on assignees of defendant, *pendente lite,* 22 Cal. 206; Forcible Entry, does not lie on eviction by legal process, 29 Cal. 216.

Howard v. Mitchell, 14 Mass. 241. Cited, Pleading, estoppel by deed or matter of record must be specially pleaded, 26 Cal. 38.

Howard v. Moffatt, 2 Johns. Ch. 206. Cited, Alimony, when granted, 38 Cal. 278.

Howard v. Priest, 5 Met. 582. Cited, Partnership, tenure in trust of partnership property, 25 Cal. 105; 28 Cal. 580.

Howard v. Robinson, 5 Cush. 119. Commented on, Mortgage, as a lien or security, 18 Cal. 488; assignment of mortgage without assignment of debt null, 21 Cal. 623.

Howard v. Shaw, 8 Mees. & W. 118. Cited, Vendor and Vendee, vendee in possession, when not liable to action for rents and profits, 22 Cal. 616.

Howard v. Shores, 20 Cal. 277. Cited, Set-off, equitable set-off may be enforced, 23 Cal. 627.

Howard v. Valentine, 20 Cal. 282. Cited, Jurisdiction, of justices' courts, in actions of forcible entry and detainer, 1 Nev. 141; antecedent rents not recoverable, 1 Nev. 447.

Howe v. Adams, 28 Vt. 541. Cited, Judgment, lien of, cannot attach to homestead, 16 Cal. 220.

Howe v. Bass, 2 Mass. 380. Cited, Deed, construction of description in, 12 Cal. 165.

Howe v. Blanden, 21 Vt. 315. Cited as not in point, Execution, 38 Cal. 655.

Howe v. Earl of Dartmouth, 7 Ves. Jr. 147. Cited, Will, construction of legacy, of personal estate, 31 Cal. 602, 610.

Howe v. Howe Machine Co., 50 Barb. 241. Cited, Trade Marks, law in relation to, 35 Cal. 75.

Howe v. Huntington, 15 Me. 350. Cited, Contract, reasonable time for performance, a question of law, 30 Cal. 558.

Howe v. Independence Co., 29 Cal. 72. Qualified, Appeal, orders on motion to set aside default in discretion of court, 29 Cal. 424; costs to be imposed as a condition to opening default, 29 Cal. 427; 36 Cal. 289.

Howe, Petition of, 1 Paige, 125. Cited, Mortgage, equitable mortgage, how created, 31 Cal. 327; 32 Cal. 389.

Howe v. Scannell, 8 Cal. 325. Overruled, Witness, exception to rule of competency of vendor to impeach his own sale, 23 Cal. 446.

Howell v. McCoy, 3 Rawle, 256. Cited, Water Rights, protection to, 23 Cal. 487.

Howell v. Ransom, 11 Paige, 538. Cited, Attorney and Client, rule as to transactions between, 33 Cal. 440, 442.

Howson v. Hancock, 8 Term Rep. 575. Cited, Contract, no remedy on illegal or immoral contract, 37 Cal. 175; recovery of money staked on wager, 37 Cal. 673.

Hoxey v. County of Macoupin, 3 Ill. 36. Cited, Judgment, entry of several judgment against one defendant in action brought jointly is a discharge of other defendants, 6 Cal. 181, 182.

Hoxie v. Carr, 1 Sum. 173. Cited, Partnership, tenure of real estate, 28 Cal. 580.

Hoyt v. Commissioners of Taxes, 23 N. Y. 240. Approved, Taxation, *situs* of personal property, 29 Cal. 542, 544, 547.

Hoyt v. Dimon, 5 Day. 479. Cited, Appeal, error, without injury, not sufficient cause for reversal, 26 Cal. 467.

Hoyt v. French, 24 N. H. 198. Cited, Surety, on note, when discharged by agreement for delay, 10 Cal. 425.

Hoyt v. Gelston, 13 John. 139. Cited, Injunction, appeal from order dissolving, does not operate as a revival, 15 Cal. 110.

Hoyt v. Howe, 3 Wis. 752. Statutes distinguished, Judgment, no lien on homestead, 16 Cal. 219.

Hoyt v. Sheldon, 3 Bosw. 267. Cited, Corporation, deed executed by, presumed valid, 37 Cal. 598.

Hoyt v. Swift, 13 Vt. 129. Cited, Attachment, equitable demands not subject to garnishment, 35 Cal. 386.

Hoyt v. Thompson, 5 N. Y. 335. Reversing S. C. 3 Sand. 416. Approved, Maintenance, unknown to statutes of State, 22 Cal. 95; Assignment, right of action for conversion is assignable, 22 Cal. 142; Corporation, validity of deed of, presumed, 37 Cal. 598.

Hubbard v. Barry, 21 Cal. 321. Cited, Ejectment, action maintainable on right of entry and possession, 38 Cal. 43; in action on prior possession defendant cannot justify by showing true title outstanding, 24 Cal. 348; 29 Cal. 129; 38 Cal. 370; Van Ness Ordinance, as a rule of property, 28 Cal. 223.

Hubbard v. Cummings, 1 Greenl. 11. Cited, Infancy, ratification of purchase by, 24 Cal. 216.

Hubbard v. Elmer, 7 Wend. 446. Cited, Principal and Agent, when principal bound by acts of special agent, 24 Cal. 140.

Hubbard v. Sullivan, 18 Cal. 508. Construed, San Francisco, Van Ness ordinance, possession under, 19 Cal. 25; as a rule of property, 28 Cal. 223; tenure of lands by city, in trust, 42 Cal. 557.

Hubbell v. Carpenter, 5 N. Y. 171. Cited, Sureties on Note, when not discharged by time given to debtor, 10 Cal. 426.

Hubbly v. Brown, 16 John. 70. Cited, Costs, of former action on negotiable instrument, when recoverable against indorser, 22 Cal. 250.

Huber v. Gazley, 18 Ohio, 18. Cited, Dedication, by deed, when ineffectual, 42 Cal. 553.

Huddleston v. Briscoe, 11 Ves. Jr. 596. Cited, Revenue Stamp, what must be shown to defeat recovery for want of stamp on instrument, 34 Cal. 175.

Hudson v. Doyle, 6 Cal. 101. Cited, Nuisance, action for relief from, 30 Cal. 576.

Hudson v. Hudson, 1 Atk. 460. Commented on, Executors and Administrators, representation entire, act of one is act of all, 24 Cal. 500; 1 Wend. 617; 4 Rawle, 156; 18 Conn. 121.

Huffman v. Hulbert, 13 Wend. 376. Cited, Surety, on undertaking, discharged by agreement for extension of time, 26 Cal. 541.

Huffman v. San Joaquin Co., 21 Cal. 426. Cited, County, not liable for injuries from defective bridge or highway, 25 Cal. 315.

Hughes v. Buckingham, 5 Smedes & M. 648. Commented on, Constitutional Construction, term of office, 11 Cal. 87, 88; 12 Cal. 390.

Hughes v. Bucknell, 8 Car. & P. 566. Cited, Mortgage, relation between purchaser and tenant of mortgagor, 16 Cal. 590.

Hughes v. Davis, 40 Cal. 117. Deed, as a mortgage, absolute deed, conveys legal title, though shown to be a mortgage, 40 Cal. 63.

Hughes v. Devlin, 23 Cal. 501. Commented on, Public Domain, tenure of mineral lands, vested rights of miners, 42 Cal. 483.

Hughes v. Edwards, 9 Wheat. 489. Cited, Aliens, power of inheritance, under treaty, 5 Cal. 382, 386; 12 How.

108; Mortgage, what determines conveyance to be a mortgage, 8 Cal. 430, 435; 33 Cal. 333.

Hughes v. Kline, 30 Penn. St. 227. Cited, Street Assessment, failure to appeal to board is acquiescence in approval of work, 29 Cal. 87.

Hulett v. Swift, 33 N. Y. 571; affirming S. C. 42 Barb. 230. Cited, Innkeepers, liability for loss of property of guest, 33 Cal. 600, 602, 607.

Hull v. Carnley, 11 N. Y. 506. Cited, Chattel Mortgage, validity, on what depends, 23 Cal. 301.

Hull v. Sacramento V. R. R. Co., 14 Cal. 387. Cited, Railroads, proof of negligence, resulting in fire communicated by sparks, 55 Ill. 202. Commented on, 37 Mo. 297. Denied, 30 Iowa, 422.

Hull v. Oneida County, 19 John. 259. Cited, Mandamus, principles governing its issuance, 3 Cal. 173; 41 Cal. 77; cannot control discretion, 4 Cal. 179; 10 Cal. 376.

Hull v. Vaughan, 6 Price, 157. Cited, Vendor and Vendee, right of possession in vendee, under contract of sale, 22 Cal. 617.

Hulme v. Coles, 2 Sim. 12. Cited, Sureties, on official bond, release of, by agreement to extend time, 29 Cal. 100.

Hulme v. Tenant, 1 Brown Ch. 16. Cited, Married Woman, control over her separate estate, 23 Cal. 565. Commented on, 16 Md. 554; 13 Wis. 129; 15 Wis. 375; 31 Ind. 94.

Hultz v. Wright, 16 Serg. & R. 346. Commented on, Written Instruments, parol evidence admissible to prove fraudulent procurement and use, 13 Cal. 127.

Humbert v. Trinity Church, 24 Wend. 587; affirming S. C. 7 Paige, 195. Approved, Pleading, facts, bringing plaintiff within the exception to the statute of limitations, must be specially pleaded, 9 Cal. 425; 19 Cal. 481. Cited, Tenants in Common, possession of one presumed to be possession of all, 23 Cal. 247; 24 Cal. 376.

Humble v. Mitchell, 2 Rail. Cas. 70. Cited, Specific Performance, when will be enforced, on sale of shares of stock, 23 Cal. 392.

Hume v. Scott, 3 A. K. Marsh. 260. Cited, Witness, rule of examination on impeachment of, 27 Cal. 636; 12 How. 555.

Humphreys v. Collier, 2 Ill. 52.   Cited, Pleading, election of plaintiff on joint and several contract, 6 Cal. 181.

Humphreys v. Crane, 5 Cal. 173.   Cited, Surety, on note, liabilities of, 9 Cal. 561; 10 Cal. 289.   Commented on, 6 Cal. 397; not discharged by mere neglect to sue, 9 Cal. 23; 24 Cal. 165; 26 Cal. 543; Parties, on joint and several contracts, administrator cannot be joined with survivor, 6 Cal. 643.

Humphreys v. McCall, 9 Cal. 59.   Cited, Pleading, denials to verified complaint must be specific, 9 Cal. 473; 10 Cal. 232; 13 Cal. 371; 32 Cal. 607.

Humphreys v. Newman, 51 Me. 40.   Cited, Husband and Wife, conveyance to married woman, presumptions, 30 Cal. 56; 31 Cal. 449.

Humphries v. Brogden, 12 Q. B. 739.   Cited, Injunction, equitable protection of real property from injury by adjoining landholders, 35 Cal. 549.

Hunsaker v. Borden, 5 Cal. 288.   Construed, County, actions by, and against, 18 Cal. 59; State, remedy of creditors of, 34 Cal. 290, 291; of creditors of county, 39 Cal. 275.

Hunt v. Adams, 5 Mass. 358.   Cited, Negotiable Instrument, obligation of surety, 10 Cal. 291.

Hunt v. Bridgham, 2 Pick. 581.   Cited, Surety, on note, mere delay without fraud will not discharge, 10 Cal. 425.

Hunt v. Comstock, 15 Wend. 665.   Commented on, Lease, contract construed as, 25 Cal. 66; Landlord and Tenant, demand to fix liability for unlawful detainer, 33 Cal. 406.

Hunt v. Holden, 2 Mass. 168.   Cited, Statutory Construction, "month" defined, 31 Cal. 176.

Hunt v. Hunt, 14 Pick. 374.   Disapproved, Mortgage, transfer of, 5 Cal. 336.

Hunt v. Knickerbacker, 5 John. 327.   Cited, Specific Performance, acts prohibited by law will not be enforced, 38 Cal. 310.

Hunt v. Lewin, 4 Stewt. & P. 138.   Cited, Foreclosure, action lies within four years though the debt secured may be already barred, 22 Cal. 626.

Hunt v. Livermore, 5 Pick. 395.   Cited, Contracts, to convey real property, covenants independent, 35 Cal. 663.

Hunt v. Loucks, 38 Cal. 372. Cited, Execution, presumptions in favor of validity of sales under, 13 Wall. 514.

Hunt v. Porter, Cal. Sup. Ct. Oct. T. 1856 (not reported.) Approved, Appeal, presumptions in favor of judgment, where averments in pleading are defective, 10 Cal. 562.

Hunt v. Rousmaniere's Admrs., 1 Pet. 1; S. C. 8 Wheat. 174. Cited, Principal and Agent, death of principal revokes authority of agent, 15 Cal. 18; powers when irrevocable, 32 Cal. 617; Equity, relieves from mistakes, 19 Cal. 673; 9 How. 92. Commented on, 9 Conn. 100; 5 Cranch, C. C. 161; 15 Wall. 144.

Hunt v. San Francisco, 11 Cal. 250. Cited, Pleading, defects cured by default on verdict, 30 Cal. 488.

Hunt v. Silk, 5 East, 449. Cited, Contract, rescission of, equitable doctrine, 15 Cal. 458; 29 Cal. 594; 34 Cal. 144.

Hunt v. Stiles, 10 N. H. 466. Cited, Mortgage securing several notes, equitable doctrine on foreclosure, 23 Cal. 30.

Hunt v. Test, 8 Ala. 713. Cited, Contract, measure of damages on breach of, 4 Cal. 394.

Hunt v. United States, 1 Gall. 32. Cited, Surety, when not discharged by agreement for delay, 10 Cal. 425.

Hunt v. Van Alstyne, 25 Wend. 605. Commented on, Statute, impeachment of, 2 Cal. 170; 30 Cal. 259, 261, 266.

Hunt v. Wallis, 6 Paige, 371. Cited, Default, practice on opening, 29 Cal. 426.

Hunt v. Waterman, 12 Cal. 301. Cited, Vendor's Lien, waived by taking other security, 3 Or. 419.

Hunt v. Wickwire, 10 Wend. 104. Cited, Justice of Peace, has no power to vacate judgment of dismissal for nonappearance and reinstate case, 29 Cal. 316.

Hunt's Lessee v. McMahan, 5 Ohio, 134. Cited, Settler's Act, liability for rents on eviction by paramount title, 7 Cal. 24.

Hunter v. Atkins, 3 Myl. & K. 113. Cited, Attorney and Client, transactions between, how governed, 33 Cal. 440.

Hunter v. Hemphill, 6 Mo. 106. Cited, Preëmption, validity of, cannot be questioned by party not in privity with paramount source of title, 33 Cal. 458.

Hunter v. Martin, 4 Munf. 1. Approved, Constitutional Construction, appellate jurisdiction of U. S. supreme court, 11 Cal. 182, 184.

Hunter v. Town of Marlboro, 2 Wood. & M. 168. Cited, Specific Performance, time not of essence of contract, 40 Cal. 11.

Hunter v. Watson, 12 Cal. 363. Cited, Title, possession of tenant as notice of landlord's title, 13 Cal. 512. Construed, Conveyance, possession as notice of, 17 Cal. 304; 18 Cal. 367. Approved, 19 Cal. 676; 21 Cal. 628; 22 Cal. 335; 26 Cal. 419; 36 Cal. 271. Commented on, 29 Cal. 490. Cited, Power of Attorney, construction of, 16 Cal. 512; Deed, validity of, 17 Cal. 56; 14 Mich. 225; Witness, privileged communications, 23 Cal. 333.

Huntington, Town of, v. Nicoll, 3 John. 566. Commented on, Bill of Peace, will not lie in favor of party out of possession, 6 Cal. 40.

Huntington, Town of, v. Town of Charlotte, 15 Vt. 46. Cited, Judgment, validity of, how impeached, 30 Cal. 446.

Hurd v. Rutland and Burlington R. R. Co., 25 Vt. 116. Cited, Railroads, liability for injuries to cattle, 33 Cal. 236.

Hurlburd v. Bogardus, 10 Cal. 518. Cited, Statute of Frauds, insufficient delivery and change of possession, on sale of chattel, 1 Nev. 224; 2 Nev. 293.

Hurlburt, Ex parte, 8 Cow. 138. Cited, Appeal, sufficiency of undertaking on, 13 Cal. 509.

Hurlburt v. Jones, 25 Cal. 229. Cited, Appeal, objections to defective findings cannot be raised for first time in appellate court, 29 Cal. 142.

Hurlbutt v. Butenop, 27 Cal. 50. Cited, Taxation, tax deed void from invalid assessment, 30 Cal. 619; assessment void for want of dollar marks, 31 Cal. 135; Lis Pendens, effect of filing, 34 Cal. 615. Cited, Evidence, when certified copy of deed admissible, 38 Cal. 449.

Hurt v. State, 25 Miss. 378. Cited, Criminal Procedure, conviction for manslaughter as an acquittal for murder, 4 Cal. 377. Approved, effect of former acquittal, Id. 379.

Husbands v. Vincent, 5 Har. Del. 268.   Cited, Pleading, demand in action for payment of money, when need not be averred, 22 Cal. 278.

Huse v. Merriam, 2 Greenl. 375.   Cited, Taxation, assessment, when void, 10 Cal. 404; for want of valuation, 27 Cal. 57.

Hussey v. Thornton, 4 Mass. 405.   Cited, Conditional Sale, of personal property, rights of second vendee, 36 Cal. 158; 3 Gray, 547.

Huston v. Curl, 8 Tex. 239.   Cited, Husband and Wife, common property, 12 Cal. 224.   Approved, Presumption as to property acquired during marriage, 12 Cal. 252; 28 Cal. 42; 30 Cal. 38.

Hutcheson v. Priddy, 12 Gratt. 85.   Cited, Probate Proceedings, not subject to collateral attack, 18 Cal. 505.

Hutchins v. Hutchins, 7 Hill, 104.   Approved, Conspiracy, when civil action for damages lies, 25 Cal. 560.

Hutchinson v. Bours, 6 Cal. 383.   Cited, Factor, powers of, to sell or pledge, 7 Cal. 30.   Approved, Rule that factor cannot pledge, confined to technical factors, 11 Cal. 402.   Overruled, Factor cannot pledge, 19 Cal. 73. Doubted, McAll. 411.

Hutchinson v. Bours, 13 Cal. 52.   Cited, Judgment, may be entered in vacation, 28 Cal. 340.

Hutchinson v. Burr, 12 Cal. 103.   Followed, Injunction, necessary parties to enjoin issuance of county bonds, 12 Cal. 106.

Hutchinson v. Hunter, 7 Penn. St. 140.   Cited, Sale and Delivery, chattels mingled with others, 27 Cal. 463.

Hutchinson v. Moody, 18 Me. 393.   Cited, Surety, on note, when released by delay of creditor, 10 Cal. 425.

Hutchinson v. Perley, 4 Cal. 33.   Approved, Ejectment, on prior possession, proof sufficient, 4 Cal. 78; possession *prima facie* evidence of title, 7 Cal. 579; 9 Cal. 427.   Cited, McAll. 232.

Hutchinson v. Wetmore, 2 Cal. 310.   Approved, Contract, entire contract for services, 17 Ohio St. 476.

Hutchinson v. Y. N. & B. Railway Co., 5 Exc. 341.   Cited, Master and Servant, liability of master for injury to servant, 6 Cal. 210.

Hutton v. Duey, 3 Penn. St. 100. Commented on, Husband and Wife, deeds of separation valid, 9 Cal. 493.

Hutton v. Frisbie, 37 Cal. 475. Followed, in Knowles *v.* Greenwood; True *v.* Tormey; Fowler *v.* Frisbie; True *v.* Thomas; Dixon *v.* Brownlie; Martin *v.* Frisbie; Brown *v.* Frisbie; and Whitney *v.* Thomas, decided at the Cal. Sup. Ct. July T. 1869 (not reported.) Cited, Preëmption Rights, after execution and sale of prior possessory rights, 40 Cal. 298; 41 Cal. 329; preëmption of lands included in Suscol Rancho, 41 Cal. 625. Approved, power of congress to withdraw land from preemption, 41 Cal. 493; Id. 626; Id. 638; 9 Wall. 195.

Hutton v. Reed, 25 Cal. 478. Approved, New Trial, statement to contain the grounds of error relied on, 27 Cal. 410; 28 Cal. 261; Id. 265; Id. 413; 32 Cal. 316; Id. 316; 36 Cal. 120; 37 Cal. 385; 38 Cal. 280; 5 Nev. 262; or, on failure, the order will be affirmed, or appeal dismissed, see same cases; Appeal, office of statement, 27 Cal. 112; 28 Cal. 296; 33 Cal. 554; 34 Cal. 605; must contain grounds relied on, 25 Cal. 515; 26 Cal. 524; 28 Cal. 165; on appeal on judgment roll, no statement is required, 34 Cal. 34; 36 Cal. 232; judgment affirmed where no briefs were filed in time, 28 Cal. 489.

Hutton v. Schumaker, 21 Cal. 453. Cited, Ejectment, on prior possession, actual possession to be shown, 32 Cal. 20, 22; 4 Nev. 68, 69.

Huyett v. Philadelphia & Reading R. R. Co., 23 Penn. St. 373. Commented on, Negligence, Railroads, liability for injuries from sparks, 9 Cal. 257; 14 Cal. 389.

Hyatt v. Argenti, 3 Cal. 151. Cited, Personal Property, mortgage and pledge of, in general, 8 Cal. 150; legal title in pledged goods, 8 Cal. 151, 152; Contracts, how construed, 46 Miss. 569.

Hysinger v. Baltzell, 3 Gill & J. 158. Commented on, Statute of Limitations, "return" construed, 16 Cal. 97.

Iglehart v. Armiger, 1 Bland. Ch. 523. Cited, Vendor's Lien, not assignable, 21 Cal. 177.

Illidge v. Goodwin, 5 Car. & P. 190. Cited, Negligence, action for injuries from, when it lies, 37 Cal. 423.

Illinois Cent. R.R. v. United States, 20 Law Rep. 630. Cited, State Sovereignty, Eminent Domain, 18 Cal. 252.

Ilott v. Wilkes, 3 Barn. & Ald. 304; S: C. 5 Eng. C. L. 295. Cited, Negligence, action for injuries from, when it lies, 18 Cal. 357; 14 Conn. 10.

Ilsley v. Jewett, 3 Met. 439. Cited, New Promise, effect of, on statutory bar, 19 Cal. 483.

Imlay v. Carpentier, 14 Cal. 173. Cited, Judgment, remedy by motion, against void judgment, 14 Cal. 159; 17 Cal. 86; 37 Cal. 228; Insolvency, discharge of debt equally a discharge of judgment on that debt, 19 Cal. 170.

Imley v. Beard, 6 Cal. 666. Approved, Appeal, does not lie from order procured on party's own motion or by consent, 22 Cal. 456; 42 Cal. 518; 1 Nev. 96.

Indian Canon R. Co. v. Robinson, 13 Cal. 519. Cited, Franchises, grant of franchise when not exclusive, 21 Cal. 252; 22 Cal. 423. Approved, 25 Cal. 288.

Indiana Cent. R. R. Co. v. Hunter, 8 Ind. 75. Cited, Condemnation of land for railroad purposes, benefits to be considered in estimate of damage, 31 Cal. 374.

Indianopolis and C. R. R. Co. v. Kinney, 8 Ind. 402. Commented on and qualified, Railroads, liability for injuries to cattle, 18 Cal. 355.

Ingalls v. Bills, 9 Met. 1. Cited, Negligence, liability for personal injuries, 28 Cal. 628. Commented on, 13 N. Y. 25; 11 Gratt. 715.

Inge v. Murphy, 10 Ala. 885. Cited, Common Law, where presumed to exist, 15 Cal. 252.

Ingersoll v. Truebody, 40 Cal. 603. Approved, Husband and Wife, presumptions as to conveyance to wife, 42 Cal. 361.

Ingersoll v. Van Bokkelin, 7 Cow. 670. Cited, Conversion, measure of recovery in action by pledgee, 34 Cal. 606.

Ingoldsby v. Juan, 12 Cal. 564. Commented on, Husband and Wife, conveyance by wife, 13 Cal. 497; 25 Cal. 383; 30 Cal. 516, 517. Cited, 32 Cal. 383; Validity of conveyance of lands, 24 Cal. 176. Explained and affirmed, 31 Cal. 400, 403, 405; Acknowledgment, sufficiency of, 36 Cal. 203.

Ingraham v. Baldwin, 9 N. Y. 45. Cited, Ejectment, effect of denial of. landlord's title, 27 Cal. 105. Commented on, Tenant when estopped from denying landlord's title, 33 Cal. 251; 35 Cal. 571. Cited, Demand, when essential in actions for recovery of property, 38 Cal. 512.

Ingraham v. Geyer, 13 Mass. 146. Cited, Assignment, in trust, made in foreign State, how tested, 13 Cal. 278; 11 Wheat. 100, note. Commented on, 6 Pick. 306; 2 Wall. Jr. 133; 32 Vt. 458.

Ingraham v. Gildemeester, 2 Cal. 88, 161. Construed, Appeal, review of rulings on questions of law, 14 Cal. 38. Cited, Judgment, can be taken only against those served with process, 16 Cal. 68.

Ingraham v. Phillips, 1 Day, 117. Cited, Attachment, lien of, 29 Cal. 372.

Inhabitants, etc., v. String, 5 Halst. 323. Cited, Corporation, omission of part of name of, will not affect rights, 39 Cal. 515.

Inhabitants, etc., in Winthrop v. Benson, 31 ' e. 384. Approved, Title, by adverse possession under statute, 36 Cal. 540.

Inman v. Foster, 8 Wend. 602. Cited, Libel and Slander, evidence not admissible, 41 Cal. 384. Doubted, 6 Hill, 521. Commented on, 44 N. Y. 270; 29 Me. 246.

Innes v. Agnew, 1 Ohio, 387. Cited, Covenants, when covenants in deed are personal, 37 Cal. 189.

Innis v. Steamer Senator, 1 Cal. 459. Commented on and distinguished, Evidence, inadmissible testimony, 5 Cal. 414. Cited, declarations, when no part of *res gestæ*, 9 Cal. 256; 14 Cal. 37.

Iron Factory Co. v. Richardson, 5 N. H. 295. Cited, Services, contract for, construed, 5 Cal. 475.

Iron Mountain Co. v. Haight, 39 Cal. 540. Followed, Mandamus, 39 Cal. 662.

Irvine v. Elnon, 8 East, 54. Cited, Arbitration, effect of alteration in award, 23 Cal. 368.'

Irvine, Adm. v. Withers, 1 Stewt. 234. Cited, Negotiable Instruments, place of payment not of essence of contract, 11 Cal. 324.

Irving v. Motley, 7 Bing. 543; S. C. 5 Moore & P. 380. Cited, Fraud, sale procured by, passes no title to property, 12 Cal. 462.

Irwin v. Bacchus, 25 Cal. 214. Approved, Probate, judgment on bond conclusive on principal and sureties alike, 32 Cal. 120, 121, 122, 123, 130. Cited, 7 Nev. 173.

Distinguished, Id. 153; 33 Cal. 170. Applied to undertaking on appeal, 38 Cal. 601.

Irwin v. Dixion, 9 How. 10. Approved, Dedication, to public use, assent how shown, 14 Cal. 649. Cited, 22 Cal. 489; by sale of lots on plat, 35 Cal. 501; by deed, when ineffectual, 42 Cal. 553.

Irwin v. Phillips, 5 Cal. 146. Cited, Public Domain, right of miners to enter upon, 5 Cal. 398; 6 Cal. 46. Commented on, Priority of appropriation, a rule of property, 8 Cal. 141, 143; 22 Cal. 453, 455; right in ditch property, 6 Cal. 558; Judicial Notice, political and social condition, 7 Cal. 325.

Irwin v. Scriber, 18 Cal. 499. Referred to, Probate, exclusiveness of probate jurisdiction over wills, 18 Cal. 481. Commented on, Character of jurisdiction, 19 Cal. 209. Cited, Proceedings, not subject to collateral attack, 22 Cal. 73; Id. 276; intendments in favor of action of court, 28 Cal. 185.

Isaac v. Swift, 10 Cal. 71. Cited, Judgment Lien, pending appeal, 25 Cal. 351. Approved, Execution cannot extend lien, 37 Cal. 133, 141; continuance of lien governed strictly by statute, 29 Cal. 372.

Isaacs v. Steel, 4 Ill. 97. Distinguished, Preëmption Rights, 37 Cal. 498, 517.

Isbell v. N. Y. & N. H. R. R. Co., 27 Conn. 393. Approved, Negligence, rule releasing from liability for contributory negligence, 37 Cal. 420.

Israel v. Douglas, 1 H. Black. 242. Commented on, Assignment, order as an equitable assignment, 14 Cal. 407. Doubted, 15 N. H. 135; 12 Leigh, 225.

Iverson v. Shorter, 9 Ala. 713. Commented on, Statutory Construction, statutes not to be construed retrospectively, 4 Cal. 136, 161; power of repeal, 15 Cal. 523; 10 Iowa, 487. Disapproved, 30 Tex. 733.

Ives v. Carter, 24 Conn. 392. Approved, Action, election of remedy where breach of contract is a tort, 18 Cal. 534.

Ives v. Cress, 5 Penn. St. 118. Cited, Vendor and Vendee, when vendor liable for rents and profits in ejectmet by vendee, 22 Cal. 617.

Ives v. Finch, 22 Conn. 101. Cited, Appeal Bond, validity of, 13 Cal. 509.

Izon v. Gorton, 7 Scott. 546. Cited, Lease, covenant by lessor to build, construed, 39 Cal. 153.

Jack v. Dougherty, 3 Watts, 151. Cited, Deed, parol proof of consideration, 6 Cal. 137.

Jackman v. Hallock, 1 Ohio, 318. Cited, Vendor's Lien, not assignable, 21 Cal. 177.

Jackman v. Mitchell, 13 Ves. Jr. 581. Cited, Equity, power of, to order cancellation of written instrument, when exercised, 10 Cal. 576.

Jacob v. City of Louisville, 9 Dana, 114. Cited, Eminent Domain, rule of compensation, on condemnation, 31 Cal. 373.

Jacobs v. Kruger. See People v. Kruger.

Jacomb v. Harwood, 2 Ves. Sr. 267. Cited, Executors and Administrators, representation entire, act of each is the act of all, 24 Cal. 500.

Jacks v. Day. See People v. Day.

Jackson v. Allen, 3 Cow. 220. Cited, Landlord and Tenant, receipt of rent, waives forfeiture, 25 Cal. 394.

Jackson v. Ayers, 14 John. 224. Commented on, Estoppel, of tenant, 33 Cal. 252. Doubted, 35 Cal. 570.

Jackson v. Barringer, 15 John. 471. Cited, Deed, description in, how construed, 12 Cal. 164, 165.

Jackson v. Bartlett, 8 John. 361. Cited, Judicial Sale, title of purchaser cannot be collaterally impeached, 9 Cal. 429; voidable execution not subject to collateral attack, 38 Cal. 382.

Jackson v. Betts, 9 Cow. 208. Cited, Evidence, secondary evidence of lost instrument, 9 Cal. 451.

Jackson v. Bodle, 20 John. 184. Cited, Principal and Agent, authority for act of principal presumed from benefit derived by principal, 4 Cal. 169.

Jackson v. Boneham, 15 John. 226. Cited, Evidence, identity of name as identity of person, 28 Cal. 218, 221.

Jackson v. Bowen, 7 Cow. 13. Cited, Mortgage, how debt is evidenced, not of essence of contract, 15 Cal. 644.

Jackson v. Bradford, 4 Wend. 619. Cited, Conveyance, without warranty does not operate on after-acquired title, 14 Cal. 628.

19

Jackson v. Bronson, 19 John. 325. Commented on, Mortgage, a mere security, assignment of, without the debt, a nullity, 9 Cal. 408; Id. 428; 21 Cal. 623; 30 Cal. 688.

Jackson v. Bronson, 7 John. 227. Cited, Landlord and Tenant, receipt of rent, waives forfeiture, 25 Cal. 394.

Jackson v. Buel, 9 John. 298. Cited, Ejectment, when action lies, 38 Cal. 572.

Jackson v. Bull, Johns. Cas. 81. Disapproved, Deed, effect of conveyance without warranty on after-acquired title, 14 Cal. 628.

Jackson v. Bulloch, 12 Conn, 53. Cited, Law of Nations, national comity, right of transit, 9 Cal. 163.

Jackson v. Burgott, 10 John. 456. Commented on, Conveyance, effect of actual notice of prior unrecorded deed, 12 Cal. 374; 26 Cal. 87.

Jackson v. Burton, 1 Wend. 341. Cited, Vendor and Vendee, vendor in possession as tenant of vendee, 37 Cal. 374.

Jackson v. Bush, 10 John. 223. Cited, Estoppel, of execution defendant, as to purchaser's title, 23 Cal. 399.

Jackson v. Cadwell, 1 Cow. 622. Cited, Conveyances, purpose and intent of recording act, 6 Cal. 314; Exceptions, objections to admission or exclusion of evidence, must be specific, 10 Cal. 268; 12 Cal. 245; exceptions to be taken on facts not denied, 34 Cal. 686; Execution, title of purchaser at sale under, 38 Cal. 377, 380; Appeal, restitution on reversal of judgment, 14 Cal. 679.

Jackson v. Campbell, 5 Wend. 572. Cited, Corporate Deed, validity of, 37 Cal. 598; 2 Black. 716.

Jackson v. Carpenter, 11 John. 539. Commented on, Infancy, ratification of contract by, 24 Cal. 213; 10 Pet. 73.

Jackson v. Catlin, 2 John. 248. Cited, Deed, as an escrow, 30 Cal. 212.

Jackson v. Chamberlain, 8 Wend. 620. Cited, Conveyances, purchase of judgment creditor at his own sale, 12 Cal. 377.

Jackson v. Chew, 12 Wheat. 153. Approved, Stare Decisis, local adjudication as a rule of property, 15 Cal. 603, 605; 5 Pet. 155; 3 How. 476; 4 How. 379; 8 How. 559; 11 How. 318. Commented on, 5 Humph. 37.

Jackson v. Clark, 7 John. 217. Doubted, Power, validity of sale of real property under, how tested, 22 Cal. 590.

Jackson v. Collins, 3 Cow. 89. Approved, Sheriff's Deed, execution of, by ex-sheriff, 8 Cal. 410.

Jackson v. Cornell, 1 Sand. Ch. 348. Cited, Partnership, priority of creditor's lien on partnership property, 13 Cal. 632. Commented on, 18 Gratt. 415.

Jackson v. Cory, 8 John. 385. Cited, Deed, construction of, premises to prevail over *habendum* clause, 17 Cal. 52; conveyance to A. and company vests legal title in A. alone, 29 Cal. 412.

Jackson v. Crafts, 18 John. 110. Denied, Mortgage, tender and refusal after law day operates as a discharge, 14 Cal. 528.

Jackson v. Crawfords, 12 Wend. 533. Cited, Probate, proceedings not subject to collateral attack, 22 Cal. 63; Evidence, secondary evidence to show regularity of proceedings, 22 Cal. 64. Commented on, 1 Hill, 138.

Jackson v. Croy, 12 John. 427. Cited, Deed, parol evidence of, when inadmissible, 24 Cal. 417.

Jackson v. Cuerden, 2 Johns. Cas. 353. Commented on, Estoppel, tenant when not estopped, 35 Cal. 575.

Jackson v. Cullum, 2 Blackf. 228. Cited, Evidence, secondary, of regularity of proceedings, on loss of record, 22 Cal. 64.

Jackson v. Davis, 18 John. 7. Cited, Ejectment, estoppel of execution defendant, 23 Cal. 399.

Jackson v. Defendorf, 1 Caines, 493. Commented on, Deed, construction of description in, 12 Cal. 164.

Jackson v. DeLancy, 13 John. 537. Cited, Deed, void for uncertainty of description, 6 Cal. 312.

Jackson v. Delancey, 4 Cow. 427. Cited, Conveyances, purpose and intent of recording act, 6 Cal. 314.

Jackson v. Demont, 9 John. 55. Cited, Ejectment, new matter must be specially pleaded, 30 Cal. 474.

Jackson v. Denn, 5 Cow. 200. Doubted, Ejectment, on prior possession, 1 Cal. 309. Cited, 4 Cal. 79.

Jackson v. Deyo, 3 John. 422. Approved, Landlord and Tenant, when notice to quit not necessary, 16 Cal. 90; 24 Cal. 145.

Jackson v. Dickenson, 15 John. 309. Cited, Sheriff's Deed, title by relation, 31 Cal. 304.

Jackson v. Dieffendorf, 3 John. 269. Cited, Title, by adverse possession, 34 Cal. 382; 36 Cal. 541.

Jackson v. Dunsbagh, 1 Johns. Cas. 92. Doubted, Conveyances, purpose and intent of recording act, 6 Cal. 313.

Jackson v. Eaton, 20 Johns. 478. Cited, Deed, title of purchaser under quitclaim deed, 11 Cal. 160.

Jackson v. Elston, 12 John. 454. Cited, Lands, constructive possession under deed, 25 Cal. 135.

Jackson v. Feather Riv. Wat. Co., 14 Cal. 18. Cited, Mining Claim, parol sale, sufficiency of transfer of, 23 Cal. 179; Id. 222; Id. 576. Doubted, 30 Cal. 363. Approved, Error, *prima facie* an injury to party against whom made, 25 Cal. 167; 39 Cal. 612. Cited, Witness, rule of cross-examination, 25 Cal. 213; 33 Cal. 648; 7 Nev. 390.

Jackson v. Ferris, 15 John. 345. Commented on, Will, power of sale under, 32 Cal. 439; 5 How. 272.

Jackson v. Fish, 10 John. 456. Cited, Deed, consideration may be proved by parol, 26 Cal. 474.

Jackson v. Freer, 17 John. 29. Cited, Boundaries, acquiescence in division line, 25 Cal. 626.

Jackson v. French, 3 Wend. 339. Cited, Witness, privileged communications, 5 Cal. 451.

Jackson v. Frost, 5 Cow. 346. Cited, Title, what constitutes color of title, 33 Cal. 676.

Jackson v. Gardner, 8 John. 394. Cited, Deed, construction of, 25 Cal. 182.

Jackson v. Graham, 3 Caines, 188. Cited, Estoppel, of execution defendant as to purchaser's title, 23 Cal. 399.

Jackson v. Gridley, 18 John. 104. Cited, Witness, examination as to competency, 10 Cal. 67.

Jackson v. Griswold, 4 Hill, 522. Commented on, Surety, on official bonds, not concluded by judgment in action against principal alone, 14 Cal. 206.

Jackson v. Groat, 7 Cow. 285. Approved, Assignment, the valuable privilege of preemption assignable, 9 Cal. 677. Cited, Covenant, of privilege of purchase in lessee, valid, 16 Cal. 513.

Jackson v. Gumaer, 2 Cow. 552.   Cited, Acknowledgment, of deed, sufficiency, on what depends, 8 Cal. 584.

Jackson v. Halstead, 5 Cow. 219.   Cited, Instructions, actual possession, construed, 19 Cal. 690.

Jackson v. Harder, 4 John. 203.   Doubted, Ejectment, on prior possession, 1 Cal. 309.

Jackson v. Harrison, 17 John. 66.   Cited, Landlord and Tenant, demand for rent to establish forfeiture, 3 Cal. 283.   Doubted, 8 Minn. 284.

Jackson v. Harsen, 7 Cow. 323.   Cited, Vendor and Vendee, vendor retaining possession is tenant of vendee, 37 Cal. 374.

Jackson v. Hazen, 2 John. 22.   Doubted, Ejectment, on prior possession, 1 Cal. 309.

Jackson v. Henry, 10 John. 186.   Cited, Statute of Frauds, title of innocent purchasers, 12 Cal. 498; voidable conveyances not subject to impeachment by stranger, 29 Cal. 36.

Jackson v. Hills, 8 Cow. 290.   Cited, Ejectment, sub-lessees of defendant bound by judgment in, 22 Cal. 207.

Jackson v. Housel, 17 John. 283.   Cited, Property, what it includes, 9 Cal. 142; 31 Cal. 637.

Jackson v. Hubble, 1 Cow. 613.   Cited, Conveyance, bill of sale of real estate without warranty, 11 Cal. 160; 14 Cal. 628.

Jackson v. Hudson, 3 John. 375.   Cited, Deed, construction of, 25 Cal. 182.

Jackson v. Ireland, 3 Wend. 99.   Cited, Deed, construction of, premises to prevail over *habendum* clause, 17 Cal. 51.

Jackson v. Ives, 9 Cow. 661.   Cited, Ejectment, to be brought against parties in possession, 9 Cal. 270.

Jackson v. King, 5 Cow. 237.   Cited, Exceptions, objections to evidence to be taken at the trial, 16 Cal. 555.

Jackson v. Kisselbrack, 10 John. 335.   Cited, Written Instruments, construction of, 7 Cal. 413.

Jackson v. Lamphire, 3 Pet. 280.   Commented on, Conveyances, power of legislature to pass recording acts, 7 Cal. 487, 501; 9 Cal. 513; 2 How. 613; 13 Wall. 71.

Jackson v. Lawton, 10 John. 23. Commented on, Patent, not subject to collateral attack, 14 Cal. 365; Id. 469; 11 Wheat. 384.

Jackson v. Leek, 19 Wend. 339. Cited, Notice, to agent is notice to principal, 31 Cal. 165.

Jackson v. Legrange, 19 John. 386. Cited, Will, attestation to, presumptions, 10 Cal. 479.

Jackson v. Leonard, 9 Cow. 653. Cited, Title, successive possessions, when may be added, 37 Cal. 354.

Jackson v. Livingston, 7 Wend. 136. Cited, Deed, when grantee enters under, as tenant in common, 24 Cal. 110; 37 Cal. 520.

Jackson v. Lodge, 36 Cal. 28. Approved, Deed, as mortgage, may be shown by parol, 37 Cal. 454. Cited, Absolute deed conveys legal title, though intended as a mortgage, 40 Cal. 120.

Jackson v. Loomis, 18 John. 81. Cited, Deed, construction of, 24 Cal. 446.

Jackson v. Lucett, 2 Caines, 363. Cited, Deed, construction of calls in, 32 Cal. 230.

Jackson v. Lunn, 3 Johns. Cas. 109. Cited, Alienage, incapacities under common law, 12 Cal. 456; 3 Wheat. 13, note c; 6 Pet. 121.

Jackson v. Luquere, 5 Cow. 221. Cited, Will, attestation to, presumptions, 10 Cal. 479.

Jackson v. Marsh, 6 Cow. 281. Cited, Equity, relieves from mistakes, 12 Cal. 212.

Jackson v. May, 16 John. 184. Cited, Ejectment, when action lies, 38 Cal. 572.

Jackson v. McChesney, 7 Cow. 361. Denied, Evidence, recitals of consideration in deed, 26 Cal. 86. Doubted, 10 N. Y. 528.

Jackson v. McConnel, 11 John. 424. Cited, Ejectment, new matter must be specially pleaded, 30 Cal. 474.

Jackson v. McConnell, 19 Wend. 175. Approved, Deed, construction of, 12 Cal. 164.

Jackson v. McLeod, 12 John. 182. Cited, Landlord and Tenant, when tenant not entitled to notice to quit, 38 Cal. 564.

Jackson v. Miller, 7 Cow. 747. Rule distinguished, Landlord and Tenant, tenant at will entitled to notice to quit, 24 Cal. 145.

Jackson v. Moncrief, 5 Wend. 26. Cited, Vendor and Vendee, vendee entitled to possession under contract of sale, 22 Cal. 616. Rule distinguished, Vendee entitled to notice to quit before action by vendor for possession, 24 Cal. 145.

Jackson v. Moore, 6 Cow. 706. Cited, Deed, construction of, 12 Cal. 164; 22 How. 19.

Jackson v. Morse, 16 John. 197. Cited, Ejectment, when defendant may set up outstanding title, 13 Cal. 595.

Jackson v. Murray, 12 John. 201. Denied, Deed, without warranty, an estoppel, 14 Cal. 628.

Jackson v. Myers, 3 John. 388. Cited, Ejectment, on prior possession, showing required, 1 Cal. 310; 4 Cal. 79. Commented on, Deed, construction of, 7 Cal. 414. Cited, 30 Cal. 347. Distinguished, 3 Wash. C. C. 376. Cited, Cloud on Title, action to set aside void conveyance, when not barred by statute, 32 Cal. 264.

Jackson v. Neely, 10 John. 374. Commented on, Evidence, preliminary proof, of lost instrument, 2 Cal. 30.

Jackson v. Newton, 18 John. 355. Cited, Dissenting opinion, Hastings, C. J., Indian Titles, 1 Cal. 290; colorable title under void deed, 1 Cal. 319. Cited, Execution, sale in mass of real property, void, 21 Cal. 59.

Jackson v. Ogden, 4 John. 140. Approved, Boundaries, acquiescence in division line, 25 Cal. 626. Commented on, Id. 631. Distinguished, 5 Minn. 261.

Jackson v. Oltz, 8 Wend. 440. Cited, Title by adverse possession, 34 Cal. 381; 36 Cal. 541.

Jackson v. Page, 4 Wend. 588. Commented on, Execution, amendable execution, not void, 38 Cal. 380.

Jackson v. Parkhurst, 5 John. 128. Cited, Landlord and Tenant, when tenant at sufferance not entitled to notice to quit, 38 Cal. 564.

Jackson v. Pesked, 1 Maule & S. 234. Cited, Pleading, errors cured by verdict, 9 Cal. 270.

Jackson v. Pierce, 10 John. 414. Cited, Action, lies on express promise to pay debt of another, 37 Cal. 537.

Jackson v. Port, 17 John. 482. Cited, Indemnity, measure of relief on bond of, 25 Cal. 172.

Jackson v. Post, 15 Wend. 588. Cited, Conveyances, *bona fide* purchasers, who are, 12 Cal. 377; 41 Cal. 50.

Jackson v. Pratt, 10 John. 381. Cited, Execution, amendable executions not void, 38 Cal. 381; validity of sheriff's deed, 38 Cal. 659.

Jackson v. Ramsay, 3 Cow. 75. Approved, Performance, doctrine of relation as to acts of, 4 Cal. 414; Ejectment, new matter, as title acquired pending action must be specially pleaded, 30 Cal. 474; title under execution sale, doctrine of relation, 31 Cal. 304.

Jackson v. Reeves, 3 Caines, 293. Cited, Description of Land, construction, 25 Cal. 298.

Jackson v. Rich, 7 John. 194. Cited, Ejectment, new matter must be specially pleaded, 30 Cal. 474.

Jackson v. Rightmyre, 16 John. 314. Cited, Ejectment, who bound by judgment, 22 Cal. 207. Distinguished, 30 Cal. 201. Approved, Title, by adverse possession under statute, 34 Cal. 382; 36 Cal. 541. Cited, Principal and Agent, ratification by principal, 30 Cal. 414.

Jackson v. Roberts, 7 Wend. 83. Cited, Execution, setting aside sale under, 14 Cal. 678.

Jackson v. Roberts' Exrs., 11 Wend. 422. Cited, Evidence, parol evidence of deed when and when not admissible, 24 Cal. 417, 418; Execution, application of assets, 37 Cal. 136.

Jackson v. Robins, 16 John. 537. Cited, Judicial Sale, validity of, not subject to collateral attack, 9 Cal. 429; 38 Cal. 382; 14 Md. 135.

Jackson v. Root, 18 John. 60. Cited, Evidence, subscribing witness, when to be produced, 12 Cal. 308.

Jackson v. Rosevelt, 13 John. 97. Cited, Conveyance, validity of, what essential, 6 Cal. 312.

Jackson v. Rowland, 6 Wend. 666. Cited, Estoppel, when lessee not estopped, 33 Cal. 245; 38 Cal. 124.

Jackson v. Schoonmaker, 2 John. 230. Cited as overruled, Adverse Possession, what insufficient to establish, 1 Cal. 310, 321. Commented on, Actual Possession, essential, 19 Cal. 690; 32 Cal. 20. Cited, Deed, void for uncertainty, 17 Cal. 52.

Jackson v. Schutz, 18 John. 174. Cited, Lease, covenant of privilege of purchase in lessee, 9 Cal. 676. Approved, construction of covenant, 16 Cal. 513. Cited, when receipt of rent waives forfeiture, 25 Cal. 394.

Jackson v. Scoville, 5 Wend. 96. Cited, Ejectment, conclusiveness of general verdict, 4 Cal. 80.

Jackson v. Sebring, 16 John. 515. Cited, Conveyances, covenant to stand seized to uses, 6 Cal. 314. Commented on, 16 Ohio St. 660.

Jackson v. Sharp, 9 John. 162. Cited, Notice, to agent is notice to principal, 31 Cal. 165.

Jackson v. Shearman, 6 John. 19. Commented on, Evidence, parol evidence as to title, 26 Cal. 41, 44.

Jackson v. Sheldon, 5 Cow. 448. Cited, Landlord and Tenant, receipt of rent waives forfeiture, 25 Cal. 394.

Jackson v. Sill, 11 John. 201. Cited, Wills, cannot be varied or contradicted by parol, 35 Cal. 340.

Jackson v. Sisson, 2 Johns. Cas. 321. Cited, Deed, executed to A. and company vests fee in A., 29 Cal. 411.

Jackson v. Smith, 7 Cow. 717. Commented on, dissenting opinion, Sawyer, J., Estoppel, of tenant, 33 Cal. 252.

Jackson v. Spear, 7 Wend. 401. Cited, Estoppel, when tenant released from, 30 Cal. 201; tenant when not estopped, 35 Cal. 575.

Jackson v. Stanford, 19 Geo. 14. Approved, Deed, validity of deed executed by part of grantors, 22 Cal. 501.

Jackson v. Stanley, 2 Ala. 326. Cited, Attachment Bond, substitution of new bond, 15 Cal. 33.

Jackson v. Sternberg, 20 John. 50. Cited, Sheriff's Deed, conclusiveness of recitals in, 24 Cal. 418.

Jackson v. Sternbergh, 1 Johns. Cas. 153. Commented on, Validity of title, on what depends, 11 Cal. 248.

Jackson v. Stiles, 4 John. 493. Cited, Ejectment, landlord admitted to defend, 22 Cal. 205.

Jackson v. Stiles, 6 Cow. 594. Cited, Ejectment, landlord admitted to defend, 22 Cal. 205.

Jackson v. Stone, 13 John. 447. Cited, Judgment, for recovery of property not a bar to subsequent action for its use, 10 Cal. 521; sub-lessees of defendant bound by judgment in ejectment, 22 Cal. 207.

Jackson v. Swart, 20 John. 85. Commented on, Deed, intention of grantee to control, 30 Cal. 26, 27; 4 How. 376.

Jackson v. Tibbits, 9 Cow. 241. Commented on, Ejectment, ouster by tenant in common, 27 Cal. 559.

Jackson v. Topping, 1 Wend. 388. Cited, Deed, conditions in, when void, 17 Cal. 52. Commented on, Forfeiture on breach of condition, 25 Cal. 241.

Jackson v. Town, 4 Cow. 599. Cited, Conveyances, *bona fide* purchasers within registration act, 12 Cal. 377.

Jackson v. Tuttle, 9 Cow. 233. Cited, Judgment, who bound by, in ejectment, 22 Cal. 206.

Jackson v. Twentyman, 2 Pet. 136. Cited, Jurisdiction, of federal courts, 22 Cal. 85.

Jackson v. Van Dalfsen, 5 John. 43. Cited, Mortgage, title of mortgagee at his own sale under power contained in mortgage, 21 Cal. 329; of trustee, 29 Cal. 34.

Jackson v. Vanderheyden, 17 John. 167. Cited, Sheriff's Deed, conclusiveness of, 24 Cal. 417.

Jackson v. VanValkenburg, 8 Cow. 260. Cited, Conveyance, possession as notice of, 29 Cal. 488.

Jackson v. Van Zandt, 12 John. 174. Cited, Statutory Construction, statutes to be construed prospectively, 27 Cal. 159.

Jackson v. Vickory, 1 Wend. 406. Cited, Will, attestation to, presumptions, 10 Cal. 479.

Jackson v. Vosburgh, 9 John. 270. Cited, Evidence, parol evidence inadmissible, as to title, 26 Cal. 41.

Jackson v. Waldron, 13 Wend. 178. Cited, Estoppel, by deed, 14 Cal. 628. Evidence, proof of handwriting of witnesses, 26 Cal. 411.

Jackson v. Walker, 7 Cow. 637. Cited, Ejectment, prior possession with color of title must prevail, 4 Cal. 79.

Jackson v. Walker, 4 Wend. 462. Cited, Execution, validity of title of purchaser, on what depends, 12 Cal. 134; Judgment, when amendable, is not void, 38 Cal. 380.

Jackson v. Walsh, 14 John. 407. Cited, Mortgage, purchase by mortgagee at sale under power not void, 21 Cal. 329.

Jackson v. Waters, 12 John. 365. Cited, Title, what will not constitute color of title, 33 Cal. 676; 8 Cow. 613.

Jackson v. Wendell, 5 Wend. 142. Cited, Deed, construction of calls in, 34 Cal. 344.

Jackson v. Wheeler, 6 John. 272. Cited, Landlord and Tenant, when notice to quit not necessary, 16 Cal. 90.

Jackson v. Willard, 4 John. 41. Commented on, Mortgage, interest of mortgagee in possession, 21 Cal. 622. Cited, Mortgage a mere security, 36 Cal. 58; assignment of mortgage without the debt a nullity, 30 Cal. 688; payment of debt extinguishes lien, 36 Cal. 41.

Jackson v. Winslow, 9 Cow. 13. Cited, Deed, without warranty does not convey after-acquired title, 11 Cal. 160; notice to agent is notice to principal, 31 Cal. 165.

Jackson v. Wiseburn, 5 Wend. 136. Cited as inapplicable, Amendments, 3 Cal. 119.

Jackson v. Wood, 7 John. 290. Approved, Title, Indians incapable of passing titles, 1 Cal. 284; 6 Pet. 121.

Jackson v. Woodruff, 1 Cow. 276. Cited, Adverse Possession, what necessary to constitute, 19 Cal. 690; Color of Title, what constitutes, 33 Cal. 323; Id. 676.

Jackson v. Wright, 14 John. 193. Cited, Conveyance, without warranty, what interest passes, 11 Cal. 160. Approved, 14 Cal. 628.

Jackson v. Wright, 4 John. 75. Cited, Alien, proof of alienage, 30 Cal. 188.

Jaffrey v. Cornish, 10 N. H. 505. Cited, Promissory Note, effect of payment by note, 12 Cal. 323.

Jameison v. Calhoun, 2 Spear, 19. Approved, Indemnity, agreements to indemnify, for commission of trespass, void, 18 Cal. 624.

James v. Chalmers, 5 Sand. 52. Affirmed, 6 N. Y. 209. Cited, Parties, holder of note may maintain action, 9 Cal. 247.

James, Estate of, 23 Cal. 415. Cited, Homestead, jurisdiction as to title by inheritance, in district court, 41 Cal. 36.

James v. Fisk, 9 Smedes & M. 144. Cited, Married Woman, conveyance by, validity on what depends, 13 Cal. 498.

James v. Hayward, 4 Croke, 184. Approved, Nuisance, right to abate a common nuisance, 1 Cal. 466.

James v. Landon, 1 Croke, 36. Cited, Estoppel, tenant released from, on surrender of possession, 30 Cal. 201.

James v. O'Driscoll, 2 Bay, 101. Cited, Services, no action lies for gratuitous services, 22 Cal. 510.

James v. Post, Cal. Sup. Ct. Jan. T. 1856 (not reported.) Cited, Guaranty, on charter party, valid, 7 Cal. 34.

James v. Vanderheyden, 1 Paige, 385. Commented on, Deed, deposited with third party, when not an escrow, 30 Cal. 213.

James v. Williams, 31 Cal. 211. Cited, Findings, opinions no part of findings, 38 Cal. 577; Appeal, findings to support judgment, will be presumed, 41 Cal. 99; 42 Cal. 617.

Jamson v. Quivey, 5 Cal. 490. Disapproved, Instructions, practice on instructions, asked for, 25 Cal. 470. .

Jansen v. Acker, 23 Wend. 480. Cited, Appeal, effect of affirmance of order granting new trial, law of the case; 26 Cal. 525; Attachment, justification of levy, 34 Cal. 351.

Janson v. Brooks, 29 Cal. 214. Approved, Forcible Entry, when action will not lie, 28 Cal. 532; unlawful entry, what constitutes, 38 Cal. 422.

Jaques v. Areson, 4 Abb. Pr. 282. Cited, Injunction, practice, on motion to dissolve, 35 Cal. 60.

Jaques v. M. E. Church, 17 John. 548. Cited, Married Woman, control of separate estate, 7 Cal. 270; power of alienation of, 7 Cal. 273; 32 Cal. 385; charging with debts, 23 Cal. 565, 566.

Jaques v. Weeks, 7 Watts, 269. Cited, Conveyances, penalty in recording act, construed, 7 Cal. 304; 10 Ark. 544.

Jarndyce v. Jarndyce, Dickens's Bleak House. Cited in illustration, Vexatious Litigation, 12 Cal. 214.

Jarvis v. Blanchard, 6 Mass. 4. Cited, Appeal, remedy under statute, exclusive, 8 Cal. 300; 26 N. H. 203.

Jarvis v. Dean, 3 Bing. 447. Cited, Dedication, to public use, what constitutes, 14 Cal. 649; 9 How. 31.

Jarvis v. Jarvis, 3 Edw. Ch. 462. Cited, Statutory Construction, statutes not construed retrospectively, 27 Cal. 159.

Jarvis v. Rogers, 13 Mass. 105. Cited, Pledge, of negotiable securities, 5 Cal. 261.

Jeanes v. Wilkins, 1 Ves. Sr. 195. Commented on, Execution, when sale under may be avoided, 38 Cal. 377.

Jeffrey v. Bigelow, 13 Wend. 518. Cited, Principal and Agent, when principal bound by unauthorized act of agent, 8 Cal. 249.

Jenkins v. Eldridge, 3 Story, 181. Commented on, Deed, as a mortgage, parol evidence of, 8 Cal. 429; 19 How. 299. Cited, Notice, what sufficient in equity, 36 Cal. 437. Commented on, Statute of Frauds, parol evidence admissible to prove fraud, 21 Cal. 101.

Jenkins v. Frink, 27 Cal. 337. Cited and practice disapproved, New Trial, striking out statement on motion for, 32 Cal. 305; motion as a step in the procedure, 32 Cal. 313; waiver of motion by failure to file statement, 41 Cal. 518.

Jenkins v. McConico, 26 Ala. 213. Cited, Husband and Wife, conveyance by wife, 13 Cal. 497.

Jenner v. Joliffe, 9 John. 381. Cited, Officers, liability for negligence, 36 Cal. 214.

Jenness v. Bean, 10 N. H. 266. Construed, Pledge, of negotiable securities, 3 Cal. 164.

Jenney v. Alden, 12 Mass. 375. Commented on, Parent and Child, deed of gift to child, 8 Cal. 123; emancipation of minor, 25 Cal. 152.

Jennings v. Loring, 5 Ind. 250. Cited, Injunction Bond, counsel fees not recoverable, 25 Cal. 174.

Jennings v. Wood, 20 Ohio, 261. Cited, Deed, record of, when not conclusive, 7 Cal. 294; 31 Cal. 321. Commented on, 5 Ohio St. 86.

Jenny Lind Co. v. Bower, 11 Cal. 194. Cited, New Trial, on ground of newly discovered evidence, 35 Cal. 688; 38 Cal. 194.

Jerome v. Ross, 7 Johns. Ch. 315. Disapproved, Eminent Domain, compensation for condemnation, 12 Cal. 529.

Jerome v. Stebbins, 14 Cal. 457. Cited, Pleading, essentials in complaint on special contract for services, 26 Cal. 21; 28 Cal. 547. Applied, To demand in actions of replevin, 3 Nev. 565.

Jerusalem, The, 2 Gall. 190. Cited, Jurisdiction, of State courts in actions brought by aliens, 1 Cal. 487; 3 Wheat. 101, note.

Jesse v. State, 20 Geo. 156. Cited, Juror and Jury, qualification of juror, 32 Cal. 47.

Jesson v. Wright, 2 Bligh. 50.   Cited, Will, construction of words in, 27 Cal. 449.   Commented on, 1 Sum. 251; 14 Geo. 575.

Jeter v. State, 1 McCord, 233.   Cited, Office, term of, 11 Cal. 88.

Jewell's Lessee v. Jewell, 1 How. 219.   Cited, Evidence, parol evidence to disprove marriage, 9 Cal. 595.

Jewett v. Palmer, 7 Johns. Ch. 65.   Cited, Deed, grantor concluded by recitals in, 26 Cal. 87.

Jewett v. Warren, 12 Mass. 300.   Cited, Pledge, consideration for, 37 Cal. 25.

John and Cherry Sts., Matter of, 19 Wend. 659.   Cited, Condemnation of Land, estimate of benefits, 32 Cal. 539.

Johns v. Church, 12 Pick. 557.   Cited, Deed, parol evidence of consideration in, 6 Cal. 137;   Replevin, when receiptor not estopped, 10 Cal. 176.

Johns v. Stevens, 3 Vt. 316.   Cited, Water Rights, title by adverse possession, 27 Cal. 366.

Johnson v. Alameda Co., 14 Cal. 106.   Cited, Eminent Domain, payment or tender of compensation a condition precedent to right of entry, 29 Cal. 117.   Commented on, 31 Cal. 548.

Johnson v. Ames, 11 Pick. 173.   Cited, Trust and Trustee, when executor held to account as trustee, 31 Cal. 25.

Johnson v. Barney, 1 Iowa, 531.   Cited, Certificates of Deposit, as promissory notes, 29 Cal. 506.

Johnson v. Beauchamp, 9 Dana, 125.   Cited, Vendor and Vendee, vendee entitled to possession, 22 Cal. 616.

Johnson v. Blackman, 11 Conn. 342.   Cited, Appeal, judgment not reversed for error without injury, 26 Cal. 467.

Johnson v. Blasdale, 1 Smedes & M. 17.   Cited, Negotiable Instruments, filling in blank in note, 8 Cal. 112.

Johnson v. Buffington, 2 Wash. Va. 116.   Cited, Patent, surplus land in grant, 3 Cal. 43; 5 Cranch, 252.

Johnson v. Burrell, 2 Hill, 238.   Cited, Statutory Construction, statutes to be construed prospectively, 27 Cal. 159.

Johnson v. Bush, 3 Barb. Ch. 207.   Commented on, Municipal Corporation, validity of deed of, 16 Cal. 640.

Johnson v. Dalton, 1 Cow. 543. Cited, Jurisdiction, of State courts in actions by aliens, 1 Cal. 487.

Johnson v. Day, 17 Pick. 106. Cited, Amendment, to officers' returns, 23 Cal. 81.

Johnson v. Dopkins, 6 Cal. 83. Cited, Appeal, interlocutory orders reviewable on appeal from judgment, 10 Cal. 528; 22 Cal. 637.

Johnson v. Erskine, 9 Tex. 1. Cited, Undertaking, execution of joint bond by principal essential to its validity, 14 Cal. 423; 21 Cal. 589.

Johnson v. Fitzhugh, 3 Barb. Ch. 360. Cited, Insolvency, discharge of debt is discharge of judgment, 14 Cal. 176.

Johnson v. Gordon, 4 Cal. 368. Followed, Jurisdiction, of Federal and State courts, in Sullivan v. Cairo, Oct. T. 1854 (not reported.) Construed and distinguished, 6 Cal. 271. Commented on, Judicial power of Federal courts not exclusive, 9 Cal. 710, 724; no supervisory power of U. S. Supreme court over State courts, 11 Cal. 184. Overruled on this point, 25 Cal. 613. Cited, 6 Ohio St. 378.

Johnson v. Gorham, 6 Cal. 195. Cited, Sheriff, refusal to pay over moneys, remedy, 10 Cal. 489; 2 Nev. 378.

Johnson v. Hudson Riv. R. R. Co., 5 Duer, 21; S. C. 20 N. Y. 65. Cited, Negligence, when action lies for injuries causing death of party, 34 Cal. 164.

Johnson v. Jones, 4 Barb. 369. Cited, Mining Stock, trustee may sell or hypothecate, 42 Cal. 147.

Johnson v. Lamping, 34 Cal. 293. Cited, Execution, validity of title of purchaser, 38 Cal. 377.

Johnson v. People, 3 Hill, 178. Cited, Witness, impeachment of, rule of examination, 27 Cal. 635.

Johnson v. Reynolds, Cal. Sup. Ct. Jan. T. 1857 (not reported.) Doubted, Execution, choses in action, levy and sale of, 13 Cal. 22; 34 Cal. 88.

Johnson v. Rich, 9 Barb. 680. Cited, Statute, validity of statute contingent on vote of electors, 17 Cal. 34; contra, 8 N. Y. 496; 3 Mich. 423.

Johnson v. Santa Clara Co., 28 Cal. 545. Cited, County, liability of, for care of indigent sick, averments essential, 4 Nev. 29.

Johnson v. Sepulveda, 5 Cal. 149. Cited, Exceptions, Practice, 3 Nev. 530. See De Johnson v. Sepulbeda, *ante*.

Johnson v. Sherman, 15 Cal. 287; S. C. July T. 1858 (not reported.) Referred to, 10 Cal. 160; 13 Cal. 124. Approved, Mortgage, a mere lien or security, no estate passes without foreclosure and sale, 16 Cal. 468; 18 Cal. 488; 21 Cal. 621; 36 Cal. 39; possession of mortgagee does not affect its nature, 21 Cal. 625; 22 Cal. 262; 24 Cal. 409; 36 Cal. 43; lien extinguished by payment of debt secured, 24 Cal. 498; Deed as Mortgage, parol evidence admissible to prove, 27 Cal. 606; 33 Cal. 332; 33 Cal. 690; 36 Cal. 42, 47, 48; 37 Cal. 454; assignment of lease, as mortgage, 36 Cal. 64.

Johnson v. State, 17 Ohio, 593. Cited, New Trial, admission of hearsay evidence as ground for, 21 Cal. 265.

Johnson v. Totten, 3 Cal. 343. Cited, Partnership, liability after dissolution, 15 Cal. 321.

Johnson v. Van Dyke, 20 Cal. 225. Commented on, Mexican Grants, statute of limitation begins to run only from issuance of patent, 26 Cal. 46; 29 Cal. 585; 33 Cal. 457, 479; 1 Saw. 560.

Johnson v. Weed, 9 John. 310. Cited, Negotiable Instrument, payment by note, effect of, 5 Cal. 330; 12 Cal. 323. Commented on, Id. 324.

Johnson v. Wetmore, 12 Barb. 433. Cited, Undertaking, for release of attachment, action on, 9 Cal. 501.

Johnson v. Whitlook, 13 N. Y. 344. Commented on, New Trial, amendment of statement, 15 Cal. 396.

Johnson v. Wide West Min. Co., 22 Cal. 479. Cited, Injunction, dissolution on answer denying all equities, 23 Cal. 84.

Johnson v. Wygant, 11 Wend. 48. Cited, Pleading, in contract with dependent promises, conditions precedent, 1 Cal. 338; 35 Cal. 663.

Johnston v. Beard, 7 Smedes & M. 217. Cited, Bond for Deed, demand essential in action on, 17 Cal. 276.

Johnston v. Searcy, 4 Yerg. 182. Cited, Surety, on note, not discharged by mere delay, 10 Cal. 425.

Johnston v. Wilson, 2 N. H. 202. Cited, Office, constitutional term of, 2 Cal. 212.

Jolland v. Stainbridge, 3 Ves. Jr. 478. Cited, Conveyances, possession as notice of title, 12 Cal. 376.

Jones v. Adair, 1 Bibb, 311. Cited, Attachment, official duty in issuance of, 25 Cal. 209.

Jones v. Atherton, 7 Taunt. 56. Cited, Execution, lien of, 8 Cal. 252.

Jones v. Block, 30 Cal. 227. Cited, Findings, of what should consist, 38 Cal. 577.

Jones v. Brooke, 4 Taunt. 464. Cited, Costs, indorser of note when liable for costs incurred by indorsee, 22 Cal. 250.

Jones v. Butler, 30 Barb. 641. Cited, Infancy, ratification and avoidance of contracts by, 24 Cal. 215.

Jones v. Butler, 20 How. Pr. 189. Cited, Pleading, demand for relief, 37 Cal. 324.

Jones v. Chiles, 2 Dana, 25. Cited, Ejectment, who bound by judgment in, 22 Cal. 206. Commented on, who turned out under writ of possession, 29 Cal. 136; 36 Cal. 460; possession by entry of tenant under deed to landlord, 38 Cal. 492.

Jones v. Conoway, 4 Yeates, 109. Cited, Statute of Limitations, fraudulent concealment to avoid, 8 Cal. 460.

Jones v. Cook, 1 Cow. 309. Cited, Attachment, duty of sheriff as to, 28 Cal. 286.

Jones v. Darch, 4 Price, 300. Cited, Infancy, validity of contract by infant, 24 Cal. 209.

Jones v. Frost, 28 Cal. 245. Approved, Pleading, amended complaint supersedes the original, 33 Cal. 501; 8 Nev. 60.

Jones v. Frost, Jac. 466. Cited, Will, jurisdiction to test validity of, 20 Cal. 266.

Jones v. Gale's Cur'x, 4 Mart. 635. Approved, Judicial Notice, official signatures, 32 Cal. 108.

Jones v. Gardner, 10 John. 266. Cited, Contracts to convey land, covenants dependent, 35 Cal. 663.

Jones v. Hacker, 5 Mass. 264. Cited, Judgment, restoration of rights on reversal of, 14 Cal. 679.

Jones v. Henry, 3 Litt. 428. Cited, Vendor and Vendee, liability of fraudulent vendee to creditors of vendor, 23 Cal. 236.

Jones v. Jones, 10 Barn. & C. 718. Cited, Ejectment, tenant at will entitled to notice to quit, 24 Cal. 145.

20

Jones v. Jones, 3 Mer. 171; S. C. 7 Price, 663. Commented on, Will, jurisdiction on probate of, 20 Cal. 267. Cited, 20 Cal. 266; relief from fraudulent will, 2 How. 645.

Jones v. Jones, 15 Tex. 143. Cited, Estates of deceased persons, priority of claim of partnership debts, 17 Cal. 537.

Jones v. Judd, 4 N. Y. 411. Commented on, Contract, damages on breach of entire contract for services, 35 Cal. 242, 245. Distinguished, 26 N. Y. 284.

Jones v. Martin, 16 Cal. 165. Cited, Conveyances, record of official seal, 36 Cal. 203.

Jones v. Moore, 5 Bin. 573. Cited, New Promise, what sufficient to avoid statute, 36 Cal. 185.

Jones v. Morehead, 3 B. Mon. 377. Cited, Husband and Wife, conveyance of wife's separate estate, 12 Cal. 578.

Jones v. Morgan, 1 Bro. Ch. 219. Commented on, Will, construction of, 27 Cal. 446.

Jones v. Parsons, 25 Cal. 100. Cited, Partnership, tenure of real estate, 28 Cal. 580; liability for partnership debts, Id. 581, 587.

Jones v. People, 14 Ill. 196. Cited, Sunday Laws, statutes of binding force, 18 Cal. 681.

Jones v. Perry, 2 Esp. 482. Cited, Negligence, liability for injuries by ferocious animal, 41 Cal. 141.

Jones' Heirs v. Perry, 10 Yerg. 59. Cited, Constitutional Construction, protection of inherent rights, 22 Cal. 318.

Jones v. Petaluma, 36 Cal. 230. Approved, Pleading, denials "upon" information and belief sufficient, 38 Cal. 163. Commented on, Dedication to Public Use, construction of town lands act, 38 Cal. 558. Cited, Estoppel, former judgment, as a bar, 41 Cal. 227.

Jones v. Post, 4 Cal. 14; S. C. 6 Cal. 102. Cited, Witness, competency of, interest in action, 4 Cal. 408; Guaranty, when not void on consideration not expressed, 16 Cal. 153; when not within statute of frauds, 34 Cal. 675; 38 Cal. 135. Commented on and approved, 27 Cal. 83.

Jones v. Price, 1 East, 81. Cited, Arrest and Bail, bail as a waiver of process, 6 Cal. 59.

Jones v. Pugh, 1 Phil. Ch. 96. Cited, Witness, privileged communications, 29 Cal. 62, 66.

Jones v. Read, 1 La. An. 200. Cited, Judicial Sales, administrator's sale judicial, 9 Cal. 196.

Jones v. Reed, 1 Johns. Cas. 20. Cited, Pleading, jurisdictional facts, in collateral actions, 33 Cal. 536.

Jones v. State, 1 Geo. 610. Commented on, Witness, competency of accomplice, 5 Cal. 185. Cited, 20 Cal. 440. Denied, 14 Mich. 307.

Jones v. Stevens, 11 Price, 235. Cited, Libel and Slander, evidence in mitigation not admissible, 41 Cal. 384. Doubted, 8 Leigh, 549; 20 Vt. 237.

Jones v. Thompson, 12 Cal. 191. Cited, Execution, on partnership property on judgment against partner, 38 Cal. 615.

Jones v. Thurmond's Heirs, 5 Tex. 318. Commented on, Exceptions, to charge of court practice, 26 Cal. 266.

Jones v. Tipton, 2 Dana, 295. Cited, Vendor and Vendee, vendee in possession when not liable for rents and profits, 22 Cal. 616.

Jones v. United States, 7 How. 681. Cited, Debtor and Creditor, application of payments, 14 Cal. 449.

Jones v. VanPatten, 3 Ind. 107. Commented on, Exceptions to instructions, when to be taken, 26 Cal. 267.

Jones v. Wight, 5 Ill. 338. Cited, Judgment, by default, entry of, on joint and several obligation, when irregular, 6 Cal. 182; 7 Cal. 448.

Jones v. Wilde, 5 Taunt. 183. Cited, Ejectment, who bound by judgment in, 22 Cal. 207.

Jones v. Williams, 5 Adol. & E. 297. Commented on, Mortgage, relation of mortgagor in possession and mortgagee, 14 Cal. 633.

Jordan v. Corey, 2 Ind. 385. Denied, Acknowledgment of Deeds, authority of notary public, 11 Cal. 298.

Jordan v. Giblin, 12 Cal. 100. Cited, Summons, statutory provisions for publication of, to be strictly pursued, 20 Cal. 82; 30 Cal. 617.

Joslyn v. Smith, 13 Vt. 353. Cited, Surety, on note, when discharged by agreement for delay, 10 Cal. 425.

Jourdan v. Jourdan, 9 Serg. & R. 270. Cited, Acknowledgment of Deeds, powers of notary, 11 Cal. 298.

Joy v. Adams, 26 Me. 330.   Commented on and rule distinguished, Mortgage, remedy when barred under statute, 18 Cal. 490; 42 Cal. 502.

Joy v. Sears, 9 Pick. 4.   Cited and applied, Statute of Frauds, sale and delivery of ship and cargo, 37 Cal. 638.

Joyce v. Joyce, 5 Cal. 449.   Approved, Sheriff's return, in name of deputy, a nullity, 23 Cal. 403.   Cited, Appeal, when judgment by default will be reversèd, 3 Nev. 385.

Joyce v. McAvoy, 31 Cal. 287.   Cited, Cloud on Title, when action lies to remove, 34 Cal. 389.

Juan v. Ingoldsby, 6 Cal. 439.   Approved, Appeal, interlocutory orders appealable only in special cases, 10 Cal. 528.

Judah v. American L. S. Ins. Co., 4 Ind. 334.   Cited, Corporation, acts required on formation of, to be liberally construed, 22 Cal. 440, 441.

Judd v. Ives, 4 Met. 401.   Commented on, Insolvency, effect of passage of Bankrupt Act on State jurisdiction, 37 Cal. 211, 213.

Judges of Oneida C. P. v. People, 18 Wend. 89.   Cited, Condemnation of Land, proceedings before district judge are judicial, 18 Cal. 260; Mandamus, when it will not lie, 24 Cal. 84; 28 Cal. 640.

Judson v. Atwill, 9 Cal. 477.   Cited, Insolvency, proceedings special, no intendments as to jurisdiction, 31 Cal. 169; name of creditor to appear in schedule, 33 Cal. 538.

Judson v. Love, 35 Cal. 463.   Cited, Appeal, dismissal of, on death of party, 40 Cal. 96.

Julia v. McKinney, 3 Mo. 270.   Cited, State Sovereignty, right of transit with slave property, 9 Cal. 163, 164, 165.

Jumel v. Jumel, 7 Paige, 591.   Cited, Mortgage, purchase of equity of redemption, 14 Cal. 34.   Commented on, 29 Barb. 531.

Jungerman v. Bovee, 19 Cal. 354.   Cited, Written Instruments, contemporaneous parol agreements not admissible to contradict, 31 Iowa, 502.

Kane v. Bloodgood, 7 Johns. Ch. 90. Cited, Trust and Trustee, express trust how created, 27 Cal. 279; 12 How. 155; application of statute of limitations to trust estates, 40 Cal. 567, 570; 10 Wheat. 180, note *a;* 3 Pet. 52; 10 Tex. 252; statute runs from discovery of fraud, 9 Cal. 425; 34 Cal. 258; 36 Cal. 433; 5 How. 276.

Kane v. Cook, 8 Cal. 449. Cited, Foreign Judgment, when not binding *in personam,* 31 Iowa, 403; 7 Wall. 149.

Kane v. Hood, 13 Pick. 281. Cited, Contract, to convey real estate, covenants dependent, 35 Cal. 663.

Kane v. Sanger, 14 John. 89. Cited, Covenants, in deed, when personal, 37 Cal. 189.

Kane v. Whittick, 8 Wend. 219. Cited, Decree, when not executory, 9 Cal. 635.

Karth v. Light, 15 Cal. 324. Referred to, Appeal, dismissal of, for want of prosecution, effect of, 16 Cal. 207. Cited, 29 Cal. 138; 7 Nev. 119; 5 Kan. 279. Commented on, when not a bar to second appeal, 1 Colorado, 184, 189.

Kashaw v. Kashaw, 3 Cal. 312. Distinguished, Husband and Wife, domicil, 5 Cal. 281. Approved, 5 Cal. 257. Cited, Division of common property on divorce, 20 Wis. 590.

Kater v. Steinruck's Admr., 40 Penn. St. 501. Construed, Chattel Mortgage, 35 Cal. 415.

Kazer v. State, 5 Ohio, 280. Cited, Criminal Procedure, record of, conviction of principal, not admissible on trial of accessory, 10 Cal. 70.

Kea v. Robeson, 5 Ired. Eq. 373. Cited, Deed, void for uncertainty of description, 6 Cal. 312.

Keane v. Cannovan, 21 Cal. 291. Cited, Title, constructive possession under color of title, 23 Cal. 437; 38 Cal. 487. Commented on, 25 Cal. 138; admissibility of deed to prove possession, Id. 141; 38 Cal. 488. Cited, Abandonment a question of intent, 30 Cal. 636. Commented on, 36 Cal. 339, 340; Evidence, payment of taxes not evidence as to title, 30 Cal. 637; evidence *aliunde* of description of property in tax deed not admissible, 38 Cal. 224.

Kearney v. Boston & W. R.R., 9 Cush. 108. Cited, Action, civil action for death of person, exclusively statutory, 25 Cal. 435.

Kearney, Ex parte, 7 Wheat. 38. Cited, Legislature, power over contempts not revisable by judiciary, 29 Cal. 400.

Kearsing v. Kilian, 18 Cal. 491. Cited, Deed, redelivery of, does not revest title, 34 Cal. 38; 37 Cal. 207.

Kearslake v. Morgan, 5 Term Rep. 513. Cited, Debt, payment by note, effect of, 12 Cal. 322; 3 Cranch, 317.

Keasy v. Louisville, 4 Dana, 154. Cited, Condemnation of Land, compensation, estimate of benefits, 31 Cal. 373.

Keates v. Cadogan, 2 Eng. L. & E. 320. Commented on, Landlord and Tenant, obligations of lessors, 33 Cal. 347.

Keating v. Price, 1 Johns. Cas. 22. Cited, Contract, performance as to time may be waived by parol, 39 Cal. 175; 4 Wheat. 93, note.

Keaton v. Greenwood, 8 Geo. 103. Cited, Trust and Trustee, statute of limitations runs from disavowal of trust, 36 Cal. 433.

Keay v. Goodwin, 16 Mass. 1. Construed, Tenants in Common, right of possession, 27 Cal. 547; ouster by, a question of intent, Id. 558.

Keech v. Hall, 1 Doug. 21. Cited, Foreclosure, purchaser at sale may eject tenant of mortgagor, 16 Cal. 590.

Keech v. Sandford, 1 Lead. Cas. in Eq. 32. Cited, Tenant in Common, may purchase outstanding title, right of participation in burdens and benefits, 39 Cal. 133.

Keeler v. Field, 1 Paige, 312. Doubted, Vendor and Vendee, rights of purchaser from vendee on conditional sale, 36 Cal. 158. Construed, 40 N. Y. 318.

Keeler v. Taylor, 53 Penn. St. 467. Cited, Contract, in restraint of trade, when void, 36 Cal. 358.

Keen v. Sprague, 3 Greenl. 77. Cited, Parent and Child, emancipation of minor, 25 Cal. 152.

Keener v. State, 18 Geo. 228. Cited, Criminal Procedure, threats of defendant as evidence, 34 Cal. 206.

Keeney v. Good, 21 Penn. St. 349. Commented on, Husband and Wife, separate property of wife, burden of proof, 12 Cal. 254; 30 Cal. 43.

Keeran v. Allen, 33 Cal. 542. Affirmed, State Lands, evidence that lands are swamp and overflowed, 34 Cal. 584, 586.

Keeran v. Griffith, 31 Cal. 461. Referred to, State Lands, swamp and overflowed, 33 Cal. 547. See Kernan *v.* Griffith.

Kegans v. Allcorn, 9 Tex. 25. Commented on, Probate Proceedings, 19 Cal. 218.

Kelley v. Fowler, Wilm. Notes, 298. Cited, Stare Decisis, as a rule of property, 15 Cal. 620.

Keith v. Reynolds, 3 Greenl. 393. Cited, Deed, construction of calls in, 25 Cal. 144.

Keithler v. State, 10 Smedes & M. 192. Cited, Criminal Procedure, record of conviction of principal inadmissible on trial of accessory, 10 Cal. 70.

Keithley v. Borum, 2 How. Miss. 683. Cited, Process, presumptions favor due execution of mesne process, 11 Cal. 248.

Keller v. Hicks, 22 Cal. 457. Cited, County Warrants, not negotiable, 23 Cal. 126.

Keller v. Hyde, 20 Cal. 593. Cited, County Treasurer, not bound to pay warrants not legally chargeable, 22 Cal. 461; 23 Cal. 451.

Kelleran v. Brown, 4 Mass. 443. Commented on, Conveyance, when a mortgage, 10 Cal. 208; 8 Greenl. 251.

Kellersberger v. Kopp, 6 Cal. 563. Cited, Homestead, cannot be established on property held in joint tenancy, 23 Cal. 517; 27 Cal. 425; 32 Cal. 483.

Kelley v. Munson, 7 Mass. 319. Cited, Estates of Deceased, proceeds of goods assigned no part of assets, 22 Cal. 518.

Kellinger, Matter of, 9 Paige, 62. Commented on, Taxation, of money in hands of county treasurer, 30 Cal. 244.

Kellogg, Ex parte, 6 Vt. 509. Cited, Judgment, by default, entered in wrong name, not void, 30 Cal. 206.

Kellogg v. Forsyth, 24 How. 186. Cited, Ejectment, conduct of defense by landlord, 21 Cal. 620.

Kellogg v. Paine, 8 How. Pr. 329. Commented on, Bill of Items, practice, 17 Cal. 282.

Kellogg v. Schuyler, 2 Den. 73. Cited, Assignment, cause of action for tort not assignable, 22 Cal. 178.

Kelly v. Adair, 1 Bibb, 311. Cited, Attachment, duties of officers, 25 Cal. 209.

Kelly v. Mayor, etc., of N. Y., 11 N. Y. 432. Commented on, Municipal Corporations, doctrine of *respondeat superior* not to apply, 8 Cal. 493.

Kelly v. Natoma Wat. Co., 6 Cal. 105. Distinguished, Water Rights, 7 Cal. 49. Commented on, Test of priority of appropriation, 7 Cal. 262; 37 Cal. 312. Cited, Interest acquired by appropriation, 29 Cal. 206.

Kelly v. State, 3 Smedes & M. 518. Cited, Criminal Procedure, proof of intoxication as to the question of intent, 29 Cal. 683.

Kelly v. Taylor, 23 Cal. 11. Approved, Estoppel, in pais, applies to title to mining lands, 1 Colorado, 563.

Kelly v. Van Austin, 17 Cal. 564. Cited, Default, act of clerk, in entry of, ministerial, 27 Cal. 497. Approved, 28 Cal. 651; 30 Cal. 198; 32 Cal. 636; 3 Or. 251; when judgment by default in action against defendants severally liable is void, 30 Cal. 205; Id. 534.

Kelsey v. Abbott, 13 Cal. 609. Cited, Taxation, assessment must be certain as to person taxed, 32 Cal. 332; may be made to owners known or "unknown," 28 Cal. 615; 30 Cal. 538; right of action to enforce payment, 16 Cal. 344. Construed, Tax Title, party in possession, whose duty it is to pay tax, purchases at tax sale as trustee of party assessed, 14 Cal. 34. Approved, 27 Cal. 318; 36 Cal. 146; Id. 326; 38 Cal. 223; 39 Cal. 356.

Kelsey v. Dunlap, 7 Cal. 160. Cited, Acknowledgment, of deeds, essentials of certificate, 8 Cal. 584.

Kelsey v. Trustees of Nevada, 18 Cal. 629. Approved, Taxation, power of legislature, 19 Wis. 516.

Kemp v. Westbrook, 1 Ves. Sr. 278. Cited, Chattel Mortgage, equity of redemption, 27 Cal. 270; Trust and Trustee, when statute begins to run, 36 Cal. 433, 440.

Kemper v. McClelland's Lessee, 19 Ohio, 308. Cited, Taxation, validity of tax sale, on what depends, 10 Cal. 404; 36 Cal. 73.

Kempshall v. Stone, 5 Johns. Ch. 193. Cited, Vendor and Vendee, election of remedy in vendor on breach of contract, 14 Cal. 73.

Kendall v. Almy, 2 Sum. 295. Cited, Specific Performance, when will not be decreed, 33 Cal. 133; 39 Cal. 302.

Kendall v. Lawrence, 22 Pick. 542. Cited, Contract, or judgment, void in part is void *in toto,* 7 Cal. 355; Conveyance, open and notorious possession as notice of title, 29 Cal. 490; 31 Cal. 185.

Kendall v. Miller, 9 Cal. 591. Cited, Estates of Deceased Guardian, powers of, 35 Cal. 345. Approved, Sale of property of ward, invalid, 42 Cal. 293.

Kendall v. United States, 12 Pet. 524. Commented on, Mandamus, when it lies, 7 Cal. 72; 16 Cal. 42; 39 Cal. 210; 3 How. 795; 6 How. 102; 11 How. 289, 292; 22 How. 183; 9 Wall. 312; proceedings, a civil action, 27 Cal. 684; 24 How. 97; Government, relative powers of departments of, 39 Cal. 219; 7 How. 53.

Kendall v. Vallejo, 1 Cal. 371. Cited, Pleading, new matter must be specially pleaded, 10 Cal. 30.

Kendall v. Washburn, 14 How. Pr. 380. Cited, Summons, statutory provisions as to service by publication to be strictly pursued, 20 Cal. 82; 27 Cal. 314.

Kendrick v. Delafield, 2 Caines, 67. Cited, New Trial, surprise, what must be shown, 1 Cal. 433.

Kennard v. Adams, 11 B. Mon. 102. Cited, Insolvency, preference of creditors, 10 Cal. 277; Id. 494; 19 Cal. 46.

Kennedy v. Baylor, 1 Wash. (Va.) 162. Cited, Pleading, verity of, practice, 1 Cal. 142.

Kennedy v. Brent, 6 Cranch, 187. Cited, Process, duty of officer in execution of, 13 Cal. 340.

Kennedy v. Hamer, 19 Cal. 374. Cited, Appeal, restitution on reversal, 1 Nev. 104.

Kennedy's Exrs. v. Jones, 11 Ala. 63. Cited, Dedication, to public use, what constitutes, 22 Cal. 489.

Kennedy v. Raguet, 1 Bay, 484. Cited, Attachment, construction of statute, 29 Cal. 367. Statute distinguished, Id. 378.

Kennedy v. Scovil, 12 Conn. 317. Cited, Water Rights, interest acquired, 29 Cal. 207.

Kennon v. Dickens, 1 Taylor (Conf. Rep.) 435. Cited, Interest, on interest after due, 29 Cal. 392.

Kennon v. Ficklin, 6 B. Mon. 415. Cited, Attachment, priority of lien, 25 Cal. 209.

Kenny v. Udall, 5 Johns. Ch. 464.   Cited, Alimony, 38 Cal. 278.

Kent v. Allen, 24 Mo. 98.   Cited, Evidence, opinions of witnesses not evidence, 29 Cal. 412.

Kent v. Elstob, 3 East, 18.   Cited, Arbitration, validity of award, 2 Cal. 77.

Kent v. Laffan, 2 Cal. 595.   Cited, Redemption, Statutory right of, 9 Cal. 412; 21 Cal. 395; 22 Cal. 650.

Kent v. Snyder, 30 Cal. 666.   Cited, Pleading, facts constituting fraud must be specially stated, 39 Cal. 125.

Kenyon v. Welty, 20 Cal. 637.   Cited, Equity, relief from mistake, 27 Ark. 615.

Kercheval v. Ambler, 4 Dana, 167.   Cited, Writ of restitution, return conclusive, 20 Cal. 47.

Kercheval v. Swope, 6 Mon. 362.   Cited, Specific Performance, defense of forfeiture, 40 Cal. 13.

Kerlin v. West, 3 Green Ch. 449.   Cited, Injunction, when action lies, 27 Cal. 646.

Kernan v. Griffith, 27 Cal. 87; S. C. *Sub nom* Keeran v. Griffith, 31 Cal. 461. Affirmed, S. C. 34 Cal. 580. Cited, State Lands, validity of legislative grant, 27 Cal. 327; 3 Or. 397; oral testimony admissible to prove lands to be swamp and overflowed, 28 Cal. 603; 29 Cal. 319. Approved, 29 Cal. 322. Affirmed, 34 Cal. 584. Referred to, 33 Cal. 545; what constitutes swamp and overflowed lands, 33 Cal. 547, 548.

Kerns v. Swope, 2 Watts, 75.   Cited, Conveyance, insufficient, from defective description, 6 Cal. 315.

Kerr v. Gilmore, 6 Watts, 405.   Commented on, Conveyance, when a mortgage, 10 Cal. 209, 211; 6 Penn. St. 391.

Kerr v. Merchants' Exchange Co., 3 Edw. Ch. 315.   Cited, Lease, when terminated by destruction of structure, 38 Cal. 90.

Kerrich v. Bransby, 7 Bro. Cas. in Parl. 437.   Cited, Probate, jurisdiction of probate court exclusive, 20 Cal. 266.

Kerridge v. Hesse, 9 Carr. & P. 200.   Cited, Corporation, contract waiving personal liability of stockholders, 22 Cal. 389.

Kershaw v. Thompson, 4 Johns. Ch. 609. Commented on, Writ of Assistance, remedy by, in foreclosure, 11 Cal. 192; 18 Cal. 143; 21 Cal. 33.

Kerwhaker v. Cleveland C. and C. R.R. Co., 3 Ohio St. 172. Cited, Railroads, liability for injuries caused by negligence, 37 Cal. 423.

Ketcham v. Zerega, 1 E. D. Smith, 553. Approved, Pleading, inconsistent defenses when may be set up in verified answer, 22 Cal. 680.

Ketchum v. Crippen, 31 Cal. 365. Approved, Appeal does not lie from order striking out statement on new trial, 32 Cal. 75; Id. 160; Id. 305; Id. 326. Commented on, 34 Cal. 483; when appeal lies, 42 Cal. 113; Id. 117.

Ketchum v. Evertson, 13 John. 364. Cited, 9 Cal. 146.

Kewen v. Bidleman, Cal. Sup. Ct. April T. 1852 (not reported.) Cited, Jurisdiction Court loses power over its judgment, on expiration of term, 3 Cal. 134. Commented on, 6 Cal. 22.

Key v. Goodwin, 4 Moore & P. 341. Cited, Statutes, effect of repeal, 4 Cal. 135, 165.

Keyes v. Wood, 21 Vt. 331. Cited, Mortgage, assignment of part of debt carries *pro rata* of security, 6 Cal. 483; rights of holders of several mortgage securities, 23 Cal. 30.

Kidd v. Laird, 15 Cal. 161. Commented on, Verdict, general verdict, as an estoppel, 15 Cal. 148. Cited, 22 Cal. 222; 23 Cal. 375; 28 Cal. 516; Pleading, several defenses, 22 Cal. 681; Water Rights, appropriation of water, 19 Cal. 616; 29 Cal. 206; 37 Cal. 311.

Kidder v. Hunt, 1 Pick. 328. Cited, Money paid on contract, may be recovered back, 33 Cal. 195.

Kidder v. Inhab. of Dunstable, 11 Gray, 342. Cited, Evidence, in chief, confined to matters in issue, 36 Cal. 580.

Kierski v. Mathews, 25 Cal. 591. Cited, Legal Tender Act, constitutional, 38 Cal. 254.

Kilburn v. Ritchie, 2 Cal. 145. Cited, Appeal, error must be affirmatively shown, 5 Cal. 410; Ejectment, when tenant not entitled to notice and demand, 22 Cal. 229.

Kilburn v. Woodworth, 5 John. 37. Cited, Foreign judgment when not binding *in personam*, 8 Cal. 457.

Kilby v. Wilson, Ry. & M. 178. Cited, Fraud, avoids contract of sale, 12 Cal. 462.

Kildare, Earl of, v. Sir M. Eustace, 1 Vern. 419. Cited, Specific Performance, enforcement of trust, 38 Cal. 200.

Kile v. Tubbs, 23 Cal. 431; S. C. 28 Cal. 402; 32 Cal. 332. Cited, Preëmption, claim of preëmptioner, 29 Cal. 321; Ejectment, evidence of title in, 36 Cal. 562; constructive possession under color of title, 38 Cal. 487, 489; Appeal, new trial, when not granted for insufficiency of evidence, 4 Nev. 307; 5 Nev. 421; State Lands, parol evidence of swamp lands admissible, 28 Cal. 603.

Kiler v. Kimball, 10 Cal. 267. Approved, Exceptions, to admissions of evidence must be specific, 12 Cal. 245; 16 Cal. 248; 18 Cal. 324; 23 Cal. 264; 24 Cal. 177; 27 Cal. 474; 34 Cal. 585; 3 Nev. 557; 6 Nev. 383; 7 Nev. 415. Cited, Parol evidence of mining regulations, practice, striking out, 23 Cal. 248; Nonsuit, grounds of motion must appear, 12 Cal. 429.

Kilgore v. Bulkley, 14 Conn. 362. Cited, Negotiable Instruments, certificates of deposit, 29 Cal. 506.

Killey v. Scannell, 12 Cal. 73. Denied, Replevin, demand, 3 Nev. 563. Approved, 8 Min. 79.

Killey v. Wilson, 33 Cal. 690. Cited, Deed, redelivery of, does not revest title, 34 Cal. 38; 37 Cal. 207; possession as notice of conveyance, 36 Cal. 272.

Kimball v. Blaisdell, 5 N. H. 533. Cited, Conveyance, without warranty, effect of, 14 Cal. 628.

Kimball v. Cunningham, 4 Mass. 502. Cited, Fraudulent Contract, rescission of, 29 Cal. 593.

Kimball v. Fenner, 12 N. H. 248. Cited, Deed, recitals conclusive as to grantor, 26 Cal. 87.

Kimball v. Gearhart, 12 Cal. 27. Cited, Water Rights, diligence in construction of ditches, 12 Cal. 431. Commented on, 37 Cal. 311, 312, 314; Exceptions, general objection to evidence is insufficient, 18 Cal. 327; Appeal, new trial not granted where verdict is against weight of evidence, 33 Cal. 68.

Kimball v. Lamson, 2 Vt. 138. Cited, Statutory Construction, 21 Cal. 396; "month defined," 31 Cal. 176.

Kimball v. Lohmas, 31 Cal. 154. Approved, Land, adverse possession, what constitutes, 38 Cal. 80. Cited, Constructive possession by entry under deed, Id. 673. Commented on, Replevin, for timber severed from realty, 39 Cal. 417.

Kimball v. Plant, 14 La. 511. Cited, Negotiable Instruments, certificates of deposit, 9 Cal. 418.

Kimball v. Semple, 25 Cal. 440. Cited, Deed, construction of covenants in, 30 Cal. 348; Ejectment, patents as evidence, 40 Cal. 667; evidence of prior Mexican grant, Id. 668.

Kimball v. Semple, 31 Cal. 657. Cited, New Trial, exhibits referred to in statement, 40 Cal. 147.

Kimball v. Semple, Cal. Sup. Ct. Jan. T. 1870 (not reported.) Commented on, Appeal, from order, 42 Cal. 114, 115.

Kime v. Brooks, 9 Ired. 219. Cited, Deed, execution of, by attorney, 21 Cal. 392.

Kimmel v. Willard's Admr., 1 Doug. Mich. 217. Cited, Mortgage, payment by instalments, effect of foreclosure, 23 Cal. 31.

Kincaid v. Howe, 10 Mass. 203. Cited, Name, additions no part of name, 28 Cal. 222.

Kincaid v. Neall, 3 McCord, 201. Cited, Attachment, irregularities not to invalidate, 18 Cal. 155.

Kinder v. Macy, 7 Cal. 206. Cited, Fraud, facts to be averred in actions for relief, 17 Cal. 580; 19 Cal. 289; 23 Cal. 77; 29 Cal. 60; 30 Cal. 674; Insolvency, when *bona fide* sale not fraudulent, 23 Cal. 550.

Kinder v. Shaw, 2 Mass. 398. Cited, Factor, cannot pledge, pledgee bound to know factor's powers, 19 Cal. 72, 75; conversion by bailee, 25 Cal. 559.

King v. Baldwin, 2 Johns. Ch. 554; S. C. 17 John. 384. Cited as overruled in 4 Hill, 650; Surety, discharge of, 5 Cal. 176; 9 Cal. 562. Commented on, 24 Cal. 164.

King v. Berry's Exrs., 2 Greene Ch. 44. Cited, Parties to equitable action, 31 Cal. 427.

King v. Brown, 2 Hill. 485. Cited, Action, lies for recovery back of money paid or value of services on void contract, 33 Cal. 195; 38 Cal. 110; 2 Hilt. 11; 5 Minn. 321; 1 Zab. 116, note.

King v. Chase, 15 N. H. 9. Cited, Res Adjudicata, facts in issue, and facts in controversy, 20 Cal. 486; 26 Cal. 494; 29 Cal. 521; 36 Cal. 37.

King v. Davis, 34 Cal. 100. Cited, Pleading, objections to defective pleading, when to be taken, 37 Cal. 336.

King v. Dunn, 21 Wend. 253. Cited, Appeal, death of appellant after argument, practice, 20 Cal. 69.

King v. Gunnison, 4 Penn. St. 172. Cited, Probate, sales are judicial, 9 Cal. 196, 197.

King v. Hall, 5 Cal. 82. Approved, Injunction, when will not lie, 13 Cal. 598.

King v. Harrison, 15 East, 612. Cited, Execution, may be amended, 38 Cal. 376, 381.

King v. Holmes, 11 Penn. St. 457. Cited, Negotiable Instruments, notice of dishonor, 8 Cal. 634.

King v. Mayor of N. Y., 36 N. Y. 182. Cited, Appeal, in special cases, 42 Cal. 56.

King v. Melling, 2 Lev. 58; S. C. 1 Ventr. 225. Cited, Will, construction of, 27 Cal. 445.

King v. Norman, 4 Com. B. 883. Cited, Surety, on official bond, effect of judgment against, 14 Cal. 207.

King v. Paddock, 18 John. 143. Cited, Presumption, when presumption of life ceases, 8 Cal. 64.

King v. Randlett, 33 Cal. 318. Cited, Mining Claims, title to, cannot be passed by parol, 35 Cal. 653.

King v. Richards, 6 Whart. 418. Cited, Bailment, action by bailor, proof of title in third party, 9 Cal. 574.

King v. Smith, 2 Hare, 239. Cited, Mortgage, rights of mortgagor in possession, 27 Cal. 436.

King, The, v. Arundel, Hob. 244. Cited, Statute, record of statute, enrollment, 30 Cal. 256, 257.

King, The, v. Bagshaw, 7 Term Rep. 363. Cited, Powers, special statutory powers to be strictly pursued, 19 Cal. 59.

King, The, v. College of Physicians, 7 Term Rep. 282. Commented on, Judicial Decisions, *obiter dictum,* 9 Cal. 732.

King, The, v. Corporation of Bedford Level, 6 East, 356. Commented on, Mandamus, 3 Cal. 176. Cited, Principal and Agent, authority of agent ceases on death of principal, 15 Cal. 18.

King, The, v. Hunt, 4 Barn. & Ald. 430. Cited, New Trial, insufficient grounds for, 9 Cal. 537.

King, The, v. Inhab. of Castell Careinion, 8 East, 77. Cited, Witness, impeachment, practice, 39 Cal. 450.

King, The, v. Inhab. of Longnor, 4 Barn. & Adol. 647. Cited, Deed, signature affixed by third person, at grantor's request, valid, 22 Cal. 565.

King, The, v. Justices of Monmouthshire, 7 Dowl. & R. 334. Commented on, Mandamus, when it lies, 24 Cal. 83; 29 Cal. 309.

King, The, v. Marquis of Stafford, 3 Term Rep. 646. Cited, Mandamus, when it will not lie, 3 Cal. 173.

King, The, v. Moor, 2 Mod. 129. Cited, Revenue, action lies for duties, 16 Cal. 529.

King, The, v. Severn and Wye R. Co., 2 Barn. & Ald. 646. Cited, Mandamus, remedy by, 10 Cal. 215.

King, The, v. West Riding of York, 7 East, 588. Cited, Bridge, structure, as property, 24 Cal. 488.

King, The, v. Wilkes, 2 Wils. 151. Cited, Criminal Procedure, commitment, what to state, 19 Cal. 136.

See Rex.

Kingdon v. Bridges, 2 Vern. 67. Cited, Husband and Wife, gift to wife, 12 Cal. 255.

Kingsley v. Wallis, 14 Me. 57. Cited, Trial, reasonable time for performance a question of law, 30 Cal. 558.

Kingston v. Long, 4 Doug. 9, 26 Eng. C. L. 193. Cited, Assignment, legal effect of order, 8 Cal. 105.

Kinsler v. Clarke, 2 Hill Ch. S. C. 618. Approved, Injunction, lies to restrain trespass, 7 Cal. 322, 323.

Kinsman's Lessee v. Loomis, 11 Ohio, 475. Cited, Conveyance, without warranty, effect of, 14 Cal. 628.

Kip v. Bank of New York, 10 John. 63. Cited, Estates of Deceased, trust property no part of assets, 13 Cal. 121.

Kip v. Brigham, 7 John. 168. Cited, Bond of Indemnity, breach of, 32 Cal. 25.

Kipp v. Fullerton, 4 Minn. 473. Cited, Presumptions, as to records of court, 34 Cal. 421, 428.

Kirby v. State, 7 Yerg. 259. Cited, Criminal Procedure, evidence of declarations of deceased, 24 Cal. 643.

Kirk v. State, 14 Ohio, 512. Cited, Criminal Procedure, recalling jury for additional charge, 29 Cal. 629.

Kirk v. Williams' Ex., 2 Mon. 135. Cited, Sovereignty, relative powers of Federal and State government, 2 Cal. 434.

Kirkaldie v. Larrabee, 31 Cal. 455. Cited, Public Lands, after-acquired title in mortgagor, 34 Cal. 554; 42 Cal. 179.

Kirkham v. Dupont, 14 Cal. 559. Cited, Foreclosure, subsequent incumbrancers not necessary parties, 23 Cal. 32; 40 Cal. 235; effect of decree, 40 Cal. 238.

Kirksey v. Dubose, 19 Ala. 50. Dictum denied, Attachment, justification of sheriff, what must be shown, 7 Cal. 566.

Kisling v. Shaw, 33 Cal. 425. Cited, Witness, incompetency of, where adverse party is representative of deceased, 36 Cal. 512; San Francisco, tenure of pueblo lands, in trust, 42 Cal. 557.

Kisten v. Hildebrand, 9 B. Mon. 72. Cited, Inn, what constitutes, 33 Cal. 596.

Kitchell v. Madison Co., 5 Ill. 163. Commented on, County, liability for services rendered, 30 Cal. 239.

Kite v. Commonwealth, 11 Met. 581. Commented on, Larceny, charges in indictment, 27 Cal. 403.

Kittle v. Pfeiffer, 22 Cal. 484. Cited, Dedication, to public use, by selling lots on plat, 35 Cal. 501.

Kittredge v. Warren, 14 N. H. 509. Cited, Attachment, lien of, 29 Cal. 372, 374, 376; enforcement of, against administrators, Id. 374. Commented on, Proceedings, 7 How. 621.

Kittridge v. Stevens, 16 Cal. 381. Referred to on second appeal, Orders, finality of, 23 Cal. 283.

Klein v. Alton & S. R. R. Co., 13 Ill. 514. Cited, Legislature, may authorize county aid to railroads, 13 Cal. 188.

Kleine v. Catara, 2 Gall. 61. Cited, Arbitration, award, when will be set aside, 2 Cal. 78. Doubted, Conclusiveness of award, 6 Greenl. 26. Commented on, 1 Handy, 345.

Kline v. Beebe, 6 Conn. 505. Cited, Infancy, ratification by acquiescence, 24 Cal. 214, 216.

Kline v. Central P. R.R. Co., 37 Cal. 400; S. C. 39 Cal. 587. Cited, Respondeat Superior, when act of agent binds principal, 38 Cal. 634; 57 Me. 255. Approved, Negligence, limitation in doctrine of contributory negligence, 40 Cal. 19.

Kline v. Chase, 17 Cal. 596. Cited, Judicial Sale, purchaser entitled to rents and profits, 37 Cal. 432. Referred to, 18 Cal. 115, note.

Klink v. Cohen, 13 Cal. 623. Approved, Pleading, inconsistent defenses in answer, practice, 25 Cal. 37; objections not taken by demurrer, waived, 7 Nev. 83.

Knight's Case, 1 Salk. 329. Cited, Record, what constitute court records, 34 Cal. 423.

Knight, Estate of, 12 Cal. 200. Cited, Executors and Administrators, duties and liabilities on use of funds, 26 Cal. 61; 39 Cal. 188.

Knight v. Fair, 9 Cal. 117. Approved, Execution, lien of purchaser at sale, 9 Cal. 413. Cited, Legal Title does not pass till delivery of deed, 31 Cal. 301.

Knight v. Fox, 5 Exc. 721. Reviewed, Respondeat Superior, when doctrine does not apply, 8 Cal. 491.

Knight v. Smythe, 4 Maule & S. 348. Cited, Estoppel, tenant released from, on surrender of possession, 30 Cal. 201; 33 Cal. 244.

Knight v. Truett, 18 Cal. 113. Cited, Execution, purchaser at sale entitled to rents and profits, 37 Cal. 432. Referred to, 17 Cal. 597, note.

Knobell v. Fuller, Peake Add. Cas. 139. Denied, Libel and Slander, evidence in mitigation, 41 Cal. 384.

Knott v. Morgan, 2 Keen, 213. Cited, Trade Marks, protection of, 35 Cal. 82. Commented on, 4 McLean, 518.

Knowles, Ex parte, 5 Cal. 300. Denied, Naturalization, jurisdiction to issue papers, 39 Cal. 101.

Knowles v. Calderwood, Cal. Sup. Ct. (not reported.) Referred to, 12 Cal. 215.

Knowles v. Inches, 12 Cal. 212. Approved, Appeal, irrelevant matter in transcript, practice, 15 Cal. 358. Referred to, 25 Cal. 170. Distinguished, 34 Cal. 566.

Knowles v. Joost, 13 Cal. 620. Cited, Mechanic's Lien Act, construed, 16 Cal. 127.

21

Knowles v. Yeates, 31 Cal. 82. Approved, Jurisdiction, on appeal, attaches in cases of contested election, 31 Cal. 263. Disapproved, Appeal, in special cases, 42 Cal. 64, 69.

Koch v. Briggs, 14 Cal. 256. Cited, Mortgage, a mere security, 16 Cal. 468; 21 Cal. 621; rights of foreclosure and redemption, reciprocal, 24 Cal. 410. Distinguished, Deed, of trust, 22 Cal. 124.

Koehler v. Black Riv. F. I. Co., 2 Black, 717. Cited, Corporation, conveyance by, when presumed valid, 37 Cal. 597.

Kohler v. Kohler, 2 Edw. Ch. 69. Cited, Equity, relief from sales under decree, 16 Cal. 470; Id. 564, 565.

Kohler v. Smith, 2 Cal. 597. Approved, Interest, stipulated rate in contract continues after maturity, 5 Cal. 417; 18 Iowa, 327; 16 Wis. 546; 2 Nev. 207.

Kohler v. Wells, 26 Cal. 606. Approved, Evidence, degree required in proof of negative, 1 Saw. 455.

Kohlman v. Wright, 6 Cal. 230. Cited, Insolvency, jurisdiction of supreme court, 28 Cal. 117; collateral attack on judgment, 34 Cal. 24.

Kohner v. Ashenauer, 17 Cal. 578. Commented on, Husband and Wife, gift from husband, 31 Cal. 446; Id. 653.

Koon, Ex parte, 1 Denio, 645. Cited, Mandamus, when will issue, 24 Cal. 84.

Koppikus v. State Capitol Commissioners, 16 Cal. 248. Approved, Condemnation of Land, statutes directing compensation to be assessed by commissioners constitutional, 19 Cal. 596; 24 Cal. 454; 8 Nev. 290. Cited, Appeal in special cases, 42 Cal. 68. Commented on, Legislature, power of, over taxation and appropriation, 27 Cal. 207, 208, 219; 5 Nev. 26.

Kortright v. Cady, 21 N. Y. 365. Commented on, Tender, effect of, as a discharge of liability, 26 Cal. 545; of mortgage debt, 32 Cal. 171; 37 Cal. 226. Cited, Mortgage, legal title, how affected, 35 Cal. 414.

Kramer v. Cleveland and P. R.R. Co., 5 Ohio St. 140. Cited, Eminent Domain, compensation for condemnation, as a condition precedent, 31 Cal. 559, 562.

Kreutz v. Livingston, 15 Cal. 344. Cited, Money had and received, when action lies for, 22 Cal. 463.

Krom v. Hogan, 2 Code Rep. 144. Cited, Injunction, motion to dissolve, practice, 35 Cal. 59.

Kuhland v. Sedgwick, 17 Cal. 123. Cited, Pleading, insufficient denials, 22 Cal. 168; 26 Cal. 418; 31 Cal. 194.

Kundolf v. Thalheimer, 12 N. Y. 593; reversing 17 Barb. 506. Cited, Special cases defined, 15 Cal. 92; 19 Cal. 574.

Kunkle v. Wolfersberger, 6 Watts, 126. Cited, Deed as a mortgage, parol proof of, Id. 430, 434.

Kyburg v. Perkins, 6 Cal. 674 Cited, Alcalde's Records, as evidence, 31 Cal. 519; 6 Wall. 430.

Kyle, Ex parte, 1 Cal. 331. Approved, Attorney, has no lien on judgment for his services, 2 Cal. 509; 11 Cal. 103; 38 Ala. 532; 46 Ill. 485; 44 Miss. 519. Commented on, Id. 530, 531.

Kyle v. Laurens R.R. Co., 10 Rich. 382. Cited, Common Carriers, contract for transportation through, 31 Cal. 53.

Labbe's Heirs v. Abat, 2 La. 548. Cited, Husband and Wife, validity of agreement of separation, 9 Cal. 495; of agreement for division of common property, 26 Cal. 570; of donation, 26 Cal. 574. Commented on, of contracts between, under Spanish law, Id. 567.

Lacey v. Collins, 2 South. 489. Distinguished, Assignment, assignee of account may sue, 6 Cal. 248.

Lachman v. Clark, 14 Cal. 131. Approved, Taxation, lands outside of cities, how listed, 22 Cal. 371, 372.

Lacon v. Hooper, 6 Term Rep. 226. Disapproved, Statutory Construction, definition of "month," 31 Cal. 176.

Ladd v. Stevenson, 1 Cal. 18. Cited, Pleading, new matter must be specially pleaded, 10 Cal. 30; Ejectment, prior possession sufficient to maintain, McAll. 231.

Lafayette, City of, v. Cox, 5 Ind. 38. Commented on, Constitutional Construction, legislature may invest municipality with power to make internal improvements, 13 Cal. 185, 186.

Lafayette, Heirs of, v. Kenton, 18 How. 197. Commented on, Patent, construction of, 40 Cal. 672.

Lafayette and Indianopolis R.R. Co. v. Shriner, 6 Ind. 141. Cited, Railroad, liability for injury to cattle, 18 Cal. 355.

Laffan v. Naglee, 9 Cal. 662. Commented on and distinguished, Lease, with power of lessee to purchase, 14 Cal. 444; 16 Cal. 513.

Lafonta, Ex parte, 2 Rob. 495. Cited, Judicial Notice, not taken of foreign laws, 15 Cal. 254.

Laforge v. Magee, 6 Cal. 650. Approved, Statute, postponing payment of county warrants, invalid, 6 Nev. 37.

La Frombois v. Jackson, 8 Cow. 588. Disapproved, Title, Indians cannot pass title, 1 Cal. 290. Commented on, what sufficient to constitute color of title, 1 Cal. 319. Cited, 21 Cal. 490; 33 Cal. 676.

Laimbeer v. New York, 4 Sand. 110. - Cited, Street Improvements, liability for, 31 Cal. 678.

Lake Merced Wat. Co. v. Cowles, 31 Cal. 215. Denied, Condemnation, proceedings as to rival corporations, 36 Cal. 646.

Lake v. Williamsburg, 4 Denio, 520. Commented on, Municipal Corporations, liability on contracts express or implied, 16 Cal. 271.

Lamar v. Minter, 13 Ala. 31. Cited, Constitutional Construction, validity of Settler's Act, 7 Cal. 25.

Lambert v. Smith, 3 Cal. 408. Cited and distinguished, Reference, report of referee, 30 Cal. 285.

Lamoure v. Caryl, 4 Denio, 370. Cited, Justices' Courts, jurisdiction as to counter-claim, 23 Cal. 63.

Lamping v. Hyatt, 27 Cal. 99. Distinguished, Judgment, gold coin judgments, 28 Cal. 292; 29 Cal. 275. Referred to, 34 Cal. 298. Cited, Relief granted in case of default, 29 Cal. 168. Commented on, when judgment, by default, amendable, 30 Cal. 535; when void, 33 Cal. 322.

Lancaster v. Walsh, 4 Mees. & W. 16. Cited, Reward, action lies for, 14 Cal. 137.

Landecker v. Houghtaling, 7 Cal. 391. Cited, Fraud, evidence of vendor's intent admissible, 8 Cal. 113; 36 Cal. 207; 1 Nev. 262.

Landers v. Bolton, 26 Cal. 393. Referred to, Abatement, pendency of action to quiet title will not abate action of ejectment, 27 Cal. 105; stipulations as to evidence, Id. 105, 106. Cited, Pleading, denials must be specific, 28 Cal. 172; 29 Cal. 191; 31 Cal. 195; 38 Cal. 290; Evidence, copies of recorded deeds as, 27 Cal. 245; of handwriting of party executing deed, 27 Cal. 310; Conveyance, possession under unrecorded deed as notice of title, 34 Cal. 38; 36 Cal. 272.

Landes v. Brant, 10 How. 348. Commented on, Patent, doctrine of relation applicable to, 13 Cal. 419; 20 Cal. 161. Cited, 10 How. 328; 21 How. 305; 22 How. 341.

Landis v. Dayton, Wright, 659. Approved, Verdict, polling jury in civil action, 20 Cal. 71.

Landis v. Turner, 14 Cal. 575. Cited, Witnesses, assignors as, 17 Cal. 573.

Landsberger v. Gorham, 5 Cal. 450. Cited, Witness, confidential communications, 23 Cal. 333.

Lane v. Bommelmann, 21 Ill. 147. Approved, Taxation, assessment for taxes, 31 Cal. 135.

Lane v. Clark, Clarke Ch. 316. Cited, Equity, relief from order or decree, 8 Cal. 36.

Lane v. Crombie, 12 Pick. 176. Denied, Negligence, burden of proof, 34 Cal. 164.

Lane v. Dorman, 4 Ill. 238. Cited, Constitutionality of Statute, judicial inquiry, 26 Cal. 228.

Lane v. Gluckauf, 28 Cal. 288. Approved, Specific Contract Act, construction of, 32 Cal. 130. Distinguished, Contract, payment in alternative, 29 Cal. 275, 277. Applied, 33 Cal. 473; 6 Nev. 50; Judgment, by default, for gold coin, must correspond with prayer for relief, 29 Cal. 168; interest allowed on, 28 Cal. 631; on trial of issues, what relief may be granted, 32 Cal. 88; when demand for relief not essential, 37 Cal. 324.

Lane v. Hitchcock, 14 John. 213. Cited, Mortgage, action by mortgagee for injury impairing security, 24 Cal. 473. Commented on, 16 Mo. 355.

Lane v. Mullins, 1 Gale & D. 712. Cited, Revenue Stamp, want of, on note, as a defense, what must be shown in answer, 34 Cal. 175.

Lane v. Shears, 1 Wend. 433. Cited, Conveyance, when construed as a mortgage, 36 Cal. 39; 38 Cal. 199. Commented on, Mortgage, a mere security, Id. 40, 58; payment of debt extinguishes lien, Id. 41.

Lane v. Vick, 3 How. 464. Commented on, Stare Decisis, as a rule of property, 15 Cal. 604.

Lang v. Scott, 1 Blackf. 405. Cited, Rights and Remedies, when statutory, are not exclusive, 7 Cal. 129.

Langdon v. Astor's Exrs., 16 N. Y. 9; reversing S. C. 3 Duer, 477. Cited, Nuisance, right to abate, 5 Cal. 122.

Langdon v. Buel, 9 Wend. 80. Cited, Chattel Mortgage, legal effect and operation of, 27 Cal. 269; 36 Cal. 428; pledge construed, 35 Cal. 411.

Langdon v. Keith, 9 Vt. 299. Cited, Mortgage, securing several notes, 23 Cal. 30.

Langendyck v. Burhans, 11 John. 461. Cited, Tenant in Common, when may recover rents and profits from co-tenant, 29 Cal. 333.

Langenour v. French, 34 Cal. 92. Cited, Insolvency, validity of discharge, 36 Cal. 27.

Langley v. Warner, 3 How. Pr. 363. Commented on, Appeal, undertaking, 15 Cal. 386.

Langton v. Horton, 1 Hare, 549. Cited, Assignment, of thing, not *in esse*, 30 Cal. 86.

Lansdale's Admrs., etc., v. Cox, 7 Mon. 401. Cited, Sureties, contribution between, 20 Cal. 135.

Lansing v. Lansing, 8 John. 454. Approved, Wagers, upon elections, void, as against public policy, 37 Cal. 672.

Lansing v. McKillip, 3 Caines, 286. Cited, Pleading, consideration, on special promise, 34 Cal. 147.

Lansing v. Smith, 8 Cow. 146; S. C. 4 Wend. 9. Cited, Nuisance, special damages must be particularly stated in complaint, 41 Cal. 565.

Lansingh v. Parker, 9 How. Pr. 288. Cited, Pleading, several defenses in answer, 22 Cal. 680.

Lapham v. Barnes, 2 Vt. 213. Cited, Principal and Surety, recourse of surety for money paid, 20 Cal. 136.

Lapham v. Curtis, 5 Vt. 371. Cited, Negligence, liability for damage on breakage of dam, 10 Cal. 418.

Laroo v. Casaneuava, 30 Cal. 560. Cited, Pleading, averments of evidence, irrelevant, 32 Cal. 456; 36 Cal. 233; Jurisdiction, power of judge at chambers, limited by statute, 34 Cal. 332; 35 Cal. 691.

Large v. Penn, 6 Serg. & R. 488. Cited, Deed, construction of description in, 12 Cal. 165.

Larrabee v. Baldwin, 35 Cal. 155. Cited, Corporation, liability of stockholder, 38 Cal. 534.

Larue v. Gaskins, 5 Cal. 507. Distinguished, Mandamus, when it lies, 22 Cal. 38. Commented on, Forcible Entry, trial of title in action, 23 Cal. 520.

Lasky v. Davis, 33 Cal. 677. Overruled, Appeal, review of order on motion to retax costs, 41 Cal. 441. See dissenting opinion, Rhodes, C. J., Id. 443.

Lassen v. Vance, 8 Cal. 271. Distinguished, Homestead, lien on, 16 Iowa, 154.

Latham v. Edgerton, 9 Cow. 227. Cited, Appeal Bonds, sufficiency of, 13 Cal. 509.

Lathrop v. Brittain, 30 Cal. 680. Cited, Office, of sheriff and of tax collector, distinct, 38 Cal. 77.

Lathrop v. Cook, 14 Me. 414. Commented on, Attachment, when receiptor of property not estopped, 10 Cal. 176.

Lathrop v. Mills, 19 Cal. 513. Commented on and approved, Constitutionality of Statute, statute to quiet land titles, 22 Cal. 109; 36 Cal. 633; validity of statute, part unconstitutional, 24 Cal. 547.

Lattimer v. Ryan, 20 Cal. 628. Cited, Jurisdiction, courts cannot set aside judgment after adjournment of term, 25 Cal. 52; 28 Cal. 338; Judgment, by default, measure of relief, 27 Cal. 103; 29 Cal. 168; 1 Nev. 317.

Laugher v. Pointer, 5 Barn. & C. 579. Commented on, Respondeat Superior, when doctrine does not apply to owner of carriage, 8 Cal. 495; 24 How. 124.

Laughlin v. Marshall, 19 Ill. 390. Cited, Negotiable Instruments, certificates of deposit, 29 Cal. 506.

Laughman v. Thompson, 6 Smedes & M. 259. Cited, Probate Sales, authority of court restricted by statute, 20 Cal. 312.

Laughton v. Atkins, 1 Pick. 535. Commented on, Probate, proceedings conclusive, 18 Cal. 480.

Lavergne's Heirs v. Elkins' Heirs, 17 La. 220. Cited, Title, under grant, when it vests, delivery not essential, 31 Cal. 513, 514.

Laverty v. Burr, 1 Wend. 529. Cited, Surety, on note, partner as surety, burden of proof, 37 Cal. 117.

Law v. Merrills, 6 Wend. 268. Cited, Evidence, of declarations and admissions, 26 Cal. 44.

Lawrence v. Bolton, 3 Paige, 294. Cited, Pleading, supplemental complaint, 27 Cal. 313.

Lawrence v. Dale, 3 Johns. Ch. 23. Cited, Fraud, when equity will not relieve from, 17 Cal. 384.

Lawrence v. Fast, 20 Ill. 338. Approved, Taxation, assessment invalid for want of valuation, 31 Cal. 135.

Lawrence v. Fulton, 19 Cal. 683. Approved, Abandonment, lapse of time as an element of, 36 Cal. 338. Commented on, Ejectment, what constitutes actual possession, 4 Nev. 67.

Lawrence v. Hunt, 10 Wend. 81. Cited, Judgment, conclusiveness of, 26 Cal. 494; limitation of bar of, 26 Cal. 505.

Lawrence v. Mayor, etc., of New York, 2 Denio, 491, note *a*. Cited, Condemnation, destruction of building to stop conflagration, not a condemnation requiring compensation, 1 Cal. 356.

Lawrence v. Montgomery, 37 Cal. 183. Cited, Covenant, of seizin, a personal covenant, 41 Cal. 484, 485.

Lawrence v. Taylor, 5 Hill, 107. Cited, Agreements, to convey, promises are dependent, conditions precedent to action, 1 Cal. 338; 32 Cal. 654.

Lawrence v. Trustees of Leake & Watts's Orphan House, 2 Denio, 577. Cited, Estates of Deceased, order of payment of debts, 26 Cal. 67.

Lawrence v. Wardwell, 6 Barb. 423. Cited, Negligence, when loss of profits as an element of damage, 26 Cal. 307.

Lawrenson v. Butler, 1 Scho. & L. 13. Commented on, Specific Performance, when will be decreed, 40 Cal. 67; 1 Stoct. Ch. 343.

Laws v. Thompson, 4 Jones, N. C. 104. Commented on, Judicial Sale, rights of purchaser at, 24 Cal. 607.

Lawson v. Crutchfield, 7 Ark. 48. Commented on, Probate, grant of letters not subject to collateral attack, 18 Cal. 507.

Lawson v. Ripley, 17 La. 238. Cited, Husband and Wife, community property, 14 Cal. 606; 26 Cal. 568.

Lawson v. Shotwell, 27 Miss. 630. Cited, dissenting opinion Sprague, J., Alimony, inseparable from divorce, 38 Cal. 277.

Lawton v. Erwin, 9 Wend. 237. Cited, Pleading, when jurisdictional facts to be pleaded, 33 Cal. 536.

Lawton v. Gordon, 34 Cal. 36. Cited, Deed, redelivery of, does not revest title, 37 Cal. 207; Fraudulent Conveyance, valid as between grantor and grantee, 28 Wis. 648.

Lawton v. Lawton, 3 Atk. 13. Commented on, Fixtures, as between heir and executor, 10 Cal. 264; 41 N. H. 514; removal of trade fixtures, 14 Cal. 68.

Lawton v. Salmon, 1 H. Black, note *b*, 259. Commented on, Fixtures, what constitutes, 14 Cal. 66.

Lay v. Neville, 25 Cal. 545. Approved, Sale and Delivery, what constitutes a delivery, 29 Cal. 472.

Layton v. New Orleans, 12 La. An. 515. Cited, Street Improvement, constitutionality of act for extension of street, 41 Cal. 532.

Lazard v. Wheeler, 22 Cal. 139. Approved, Assignment, claims for damages, assignable, 32 Cal. 594.

Leach v. Day, 27 Cal. 643. Cited, Injunction, to restrain trespass, when will be granted, 32 Cal. 594; 37 Cal. 307.

Leaper v. Tatton, 16 East, 420. Practice distinguished, New Promise, must be specially pleaded, 19 Cal. 482; 4 Leigh, 531; 19 Ill. 198.

Learned v. Bryant, 13 Mass. 223. Commented on, Claim and Delivery, bailee of sheriff not estopped, 10 Cal. 175.

Learned v. Vandenburgh, 8 How. Pr. 77. Cited, Attachment, application to compel payment of proceeds by sheriff to be made by motion, 8 Cal. 573.

Learned v. Welton, 40 Cal. 349. Affirmed and followed, Deed by Trustee, in Taylor *v.* Welton, No. 2550, and Butler *v.* Welton, No. 2551, same term (not reported.)

Leavenworth v. Brockway, 2 Hill, 201. Cited, Contract, made in foreign country, presumptions as to law o , 13 Cal. 278; 21 Cal. 226.

Leavitt v. Palmer, 3 N. Y. 19. Cited, Contract, no remedy on unlawful contract, 29 Cal. 271; but good part may be enforced, Id. 272; Negotiable Instruments, certificate of deposit, 35 Cal. 120.

Leavitt v. Savage, 16 Me. 72. Cited, Surety, on note, not discharged by mere delay, 10 Cal. 425.

Lecompte v. United States, 11 How. 115. Cited, Grant, validity of floating grant, 3 Cal. 42.

LeCroy v. Eastman, 10 Mod. 499. Approved, Bailment, right of owner to recover specific property, 42 Cal. 105.

Ledley v. Hays, 1 Cal. 160. Cited, Master and Servant, possession of servant is possession of master, 8 Cal. 617; Trespass, by sheriff, demand not necessary, 12 Cal. 495. Approved, 30 Cal. 191; 38 Cal. 584.

Ledoux v. Black, 18 How. 475. Commented on, Mexican Grant, segregation by survey essential, 13 Cal. 413. Commented on, Id. 417.

Lee v. Bank of United States, 9 Leigh, 218. Commented on, Husband and Wife, conveyance of wife's equitable estate, 13 Cal. 497.

Lee v. Evans, 8 Cal. 424. Approved, Deed, as a mortgage, parol evidence of, when admissible, 9 Cal. 548, 552. Commented on, 10 Cal. 160. Overruled, as to restriction to admission of, 13 Cal. 124. Cited, Mortgage, once a mortgage, always a mortgage, 14 Cal. 246; Written Instrument, as evidence of relation of parties thereto, 9 Cal. 640; Statutory Construction, exceptions in statute, how construed, 10 Cal. 45; legal presumptions as to statute, 10 Cal. 191.

Lee v. Figg, 37 Cal. 328. Approved, Judgment, by confession, not subject to collateral attack, 1 Saw. 246; 3 Or. 413.

Lee v. Fox, 6 Dana, 172. Cited, Tenant in Common, purchase of outstanding title inures to benefit of co-tenant, 33 Cal. 43; election to participate, to be made in reasonable time, 39 Cal. 133.

Lee v. Lee, 6 Gill & J. 316. Cited, Contract, for services, when no action lies, 22 Cal. 510.

Lee v. McDaniel, 1 A. K. Marsh. 234. Cited, Land, possession under deed by entry of tenant, 38 Cal. 491.

Lee v. Newkirk, 18 Ill. 550. Cited, Execution, when void, 38 Cal. 378.

Lee v. Risdon, 7 Taunt. 188.   Cited, Fixtures, removal of, by tenant, 14 Cal. 68.   Approved, 17 Vt. 411.

Lee v. Tillotson, 4 Hill, 27.   Commented on, Judgment, rendition of, defined, 28 Cal. 422.

Leech v. West, 2 Cal. 95.   Distinguished, Appeal, waiver of right of, 6 Cal. 478.   Approved, Statement, waived by failure to make it in time, 3 Or. 565.

Lees v. Nuttall, 1 Russ & M. 53.   Commented on, Resulting Trust, verbal agreement, when not within statute of frauds, 21 Cal. 100; 35 Cal. 488; 3 Story, 220; 3 Sum. 468.   Distinguished, 13 Ill. 234; 16 Vt. 508.

Leese v. Clark, 29 Cal. 664.   Cited, Ejectment, who should be removed under writ of restitution, 34 Cal. 487, 490. Approved, 36 Cal. 150.

Leese v. Clark, 3 Cal. 17; S. C. 18 Cal. 535; 20 Cal. 387. Approved, Mexican Grants, that ejectment will not lie till confirmation of, by territorial deputation, 3 Cal. 48. Distinguished, 3 Cal. 46.   Commented on, 6 Cal. 269; McAll. 163; and overruled, 10 Cal. 621; judicial delivery by survey and measurement essential to vest perfect title, 24 Cal. 87.   Cited, 26 Cal. 628; 38 Cal. 66; construction of congressional acts, as to survey, 28 Cal. 95.   Affirmed, Presentation to board of commissioners of grant by Governor to lands within pueblo, essential, 30 Cal. 506; 31 Cal. 131.   Cited, Conclusiveness of Confirmation, survey and patent, 19 Cal. 458; patent takes effect by relation, 20 Cal. 160; 27 Cal. 168; 34 Cal. 253; 35 Cal. 88; 1 Saw. 566.   Approved, 38 Cal. 71.   Cited, Confirmed Survey takes effect by relation, 34 Cal. 253; 35 Cal. 88; third persons, not concluded, who are, 24 Cal. 669; 26 Cal. 627; 1 Saw. 569; patent not subject to collateral attack, 22 Cal. 111.   Affirmed and law of case announced, 20 Cal. 415.   Cited, 1 Saw. 576, 577; Pueblo Lands, tenure of, 42 Cal. 556.   Cited as inapplicable, Alcalde Grants, 8 Cal. 198; Powers of Alcaldes to make grants, 1 Saw. 575.   Cited, Stare Decisis, as a rule of property, 15 Cal. 598, 606; Appeal, loss of jurisdiction on filing remittitur, 22 Cal. 25; 24 Cal. 58.

Leet v. Wadsworth, 5 Cal. 404.   Rule limited, Factor, has no power to pledge, 6 Cal. 385.   Commented on, McAll. 411.

Leet v. Wilson, 24 Cal. 398.   Cited, Exceptions, grounds of objection to evidence should be stated, 3 Nev. 557; 7 Nev. 415; 24 Wis. 72.

Lefevre, Appeal of, 32 Cal. 565. Instanced, Appeal, in special cases, 42 Cal. 68.

Le Fevre v. LeFevre, 4 Serg. & R. 241. Cited, Pleading, parol agreement as a defense in action on specialty, 4 Cal. 316.

Le Fevre v. Lloyd, 5 Taunt. 749. Cited, Contract, drawn by agent, when agent liable, 13 Cal. 48. Distinguished, 11 Rich. S. C. 214.

Lefevre v. Mayor of Detroit, 2 Mich. 587. Cited, Street Assessments, on whom made, 31 Cal. 684.

Leffingwell v. Griffing, 29 Cal. 192. Cited, Appeal, non-appealable orders, 31 Cal. 367. Approved, 32 Cal. 75; Id. 160; Id. 305. Commented on, 42 Cal. 117.

Leffingwell v. Warren, 2 Black, 599. Approved, Title, by adverse possession, 34 Cal. 383; 36 Cal. 541.

Leggett v. Dubois, 5 Paige, 114. Commented on, Resulting Trust, when it arises, 22 Cal. 579.

Leggett v. New Jersey Manf. & B. Co., 1 Sax. Ch. 559. Cited, Corporation, validity of deed of, seal as evidence, 16 Cal. 639; 37 Cal. 598.

Leggett v. Raymond, 6 Hill, 639. Cited, Guaranty, on note, sufficiency of, 7 Cal. 34.

LeGuen v. Gouverneur, 1 Johns. Cas. 436. Approved, Judgment, conclusiveness of, 24 Cal. 604; 25 Cal. 272; 27 Cal. 169; 15 Ill. 457. Limited, 38 Cal. 647.

Lehman v. Southerland, 3 Serg. & R. 145. Cited, Office, term of, 6 Cal. 292.

Leigh's Case, 1 Munf. 468. Cited, Attorney-at-Law, not a public officer, 22 Cal. 315. Commented on, 1 W. Va. 300.

Leighton v. Leighton, 1 P. Wms. 672. Cited, Bill of Peace, possession requisite to give right of action, 6 Cal. 40.

Leighton v. Wales, 3 Mees. & W. 545. Cited, Contract, liquidated damages in, 9 Cal. 587.

Leighton v. Walker, 9 N. H. 59. Cited, Statute, repeal by implication, 10 Cal. 316.

Leitch v. Hollister, 4 N. Y. 211. Commented on, Insolvency, assignment in trust, valid, 10 Cal. 276; 26 Cal. 327.

Leland v. Wilkinson, 10 Pet. 294. Cited, Statute, validity of confirmatory statutes, 16 Cal. 238.

Leman v. Whitley, 4 Russ. 423. Commented on, Resulting Trust, not implied as between parent and child, 16 Cal. 356. Cited, Equity, relief from mistake, 28 Cal. 637, 638. Distinguished, 22 Cal. 580.

Lemar v. Miles, 4 Watts, 330. Cited, Fixtures, what pass on sale of property, 14 Cal. 68.

Lemon v. Craddook, Litt. Sel. Cas. 252. Commented on, Execution, deed to be made by retiring sheriff, 8 Cal. 409.

Lemon v. Trull, 13 How. Pr. 248. Cited, Pleading, counterclaim in answer, 26 Cal. 306.

Lench v. Lench, 10 Ves. Jr. 511. Cited, Evidence, of declarations and admissions, 26 Cal. 44; of implied trust, 27 Cal. 112.

Le Neve v. Le Neve, 1 Ves. Sr. 64; S. C. 3 Atk. 646. Cited, Notice to agent is notice to principal, 31 Cal. 165; possession of land as notice of conveyance, 31 Cal. 185; 37 Cal. 206; 11 How. 395.

Lent v. Morrill, 25 Cal. 492. Referred to, 24 Cal. 242; Conveyance of mortgaged premises, effect of, 36 Cal. 20.

Lent v. Shear, 26 Cal. 361. Cited, Foreclosure, action when barred, 33 Cal. 97; 42 Cal. 503; Conveyance of mortgaged premises, effect of, 36 Cal. 20.

Leonard v. Darlington, 6 Cal. 123. Cited, Pueblo Lands, grants of, 8 Cal. 201.

Leonard v. Leonard, 14 Pick. 283. Cited, Probate, proceedings not subject to collateral attack, as to jurisdictional facts, 7 Cal. 234; 18 Cal. 507.

Leonard v. Pitney, 5 Wend. 30. Denied, Statute of Limitations, in case of fraudulent concealment, 8 Cal. 459; 2 Black, 605. Commented on, Action, for deceit, 9 Cal. 227.

Leonard v. Vredenburg, 8 John. 29. Cited, Guaranty, consideration, 9 Cal. 334; 38 Cal. 135. Commented on, 2 McLean, 110. Approved, 26 Wis. 185.

Le Roy v. Mayor of New York, 20 John. 430. Approved, Certiorari, when it lies, 16 Cal. 209. Doubted, 2 Hill, 11.

LeRoy v. Rassette, 32 Cal. 171. Cited, New Trial, right to move waived by failure to file statement, 41 Cal. 518; 42 Cal. 32.

LeRoy v. Rogers, 30 Cal. 229. Cited, Title by adverse possession, 34 Cal. 382.

LeSage v. Coussmaker, 1 Esp. 187. Cited, Services, when no action lies for, 22 Cal. 510.

Les Bois v. Bramell, 4 How. 449. Cited, Grant, validity of floating grant, 3 Cal. 42; private survey ineffectual, 13 Cal. 416; 14 Cal. 359; 4 How. 448.

Lessieur v. Price, 12 How. 59. Cited, State Lands, legislative grant effectual to pass title, 27 Cal. 327, 328; 15 How. 447; 22 How. 159.

Lessieur v. Price, 12 How. 77. Cited, State Lands, title in State, when it vests, 25 Cal. 256.

Lester v. Garland, 15 Ves. Jr. 248. Cited, Time, computation of, 8 Cal. 416.

Lester v. Jewett, 11 N. Y. 453. Cited, Contract, to convey real estate, covenants dependent, 35 Cal. 663.

Lestrade v. Barth, 19 Cal. 660; S. C. 17 Cal. 285. Commented on, New Trial, surprise, 19 Cal. 36. Cited, Title, adverse possession as notice of conveyance, 21 Cal. 628; 26 Cal. 419; 29 Cal. 490; 31 Cal. 184; 36 Cal. 271; Equity, will relieve from mistakes, 23 Cal. 124. Approved, Ejectment, equitable defenses may be pleaded, 24 Cal. 141; 25 Cal. 597; 26 Cal. 39; 42 Cal. 352; 4 Nev. 460; 13 Wall. 103.

Lett v. Morris, 4 Sim. 607. Cited, Assignment, effect of order for money, 14 Cal. 407.

Letter v. Putney, 7 Cal. 423. Cited, Exceptions, to instructions, when to be taken, 26 Cal. 267; 3 Nev. 520.

Letters v. Cady, 10 Cal. 533. Cited, Marriage, sufficiency of proof of where marriage is foundation of claim, 26 Cal. 133; 1 Saw. 120; Pleading, insufficient averments in complaint, 7 Nev. 172.

Levering v. Mayor of Memphis, 7 Humph. 553. Cited, Corporation, validity of deed by, 16 Cal. 639; 37 Cal. 598.

Levering v. Rittenhouse, 4 Whart. 130.   Cited, Statute of Limitations, construction of, 35 Cal. 638.

Levinson v. Schwartz, 22 Cal. 229.   Cited, Replevin, demand essential, 3 Nev. 565.

Levy v. Brown, 11 Ark. 16.   Commented on, New Trial, surprise, 24 Cal. 88; 3 Mo. 600.

Levy v. Getleson, 27 Cal. 685.   Commented on, Appeal, settlement of statement, 31 Cal. 337; statement may be stricken out, 32 Cal. 326; non-appealable orders, 33 Cal. 678.   Overruled, order on motion to retax costs, when appealable, 41 Cal. 441, 443.

Levy v. Pope, Mood & M. 410.   Cited, Attorney and Counsel, as privileged witness, 36 Cal. 508.

Lewis v. Clarkin, 18 Cal. 399.   Referred to, Judgment, several, against joint debtors, 18 Cal. 404; 39 Cal. 95.

Lewis v. Covillaud, 21 Cal. 178.   Referred to in syllabus, Statute of Frauds, express promise when not within, not cited, 22 Cal. 188.   Referred to and discussed, 25 Cal. 346, 347, 350, 354.   Cited, Vendor's Lien, not assignable, 36 Cal. 321; 26 Ark. 396; Id. 645.

Lewis v. Dubose, 29 Ala. 219.   Cited, Attachment, debtor and tortfeasor, 34 Cal. 300.

Lewis v. Fullerton, 1 Rand. 15.   Cited, Manumission, of slave, 2 Cal. 443.

Lewis v. Garrett's Adm., 5 How. Miss. 434.   Cited, Constitutional Construction, right of trial by jury, 2 Cal. 247.

Lewis v. Holloway, 6 Binn. 216.   Cited, Constitutional Construction, 2 Cal. 445.

Lewis v. Johns, 24 Cal. 98.   Affirmed, Trespass, under legal process, 34 Cal. 635.

Lewis v. Kendall, 6 How. Pr. 59.   Cited, Pleading, inconsistent defenses, 13 Cal. 625.

Lewis v. Lyman, 22 Pick. 437.   Cited, Contract, cropping on shares, construction of, 17 Cal. 546; 25 Cal. 66.

Lewis v. Myers, 3 Cal. 475.   Cited, Trial, when consideration, an essential fact, 23 Cal. 539.

Lewis v. Rigney, 21 Cal. 268.   Cited, Jurisdiction, over judgment, lost on adjournment of term, 28 Cal. 338.

Lewis v. San Antonio, 7 Tex. 288. Cited, Wills, law of forum, as to proof of execution, 10 Cal. 479. Commented on, Pueblo Lands, title to, 15 Cal. 560, 596.

Lewis v. Stein, 16 Ala. 214. Cited, Water Rights, prior appropriation entitled to protection of, 23 Cal. 487.

Lewis v. Thompson, 3 Cal. 266. Cited, Officer, acts of deputy must be in name of principal, 23 Cal. 403.

Lewis v. Tobias, 10 Cal. 574. Approved, Injunction, when will not be granted, 13 Cal. 597.

Lewis v. Woodworth, 2 N. Y. 512. Cited, Tenants in Common, when not bound by several act of co-tenant, 6 Cal. 621.

Lexington v. Clarke, 2 Ventr. 223. Cited, Contract, void in part is void *in toto*, 38 Cal. 109.

Lexington v. McGuillan's Heirs, 9 Dana, 521. Cited, Municipal Corporations, statutory right to cause repair of streets, 12 Cal. 478.

Libby v. Burnham, 15 Mass. 144. Cited, Street Improvements, duty of superintendent, 36 Cal. 413.

License Cases, 5 How. 504. Cited, State Sovereignty, power of taxation, 1 Cal. 236; statutes providing for issuance of licenses not unconstitutional, 1 Cal. 239. Applied to foreign miners' licenses, 1 Cal. 244. Commented on, Id. 247. Cited, Concurrent powers of State and Federal, over commerce, 4 Cal. 61. Construed, power as to police regulations, 20 Cal. 580. Reviewed, 7 How. 470.

Lichtenthaler v. Thompson, 13 Serg. & R. 157. Cited, Surety, on undertaking, when discharged, 26 Cal. 542; 29 Cal. 198.

Lick v. Diaz, 30 Cal. 65. Referred to on second appeal, 37 Cal. 440.

Lick v. Faulkner, 25 Cal. 404. Approved, Legal Tender, constitutionality of legal tender act, 25 Cal. 504; Id. 570; Id. 593; 26 Cal. 47; Id. 662; 27 Cal. 161; 38 Cal. 254. Cited, Legislature, discretionary powers of, 27 Cal. 224; 1 Nev. 585; 42 Ala. 574.

Lick v. Madden, 36 Cal. 208; S. C. 25 Cal. 202. Cited, Officer, liability for malfeasance, omission, or neglect, 29 Iowa, 346.

Lick v. O'Donnell, 3 Cal. 59. Cited, Deed, when grantee becomes tenant in common, 24 Cal. 111; 37 Cal. 520.

Lick v. Stockdale, 18 Cal. 219. Cited, Judgment, validity, on what depends, 34 Cal. 614. Commented on, 1 Saw. 323, 325, 327.

Lickbarrow v. Mason, 2 Term Rep. 63. Approved, Bill of Lading, how far a negotiable instrument, 1 Cal. 79, 81. Commented on, Equity, maxim as to burden of loss, 26 Cal. 44.

Lies v. De Diablar, 12 Cal. 327. Cited, Homestead, right of, defined, 22 Cal. 638; Mortgage, by husband, void, 13 Iowa, 583.

Life & Fire Ins. Co. of N. Y. v. Adams, 9 Pet. 602. Cited, Mandamus, direction to inferior tribunal, 28 Cal. 641.

Life and F. Ins. Co. v. Mechanic F. Ins. Co. of N. Y., 7 Wend. 31. Cited, Exceptions, to instructions, when to be taken, 26 Cal. 266.

Lightstone v. Laurencel, 4 Cal. 277. Cited, Negotiable Instruments, uniform liability of promisors on note, 6 Cal. 397; 9 Cal. 23; Surety, on note, 7 Cal. 538; guarantor entitled to notice, 16 Cal. 153.

Like v. Thompson, 9 Barb. 315. Cited, Wagers, when money staked may be recovered back, 37 Cal. 674.

Lilly v. Ewer, 1 Doug. 72. Cited, Evidence, admissible in construing written instruments, 34 Cal. 629.

Lincoln v. Battelle, 6 Wend. 475. Cited, New Promise, original debt as consideration, 42 Cal. 499.

Lincoln v. Blanchard, 17 Vt. 464. Cited, Judgment, against principal, when conclusive on surety, 14 Cal. 204.

Lincoln v. Saratoga and S. R.R. Co., 23 Wend. 425. Commented on, Evidence, opinions of witnesses, when inadmissible, 10 Cal. 342.

Lindenberger v. Beall, 6 Wheat. 104. Cited, Negotiable Instruments, notice of dishonor, 8 Cal. 634.

Lindsay v. Jackson, 2 Paige, 581. Cited, Set-off, when equitable set-off will be enforced, 11 Cal. 102; 23 Cal. 628.

Lindsay v. Lindsay, 11 Vt. 521. Cited, Trial, delivery of conveyance a question of fact, 5 Cal. 318.

Lindsay v. Lynch, 2 Scho. & L. 1. Approved, Specific Performance, of void contract, cannot be enforced, 4 Cal. 92; nor of contract, vague or indefinite, 33 Cal. 133.

22

Lindsay's Exrs. v. Armfield, 3 Hawks, 548.   Cited, Process, duty of officers in execution of, 13 Cal. 339.

Lindsey v. Gordon, 13 Me. 60.   Cited, Contract, when right to rescind is waived, 1 Cal. 341.

Lindsey v. McClelland, 1 Bibb. 262.   Cited, Jurisdiction, cannot be conferred by consent, 29 Cal. 463.

Lineker v. Ayeshford, 1 Cal. 75.   Distinguished, Agent, cannot maintain action in his own name, 1 Cal. 94.

Lining v. Bentham, 2 Bay, 1.   Commented on, Contempt, power of court in cases of, 1 Cal. 153, 154.

Linn v. Ross, 10 Ohio, 412.   Cited, Landlord and Tenant, covenant to rebuild not implied, 39 Cal. 153.

Linn v. Twist, 3 Cal. 89.   Denied, New Trial, reference to evidence in statement, 9 Cal. 210.

Lin Sing v. Washburn, 20 Cal. 534.   Cited, State Sovereignty, invalidity of passenger tax by State, 34 Cal. 498.

Linton v. Porter, 31 Ill. 107.   Approved, Warranty, no breach of, till vendee's possession is disturbed, 41 Cal. 116.

Linville v. Earlywine, 4 Blackf. 469.   Cited, Libel and Slander, essentials in complaint, 41 Cal. 481.

Lion v. Burtiss, 20 John. 483.   Commented on, Stare Decisis, as a rule of property, 15 Cal. 605; 3 Paige, 281.

Lisman v. Early, 15 Cal. 199.   Approved, Evidence, practice on admission of, discretion of court, 42 Cal. 442.

Litchfield v. Burwell, 5 How. Pr. 346.   Cited, Service of Process, proof of, 9 Cal. 321.

Litchfield v. McComber, 42 Barb. 289.   Commented on, Street Assessments, personal liability for, 31 Cal. 259; Id. 678.

Litt v. Cowley, 7 Taunt. 169. Cited, Common Carrier, right of stoppage *in transitu,* how exercised, 37 Cal. 632.

Little v. Bishop, 9 B. Mon. 240.   Cited, Ejectment, judgment by default, 10 Cal. 378.

Little v. Dawson, 4 Dall. 111.   Cited, Services, when no action lies for, 22 Cal. 510.

Little v. Greenleaf, 7 Mass. 236.   Cited, Taxation, *situs* of personal property, 23 Cal. 139.

Little v. Harvey, 9 Wend. 157. Commented on, Judgment Lien, not extended by execution, 10 Cal. 80; 37 Cal. 133.

Little v. Larrabee, 2 Greenl. 37. Approved and applied, Verdict, power of court to amend, 3 Cal. 139.

Little v. Little, 13 Pick. 426. Approved, Consideration, sufficient for express promise, 13 Cal. 832.

Little v. Pearson, 7 Pick. 301. Cited, Vendor and Vendee, when action for rents lies against vendee, 22 Cal. 616.

Little v. Wyatt, 14 N. H. 25. Cited, Evidence, entries in book as, 14 Cal. 576.

Little Miami R. R. Co. v. Collett, 6 Ohio St. 182. Cited, Eminent Domain, compensation on condemnation, 31 Cal. 373.

Littlepage v. Fowler, 11 Wheat. 215. Commented on, Deed, description in, 25 Cal. 451.

Lively v. Ball, 2 B. Mon. 54. Cited, Appeal, judgment not reversed for errors without injury, 26 Cal. 467.

Live Yankee Co. v. Oregon Co., 7 Cal. 40. Approved, New Trial, when not granted, on evidence newly discovered, 22 Cal. 163; 3 Or. 43; on ground of surprise, 29 Cal. 609.

Livingston v. Ackeston, 5 Cow. 531. Cited, Services, when promise for remuneration is implied, 22 Cal. 511.

Livingston v. Hollenbeok, 4 Barb. 9. Cited, Cloud on Title, when equity will set aside deed, 15 Cal. 134.

Livingston v. Jefferson, 1 Brock. 203. Cited, Judiciary, power of, in construction of statutes, 9 Cal. 512.

Livingston v. Livingston, 4 Paige, 111. Cited, Injunction, dissolution on bill and answer, practice, 9 Cal. 553; 35 Cal. 60.

Livingston v. Livingston, 6 Johns. Ch. 497. Commented on, Injunction to restrain trespass, 7 Cal. 323, 329. Reviewed, 2 Mich. 582.

Livingston v. Mayor of N. Y., 8 Wend. 85. Approved, Constitutional Construction, right of trial by jury, 16 Cal. 254; as to special proceedings, 24 Cal. 454. Cited, Compensation on condemnation of land, estimate of benefits, 31 Cal. 374; Dedication to Public Use, streets in cities, 22 Cal. 490. Approved, 35 Cal. 500.

Livingston v. Peru Iron Co., 9 Wend. 511.   Distinguished, Title, by actual possession, 25 Cal. 131; what constitutes color of title, 33 Cal. 676.

Livingston v. Platner, 1 Cow. 175.   Cited, Pleading, treble damages under statute must be expressly demanded, 5 Cal. 240.

Livingston v. Rogers, 1 Caines, 584.   Cited, Contract, containing mutual covenants, execution of, 21 Cal. 69.

Livingston v. Roosevelt, 4 John. 251.   Cited, Partnership, notice of limitation to personal liability, 22 Cal. 389.

Lloyd v. Callett, 4 Bro. C. C. 469.   Commented on, Contract, time as essence of, 10 Cal. 329.

Lloyd v. Gordon, 2 Harr. & McH. 254.   Commented on, Ejectment, ouster by tenant in common, 27 Cal. 555.

Lloyd v. Hough, 1 How. 153.   Commented on, Use and Occupation, action when it lies, 35 Cal. 194.

Lloyd v. Lynoh, 28 Penn. St. 419.   Cited, Tenant in Common, purchase of outstanding title by, 39 Cal. 133.

Lloyd v. Mayor, etc., of N. Y., 5 N. Y. 369.   Commented on, Municipal Corporation, powers of, 7 Cal. 376. Cited, Contracts of, how construed, 16 Cal. 270.

Lloyd v. Taylor, 1 Dall. 17.   Commented on, Married Woman, validity of conveyance by, 1 Cal. 499.

Locke v. Whiting, 10 Pick. 279.   Cited, Deed, parol evidence of, when not admissible, 24 Cal. 417.

Lockey v. Lockey, Finch Pre. Ch. 518.   Cited, Statute of Limitations, when it runs in favor of trustee, 40 Cal. 567.

Lockwood v. Barnes, 3 Hill, 128.   Cited, Statute of Frauds, action on contract under, 33 Cal. 195.

Lockwood v. Canfield, 20 Cal. 126.   Cited, Resulting Trust, may be proved by parol, 22 Cal. 579.

Lockwood v. Perry, 9 Met. 440.   Approved, Replevin, right of possession obtained under writ, 11 Cal. 274, 277.

Lockwood v. St. Louis, 24 Mo. 21.   Cited, Street Assessments, liability for, 28 Cal. 359.

Lockwood v. Younglove, 27 Barb. 506.   Cited, Execution, claim of exemption, how asserted, 22 Cal. 506.

Lodge v. Turman, 24 Cal. 385.   Cited, Deed, as a mortgage, parol evidence of, 33 Cal. 332; 36 Cal. 62.

Loohr v. Latham, 15 Cal. 418.. Cited, Change of place of trial, convenience of witnesses, practice, 22 Cal. 131; Id. 538.

Logan v. Hillegass, 16 Cal. 200. Referred to, Judgment, by default, remedy for, when void and voidable, 14 Cal. 159. Approved, Arrest of process under void judgment, 19 Cal. 708; 31 Cal. 172; setting aside, remedy by motion exclusive, 37 Cal. 228; Id. 529; showing required, 23 Cal. 129.

Logan v. Logan, 2 B. Mon. 142. Approved, Alimony, without divorce, 38 Cal. 270.

Logan v. Mathews, 6 Penn. St. 417. Cited, Consideration, for payment of interest, 6 Cal. 130.

Logansport v. Dunn, 8 Ind. 378. Cited, Dedication, to public use, by sale of lots with plat, 35 Cal. 501.

Lombard v. Cobb, 14 Me. 222. Cited, Agency, several action maintainable for expenses incurred, 12 Cal. 128.

London v. Perkins, 3 B. P. C. by Toml. 602. Commented on, Bill of Peace, when it lies, 6 Cal. 39.

Long v. Beard, 3 Murph. 57. Cited, Ferry Franchise, protection from invasion of, 6 Cal. 595, 598.

Long v. Dollarhide, 24 Cal. 218. Cited, Deed, recitals in, on whom conclusive, 26 Cal. 86; declarations of grantor when not admissible to impeach, 38 Cal. 282, 284. Approved, Conveyances, construction of recording act as to priority of record, 6 Nev. 391; Partition, by parol, 27 Cal. 425.

Long v. Majestre, 1 Johns. Ch. 305. Cited, Parties, in supplementary proceedings against insolvent, 7 Cal. 204; 14 How. 34.

Long v. Morton, 2 A. K. Marsh. 39. Commented on, Ejectment, who bound by judgment, 22 Cal. 206; 9 How. 49.

Long v. Neville, 29 Cal. 131; S. C. 36 Cal. 455. Cited, Ejectment, who not liable to dispossession, 34 Cal. 490; 35 Cal. 129; 36 Cal. 460; 37 Cal. 348; 31 Wis. 543.

Long v. Rodgers, 19 Ala. 321. Cited, Instructions, modification of, not error, 25 Cal. 471.

Long v. Short, 1 P. Wms. 403. Cited, Will, construction of devise, 31 Cal. 611. Doubted, 9 Gratt. 549.

Longendyke v. Longendyke, 44 Barb. 366. Cited, Parties, action may be maintained by wife against husband, 36 Cal. 452.

Long Isl. R. R. Co. v. Conklin, 29 N. Y. 572. Cited, Tenant in Common, grantee of specific quantity may maintain ejectment, 37 Cal. 521.

Long's Lessee v. Pellett, 1 Harr. & McH. 531. Cited, Evidence, hearsay, when admissible, 15 Cal. 281.

Longwith v. Butler, 8 Ill. 32. Cited, Mortgage, power of sale in mortgagee, 17 Cal. 593.

Longworth v. Taylor, 1 McLean, 395. Cited, Title, equitable title, how lost, 40 Cal. 571.

Lonsdale v. Brown, 4 Wash. C. C. 148. Cited, New Trial, when verdict will not be set aside, 15 Cal. 182; Contract, construction of, 22 Cal. 94.

Loomer v. Wheelwright, 3 Sand. Ch. 135. Cited, Married Woman, mortgage on separate property for debt of another, 20 Cal. 675.

Loomis v. Bedel, 11 N. H. 74. Cited, Covenant, what sufficient eviction to constitute a breach, 39 Cal. 367, 368.

Loomis v. Brown, 16 Barb. 325. Cited, Judgment, of dismissal, effect of, 18 Cal. 627.

Loomis v. Marshall, 12 Conn. 76. Cited, Partnership, what necessary to constitute, 38 Cal. 213.

Loomis v. McClintock, 10 Watts, 274. Cited, Power, execution of, 32 Cal. 444.

Loomis v. Terry, 17 Wend. 496. Cited, Negligence, liability for injury by ferocious animal, 41 Cal. 141.

Lord v. Baldwin, 6 Pick. 348. Cited, Assignment, in trust, obligations of assignee, 6 Cal. 353.

Lord v. Morris, 18 Cal. 482. Cited, Mortgage, a mere security, 21 Cal. 623; Foreclosure, grantee a necessary party, 25 Cal. 161; Id. 499. Approved, Action barred when debt secured is barred, 21 Cal. 501; 24 Cal. 498; 26 Cal. 144; Id. 365, 369; 42 Cal. 501, 503; contra, 1 Nev. 621; 1 McAll. 497; revival of remedy by new promise on debt, 22 Cal. 102; mortgagor after disposal of premises loses all power, 26 Cal. 369; 36 Cal. 20. Cited, Statute of Limitations, applies to equitable actions, 23 Cal. 34; 24 Cal. 409; 4 Nev. 289; who may plead statute in bar, 23 Cal. 25; Id. 143.

Lord v. Sherman, 2 Cal. 498. Cited, Power, to convey lands, requisites of, 17 Wis. 612.

Lord v. Veazie, 8 How. 254. Cited, Appeal, questions not presented in good faith will not be reviewed, 30 Cal. 325.

Lord Carrington v. Payne, 5 Ves. Jr. 411. Cited, Will, proof of attestation to, 10 Cal. 479.

Lord Inchiquin v. O'Brien, 1 Wils. 82. Cited, Will, construction of devise, 31 Cal. 600.

Lord Mohun's Case, 1 Salk. 104. Cited, Criminal Procedure, bail in murder cases, 19 Cal. 544.

Lord Rancliffe v. Parkyns, 6 Dow. 202; S. C. 2 Jur. N. S. 457. Cited, Will, attestation to, 10 Cal. 479.

Lord St. John v. Lady St. John, 11 Ves. Jr. 526. Cited, Husband and Wife, agreements for separation valid, 9 Cal. 492.

Loring v. Boston, 7 Met. 409. Cited, Reward, action lies for, 14 Cal. 137.

Loring v. Brackett, 3 Pick. 403. Cited, Release, obtained by fraud, no bar to action, 23 Cal. 351.

Loring v. Illsley, 1 Cal. 24. Cited, Appeal, jurisdiction over cases brought in court of first instance, 1 Cal. 35. Commented on, Order and final judgment distinguished, 1 Cal. 136; Id. 139. Cited, Judgment, conclusiveness of, 22 Cal. 222.

Lorraine v. Long, 6 Cal. 452. Approved, Judgment, when not conclusive as to, equitable defense, 30 Cal. 311.

Lott v. Keach, 5 Tex. 394. Cited, Husband and Wife, presumptions as to common property, 12 Cal. 224, 253.

Lott v. Prudhomme, 3 Rob. 293. Cited, Mexican Grant, effect of location and survey, 13 Cal. 417; title vests on execution of patent, 31 Cal. 513.

Loucks v. Edmondson, 18 Cal. 203. Approved, Appeal from order on new trial, statement on, 23 Cal. 549; striking out statement, 32 Cal. 326.

Loudon v. Robertson, 5 Blackf. 277. Cited, Probate Sale, *caveat emptor* the rule, 9 Cal. 197.

Louisville v. Grey, 1 Litt. 147. Cited, Alien, right of inheritance, 12 Cal. 456.

Louisville & C. & C. R.R. Co. v. Letson, 2 How. 497. Cited, Corporations, as citizens, 22 Cal. 538; 14. How. 100; 15 How. 248.

Louisville & F. R.R. Co. v. Milton, 14 B. Mon. 61. Doubted, Railroads, liability for injury to cattle, 18 Cal. 356. Approved, 2 Met. 183.

Love v. Robertson, 7 Tex. 6. Cited, Husband and Wife, presumption as to common property, 12 Cal. 252. Reviewed, 30 Cal. 37, 38.

Love v. Sierra Nevada L. W. & M. Co., 32 Cal. 639. Cited, Powers, equitable relief from defective execution of, 41 Cal. 349.

Love v. Watkins, 40 Cal. 547. Reviewed and affirmed, Ejectment, does not lie against vendee in possession, on conditions performed, 41 Cal. 350, 351; 42 Cal. 396.

Lovell v. St. Paul, 10 Minn. 291. Cited, Street Assessments, enforcement of, 31 Cal. 686.

Lovely v. Caldwell, 4 Ala. 684. Cited, Attachment, will not lie on money assigned by order, 12 Cal. 98; 19 How. 252.

Loveridge v. Botham, 1 Bosanq. & P. 49. Cited, Tenant in Common, entitled to pay for services under agreement, 18 Cal. 634.

Lovering v. Fogg, 18 Pick. 540. Cited, Deed and defeasance as a mortgage, 33 Cal. 332.

Lovet v. Price, Wright, 89. Cited, Services, implied promise as to remuneration, 22 Cal. 510.

Lovett v. Salem & S. D. R. R. Co., 9 Allen, 557. Cited, Negligence, liability for personal injuries, compulsion construed, 37 Cal. 405.

Lovett v. Steam Sawmill Asso., 6 Paige, 54. Cited, Corporation, validity of deed of, seal as evidence of authority, 16 Cal. 639; 37 Cal. 598.

Low v. Adams, 6 Cal. 277. Cited, Judgment, not subject to collateral attack, 12 Cal. 133. Approved, Attachment, nature of remedy, 29 Cal. 372.

Low v. Allen, 26 Cal. 141. Cited, Mortgage, when barred by statute, 26 Cal. 366; 42 Cal. 503; on joint mortgage, 36 Cal. 20.

Low v. Archer, 12 N. Y. 279. Cited, Deed, as a mortgage, evidence to establish, 36 Cal. 46.

Low v. Carter, 1 Beav. 426. Cited, Husband and Wife, presumptions as to property acquired during marriage, 12 Cal. 255.

Low v. Henry, 9 Cal. 538. Overruled, Deed, as a mortgage, admissibility of parol evidence, 13 Cal. 124. Approved, Pleading, pleader held to his assumptions, 36 Cal. 178.

Low v. Marysville, 5 Cal. 214. Dictum denied, Municipal Corporations, investiture with rights and privileges by special acts, 22 Cal. 428.

Low v. Rice, 8 John. 409. Cited, Appeal, filing of notice indispensable, 29 Cal. 463.

Low v. Wyman, 8 N. H. 536. Commented on, Insolvency, pledge by debtor, 10 Cal. 275.

Lowe v. Alexander, 15 Cal. 296. Distinguished, Judgment, of justice's court, collateral attack, 16 Cal. 392; 17 Cal. 297. Commented on, 18 Cal. 130; jurisdiction not presumed, showing required, 23 Cal. 403. Cited, 1 Nev. 198; defective proof to render process void, 1 Nev. 98; 2 Nev. 111. Approved, Certiorari, inferior tribunals to certify records, 32 Cal. 53; 34 Cal. 362. Cited, Currey, C. J. and Sanderson, J. dissenting, what certified record should show, 32 Cal. 585; 34 Cal. 326.

Lowe v. Jolliffe, 1 W. Black. 365. Commented on, Witness, competency of, to prove will, 1 Cal. 506.

Lowe v. Govett, 3 Barn. & Ad. 863. Cited, Tide Waters, usual high water mark, 18 Cal. 21.

Lowe v. Morgan, 1 Bro. Ch. 368. Cited, Mortgage, with power of sale, 22 Cal. 125. Reviewed, 2 Ohio St. 20.

Lowe v. Peers, 4 Burr. 2225. Cited, Contract, liquidated damages in, 9 Cal. 587.

Lowell v. Boston & L. R. R. Co., 23 Pick. 24. Denied, Respondeat Superior, injuries resulting from negligent and unskilful construction, 8 Cal. 497; 22 Mo. 547; 36 Mo. 218. Commented on, 3 Gray, 352. Cited, Contracts, no remedy on illegal contract, 37 Cal. 175.

Lowell v. Flint, 20 Me. 401. Cited, Officers, legal presumptions in favor of their authority, 3 Cal. 453.

Lowell v. French, 6 Cush. 223. Cited, Street Improvements, enforcement of assessment, 31 Cal. 684.

Lowell v. Hadley, 8 Met. 194. Cited, Street Assessment, acts of superintendent not subject to collateral attack, 29 Cal. 87.

Lowell v. Parker, 10 Met. 314. Cited, Official Bond, judgment, against principal, conclusiveness on surety, 14 Cal. 206.

Lower v. Knox, 10 Cal. 480. Cited, Appeal, judgment not reviewable on appeal from order, 15 Cal. 198.

Lowry v. Stowe, 7 Port. 483. Cited, Attachment, substitution of new bond, 15 Cal. 32.

Lowry v. Tew, 3 Barb. Ch. 407. Cited, Specific Performance, what constitutes part performance, 10 Cal. 159; 19 Cal. 461.

Loyd v. Anglin's Lessee, 7 Yerg. 428. Statute distinguished, Execution, validity of sale under, 38 Cal. 655.

Loyless v. Howell, 15 Geo. 554. Cited, Injunction, dissolution on bill and answer, in discretion, 39 Cal. 167.

Lubeck v. Bullock, 24 Cal. 338. Cited, Appeal, new trial, not granted where testimony was conflicting, 4 Nev. 307; 5 Nev. 421.

Lucas v. Allen, Cal. Sup. Ct. April T. 1855 (not reported.) Cited, Contempt, when party not liable, 6 Cal. 318.

Lucas v. Governor, 6 Ala. 826. Cited, Judgment, against principal, when not conclusive on surety, 14 Cal. 207.

Lucas v. Lucas, 1 Atk. 270. Cited, Husband and Wife, property acquired pending marriage, 12 Cal. 255.

Lucas v. Payne, 7 Cal. 92. Cited, Witnesses, competency of party to record, 8 Cal. 579; 9 Cal. 103; 10 Cal. 124. Approved, Statutory Construction, general words controlled by specific exceptions, 11 Cal. 339.

Lucas v. San Francisco, 7 Cal. 463; S. C. 28 Cal. 591. Commented on, Municipal Corporations, liability on contracts, express or implied, 16 Cal. 272. Referred to on second appeal, and law of case announced, 28 Cal. 592. Cited, Findings, in support of judgment presumed, 31 Cal. 213; 42 Cal. 617.

Luckhart v. Ogden, 30 Cal. 547. Approved, Contract, time for performance may be waived by parol, 39 Cal. 175.

Luco v. United States, 23 How. 515. Referred to, Rejection of Mexican Grant, 39 Cal. 342.

Luddington v. Peck, 2 Conn. 702. Cited, Execution, when voidable, 38 Cal. 379.

Ludlow v. Kidd, 4 Ohio, 244. Cited, Fraud, equitable relief against fraudulent vendee, 23 Cal. 236. Denied, 1 Ohio St. 7.

Ludlow v. Lansing, 1 Hop. Ch. 264. Cited, Foreclosure, remedy by writ of assistance, 11 Cal. 193.

Luffborough v. Parker, 12 Serg. & R. 48. Commented on, Deed, evidence of execution of, 20 Cal. 159.

Lumm v. State, 3 Ind. 294. Cited, Criminal Procedure, admission to bail, 19 Cal. 547.

Lunt v. Adams, 17 Me. 230. Commented on, Negotiable Instruments, presentment and demand, 8 Cal. 633.

Lunt v. Holland, 14 Mass. 149. Cited, Deed, description of land in, 10 Cal. 626; 24 Cal. 444.

Lupin v. Marle, 2 Paige, 169. Cited, Fraud, vitiates sale of goods, 8 Cal. 213; 12 Cal. 462.

Lupton v. Lupton, 3 Cal. 120. Commented on, Equity, when relief obtained, 29 Cal. 55.

Lupton v. White, 15 Ves. Jr. 432. Commented on, Principal and Agent, conversion of goods, rights of principal, 9 Cal. 660, 661; 11 Cal. 151.

Lurvey v. Wells, 4 Cal. 106. Explained, New Trial, effect of motion, 25 Cal. 16; 28 Cal. 71.

Lush v. Druse, 4 Wend. 313. Commented on, Deed, construction of calls in, 36 Cal. 619.

Luther v. Borden, 7 How. 1. Commented on, Constitutional Law, political powers, exercise of, not subject to judicial review, 23 Cal. 176; 27 Cal. 223.

Lutz v. Ey, 3 E. D. Smith, 621. Cited, Pleading, complaint on special contract, 26 Cal. 22.

Lycoming v. Union, 15 Penn. St. 166. Cited, Statutory Construction, 17 Cal. 562.

Lyddal v. Weston, 2 Atk. 19. Cited, Trial, rule of determination in questions of title, 25 Cal. 80.

Lyde v. Russell, 1 Barn. & Ad. 394. Cited, Fixtures, right of removal by tenant, 14 Cal. 68, 72.

Lyell v. Superv. of St. Clair Co., 3 McLean, 580. Commented on, County, liability of, to action, 15 Cal. 585.

Lyle v. Barker, 5 Bin. 457. Cited, Conversion, measure of damages in action by bailee, 34 Cal. 606.

Lyle v. Ducomb, 5 Bin. 585. Cited, Mortgage, to secure future advances, valid, 35 Cal. 309; 23 How. 27.

Lyle v. Rollins, 25 Cal. 437. Cited, Action, to determine adverse claims, possession of plaintiff a material averment in complaint, 34 Cal. 559; possession by plaintiff essential, Id. 565; 37 Cal. 307; 39 Cal. 18. Commented on, 39 Cal. 21. Cited, Ejectment, to be brought against party in possession, 28 Cal. 536; Appeal, judgment not disturbed where there is a conflict of evidence, 32 Cal. 537; 35 Cal. 37; but new trial will be granted where findings are unsupported by evidence, 32 Cal. 235.

Lyles v. Caldwell, 3 McCord, 225. Cited, Probate Proceedings, decree conclusive, 25 Cal. 223.

Lyman v. Fiske, 17 Pick. 231. Cited, Taxation, *situs* of personal property, 23 Cal. 139.

Lynch v. Baxter, 4 Tex. 431. Cited, Judicial Sales, administrators' sales judicial, 9 Cal. 196.

Lynch v. Dalzell, 4 Bro. Parl. Cas. 431. Cited, Insurance policy void for want of interest of insurer, 30 Cal. 89; assignment of, 38 Cal. 542.

Lynch v. Dunn, 34 Cal. 518. Cited, Appeal, filing and serving notice of, 8 Nev. 178.

Lynch, Ex parte, 2 Hill. 45. Cited, Mandamus, when it lies, 16 Cal. 212; 21 Cal. 700.

Lynch v. Livingston, 6 N. Y. 433. Cited, Officers, presumptions as to official acts, 32 Cal. 278. Commented on, 46 Mo. 407.

Lynch v. McHugo, 1 Bay, 33. Cited, Evidence, when book of account not admissible, 17 Cal. 466.

Lynch v. Nurdin, 1 Q. B. 29. Cited, Negligence, liability for injuries by defective structure, 12 Cal. 559. Commented on, Rule as to contributory negligence, 18 Cal. 356; 16 Ill. 202; 27 Ind. 515.

Lynde v. Noble, 20 John. 80. Cited, Certiorari, when it may issue, 40 Cal. 480.

Lyon v. Hancock, 35 Cal. 372. Commented on, Evidence, proof of threats, 37 Cal. 702.

Lyon v. Hunt, 11 Ala. 295. Cited, Cloud on Title, action lies to remove, 2 Cal. 589.

Lyon v. Lyon, 21 Conn. 185. Cited, Divorce, allowance to wife pending action may be enforced, 18 Cal. 64.

Lyon v. Richmond, 2 Johns. Ch. 59. Commented on, Equity, will not relieve from mistake of law, 20 Cal. 642.

Lyon v. Sandford, 5 Conn. 544. Cited, Foreclosure, subsequent incumbrancers necessary parties, 10 Cal. 552, 553.

Lyon v. Sundius, 1 Camp. 423. Commented on, Negotiable Instruments, place of acceptance in bill, 11 Cal. 324.

Lyons v. Leimback, 29 Cal. 139. Cited, Findings, presumed in support of judgment where no exceptions are taken, 28 Cal. 597; 31 Cal. 213; 33 Cal. 676; 42 Cal. 617; 4 Nev. 337.

Lysney v. Selby, 2 Ld. Ray. 1118. Commented on, Fraudulent Representations, 9 Cal. 228.

Lytle v. State of Arkansas, 9 How. 314; S. C. 22 How. 193. Commented on, Preëmption, claim defined, 29 Cal. 320; 30 Cal. 653; 37 Cal. 496, 515, 516. Approved, Limitation to lands subject to location, 37 Cal. 485, 489. Cited, Performance of conditions, 37 Cal. 512; relief from fraudulent preëmption, 42 Cal. 615; 14 How. 379; 20 How. 8; 1 Black, 139, 203; 2 Black, 559; 13 Wall. 85.

Mackalley's Case, 9 Coke, 61. Cited, Criminal Procedure, arrest without warrant, 27 Cal. 578.

Mackay v. Bloodgood, 9 John. 285. Cited, Deed, execution by agent, 21 Cal. 392.

Mackay v. Dillon, 4 How. 421. Cited, Survey, private survey of no binding effect, 13 Cal. 416; 14 Cal. 359; 18 Mo. 291; 8 How. 339.

Macbeath v. Haldimand, 1 Term Rep. 181. Cited, Principal and Agent, when agent personally liable on contract, 13 Cal. 48; public agents not liable on contracts, 15 Cal. 457. Commented on, 1 Cal. 113. Approved, 1 Cranch, 364. Cited, 2 Wheat. 57, note a; 4 How. 148.

Mackinloch v. Blyth, 8 Moore, 211; S. C. 1 Bing. 269. Cited, Arbitration, costs on award, 23 Cal. 368.

Maclay v. Love, 25 Cal. 367; 35 Cal. 398. Cited, Husband and Wife, statute construed, wife's power of alienation,

32 Cal. 385; Sole Trader Act construed, 29 Cal. 566; conveyance by wife of separate estate, 30 Cal. 518; 40 Cal. 560. Commented on, 30 Cal. 142; Id. 517; 31 Cal. 644; Id. 655. Cited, Married Woman, incapable of contracting, 31 Cal. 478; 38 Cal. 256; 40 Cal. 558; charging separate estate of, 38 Cal. 233. Distinguished, 26 Cal. 446. Cited, Pleading, essential averments in complaint on note of husband and wife, 29 Cal. 122; Statutory Construction, striking out part of section, 29 Iowa, 399.

Macomber v. Parker, 14 Pick. 497. Cited, Pledge, possession by pledgee of property owned in common, 29 Cal. 559. Commented on, 30 Cal. 87; 10 Met. 489.

Mackreth v. Symmons, 15 Ves. Jr. 329; S. C. 2 Lead. Cas. in Eq. 274; 1 Lead. Cas. in Eq. 270. Cited, Vendor's Lien, defined, 21 Cal. 177; 4 Wheat. 292; not lost by taking notes of vendee, 8 Cal. 403; lost by taking mortgage security, 12 Cal. 305. Dictum denied, 17 Ohio, 536; not assignable, 21 Cal. 177; enforcement of, 35 Cal. 205, 206; priority of, over creditors, 35 Cal. 207.

Macy v. Goodwin, 6 Cal. 579. Cited, Evidence, secondary evidence of lost instrument, 12 Cal. 105; 31 Cal. 107.

Maddox v. Graham, 2 Met. Ky. 56. Cited, Supervisors, payment of county indebtedness, 21 Cal. 702. Commented on, Mandamus, to enforce duty of, Id. 702.

Madison, etc., Plank R. Co. v. Reynolds, 3 Wis. 287. Cited, Corporation, powers of, 22 Cal. 629.

Maeris v. Bicknell, 7 Cal. 261. Commented on, Water Rights, appropriation of water, 21 Cal. 381; limitation of right to use of water, 32 Cal. 32, 33; 37 Cal. 312. See Marius v. Bicknell.

Magee v. Calaveras Co., 10 Cal. 376. Cited, Office, certificate of election only *prima facie* evidence of right to, 20 Cal. 53; remedy, to test right to, 24 Cal. 127.

Magee v. Mokelumne Hill Co., 5 Cal. 258. Cited, Corporation, constitutional prohibition from issuing bills for circulation as money, 6 Cal. 7; Appeal, papers not embodied in statement, no part of record, 28 Cal. 296.

Magor v. Chadwick, 11 Adol. & E. 571. Cited, Nuisance, appropriator of water entitled to protection, 23 Cal. 488.

Magraw v. McGlynn, 26 Cal. 420. Commented on, Probate, decree of court in gold coin, against execution, 32 Cal. 127; conclusive on sureties, 32 Cal. 130; when erroneous to decree payment in gold coin, 39 Cal. 70. Referred to, 8 Wall. 639.

Mahala v. State, 10 Yerg. 532. Cited, Criminal Procedure, when discharge of jury operates as an acquittal, 38 Cal. 478; 5 Cold. 314. Denied, 41 Cal. 217; 3 Sneed, 478.

Maher v. Overton, 9 La. 115. Commented on, Principal and Agent, note drawn by agent, 7 Cal. 542.

Mahler v. Newbauer, 32 Cal. 168. Cited, Mortgage, tender of mortgage debt, 37 Cal. 226.

Mahlstadt v. Blanc, 34 Cal. 577. Approved, Pleading, amended complaint takes place of original, 36 Cal. 377.

Mahon v. N. Y. Cent. R. Co., 24 N. Y. 659. Cited, Railroad, cannot appropriate public highway without condemnation and compensation, 32 Cal. 510.

Mahone v. Mahone, 19 Cal. 626. Cited, Divorce, on ground of cruelty, 23 Iowa, 441.

Mahoney v. Van Winkle, 21 Cal. 552; S. C. 33 Cal. 448. Approved, Mexican Grant, of tract within exterior boundaries, confirmee entitled to possession as tenant in common, and may maintain ejectment, 24 Cal. 280; Id. 580; 27 Cal. 564; 31 Cal. 493; 33 Cal. 108; 1 Wall. 373; 1 Saw. 560. Explained, selection and location by grantee, 24 Cal. 282; segregation by location and survey, 24 Cal. 578; 38 Cal. 66.

Mahoney v. Wilson, 15 Cal. 42. Approved, Reference, failure to prosecute motion to set aside report of referee is an abandonment of motion, 15 Cal. 303, 304. Referred to, Ejectment, 37 Cal. 392, 396, 397, 398, 399.

Mahurin v. Brackett, 5 N. H. 9. Commented on, Amendment, of officer's return, 23 Cal. 81.

Maize v. State, 4 Ind. 342. Commented on, Judiciary, power of, review as to constitutionality of statute, 41 Cal. 159. Doubted, that part of act may be held unconstitutional, 11 Ind. 485.

Makepeace v. Harvard College, 10 Pick. 298. Cited, Written Instruments, several papers construed as one, 12 Cal. 577. Commented on, 20 Iowa, 539.

Mallan v. May, 11 Mees. & W. 653. Cited, Contract, in partial restraint of trade, valid, 36 Cal. 358.

Mallory, Matter of, 2 Cow. 531. Commented on, County, liability of, for services rendered, 30 Cal. 239.

Mallory v. Norton, 21 Barb. 424. Commented on, Set-off, when judgments cannot be set-off, 18 Cal. 389; 22 Cal. 178.

Malone v. Samuel, 3 A. K. Marsh. 350. Cited, Amendment, to officers' returns, 23 Cal. 81.

Maloy v. City of Marietta, 11 Ohio St. 637. Cited, Street Assessments, power of legislature to direct mode of, 28 Cal. 352, 369.

Mamlock v. White, 20 Cal. 598. Cited, Attachment, justification for levy, 34 Cal. 350.

Mammatt v. Mathew, 10 Bing. 506. Cited, Arrest and Bail, irregularities waived by bail, 6 Cal. 59.

Manahan v. Gibbons, 19 John. 109. Cited, Common Law, rule as to action on joint liability, 1 Cal. 169.

Manchester v. Doddridge, 3 Ind. 360. Cited, Tenant in Common, what constitutes ouster by, 24 Cal. 376.

Mandeville v. Welch, 5 Wheat. 277. Cited, Assignment, of unaccepted bill of exchange, 12 Cal. 98. Commented on, 2 McCart. 28; 5 Pet. 598; demands assigned in parts, 38 Cal. 519; 5 Pet. 394.

Manice v. Mayor of New York, 8 N. Y. 120. Cited, Street Assessments, validity of, 31 Cal. 674.

Mann v. Eckford's Exrs., 15 Wend. 502. Cited, Appeal, bond, sufficient averment in action on, 9 Cal. 285; Corporation, powers of, 22 Cal. 629.

Mann v. Glover, 2 Green N. J. 195. Cited, Juror and Jury, grounds of challenge, 12 Cal. 492; 16 Cal. 131. Commented on, 1 Dutch. 588.

Mann v. Mann, 1 Johns. Ch. 231. Cited, Wills, cannot be varied or contradicted by parol, 35 Cal. 340.

Mann v. Morewood, 5 Sand. 557. Cited, Pleading, material averments, 11 Cal. 168.

Mann v. Rogers, 35 Cal. 316. Approved, Judgment, in ejectment, of what conclusive, 36 Cal. 134. Cited, Homestead, actual residence essential, 41 Cal. 83.

Mann's Appeal, 1 Penn. St. 24. Cited, Conveyances, recording act construed, 12 Cal. 377.

Manning v. Fifth Parish in Gloucester, 6 Pick. 10. Cited, Eminent Domain, legislature exclusive judge of public necessity, 18 Cal. 252.

Manning's Case, 8 Coke, 97. Commented on, Execution, amendment of, 38 Cal. 377.

Manrow v. Durham, 3 Hill, 584. Commented on, Guarantor on Note, liability of, 7 Cal. 34; 1 Nev. 385; 3 Wis. 697; 3 Mich. 194; 2 N. Y. 228; 8 N. Y. 207.

Manfield v. Maitland, 4 Barn. & Ald. 582. Cited, Freight, advanced, may be recovered back on failure of transportation, 6 Cal. 370, 371.

Mansfield v. Dorland, 2 Cal. 507. Approved, Attorney and Counsel, has no lien on judgment; 11 Cal. 103.

Mansfield, Earl of, v. Blackburne, 6 Bing. N. C. 426. Cited, Fixtures, removal by tenant, 14 Cal. 70.

Mansony, Ex parte, 1 Ala. 99. Cited, Specific Performance, enforcement of agreement, 19 Cal. 461.

Manufacturers' and M. Bk. v. Gore, 15 Mass. 75. Cited, Felony, conviction of, as a suspension of civil rights, 1 Cal. 435.

Manufacturers' & M. Bk. v. St. John, 5 Hill, 497. Cited, Confession of Judgment, statute to be strictly pursued, 20 Cal. 687.

Marbury v. Madison, 1 Cranch, 137. Commented on, Supreme court has no original jurisdiction, 1 Cal. 146, 147; 3 Cal. 390; 4 Cranch, 102; 6 Wheat. 400. Cited, 11 Wheat. 472, note *a;* 12 Pet. 617; 5 How. 191; 7 How. 197; 14 How. 165. Commented on, Mandamus, when it lies against public officer to enforce official duty, 7 Cal. 80; 16 Cal. 41, 44, 52; 30 Cal. 601; 39 Cal. 210; dissenting opinion, Temple, J. 217, 218, 223; 7 Wall. 349. Commented on, Office, removal from, and appointment to, 6 Cal. 292, 293; 10 Cal. 44, 47; 32 Cal. 79. Cited as to mandamus, 2 Wheat. 370, note *a;* 6 Wheat. 604; 5 Pet. 200, 208; 11 How. 292. Cited, Grant, delivery of conveyance has no application to government grants, 31 Cal. 513.

Marchant v. Langworthy, 6 Hill, 646. Cited, Statutory Construction, time as a directory provision, 30 Cal. 527.

23

Marcy v. Clark, 17 Mass. 330. Commented on, Corporations, personal liability of stockholders, 14 Cal. 267.

Marcy v. Marcy, 6 Met. 360. Commented on, Tenant in Common, ouster by co-tenant, 27 Cal. 547, 555, 558.

Marden v. Babcock, 2 Met. 99. Cited, Deed and Defeasance, construction of, 33 Cal. 332.

Mardis' Adrs. v. Shackleford, 4 Ala. 493. Cited, Evidence, proof of handwriting, rule of admission, 26 Cal. 412.

Marine Ins. Co. v. Hodgson, 7 Cranch, 332. Cited, Fraud, when equity will not grant relief, 27 Cal. 169; 8 How. 161.

Mariner v. Coon, 16 Wis. 465. Cited, Execution, irregular executions when not void, 38 Cal. 379, 382.

Mariner v. Saunders, 10 Ill. 113. Cited, Acknowledgment, of conveyance by married woman, essential to its validity, 7 Cal. 275.

Marius v. Bicknell, 10 Cal. 217. See S. C. *Sub nom.* Maeris *v.* Bicknell.

Markle v. Hatfield, 2 John. 455. Cited, Money, fraudulently received, action to recover back, 22 Cal. 463.

Markwald v. Creditors, 7 Cal. 213. Cited, Common Carriers, right of stoppage *in transitu*, 23 Cal. 510; 37 Cal. 632.

Marlin v. Willink, 7 Serg. & R. 297. Cited, Vendor and Vendee, right of possession in vendee, 22 Cal. 617; 40 Cal. 567.

Marlow v. Marsh, 9 Cal. 259. Cited, Appeal, engrossment of amended statement, 9 Cal. 291; 10 Cal. 300; 23 Cal. 462; 31 Cal. 662.

Marquand v. Webb, 16 John. 89. Cited, Error, injury presumed from admission of incompetent testimony, 38 Cal. 283, 285.

Marquat v. Marquat, 12 N. Y. 336. Cited, Verdict, relief granted on, 37 Cal. 324.

Marquez v. Frisbie, 41 Cal. 624. Approved, Public Lands, withdrawal of, from right of preëmption, 41 Cal. 638.

Marquis of Winchester's Case, 3 Coke, 5. Cited, Judicial Decisions, reasons for, no part of, 13 Cal. 26.

Marriot v. Davey, 1 Dall. 164. Cited, Mortgage, subrogation of second mortgagee, 10 Cal. 385.

Mars v. McKay, 14 Cal. 127. Cited, Mechanic's Lien, rights of intervenors in action, 6 Nev. 290; 8 Nev. 231.

Marsh v. Chesnut, 14 Ill. 223. Cited, Taxation, assessment when to be levied, 34 Cal. 442.

Marsh v. Gold, 2 Pick. 284. Approved, Indemnity, right of sheriff to demand indemnity on execution of process, 36 Cal. 459, 461.

Marsh v. N. Y. & E. R. R. Co., 14 Barb. 364. Doubted, Negligence, injuries to cattle, negligence of owners, 18 Cal. 356. Overruled, 13 N. Y. 51.

Marsh v. Pier, 4 Rawle, 289. Cited, Judgment, conclusiveness of, 26 Cal. 494.

Marsh v. Rice, 1 N. H. 168. Cited, Mortgage, subrogation of second mortgagee, 10 Cal. 385.

Marshall v. Baltimore & Ohio R. R. Co., 16 How. 314. Cited, Contract, when void as against public policy, 38 Cal. 340.

Marshall v. Betner, 17 Ala. 832. Cited, Damages, when counsel fees recoverable, 25 Cal. 173.

Marshall v. Beverley, 5 Wheat. 313. Cited, Parties in equitable action, 31 Cal. 427.

Marshall v. Dupey, 4 J. J. Marsh. 388. Common law rule distinguished, Judgment, in ejectment, conclusiveness of, 14 Cal. 468.

Marshall v. Ferguson, 23 Cal. 65. Cited, Statute of Frauds, contracts for sale of growing crops not within, 37 Cal. 636.

Marshall v. Harwood, 5 Md. 423. Principle adopted, Office, constitutional term of, 11 Cal. 88; 12 Cal. 390.

Marshall v. Hosmer, 4 Mass. 60. Cited, Indemnity, officer entitled to, on execution of process, 36 Cal. 459.

Marshall v. Mullen, 3 Rob. 328. Cited, Husband and Wife, common property, 30 Cal. 35.

Marshall v. Shafter, 32 Cal. 176. Cited, Ejectment, when judgment in, is an estoppel, 36 Cal. 514; 41 Cal. 227; construction of "claim" as applied to allegation of title to public lands, 41 Cal. 29; plea of title, after general issue, may be omitted, 42 Cal. 349; sufficient proof of ouster, 41 Cal. 610.

Marston v. Baldwin, 17 Mass. 605.   Cited, Fraud, ownership of goods not changed on sale procured by, 12 Cal. 462.

Martin v. Bank of U. S., 4 Wash. C. C. 253.   Cited, Secondary evidence of lost note admissible, 10 Cal. 149.

Martin v. Broach, 6 Geo. 21.   Cited, Constitutional Construction, title to act, 2 Cal. 299.

Martin v. Draher, 5 Watts, 544.   Cited, Debtor and Creditor, application of payments, 14 Cal. 449.

Martin v. Hunter's Lessee, 1 Wheat. 304.   Denied, State Sovereignty, appellate power of U. S. supreme court, 4 Cal. 369; 11 Cal. 184; 2 Hill, 166.   Cited, 7 Wheat. 208, note *a;* 12 How. 124; 22 How. 203.   Approved, Powers of Federal Judiciary, 9 Cal. 723, 724; 26 Cal. 613.   Cited, 5 Wheat. 69, note *a;* 49, note *b;* 5 Wheat. 106; 6 Wheat. 423; 5 Pet. 202; 11 How. 607; 12 How. 315; 4 Wall. 428.   Denied, Rice, 414.   Cited, Concurrent judicial powers of State courts, 5 Cal. 301; 9 Cal. 713; Appeal, conclusiveness of final judgment on appeal, law of the case, 15 Cal. 83; 20 Cal. 419. Approved, 25 Cal. 419.   Cited, 12 Pet. 492; 1 How. 149; 3 How. 425, 426; 6 How. 40; 15 How. 466.

Martin v. Johnson, 5 Mart. O. S. 655.   Commented on, Title, Indians cannot pass title, 1 Cal. 291.

Martin v. Maverick, 1 McCord, 27.   Cited, Verdict, assent when conclusive on jury, 20 Cal. 71.

Martin v. McFadin, 4 Litt. 240.   Cited, Pleading, complaint, under statute of frauds, 29 Cal. 599.

Martin v. Mott, 12 Wheat. 19.   Cited, Constitutional Construction, action of political department not subject to review by judiciary, 23 Cal. 176; 27 Cal. 223.

Martin v. Porter, 5 Mees. & W. 352.   Commented on, Trespass, measure of damages, 23 Cal. 310.

Martin v. San Francisco, 16 Cal. 285.   Cited, Negotiable Instruments, auditors' warrants not negotiable, 23 Cal. 126.

Martin v. Travers, 12 Cal. 243.   Approved, Exceptions, point of objection must be stated, 18 Cal. 324; 24 Cal. 403; 25 Cal. 243; 34 Cal. 558; 3 Nev. 557; 7 Nev. 415; 24 Wis. 72.   Cited, Appeal, right of, from *ex parte* order, 33 Cal. 392.

Martin v. Wade, 37 Cal. 168. Cited, Contract, in violation of statute, void, 31 Wis. 254.

Martin v. Wilson, 1 N. Y. 240. Cited, Appeal, jurisdiction of supreme court lost after filing remittitur, 1 Cal. 195. Approved, 24 Cal. 58.

Martin v. Winslow, 2 Mason, 241. Cited, Negotiable Instruments, when presumptively dishonored, 39 Cal. 352.

Martin's Exrs. v. Martin, 25 Ala. 201. Commented on, Stare Decisis, 15 Cal. 603.

Martin's Heirs v. Martin, 22 Ala. 86. Cited, Marriage, sufficient proof of, in cases where marriage is not foundation of claim, 26 Cal. 133.

Martinez v. Gallardo, 5 Cal. 155. Cited, Appeal, second appeal, when may be taken, 20 Wis. 646.

Martini v. Coles, 1 Maule & S. 140. Commented on, Factor, cannot pledge, 11 Cal. 401; 19 Cal. 73; 11 How. 225.

Marvin v. Bennett, 26 Wend. 169. Cited, Deed, mistake in quantity, when equity will relieve from, 29 Cal. 178.

Mary F. v. Samuel F., 1 N. H. 198. Cited, Divorce, wilful neglect, 9 Cal. 476.

Marysville v. Buchanan, 3 Cal. 212. Approved, Judgment, entry of, on filing remittitur, and issue of execution thereon, 12 Cal. 468; 20 Cal. 55.

Marzetti v. Williams, 1 Barn. & Ad. 415. Cited, Pleading, averment of special damage not essential in action for breach of contract, 10 Cal. 464.

Marziou v. Pioche, 8 Cal. 522. Cited, Assignment, of debt, in parcels, 38 Cal. 519.

Marziou v. Pioche, 10 Cal. 545. Cited, Appeal, judgment on, directions in, 30 Cal. 463.

Mask v. State, 36 Miss. 77. Cited, Instructions, practice, 30 Cal. 450.

Mason v. Brook, 12 Ill. 273. Cited, Married Woman, acknowledgment of deed by, essential to its validity, 7 Cal. 275.

Mason v. Chambers, 4 Litt. 253. Cited, Covenant, in deed, breach of, not available as a defense while vendee retains possession, 5 Cal. 265.

Mason v. Cronise, 20 Cal. 211. Cited, Pleading, when statute of limitations may be presented by demurrer, 23 Cal. 353.

Mason v. Denison, 15 Wend. 64. Denied, Execution, in action against joint debtors, 39 Cal. 96.

Mason v. Haile, 12 Wheat. 370. Cited, Legislature, power of special legislation, 17 Cal. 562.

Mason v. Rumsey, 1 Camp. 384. Cited, Contract, execution of, by agent, 13 Cal. 48. Commented on, 12 Leigh, 47.

Mason v. Thompson, 9 Pick. 280. Commented on, Innkeepers, liability for loss, 1 Cal. 229; 33 Cal. 600.

Mason v. Waite, 17 Mass. 558. Cited, Wagers, rights and duties of stakeholder, 11 Cal. 350; 15 Cal. 347.

Masser v. Strickland, 17 Serg. & R. 354. Denied, Sureties, when concluded by judgment against principal, 14 Cal. 206.

Massie v. Watts, 6 Cranch, 148. Cited, Specific Performance, when jurisdiction of action attaches, 38 Cal. 201; 6 Wheat. 558; 5 Pet. 79; 15 How. 243.

Masson v. Bovet, 1 Denio, 69. Cited, Contract, when cannot be rescinded, 15 Cal. 458.

Masten v. Deyo, 2 Wend. 429. Commented on and construed, Trial, want of probable cause a mixed question, 29 Cal. 650.

Masters of Bedford Charity, Matter of, 2 Swanst. 520. Cited, Attorney-General, actions by, when relator not necessary party, 25 Cal. 249.

Masters v. Eastis, 3 Port. 368. Cited, Ejectment, may be maintained by preëmptioner, 38 Cal. 44.

Masters v. Masters, 1 P. Wms. 424. Cited, Will, construction of devise, 31 Cal. 611.

Masterton v. Mayor of Brooklyn, 7 Hill, 61. Cited, Damages, when loss of profits an element of, 26 Cal. 307. Approved on breach of entire contract, 35 Cal. 242, 243; 38 Cal. 664; 13 How. 344.

Mastick v. Thorp, 29 Cal. 444. Cited, New Trial, absence at trial not a ground for, 33 Cal. 36, 38.

Matchin v. Matchin, 6 Penn. St. 332. Commented on, Divorce, effect of confessions, 13 Cal. 94.

Mateer v. Brown, 1 Cal. 221. Cited, Evidence, when declarations of agent admissible against principal, 1 Cal. 461; 9 Cal. 256; Appeal, jurisdiction lost on filing remittitur, 22 Cal. 25; 24 Cal. 58; Nonsuit, when it will be granted, 26 Cal. 525; grounds of, must be specifically stated, 27 Cal. 474. Commented on, Innkeeper, liability of, 33 Cal. 598, 600, 602.

Mather v. Trinity Church, 3 Serg. & R. 509. Approved, Trial, title cannot be tried in replevin for chattel severed from realty, 28 Cal. 610.

Mathewson v. Sprague, 1 Curt. 457. Cited, Probate Court, jurisdiction exclusive, 18 Cal. 481.

Matoon v. Eder, 6 Cal. 57. Cited, Sureties, on undertaking, when liability attaches, 7 Cal. 570. Commented on, Arrest and Bail, when writ of arrest will issue, 36 Cal. 167.

Matthews v. Zane, 7 Wheat. 164. Cited, Statutory Construction, when act takes effect, 37 Cal. 218.

Mattox v. Mattox, 2 Ohio, 234. Cited, Divorce, doctrine of recrimination applies, 10 Cal. 257.

Mauge v. Heringhi, 26 Cal. 577. Cited, Pledge, sale of property in satisfaction of debt, 27 Cal. 271; 36 Cal. 429.

Maure v. Harrison, 1 Eq. Ab. 93. Commented on, Mortgage, trust created under, 13 Cal. 122.

Mauri v. Heffernan, 13 John. 57. Cited, Sureties, action for contribution, 20 Cal. 136; Evidence, proof of execution of promissory note, 22 Cal. 484.

Maury v. Waugh, 1 A. K. Marsh. 452. Cited, Lands, possession acquired under deed by entry of tenant, 38 Cal. 491.

Maverick v. Lewis, 3 McCord, 211. Cited, Contract, cropping contract construed, 17 Cal. 546.

Maxfield v. Johnson, 30 Cal. 545. Cited, Jurisdiction, amount in controversy, test of, 34 Cal. 34.

Maxim v. Morse, 8 Mass. 127. Cited, New Promise, debt sufficient consideration, 19 Cal. 484.

Maxwell v. Dulwich College, 4 L. J. N. S. Ch. 131. Cited, Corporation, contract of, 4 Cal. 147.

May v. Baker, 15 Ill. 90. Commented on, Attachment, equitable demands not subject to garnishment, 35 Cal. 386.

May v. Hanson, 5 Cal. 360. Cited, Common Carriers, ferryman liable for loss of property, 22 Cal. 535; 23 Iowa, 94; burden of proof as to negligence of plaintiff, 7 Cal. 255.

Maybury v. Jones, 4 Yeates, 21. Cited, Execution, sale of real property, 23 Cal. 279.

Mayburry v. Brien, 15 Pet. 21. Cited, Title, transitory seizin by purchase and mortgage back passes no estate, 8 Cal. 274.

Maye v. Tappan, 23 Cal. 306. Cited, Trespass, on mining claim, estimate of damages in action, 30 Cal. 485.

Mayfield v. Morris, 10 La. 442. Cited, Possessory action under civil law, 1 Cal. 289; possession sufficient to maintain, 1 Cal. 289, 320.

Mayfield v. Wadsley, 3 Barn. & C. 361; S. C. 5 Dowl. & R. 228. Cited, Contract, entire contract indivisible, 15 Cal. 257.

Mayhew v. Norton, 17 Pick. 357. Cited, Deed, description in, rule of construction, 26 Cal. 632.

Mayhew v. Prince, 11 Mass. 53. Commented on, Negotiable Instrument, execution by agent, 7 Cal. 539.

Mayhew v. Robinson, 10 How. Pr. 162. Cited, Evidence, burden of proof as to new matter on defendant, 10 Cal. 558; Pleading, several defenses may be set up, 22 Cal. 679.

Maynard v. Hunt, 5 Pick. 240. Cited, Mortgage, tender and refusal after law day not a discharge of lien, 14 Cal. 529.

Maynard v. Maynard, 10 Mass. 456. Cited, Deed, delivery of, a question of intention, 5 Cal. 319; 34 N. H. 474; 6 Minn. 78.

Mayne v. Jones, 34 Cal. 483. Cited, Writ of Possession, execution of, 36 Cal. 150.

Mayo v. Ah Loy, 32 Cal. 477. Cited, Judgment, when void, 33 Cal. 322; conclusiveness of judgment in tax suits, 36 Cal. 222. Commented on, 39 Cal. 440.

Mayo v. Madden, 4 Cal. 27. Distinguished, Pleading, joinder of causes of action, 7 Cal. 126.

Mayo v. Mazeau, 38 Cal. 442. Approved, Sacramento City, deed including site of, 41 Cal. 487; 42 Cal. 392.

Mayor, etc., v. Patten, 1 Am. Lead. Cas. 268; 4 Cranch, 317. Cited, Debtor and Creditor, application of payments, 33 Cal. 657.

Mayor, etc., v. Commrs. of Spring Garden, 7 Penn. St. 348. Commented on, Water Rights, what grant includes, 29 Cal. 207.

Mayor, etc., of Albany v. Trowbridge, 5 Hill, 71. Approved, Pleading, unskilful performance to be specially pleaded, 1 Cal. 372.

Mayor, etc., of Alexandria v. Patton, 4 Cranch, 317. Cited, Debtor and Creditor, application of payments, 14 Cal. 449; 33 Cal. 657; 7 How. 691.

Mayor, etc., of Baltimore v. Green Mountain Cemetery, 7 Md. 517. Cited, Street Assessments, power of legislature to impose burden, 28 Cal. 352. Reviewed, Id. 358; enforcement by action, 31 Cal. 682.

Mayor, etc., of Baltimore v. Howard, 6 Har. & J. 383. Commented on, Street Assessment, enforcement of, 31 Cal. 681.

Mayor, etc., of Baltimore v. Lefferman, 4 Gill, 425. Commented on, Money paid under duress, when recoverable, 18 Cal. 271, 272.

Mayor of Colchester v. Brooke, 7 Q. B. (53 Eng. C. L.) 339. Cited, Negligence, liability for injuries, contributory negligence, 37 Cal. 423.

Mayor of Ludlow v. Charlton, 6 Mees. & W. 815. Cited, Corporations, how bound under common law, 7 Cal. 381.

Mayor, etc., of New York, Matter of, 11 John. 77. Commented on, Street Assessments, 28 Cal. 358.

Mayor, etc., of New York v. Bailey, 2 Denio, 433. Cited, Negligence, liability for injuries from defective structure, 10 Cal. 418; 29 Cal. 250. See Bailey *v.* Mayor, etc., of New York.

Mayor, etc., of New York v. Butler, 1 Barb. 325. Cited, Conditions Precedent, performance and non-performance, 7 Cal. 442.

Mayor, etc., of New York v. Colgate, 12 N. Y. 140. Commented on, Street Assessments, enforcement of, 31 Cal. 672, 679.

Mayor, etc., of New York v. Furze, 3 Hill, 612. Cited, Officers, power of, enjoined as a duty, 30 Cal. 437.

Mayor, etc., of New York v. Lord, 17 Wend. 285. Affirmed, 18 Wend. 126. Distinguished, Municipal Corporations, statute liability, 1 Cal. 358.

Mayor of Norwich v. Norfolk R. R. Co., 30 Eng. L. & E. 128. Commented on, Pleading, defense of *ultra vires* by corporation, 37 Cal. 580.

Mayor of Poole v. Whitt, 15 Mees. & W. 571. Commented on, Taxation, municipal property not liable to, 15 Cal. 585.

Mayor of Thetford's Case, 1 Salk. 192. Commented on, Mandamus, pleading and proceedings in, 27 Cal. 672, 673; validity of acts of corporation *in pais*, 12 Wheat. 95.

Mayor of York v. Pilkington, 1 Atk. 283. Commented on, Bill of Peace, 6 Cal. 39.

Mays v. Cincinnati, 1 Ohio St. 268. Cited, Money paid, under mistake of law, not recoverable, 18 Cal. 271; what constitutes compulsory payment, Id. 272.

Maze v. Miller, 1 Wash. C. C. 328. Cited, Debt, effect of payment by check or note, 12 Cal. 323.

McAfee v. Keirn, 7 Smedes & M. 780. Approved, Public Lands, preëmption rights, 37 Cal. 497, 516.

McAllister v. Albion P. R. Co., 10 N. Y. 353. Cited, Appeal, finality of judgment, 42 Cal. 56.

McAllister v. Strode, 7 Cal. 428. Cited, Insolvency, requirements of act to be strictly followed, 9 Cal. 478; no intendments in favor of jurisdiction, 31 Cal. 169.

McArthur v. Hoysradt, 11 Paige, 495. Cited, Supplementary Proceedings, parties, 7 Cal. 204.

McArthur v. Sears, 21 Wend. 190. Cited, Damages by the Elements, what constitute "acts of God," 35 Cal. 423.

McAuley v. York Min. Co., 6 Cal. 80. Commented on, Witness, incompetency, from interest, 14 Cal. 266; 20 Cal. 615; 23 Cal. 329.

McBride v. Choate, 2 Ired. Eq. 610. Denied, Sureties on administrator's bond, proceedings against administrator as evidence, 25 Cal. 222.

McBride v. Floyd, 2 Bailey, 209. Cited, Attachment, equities in favor of most diligent, 8 Cal. 573.

McCabe v. Grey, 20 Cal. 509. Cited, Assignment, assignees of judgment take subject to right of set-off, 23 Cal. 626; Conveyances, construction of recording act, 6 Nev. 391.

McCabe v. Worthington, 16 How. 86. Cited, Public Lands, segregation necessary to perfect title under Mexican grant, 30 Cal. 508.

McCain v. Wood, 4 Ala. 264. Cited, Deed, recitals in, conclusive on grantor, 26 Cal. 87.

McCall v. Byram Manf. Co., 6 Conn. 427. Commented on, Office, holding over, 28 Cal. 52.

McCann v. Beach, 2 Cal. 25. Approved, Evidence, secondary evidence of lost deed, practice, 6 Cal. 462; Id. 581; 10 Cal. 148; Depositions, by whom taken, 2 Cal. 33.

McCann v. Lewis, 9 Cal. 246. Approved, Judgment, rule as to interest in, 32 Cal. 88.

McCann v. Sierra Co., 7 Cal. 121. Approved, Eminent Domain, compensation on condemnation, 9 Cal. 599; 12 Cal. 528, 531; 31 Cal. 546; payment or tender a condition precedent to exercise of right, 29 Cal. 117; condemnation without compensation may be enjoined, 27 Cal. 647; Action, against county, condition precedent to right of, 28 Cal. 431.

McCann v. State, 9 Smedes & M. 465. Cited, Verdict, separation of jury a ground for setting aside, 21 Cal. 341; presumptions against purity of verdict from improper influences on juror, 39 Cal. 375. Commented on, 8 Gratt. 648.

McCarthy v. White, 21 Cal. 495. Approved, Mortgage, remedy barred when debt is barred, but may be revived by new promise, 22 Cal. 102; 24 Cal. 409; Id. 498; 26 Cal. 144. Affirmed on principle of stare decisis, 26 Cal. 365, 367; remedy revived by new promise, 22 Cal. 102. Cited, Statute of limitations applies equally to equitable as to legal actions, 23 Cal. 34; subsequent grantees and incumbrancers may plead statute, 23 Cal. 25; Id. 143; 26 Cal. 144.

McCartney v. FitzHenry, 16 Cal. 184. Cited, Exceptions to rulings must be taken at trial, 34 Cal. 586.

McCarty v. Beach, 10 Cal. 461. Approved, Seal, imports a consideration, 17 Cal. 101.

McCarty v. Vickery, 12 John. 348.   Denied, Fraud, effect of fraudulent sale on title to property, 12 Cal. 462. Doubted, 3 Hill, 350.

McCaskill v. Elliot, 5 Strob. 196.   Cited, Negligence, liability for injuries by ferocious animal, 41 Cal. 141.

McCauley v. Brooks, 16 Cal. 11.   Approved, Constitutional Construction, distribution of powers of government, 17 Cal. 557; mandamus lies, to executive officer, to compel performance of duties strictly ministerial, 18 Cal. 675; 30 Cal. 603; 32 Cal. 278; 39 Cal. 210; 41 Cal. 77.   Cited, State Indebtedness, creditors, rights of, under contracts made with State, 16 Cal. 194; 39 Cal. 274; on what to rely for payment, 34 Cal. 290; Legislature, power of taxation, 27 Cal. 209; of appropriation of moneys, 27 Cal. 219; validity of funding acts, 19 Cal. 184; Legislature has no power to destroy or impair vested rights, 16 Cal. 194.   Commented on, validity of act making appropriations, 5 Nev. 25.

McCauley v. United States, 1 Morris, Iowa, 486.   Commented on, Criminal Procedure, effect of plea of "guilty," 6 Cal. 547.

McCauley v. Weller, 12 Cal. 500.   Cited, Eminent Domain, compensation a condition precedent to right of condemnation, 13 Cal. 314; 24 Cal. 435; 29 Cal. 117. Distinguished, 31 Cal. 547, 548.   Approved, Change of place of trial, disqualification of judge, when not a ground for, 24 Cal. 35.

McChesney's Lessee v. Wainwright, 5 Ohio, 452.   Cited, Deed, void for uncertainty in description, 6 Cal. 312.

McClellan v. Crook, 7 Gill, 333.   Cited, New Trial, law of the case conclusive, 20 Cal. 417.

McClintock v. Bryden, 5 Cal. 97.   Distinguished, Public Lands, occupation of mineral lands, 5 Cal. 310.   Limited, 6 Cal. 46.   Cited, Right to mine, 7 Cal. 324. Adhered to, 11 Cal. 14.   Cited and explained, 23 Cal. 456.

McCloud v. O'Neall, 16 Cal. 392.   Approved, New Trial, question as to the competency of a witness cannot be raised on motion, 21 Cal. 641; Exceptions to introduction of incompetent evidence must be taken at the trial, 23 Cal. 60; 29 Cal. 223.

McClung v. Ross, 5 Wheat. 116.   Approved, Tenant in

Common, what insufficient to constitute an ouster by, 24 Cal. 379.

McCluny v. Silliman, 2 Wheat. 369. Cited, Jurisdiction, supreme court has not original jurisdiction in mandamus, 1 Cal. 147.

McClure v. Colclough, 5 Ala. 65. Commented on, Appeal, restitution of rights on reversal, 18 Cal. 290.

McCollum, Ex parte, 1 Cow. 564. Cited, Statutory Construction, intendments in support of their validity, 25 Cal. 569, 572.

McCollum v. Hubbert, 13 Ala. 282. Cited, Execution, amendment of, to conform to judgment, 38 Cal. 376, 381.

McComble v. Davies, 6 East, 538. Cited, Factor, cannot pledge, 19 Cal. 72.

McCombs v. Akron, 15 Ohio, 474. Cited, Municipal Corporations, liability on contracts, express and implied, 16 Cal. 270.

McConihe v. N. Y. & E. R. R., 20 N. Y. 495. Cited, Injunction Bond, fees of counsel, when recoverable, 25 Cal. 174.

McConnel v. Swailes, 3 Ill. 571. Cited, Action, on joint contract, plaintiff concluded by election to sue jointly, 6 Cal. 182.

McConnell v. Bowdry's Heirs, 4 Mon. 392. Cited, Principal and Agent, ratification of deed made by attorney, 22 Cal. 592. Commented on, Estoppel, of tenant, 33 Cal. 249. Denied, 35 Cal. 569.

McConnell v. Denver, 35 Cal. 365. Distinguished, Corporation, promissory note of, 42 Cal. 194.

McConnell v. Lexington, 12 Wheat. 582. Cited, Dedication, to public use, evidence of, 14 Cal. 649; ownership and dedication, 15 Cal. 548; 7 How. 31.

McCoon v. Smith, 3 Hill, 147. Cited, Estoppel, doctrine not to apply to infants, 25 Cal. 153.

McCormick v. Barnum, 10 Wend. 105. Cited, Boundary, acquiescence in division line, 25 Cal. 627.

McCormick v. Brown, 36 Cal. 180. Approved, New Promise, sufficiency of acknowledgment, 36 Cal. 192; 5 Nev. 216; judgment in action on, 39 Cal. 438.

McCormick v. Lafayette, 1 Ind. 52.   Cited, Eminent Domain, compensation a condition precedent to exercise of right of condemnation, 31 Cal. 559.

McCormick v. Sisson, 7 Cow. 715.   Commented on, Malicious Prosecution, want of probable cause, 29 Cal. 650; when action lies, 29 Cal. 657.

McCosker v. Brady, 1 Barb. Ch. 329.   Affirmed, 1 N. Y. 214.   Cited, Costs, disclaimer of interest, when not exemption from liability for, 17 Cal. 270.

McCoy v. Trustees of Dickenson College, 5 Serg. & R. 254. Cited, Title, successive possession, when cannot be added, 37 Cal. 354.

McCracken v. Hayward, 2 How. 608.   Approved, Constitutional Construction, statutes altering remedy on contract, unconstitutional, 2 Cal. 549, 550, 552; 10 Cal. 308; 16 Cal. 31; 6 How. 328, 332; 15 How. 319; law in existence as part of contract, 4 Cal. 139, 155; 7 Cal. 496; 15 Cal. 528.   Doubted, that remedy constitutes part of contract, 3 McLean, 546; 2 Minn. 97; 38 Geo. 358.   Restricted, 11 N. Y. 292.   Distinguished, 2 Kan. 403; 8 Watts & S. 50.

McCracken v. San Francisco, 16 Cal. 591.   Cited, Lands, constructive possession under color of title, 23 Cal. 437.   Approved, Adverse Possession, what constitutes, 38 Cal. 81; Estoppel, *in pais*, what essential to, 38 Cal. 316; 22 Ind. 95.   Cited, Municipal Corporations, validity of ordinance, on what depends, 23 Cal. 318; of contract, on what depends, 20 Cal. 102; 3 Wall. 669; 10 Wall. 684; subsequent ratification, 31 Cal. 28.   Distinguished, effect of ordinance, 31 Cal. 590.   Referred to, San Francisco, sale of city slip property, 27 Cal. 416.   Approved, Appropriation of proceeds of sale not a ratification of order of sale, 18 Cal. 608; 21 Cal. 362; city liable for value of property appropriated, 33 Cal. 140, 141.   Cited, Tenure of real property of pueblo, 42 Cal. 557.

McCrea v. Purmort, 16 Wend. 460; S. C. 5 Paige, 620. Approved, Evidence, consideration clause in deed may be explained by parol, 6 Cal. 137; 20 Cal. 676; 21 Cal. 51; 30 Cal. 23; Id. 57; 36 Cal. 370, 371.   Commented on, 2 Denio, 316.   Cited, Release, extinguishes debt, 38 Cal. 532.

McCreary v. Commonwealth, 29 Penn. St. 323.   Cited,

Criminal Procedure, discharge of jury, as an acquittal, 41 Cal. 216.

McCredie v. Senior, 4 Paige, 378. Commented on, Insolvency, partnership property, 7 Cal. 198.

McCulloch v. Maryland, 4 Wheat. 316. Approved, Constitutional Construction, supremacy of Federal Government as to delegated powers, 20 Cal. 571; 25 Cal. 418, 419, 421, 432; 2 Black, 632; 7 How. 407. Doubted, 6 Ohio St. 423; legislative discretion as to means for exercise of powers conferred, 24 Cal. 663; 27 Cal. 224; 36 Cal. 669; 19 How. 542. Cited, State Sovereignty, limitation to power of taxation, 1 Cal. 236; 28 Cal. 354; 41 Cal. 166; 4 Pet. 563; 12 Wheat. 449; 7 How. 538. Commented on, 9 Wheat. 765; 4 Pet. 563; 5 How. 593. Cited, Treaty, as supreme law, 25 Cal. 418.

McCulloch v. State, 11 Ind. 424. Cited, Constitutionality of statute, 22 Cal. 386.

McCullough, Ex parte, 35 Cal. 97. Cited, Habeas Corpus, office of writ, 41 Cal. 220.

McCullough v. Mayor, etc., of Brooklyn, 23 Wend. 457. Cited, Mandamus lies to enforce duty of public officers, 10 Cal. 215; 28 Cal. 71. Distinguished, Municipal Corporations, liability of, 16 Cal. 263, 271. Cited, Street Improvements, assessment of expense for, 31 Cal. 676.

McCullough v. Moss, 5 Denio, 567. Commented on, Corporation, validity of corporation contract, 33 Cal. 18, 21; 22 N. Y. 302.

McDaniel v. Moody, 3 Stewt. 314. Cited, Fixtures, what are, 14 Cal. 68.

McDaniel v. State, 8 Smedes & M. 401. Commented on, Criminal Procedure, evidence of character of accused, 5 Cal. 130; 7 Cal. 130; instructions to jury, 6 Cal. 547.

McDermott v. Douglass, 5 Cal. 89. Cited, Appeal, from justice's court, fees of justice, 6 Cal. 287.

McDermott v. Isbell, 4 Cal. 113. Cited, Replevin, insufficient defense in action on bond, 2 Or. 319.

McDevitt v. Sullivan, 8 Cal. 592. Cited, Judicial Sale, purchaser entitled to rents, 18 Cal. 115; 37 Cal. 431.

McDonald v. Askew, 29 Cal. 200. Cited, Water Rights, defined, 37 Cal. 311.

McDonald v. Badger, 23 Cal. 393. Cited, Sheriff's Deed, validity of, 38 Cal. 658.

McDonald v. Bear Riv. and Aub. W. & M. Co., 13 Cal. 220; S. C. 15 Cal. 145. Cited, Res Adjudicata, judgment of, what conclusive, 22 Cal. 222; 23 Cal. 375; 26 Cal. 494; Statute of Limitations, questions as to, must be presented at the trial, 31 Cal. 229. Cited, Principal and Agent, contract made by agent, 32 Cal. 654; 2 Nev. 13. Cited, Pleading, in action for diversion of water, 7 Nev. 327.

McDonald v. Griswold, 4 Cal. 352. Cited as inapplicable, County, payment of indebtedness of, 5 Cal. 334. Construed, 16 Cal. 34.

McDonald v. Katz, 31 Cal. 167. Cited, Insolvency, necessary steps in proceedings, 39 Cal. 142.

McDonald v. Maddux, 11 Cal. 187. Cited as inapplicable, County, redemption of county warrants, 18 Cal. 198. Explained, Payment of county indebtedness, 16 Cal. 34; 19 Cal. 184.

McDonough v. Childress, 15 La. 556. Cited, Real Actions, under civil law, actual possession, 1 Cal. 270; Id. 289; Id. 320.

McDougall v. Bell. See People *v.* Bell.

McDowel v. Delap, 2 A. K. Marsh. 33. Cited, Pleading, under statute of frauds, 29 Cal. 599.

McDowell v. Bank of Wilmington, 1 Harr. Del. 27. Cited, Corporation, transfer of unpaid shares of stock, 9 Cal. 115.

McElwain v. Willis, 9 Wend. 548. Cited, Fraudulent Conveyance, creditors at large cannot impeach, 27 Cal. 316.

McEwen v. Johnson, 7 Cal. 258. Cited, Findings, sufficiency of, 14 Cal. 418. Distinguished, 19 Cal. 105; conclusiveness of, 35 Cal. 35; special verdicts, practice, 30 Cal. 286.

McFadden v. Kingsbury, 11 Wend. 667. Doubted, Written Instruments, parol evidence of, 9 Cal. 594.

McFadden v. O'Donnell, 18 Cal. 160. Approved, Attachment, remedy of garnishee in action by attachment debtor, 22 Cal. 669.

McFarlan v. Triton Ins. Co., 4 Denio, 392. Cited, Corporation, immaterial irregularities on formation of, 22 Cal. 440; not subject to collateral inquiry, Id. 441.

McFarland v. Gwin, 3 How. 717. Cited, Statutory Construction, existing law a part of the contract, 7 Cal. 496; Execution, of process, completion of, after expiration of office, 37 Cal. 150.

McFarland v. Pico, 8 Cal. 626. Cited, Negotiable Instruments, action on, when premature, 18 Cal. 381.

McFarland's Admrs. v. Clark, 9 Dana, 134. Cited, New Trial, on ground of surprise, 24 Cal. 88.

McFerran v. Powers, 1 Serg. & R. 102. Cited, Customs and usage as law, 1 Cal. 499.

McGarrahan v. Maxwell, 28 Cal. 75. Cited, Appeal, from order dissolving injunction, effect of, 10 Wall. 297.

McGarrity v. Byington, 12 Cal. 426. Cited, Mines and Mining Claims, right perfected by posting notice, 18 Cal. 588; forfeiture depends on local rules, 36 Cal. 219. Commented on, Ejectment, from mining claim, on prior possession, 24 Cal. 347. Approved, Appeal, grounds of motion for nonsuit must appear on the record, 27 Cal. 474; error in granting or refusing new trial must affirmatively appear, 33 Cal. 525.

McGarvey v. Little, 15 Cal. 27. Cited, Judgment, when joint judgment is erroneous, 28 Cal. 35.

McGatrick v. Wason, 4 Ohio St. 566. Approved, Employer and Employé, when employer not liable for injuries from defective machinery, 31 Cal. 380.

McGee v. Anderson, 1 B. Mon. 187. Cited, Execution, election by debtor of property exempt, 22 Cal. 507.

McGee v. McGee, 10 Geo. 482. Cited, Alimony inseparable from divorce, opinion of Sprague, J. dissenting, 38 Cal. 277.

McGee v. Metcalf, 12 Smedes & M. 535. Cited, Surety, on specialty, when discharged, 10 Cal. 426.

McGennis v. Allison, 10 Serg. & R. 199. Cited, Evidence, handwriting of subscribing witness, 26 Cal. 411.

McGinn v. Worden, 3 E. D. Smith, 355. Cited, Assignment, right of action for wrongful detention of property is assignable, 22 Cal. 142.

McGintry v. Reeves, 10 Ala. 137. Cited, Vendor and Vendee, vendor concluded by recitals in deed, as to rights of vendee, 22 Cal. 503; 26 Cal. 87.

24

McGovern v. Payn, 32 Barb. 84. Cited as inapplicable, Sheriff, duties of, 28 Cal. 286.

McGowan v. Branch Bk. of Mobile, 7 Ala. 823. Cited, Mortgage, power of sale in, not to affect right to foreclose, 22 Cal. 125.

McGowan v. McGowan, 14 Gray, 121. Cited, Resulting Trust, when it arises, 25 Cal. 326.

McGreary v. Osborne, 9 Cal. 119. Cited, Fixtures, when and when not part of realty, 40 N. Y. 294.

McGregor v. Deal and Dover R. Co., 17 Jur. 21; S. C. 16 Eng. L. & E. 180. Commented on, Corporation, contract *ultra vires,* 37 Cal. 581.

McGrew v. McLanahan, 1 Penn. 44. Approved, Foreclosure, on instalment, extinguishes mortgage, 23 Cal. 31.

McHendry v. Reilly, 13 Cal. 75. Cited, Homestead, on land subject to vendor's lien, 5 Nev. 238.

McHenry v. Moore, 5 Cal. 90. Cited, Findings, in equity case, not disregarded on appeal, 18 Cal. 449.

McInstry v. Tanner, 9 John. 135. Cited, Office, entry into, under color of right cannot be collaterally questioned, 29 Cal. 485.

McIntire v. State, 5 Blackf. 384. Cited, Condemnation of Land, benefits considered in award of compensation, 31 Cal. 374.

McIntyre v. Chappell, 4 Tex. 187. Commented on, Husband and Wife, separate property, 30 Cal. 37, 38.

McIntyre v. Trumbull, 7 John. 35. Cited, Officer, when liable for wrongful acts of deputy, 14 Cal. 199.

McIntyre v. Willis, 20 Cal. 177. Cited, Appeal, effect of failure to make statement, 22 Cal. 266.

McIver v. Ragan, 2 Wheat. 25. Commented on, Statute of Limitations, construction as to exceptions in, 35 Cal. 640; 9 How. 529. Cited, 21 How. 238; 14 Wall. 146.

McIver v. Walker, 9 Cranch, 173. Cited, Patent, evidence admissible to explain, 10 Cal. 626.

McKay v. Petaluma Lodge, Cal. Sup. Ct. Apl. T. 1866 (not reported.) Referred to, Estoppel, by judgment, 41 Cal. 226.

McKee v. Greene, 31 Cal. 418. Cited, Land, constructive possession, under deed, 38 Cal. 487.

McKee v. Judd, 12 N. Y. 622.   Approved, Assignment, right of action for conversion, assignable, 22 Cal. 142; 32 Cal. 593.

McKeen v. Delancey's Lessee, 5 Cranch, 22.   Cited, Stare Decisis, applied to customs and usages, 1 Cal. 499; to construction of statutes, 12 Wheat. 168; to construction of constitution, 14 How. 504.

McKellar v. Bowell, 4 Hawks, 34.   Commented on, Sureties on Bond, when not concluded by decree against principal, 14 Cal. 205; 25 Cal. 222.

McKenney v. Whipple, 21 Me. 98.   Cited, Negotiable Instruments, demand at place of payment not of essence of contract, 11 Cal. 321.

McKenty v. Gladwin, 10 Cal. 227.   Approved, Fraudulent Contracts, note void where part of consideration is illegal, 13 Cal. 79.   Cited, 27 Cal. 235.   Commented on, 13 Cal. 334.   Cited, Conveyance void in part is void *in toto,* 23 Cal. 236.   Applied, 35 Cal. 308.

McKeon v. Bisbee, 9 Cal. 137.   Approved, Mining Claim, interest in, taxable property, 12 Cal. 70; 23 Cal. 506.

McKiernan v. Patrick, 4 How. Miss. 333.   Cited, Attorney and Counsel, presumed *prima facie* to have authority in conduct of action, 17 Cal. 433; 39 Cal. 685.   Commented on, 35 Cal. 540.

McKinley v. Smith, Hard. Ky. 167.   Cited, New Trial, objections to competency of juror not cured by verdict, 9 Cal. 311.

McKinley v. Tuttle, 34 Cal. 235.   Referred to on second appeal, 42 Cal. 576.

McKinney v. McKinney, 12 How. Pr. 24.   Cited, Bill of Particulars, practice, 32 Cal. 637.

McKinney v. Neil, 1 McLean, 540.   Cited, Negligence, liability for personal injuries, 28 Cal. 628.

McKinney v. Smith, 21 Cal. 374.   Denied, Water Rights, limitation of use to original purposes of appropriation, 32 Cal. 33.   Cited, Rights of prior appropriator, 37 Cal. 313.

McKinstry v. Solomons, 2 John. 57.   Cited, Arbitration and Award, selection of umpire, 23 Cal. 367.

McKircher v. Hawley, 16 John. 289.   Cited, Land, actual possession, presumptions arising from, 21 Cal. 490.

Cited, Foreclosure, relation of purchaser at sale and tenant in possession, 16 Cal. 590.

McKnight v. Dunlop, 4 Barb. 36. Cited, Judgment, limitation of bar of, 26 Cal. 505; what constitutes record of, 34 Cal. 423.

McKune v. McGarvey, 6 Cal. 497. Cited, Married Woman, rights and liabilities under Sole Trader Act, 7 Cal. 458; 29 Cal. 566.

McKyring v. Bull, 16 N. Y. 297. Cited, Pleading, new matter must be specially set up, 27 Cal. 367. Approved, 22 Wis. 359; so as to counter-claim, 26 Cal. 306.

McLain v. State, 10 Yerg. 241. Commented on, New Trial, incompetency of juror not cured by verdict, 9 Cal. 310; separation of jury a ground for, 21 Cal. 340.

McLaren v. Hutchinson, 18 Cal. 80. Reversed, S. C. 22 Cal. 189. Doubted, Agreement, between parties, to pay debt of either, may be enforced by creditor, 21 Cal. 189.

McLaren v. Pennington, 1 Paige, 107. Cited, Corporation, power of self-dissolution, 38 Cal. 172.

McLarren v. Spalding, 2 Cal. 510. Disapproved, Pleading, general denial put in issue only the allegations of complaint, accord and satisfaction must be specially pleaded, 10 Cal. 30; 21 Cal. 50.

McLaughlin v. Bank of Potomac, 7 How. 220. Denied, Surety on official bond, when judgment against principal, not evidence against, 14 Cal. 206.

McLaughlin v. Piatti, 27 Cal. 451. Cited, Specific Performance, of contract for personal property, may be enforced, 38 Cal. 454.

McLaurin v. Thompson, 1 Dudley, S. C. 335. Cited, Administrators, revocation of letters, 10 Cal. 117.

McLean v. Barnard, 1 Root, 462. Cited, Will, competency of witness to, 1 Cal. 506.

McLean v. Hugarin, 13 John. 184. Cited, Jurisdiction, of justice's court, evidence *aliunde* the record when admissible, 34 Cal. 327.

McLean, Succession of, 12 La. An. 222. Commented on, Husband and Wife, common property liable for debts of community, 17 Cal. 540.

McLendon v. Jones, 8 Ala. 298. Approved, Pleading, supplying place of, when lost, 27 Cal. 523.

McLeran v. Shartzer, 5 Cal. 70. Doubted, Appeal, waiver of service of notice, 2 Nev. 43.

McMahon v. Burchell, 3 Hare, 97; S. C. 2 Phill. 127. Cited, Tenant in Common, when liable to action for use and occupation, 12 Cal. 421. Limited, 44 Vt. 344.

McManus v. Crickett, 1 East, 108. Cited, Master, when chargeable with acts of servant, 38 Cal. 634. Distinguished, 38 Miss. 278.

McMechan v. Griffing, 3 Pick. 149. Cited, Conveyance, possession as notice of, 29 Cal. 490; 31 Cal. 185. Commented on, 2 Sum. 556.

McMillan v. Dana, 18 Cal. 339. Approved, Attachment, liability on bond for release of property, 2 Nev. 152.

McMillan v. Reynolds, 11 Cal. 372. Cited, Judgment, invalid, from defective service, 27 Cal. 299; by defective affidavit of service, 33 Cal. 514; by failure to serve copy of complaint, 35 Cal. 300.

McMillan v. Richards, 9 Cal. 365. Approved, Attachment, indebtedness on negotiable instrument not subject to levy, 10 Cal. 340; certificates of deposit are negotiable instruments, 22 Cal. 249; 35 Cal. 120; Mortgage, a mere security, legal title remains in mortgagor, 13 Cal. 14; 15 Cal. 293; 16 Cal. 467; 17 Cal. 592; 18 Cal. 488; 21 Cal. 621; 22 Cal. 262; 33 Cal. 264; 35 Cal. 413; 36 Cal. 39, 42, 58, 59; 39 Cal. 254, 255; 13 Mich. 396; holder of mortgage cannot obtain title without purchase at foreclosure sale, 9 Cal. 428. Explained and limited on this point, 26 Cal. 602. Approved, Payment of debt operates as extinguishment of lien, 21 Cal. 623; when debt is barred by statute, remedy on mortgage is barred, 24 Cal. 498; Foreclosure, clause in decree as to equity of redemption a useless formula, 11 Cal. 317; title of purchaser at sale under decree, pending redemption, 10 Cal. 531; legal title does not pass till delivery of sheriff's deed, doctrine of relation, 16 Cal. 469; 31 Cal. 301; all judicial sales alike subject to right of redemption, 21 Cal. 395; 22 Cal. 650. Cited, Redemption effected by payment, under protest, 14 Cal. 240; Money Paid, action lies for money paid under compulsion, 16 Cal. 170; 18 Cal. 274; Judgment, entry of, a ministerial act, and may be in vacation, 13 Cal. 52. Approved, 20 Cal. 55; 28 Cal. 36; Id. 340;

lien of, on what attaches, 14 Cal. 434. Referred to and commented on, *Res Adjudicata*, former judgment as an estoppel, 32 Cal. 189, 190, 192, 197, 199, 200.

McMillan v. Vanderlip, 12 John. 165. Cited, Services, action for, on entire contract, 2 Cal. 312.

McMinn v. Bliss, 31 Cal. 122. Cited, Statutory Construction, conflicting statutes how construed, 35 Cal. 708; Forcible Entry and Detainer, gist of action, 8 Nev. 88.

McMinn v. Mayes, 4 Cal. 209. Commented on, Ejectment on prior possession, evidence admissible, 9 Cal. 5.

McMinn v. O'Connor, 27 Cal. 238. Approved, Evidence, proof of handwriting of party to written instrument, 27 Cal. 310; secondary evidence, when admissible, 38 Cal. 449. Commented on, Pleading, title acquired, *pendente lite*, to be set up in supplemental answer, 30 Cal. 473. Cited, 37 Cal. 129; Id. 153; or by amendment, 39 Cal. 356; so as to new matter generally, 31 Cal. 336; Judicial Sale, title vests only on delivery of sheriff's deed, 31 Cal. 301. Approved, Judgment, when subject to collateral attack, 31 Cal. 348.

McMinn v. Whelan, 27 Cal. 300. Approved, Judgment, when subject to collateral attack, 27 Cal. 246; 31 Cal. 348. Commented on and qualified, 34 Cal. 402. Cited, Jurisdiction, cannot be acquired by mere assertion, applied to contracts of municipal corporations, 29 Cal. 188; New Trial, settlement of statement on, 32 Cal. 318; Tax Title, cannot be acquired by party whose duty it is to pay tax, 36 Cal. 146; Id. 326; 38 Cal. 222; 39 Cal. 356. Approved, Trial, conduct of judge at, 7 Nev. 383.

McMurray v. Gifford, 5 How. Pr. 14. Cited, Pleading, allegation of ownership insufficient, 11 Cal. 168; frivolous denial of, 32 Cal. 573.

McNair v. Hunt, 5 Mo. 301. Cited, Estates of Deceased, jurisdiction of courts prior to passage of probate act, 37 Cal. 92.

McNairy v. Bell, 1 Yerg. 502. Cited, Negotiable Instruments, presentment and demand at place fixed, not of essence of contract, 11 Cal. 323.

McNally v. Mott, 3 Cal. 235. Cited, Judgment, against party not named in the record, void, 7 Cal. 587; 37 Cal. 348.

McNamara v. King, 7 Ill. 432. Approved, New Trial, verdict, when set aside for excessive damages, 24 Cal. 517.

McNeil v. Borland, 23 Cal. 144. Approved, Mechanic's Lien, proceedings to enforce, are special, 23 Cal. 458.

McNeven v. Livingston, 17 John. 437. Cited, Fraud, waiver of fraud and of right to rescind contract, 17 Cal. 384.

McNutt v. Livingston, 7 Smedes & M. 641. Cited, Officers, duties and liabilities of, on issuance of writs, 36 Cal. 214.

McPherson v. Cunliff, 11 Serg. & R. 422. Cited, Probate, validity of probate sales, 7 Cal. 235; 2 Pet. 167.

McQuade v. Whaley, 29 Cal. 612. Cited, Appeal, a summary of the pleadings, if agreed to, is sufficient, in transcript, 36 Cal. 130.

McQueen v. Middletown Manf. Co., 16 John. 5. Cited, Service, of process, on corporation, at common law, 38 Cal. 154.

McQuillen v. State, 8 Smedes & M. 587. Cited, Verdict, in criminal action, when null, 28 Cal. 331.

McRae v. McLean, 3 Port. 138. Commented on, Replevin, possession obtained by plaintiff not a discharge of lien of attachment, 11 Cal. 274.

McVay v. Bloodgood, 9 Port. 547. Cited, Mortgage, securing several notes, holders entitled to *pro rata* interest, 23 Cal. 30.

McVickar v. Wolcott, 4 John. 510. Distinguished, Appeal, jurisdiction on, 1 Cal. 136.

Meacham v. Fitchburg Railroad Co., 4 Cush. 291. Cited, Eminent Domain, benefits to be estimated on compensation for condemnation, 31 Cal. 374.

Mead v. Elmore, Cal. Sup. Ct. July T. 1868 (not reported.) Approved, Corporation, transfers of stock of, 40 Cal. 625.

Mead v. Keeler, 24 Barb. 20. Cited, Corporation, immaterial defects in formation, 22 Cal. 440.

Meagher v. Gagliardo, 35 Cal. 602. Distinguished, Stipulation, agreement setting day for trial, 38 Cal. 629.

Mears v. Graham, 8 Blackf. 144. Cited, Negotiable Instrument, construction of, 39 Cal. 350.

Mechanics' Bank v. Bank of Columbia, 5 Wheat. 326. Approved, Principal, when liable for acts of agent, 24 Cal. 140; 8 How. 469.

Mechanics' Bank v. N. Y. and N. H. R. R. Co., 13 N. Y. 599. Cited, Corporation, certificates of stock as evidence of title to corporate property, 37 Cal. 30; 42 Cal. 99.

Mechanics' Bank v. Seton, 1 Pet. 299. Cited, Specific Performance, of agreement for transfer of stock, 23 Cal. 392, 393; Notice, to agent is notice to principal, 31 Cal. 165. Approved, Parties necessary in equitable action, 31 Cal. 427; 19 How. 115.

Mechelen v. Wallace, 7 Adol. & E. 49. Cited, Contract, void in part is void *in toto,* 40 Cal. 348.

Meeker v. Harris, 19 Cal. 278. Distinguished, Pleading, averments in complaint to set aside fraudulent deed, 29 Cal. 60. Commented on, 34 Cal. 106.

Meeker v. Meeker, 16 Conn. 387. Commented on, Deed, construction of consideration clause in, 30 Cal. 26.

Meeker v. Williamson, 4 Mart. 625. Cited, Real actions under civil law, title by possession, sufficient, 1 Cal. 269. Commented on, Issue of title in action, 1 Cal. 270.

Meeker v. Wilson, 1 Gall. 419. Commented on, Statute of Frauds, change of possession on mortgage or sale of chattel, 29 Cal. 476.

Meeks v. Hahn, 20 Cal. 620. Cited, Executors and Administrators, sole right to maintain ejectment till estate distributed, 21 Cal. 91; Id. 209; Id. 348; 23 Cal. 29; title vests in heir, on death of ancestor, but administrator entitled to possession, 31 Cal. 604; 42 Cal. 463; of personal property, 29 Cal. 510. Statutes distinguished, 28 Wis. 230.

Meerholz v. Sessions, 9 Cal. 277. Cited, Appeal, order by consent not renewable, 11 Cal. 405.

Megerle v. Ashe, 27 Cal. 322. Affirmed, S. C. 33 Cal. 74. Cited, State Lands, selection and location vests title, which title passes by State patent, 33 Cal. 262. Approved, 34 Cal. 514; location of State warrants, on unsurveyed lands, void, 34 Cal. 512. Cited, Ejectment, conflicting patents, admissible in evidence, 37 Cal. 389; Preemption, time of filing preemption claim, 40 Cal. 170; 42 Cal. 618; right must be proved, 40 Cal. 377;

indorsement on declaration as evidence, 42 Cal. 608. Explained, Estoppel, waiver of, 39 Cal. 481.

Meiggs v. Scannell, 7 Cal. 405. Cited, Attachment, on vessels, lien when it attaches, 8 Cal. 422.

Melcher v. Kuhland, 22 Cal. 522. Approved, Married Woman, Sole Trader Act construed, 29 Cal. 566.

Melen v. Andrews, Mood. & M. 336. Cited, Evidence, party not bound by statements of witnesses, not denied, 22 Cal. 238.

Mellen v. Boarman, 13 Smedes & M. 100. Cited, Probate Sales, *caveat emptor* applies, 9 Cal. 197.

Mellon v. Croghan, 3 Mart. N. S. 423. Cited, Negotiable Instruments, place of payment not of essence of contract, 11 Cal. 324.

Melvin v. Proprietors of Locks, etc., 5 Met. 15. Cited, Title, by adverse possession, successive possession when cannot be added, 37 Cal. 354.

Mena v. Le Roy, 1 Cal. 216. Cited, Alcalde, powers of, 1 Cal. 508; 2 Black, 210.

Menard's Heirs v. Massey, 8 How. 293. Cited, Mexican Grants, execution of government trust under treaty, 3 Cal. 26; submission of claim to board of commissioners, 3 Cal. 42. Referred to, Validity of grant, 11 How. 562; 13 How. 258; 19 How. 82; Id. 336.

Mendocino Co. v. Lamar, 30 Cal. 627. Distinguished, Recognizance, liability on, 2 Or. 319.

Merced Min. Co. v. Fremont, 7 Cal. 130; S. C. 7 Cal. 317. Cited, Public Lands, appropriation for mining purposes, vested interest in miners, 9 Cal. 142. Approved, 10 Cal. 183; 12 Cal. 70; 14 Cal. 313; Quieting Title, action may be brought by miner in possession, 15 Cal. 263; 23 Cal. 506. Approved, 35 Cal. 34. Cited, Injunction, in trespass on, and to restrain waste, sufficiency of complaint, 8 Cal. 397; 10 Cal. 238; 32 Cal. 594. Commented on, McAll. 317, 366; Appeal, effect of, from order dissolving injunction on, 15 Cal. 110; 10 Wall. 297.

Mercein v. Andrus, 10 Wend. 463. Cited, Negotiable Instruments, effect of notice, of accommodation indorsement by one partner of firm, 37 Cal. 118.

Mercer v. Jones, 3 Camp. 477. Erroneously cited, Conversion, measure of damages where property has a fixed value. Criticism of Abbott, C. J., in 1 Carr. & P. 626, quoted erroneously as opinion of Ld. Ellenborough in Mercer v. Jones, and adopted, where value is fluctuating, 9 Cal. 563; 33 Cal. 119; 3 Sand. 635; 40 Miss. 361. Rule qualified, 39 Cal. 420.

Mercer v. Watson, 1 Watts, 330. Cited, Statutory Construction, province of judiciary, 17 Cal. 562; constitutionality of remedial statutes, 30 Cal. 144; Title, by adverse possession, when successive possessions cannot be added, 37 Cal. 354.

Merchants' Bank v. Spicer, 6 Wend. 443. Cited, Deed, executed in wrong name, valid, 25 Cal. 81.

Meredith v. Richardson, 10 Ala. 828. Cited, Attachment, bond for release, parol proof of recitals in, 13 Cal. 556.

Merle v. Mathews, 26 Cal. 455. Cited, Appeal, errors without injury no ground for reversal, 28 Cal. 192; Contract, validity of, under Mexican law, 30 Cal. 73; 11 Wall. 578; Alien, rights of, under common law and civil law, 32 Cal. 386.

Merrick's Estate, 8 Watts & S. 402. Cited, Estates of Deceased, money received for sale of goods on *del credere* commission, no part of assets, 22 Cal. 518.

Merrifield v. Bachelder, Cal. Sup. Ct. Jan. T. 1854 (not reported.) Construed, Fraud, title of purchaser without notice of fraud, valid, 12 Cal. 497.

Merrifield v. Cooley, 4 How. Pr. 272. Denied, judgment, recovery on joint contract, 1 Cal. 169, 173.

Merrill v. Gorham, 6 Cal. 41. Approved, Offices, of tax collector and sheriff may be held by same person, 9 Cal. 292; 14 Cal. 16. Commented on, Equity, when relief obtainable in, 29 Cal. 55. Cited, Statutory Construction, consolidation of offices, before election of incumbent, unconstitutional, 34 Cal. 476; repeal by implication not favored, laws to be construed together, 35 Cal. 708.

Merrills v. Swift, 18 Conn. 257. Cited, Powers, ratification by principal, when presumed, 4 Cal. 169.

Merrills v. Tariff Manf. Co., 10 Conn. 384. Commented on, Corporation, liability of, for malicious injury, 34 Cal. 54.

Merrimac Manf. Co. v. Garner, 2 Abb. Pr. 318; S. C. 4 E. D. Smith, 387. Cited, Injunction, practice on motion to dissolve, 35 Cal. 59, 65.

Merritt v. Brinkerhoff, 17 John. 306. Cited, Water Rights, by priority of appropriation, 23 Cal. 486.

Merritt v. Earle, 29 N. Y. 115. Cited, Damages, by the elements, "acts of God" defined, 35 Cal. 423.

Merritt v. Judd, 14 Cal. 59. Commented on, Public Land, claim to mining land as property, 23 Cal. 505; 42 Cal. 482. Cited, Fixtures, what constitute, 6 Nev. 248; 7 Nev. 42; 40 N. Y. 294.

Merritt v. Lambert, 10 Paige, 352. Approved, Mortgage, tender and refusal, not a discharge of lien, 14 Cal. 529. Cited, Attorney-at-Law, not public officer, 22 Cal. 315.

Merritt v. Seaman, 6 N. Y. 168. Approved, Exceptions, when general objection to evidence is available, 18 Cal. 324.

Mervin v. Kumbel, 23 Wend. 293. Cited, Execution, joint property, statutory construction, 39 Cal. 96. Denied, Judgment, against party not served cannot be enforced, 39 Cal. 97. Commented on, 18 N. Y. 569.

Mesick v. Sunderland, 6 Cal. 297. Commented on, Conveyances, penalty in recording act construed, 7 Cal. 303. Doubted, Actual Notice, effect of, Id. 306. Explained, 7 Cal. 489. Criticised as to construction of recording act, 10 Cal. 107.

Messinger v. Kintner, 4 Bin. 97. Cited, Probate, jurisdiction as governed by domicil, 7 Cal. 236.

Metcalf v. Bingham, 3 N. H. 459. Cited, Roads and Highways, constitutionality of statute opening private roads, 32 Cal. 255.

Metcalf v. Clark, 8 La. An. 287. Commented on, Husband and Wife, property recorded in name of wife, 30 Cal. 36; burden of proof as to separate estate of wife, 30 Cal. 44; on conveyance to wife, construction of, 30 Cal. 55.

Methodist Churches, etc., v. Barker, 18 N. Y. 463. Approved, Injunction Bond, liability on, attaches on dismissal of action, 18 Cal. 628.

Methodist E. Church v. Jaques, 3 John. Ch. 77. See Jaques v. M. E. Church, *ante.*

Metropolitan Bank v. Van Dyck, 27 N. Y. 400. Approved, Legal Tender Notes, validity of act, 27 Cal. 161.

Meuser v. Risdon, 36 Cal. 239. Commented on, Street Improvements, order for street work, 41 Cal. 501.

Meyer v. Gorham, 5 Cal. 322. Cited, Chattel Mortgage, statute to be strictly construed, 23 Cal. 301.

Meyer v. Kalkmann, 6 Cal. 582. Disapproved, Superior Court, of San Francisco, jurisdiction, on issuance of process, 10 Cal. 294; 14 Cal. 158. Referred to, 20 Cal. 640. Commented on, 30 Cal. 579; 39 Cal. 519; Judgment, on partnership accounting, 17 Cal. 162.

Meyer v. Kinzer, 12 Cal. 247. Approved, Husband and Wife, presumption that property acquired by either, after marriage, is common property, 12 Cal. 224. Cited, 13 Cal. 470; 15 Cal. 131; 16 Cal. 557; 17 Cal. 581; 21 Cal. 91; 22 Cal. 288; 23 Cal. 241; Id. 398; 26 Cal. 420; 28 Cal. 42; 30 Cal. 42, 55, 61; burden of proof as to acquisition by gift, bequest, etc., see above citations.

Meyer v. Kohlman, 8 Cal. 44. Cited, Insolvency, proceedings special, no intendments in favor of jurisdiction, 31 Cal. 169.

Meyer v. Kohn, 29 Cal. 278. Referred to on second appeal, Judgment in gold coin, 33 Cal. 486.

Mezes v. Greer, McAll. 401; S. C. 24 How. 268. Cited, Boundaries, proof of, in ejectment, 35 Cal. 154. See Greer v. Mezes, *ante.*

Miami Exporting Co. v. Bank of U. S., Wright, 249. Cited, Conveyance, when a mortgage, 8 Cal. 430; parol evidence of, admissible, 13 Cal. 129; once a mortgage always a mortgage, 8 Cal. 434.

Michoud v. Girod, 4 How. 503. Commented on, Trust, purchase by administrator at his own sale, voidable but not void, 29 Cal. 37. Cited, 8 How. 152.

Mickles v. Haskin, 11 Wend. 125. Cited, Sureties, levy of execution as satisfaction of judgment and discharge of sureties, 8 Cal. 30; 23 Cal. 100.

Mickles v. Rochester City Bank, 11 Paige, 118. Cited, Corporation, stockholders no power to execute conveyance, 33 Cal. 19.

Middleton v. Findla, 25 Cal. 76. Cited, Principal and Agent, agent entitled to commissions on sale of property, 29 Cal. 395; conveyance may be executed by grantor in any name, 38 Cal. 49.

Middleton v. Fowler, 1 Salk. 282. Cited, Master and Servant, when master liable for act of servant, 38 Cal. 634.

Middleton v. Franklin, 3 Cal. 238. Cited, Nuisance, when a question of fact, 30 Cal. 384; when injunction lies to restrain, 47 N. H. 78.

Middleton v. Low, 30 Cal. 596. Cited, Mandamus, when will issue to governor, 39 Cal. 210, 219.

Middleton v. Perry, 2 Bay, 539. Cited, Deed, parol evidence admissible to explain, 10 Cal. 625.

Midhurst v. Waite, 3 Burr. 1259. Cited, Officers, may act by deputy, 35 Cal. 713.

Mier v. Cartledge, 2 Code Rep. 125; S. C. 4 How. Pr. 115. Reversed in part, 8 Barb. 75. Cited, Pleading, general denial to verified complaint, insufficient, 1 Cal. 196.

Miles v. Berry, 1 Hill, S. C. 296. Denied, Statute of Limitations, fraudulent concealment, effect of, 8 Cal. 460.

Miles v. Caldwell, 2 Wall. 35. Cited, Judgment, limitation of bar of, 26 Cal. 514.

Miles v. Cattle, 7 Bing. 743; 19 Eng. 333. Distinguished, Bailment, liability of bailee for loss of property, 33 Cal. 604.

Miles v. Johnson, 1 McCord, 157. Cited, Ferrymen, duties and liabilities as common carriers, 5 Cal. 364.

Miles v. Knott, 12 Gill & J. 442. Cited, Execution, when erroneous, but not void, 38 Cal. 380.

Miles v. Williams, 1 P. Wms. 249. Commented on, Statutory Construction, general rule, 13 Cal. 95.

Milhau v. Sharp, 15 Barb. 193; S. C. 27 N. Y. 611. Commented on, Municipal Corporations, powers of, 7 Cal. 376. Cited, Liability on its contracts, 16 Cal. 270; grant of franchise for street railroad, 32 Cal. 512.

Millar v. Taylor, 4 Burr. 2319. Cited, Forfeiture, created by statute, enforcement of, 33 Cal. 217.

Millard v. Hathaway, 27 Cal. 119. Cited, Resulting Trust, how created, 35 Cal. 487. Distinguished, 40 Cal. 637. Cited, Enforcement of, what must be shown, 38 Cal. 193. Commented on, 7 Kan. 478; 48 Mo. 596.

Millard v. Hewlett, 19 Wend. 301. Cited, Infancy, ratification of contract by infant, 24 Cal. 213.

Miller v. Austen, 13 How. 218. Commented on, Negotiable Instruments, certificates of deposit, 29 Cal. 505.

Miller v. Bear, 3 Paige, 466. Cited, Specific Performance, waiver of forfeiture in contract, 40 Cal. 13; Vendor in possession holds as trustee of vendee, 40 Cal. 571.

Miller v. Brinkerhoff, 4 Denio, 120. Cited, Jurisdiction, process and proceedings, when void and when voidable, 31 Cal. 349, 350.

Miller v. Cullum, 4 Ala. 576. Cited, Deed, description by reference to plan, 24 Cal. 444.

Miller v. Dennett, 6 N. H. 109. Cited, Statutory Construction, statutes not to be construed retrospectively, 4 Cal. 136.

Miller v. Dobson, 6 Ill. 572. Denied, Witness, competency of vendor, 23 Cal. 446.

Miller v. Drake, 1 Caines, 45. Cited, Pleading, under statute of frauds, 29 Cal. 599.

Miller v. Earle, 24 N. Y. 111. Cited, Judgment by confession, collateral attack, 37 Cal. 336.

Miller v. Ewer, 27 Me. 509. Cited, Deed, by corporation, under seal, *prima facie* valid, 16 Cal. 640. Explained, 36 Vt. 750; 35 Mo. 25.

Miller v. Ewing, 6 Cush. 34. Cited, Deed, when warranty not an estoppel, as to after-acquired title, 25 Cal. 452.

Miller v. Ewing, 8 Smedes & M. 421. Cited, Judgment, recital of appearance, in record, not conclusive, 13 Cal. 561.

Miller, Ex parte, 2 Hill, 418. Cited, Water Rights, interest acquired by purchase, 29 Cal. 207.

Miller v. Foutz, 2 Yeates, 418. Distinguished, Sureties, on replevin bond, measure of liability, 7 Cal. 572.

Miller v. Gunn, 7 How. Pr. 159. Cited, Appeal, death of appellant, after argument, effect of, 20 Cal. 69.

Miller v. Manice, 6 Hill, 114. Cited, Pleading, defenses in action, 10 Cal. 27. Approved, Judgment, limitation of bar of, 38 Cal. 647.

Miller v. McBrier, 14 Serg. & R. 382. Commented on, Estoppel, when tenant not estopped, 33 Cal. 253. Cited, 35 Cal. 571.

Miller v. Meetoh, 8 Penn. St. 417. Commented on, Power of sale in will, construction of, 32 Cal. 443, 444.

Miller v. Miller, 33 Cal. 353. Cited, Divorce, award of common property in, 4 Nev. 472.

Miller v. Miller, 10 Tex. 332. Cited, Probate Proceedings, review of, 7 Cal. 237.

Miller v. Newton, 23 Cal. 554. Disapproved, Married Woman, separate estate how charged, 25 Cal. 375.

Miller v. Plumb, 6 Cow. 665. Cited, Fixtures, what constitute, 10 Cal. 264.

Miller v. Race, 1 Burr, 457; S. C. 1 Smith's Lead. Cas. 251. Cited, Pledge, liability of bailee, 6 Cal. 647.

Miller v. Sacramento Co., 25 Cal. 93. Cited as not in point, Office and Officers, 28 Cal. 57; office, what constitutes, 28 Cal. 388; judicial functions of officer, what are, 29 Cal. 85; powers and duties of officers, 34 Cal. 541.

Miller v. Sanderson, 10 Cal. 489. Cited, Officer, remedy against, for breach of duty, 31 Ill. 320.

Miller v. Steen, 30 Cal. 402; S. C. 34 Cal. 138. Cited, New Trial, motion for, is exclusive remedy for review of findings, 38 Cal. 531, 536; Specific Performance, time not of essence of contract, 40 Cal. 11.

Miller v. Stem, 2 Penn. St. 286. Cited, Surety, on specialty, when discharged by agreement for delay, 10 Cal. 426.

Miller v. Stewart, 24 Cal. 502. Cited, Instructions, charging matters of fact erroneous, 33 Cal. 305.

Miller v. Stewart, 9 Wheat. 680. Construed, Surety, contract of, to be strictly construed, 17 Cal. 508. Cited, 6 How. 299; 21 How. 76.

Miller v. Thomas, 14 Ill. 428. Cited, Ejectment, measure of damages for rents and profits, 7 Cal. 25. Commented on, Mortgage, by deed and defeasance, 13 Cal. 129.

Miller v. Thompson, 3 Port. 196. Cited, Conveyance, when void for fraud, 13 Cal. 72.

Miller v. Van Tassel, 24 Cal. 458. Approved, Warranty, by vendor of chattel, on possession, implied, 41 Cal. 113.

Miller v. Watson, 5 Cow. 195. Cited, Vendor and Vendee, payment of purchase money cannot be resisted without an eviction, 5 Cal. 264.

Milligan v. Wedge, 12 Adol. & E. 737. Commented on, Respondeat Superior, when rule applies, 8 Cal. 489, 496; 19 N. H. 440. Cited, 24 How. 124.

Millikin v. Cary, 5 How. Pr. 272; S. C. 3 Code R. 250. Cited, Injunction, practice on motion to dissolve, 35 Cal. 59.

Million v. Riley, 1 Dana, 359. Affirmed, 5 Dana, 274. Cited, Execution, effect of levy on property exempt, 15 Cal. 615.

Mills v. Bank of United States, 11 Wheat. 431. Commented on, Negotiable Instruments, notice to indorser, 14 Cal. 163; sufficiency of statement in notice, 24 Cal. 383; 9 Pet. 46.

Mills, Case of, 1 Mich. 392. Cited, Attorney-at-Law, when will be stricken from roll, 22 Cal. 320.

Mills v. Duryee, 7 Cranch, 481. Cited, Judgment, impeachment of, validity of, 30 Cal. 446; 3 Wheat. 235. Commented on, 13 Pet. 326. Construed, 2 Paine, 508; 2 Swan, 560; 37 N. H. 474.

Mills v. Fowkes, 5 Bing. N. C. 455. Cited, Debtor and Creditor, application of payments, 14 Cal. 449; 7 How. 691.

Mills v. Gleason, 21 Cal. 274. Commented on, Replevin Bond, complaint in action on, 24 Cal. 152.

Mills v. Spencer, 1 Holt, 533; S. C. 3 Eng. C. L. 211. Cited, Libel, evidence in mitigation not admissible, 41 Cal. 384.

Mills v. Tukey, 22 Cal. 373. Distinguished, Writ of Assistance, 23 Cal. 403.

Mills v. Wilkins, 6 Mod. 62. Cited, Statutory Construction, title of act, 9 Cal. 522; 20 Cal. 582.

Milnes v. Slater, 8 Ves. Jr. 305. Cited, Will, construction of devise, 31 Cal. 610.

Miner v. Bradley, 22 Pick. 459. Cited, Contract, entire contract indivisible, 15 Cal. 256. Distinguished, 49 N. H. 129.

Miner v. Clark, 15 Wend. 425. Cited, Ejectment, notice of action necessary to bind party by judgment, 9 Cal. 226.

Miners' Ditch Co. v. Zellerbach, 37 Cal. 543. Commented on, Corporations, power of disposal of corporate property, 38 Cal. 171. Distinguished, 38 Cal. 316. Commented on, Different kinds of corporations, 7 Kan. 521.

Minier, Ex parte, 2 Hill, 411. Cited, Fees of Office, statutory construction, 26 Cal. 119.

Minnichite v. Ramirez, Cal. Sup. Ct. July T. 1857 (not reported.) Cited, Arbitration and Award, jurisdiction, 9 Cal. 146.

Minor v. Mechanics' Bank, 1 Pet. 46. Commented on, Judgment, several judgment on joint liability, 1 Cal. 171. Cited, Actions, matters of form to yield to substantial purposes of justice, 1 Cal. 286; Id. 314; 5 How. 64.

Minturn v. Baylis, 33 Cal. 129. Cited, Specific Performance, not enforced where contract is vague and uncertain, 39 Cal. 301.

Minturn v. Brower, 24 Cal. 644. Cited, Mexican Grant, legal title does not vest till confirmation and segregation, 26 Cal. 123. Approved, Distinction as to perfect titles, 29 Cal. 107; 30 Cal. 507; 35 Cal. 431; what constitutes a perfect title, Id. 508. Commented on, 39 Cal. 236, 237; 13 Wall. 489; Third Persons, not concluded by confirmation and patent, who are, 26 Cal. 627.

Minturn v. Burr, 16 Cal. 107; S. C. 20 Cal. 48. Cited, Forcible Entry and Detainer, insufficient statement of facts, 27 Cal. 375. Approved, Actual Possession, what constitutes, 38 Cal. ~~420.~~ 410

Minturn v. Hays, 2 Cal. 590. Approved, Injunction, will not lie to restrain collection of tax, 2 Neb. 438; 7 Kan. 231.

Minturn v. Larue, 1 McAll. 370. Cited, Corporation, powers of, under charter or legislative grant of franchise, 13 Cal. 547.

Mirehouse v. Scaife, 2 Mylne & C. 695. Cited, Will, construction of devise, 31 Cal. 610; 16 How. 11.

Missouri Institute v. How, 27 Mo. 211. Cited, Dedication, to public use, by deed, when ineffectual, 42 Cal. 553.

Mitchel v. Reynolds, 1 P. Wms. 181. Commented on, Contract, in restraint of trade, when invalid, 6 Cal. 261; 36 Cal. 358.

Mitchel v. United States, 9 Pet. 711; S. C. 15 Pet. 86. Cited, National Law, laws of ceded territory, 2 Cal. 48; 18 Cal. 23; 9 How. 445; rights protected by treaty, 24 Cal. 660, 664; Military reserves in pueblo grants,

25

15 Cal. 543; 21 How. 449; Title, legal seizin and possession under perfect title, 24 Cal. 660.

Mitchell v. Churchman's Lessee, 4 Humph. 218. Cited, Instructions, misapprehension of jury, 11 Cal. 142.

Mitchell v. Cotton, 3 Fla. 134. Cited, Surety, on note, when discharged by agreement of creditor with debtor for delay, 10 Cal. 426.

Mitchell v. Crassweller, 13 Com. B. 237. Cited, Master, when liable for acts of servant, 38 Cal. 634.

Mitchell v. Culver, 7 Cow. 337. Cited, Negotiable Instruments, filling blank in, not an alteration, 8 Cal. 112.

Mitchell v. Davis, 20 Cal. 45. Referred to on second appeal, Forcible Entry and Detainer, 23 Cal. 382.

Mitchell v. DeRoche, 1 Yeates, 12. Cited as not in point, Vendor and Vendee, right of possession of vendee, 22 Cal. 619.

Mitchell v. Hazen, 4 Conn. 495. Cited, Probate, administrator's sale, *caveat emptor* applies, 9 Cal. 197.

Mitchell v. Hockett, 25 Cal. 538. Cited, Judicial Sale, conclusiveness of recitals in sheriff's deed, 30 Cal. 288.

Mitchell v. Lenox, 2 Paige, 280. Cited, Pleading, objections to non-joinder may be taken by demurrer or answer, 8 Cal. 516.

Mitchell v. Lipe, 8 Yerg. 179. Cited, Attachment, on real estate, lien of, 11 Cal. 248. Statutes distinguished, Judicial Sale, validity of purchaser's title, 38 Cal. 655.

Mitchell v. Oakley, 7 Paige, 68. Cited as inapplicable, Negotiable Instruments, equitable relief from fraudulent note, 9 Cal. 102.

Mitchell v. Reed, 9 Cal. 204. Cited, Estoppel, owner of property attached for debt of third person, when estopped from setting up title, 9 Cal. 606; 51 N. H. 294.

Mitchell v. Sheppard, 13 Tex. 484. Cited, Vendor and Vendee, vendee in possession, trustee of vendor, statute, does not run, 40 Cal. 572.

Mitchell v. Stavely, 16 East, 58. Commented on, Arbitration and Award, effect of omissions in award, 12 Cal. 340. Explained, 8 Leigh, 613. Distinguished, 3 Zab. 97.

Mitchell v. Steelman, 8 Cal. 363. Approved, Commerce, power of congress, to regulate, is exclusive, when exercised, 34 Cal. 498; 7 Wall. 656.

Mitchell v. Thompson, 1 McLean, 96. Cited, Statute of Limitations, fraudulent concealment, effect of, 8 Cal. 460.

Mitchell v. Warner, 5 Conn. 497. Cited, Covenants of seizin and right to convey are personal, 37 Cal. 189.

Mitchell v. Winslow, 2 Story, 630. Commented on, Assignment, of contingent rights, in equity, 30 Cal. 86, 90. Doubted, 28 Mo. 413. Denied, 10 Wis. 403.

Mitchell v. Worden, 20 Barb. 253. Cited, Fraud, vitiates sale of chattels, 8 Cal. 213. Commented on, Effect of concealment of insolvency, 8 Cal. 214.

Mitchum v. State, 11 Geo. 615. Cited, Evidence, declarations when part of the *res gestœ*, 35 Cal. 51.

Mizell v. Herbert, 12 Smedes & M. 547. Denied, Witness, competency, vendor of chattel, 23 Cal. 446.

Moadinger v. Mechanics' F. Ins. Co. of N. Y., 2 Hall, 527. Cited, New Trial, modification of instructions not a sufficient ground for, 36 Cal. 176.

Moale v. Hollins, 11 Gill & J. 11. Cited, Judgment, on joint obligation, 6 Cal. 181.

Mobile Cotton Press v. Moore, 9 Port. 679. Cited, Jurisdiction, power of restitution on reversal, 14 Cal. 678.

Mobile and Ohio R. R. Co. v. State, 29 Ala. 573. Commented on, Constitutionality of statute, validity of statutes in part unconstitutional, 22 Cal. 394.

Moers v. City of Reading, 21 Penn. St. 188. Cited, Legislature, statutes dependent for their effect on vote of electors, valid, 13 Cal. 188. Approved, 17 Cal. 31; 25 646; validity of statutes in the alternative, 13 Cal. 358; 17 Cal. 33, 34; authority to raise money by exercise of taxing power, constitutional, 13 Cal. 355.

Moffit v. State, 2 Humph. 99. Approved, Criminal Procedure, accomplice a competent witness, 5 Cal. 185; 20 Cal. 440.

Mogg v. Mogg, 1 Mer. 654. Cited, Injunction, to restrain trespass, 7 Cal. 323.

Mohawk Bank v. Broderick, 13 Wend. 133. Cited, Negotiable Instruments, presumptive dishonor, what is reasonable time, 40 Cal. 115.

Mohawk and H. R. R. Co., Matter of, 19 Wend. 139. Cited, Election, what irregularities will not invalidate, 12 Cal. 361.

Mohler's Appeal, 5 Penn. St. 418. Denied, Parties, to suit in foreclosure, 14 Cal. 218.

Moies v. Bird, 11 Mass. 438. Cited, Negotiable Instruments, effect of superscribing "surety" by indorser, 10 Cal. 291.

Mokelumne Hill Co. v. Woodbury, 14 Cal. 265; S. C. 10 Cal. 185, 187, 188. Referred to, 13 Cal. 635. Cited, Witness, member of corporation when incompetent, 20 Cal. 615; 23 Cal. 329; Corporations, how regarded as to liability of stockholders, 22 Cal. 388; stockholders liable as principals, 39 Cal. 654; 14 Wis. 701. Commented on, 34 Cal. 505; minor irregularities in formation of corporation, not to invalidate existence of, 22 Cal. 440, 441; substantial compliance with statute sufficient, 29 Cal. 127.

Moline, Ex parte, 19 Ves. Jr. 216. Cited, Negotiable Instruments, notice of dishonor, when may be given, 8 Cal. 634.

Molyn, Case of Sir John, 6 Coke, 6. Cited, Grants, from government, how construed, 13 Cal. 453.

Moncrief v. Ward, 16 Abb. Pr. 354, note. Commented on, Married Woman, when liable for costs of suit, 26 Cal. 445.

Monell v. Colden, 13 John. 396. Cited, Coveyance, without warranty, no action lies for false representations as to title, 9 Cal. 227.

Monell v. Dennison, 17 How. Pr. 422. Approved, Probate, conclusiveness of decisions, 18 Cal. 504.

Monell v. Lawrence, 12 John. 521. Cited, Notice, judgments and decrees as notice, 23 Cal. 38.

Monroe v. Douglass, 5 N. Y. 447. Commented on, Judicial Notice, not taken of foreign laws, 15 Cal. 254.

Monroe v. State, 5 Geo. 142. Cited, New Trial, objections to competency of juror not cured by verdict, 9 Cal. 311.

Montacute v. Maxwell, 1 P. Wms. 618. Approved, Statute of Frauds, parol proof when admissible under, 21 Cal. 101. Commented on, 3 Story, 290.

Montague v. Commonwealth, 10 Gratt. 767. Approved, Juror and Jury, court may excuse juror of its own motion, 32 Cal. 45.

Montalet v. Murray, 4 Cranch, 46. Cited, Jurisdiction, of federal courts, 22 Cal. 85; 5 How. 291; 19 How. 402.

Monte Allegre, 9 Wheat. 616. Approved, Judicial Sales, *caveat emptor* applies, 24 Cal. 607. Commented on, Warranty, warranty not implied, on sale of chattels by agent, 25 Cal. 81. Cited, 8 How. 468.

Montgomerie v. Marquis of Bath, 3 Ves. Jr. 560. Denied, Parties, in foreclosure, 14 Cal. 218.

Montgomery v. Dillingham, 3 Smedes & M. 647. Cited, Surety, on note, mere delay of creditor will not discharge surety, 10 Cal. 425.

Montgomery v. Hunt, 5 Cal. 366. Cited, Trial, change of possession under statute of frauds, when a question of fact, and when of law, 23 Cal. 584.

Montgomery v. Middlemiss, 21 Cal. 103. Followed, Writ of Assistance, purchaser at foreclosure sale entitled to, 21 Cal. 108. Cited, Foreclosure, conclusiveness of decree, 23 Cal. 35.

Montgomery v. State, 11 Ohio, 424. Cited, Criminal Procedure, evidence of dying declarations, 35 Cal. 52.

Montgomery v. Tutt, 11 Cal. 190; S. C. 11 Cal. 307. Cited, Mortgage, estate in mortgagor till foreclosure and sale, 16 Cal. 468; Foreclosure, subsequent incumbrancers should be made parties, 13 Cal. 70; 15 Cal. 527; 21 Cal. 91; 40 Cal. 235, 238; purchaser after *lis pendens* filed not a necessary party, 28 Cal. 203; Decree, conclusive only on parties to action, 24 Cal. 512, and see above citations; Judgment, compound interest not allowed unless under express agreement, 29 Cal. 392; Writ of Assistance, rights of purchaser at judicial sale, 16 Cal. 158; 18 Cal. 143. Approved, 21 Cal. 107.

Montgomery Co. Bank v. Albany City Bank, 7 N. Y. 459. Cited, Pleading, objection to defects when to be taken, 10 Cal. 560.

Montgomery's Lessee v. Dickey, 2 Yeates, 212. Doubted, Evidence, admission of deposition of living witness, 15 Cal. 281.

Montrose v. Conner, 8 Cal. 344. Cited, Mechanic's Lien, sufficiency of description in notice, McAll. 521.

Moodalay v. Morton, 1 Bro. Ch. 469. Cited, Corporations, liability on contracts, 16 Cal. 269.

Moody v. McDonald, 4 Cal. 297. Cited, Negligence, measure of damages, 57 Me. 256.

Moody v. Payne, 2 Johns. Ch. 548. Cited, Execution, levy and sale of interest in partnership property, 12 Cal. 198. Denied, 1 Green Ch. 168; 12 Ohio St. 651; 19 Vt. 291. Commented on, 1 Stoct. 468.

Mooers v. Wait, 3 Wend. 104. Cited, Fixtures, subsequently annexed to mortgaged premises, pass by sheriff's deed, 10 Cal. 265.

Moon v. Rollins, 36 Cal. 333. Cited, Title, by prior possession and appropriation, 1 Saw. 621.

Moor v. Risdell, 1 Ld. Ray. 243. Cited, Record, what constitute court records, 34 Cal. 423; conclusiveness of, Id.

Moore v. Brown, 11 How. 414. Cited, Statutory Construction, validating acts, 16 Cal. 237; 13 How. 478. Doubted, 25 Wis. 464.

Moore v. Cable, 1 Johns. Ch. 385. Cited, Redemption, when barred by statute, 23 Cal. 34.

Moore v. Cooper, 1 Spear. 87. Denied, Contract, liability of agent on contract signed by him, 13 Cal. 235; 1 Rich. 503.

Moore v. Earl of Plymouth, 3 Barn. & Ald. 66. Cited, Deed, construction of restriction in *habendum* clause, 17 Cal. 52.

Moore v. Evans, 14 Barb. 524. Cited, Common Carriers, receipt construed as a contract, 27 Cal. 38.

Moore v. Goslin, 5 Cal. 266. Affirmed, Forcible Entry and Detainer, statutory remedy for unlawful entry construed, 5 Cal. 159. Cited, Actual possession, 16 Wis. 578; 24 Wis. 405.

Moore v. Herndon, 5 Blackf. 168. Cited, Appeal, does not lie from judgment entered on motion of appellant, 6 Cal. 666.

Moore v. Hillebrant, 14 Tex. 312. Cited, Probate Proceedings, trial of issues, 7 Cal. 239.

Moore v. Hylton, 1 Dev. Eq. 433. Cited, Injunction, granting or dissolving, in discretion, 39 Cal. 167.

Moore v. Illinois, 14 How. 13. Cited, Counterfeiting, constitutionality of State laws relating thereto, 34 Cal. 186. Distinguished, Criminal jurisdiction of State courts, 38 Cal. 150.

Moore v. Luce, 29 Penn. St. 260. Cited, Title, by adverse possession, 34 Cal. 383; 2 Black, 605.

Moore v. Martin, 38 Cal. 428. Cited, Judicial Sale, purchaser's title at sheriff sale, on what depends, 38 Cal. 654; Judgment, validity, on what depends, 41 Cal. 83.

Moore v. Murdock, 26 Cal. 514. Cited, Pleading, matters of evidence, not issuable facts, 33 Cal. 96; Id. 128.

Moore v. Patch, 12 Cal. 265. Affirmed, Taxation, publication of delinquent list, 12 Cal. 274. Cited, Enforcement of duty to pay tax, 16 Cal. 344. Explained, Tax as a debt, 20 Cal. 351. Approved, Validity of special validating statutes, 17 Cal. 553.

Moore v. Platte Co., 8 Mo. 467. Cited, Contract, penalty in building contract, 9 Cal. 587.

Moore v. Protection Ins. Co., 29 Me. 97. Cited, New Trial, when granted for fraud and false swearing, 36 Cal. 176.

Moore v. Small, 9 Penn. St. 194. Cited, Title, by adverse possession, when successive possessions cannot be added, 37 Cal. 354.

Moore v. Smaw, 17 Cal. 199. Referred to, Public Lands, ownership of, 14 Cal. 374; paramount title to mineral lands, 18 Cal. 435; patent conveys title to metals and minerals contained in, 19 Cal. 497.

Moore v. Smith, 14 Serg. & R. 388. Cited, Evidence, when party bound by his declarations and admissions, 22 Cal. 238.

Moore v. Starks, 1 Ohio St. 369. Cited, Judgment, collateral attack on, 34 Cal. 428.

Moore v. Tice, 22 Cal. 513. Cited, Ejectment, defense of after-acquired title, 23 Cal. 242. Explained, 30 Cal. 474.

Moore v. Wilkinson, 13 Cal. 478. Affirmed, 13 Cal. 489. Approved, Mexican Grants, conclusiveness of survey and patent, 14 Cal. 361; 15 Cal. 366; 20 Cal. 424; Third persons not concluded, who are, 2 Or. 268; 3

Or. 113; 1 Saw. 569; patent not subject to collateral attack, 14 Cal. 469; 20 Cal. 424; 22 Cal. 111; title under, patent takes effect by relation, 18 Cal. 26; Id. 571; 20 Cal. 160; 34 Cal. 253; 35 Cal. 88. Cited, Claimants how far estopped, 1 Saw. 563; survey of grant a political right, 38 Cal. 66. Construed, Location and survey of grant, 18 Cal. 202. Cited, Ejectment, value of improvements when not a set-off, 18 Cal. 696.

Moraga v. Emeric, 4 Cal. 308. Cited, Appeal, does not lie from decision on demurrer, 30 Cal. 529; 32 Cal. 314.

Moran v. Baudin, 2 Pet. Adm. 415. Cited, Jurisdiction, in State courts, where both parties are aliens, 1 Cal. 487.

Moran v. Palmer, 13 Mich. 367. Cited, Cloud on Title, when action lies to remove, 39 Cal. 22.

More v. Bonnet, 40 Cal. 251. Cited, Contract, entire contract, void in part is void *in toto*, 40 Cal. 348.

More, Case of Sir W., Cro. Eliz. 26. Cited, Will, construction of power of sale in, 32 Cal. 440.

More v. DelValle, 28 Cal. 170. Cited, Appeal, minutes no part of transcript, unless made so by statement, 33 Cal. 173; Id. 553.

More v. Thayer, 10 Barb. 259. Cited, contra, Attachment lien destroyed by death of defendant, dissenting opinion Shafter, J., 29 Cal. 371.

Morecock v. Dickins, Amb. 678. Commented on, Stare Decisis, as a rule of property, 15 Cal. 621.

Morenhout v. Higuera, 32 Cal. 289. Approved, Partition, issues of title may be tried in action, 33 Cal. 465. Affirmed, Id. 468. Cited, 35 Cal. 598; Grantees, necessary parties, 36 Cal. 116. Commented on, Relation of parties and right of appeal, 38 Cal. 642.

Morewood v. Wood, 4 Term Rep. 157. Cited, Evidence, admission of hearsay evidence, 3 Cal. 45.

Morgan v. Groff, 4 Barb. 524. Approved, Wagers on elections, disaffirmance, and recovery of money staked, 37 Cal. 674.

Morgan v. Insurance Co. of N. A., 4 Dall. 455. Cited, Charter Party, when charterer not liable for demurrage, 1 Cal. 485.

Morgan v. Powell, 3 Q. B. 278. Cited, Trespass on mining claim, measure of damages, 23 Cal. 310.

Morgan, Succession of, 12 La. An. 153. Cited, Husband and Wife, common property acquired during marriage, 14 Cal. 606.

Morgan v. Overman S. M. Co., 37 Cal. 534. Cited, Express Promises, action lies on promise to pay creditor's demand, 1 Saw. 631.

Morgan v. Varick, 8 Wend. 587. Cited, Replevin, lies for fixtures wrongfully severed from mortgaged property, 10 Cal. 265.

Morley v. Attenborough, 3 Exch. 507. Denied, Warranty, implied on sale of chattels by party in possession, 41 Cal. 113.

Morley v. Dickinson, 12 Cal. 561. Distinguished, Execution, release of levy on note of debtor taken in satisfaction, 14 Cal. 666. Cited, Levy, as a satisfaction of judgment, 23 Cal. 100.

Morley v. Elkins, 37 Cal. 454. Cited, Appeal, to county court, practice, 40 Cal. 647.

Morphett v. Jones, 1 Swanst. 181. Cited, Specific Performance, of verbal contract, when decreed, 10 Cal. 158.

Morrell v. Dickey, 1 Johns. Ch. 153. Cited, Wills, construction of, 36 Cal. 82.

Morrill v. Chapman, 35 Cal. 85. Cited, Appeal, findings in support of judgment, implied, 38 Cal. 421.

Morrill v. Morrill, 26 Cal. 288. Cited, Pleading, insufficient denials, 26 Cal. 418; 28 Cal. 567; equivalent to admissions, 38 Cal. 290.

Morris v. Colman, 18 Ves. Jr. 437. Cited, Contracts, in total restraint of trade, invalid, 36 Cal. 358.

Morris v. Davies, 5 Clark & F. 163. Commented on, Parent and Child, presumption of legitimacy, 13 Cal. 101.

Morris v. DeCelis, 41 Cal. 331. Cited, Appeal, from order striking out statement on new trial, 42 Cal. 118; parties entitled to hearing on motion, 42 Cal. 367.

Morris v. Morris, 2 Bibb, 311. Cited, Evidence, parol evidence of declarations and admissions, 26 Cal. 44.

Morris v. Morris, 14 Cal. 76. Cited, Divorce, extreme cruelty defined, 22 Cal. 360; 4 Nev. 398.

Morris v. Morris, Wright, 630. Cited, Divorce, for fraudulent concealment of pregnancy, 13 Cal. 104.

Morris v. Mowatt, 2 Paige, 586. Approved, Foreclosure, judgment creditor not concluded by decree unless made a party, 24 Cal. 511, 512.

Morris v. Nixon, 1 How. 118. Commented on, Deed, as mortgage, parol proof admissible, 8 Cal. 429; 13 Cal. 130; 12 How. 147; 19 How. 299.

Morris v. People, 3 Denio, 392. Cited, Taxation, legislative powers of, 13 Cal. 355; Statutory Construction, intendments in support of validity, 25 Cal. 569.

Morris v. Wadsworth, 17 Wend. 103. Cited, Evidence, official certificates as, 16 Cal. 554.

Morris Canal Co. v. Emmett, 9 Paige, 168. Cited, Equity, when will relieve from mistake, 29 Cal. 179.

Morris C. and B. Co. v. Jersey City, 1 Beasl. 227. Cited, Injunction, discretion of court in granting or dissolving, 39 Cal. 167.

Morris C. and B. Co. v. Townsend, 24 Barb. 665. Cited, Eminent Domain, through whom right of, may be exercised, 18 Cal. 251, 252.

Morris and Essex R. R. Co. v. Newark, 2 Stockt. Ch. 352. Cited, Street Railroad, right of, to lay track, 35 Cal. 333.

Morrison v. Bowman, 29 Cal. 377. Commented on, Pleading, significancy of prayer in complaint, 37 Cal. 304.

Morrison v. Dapman, 3 Cal. 255. Commented on, Amendment of Judgment, 25 Cal. 53; 9 Cal. 173; Id. 352; jurisdiction lost on adjournment of term, 25 Cal. 52; 28 Cal. 338; 15 Wis. 210.

Morrison v. Gray, 2 Bing. 260. Denied, Assignment, legal property in chose in action assigned, 1 Cal. 82, 83.

Morrison v. McMillan, 4 Litt. 210. Cited, Trust, presumptions in favor of regularity in execution of trust, 22 Cal. 591.

Morrison v. Rossignol, 5 Cal. 64. Cited, Specific Performance, not decreed on contract vague or indefinite, 33 Cal. 133; 39 Cal. 301

Morrison v. Semple, 6 Binn. 94. Cited, Property, defined, 31 Cal. 637.

Morrison v. Springer, 15 Iowa, 304. Commented on, Constitutionality of Statute, soldier's vote, 26 Cal. 201.

Morrison v. Wilson, 13 Cal. 494; S. C. 30 Cal. 344. Cited, Married Woman, conveyance of separate estate, 16 Cal. 290; 25 Cal. 374; 30 Cal. 142; Id. 517; 31 Cal. 645; Id. 654; Ejectment, equitable title may be interposed, in defense, 24 Cal. 141; 4 Nev. 460. Commented on and explained, 30 Cal. 311; 40 Cal. 566; Deed, quit claim deed does not pass after-acquired title, 33 Cal. 289; 20 Iowa, 436.

Morrow v. Weed, 4 Iowa, 77. Practice distinguished, Judgment Roll, court records, 34 Cal. 427, 428.

Mors v. Slew, 3 Keb. 72; S. C. 25 Eng. L. & E. 287. Commented on, Common Carriers, contract construed, 31 Cal. 58.

Morse v. Dewey, 3 N. H. 535. Cited, Execution, amendment of, 38 Cal. 381.

Morse v. Godfrey, 3 Story, 364. Cited, Conveyance, passing only an equity, 11 Cal. 160.

Morse v. McCarty, Cal. Sup. Ct. July T. 1856 (not reported.) Cited, Homestead, estate a joint tenancy, 7 Cal. 346; conveyance of, 8 Cal. 74.

Morse v. Shattuck, 4 N. H. 229. Commented on, Deed, parol evidence, not admissible to contradict consideration, 30 Cal. 24. Cited, Admissibility of parol evidence as to consideration, 36 Cal. 370.

Morse v. Welton, 6 Conn. 547. Cited, Parent and Child, emancipation of minor, 25 Cal. 152.

Morss v. Stone, 5 Barb. 516. Distinguished, Debtor and Creditor, transfer of property in trust, 39 Cal. 287.

Mortimer v. Mortimer, cited in 2 Hagg. Ecc. Rep. 410. Commented on, Divorce, confessions as evidence, 13 Cal. 94.

Mortin v. Shoppee, 3 Carr. & P. 374. Cited, Assault, what constitutes, 27 Cal. 634.

· **Morton v. Edwin**, 19 Vt. 77. Statute distinguished, Execution, validity of purchaser's title, on what it depends, 38 Cal. 655.

Morton v. Folger, 15 Cal. 275. Approved, Evidence, declarations, hearsay evidence, as to boundaries, when admissible, 16 Cal. 428.

Morton v. Naylor, 1 Hill, 583. Commented on, Assignment, order for money, 14 Cal. 407.

Morton v. Robards, 4 Dana, 258. Commented on, Conveyances, construction of recording act, 7 Cal. 309.

Morton v. Solambo Min. Co., 26 Cal. 527. Cited, Evidence, mining rules and customs, 26 Cal. 272.

Mosely v. Tift, 4 Fla. 402. Cited, Taxation, duty imposed on sale of goods at auction, 16 Cal. 523.

Moses v. Mead, 1 Denio, 378. Commented on, Warranty, not implied on sale of chattels, 5 Cal. 473.

Moses v. Murgatroyd, 1 Johns. Ch. 128. Commented on, Assignments, in trust, rights of creditors, 13 Cal. 121.

Moses v. Pittsburg, F. W. & C. R. R. Co., 21 Ill. 516. Cited, Street Railroad, right of, to lay track, 35 Cal. 333.

Moses Taylor, The, 4 Wall. 411. Explained, Jurisdiction, congress may vest exclusive jurisdiction in federal courts as to maritime contracts, 42 Cal. 472. Cited, Admiralty jurisdiction, 46 Ill. 513.

Mosley v. Ward, 11 Ves. Jr. 581. Cited, Estates of Deceased, duty of administrator as to surplus funds, 37 Cal. 429.

Moss v. Adams, 4 Ired. Eq. 42. Cited, Debtor and Creditor, application of payments, 14 Cal. 449.

Moss v. McCullough, 5 Hill, 131. Cited, Sureties, judgment against principal as evidence against, 14 Cal. 205. Doubted, 4 McLean, 579.

Moss v. Hall, 5 Exch. 46. Cited, Surety on note, when discharged by agreement for delay, 10 Cal. 426.

Moss v. Oakley, 2 Hill, 265. Cited, Sureties, liability of, when it attaches, 14 Cal. 206; 19 Wis. 437.

Moss v. Rossie Lead Min. Co., 5 Hill, 137. Cited, Corporation, ratification of unauthorized contract of agent, 10 Cal. 400. Commented on, 16 Cal. 265, 271; authority of corporation to contract, 40 N. H. 235; not subject to collateral inquiry, 22 Cal. 630.

Moss v. Scott, 2 Dana, 275. Cited, Lands, actual possession of, 25 Cal. 132.

Moss v. Shear, 30 Cal. 467; S. C. 25 Cal. 38. Cited, Tax Title, purchaser at tax sale, whose duty it is to pay tax, gains no advantage, 27 Cal. 318; 33 Cal. 425; 36 Cal. 146; Id. 326; 38 Cal. 223; 39 Cal. 356; 6 Kan. 332; 7 Kan. 122; Taxation, assessments on real estate, when invalid, 28 Cal. 615; 30 Cal. 538; 32 Cal. 332. Commented on, 29 Cal. 328. Cited, Ejectment, new matter arising, *pendente lite* must be set up by supplementary answer, 31 Cal. 336; so as to title acquired, 37 Cal. 129; Id. 153; Id. 339; 39 Cal. 356; claim to value of improvements as a set-off must be specially pleaded, 31 Cal. 496; conveyance by plaintiff does not necessarily defeat action, 34 Cal. 92; Deed, sufficiency of calls in, 38 Cal. 486.

Moss v. Warner, 10 Cal. 296. Cited, Foreclosure, necessary parties, 13 Cal. 70; Homestead, residence of family, *prima facie,* impresses character of estate, 37 Cal. 372; temporary removal not an abandonment, 46 N. H. 52; 47 N. H. 50.

Mossman v. Higginson, 4 Dall. 12. Cited, Jurisdiction, of federal courts, 22 Cal. 85; 2 How. 17.

Mott v. Burnett, 2 E. D. Smith, 50. Cited, Pleading, several defenses in answer, 22 Cal. 679; insufficient denials of verified complaint, 25 Cal. 196.

Mott v. Hicks, 1 Cow. 513. Approved, Principal and Agent, principal bound by contract made by agent, 7 Cal. 541; 13 Cal. 48. Cited, Witness, competency of, practice on examination, 26 Cal. 132.

Mott v. Smith, 16 Cal. 533. Cited, Mexican Grant, conclusiveness of decree of confirmation, 21 Cal. 576; of decrees of courts generally, 27 Cal. 170; Patent, not subject to collateral attack, 22 Cal. 111; Evidence, identity of name as evidence of identity of person, 28 Cal. 218; Id. 221; Married Woman, sale of separate estate by attorney, 30 Cal. 142. Commented on, Power of attorney of, 31 Cal. 645, 646; Husband and Wife, statutory construction, Id. 647, 654; 3 Nev. 285. Cited, Husband proper party in actions concerning common property, 6 Nev. 149; Principal and Agent, unauthorized deed by agent, passes no title, 28 Wis. 693.

Moulton v. Ellmaker, 30 Cal. 527. Cited, Appeal, does not lie from an interlocutory order, 32 Cal. 314; from an order sustaining demurrer, 38 Cal. 567; 4 Nev. 436; filing and serving of notice, to be contemporaneous, 8 Nev. 178.

Mount v. Chapman, 9 Cal. 294. Cited, Assignment, assignee takes subject to equities, 14 Cal. 680; Judgment, interest to be included in, 32 Cal. 88.

Mount Morris Square, Matter of, 2 Hill, 14. Cited, Certiorari, lies to review judicial acts of municipal corporations, 16 Cal. 209; 2 Dutch. 52; Appeal, in special cases, jurisdiction dependent on statutory provisions, 24 Cal. 454.

Mouys v. Leake, 8 Term Rep. 416. Cited, Execution, amendment of, allowed, 38 Cal. 376, 381.

Mowatt v. Wright, 1 Wend. 355. Cited, Money paid, under mistake of law, when may not be recovered back, 18 Cal. 271.

Mowrey v. Walsh, 8 Cow. 238. Cited, Fraud, vitiates contract of sale, 12 Cal. 462; 16 Conn. 82; *bona fide* purchaser from fraudulent vendee, 12 Cal. 498. Doubted, 1 Hill. 306; 32 Barb. 178.

Mowry v. Starbuck, 4 Cal. 274. Cited, Evidence, admission of, after close of evidence in chief, in discretion of court, 42 Cal. 442.

Moyer v. Shoemaker, 5 Barb. 319. Cited, Contract, rescission of, conditions precedent, 16 Cal. 638.

Muir v. Leitch, 7 Barb. 341. Cited, Execution, lien of judgment not extended by levy, 37 Cal. 134.

Muldrow v. Norris, 2 Cal. 74; S. C. 12 Cal. 331. Explained, Arbitration and Award, conclusiveness of award, 2 Cal. 130. Approved, Id. 325; 4 Cal. 125; Id. 207. Cited, 14 Cal. 394. Approved, Award good in part and bad in part, 9 Cal. 146. Cited, Equity will set aside for fraud, 51 N. H. 544.

Mulford's Case. See People *v.* Turner.

Mulford v. Cohn, 18 Cal. 42. Cited, New Trial at law, when equity will not grant, 33 Cal. 36, 38.

Mulford v. Estudillo, 17 Cal. 618; S. C. 23 Cal. 94; 32 Id. 131. Affirmed, 32 Cal. 135. Cited, Evidence, contrary to admissions in pleadings not admissible, 42 Cal. 238.

Mulford v. Le Franc, 26 Cal. 88. Cited, Statute of Limitations, as to Mexican grants, 31 Cal. 229; Deed, construction of, 34 Cal. 627; 11 Wall. 576.

Mulherrin v. Hannum, 2 Yerg. 81. Cited, Negotiable Instruments, place of payment in note, 11 Cal. 323.

Mulholland v. Heyneman, 19 Cal. 605. Cited, Default, orders setting aside judgment by, in discretion, 29 Cal. 424; New Trial, motions for, addressed to discretion of court, 33 Cal. 525.

Muller v. Boggs, 25 Cal. 175. Approved, Officers, power of deputy to take acknowledgment of homestead declaration, 36 Cal. 203; Deed, construction of, 36 Cal. 617.

Mumford v. Brown, 1 Wend. 52. Construed, Tenant in Common, ouster by, 27 Cal. 547.

Mumford v. McKay, 8 Wend. 442. Cited, Title, by adverse possession, 34 Cal. 382.

Mumford v. McPherson, 1 John. 414. Commented on, Warranty, of chattels, proof of, 24 Cal. 464.

Mumma v. Potomac Co., 8 Pet. 281. Cited, Corporation, power of self-dissolution, 38 Cal. 172.

Munch v. Williamson, 24 Cal. 167. Cited, New Trial, waiver of motion by failure to file statement, 28 Cal. 154; 41 Cal. 518.

Munford v. Overseers of the Poor, 2 Rand. 313. Commented on, Sureties, on official bond, judgment against principal as evidence, 14 Cal. 205.

Municipality No. 2 v. White, 9 La. An. 446. Cited, Street Assessment, not a tax, 27 Cal. 620; power of legislature to direct, 28 Cal. 352. Commented on, 28 Cal. 371.

Municipality No. 3 v. Hart, 6 La. An. 570. Cited, Execution, taxes exempt from execution, 15 Cal. 595.

Munn v. Baker, 2 Stark. 255; 3 Eng. C. L. 399. Cited, Common Carriers, construction of contract, 27 Cal. 38.

Munn v. President, etc., of the Commission Co., 15 John. 44. Cited, Negotiable Instruments, action by indorsee against indorser, 16 Cal. 160.

Munns v. Dupont, 1 Am. Lead. Cas. 200; 3 Wash. C. C. 31. Cited, Malicious Prosecution, want of probable cause a mixed question of law and fact, 29 Cal. 652.

Munroe v. Cooper, 5 Pick. 412. Cited, Negotiable Instruments, presumptions as to consideration, 10 Cal. 526.

Munroe v. Leach, 7 Met. 274. Cited, Negligence, when action lies for injury by, 37 Cal. 422.

Munroe v. Thomas, 5 Cal. 470. Approved, Franchises, ferry franchise not subject to levy and sale on execution, 7 Cal. 287; 24 Cal. 487; franchises not assignable without consent of grantor, 41 Cal. 510. Cited, Franchise, a mere personal trust, 2 Or. 238.

Munroe v. Ward, 4 Allen, 150. Cited, Cloud on Title, when action lies to remove, 39 Cal. 22.

Munson v. Newson, 9 Tex. 109. Cited, Probate Proceedings, jurisdiction, 7 Cal. 237.

Murden v. Priment, 1 Hilt. 76. Commented on, Counterclaim, what constitutes, 35 Cal. 281.

Murdock v. Chenango Co. M. Ins. Co., 2 N. Y. 216. Cited, Insurance, party insured must have interest in property, 30 Cal. 89.

Murdook v. De Vries, 37 Cal. 527. Referred to, Judgment, collateral attack, 41 Cal. 256.

Murdook v. Murdook, 7 Cal. 511. Commented on, Contract, for services, when right to recover vests on implied contract, 8 Cal. 123; 42 Cal. 468.

Murphy v. Napa Co., 20 Cal. 497. Cited, County, liability on implied contract, 31 Iowa, 392.

Murphy v. Wallingford, 6 Cal. 648. Approved, Ejectment, possession insufficient to give right of action, 7 Cal. 302, 309. Commented on, 4 Nev. 69.

Murray v. Barlee, 3 Mylne & K. 209; S. C. 4 Sim. 82. Commented on, Married Woman, charging separate estate of, 23 Cal. 565; 25 Cal. 377.

Murray v. Blatchford, 1 Wend. 583. Commented on, Executors and Administrators, powers and duties of, 24 Cal. 500.

Murray v. East India Co., 5 Barn. & Ald. 204. Cited, Statute of Limitations, suspended by death of party, 35 Cal. 638.

Murray v. Gibson, 15 How. 421. Cited, Statutory Construction, statutes not to be construed retrospectively, 10 Cal. 572.

Murray v. S. C. Railroad Co., 1 McMull. 398. Denied, Negligence, liability of common carrier for loss and injury, 6 Cal. 471.

Murray v. Walker, 31 N. Y. 399. Commented on, Mortgage, by deed and defeasance, 36 Cal. 41, 51.

Murray's Lessee v. Hoboken Land and Imp. Co., 18 How. 272. Cited, Statutory Construction, special legislation, 17 Cal. 562; legislature cannot interfere with inherent rights, 22 Cal. 318.

Muschamp v. Lancaster and Preston Railway, 8 Mees. & W. 421. Cited, Common Carriers, contract for transportation through, 31 Cal. 52, 54. Denied, 1 Gray, 505; 23 Vt. 209; 23 Conn. 474.

Musgrove v. Perkins, 9 Cal. 211. Approved, Trial, granting of continuance, in discretion of court, 11 Cal. 162; 20 Cal. 181; 28 Cal. 590.

Mussen v. Price, 4 East, 147. Commented on, Action, on special contract, 26 Cal. 22.

Mutual Ins. Co. v. Supervisors of Erie, 4 N. Y. 442. Approved, Corporations, bonds deposited with controller, part of capital stock, 29 Cal. 546.

Muzzy v. Whitney, 10 John. 226. Cited, Partnership, intention necessary to constitute, 38 Cal. 213.

Myers v. English, 9 Cal. 341. Approved, Constitutional Construction, obligation of contracts, 22 Cal. 320.

Myers v. Mott, 29 Cal. 359. Cited, Attachment, death of defendant destroys lien, 42 Cal. 133.

Myers v. South Feather Riv. W. Co., 10 Cal. 580. Referred to in same case, 14 Cal. 274.

Nagel v. Nagel, 12 Mo. 53. Commented on, Divorce, dismissal of action for mutual criminality, 10 Cal. 257.

Nagle v. Macy, 9 Cal. 426. Cited, Mortgage, a mere security, 15 Cal. 293; 16 Cal. 468; 18 Cal. 488; 21 Cal. 621; 36 Cal. 39, 42; Foreclosure, purpose of action, 21 Cal. 33; when debt is barred remedy by action is barred, 24 Cal. 498; jurisdiction of person presumed, 33 Cal. 512; execution not stayed by death of party after entry of decree, 14 Cal. 641.

Naglee v. Lyman, 14 Cal. 450. Referred to, Negotiable Securities, 14 Cal. 98; when holder not subject to equities, 6 Nev. 318.

Naglee v. Minturn, 8 Cal. 540. Approved, Partnership, proceedings on dissolution, 9 Cal. 337.

Naglee v. Pacific Wharf Co., 20 Cal. 529. Affirmed on principle of stare decisis, Corporation, transfer of stock, 35 Cal. 655; 40 Cal. 625.

Naglee v. Palmer, 7 Cal. 543. Distinguished, Set-off, as to actions at law and in equity, 19 Cal. 659. Cited, Set-off in Equity, 23 Cal. 627.

26

Naglee v. Wilson, Cal. Sup. Ct. Oct. T. 1867 (not reported.) Affirmed, Insolvency, validity of discharge, 36 Cal. 27.

Napa Val. R.R. Co. v. Napa Co., 30 Cal. 437. Cited, Legislature, power of, over local taxation and appropriation of revenues, 35 Cal. 633; 27 Ark. 614. Approved, Action of legislature empowering counties to subscribe for railroad stock not open to judicial review, 41 Cal. 169, 178; Mandamus, lies to compel performance of public duty, 36 Cal. 604.

Nassau Street, Matter of Improving, 11 John. 79. Cited, Street Assessments, how made, 31 Cal. 678.

Nathan v. Louisiana, 8 How. 73. Commented on, State Sovereignty, power of taxation, 4 Cal. 58.

Natoma Wat. and Min. Co. v. Clarkin, 14 Cal. 544. Cited, Injunction, to restrain waste, pending ejectment, 15 Cal. 264. Approved, Motion for Dissolution, practice, 16 Cal. 85. Commented on, Pleadings in Action, 32 Cal. 595, 596. Cited, Evidence, secondary, of Mexican grant, 19 Cal. 95; Patent, not subject to collateral attack, 22 Cal. 111; as evidence of title by confirmation and segregation, 33 Cal. 456. Approved, Corporation, exercise of powers by, not subject to collateral inquiry, 22 Cal. 430. Cited, Id. 630; Appeal, objections to evidence confined on appeal to grounds taken at trial, 6 Nev. 383.

Natoma Wat. & Min. Co. v. Parker, 16 Cal. 83. Approved, Injunction, right of motion to dissolve, 15 Cal. 117.

Naylor v. Collinge, 1 Taunt. 19. Cited, Fixtures, right of removal by tenant, 14 Cal. 70.

Naylor v. Moody, 3 Blackf. 92. Cited, Surety, on note, not discharged by mere delay, 10 Cal. 425.

Ned v. State, 7 Port. 187. Cited, Criminal Procedure, when discharge of jury equivalent to acquittal, 38 Cal. 478. Commented on, 41 Cal. 216.

Needham v. San Francisco & S. J. R. R. Co., 37 Cal. 409. Approved, Negligence, limitation of rule as to contributory negligence, 37 Cal. 406; 40 Cal. 19; Id. 453.

Needles v. Howard, 1 E. D. Smith, 55. Commented on, Bailment, liability of innkeeper for loss of property, 33 Cal. 599.

Neel v. Hughes, 10 Gill & J. 7. Cited, Deed, invalidity of, for insufficient description, 6 Cal. 312.

Negus, Matter of, 7 Wend. 499. Cited, Indemnity, measure of recovery on bond of, 13 Cal. 525.

Neighbors v. Simmons, 2 Blackf. 75. Commented on, Written Instrument, when a contract, 24 Cal. 328.

Neile v. Jakle, 2 Car. & K. 709. Cited, Criminal Procedure, evidence, implied admissions, 32 Cal. 101.

Neill v. Hodge, 5 Tex. 487. Cited, Probate Procedure, effect of approval of claim against estate, 7 Cal. 239. Approved, 26 Cal. 430.

Neilson v. Blight, 1 Johns. Cas. 205. Cited, Trust, assignment in trust, rights of creditors, 13 Cal. 122.

Neilson v. Com. Mut. Ins. Co., 3 Duer, 455. Cited, Judgment, on agreed case, 20 Cal. 74.

Neinicewicz v. Gahn. See Gahn v. Neinicewicz.

Nellis v. Bradley, 1 Sand. 560. Cited, Sale and Delivery, rescission of sale by vendor, 15 Cal. 218.

Nelson v. Allen, 1 Yerg. 360. Commented on, Ejectment, value of improvements as a set-off, 7 Cal. 7.

Nelson v. Boynton, 3 Met. 396. Commented on, Guaranty, original and collateral promises, 9 Cal. 334.

Nelson v. Dubois, 13 John. 175. Cited, Pleading, under statute of frauds, 29 Cal. 599.

Nelson v. Dunn, 15 Ala. 501. Cited, Insolvency, decree as to assets of insolvent firm, 7 Cal. 548.

Nelson, Ex parte, 1 Cow. 417. Cited, Mandamus, does not lie to control discretionary powers, 10 Cal. 376.

Nelson v. Nelson, 6 Cal. 430. Approved and followed, Statute of Limitations, construction of, 10 Cal. 374.

Nelson v. Rockwell, 14 Ill. 375. Cited, Equity, relief, purchaser at execution sale, 23 Cal. 362.

Nelson's Heirs v. Clay's Heirs, 7 J. J. Marsh, 139. Cited, Tenant in Common, when not liable for rents and profits, 12 Cal. 422.

Nepean v. Doe, 2 Smith Lead. Cas. 541; 2 Mees. & W. 894. Cited, Title, by adverse possession, what must be shown, 32 Cal. 19.

Nesbitt v. Dallam, 7 Gill & J. 494. Cited, Appeal, restitution on reversal, 14 Cal. 678.

Nesmith v. Drum, 8 Watts & S. 9. Cited, Assignment, rights of assignee, 12 Cal. 98.

Nesmith v. Washington Bank, 6 Pick. 329. Cited, Corporation, lien on stock for unpaid purchase money, 9 Cal. 115.

Nevada Co. and S. C. Co. v. Kidd, 28 Cal. 673; S. C. 37 Cal. 282. Cited, Pleading, construction of, 32 Cal. 192.

Nevitt v. Bank of Port Gibson, 6 Smedes & M. 513. Cited, Corporation, authority to act not subject to collateral inquiry, 22 Cal. 630.

Nevitt v. Gillespie, 1 How. Miss. 108. Cited, Injunction, when will not be granted, 10 Cal. 529.

New Albany & S. R. R. Co. v. O'Daily, 12 Ind. 551. Cited, Street Railroad, not a nuisance, 35 Cal. 333.

Newall v. Wright, 3 Mass. 139. Rule distinguished, Mortgage, estate of mortgagee, 9 Cal. 407.

New Barbadoes Toll Bridge Co. v. Vreeland, 3 Green Ch. 157. Cited, Vendor and Vendee, vendor in possession as trustee of vendee, 40 Cal. 571.

Newburgh Turnpike Co. v. Miller, 5 Johns. Ch. 101. Reviewed, Franchises, bridge or ferry franchise entitled to protection, 6 Cal. 596.

Newbury v. Armstrong, 6 Bing. 201. Cited, Express Promise, consideration, 5 Cal. 287.

Newby v. Jackson, 1 Barn. & C. 448. Cited, Tenant at Will, when relation exists, 24 Cal. 145.

Newby v. Platte County, 25 Mo. 258. Cited, Street Improvements, power of legislature to regulate assessments for, 28 Cal. 352, 371.

Newcomb v. Butterfield, 8 John. 342. Cited, Pleading, demand for treble damages given by statute, 5 Cal. 240.

Newcomb v. Drummond, 4 Leigh, 57. Cited, Evidence, secondary, of legal records, 22 Cal. 64.

Newcomb v. Griswold, 24 N. Y. 298. Cited, Witness, impeachment of, practice, 39 Cal. 449.

Newcomb v. Presbrey, 8 Met. 406. Cited, Deed, covenant of non-claim construed, 14 Cal. 473.

Newcombe v. Leavitt, 22 Ala. 631. Cited, Title, by adverse possession, 34 Cal. 383; 36 Cal. 541; 2 Black, 605.

Newell, Ex parte, 4 Hill, 589. Commented on, Redemption, by creditor, 9 Cal. 419.

Newell v. Hamer, 4 How. Miss. 684. Cited, Surety, on note, when discharged by agreement for delay, 10 Cal. 426.

Newell v. Turner, 9 Port. 420. Cited, Contract, rescission for fraud, 17 Cal. 384.

New England Mar. Ins. Co. v. De Wolf, 8 Pick. 56. Commented on, Principal and Agent, principal bound by contract signed by agent, 13 Cal. 235.

Newhall v. Provost, 6 Cal. 85. Cited, Amendment, of sheriff's return, 45 Mo. 116.

New Jersey R.R. and T. Co. v. Suydam, 2 Harr. N. J. 25. Cited, Condemnation of Land, review of report of commissioners, 35 Cal. 260.

New Jersey St. Nav. Co. v. Merchants' Bank, 6 How. 344. Commented on, Jurisdiction, in maritime cases, 9 Cal. 726; 27 Cal. 33; 5 How. 452. Cited, 10 How. 668; 12 How. 464; 21 How. 246.

Newland v. Kean, Cal. Sup. Ct. Jan. T. 1856 (not reported.) Cited, Appeal, papers inserted in transcript, when no part of record, 11 Cal. 214; evidence in each case must correspond with allegations, 7 Cal. 57.

New London v. Brainard, 22 Conn. 552. Commented on, Municipal Corporation, powers of, 16 Cal. 271.

Newman v. Alvord, 49 Barb. 588. Cited, Trade Marks, law of, 35 Cal. 75, 76, 82.

Newman, Ex parte, 9 Cal. 502; dissenting opinion of Field, C. J. Approved, Sunday Laws, statutes constitutional, 18 Cal. 685; 15 Ind. 454. Cited, Statutory Construction, title of act, 20 Cal. 582.

Newman v. Payne, 2 Ves. Jr. 199. Cited, Attorney and Client, transactions between, 33 Cal. 440, 441.

Newnam's Lessee v. Cincinnati, 18 Ohio, 323. Cited, Judgment, collateral attack, 34 Cal. 428.

New Orleans v. United States, 10 Pet. 662. Cited, National Law, laws of ceded territory, 1 Cal. 286; 18 Cal. 23; Dedication, to public use, assent how proved, 14 Cal. 649; 22 Cal. 489; 9 How. 31; 15 How. 410. Commented on, Title to property dedicated, 15 Cal. 548, 560. Cited, Reservation, in deed, to invalidate dedication, 42 Cal. 553; 14 How. 274; San Francisco, title to city lands, 15 Cal. 595. Commented on, Tenure of pueblo lands in trust, 15 Cal. 575.

Newport, etc., v. Taylor, 16 B. Mon. 699. Cited, Dedication, to public use, by sale of lots on plat, 22 Cal. 489.

Newport Mech. Man. Co. v. Starbird, 10 N. H. 123. Cited, Corporation, minor irregularities in formation of, not to vitiate rights of, 39 Cal. 514.

Newsom v. Davis, 20 Tex. 419. Cited, Vendor and Vendee, when statute does not run against vendee in possession, 40 Cal. 572.

Newsom v. Luster, 13 Ill. 181. Cited, Evidence, secondary evidence of execution when admissible, 26 Cal. 409, 410; proof of handwriting of party, Id. 412.

Newton v. Bronson, 13 N. Y. 587. Cited, Specific Performance, when jurisdiction attaches, 38 Cal. 201.

New York v. Miln, 11 Pet. 102. Cited, State Sovereignty, 1 Cal. 236; as to police regulations, 9 Cal. 166; validity of Foreign Miners' License Act, 1 Cal. 244; power to regulate commerce in absence of congressional provisions, 8 Cal. 372. Disapproved, 20 Cal. 566. Commented on, 5 How. 584. Cited, 14 How. 574.

New York A. and B. Tel. Co. v. De Rutte, 5 Am. Law Reg. N. S. 407. Cited, Common Carrier, construction of contract for transportation through, 31 Cal. 53.

New York and S. Can. Co. v. Fulton Bank, 7 Wend. 412. Reviewed and explained, Corporations, as tenants in common of property, 2 Cal. 298.

New York Cent. R. R. Co. v. Marvin, 11 N. Y. 276. Cited, Condemnation of Land, a special proceeding, 24 Cal. 433; Appeal, when it will not lie in special cases, 24 Cal. 454; 42 Cal. 56.

New York Fire Ins. Co. v. Bennett, 5 Conn. 580. Cited, Surety, on note, burden of proof of firm liability on indorsement by partner, 37 Cal. 117, 120.

New York Fire Ins. Co. v. Ely, 5 Conn. 568. Cited, Corporation, restriction in charter, as to mode of exercising powers, 16 Cal. 620; 20 Cal. 102.

New York Ins. Co. v. Roulet, 24 Wend. 505. Commented on, Jurisdiction, concurrent in law and equity, 7 Cal. 351.

New York Life Ins. Co. v. Supervisors of N. Y., 1 Abb. Pr. 250. Limited, Tax, not a cloud on title, its enforcement, only a trespass, 12 Cal. 299.

New York Life Ins. & T. Co. v. Bailey, 3 Edw. Ch. 416. Cited, Execution, title of purchaser at sale under, 31 Cal. 302.

Nicholls v. Bowes, 2 Camp. 498. Cited, Negotiable Instruments, place of payment, 11 Cal. 324.

Nichols v. Aylor, 7 Leigh, 546. Cited, Dedication, to public use, assent necessary, 14 Cal. 649, 650; 9 How. 31.

Nichols v. Bridgeport, 23 Conn. 189. Cited, Street Assessment, legislative power to direct, 28 Cal. 352. Commented on, to provide for enforcement of, 31 Cal. 683, 688.

Nichols v. Jones, 6 How. Pr. 355. Cited, Pleading, sham answer, what is, 10 Cal. 29. Approved, Demurrer to answer, 13 Cal. 625.

Nichols v. Packard, 16 Vt. 83. Cited, Libel, extrinsic facts to be set out, 41 Cal. 481.

Nichols v. Palmer, 5 Day, 47. Cited, Husband and Wife, agreements for separation, valid, 9 Cal. 493.

Nichols v. Rensselaer Co. Mut. Ins. Co., 22 Wend. 125. Cited, Demand, on tender, when not necessary in action on an award, 23 Cal. 369.

Nichols v. Smith, 22 Pick. 316. Cited, Tenants in Common, conveyance by, 35 Cal. 588; rights of grantees, 15 Cal. 369.

Nichols v. Somerset & K. R. R. Co., 43 Me. 358. Cited, Condemnation of Land, for railroads, compensation to be provided, 31 Cal. 559.

Nicholson v. Leavitt, 4 Sand. 252. Cited, Insolvency, preferred creditor, 10 Cal. 277; Id. 494; 19 Cal. 46; Fraudulent Conveyance, complaint in action to cancel, 29 Cal. 59.

Nicholson v. Revill, 4 Ad. & El. 683. Cited, Release of one joint debtor is a release of all, 38 Cal. 532.

Nickerson v. California Stage Co., 10 Cal. 520. Commented on, Judgment, in replevin to be in alternative, 24 Cal. 151.

Nickerson v. Chatterton, 7 Cal. 568. Approved, Replevin, judgment in, to be in alternative, to hold sureties on bond, 7 Cal 390; 24 Cal. 149, Commented on and held to apply only to cases submitted to a jury, 8 Cal. 448. Cited, Possession obtained by plaintiff does not

divest title, 11 Cal. 278; pleading in action on undertaking, 9 Cal. 285; 38 Cal. 604.

Nickles v. Haskins, 15 Ala. 619.   Cited, Stare Decisis, as a
rule of property, 15 Cal. 622.

Nicol v. Mayor of Nashville, 9 Humph. 252.   Cited,
Municipal Corporations, may be empowered to subscribe for and purchase railroad stock, 13 Cal. 188.

Nicoll v. Mumford, 4 Johns. Ch. 522.   Cited, Presumption,
assent presumed from benefit derived, 13 Cal. 287.

Nicolson Pavement Co. v. Painter, 35 Cal. 699.   Followed,
Street Assessment, letting contract, 35 Cal. 695.

Nieto v. Carpenter, 7 Cal. 527.   Referred to, Mexican Grant,
same case, 21 Cal. 453.

Nightingale v. Scannell, 18 Cal. 315.   Cited, Trespass, by
sheriff, inadmissible evidence as to damage, 18 Cal.
376.

Nightingale v. Withington, 15 Mass. 272.   Cited, Negotiable Instrument, made or indorsed by infant only voidable, 24 Cal. 208, 209.   Reviewed, Id. 210.

Nill v. Comparet, 16 Ind. 107.   Cited, Foreign Judgment,
sufficiency of defense in action on, 39 Cal. 539.

Nims v. Palmer, 6 Cal. 8.   Cited, State Lands, location of
school land warrants, 7 Cal. 417.

Ninety-Nine Plaintiffs v. Vanderbilt, 1 Abb. Pr. 193.
Cited, Attorney and Counsel, authority to appear, presumed, 39 Cal. 685.

Niven v. Belknap, 2 John. 575.   Cited, Cloud on Title, when
action to remove will lie, 39 Cal. 22.

Noble v. Bosworth, 19 Pick. 314.   Cited, Fixtures, what
constitute, 14 Cal. 68.

Noble v. Holmes, 5 Hill, 194.   Commented on, Replevin,
what must be shown under plea of justification of attachment, 7 Cal. 563.   Cited, 10 Cal. 304; 34 Cal. 350.

Noble v. Paddock, 19 Wend. 456.   Cited, Witness, when
servant not a competent witness for master, 7 Cal. 256.

Noble v. Wilson, 1 Paige, 164.   Cited, Injunction, practice
on motion to dissolve, 35 Cal. 60.

Nobles v. Bates, 7 Cow. 307.   Cited, Contract, in total restraint of trade, void, 36 Cal. 358.

Noe v. Card, 14 Cal. 576. Referred to, Mexican Law, community property of husband and wife, 13 Cal. 477, note. Cited, Grant to husband constitutes separate property, 26 Cal. 565. Approved, 33 Cal. 703. Cited, Lucrative and onerous titles, 26 Cal. 566; property acquired with community funds, Id. 568; Ejectment, disclaimers unknown in, 26 Cal. 278.

Noell v. Wells, 1 Lev. 235. Cited, Judgment, when a bar to subsequent action, 20 Cal. 486.

Nolan v. Reese, 32 Cal. 484. Approved, Street Assessment, owners not parties to contract, 39 Cal. 392; fraud cannot be pleaded in defense to action for, remedy by appeal exclusive, 39 Cal. 392; 40 Cal. 520.

Nolen v. Gwyn's Heirs, 16 Ala. 725. Cited, Vendor and Vendee, vendor concluded by recitals in deed, 22 Cal. 593; 26 Cal. 87; 19 How. 251.

Noonan v. Lee, 2 Black, 507. Cited, Covenants, what constitutes sufficient eviction under, 39 Cal. 367.

Norcross v. Widgery, 2 Mass. 506. Cited, Conveyances, construction of recording act, 7 Cal. 303.

Norman v. Wells, 17 Wend. 136. Cited, Evidence, opinions of experts, 33 Cal. 237.

Norris v. City of Boston, 7 How. 283. Commented on, State Sovereignty, restriction as to regulation of commerce, 1 Cal. 236; passenger taxes, Id. 242; 20 Cal. 582; residence of aliens, 1 Cal. 246.

Norris v. Farmers' and Teamsters' Co., 6 Cal. 590. Approved, Franchise, ferry franchise entitled to protection, 7 Cal. 129; 22 Cal. 423; 18 Iowa, 335; discretion of supervisors in establishment of, cannot be collaterally attacked, 13 Cal. 12, 13.

Norris v. Harris, 15 Cal. 226. Cited, Probate Procedure, construction of statute as to sale of estates of decedent, 18 Cal. 303; 21 Cal. 31; powers of sale under will, 30 Cal. 567; presumption as to laws of foreign State, 21 Cal. 226; 32 Cal. 60; 1 Nev. 57.

Norris v. Russell, 5 Cal. 249. Distinguished as to rule under prior statute, Tax Title, sheriff's deed as evidence, 5 Cal. 321. Approved, Title, by prior possession, 25 Cal. 141.

North v. Turner, 9 Serg. & R. 244. Cited, Assignment, right of action for wrongful conversion, assignable, 22 Cal. 142. Approved, 32 Cal. 593, 594.

North American C. Co. v. Dyett, 7 Paige, 9.   See Dyett *v.* N. A. C. Co.

North Beach and M. R.R. Co., Appeal of, 32 Cal. 499. Cited, Special Cases, appeal in, where statute provided remedy by appeal, 42 Cal. 68.   Approved, Taxation, railroad franchise, as assessable property, 36 Conn. 268; 38 Id. 431.

North River Bank v. Aymar, 3 Hill, 262. Cited, Powers, when act of agent binds principal, 24 Cal. 140.

Northern Indiana R. R. Co. v. Connelly, 10 Ohio St. 159. Cited, Street Assessments, power of legislature to impose tax, 28 Cal. 352; to direct apportionment, Id. 368.

Northern Liberties v. St. John's Church, 13 Penn. St. 104. Commented on, Street Assessments, property not exempt from tax, 28 Cal. 359.   Dissenting opinion of Sawyer, J., enforcement of, 31 Cal. 683.

Northern Railroad v. Concord and C. Railway, 27 N. H. 183. Cited, Eminent Domain, exercise of right of, by legislative authority through corporate bodies, 31 Cal. 372.

Northern Turnpike R. Co. v. Smith, 15 Barb. 357. Cited, Ejectment, when action lies, 38 Cal. 572.

Northrop v. Sumney, 27 Barb. 196. Cited, Contract, rescission of, for mistake, 29 Cal. 179.

Northrop v. Wright, 24 Wend. 221; S. C. 7 Hill, 476. Cited, in dissenting opinion of Hastings, C. J., Title, color of title, under deed by Indian, 1 Cal. 290; under void deed, 1 Cal. 319; under quit claim deed, 25 Cal. 168. Approved, Tenant in Common, ouster not presumed from possession by, 23 Cal. 247.

Northwood v. Barrington, 9 N. H. 369. Cited, Election, to fill vacancy, notice essential, 11 Cal. 66.

Norton v. Beaver, 5 Ohio, 178. Cited, Cloud on Title, action lies to remove, 2 Cal. 589; Injunction, when it lies to restrain execution sale, 9 Cal. 548; 15 Cal. 133.

Norton v. Jackson, 5 Cal. 262. Cited, Injunction, when it will not lie to restrain collection of judgment, 6 Cal. 189.   Distinguished, Warranty, action on breach of, when it lies, 9 Cal. 340.   Denied, that there must be an eviction by process of law, 39 Cal. 365.

Norton v. Larco, 30 Cal. 134. Cited, Accounts, what constitute mutual accounts, 35 Cal. 126.

Norton v. Peck, 3 Wis. 714.   Cited, Eminent Domain, compensation on condemnation of lands, 31 Cal. 559.

Norton v. Woods, 22 Wend. 524.   Cited, Jurisdiction, when concurrent, conclusive where it first attaches, 21 Cal. 442.

Norton v. Young, 3 Greenl. 30.   Approved, Contract, rescision of, conditions precedent, 29 Cal. 593, 595.

Norvell v. Camm, 6 Munf. 233.   Cited, Mexican Grant, patent conclusive, 14 Cal. 469.

Norvell v. McHenry, 1 Mich. 227.   Cited, Record, what constitute court records, 34 Cal. 427.

Norway v. Rowe, 19 Ves. Jr. 144.   Cited, Injunction, insufficient averments in complaint, 7 Cal. 323; showing required to obtain, 23 Cal. 84.

Norwich v. County Commrs. of Hampshire, 13 Pick. 60. Cited, Constitutional Construction, power of taxation, 13 Cal. 355.

Norwood v. Byrd, 1 Rich. 135.   Commented on, Deed, construction of description in, 10 Cal. 628.

Norwood v. Kenfield, 30 Cal. 393; S. C. 34 Cal. 329.   Approved, Error, injury presumed from error by the court, 39 Cal. 612.   Cited, Jurisdiction, lost on expiration of term, consent cannot confer, 40 Cal. 185.

Nougues v. Douglass, 7 Cal. 65.   Cited, Mandamus, to whom it may be directed, 16 Cal. 43.   Commented on, Power of court, Id. 64.   Distinguished, Constitutional Construction, limitation of State debt, 16 Cal. 253.

Nourse v. Prime, 4 Johns. Ch. 490; S. C. 7 Johns. Ch. 69. Reviewed and compared, Bailment, sale of corporation stock by bailee, 42 Cal. 103.

Noverre v. Noverre, 1 Rob. Eccl. 428.   Cited, Divorce, confessions as evidence, 13 Cal. 98.

Noyes v. Dyer, 25 Me. 468.   Cited, Deed, constructive possession by entry under, 25 Cal. 135; construction of calls in, 38 Cal. 486.

Noyes v. Rutland & B. R. Co., 27 Vt. 110.   Cited, Common Carrier, construction of contract for transportation through, 31 Cal. 53, 61.

Nugent v. Opdyke, 9 Rob. 453.   Cited, Assignment, effect of order for money, 12 Cal. 98.

Nugent v. State, 18 Ala. 521.   Cited, Municipal Courts, jurisdiction of, 10 Cal. 295; 36 Cal. 697.

Oakland v. Carpentier, 13 Cal. 540. Cited, Municipal Corporations, construction of city charters, 18 Cal. 647; charters as restrictive of powers and mode of their exercise, 29 Cal. 186.

Oakley v. Aspinwall, 4 N. Y. 514. Commented on, Jurisdiction, cannot be conferred by consent, applied as to disqualification of judge, 24 Cal. 77; effect of disqualification of judge, 37 Cal. 192; jurisdiction of person essential to validity of judgment, 27 Cal. 314; 24 How. 203; Constitutional Construction, powers of departments of government, 41 Cal. 192.

O'Brien v. Brady, 23 Cal. 243. Cited, Appeal, order granting new trial, when reviewable, 34 Cal. 557.

O'Brien v. Hilburn, 22 Tex. 616. Approved, Husband and Wife, conveyance to wife, may be shown to be a gift, 30 Cal. 54, 63.

O'Brien v. Norwich & Worcester R. R., 17 Conn. 372. Approved, Nuisance, special damages to be shown in action for obstructing highway, 41 Cal. 451. Cited, 9 How. 28.

O'Callaghan v. Booth, 6 Cal. 63. Cited, Forcible Entry and Detainer, treble damages may be awarded in justice's court without being demanded, 6 Cal. 163; 23 Cal. 378.

O'Connor v. Blake, 29 Cal. 312. Cited, Pleading, when defense of former action pending is available, 32 Cal. 630; defense in action of replevin, 36 Cal. 110; Jurisdiction, justices of the peace cannot vacate a judgment except on motion for new trial, 35 Cal. 273.

O'Connor v. Corbitt, 3 Cal. 370. Cited, Use and Occupation, when action lies for, 5 Cal. 223; Preëmption, title based on prior equities, 23 Ind. 94.

O'Connor v. Murphy, 1 H. Black. 657. Cited, Set-off, when allowed in equity, 23 Cal. 629.

Odiorne Maxcy, 13 Mass. 181. Cited, Principal and Agent, construction of authority to agent, 14 Cal. 399; ratification of unauthorized act binds principal, 14 Cal. 400.

Odlin v. Greenleaf, 3 N. H. 270. Cited, Sureties, right of action for contribution, 20 Cal. 136.

O'Donnell v. Sweeney, 5 Ala. 467. Cited, Sunday Laws, are valid, and of binding force, 18 Cal. 681.

Offut v. Monquit, 2 La. An. 785. Denied, Execution, seizure and sale of promissory note, title of purchaser, 34 Cal. 88.

Ogden v. Blackledge, 2 Cranch, 272. Cited, Statutory Construction, statutes not to be construed retrospectively, 4 Cal. 136.

Ogden v. Saunders, 12 Wheat. 213. Cited, Constitutionality of Statutes, powers of congress, and choice of means for their exercise, 25 Cal. 421. Approved, Bankrupt Laws, State insolvent acts invalid only when congress exercises its power on the subject and creates a conflict of laws, 37 Cal. 210. Cited, 12 Wheat. 369, note *a;* 6 Pet. 346; Id. 643; 1 How. 279. Explained, 5 How. 307, 310, 316. Commented on, 35 N. H. 466; 35 Conn. 287; 11 Mich. 418; 5 Tex. 356.

Ogilvie v. Ogilvie, 1 Bradf. 356. Cited, Probate Procedure, duties of administrator as to surplus funds, 37 Cal. 429.

Ogle v. Somerset and Mt. Plesant T. Co., 13 Serg. & R. 256. Cited, Statutory Construction, statutes not to be construed retrospectively, 4 Cal. 136.

Ogle v. Vickers, 4 Adol. & E. 782. Cited, Mortgage, subsequently acquired title, by mortgagor, inures to benefit of mortgagee, 14 Cal. 634.

O'Grady v. Barnhisel, 23 Cal. 287. Approved, Tax Title, validity of tax deed, 29 Cal. 327; 32 Cal. 107.

O'Hanlon v. Perry, 9 Mo. 794. Cited, Preëmption, right of, a mere privilege, 37 Cal. 493; withdrawal of land from preëmption, 37 Cal. 502.

O'Hara v. United States, 15 Pet. 275. Cited, Mexican Grant, validity of floating grant, 3 Cal. 42.

Ohio L. Ins. and T. Co. v. Ledyard, 8 Ala. 866. Cited, Conveyances, who are *bona fide* purchasers within recording act, 12 Cal. 377. Commented on, 21 Ala. 136.

O'Keefe v. Dunn, 6 Taunt. 305. Cited, Negotiable Instruments, rights of indorsee before presumptive dishonor, 40 Cal. 116.

O'Keiffe v. Cunningham, 9 Cal. 590. Cited, Mines and Mining Rights, distinct appropriations of the same ground, 37 Cal. 315.

Olcott v. Rathbone, 5 Wend. 490. Approved, Debt, payment by note or check, effect of, 12 Cal. 323, 324; 23 Cal. 323.

Olcott v. Robinson, 21 N. Y. 150; reversing S. C. 20 Barb. 149.   Cited, Summons, publication of, computation of time, 32 Cal. 352; 34 Cal. 284; 5 Nev. 427.

Olcott v. Tioga R. R. Co., 27 N. Y. 546.   Cited, Corporation, ratification of contract by, 33 Cal. 191.

Oldham v. Ledbetter, 1 How. Miss. 43.   Commented on, Attachment, liabilities of garnishee, 11 Cal. 350.   Explained, 3 Smede & M. 295.

Oliphant v. Whitney, 34 Cal. 25.   Cited, Judgment, by default, entry of, by clerk, 8 Nev. 136.

Oliver v. Oliver, 4 Rawle, 141.   Commented on, Evidence, parol evidence of deed admissible to prove fraud, 13 Cal. 127.

Oliver v. Walsh, 6 Cal. 456.   Commented on, Witnesses, competency of assignees as, 22 Cal. 236.   Distinguished, under statutory amendment, 32 Cal. 592.

Oliverez, Matter of Carlos, 21 Cal. 415.   Approved, Constitutional Construction, jurisdiction not affected by amendment organizing new courts or counties till organization is effected, 32 Cal. 143; 34 Cal. 524; 38 Cal. 395; 1 Nev. 139.

Olivier v. Andry, 7 La. 496.   Cited, Negotiable Instruments, undertaking of indorser of certificate of deposit, 22 Cal. 249.

Olmstead v. Greenly, 18 John. 12.   Cited, Express Promise, when not within statute of frauds, 22 Cal. 190.

Olmsted v. Hotailing, 1 Hill, 317.   Cited, Fraud, vitiates sale of chattel, 8 Cal. 213.

Olympic Theater, 2 Bro. Penn. 275.   Cited, Fixtures, what constitute, 14 Cal. 66.

O'Neall v. Sims, 1 Strob. 115.   Cited, Interest, computation of, 29 Cal. 392.

O'Neil v. Garrett, 6 Iowa, 480.   Cited, Common Carrier, liability on notice of stoppage *in transitu*, 37 Cal. 632.

Opinions of Attorney-General, vol. 1, p. 459.   Cited, Office, collector of customs, tenure of office, 20 Cal. 146.

Opinions of Attorney-General, vol. 2, p. 336.   Cited, Office, commissioner of immigration, 20 Cal. 508.

Opinions of Attorney-General, vol. 4, p. 162.   Cited, Office, collector of customs, tenure of office, 20 Cal. 146.

Opinions of Attorney-General, vol. 7, p. 504. Cited, Common Law, what is, 13 Cal. 286; International Law under treaty, 13 Cal. 280.

Opinions of Attorney-General, vol. 8, p. 72. Cited, Public Lands, power in government to withdraw from right of preëmption, 37 Cal. 493, 502.

Opinions of Attorney-General, vol. 10, p. 56. Cited, Public Lands, power of government to withdraw from right of preëmption, 37 Cal. 493.

Opinions of Attorney-General, vol. 11, p. 490. Cited, Public Lands, power of government to withdraw lands from right of preëmption, 30 Cal. 652; 37 Cal. 491, 493, 502.

Opinion of Supreme Judges, 30 Conn. 591. Cited, in dissenting opinion of Sanderson, C. J., Constitutionality of Statute, statute relative to soldiers' votes, 26 Cal. 247.

Opinion of Supreme Judges, 38 Me. 597. Cited, Office, eligibility to, 10 Cal. 47; counting votes at election, 13 Cal. 153.

Opinion of Supreme Judges, 7 Mass. 524. Cited, Statutory Construction, 26 Cal. 181.

Opinion of Supreme Judges, 45 N. H. 610. Cited, Statute, validity of its passage, return of bill by governor, 39 Cal. 204.

Orange Co. Bk. v. Brown, 9 Wend. 85. Commented on, Common Carriers, liability as bailees, 33 Cal. 604.

Ord v. De La Guerra, 18 Cal. 67. Approved, Descents and Distribution, statutory rule of, 24 Cal. 77.

Ord v. McKee, 5 Cal. 515. Approved, Mortgage, an incident to the debt, 6 Cal. 483; 9 Cal. 410; when debt is barred remedy in mortgage is barred, 24 Cal. 498. Cited, 13 Mich. 396.

Organ v. State, 26 Miss. 78. Commented on, Criminal Procedure, separation of jury vitiates verdict, 5 Cal. 276.

Oriental Bk. v. Freese, 18 Me. 109. Cited, Rights and Remedies, statutory privileges, 22 Cal. 319.

Ormelade v. Coke, 3 Croke, Jac. 354. Cited, Arbitration and Award, omissions in award, 12 Cal. 341.

Ormsby v. Douglas, 5 Duer, 665. Cited, Pleading, inconsistent defenses in answer, 22 Cal. 680.

Ormsby v. Lynch, Litt. Sel. Cas. 303.   Cited, Jurisdiction cannot be conferred by consent, 29 Cal. 463.

Ormsby v. Tarascon, 3 Litt. 404.   Cited, Deed, executed under a power, validity of, how shown, 22 Cal. 590.

Orosco v. Gagliardo, 22 Cal. 83.   Doubted, Mandamus, when it will lie, 36 Cal. 288.

Orr, Estate of, 29 Cal. 101.   Cited, Homestead, enforcement of mortgage on, against heirs of mortgagor, 29 Cal. 122; survivorship right of, 30 Cal. 113; directing course of title under probate act, 35 Cal. 324; question of title where determined, 41 Cal. 36.

Orr v. Hodgson, 4 Wheat. 453.   Cited, Alien, inheritance under treaty stipulations, 5 Cal. 382; 13 Cal. 283; 8 Wheat. 489; 9 Wheat. 496.

Orser v. Hoag, 3 Hill, 79.   Cited, Alien, inheritance of, 12 Cal. 456.

Ortman v. Dixon, 13 Cal. 33.   Referred to, Water Rights, 13 Cal. 239, note.   Approved, Appropriation of Water, limited to purpose indicated, 21 Cal. 381; 37 Cal. 313; title acquired by appropriation, 2 Nev. 277; sufficiency of contract passing right to water ditch, 3 Nev. 517. Cited, Appeal, findings in equity cases not disregarded, 18 Cal. 449.

Orvis v. Kimball, 3 N. H. 314.   Commented on, Principal and Agent, ratification of contract of agent, 24 Cal. 213.

Osborn v. Bank of United States, 9 Wheat. 738.   Distinguished, Injunction, when will not issue to restrain taxation, 2 Cal. 469.   Cited, 5 Pet. 78; 21 How. 592. Commented on, Parties, State as party to action, 7 Cal. 74; 1 Pet. 122.

Osborn v. Elliott, 1 Cal. 337.   Approved, Pleading, conditions precedent in action on dependent promises, 2 Cal. 164; 35 Cal. 662; on independent promises, need not be averred, 38 Cal. 200.

Osborn v. Hendrickson, 6 Cal. 175; S. C. 7 Cal. 282; 8 Cal. 31.   Cited, Assignment, when not a release from covenant in contract, 8 Cal. 591.   Approved, Written Instrument, parol evidence not admissible to vary, 14 Cal. 307.   Cited, Appeal, dismissal of, equivalent to affirmance of judgment, 15 Cal. 327; 29 Cal. 138.   Distinguished, Judgment, interest on, 31 Cal. 470.

Osborn v. Moncure, 3 Wend. 170. Commented on, Negotiable Instruments, notice to indorser, when may be given, 8 Cal. 634.

Osborne v. Endicott, 6 Cal. 149. Cited, Statute of Frauds, bar of statute must be pleaded, to defeat a recovery, 6 Cal. 358; Resulting Trust, when it arises, 22 Cal. 578; may be proved by parol, Id. 579; 22 Cal. 593. Cited, Deed, conclusiveness of recitals in, 22 Cal. 592.

Osborne v. Huger, 1 Bay, 179. Cited, Statutory Construction, statutes not to be construed retrospectively, 4 Cal. 136.

Osgood v. Manhattan Co., 3 Cow. 612. Cited, Appeal, reversal of judgment obtained on incompetent evidence, 1 Cal. 232; injury presumed from error of law, 38 Cal. 283, 285; Evidence, declarations of vendor not competent to impair validity of vendee's title, 38 Cal. 282, 284.

Osterhout v. Shoemaker, 3 Hill, 513. Cited, Estoppel, when vendee not estopped, 18 Cal. 476. Commented on, Insanity, degree of, sufficient to avoid deed, 27 Cal. 388.

Ostrander v. Brown, 15 John. 39. Cited, Trespass, when liability does not attach, 7 Cal. 340.

Ostrander, Ex parte, 1 Denio, 679. Cited, Mandamus, writ what to direct, 28 Cal. 640.

Ostrom v. Bixby, 9 How. Pr. 57. Cited, Pleading, several defenses set up in answer, 22 Cal. 680; Sham Answer, what is, 10 Cal. 29.

Oswego v. Oswego Canal Co., 6 N. Y. 263. Commented on, Dedication, of street, what constitutes, 35 Cal. 500.

Otis v. Barton, 10 N. H. 433. Cited, Negotiable Instruments, demand at place of payment not essential, 11 Cal. 322.

Otis v. Hazeltine, 27 Cal. 80. Approved, Guaranty, promise of guarantor when not within statute of frauds, 34 Cal. 675; 38 Cal. 135, 136.

Otley v. Manning, 9 East, 59. Cited, Stare Decisis, as a rule of property, 15 Cal. 621.

Oullahan v. Starbuck, 21 Cal. 413. Cited, Appeal, order on new trial will not be disturbed where evidence is conflicting, 8 Nev. 76. Followed, Id. 121.

27

Outram v. Morewood, 3 East, 346. Cited, Estoppel, conclusiveness of verdict on judgment, 15 Cal. 182; 26 Cal. 494, 495, 501, 503, 504; 32 Cal. 198; 19 How. 267.

Overall v. Pero, 7 Mich. 316. Cited, Justice's Court, entry of judgment in, 41 Cal. 234.

Overfield v. Christie, 7 Serg. & R. 173. Cited, Title, by adverse possession, when successive possessions cannot be added, 37 Cal. 354.

Overseers of North Whitehall v. Overseers of South Whitehall, 3 Serg. & R. 117. Cited, Municipal Corporations, when liable by implication, 9 Cal. 470.

Overton's Heirs v. Woolfolk, 6 Dana, 371. Cited, Ejectment, adverse possession by tenant in common, 27 Cal. 558.

Oves v. Oglesby, 7 Watts, 106. Cited, Fixtures, what constitute, 10 Cal. 264; 14 Cal. 68.

Owen v. Fowler, 24 Cal. 192. Approved, Ejectment, what plaintiff required to allege and prove, 24 Cal. 379; 28 Cal. 539; 37 Cal. 389; action to be brought against party in possession, 28 Cal. 536.

Owen v. Frink, 24 Cal. 171. Cited, Parties, necessary parties in equity, 26 Cal. 360.

Owen v. Gooch, 2 Esp. 567. Cited, Principal, when bound by contract made by agent, 13 Cal. 48.

Owen v. Homan, 3 Eng. L. & E. 112. Commented on, Surety, on undertaking, discharge of, by contract not to sue debtor, 26 Cal. 542.

Owen v. Morton, 24 Cal. 373. Disapproved, Appeal, presumption that findings are supported by the evidence, 28 Cal. 311. Cited, Presumption that facts not found were proved, 29 Cal. 141; Ejectment, sufficient proof of ouster, 41 Cal. 610.

Owens v. Dickenson, 1 Craig & P. 48. Cited, Married Woman, charging separate estate, 23 Cal. 565.

Owens v. Jackson, 9 Cal. 322. Approved, State Lands, conclusiveness of patent to swamp lands, 27 Cal. 89; of legislative grant, 27 Cal. 327; right of State in swamp lands, 29 Cal. 322.

Owenson v. Morse, 7 Term Rep. 66. Cited, Debt, effect of payment by note, 12 Cal. 322.

Owings v. Gibson, 2 A. K. Marsh. 515. Commented on, Land, possession of landlord by entry of tenant under lease, 38 Cal. 491.

Owings v. Hull, 9 Pet. 607. Cited, Municipal Corporation, ratification by, what essential, 16 Cal. 626.

Pacheco, Estate of, 23 Cal. 476. Referred to in case with same title, Probate, grant of letters of administration, 29 Cal. 225, 226. Cited, 25 Cal. 587.

Pacheco v. Hunsacker, 14 Cal. 120. Cited, Statute of Frauds, sufficiency of delivery depends upon character of article sold, applied to growing crops, 14 Cal. 386; 25 Cal. 553; 37 Cal. 638.

Pacific Bank v. De Ro, 37 Cal. 538. Approved, Revenue Stamps, waiver of presentation, demand, notice and protest need not be stamped, 14 Wall. 375; 30 Iowa, 567.

Pacific Ins. Co. v. Conard, 1 Bald. C. C. 138. Approved, Trespass, by sheriff, measure of damages, when a question for the jury, 11 Cal. 25; 14 Cal. 557.

Pacific Railroad v. Governor of Missouri, 23 Mo. 353. Commented on, Statute, validity of enrolled statute, 30 Cal. 271, 272.

Pack v. Mayor of N. Y., 8 N. Y. 222. Commented on, Respondent Superior, doctrine does not apply between corporations and contractors, 8 Cal. 493; 2 Hill, 67.

Packard v. De La Guerra, Cal. Sup. Ct. (not reported.) Approved, Husband and Wife, rights of surviving husband on death of wife, 18 Cal. 74.

Packer v. Heaton, 9 Cal. 568. Cited, New Trial, surprise insufficient grounds for, 22 Cal. 163.

Paddock v. Beebee, 2 Johns. Cas. 117. Cited, Service, other than personal, of notices and papers, strict compliance with statute required, 30 Cal. 184.

Padelford v. Mayor, etc., of Savannah, 14 Geo. 438. Cited, Jurisdiction, appellate power of United States Supreme Court, 11 Cal. 184.

Padgett v. Lawrence, 10 Paige, 170. Cited, Name, additions to, no part of name, 28 Cal. 222.

Page v. Foster, 7 N. H. 392.   Cited, Conveyance, construction of, as mortgage, or as conditional sale, 10 Cal. 207.

Page v. Fowler, 28 Cal. 605; S. C. 37 Cal. 100; 39 Cal. 412. Cited, Law of Case, rule of, announced, 37 Cal. 105. Approved, Preëmption, power of congress to withdraw lands from right of, 37 Cal. 490, 491, 502, 503.   Affirmed, Replevin, for timber or crops cut, when action will not lie, 39 Cal. 415–418.   Commented on, Conversion, measure of damages, 8 Nev. 354.

Page v. Hardin, 8 B. Mon. 649.   Commented on, Office, term of, 6 Cal. 292; Mandamus, when may issue to executive officer, 16 Cal. 45.

Page v. Hobbs, 27 Cal. 483.   Cited, State Patent, conclusiveness of, 28 Cal. 101; 38 Cal. 83.   Approved, what must be proved by party impeaching validity of, 33 Cal. 90. Cited, 38 Cal. 501; 40 Cal. 377.   Distinguished, 28 Cal. 408.   Commented on, Public Lands, power of congress to withdraw lands from right of preëmption, 28 Cal. 609; 30 Cal. 650; 37 Cal. 490, 491, 502.   Affirmed on principle of *stare decisis,* 37 Cal. 503.

Page v. Inhabitants of Danvers, 7 Met. 327.   Approved, New Trial, verdict not set aside for irregularities not going to merits of trial, 9 Cal. 537.

Page v. Page, 8 N. H. 187.   Cited, Resulting Trust, when it arises, 27 Cal. 140, 144.

Page v. Page, 15 Pick. 368.   Commented on, Evidence, secondary evidence of lost instrument, when admissible, 9 Cal. 449.

Page v. Rogers, 31 Cal. 293.   Commented on, Execution, title of execution purchaser before redemption, 31 Cal. 594.   Cited, 36 Cal. 397; entitled to rents pending redemption, 38 Cal. 425; Mortgage, when conditional sale construed as, 33 Cal. 333.

Page v. Scheibel, 11 Mo. 187.   Commented on, Grant, construction of description of land in, 10 Cal. 626.

Paige v. O'Neal, 12 Cal. 483.   Referred to, 13 Cal. 640. Cited, Vendor and Vendee, declarations of vendor after sale not admissible to impeach validity of sale, 15 Cal. 52; 36 Cal. 207.   Cited, Fraudulent Conveyance, valid as between parties, 19 Cal. 576; Id. 622; New Trial, insufficient ground for, 23 Cal. 337.   Commented on, Pleading, defects cured by verdict, 23 Cal. 360; Defects, in order, in summons, 41 Cal. 317. Approved, Juror and Jury, challenge of juror, grounds must be stated, 2 Nev. 231. Cited, 6 Nev. 129.

Pain v. Packard, 13 John. 174. Denied, Surety, on note, discharged by refusal of creditor to sue after request, 5 Cal. 175; 9 Cal. 561; 24 Cal. 164; 2 McLean, 457; 2 Johns. Ch. 563; 4 Pick. 384; 4 Vt. 135; 1 Zab. 634. Commented on, 5 Minn. 318; 13 Ill. 384; 9 Ind. 247, note; 3 Wheat. 155, note.

Paine v. Linhill, 10 Cal. 370. Cited, Appeal, statement when not required, 17 Cal. 514.

Paine v. McIntier, 1 Mass. 69. Cited, Deed, admissibility of parol evidence of, 24 Cal. 417.

Paine v. Meller, 6 Ves. Jr. 349. Commented on, Specific Performance, lapse of time, relief in equity, 10 Cal. 329. Cited, Rights of vendee under agreement, 22 Cal. 618.

Paine v. Tilden, 20 Vt. 554. Cited, Witnesses, party as witness, practice, 17 Cal. 604.

Palmer v. Boling, 8 Cal. 384. Approved, Taxation, of land, sufficiency of description in assessment, 13 Cal. 328; 22 Cal. 372; 33 Cal. 157. Distinguished, Tax Deed as evidence, 36 Cal. 73.

Palmer v. Conly, 4 Denio, 374; S. C. 2 N. Y. 184. Cited, Statutory Construction, statutes to be construed prospectively, 27 Cal. 159.

Palmer v. Cross, 1 Smedes & M. 48. Commented on, Husband and Wife, alienation of wife's separate estate, 13 Cal. 497.

Palmer v. Goodwin, 5 Cal. 458. Cited, Negotiable Instrument, holder of note, presumptions as to *bona fides*, 40 Cal. 116.

Palmer v. Grand Junction Railway Co., 4 Mees. & W. 749. Cited, Common Carrier, liabilities of, for injuries, 27 Cal. 429.

Palmer v. Haight, 2 Barb. 210. Cited, Witness, impeachment of, 16 Cal. 179.

Palmer v. Hughes, 1 Blackf. 328. Denied, Negotiable Instruments, presentation at place of payment of note, 11 Cal. 324; 20 Ind. 8.

Palmer v. McCafferty, 15 Cal. 334. Approved, Evidence, practice on introduction of, 6 Nev. 359.

Palmer v. Melvin, 6 Cal. 651. Approved, Pleading, essentials of complaint in action on undertaking, 7 Cal. 570; 9 Cal. 37; Id. 501.

Palmer v. Vance, 13 Cal. 553. Cited, Equity, relieves from mistakes, parol proof admissible to explain, 23 Cal. 124; Undertaking, liability of sureties on statutory undertaking, 2 Nev. 311.

Palmerton v. Huxford, 4 Denio, 166. Cited, Principal and Agent, ratification of sale by agent, 22 Cal. 594.

Palmyra, The, 10 Wheat. 502; S. C. 12 Wheat. 1. Cited, Appeal, finality of decree, 9 Cal. 635; 15 How. 467; 19 How. 284.

Palmyra v. Morton, 25 Mo. 593. Commented on, Street Assessment, apportionment of, 28 Cal. 371; 31 Cal. 685.

Panaud v. Jones, 1 Cal. 488. Cited, Mexican Law, validity of execution of will under, 6 Cal. 160. Commented on, 1 McAll. 255; husband's power over community property, 8 Cal. 510; 11 Cal. 169; 13 Cal. 470; 14 Cal. 612; Descents and Distribution, 17 Cal. 536. Cited, Customs and Usages, as rules of property, 10 Cal. 478; 22 Cal. 71; 31 Cal. 522; 23 How. 365.

Pangburn v. Bull, 1 Wend. 345. Cited, Malicious Prosecution, want of probable cause the gist of the action, 29 Cal. 648. Commented on, Probable cause a mixed question, Id. 650.

Panton v. Holland, 17 John. 92. Cited, Negligence, right of party to reasonable use of property, 7 Cal. 340.

Panton v. Jones, 3 Camp. 372. Cited, Estoppel, of tenant, 33 Cal. 251.

Pardee v. Drew, 25 Wend. 459. Cited, Bailment, liability of carrier as bailee, 33 Cal. 604.

Parishes of St. John Baptist and St. James, 1 Strange, 594. Cited, Pleading, conditions precedent, non-performance how averred, 7 Cal. 572.

Park v. Carnley, 7 How. Pr. 355. Cited, Change of Place of Trial, practice, 15 Cal. 420.

Parker v. Adams, 12 Met. 415. Cited, Negligence, rule of contributory negligence, 37 Cal. 422.

Parker v. Barker, 2 Met. 423. Commented on, Estoppel *in pais*, what constitutes, 26 Cal. 41.

Parker v. Bradley, 2 Hill, 584. Distinguished, Undertaking, validity of joint bonds, 14 Cal. 423.

Parker v. Chance, 11 Tex. 513. Cited, Husband and Wife, presumption as to common property through mutations and changes, 12 Cal. 253, 255; 17 Cal. 581; 30 Cal. 38.

Parker v. Claiborne, 2 Swan, 565. Cited, Mexican Grant, conclusiveness of patent, 14 Cal. 469.

Parker v. Commonwealth, 6 Penn. St. 507. Distinguished, Constitutionality of Statute, dependent for effect on vote of electors, 17 Cal. 32.

Parker v. Ellis, 2 Sandf. 223. Cited, Surety, right of contribution, 20 Cal. 136.

Parker v. Framingham, 8 Met. 267. Cited, Dedication, by sale of lots, rights of purchasers, 22 Cal. 490.

Parker v. Gordon, 7 East, 385. Cited, Negotiable Instruments, presentation and demand, 8 Cal. 632.

Parker v. Hotchkiss, 25 Conn. 321. Cited, Nuisance, prescriptive right to overflow lands, how acquired, 40 Cal. 406.

Parker v. Huntington, 2 Gray, 124. Cited, Conspiracy, damage the gist of the action, 25 Cal. 560.

Parker v. Kett, 1 Salk. 95. Commented on, Officers, powers of deputy, 25 Cal. 184, 186; 5 Pet. 351.

Parker v. Parmele, 20 John. 130. Approved, Specific Performance, want of title as a defense, 6 Cal. 573; 10 Cal. 322; 35 Cal. 663. Contra, 4 Comst. 401.

Parker v. Porter, 6 La. 169. Approved, Execution, levy on boat used to carry the mails not a penal offence, 23 Cal. 259.

Parker v. Proprietor of Locks, etc., 3 Met. 91. Cited, Ejectment, what constitutes ouster by tenant in common, 24 Cal. 376.

Parker v. Shephard, 1 Cal. 131. Cited, Appeal, lies to set aside judgment by default improperly entered, 3 Nev. 385.

Parker v. Smith, 17 Mass. 415. Cited, Dedication, by sale of lots, rights of purchasers, 22 Cal. 490.

Parker v. Totten, 10 How. Pr. 233. Cited, Pleading, facts and not legal conclusions of ownership to be alleged, 11 Cal. 168.

Parker v. Tuttle, 44 Me. 459. Cited, Negotiable Instruments, when presumptively dishonored, 39 Cal. 352.

Parkhurst v. Smith, Willes, 327. Cited, Deed, construction of intention of parties to govern, 10 Cal. 106; 26 Cal. 112.

Parkhurst v. Van Cortlandt, 1 Johns. Ch. 273. Reversed, 14 John. 15. Cited, Specific performance of verbal contract when enforceable, 10 Cal. 159; 19 Cal. 461; 24 Cal. 142.

Parkin v. Thorold, 2 Sim. N. S. 1. Affirmed, 16 Jur. 959. Cited, Specific Performance, time as essence of contract, 10 Cal. 326.

Parkist v. Alexander, 1 Johns. Ch. 397. Cited, Trust and Trustee, rights and obligations of trustee, 36 Cal. 432.

Parkman v. Welch, 19 Pick. 231. Cited, Fraudulent Conveyance, when not void as to subsequent creditors, 13 Cal. 72.

Parks v. Alta California T. Co., 13 Cal. 422. Cited, Common Carriers, telegraph companies liable as, 60 Me. 27.

Parks v. Boston, 8 Pick. 218. Cited, Street Improvements, duty of superintendent, 29 Cal. 85.

Parks v. Davis, 16 Iowa, 20. Cited, Officers, duties and liabilities of, 36 Cal. 214.

Parks v. Goodwin, 1 Mich. 35. Cited, Insolvency, discharge of debt a discharge of judgment thereon, 14 Cal. 176, 178.

Parmelee v. Oswego and Syracuse R.R. Co., 7 Barb. 599. Affirmed, 6 N. Y. 74. Commented on, State Patent, conclusiveness of, 16 Cal. 328.

Parmelee v. Hitchcock, 12 Wend. 96. Commented on, Execution, when amendable, is not void, 38 Cal. 379, 380.

Parmer v. Anderson, 33 Ala. 78. Cited, Slander, proof of malice, 39 Cal. 74.

Parnell v. Price, 3 Rich. 121. Cited, Surety in specialty, when discharged by delay of creditor, 10 Cal. 426

Parr v. Roe, 1 Q. B. 700; S. C. 41 Eng. C. L. 736. Construed and rule distinguished, Execution, municipal lands not subject to levy and sale, 15 Cal. 585.

Parrish v. Koons, 1 Pars. Sel. Cas. 79. Cited, Specific Performance, not enforceable on contract vague and indefinite, 33 Cal. 133.

Parrott v. Worsfold, 1 Jac. & W. 595. Commented on, Will, specific legacy, construction of, 31 Cal. 601.

Parsons v. Davis, 3 Cal. 421. Distinguished, Judgment, invalidity of, from want of jurisdiction, and from irregularities, 7 Cal. 64; reversal on appeal for irregularities, 16 Cal. 68.

Parsons v. Loyd, 3 Wils. 345. Cited, County Court, judgments of, not subject to collateral attack, 18 Cal. 506.

Parsons v. Monteath, 13 Barb. 353. Cited, Common Carriers, receipt of, as a contract, 27 Cal. 38.

Parsons v. Parsons, 9 N. H. 309. Cited, in dissenting opinion of Sprague, J., Alimony, inseparable from divorce, 38 Cal. 277.

Parsons v. Tuolumne Wat. Co., 5 Cal. 43. Approved, Jurisdiction of County Court, special cases defined, 5 Cal. 280. Cited, 9 Cal. 89; Id. 146; 19 Cal. 574; 23 Cal. 147; 42 Cal. 62, 68.

Partington v. Woodcock, 6 Adol. & E. 695. Cited, Foreclosure, relation between purchaser at sale and tenant of mortgagor, 16 Cal. 590.

Partridge v. Menck, 2 Barb. Ch. 101. Cited, Trade Marks, equitable protection of, 35 Cal. 65, 75.

Pasley v. Freeman, 3 Term Rep. 51; S. C. 2 Smith Lead. Cas. 55. Commented on, Principal and Agent, liability of agent for breach of confidence, 29 Cal. 146. Cited, 8 How. 154; liability of principal for fraudulent representations of agent, 39 Cal. 385; 8 How. 156. Approved, 7 Cranch, 92.

Passenger Cases, 7 How. 283. Contra, State Sovereignty, validity of statutes imposing licenses on foreign miners, 1 Cal. 244; 20 Cal. 584; power of State to impose tax, 1 Cal. 247. Approved, Statute imposing tax on passengers, 7 Cal. 171; 20 Cal. 566; 34 Cal. 498, 501, 502; 19 How. 528; 6 Wall. 48. Commented on, Power of State to regulate local commerce, 42 Cal. 588.

Patchin v. Pierce, 12 Wend. 61. Cited, Chattel Mortgage, legal effect and operation of, 27 Cal. 269; rights of mortgagee, 36 Cal. 429; Sale, by mortgagee, 27 Cal. 270.

Pate v. Bacon, 6 Munf. 219. Cited, Pleading, firm name, how set forth in complaint, 22 Cal. 358.

Paterson v. Arnold, 45 Penn. St. 410. Commented on, Water Rights, percolating waters belong to owner of soil, 42 Cal. 309.

Paterson v. Tash, 2 Strange, 1178. Cited, Factor, cannot pledge, 11 Cal. 401; 19 Cal. 72.

Patrick v. Montader, 13 Cal. 434. Distinguished, Judgment, by confession, validity of, 17 Cal. 585. Cited, Attachment, subsequent attaching creditors cannot take advantage of irregularities, 18 Cal. 155; 28 Cal. 287. Distinguished, 18 Cal. 381.

Patten v. Green, 13 Cal. 325. Commented on, Taxation, sufficiency of description of land in assessment, 22 Cal. 372; 2 Or. 209.

Patten v. Ray, 4 Cal. 287. Followed, Foreign Judgment, statute of limitations, in Taylor v. Dewey, July T. 1854 (not reported.)

Patterson v. Brindle, 9 Watts, 98. Cited, Redemption, right of, when it attaches, 4 Cal. 149.

Patterson v. Ely, 19 Cal. 28. Approved, Practice, verbal stipulations not binding, 21 Cal. 308. Cited, New Trial, surprise insufficiency of grounds, 23 Cal. -420; showing required on motion, 32 Cal. 212; Pleading, admissions in, dispense with necessity of proof, 4 Nev. 160.

Patterson v. Jenks, 2 Pet. 216. Approved, Pueblo Lands, presumption in favor of validity of, 1 Cal. 326; 15 Cal. 553; 16 Cal. 227, 228; Id. 241.

Patterson v. Keystone Min. Co., 30 Cal. 360; S. C. 23 Cal. 575. Approved, Mining Claims, conveyance of, must be by written instrument, unless made prior to act of 1860, 30 Cal. 484; 33 Cal. 321; 35 Cal. 652. Commented on, 33 Cal. 381. Cited, Evidence, the best evidence to be produced, or its absence accounted for, 33 Cal. 320; Pleading, allegations of evidence do not bind the pleader, 42 Cal. 351; 7 Nev. 327.

Patterson v. Patterson, 13 John. 379. Cited, Services, no action lies for voluntary services, 22 Cal. 510.

Patterson v. Society for Estab. Useful Manufactures, 4 Zab. 385. Cited, Street Improvements, liability under assessment, 31 Cal. 683.

Patterson v. Winn, 5 Pet. 233. Cited, Evidence, copies of public records as evidence, 13 Cal. 573; conclusiveness of government patent as evidence, 14 Cal. 467, 469; 16 Cal. 229; 38 Cal. 83. Approved, when subject to collateral impeachment, 16 Cal. 324, 330; 24 Cal. 629; 25 Cal. 250, 251.

Pattison v. Blanchard, 5 N. Y. 189. Cited, Partnership, what necessary to constitute, 38 Cal. 213.

Pattison v. Hull, 9 Cow. 751. Cited, Mortgage, securing several notes, assignee entitled to *pro rata* security, 6 Cal. 483; rights of holders may be fixed by agreement, 23 Cal. 30.

Pattison v. Johnson, 15 How. Pr. 289. Cited, Witnesses, notice for examination of party as witness, 22 Cal. 173.

Pattison v. Richards, 22 Barb. 143. Cited, Pleading, counterclaim, unliquidated damages, when may be proved, 26 Cal. 309. Commented on, What constitutes a counterclaim, 35 Cal. 281.

Pattison v. Yuba County and the S. F. and M. R. R. Co., 13 Cal. 175. Cited, Taxation, legality of statute providing for local improvements, 16 Cal. 345; Constitutionality of Statute, how determined, 22 Cal. 322. Approved, 26 Cal. 259; 41 Cal. 162; power of legislature to authorize county subscription to railroad stock, 30 Cal. 437. Affirmed on principle of stare decisis, 41 Cal. 201. Approved, 2 Neb. 499; 7 Kan. 496, 506.

Patton v. Placer Co., 30 Cal. 175. Cited, County, money in treasury presumptively belongs to the county, 31 Cal. 78; fees in hands of public officers, 36 Cal. 622.

Paul v. Silver, 16 Cal. 73. Cited, Forcible Entry and Detainer, jurisdiction on appeal, 22 Cal. 83.

Pawlet v. Clark, 9 Cranch, 331. Cited, Dedication, assent how proved, 14 Cal. 649; 15 Cal. 548; 22 Cal. 489; 14 How. 274.

Paxson v. Hale, Cal. Sup. Ct. Oct. T. 1867 (not reported.) Cited, Fees and Salaries, demand for, when to be presented, 40 Cal. 470.

Payne v. Bensley, 8 Cal. 260. Approved, Negotiable Instruments, transferred before maturity as collateral, not subject to defenses between payor and payee, 14 Cal. 98; Id. 454.

Payne v. Clark, 19 Mo. 152. Cited, Negotiable Instruments, superscription in figures of amount how construed, 39 Cal. 350.

Payne v. Commercial Bank, 6 Smedes & M. 24. Cited, Surety, on note, when discharged by agreement for delay, 10 Cal. 426.

Payne v. Gardiner, 29 N. Y. 146. Cited, Negotiable Instrument, certificate of deposit, a promissory note, 35 Cal. 120.

Payne v. P. M. S. S. Co., 1 Cal. 33. Followed, Appeal, lies from order setting aside verdict, 1 Cal. 38. Approved, Rules governing courts in setting aside verdict, 1 Cal. 41; 1 Cal. 365.

Payne v. Payne, 18 Cal. 291. Cited, Estates of Deceased, provisions in statute as to sale of estate construed, 21 Cal. 31; Id. 44; 30 Cal. 567; right of survivorship of wife in common property, 21 Cal. 91. Approved, 29 Cal. 348.

Payne v. Rodden, 4 Bibb, 304. Cited, Statute of Limitations, on warranty in sale of chattels, 41 Cal. 115.

Payne v. San Francisco, 3 Cal. 122. Cited, Statutory Construction, time for performance of official act construed, 14 Cal. 155.

Payne v. Smith, 19 Wend. 122. Cited, Arrest and Bail, waiver of irregularities by bail, 6 Cal. 59.

Payne v. Smith, 12 N. H. 34. Cited, Demand, authority to make, when to be questioned, 16 Cal. 77; Ejectment, Id. 220. Overruling, 5 Cal. 310.

Payne v. Treadwell, 16 Cal. 220. Overruling S. C. 5 Cal. 310. Cited, Ejectment, allegation of ouster essential in complaint, 6 Cal. 47. Approved, sufficiency of complaint, 19 Cal. 117; 24 Cal. 266; 26 Cal. 314; Id. 512; 38 Cal. 218; Id. 224; 39 Cal. 586; right of entry and possession sufficient to maintain action, 38 Cal. 43; 2 Nev. 69; sufficiency of description of land in complaint, 3 Wall. 494; patent as evidence, 34 Cal. 585; San Francisco, tenure to pueblo lands, 17 Cal. 462; 42 Cal. 556. Commented on, Authority of legislature over municipal lands, 18 Cal. 614; 42 Cal. 558; Alcaldes' Grants, presumed valid, 21 Cal. 41; 9 Wall. 602.

Payne v. Young, 8 N. Y. 158. Cited, Summons, insufficiency of affidavit of publication, 27 Cal. 299.

Payson v. Whitcomb, 15 Pick. 212. Cited, Negotiable Instruments, demand at place of payment not necessary, 11 Cal. 321.

Peabody v. Minot, 24 Pick. 329. Cited, Tenant in Common, conveyance by, 35 Cal. 588.

Peabody v. Phelps, 9 Cal. 213. Cited, Appeal, interlocutory order not appealable, 10 Cal. 527; Reference, time to file motion to set aside report of referee, 16 Cal. 118; order of reference, when special and when general, 30 Cal. 285. Commented on, Judgment, party not bound by judgment in ejectment without legal notice of pendency of action, 22 Cal. 208. Questioned, Vendor and Vendee, no remedy on failure of title where sale was without warranty, 22 Cal. 604.

Peabody v. Roberts, 47 Barb. 91. Cited, Foreclosure, necessary parties, 40 Cal. 238.

Peaceable v. Read, 1 East, 573. Cited, Tenant in Common, ouster by, 24 Cal. 377.

Peachy v. Ritchie, 4 Cal. 205. Cited, Arbitration and Award, impeachment of award, 14 Cal. 394.

Peachy v. Rowland, 16 Eng. L. & Eq. 443. Commented on, Respondeat Superior, when doctrine does not apply, 8 Cal. 492.

Peacock v. Bell, 1 Saund. 73. Commented on, Jurisdiction, intendments as to superior courts, 27 Cal. 313.

Peacock v. Monk, 1 Ves. Sr. 127. Cited, Deed, when consideration may be proved by parol, 26 Cal. 474.

Peacock v. Monk, 2 Ves. Sr. 190. Cited, Married Woman, charging separate estate of, 23 Cal. 565.

Peacock v. Rhodes, 2 Dougl. 633. Commented on, Negotiable Instruments, rights of holder of note, 2 Cal. 67.

Peake v. Oldham, 1 Cowp. 275. Cited, Libel and Slander, allegations in complaint, 34 Cal. 60.

Pearis v. Covillaud, 6 Cal. 617. Cited, Statute of Limitations, its application in equity, 18 Cal. 487; 23 Cal. 34.

Pearkes v. Freer, 9 Cal. 642. Cited, Change of place of trial, waiver of right of motion, 28 Cal. 246; 3 Nev. 406; 8 Nev. 186.

Pearl Street, Matter of, 19 Wend. 652. Commented on, Appeal, report of commissioners to assess damages and estimate benefits, on condemnation for street improvement, not disturbed where evidence is conflicting, 32 Cal. 538.

Pearce v. Morrice, 2 Adol. & E. 94. Cited, Trust and Trustee, purchase of administrator at his own sale, voidable, 29 Cal. 40.

Pearson v. Morgan, 2 Bro. Ch. 388. Commented on, Fraudulent Representations, recovery back of money paid under, 7 Cal. 507.

Pearson v. Parker, 3 N. H. 366. Cited, Principal and Agent, liability of principal for individual expenses of agent, 12 Cal. 128.

Pearson v. Snodgrass, 5 Cal. 478. Approved, Exceptions to admission of evidence must be taken at the trial, 7 Cal. 423.

Pease v. Barbiers, 10 Cal. 436. Cited, Homestead, wife must join husband in execution of mortgage, 31 Cal. 530.

Peck v. Acker, 20 Wend. 605. Cited, Surety, on note, when not discharged, 24 Cal. 166.

Peck v. Brummagim, 31 Cal. 440. Cited, Husband and Wife, separate property of wife, 31 Cal. 653. Approved, Deed to Wife, may be proved to be a gift, 40 Cal. 611, 612; husband may make donation to wife from common property, 42 Cal. 361.

Peck v. Courtis, 31 Cal. 207. Cited, Appeal, from orders and judgments in partition, practice, 31 Cal. 399, 403; non-appealable order, 32 Cal. 75; time within which to appeal from judgment, 32 Cal. 159; 36 Cal. 252.

Peck v. Hubbard, 11 Vt. 612. Cited, Sale and Delivery, failure of delivery under agreement creates debt, 23 Cal. 69.

Peck v. Jenness, 7 How. 612. Approved, Judgment, conclusiveness of, where jurisdiction attaches, 27 Cal. 170; 2 Black, 589. Cited, Attachment, lien of, 29 Cal. 375.

Peck v. Merrill, 26 Vt. 686. Commented on, Insolvency, assignment to preferred creditors, valid, 10 Cal. 275.

Peck v. Vandenburg, 30 Cal. 11. Cited, Appeal, from interlocutory judgments in partition, construction of statute, 31 Cal. 209. Approved, Husband and Wife, provision may be made for wife from common property, 31 Cal. 447; Deed, parol evidence admissible to show true consideration in deed, 36 Cal. 369; 41 Cal. 604.

Pedlerick v. Searle, 5 Serg. & R. 236. Cited, Title, by adverse possession, 34 Cal. 383.

Peebles v. Plainstanes, Scott's Redgauntlet. Cited, in illustration, Vexatious litigation, 12 Cal. 214.

Peebles v. Watts' Admrs., 9 Dana, 102. Cited, Will, power of sale in, on whom devolves, 32 Cal. 442.

Peirce v. City of Boston, 3 Met. 520. Cited, Tax, not a debt, 20 Cal. 350.

Peirce v. Rowe, 1 N. H. 179. Cited, Interest, on interest after due, computation of, 29 Cal. 392.

Peisch v. Dickson, 1 Mason, 11. Commented on, Contract, parol evidence when admissible to explain, 11 Cal. 198.

Pejepscut Proprietors v. Ransom, 14 Mass. 145. Cited, Presumptions, from lapse of time and acquiescence, 22 Cal. 591.

Pell v. Farquar, 3 Blackf. 331. Cited, Ejectment, representatives of legal title can maintain action, 26 Cal. 124.

Pell v. McElroy, 36 Cal. 268. Cited, Conveyances, notice of landlord's title imparted by possession of tenant, 39 Cal. 447.

Pelletreau v. Jackson, 11 Wend. 110. Cited, Conveyance, without warranty does not pass after-acquired title, 14 Cal. 628; evidence of handwriting of grantor, when admissible, 26 Cal. 410.

Peltier v. Peltier, Harr. Ch. 29. Cited in dissenting opinion of Sprague, J., Alimony, inseparable from divorce, 38 Cal. 277.

Pemberton v. King, 2 Dev. N. C. 376. Cited, Fixtures, what constitute, 14 Cal. 68.

Pemberton v. Pemberton, 13 Ves. Jr. 290. Cited, Will, decree in probate, conclusive as to validity, 20 Cal. 266.

Pena v. Vance, 21 Cal. 142. Cited, New Promise, must be in writing to take contract out of statute, 22 Cal. 102. Explained, 25 Cal. 292. Approved, 5 Nev. 214, 215.

Pendegast v. Knox, 32 Cal. 73. Cited, Appeal, does not lie from order striking out statement on new trial, 32 Cal. 305; Id. 326; 34 Cal. 483; 42 Cal. 113.

Pendleton v. Button, 3 Conn. 406. Cited, Acknowledgment, of deeds, powers and authority of notaries public, 11 Cal. 298.

Pendleton v. Fay, 2 Paige, 202. Cited, Notice, what sufficient in equity, 36 Cal. 437.

Pendock v. Mackinder, Willes, 665.   Cited, Judicial Decisions, obiter opinions, 9 Cal. 732.

Pendrell v. Pendrell, 2 Stra. 925.   Cited, Legitimacy, presumptions as to, 13 Cal. 100.

Penn v. Lord Baltimore, 1 Ves. Sr. 444; S. C. 2 Lead. Cas. in Eq. 673.   Cited, Specific Performance, jurisdiction, when it attaches, 38 Cal. 200; 6 Cranch, 158; 5 Pet. 30; Id. 79; 15 How. 243; time not of essence of contract, 40 Cal. 11, 13.

Penniman v. Rotch, 3 Met. 216.   Commented on, Accounts, mutual accounts, 30 Cal. 132.

Pennock v. Hart, 8 Serg. & R. 369.   Denied, Execution, issuance of, effect on judgment lien, 10 Cal. 82.

Pennsylvania R. R. Co. v. McCoskey's Admr., 23 Penn. St. 528.   Commented on, Water, rights of owner of soil to percolating waters, 42 Cal. 309.

Penny v. Porter, 2 East, 2.   Cited, Pleading, averment of non-performance, 7 Cal. 572.

Penobscot Boom Corp. v. Lamson, 16 Me. 224.   Cited, Corporation, power of self-dissolution, 38 Cal. 172.

Penobscot Boom Corp. v. Wilkins, 27 Me. 345.   Cited, Claim and Delivery, estoppel of receiptor of goods attached, 10 Cal. 176.

Penrose v. Griffith, 4 Binn. 231.   Cited, Deed, conclusiveness of recitals in, 24 Cal. 418; 4 Pet. 87; 11 How. 323.

Penry Admx. v. Brown, 2 Stark. 403.   Cited, Fixtures, right to, as between landlord and tenant, 14 Cal. 70.

Penton v. Robart, 2 East, 88.   Commented on, Fixtures, right of removal by tenant, 14 Cal. 69.

Pentz v. Stanton, 10 Wend. 271.   Commented on, Principal and Agent, execution of bill or note by agent, 7 Cal. 540; 13 Cal. 48.

People v. Abbot, 19 Wend. 192.   Commented on, Rape, impeachment of chastity, 6 Cal. 223.

People v. Abbott, 16 Cal. 358.   Cited, Statutory Construction, title of act, 19 Cal. 512.   Approved, 36 Cal. 602.

People v. Acosta, 10 Cal. 195.   Cited, Appeal, when new trial will be granted in criminal action, 6 Nev. 352.

People v. Adams, 3 Denio, 190.   Cited, Jurisdiction, on crime consummated within the State, 31 Cal. 114.

People v. Addison, 10 Cal. 1. Commented on, Office, when governor may fill vacancy, 37 Cal. 619.

People v. Ah Chung, 5 Cal. 103. Construed, Court of Sessions, how composed, 6 Cal. 216. Cited, 9 Cal. 234.

People v. Ah Fong, 12 Cal. 345. Cited, Criminal Procedure, charge of court, without consent of defendant, must be in writing, 14 Cal. 438; 26 Cal. 79; 37 Cal. 276; 7 Neb. 384; error not waived by failure to except, 2 Nev. 164.

People v. Ah Fung, 16 Cal. 137; S. C. 17 Cal. 377. Approved, Instructions, court cannot assume facts not proved or admitted, 17 Cal. 171; 30 Cal. 158; sufficiency of charge to jury, 30 Cal. 208.

People v. Ah Ki, 20 Cal. 177. Approved, Criminal Procedure, proof of possession of stolen property not *prima facie* evidence of larceny, 23 Cal. 51; 27 Cal. 407; 28 Cal. 427; Evidence, confessions of guilt, how admitted, 34 Cal. 224.

People v. Ah Loy, 10 Cal. 301. Approved, Criminal Procedure, new trial, when will be granted, 27 Cal. 501. Cited, 6 Nev. 352

People v. Ah Sing, 19 Cal. 598. Cited, Criminal Procedure, test of sufficiency of pleading, 28 Cal. 208. Commented on, Allegation of ownership in larceny, 41 Cal. 237.

People v. Ah Woo, 28 Cal. 205. Approved, Criminal Procedure, conjunctive allegations in indictment for forgery, 35 Cal. 508.

People v. Aikenhead, 5 Cal. 106. Cited, Sureties on Official Bond, liabilities on expiration of term, 17 Cal. 97; 8 Nev. 110.

People v. Alameda Co., 26 Cal. 642. Cited, Legislature, power of, over appropriations, 27 Cal. 209; 28 Cal. 395; 30 Cal. 438; 35 Cal. 633; 41 Cal. 530.

People v. Alameda T. R. Co., 30 Cal. 182. Cited, Service, by mail, strict compliance with statute must be shown, 35 Cal. 187.

People v. Albany, 12 John. 415. Cited, Mandamus, principles governing its issuance, 3 Cal. 173.

People v. Allegany, 15 Wend. 198. Commented on, Certiorari, principles governing its issuance, 42 Cal. 255.

People v. Allen, 6 Wend. 486. Cited, Statutory Construction, time of exercise of a power directoy in statute, 3 Cal. 126; 30 Cal. 527.

28

People v. Ames, 39 Cal. 403. Approved, Criminal Procedure, corroborating evidence required to convict on testimony of accomplice, 39 Cal. 615. Followed, 39 Cal. 661.

People v. Antonio, 27 Cal. 404. Cited, Larceny, burden of proof on guilty possession, 28 Cal. 427.

People v. Apple, 7 Cal. 289. Cited, Exceptions to admission of evidence to be taken at trial, 10 Cal. 37.

People v. Applegate, 5 Cal. 295. Cited, Jurisdiction, supreme court has no jurisdiction in cases less than felony, 7 Cal. 140; Id. 166; 30 Cal. 101; 35 Cal. 390.

People v. Arceo, 32 Cal. 40. Cited, Juror and Jury, court may excuse juror of its own motion, 32 Cal. 72.

People v. Arnold, 15 Cal. 476. Cited, Criminal Procedure, facts explanatory of conduct of defendant should be admitted in evidence, 17 Cal. 146. Commented on, 37 Cal. 684; threats of deceased, 37 Cal. 700. Cited, Objections to pannel of grand jury when to be taken, 23 Cal. 632; 28 Cal. 469; instructions to be given with reference to facts proved, 30 Cal. 207; 39 Cal. 691.

People v. Aro, 6 Cal. 207. Cited, Indictment to state acts constituting the offense, 6 Cal. 238. Approved, 9 Cal. 31; Id. 56. Cited, Murder, 9 Cal. 275. Construed, 20 Cal. 79. Denied, Requisites of indictment, 3 Nev. 465.

People v. Auditor, 2 Ill. 537. Cited, Office, law creating, may be repealed, effect of repeal, 22 Cal. 319.

People v. Backus, 5 Cal. 278. Commented on, New Trial, separation of jury as a ground for, 19 Cal. 445; Criminal Procedure, conviction for manslaughter is an acquittal for murder, 35 Cal. 391; discharge of jury as an acquittal, 38 Cal. 478.

People v. Badgley, 16 Wend. 53. Commented on, Criminal Procedure, evidence of confessions requires corroboration to convict, 31 Cal. 568.

People v. Baine, 6 Cal. 510. Denied, Office, when governor can fill vacancy, 28 Cal. 392; 37 Cal. 618.

People v. Baker, 3 Hill, 159. Cited, Indictment charging distinct offenses, discretion of court as to election, 27 Cal. 403.

People v. Baker, 1 Cal. 405. Approved, Verdict, cannot be impeached by affidavit of juror, 25 Cal. 475.

People v. Ball, 14 Cal. 101. Distinguished, Larceny, description in indictment, 15 Cal. 513.

People v. Banvard, 27 Cal. 474. Cited, Exceptions, objections to admission of evidence, 34 Cal. 585.

People v. Barbour, 9 Cal. 230. Cited, Presumptions in favor of validity of proceedings of courts of general jurisdiction, 17 Cal. 371; Criminal Procedure, repeal of statute creating criminal offense not retroactive, 19 Cal. 550, note.

People v. Barry, 31 Cal. 357. Cited, Criminal Procedure, charge of court, presumptions from record, 32 Cal. 215.

People v. Bartlett, 6 Wend. 422. Cited, Officer, acts of, under color of office, binding, 12 Cal. 361.

People v. Batchelor, 22 N. Y. 128. Cited, Legislature, power over affairs of corporation, 41 Cal. 532.

People v. Bealoba, 17 Cal. 389. Cited, Murder, charge of court in capital cases, 17 Cal. 285, note; 17 Cal. 379. Commented on, Murder in first degree, what constitutes, 25 Cal. 365.

People v. Bearss, 10 Cal. 68. Approved, Criminal Procedure, distinction between principals and accessories, abolished by statute, 20 Cal. 441.

People v. Beatty, 14 Cal. 566. Cited, Grand Jury, impannelment of, 15 Cal. 329; challenge to pannel, 15 Cal. 331; Id. 479; 23 Cal. 632; Indictment, entitling, 17 Cal. 361; sufficiency of statement of facts constituting offense, 39 Cal. 331; 27 Ark. 361.

People v. Beeler, 6 Cal. 246. Approved, Criminal Procedure, oral charge to jury without consent illegal, 8 Cal. 344; Id. 424; 37 Cal. 276; error not waived by failure to insist, 2 Neb. 164.

People v. Belencia, 21 Cal. 544. Approved, Criminal Procedure, intoxication as a subject of consideration in criminal cases, 27 Cal. 514. Cited, 19 Mich. 418.

People v. Bell, 4 Cal. 177. Cited, Mandamus, will not issue to control discretion, 7 Cal. 133. Approved, 22 Cal. 36. Commented on, When it will issue, 16 Cal. 46; Id. 63; to enforce purely ministerial duties, 41 Cal. 77; will not issue when there is a remedy at law, 11 Cal. 359.

People v. Benson, 6 Cal. 221. Cited, Criminal Procedure, evidence in cases of rape, 18 Wis. 502.

People v. Bigler, 5 Cal. 23. Cited, Statute, validity of motives of legislature not subject to judicial inquiry, 39 Cal. 202.

People v. Bircham, 12 Cal. 50. Doubted, Officers, powers conferred by statute, 34 Cal. 528.

People v. Bissell, 19 Ill. 229. Approved, Government, judicial department, powers of, 39 Cal. 221.

People v. Blackwell, 27 Cal. 65. Cited, Criminal Procedure, presumptions as to record of presentment by grand jury, 13 Fla. 657.

People v. Blake, 19 Cal. 579. Cited, Appeal, in special cases under statutory provisions, 42 Cal. 68.

People v. Board of Delegates, 14 Cal. 479. Cited, Certiorari, return of writ, 15 Cal. 301. Dissenting opinion, 32 Cal. 585; 34 Cal. 362.

People v. Board of Commrs. of Pilots, 37 Barb. 126. Cited, Certiorari, what reviewable on, 40 Cal. 480.

People v. Bodine, 7 Hill, 147. Denied, Juror and Jury, disqualification of juror, 1 Cal. 384. Commented on, Challenge for implied bias, 16 Cal. 135; change of place of trial, 21 Cal. 265.

People v. Boggs, 20 Cal. 432. Cited, New Trial, irregularities at trial, insufficient grounds for, 22 Cal. 353; 23 Cal. 633; 29 Cal. 262; so, as to irregularities in verdict, 34 Cal 190.

People v. Bond, 10 Cal. 563. Affirmed, San Francisco, treasurer to pay over moneys to commissioners of funded debt, 10 Cal. 584; 12 Cal. 300; Constitutionality of Funding Act, 14 Cal. 12; constitutional restrictions on legislature, 16 Cal. 35; funding act a contract, 19 Cal. 23. Cited, Rights of creditors cannot be impaired, 39 Cal. 274; 16 Cal. 34; 4 Wall. 550, 555; 19 Wis. 472; effect to be given to provision for sinking fund, 19 Cal. 184.

People v. Bonilla, 38 Cal. 699. Cited, Indictment, sufficiency of, for murder in first degree, 30 Wis. 440.

People v. Bonney, 19 Cal. 426. Approved, Criminal Procedure, oral instructions to jury to retire and designate the degree of guilt, not a charge, 7 Nev. 416.

People v. Boring, 8 Cal. 406. Cited, Sheriff, ex-sheriff to complete process by execution of deed, 9 Cal. 104.

People v. Bradt, 7 John. 539.   Cited, Attorney and Counsel, presumptions as to authority to appear, 8 Cal. 246.

People v. Bradwell, 2 Cow. 445.   Cited, Courts of Justice, loss of term by failure to open court, 24 Cal. 21.

People v. Brannigan, 21 Cal. 337.   Commented on, Criminal Procedure, new trial on ground of separation of jury, 22 Cal. 352; of misconduct of juror, 39 Cal. 375.

People v. Brenham, 3 Cal. 477.   Distinguished, Election, irregularities not to invalidate, 3 Cal. 122; 11 Cal. 63. Approved, as to failure to make proclamation, 5 Cal. 344.   Distinguished as to special elections, 6 Cal. 28. Doubted, 11 Cal. 63. _ Explained and limited, Id. 64.

People v. Breyfogle, 17 Cal. 504.   Approved, Official Bonds, of county treasurers, 29 Cal. 435.

People v. Broadway Wharf Co., 31 Cal. 33.   Cited, San Francisco, street improvements, construction of consolidation act, 35 Cal. 708; deed from commissioners of sinking fund conveys no title, 32 Cal. 449.

People v. Brooklyn, 1 Wend. 318.   Cited, Mandamus, when it lies, 3 Cal. 171.

People v. Brooks, 16 Cal. 47.   Cited, Condemnation of land for railroad purposes, payment or tender a condition precedent, 29 Cal. 117.   See McCauley v. Brooks.

People v. Burbank, 12 Cal. 378.   Cited, Office, term of, construction of statutes, 12 Cal. 402; Constitutionality of Statute, rule of judicial determination, 22 Cal. 308; 26 Cal. 229; 41 Cal. 160.   Approved, Constitutional Construction, 22 Cal. 311.

People v. Burgess, 35 Cal. 115.   Doubted, Burglary, sufficiency of indictment, 7 Nev. 129.

People v. Burney, 29 Cal. 459.   Cited, Appeal to Supreme Court, in criminal cases, confined to cases of felony, 30 Cal. 101; Certiorari, when it lies, 37 Cal. 457.

People v. Burr. See Blanding v. Burr.

People v. Buster, 11 Cal. 215.   Distinguished, Surety, on bond, liability of, 17 Cal. 508, 509.   Commented on, 29 Cal. 435; 31 Cal. 77.

People v. Butler, 8 Cal. 435.   Approved, Indictment, validity of, 20 Cal. 148.

People v. Byrnes, 30 Cal. 206. Cited, Criminal Procedure, instructions to correspond with evidence, practice, 32 Cal. 285; 36 Cal. 265; 39 Cal. 691; 1 Colorado, 145.

People v. Campbell, 40 Cal. 129. Cited, Indictment, against accessory, what to state, 41 Cal. 431.

People v. Carabin, 14 Cal. 438. Cited, Criminal Procedure, evidence by confessions, to be weighed by the jury, 30 Cal. 158.

People v. Carman, 18 Cal. 693. Disapproved, Jurisdiction on appeal, 35 Cal. 273.

People v. Carpenter, 7 Cal. 402. Approved, Recognizance, want of justification no defense in action against sureties, 38 Cal. 603.

People v. Cassels, 5 Hill, 164. Cited, Officer, power and jurisdiction cannot be assumed by mere assertion, 29 Cal. 188. Commented on, 30 Cal. 607. Cited, Habeas Corpus, what reviewable on, 35 Cal. 101.

People v. Cavanagh, 2 Park. Cr. Rep. 650. Cited, Habeas Corpus, judgment of conviction as authority for detention, 28 Cal. 253; sufficiency of judgment, 31 Cal. 629.

People v. Chambers, 18 Cal. 382. Approved, Criminal Procedure, possession of stolen property not alone sufficient to prove larceny, 20 Cal. 179; 23 Cal. 51; 27 Cal. 407; may be considered with other circumstances, 28 Cal. 427, 429.

People v. Champion, 16 John. 60. Approved, Mandamus, sufficiency of answer of board of supervisors, 27 Cal. 669.

People v. Chenango Co., 1 Johns. Cas. 180. Cited, Mandamus, to restore rights of attorney and counsel, 1 Cal. 191.

People v. Chisholm, 8 Cal. 29. Cited, Sureties, discharged by levy on execution, 23 Cal. 100.

People v. Chung Lit, 17 Cal. 320. Cited, Juror and Jury, objections to pannel waived by failure to take in time, 24 Cal. 234; 28 Cal. 469. Approved, Criminal Procedure, in absence of evidence, the presumptions are that instructions were in writing, 25 Cal. 535; 28 Cal. 496.

People v. Clark, 1 Cal. 406. Cited, Time, when inquiry will be made as to the point of time of an act, 1 Cal. 416;

as to passage and approval of statutes, 2 Cal. 170; 9 Md. 280; 14 Md. 200.

People v. Coffman, 24 Cal. 230. Cited, Criminal Procedure, instructions as to insanity, 39 Cal. 692. Commented on, Irregularities in formation of grand jury, 3 Nev. 75. Approved, Proof necessary to establish fact, 8 Nev. 301.

People v. Cohen, 8 Cal. 42. Commented on and limited, Indictment, description in, of property stolen, 9 Cal. 236. Approved, in larceny by bailee, 9 Cal. 315. Distinguished and limited, 15 Cal. 513. Disapproved, as to construction of "bailee" in criminal practice act, 19 Cal. 601.

People v. Cohen, 31 Cal. 210. Approved, Taxation, possessory claim to public lands, taxable, 37 Cal. 54.

People v. Coleman, 4 Cal. 46. Cited, Constitutional Construction, 38 Cal. 477; 41 Cal. 162; State Sovereignty, power of legislature, 4 Cal. 157; 10 Cal. 489; 13 Cal. 165; 22 Cal. 208; 24 Cal. 244; 40 Ala. 127. Commented on, Power, in passage of revenue laws, 18 Cal. 443; 22 Cal. 369. Disapproved, 34 Cal. 448, 461.

People v. Collins, 7 John. 549. Cited, Election, validity of, not subject to collateral inquiry, 23 Cal. 320; Evidence, identity of name, as evidence of identity of person, 28 Cal. 222.

People v. Collins, 19 Wend. 56. Approved, Appeal, when acts of inferior board or tribunal not reviewable, 7 Cal. 437.

People v. Colmere, 23 Cal. 631. Cited, Criminal Procedure, objections to pannel of grand jury when to be taken, 28 Cal. 469.

People v. Colt, 3 Hill, 432. Commented on, Indictment, sufficiency of, for murder, 9 Cal. 275; 43 Ill. 229.

People v. Columbia Com. Pleas, 1 Wend. 297. Cited, Verdict, affidavit of juror not admissible to impeach, 25 Cal. 400.

People v. Comedo, 11 Cal. 70. Cited, Appeal, assignment of errors in statement essential, 25 Cal. 483.

People v. Commrs. of Fort Edward, 11 How. Pr. 89. Cited, Pleading denial of being lawfully bound by a judgment is insufficient, 27 Cal. 675.

People v. Commrs. of Highways, 27 Barb. 94. Cited, Executive Officers, duty of governor in executing patent, 30 Cal. 607.

People v. Common Council of Brooklyn, 22 Barb. 412. Cited, Street Improvements, discretion of board of supervisors, 36 Cal. 605.

People v. Comstock, 8 Wend. 549. Cited, Criminal Procedure, discharge of jury when equivalent to an acquittal, 38 Cal. 478.

People v. Connor, 17 Cal. 354. Approved, Indictment, entitling, sufficient, 17 Cal. 370; Appeal, presumptions in favor of regularity of proceedings, until contrary is shown, 17 Cal. 371; Id. 429; 27 Cal. 67; 28 Cal. 475; error must be shown by record, 29 Cal. 415.

People v. Cook, 8 N. Y. 67; affirming 14 Barb. 259. Approved, Election, irregularities, which do not invalidate, 12 Cal. 361; 26 Cal. 214; 30 Cal. 338.

People v. Coon, 25 Cal. 635. Cited, Municipal Bonds, issuance of, in aid of railroad, 27 Cal. 674; compromise of claim against county, Id. 678; Mandamus, lies to compel issuance of bonds, 36 Cal. 604; validity of statutes authorizing issuance of, 7 Kan. 506; Legislature, power of, over municipal property, 42 Cal. 557; 27 Ark. 612.

People v. Corbett, 28 Cal. 330. Cited, Criminal Procedure, trial without arraignment invalid, 13 Fla. 634.

People v. Corlies, 1 Sand. 228. Cited, Probate Court, authority as to sale of estates, 20 Cal. 312.

People v. Cornell, 16 Cal. 187. Distinguished, Appeal, jurisdiction in criminal cases, 20 Cal. 120. Approved, confined to cases of felony, 30 Cal. 101; 35 Cal. 390, 392.

People v. Corning, 2 N. Y. 9. Cited, Criminal Procedure, when discharge of jury operates as an acquittal, 38 Cal. 478.

People v. Cortland Co., 24 How. Pr. 119. Cited, Mandamus, when it lies, 28 Cal. 432.

People v. Cottle, 6 Cal. 227. Cited, Juror and Jury, challenge for cause, grounds of, 8 Cal. 361. Commented on, 41 Cal. 642.

People v. County Court of Eldorado, 10 Cal. 19. Approved, Appeal, new trial in county court defined, 11 Cal. 328;

power of county court to order dismissal, not reviewable, 35 Cal. 214.

People v. County Judge of Placer, 27 Cal. 151. Cited, Appeal, power of county court to render judgment for costs on dismissal of, 39 Cal. 670.

People v. County Judge of San Francisco, 40 Cal. 479. Approved and followed, Certiorari, when will issue, 40 Cal. 656.

People v. Coutant, 11 Wend. 132. Approved and adopted, Office, constitutional term of, 11 Cal. 88; 12 Cal. 390.

People v. Cowles, 13 N. Y. 350. Denied, Office, constitutional term of, 11 Cal. 58.

People v. Cox, 9 Cal. 32. Cited, Indictment for Murder, sufficiency of, 27 Cal. 509.

People v. Craycroft, 2 Cal. 243. Cited, Revenue, action will not lie against keeper of gaming house for amount of license, 3 Cal. 367; Statutory Construction, when remedies by statute are merely cumulative, 7 Cal. 129; 16 Cal. 526.

People v. Cronin, 34 Cal. 191. Cited, Indictment, sufficiency of, 36 Cal. 247. Approved, 39 Cal. 56. Cited, Criminal Procedure, circumstantial evidence, degree of, necessary, 41 Cal. 67. Approved, 42 Cal. 539. Commented on, 6 Nev. 345. Cited, Charge of Court, in murder cases, 7 Nev. 384.

People v. Croton Aqueduct Board, 5 Abb. Pr. 372. Affirmed, 26 Barb. 240; 6 Abb. 42. Statute distinguished, Mandamus, rules of practice act applicable, 27 Cal. 684.

People v. Cuintano, 15 Cal. 327. Approved and followed, Criminal Procedure, objections to pannel of grand jury when to be taken, 15 Cal. 331. Cited, 3 Nev. 76.

People v. Dana, 22 Cal. 11. Affirmed, San Francisco, extent of government reservation, 22 Cal. 25.

People v. Davidson, 5 Cal. 134. Approved, Indictment, for assault to commit murder, 6 Cal. 563; 30 Cal. 218; 8 Nev. 321.

People v. Davidson, 30 Cal. 379. Cited, Nuisance, concurrent jurisdiction in actions to abate, 30 Cal. 585. Approved, Public Lands, ejectment lies to remove trespasser on tide lands, 31 Cal. 590; Tide Lands, what are, 32 Cal. 364.

People v. Davis, 21 Wend. 309. Cited, Forgery, proof of incorporation, what sufficient, 41 Cal. 654.

People v. Day, 15 Cal. 91. Cited, Special Cases, what are, 19 Cal. 574; 42 Cal. 62.

People v. De Lacey, 28 Cal. 589. Cited, New Trial, on ground of refusal of continuance, 29 Cal. 563; on ground of newly discovered evidence, 35 Cal. 688.

People v. Demint, 8 Cal. 423. Cited, Criminal Procedure, oral instructions without consent, erroneous, 14 Cal. 438; 26 Cal. 79; 37 Cal. 276; 1 Nev. 36; error not waived by failure to object, 2 Neb. 164.

People v. Denslow, 1 Caines, 177. Commented on, Officer, official discretion, 7 Cal. 437.

People v. Dick, 32 Cal. 213; S. C. 37 Cal. 277. Cited, Appeal, error in instructions must affirmatively appear, 34 Cal. 665; Criminal Procedure, circumstantial evidence, degree of certainty required, 41 Cal. 67; challenge for implied bias, what must state, 41 Cal. 430.

People v. Dill, 2 Ill. 257. Cited, Criminal Procedure, when discharge of jury operates as an acquittal, 38 Cal. 478.

People v. Dodge, 28 Cal. 445. Approved, Instructions, court may alter or amend, 32 Cal. 288. Cited, Criminal Procedure, deposition of absent witness, practice, 38 Cal. 187.

People v. Doe, 31 Cal. 220. Cited, Tax Title, tax deed as proof of title, 4 Nev. 152.

People v. Doe, 36 Cal. 220. Cited, Taxation, municipal property not subject to levy, 42 Cal. 557.

People v. Dolan, 9 Cal. 576. Approved, Indictment, sufficiency of, for murder, 10 Cal. 310; 21 Cal. 402; 27 Cal. 510. Cited, 3 Nev. 465.

People v. Doss, 39 Cal. 428. Followed, Indictment, against officer, sufficiency of description of office, 39 Cal. 433.

People v. Downer, 7 Cal. 169. Approved, Commerce, power to regulate, exclusive in congress, 20 Cal. 579; 33 Cal. 340; 34 Cal. 498.

People v. Draper, 25 Barb. 344. Cited, Legislature, power of taxation and appropriation, 18 Cal. 355.

People v. Duden, 18 Cal. 696. Cited, Fees and Salary, of office, 27 Cal. 151.

People v. Durick, 20 Cal. 94. Cited, Statutory Construction, effect of repeal of revenue act, 43 Ala. 607.

People v. Dutchess Co., 1 Hill, 50. Commented on, Mandamus, relief granted by, 27 Cal. 683.

People v. Dutchess Co., 9 Wend. 508. Cited, Supervisors, what acts of, are judicial, 16 Cal. 209.

People v. Dwinelle, 29 Cal. 635. Cited, Certiorari, what reviewable on, 8 Nev. 362.

People v. Eastman, 25 Cal. 601. Cited, Taxation, sufficiency of description in assessment, 23 Cal. 164; bonds of insurance company, assessable, 29 Cal. 546; money at interest where to be assessed, 38 Cal. 467. Commented on, 15 Wall. 324. Cited, Pleading, sufficiency of description of property in complaint, 23 Cal. 133; Id. 164.

People v. Easton, 2 Wend. 297. Cited, Redemption, right of, 9 Cal. 415.

People v. Eckert, 16 Cal. 110. Cited, Criminal Procedure, change of personnel of court during trial erroneous, 28 Cal. 475; corroborating evidence, what required, 39 Cal. 405.

People v. Edmonds, 15 Barb. 529. Cited, Mandamus, when it lies, 16 Cal. 45.

People v. Edmonds, 19 Barb. 468. Cited, Mandamus, when it lies, 16 Cal. 45.

People v. Edwards, 9 Cal. 286. Approved, Appeal, statement how prepared, 10 Cal. 301; 23 Cal. 462; 31 Cal. 661; Office, separate and distinct offices may be held by same person, 14 Cal. 16; 30 Cal. 684; 38 Cal. 77. Commented on, Official Bonds, liability of sureties on, 31 Cal. 291; 31 Ill. 278. Cited, not to depend on strict compliance with statute, 32 Cal. 148; 2 Or. 319.

People v. El Dorado Co., 8 Cal. 58; S. C. 11 Cal. 170. Cited, Supervisors, powers of, 10 Cal. 345; 7 Nev. 397; powers of a judicial nature, 24 Cal. 127; as to approval of bonds, 25 Cal. 97; examining, approving, and accepting work, 29 Cal. 85. Disapproved, that legislature could not confer mixed functions on board of supervisors, 34 Cal. 527, 531; Id. 541. Commented on, Certiorari, when it will lie, 16 Cal. 210. Cited, Review of judgments and orders of supervisors, 23 Cal. 303; on grant of ferry license, Id. 495; Municipal Courts, jurisdiction may be regulated by legislature, 22 Cal. 478; County Warrants, not negotiable, 19 Cal. 490; 23 Cal. 126; 19 Iowa, 217; 6 Kan. 518; 49 N. H. 224; 51 N. H. 359.

People v. Elkins, 40 Cal. 642. Cited, Certiorari, when it will not lie, 8 Nev. 362.

People v. Empire G. & S. M. Co., 33 Cal. 171. Cited, Taxation, description of property assessed, 34 Cal. 440; 8 Nev. 28; Exceptions, settlement of, 3 Nev. 530.

People v. English, 30 Cal. 214. Cited, Indictment, sufficiency of, 34 Cal. 663; 8 Nev. 321. Approved, Criminal Procedure, sufficiency of verdict for assault with deadly weapon, 40 Cal. 427.

People v. Evans, 29 Cal. 429. Commented on, Sureties, on official bond, liability of, on what depends, 31 Cal. 293. Cited, 32 Cal. 148.

People v. Farrell, 31 Cal. 576. Cited, Criminal Procedure, defendant as witness in his own behalf, 36 Cal. 529; presumptions as to insanity, 38 Cal. 189.

People v. Ferguson, 34 Cal. 309. Cited, Exceptions, settlement of, practice, 37 Cal. 275; 42 Cal. 538.

People v. Ferguson, 8 Cow. 102. Cited, Election, irregularities which will not invalidate, 26 Cal. 214.

People v. Ferris, 1 Abb. Pr. N. S. 197. Cited, Juror and Jury, court may excuse juror, 32 Cal. 47.

People v. Fisher, 6 Cal. 155. Cited, Change of Place of Trial, granting motion when discretionary, 23 Cal. 378.

People v. Fitch, 1 Cal. 519. Cited, Office, power to elect includes power to fill vacancy, 2 Cal. 137; 8 Cal. 15. Commented on, 1 Nev. 80; failure to approve bond presented does not create vacancy, 7 Cal. 440; when governor not authorized to fill vacancy, 7 Cal. 525; 28 Cal. 392; 13 Flor. 18.

People v. Flagg, 16 Barb. 503. Cited, Mandamus, when it will issue, 16 Cal. 45.

People v. Fletcher, 3 Ill. 482. Cited, Mandamus, when it lies to restore to office, 1 Cal. 191.

People v. Folsom, 5 Cal. 373. Cited, Alien, rights of nonresident to hold property, 32 Cal. 386; denouncement under Mexican law, 26 Cal. 477.

People v. Forbes, 22 Cal. 135. Cited, Judgment of imprisonment to commence at expiration of term valid, 24 Wis. 493.

People v. Foren, 25 Cal. 361. Cited, Murder, degrees of, 39 Cal. 697.

People v. Fowler, 9 Cal. 85. Cited, Appeal, jurisdiction of supreme court confined to felonies, 30 Cal. 101.

People v. Francis, 38 Cal. 183. Cited, Trial, continuance, what showing required, 6 Nev. 327; 7 Cal. 156.

People v. Frank, 28 Cal. 507. Cited, Indictment, charging distinct offenses, 31 Cal. 461; sufficiency of indictment for forgery, 35 Cal. 507, 508; of charge as to corporation, 41 Cal. 652; Conviction under indictment charging two offenses, 29 Cal. 631. Commented on, Conclusiveness of judgment, 29 Cal. 523.

People v. Freeland, 6 Cal. 96. Commented on, Juror and Jury, competency of grand juror, exceptions when to be taken, 6 Cal. 215. Cited, Indictment, objections to insufficiency of, when to be taken, 22 Cal. 354; 26 Cal. 115; 28 Cal. 272; 34 Cal. 308.

People v. Frisbie, 18 Cal. 402. Cited, Judgment, on joint contract, abrogation of common law rule, 18 Cal. 401, note; 39 Cal. 95.

People v. Frisbie, 26 Cal. 135. Cited, Legislature, assumption of judicial powers, 21 Wis. 503; 7 Nev. 229.

People v. Frisbie, 31 Cal. 146. Approved, Taxation, possessory claim to public land, taxable property, 37 Cal. 54.

People v. Garcia, 25 Cal. 531. Followed, Appeal, presumption that instructions were in writing, 28 Cal. 496. Cited, Indictment, sufficiency of, 30 Cal. 216; 32 Cal. 38; 34 Cal. 663.

People v. Garnett, 29 Cal. 622. Cited, Indictment, objections waived by failure to demurrer, 32 Cal. 62; 35 Cal. 118. Denied, that indictment for burglary and stealing goods charges two distinct offenses, 7 Nev. 129.

People v. Gates, 15 Wend. 159. Cited, Indictment for arson, sufficiency of, 20 Cal. 80.

People v. Gatewood, 20 Cal. 147. Cited, Appeal, error without injury, disregarded, 23 Cal. 158.

People v. Garey. See Garey *v.* People.

People v. Gerke, 5 Cal. 381. Doubted, Alien, rights of, under treaty, constitutional construction, 6 Cal. 252. Commented on, 13 Cal. 282. Cited, Constitutional Construction, 22 Cal. 312.

People v. Gerke, 35 Cal. 677. Approved, Taxation, exemption of private property from taxation, unconstitutional, 37 Cal. 55.

People v. Gibbs, 9 Wend. 29. Cited, Estates of Deceased, not liable in action for torts, 38 Cal. 23.

People v. Gibson, 17 Cal. 283. Cited, Criminal Procedure, sufficiency of charge of court, 30 Cal. 208.

People v. Gillespie, 1 Cal. 343. Followed, Superior Court of San Francisco, no jurisdiction by *quo warranto*, 1 Cal. 345. Commented on, Powers of superior court, 5 Cal. 403. Affirmed on principle of *stare decisis*, 36 Cal. 696. Commented on, 39 Cal. 518.

People v. Gilmore, 4 Cal. 376. Commented on, Criminal Procedure, conviction for lesser offense is an acquittal of greater, charged in indictment, 5 Cal. 278; 35 Cal. 391. Cited, 11 Iowa, 357; acquittal by discharge of jury, 38 Cal. 478.

People v. Glenn, 10 Cal. 32. Approved, Evidence, dying declarations as, 21 Cal. 372; how proved, 35 Cal. 52.

People v. Goldbury, 10 Cal. 312. Reviewed and explained, Appeal, dismissal for want of assignment of errors, 25 Cal. 483.

People v. Goodwin, 18 John. 187. Commented on, Criminal Procedure, when discharge of jury operates as an acquittal, 27 Cal. 398; 41 Cal. 216.

People v. Graham, 21 Cal. 261. Approved, Bill of Exceptions, on question stated, when defective, 34 Cal. 188. Cited, Criminal Procedure, granting change of venue in discretion of court, 3 Nev. 462.

People v. Gray, 10 Abb. Pr. 469. Cited, Summons, publication of, computation of time, 32 Cal. 352.

People v. Green, 2 Wend. 266. Approved and adopted, Office, constitutional term of, 11 Cal. 88; 12 Cal. 388.

People v. Green, 15 Cal. 512. Approved, Indictment, against bailee, for conversion, 19 Cal. 601.

People v. Hall, 4 Cal. 399. Cited, Witness, exclusion of colored persons, 13 Cal. 73. Commented on, 14 Cal. 146.

People v. Hardin, 37 Cal. 258. Cited, Juror and Jury, challenge for bias, what to state, 37 Cal. 279; 41 Cal. 430.

People v. Harris, 9 Cal. 571. Cited, Appeal Bonds, on appeal from justices' courts, 19 Cal. 386. Distinguished, prepayment of fees of justice, 25 Cal. 211.

People v. Harrison, 8 Barb. 560. Cited, Indictment, insufficiency of, 35 Cal. 507.

People v. Hart, Cal. Sup Ct. Oct. T. 1872. Approved, Appeal, charge in criminal case can only be brought up by bill of exceptions, 8 Nev. 139; Id. 254.

People v. Hartley, 21 Cal. 585. Commented on, Bond, construction of, 25 Cal. 530.

People v. Haskell, 5 Cal. 357. Approved, Office, legislative offices under control of legislature, 14 Cal. 17; 22 Cal. 319.

People v. Hastings, 29 Cal. 449. Approved, Taxation, valuation essential to validity of assessment, 31 Cal. 138, 140; 34 Cal. 437; Id. 576. Cited, Authority of assessor limited to district for which he is elected, 34 Cal. 476. Approved, Id. 657; 39 Cal. 358, 359; election necessary to constitutional office, 39 Cal. 11.

People v. Hayden, 6 Hill, 361. Cited, Condemnation of Land, payment or tender a condition precedent, 31 Cal. 559.

People v. Hays, 4 Cal. 127. Approved, Redemption, statute giving right of, not retroactive, 5 Cal. 402. Doubted, Right of city to redeem lands, 15 Cal. 587. Cited, payment to sheriff essential, 6 Cal. 92; Statutory Construction, statutes not to be construed retrospectively, 15 Iowa, 137.

People v. Hennessey, 15 Wend. 148. Cited, Criminal Procedure, extra judicial confessions as evidence, 31 Cal. 568.

People v. Herkimer, Com. Pleas, 4 Wend. 210. Commented on, Statutory Construction, statutes not to be construed retrospectively, 4 Cal. 138, 166.

People v. Herrick, 13 John. 82. Cited, Witness, impeachment of, evidence of conviction, 39 Cal. 450.

People v. Hester, 6 Cal. 679. Cited, Certiorari, jurisdiction of district court to issue, 7 Cal. 116. Disapproved as to issuance of writ, 8 Cal. 61; as to functions of writ, 14

Cal. 499; that supervisors do not exercise judicial functions, 34 Cal. 527, 528, 536; 7 Nev. 396.

People v. Hidden, 32 Cal. 445. Cited, Indictment, proceedings to set aside, when to be taken, 34 Cal. 308; presumptions as to regularity in formation of grand jury, 35 Cal. 48.

People v. Hill, 7 Cal. 197. Commented on, Statute, in part unconstitutional, 22 Cal. 386. Cited, 33 Cal. 219; 29 Iowa, 399; 27 Ark. 612.

People v. Hobson, 17 Cal. 424. Cited, Criminal Procedure, admissions as evidence, 25 Cal. 535; intendments in favor of regularity of proceedings in county courts, 27 Cal. 67; change of personnel of court during trial, 28 Cal. 475.

People v. Hodges, 27 Cal. 340. Commented on, Accessory, in larceny, 40 Cal. 602.

People v. Holden, 28 Cal. 123. Commented on, Constitutional Construction, residence of voter while in the service of the United States, 38 Cal. 93; 3 Or. 573. Cited, 3 Or. 240; contesting election, 12 Fla. 224.

People v. Holladay, 25 Cal. 300. Cited as inapplicable, Taxation, legalizing assessment, 28 Cal. 614; 34 Cal. 576; defective assessment cured by legislative enactment, 32 Cal. 108; 34 Cal. 437; assessment where to be made on personal property, 35 Cal. 288; on money loaned, 38 Cal. 467.

People v. Home Ins. Co., 29 Cal. 533. Cited. Taxation, assessment of money in hands of trustee, 34 Cal. 440.

People v. Honeyman, 3 Denio, 121. Commented on, Juror and Jury, challenge on ground of bias, 16 Cal. 135.

People v. Houshell, 10 Cal. 83. Cited, Appeal, record how made up in criminal case, 32 Cal. 92.

People v. Hood, 6 Cal. 236. Disapproved, Indictment, sufficiency of, in cases of arson, 20 Cal. 79. Cited, Insufficiency of disjunctive allegations, 35 Cal. 509.

People v. Houghtaling, 7 Cal. 348. Cited, Probate Procedure, claimant of specific trust fund not a creditor, 9 Cal. 658, 659; Trust and Trustee, cestui que trust, rights of, 11 Cal. 350; remedy of, against trustee, 31 Cal. 23.

People v. Hovey, 5 Barb. 118. Cited, Divorce, restraint on second marriage, 16 Cal. 378.

People v. Huber, 20 Cal. 81. Cited, Notice, statutes authorizing constructive notice to be strictly pursued, 24 Cal. 434; so, as to publication of summons, 27 Cal. 314. Approved, 31 Cal. 351, 356.

People v. Huggins, 10 Wend. 465. Cited, Recognizance, essential averments in action on, 30 Cal. 629.

People v. Hughes, 29 Cal. 257. Distinguished, Indictment, variance in name of corporation, 32 Cal. 165. Cited, Criminal Procedure, insufficient grounds for arrest of judgment, 35 Cal. 118; 6 Nev. 185.

People v. Hunter, 10 Cal. 502. Cited, Recognizance, Sureties not liable on variance between charge and indictment, 16 Iowa, 321.

People v. Hurley, 8 Cal. 390. Approved, Instructions, practice on instructions refused, 13 Cal. 173; 17 Cal. 148.

People v. Hyler, 2 Park. Cr. Rep. 571. Approved, Criminal Procedure, bail, practice on application for, 19 Cal. 545.

People v. Jackson, 24 Cal. 630. Commented on, Pleading, conditions precedent when to be pleaded, 25 Cal. 303. Cited, Insufficient Averments, 35 Cal. 448. Approved, Appeal, no reversal to allow amendment, 36 Cal. 117. Cited, Contesting Patent, what must be shown by party contesting, 40 Cal. 377. Distinguished, 8 Nev. 97.

People v. Jenkins, 17 Cal. 500. Approved, Sureties, on official bond, estopped from denying right of incumbent to office, 6 Nev. 370.

People v. Jenks, 24 Cal. 11. Cited, Criminal Procedure, peremptory challenge, when may be imposed, 37 Cal. 690; 4 Nev. 275.

People v. Jersey, 18 Cal. 337. Cited, Conversion, by bailee, when larceny, 23 Cal. 280.

People v. Jewett, 3 Wend. 314. Cited, Juror and Jury, disqualification of juror, 1 Cal. 384.

People v. Jim Ti, 32 Cal. 61. Commented on, Indictment, sufficiency of, for larceny of money, 40 Cal. 277. Cited, Substitution of true name of defendant, on trial, 8 Nev. 256.

People v. Johnson, 6 Cal. 499. Reviewed and affirmed, Constitutional Construction, limit of State debt, 7 Cal. 66.

29

People v. Johnson, 30 Cal. 98. Cited, Certiorari, what not reviewable upon, 8 Nev. 362.

People v. Jones, 17 Wend. 81. Cited, Office, vacation of, by neglect to qualify, 3 Cal. 127.

People v. Jones, 20 Cal. 50. Cited, Office, remedy by *quo warranto* for intrusion into, 24 Cal. 127; 28 Cal. 130.

People v. Jones, 31 Cal. 565; S. C. 32 Cal. 81. Referred to, Indictment for robbery, 32 Cal. 99. Cited, Criminal Procedure, evidence to be confined to the issues, 36 Cal. 526; rule of admission of testimony of defendant, 36 Cal. 529; rule as to sufficiency of evidence, 3 Nev. 467; New Trial, practice on motion for, 6 Nev. 352.

People v. Josephs, 7 Cal. 129. Denied, Evidence, of character in criminal case, 28 Cal. 396.

People v. Judd, 10 Cal. 313. Cited, Indictment, sufficiency of, on charge of murder, 27 Cal. 510; 34 Cal. 201; 3 Nev. 465.

People v. Judge of Twelfth District, 17 Cal. 547. Cited, Constitutional Construction, supremacy of legislative power, 22 Cal. 308; relative powers in Federal and State government, 41 Cal. 162; legislature may deny to one a privilege extended to another, 22 Cal. 321; 29 Cal. 271; constitutional construction as to uniform operation of general laws, 32 Cal. 527. Approved, 37 Cal. 376; 38 Cal. 710; general laws may be local and special, 37 Cal. 379; Judiciary, power to determine constitutionality of statute, 26 Cal. 229; 41 Cal. 160; principles of judicial determination, 26 Cal. 256. Followed, Mandamus, will not lie to control judicial discretion, 18 Cal. 686. Approved, 28 Cal. 169. Cited, What writ will direct, Id. 641; Statute, validity of special statute, 7 Nev. 229.

People v. Judge of Wayne Co. Ct., 1 Mich. 360. Cited, Mandamus, what writ will direct, 28 Cal. 641.

People v. Judges of Delaware C. P., 1 Johns. Cas. 180. Cited, Mandamus, when it will lie, 1 Cal. 151.

People v. Judges of Dutchess Co., 20 Wend. 658. Cited, Mandamus will not lie to control judicial discretion as to change of venue, 24 Cal. 83; as to allowance of counter-claim, 28 Cal. 169; what writ will direct, 28 Cal. 641.

People v. Judges of Madison Co., 7 Cow. 423. Cited, Appeal, sufficiency of undertaking, 13 Cal. 509.

People v. Judges of Oneida, C. P. 1 Wend. 28. Cited, Appeal, construction of undertaking on appeal, 8 Cal. 551.

People v. Keenan, 13 Cal. 581. Cited, Appeal, what subject to review, in criminal case, 42 Cal. 167.

People v. Kelley, 28 Cal. 425. Cited, Instruction, modification of, practice, 30 Cal. 450.

People v. Kelly, 6 Cal. 210. Cited, Indictment, by wrong name, substitution of true name on trial, practice, 37 Cal. 280; 8 Nev. 256; 44 Ala. 390; sufficiency of indictment, 34 Tex. 151.

People v. Kelsey, 34 Cal. 470. Cited, Office, constitutional term of, 39 Cal. 11.

People v. Kerr, 37 Barb. 357. Cited, Street Railroad, not a nuisance, 35 Cal. 333.

People v. King, 27 Cal. 507. Cited, Indictment, test of sufficiency of, 28 Cal. 208; 32 Cal. 38. Approved, 34 Cal. 200, 208; Id. 217; 37 Cal. 280; 3 Nev. 465. Cited, Instructions in criminal case should not be refused, 30 Cal. 155; 32 Cal. 436; to be given with reference to facts proved, 30 Cal. 207; 39 Cal. 691; 1 Colorado, 144; charge as to matter of fact erroneous, 33 Cal. 305; 3 Nev. 339; charge under the common law, 36 Cal. 266; Intoxication, proof of, 29 Cal. 683; where error is not shown, instructions presumed correct, 34 Cal. 665; review of instructions on appeal, 32 Cal. 215; 38 Cal. 143.

People v. King, 28 Cal. 265. Approved, Criminal Procedure, judgment, sufficiency of, as to certainty of time, 29 Cal. 262; entry of plea of not guilty after demurrer overruled, 29 Cal. 563; objections to indictment when to be taken, 34 Cal. 308. Cited, Statutory Construction, 31 Cal. 114.

People v. Kingman, 24 N. Y. 559. Cited, Dedication, to public use, *cul de sac*, 35 Cal. 498.

People v. Koeber, 7 Hill, 40. Cited, Pleading, jurisdictional facts in special cases to be pleaded in collateral action, 33 Cal. 536; 30 Ind. 65.

People v. Kohle, 4 Cal. 198. Cited, Juror and Jury, challenge in criminal cases, 10 Cal. 59.

People v. Kruger, 19 Cal. 411. Approved, San Francisco, construction of beach and water lot act; 22 Cal. 20.

People v. Labra, 5 Cal. 183.   Approved, Criminal Procedure, competency of accomplice as witness, 20 Cal. 440.

People v. Lafarge, 3 Cal. 130.   Commented on, Judgment, relief from practice, 6 Cal. 22; 22 Cal. 337.

People v. Lake County, 33 Cal. 487.   Cited, Supervisors, discretionary powers of, under special statute, 36 Cal. 604.

People v. Lambier, 5 Denio, 9.   Cited, Dedication, by sale of lots on map, 22 Cal. 489.

People v. Langdon, 8 Cal. 1.   Cited, Office, constitutional term of, 10 Cal. 46.   Disapproved, Vacancy and power of appointment, 37 Cal. 617, 621, 625, 650.   Cited, Restriction of appointing power, 3 Or. 535, 538; 13 Fla. 18.

People v. Lawrence, 6 Hill, 244.   Cited, Supervisors, powers of, under special statute, 16 Cal. 211; quasi-judicial powers, 18 Cal. 149; Mandamus, when writ will issue to compel payment of claim, 20 Cal. 595.

People v. Lawrence, 36 Barb. 181.   Commented on, Street Improvements, apportionment of expense, 32 Cal. 520.

People v. Lawrence, 21 Cal. 368.   Cited, Criminal Procedure, objections to indictment waived by plea, 22 Cal. 354; 28 Cal. 272; 34 Cal. 308; indorsement on indictment not essential to its validity, 27 Cal. 67.

People v. Laws, 3 Abb. Pr. 450.   Cited, Sureties, on administrator's bond, when bound, 25 Cal. 222.

People v. Lee, 5 Cal. 353.   Criticised, Change of place of trial, 6 Cal. 155.   Doubted, 21 Cal. 265; 3 Nev. 462.

People v. Lee, 14 Cal. 510; S. P. 17 Cal. 76.   Referred to, Criminal Procedure, delay in settlement of statement on appeal, 14 Cal. 438.   Cited, 34 Cal. 188; 1 Nev. 460; 8 Nev. 145; Evidence, proof of dying declarations, 35 Cal. 52; New Trial, insufficient grounds for, 19 Cal. 445.

People v. Lemmon, 5 Sand. 711.   Commented on, Constitutional Construction, right of transit through State, 9 Cal. 163.

People v. Levison, 16 Cal. 98.   Cited, Criminal Procedure, possession of stolen property not alone sufficient to convict for larceny, 18 Cal. 384; review of errors on appeal, 27 Cal. 514; 32 Cal. 215; 34 Cal. 665; 38 Cal. 143; instructions, as to matters of fact, erroneous, 30 Cal. 158.

People v. Lewis, 36 Cal. 531. Cited, New Trial, when verdict not sustained by evidence, 6 Nev. 352.

People v. Littlefield, 5 Cal. 355. Cited, Indictment, sufficiency of, 28 Cal. 211; 34 Tex. 151.

People v. Livingston, 6 Wend. 526. Commented on, Statutory Construction, statutes not to be construed retrospectively, 4 Cal. 138. Cited, Power of legislature over statutory privileges, 22 Cal. 319; effect of repeal of remedial statutes, 4 Cal. 165; 15 Cal. 523.

People v. Lloyd, 9 Cal. 54. Followed, Indictment for murder, essential averments, 9 Cal. 33. Explained, 27 Cal. 509. Cited, 28 Cal. 211. Commented on, 3 Nev. 465.

People v. Lembard, 17 Cal. 316. Denied, Criminal Procedure, admissibility of evidence of character, 28 Cal. 396.

People v. Long, 39 Cal. 694. Cited, Appeal, presumption that evidence warranted charge to jury, 29 Wis. 169.

People v. Lopez, 26 Cal. 112. Cited, Criminal Procedure, objections to indictment waived by plea, 28 Cal. 272; 29 Cal. 563; 34 Cal. 308.

People v. Love, 25 Cal. 520. Cited, Sureties, on official bond, several liability, 29 Cal. 436; 24 Wis. 613; separate judgment, 29 Cal. 643; Official Bonds, separate bonds required for distinct offices held by same person, 38 Cal. 77; Office, sheriff and tax collector, distinct offices, 30 Cal. 684.

People v. Macomb Co., 3 Mich. 475. Cited, Mandamus, to enforce ministerial duty, 41 Cal. 77.

People v. Maguire, 26 Cal. 635. Cited, Appeal in Criminal Case, statement when required, 37 Cal. 457.

People v. Mahoney, 18 Cal. 180. Approved, Change of place of trial insufficient grounds for, in criminal cases, 24 Cal. 35; 28 Cal. 495; 3 Nev. 434. Cited, Juror and Jury, challenge for implied bias, 27 Cal. 512. Commented on, 3 Nev. 460.

People v. Manhattan Co., 9 Wend. 351. Cited, Corporation, due organization of, not subject to collateral inquiry, 22 Cal. 441.

People v. March, 6 Cal. 543; S. C. Cal. Sup. Ct. 1855. Denied, Criminal Procedure, that defendant waive objection to incompetency of juror, 6 Cal. 411. Approved, Defendant may be tried anew on reversal of former judgment, 28 Cal. 461; effect of general verdict of guilty, 1 Colorado, 135.

People v. Marin Co., 10 Cal. 344. Cited, Supervisors, powers and duties of, 7 Nev. 397; judgments and orders of board, how renewable, 23 Cal. 303; approval or disapproval of bonds, 25 Cal. 97, 99; 29 Cal. 435; on appeal by, no bonds necessary, 32 Cal. 656.

People v. Mariposa Co., 31 Cal. 196. Cited, Taxation, insufficient description in assessment, 39 Cal. 673.

People v. Martin, 6 Cal. 477. Approved, Appeal in Criminal Case, defendant not absolutely concluded by failure of settlement of statement within time, 14 Cal. 437. Cited, Presumption as to regularity of proceedings of courts of general jurisdiction, 17 Cal. 371.

People v. Martin, 12 Cal. 409. Approved, Election, proclamation necessary in cases of special elections, 14 Cal. 187.

People v. Martin, 32 Cal. 91. Cited, Indictment, sufficiency of, 34 Cal. 663; Appeal in Criminal Case, assignment of errors, practice, 40 Cal. 287; report of evidence no part of bill of exceptions, 42 Cal. 538.

People v. Mather, 4 Wend. 229. Doubted, Juror and Jury, disqualification of juror, 1 Cal. 384; 6 Ind. 171. Rule restricted, Witness, impeachment of, 27 Cal. 635.

People v. Mauran, 5 Denio, 389. Cited, Ejectment, when action will lie, 38 Cal. 572.

People v. May, 3 Mich. 598. Disapproved, District Attorney, eligibility to office, 32 Cal. 300.

People v. Mayhew, 26 Cal. 655. Cited, Judicial Sale, lien of purchaser, 30 Cal. 137; Legal Tender, constitutionality of legal tender act, 38 Cal. 254.

People v. Mayor, etc., of Brooklyn, 4 N. Y. 419. Approved, Taxation, apportionment of tax, power of legislature, 12 Cal. 84, 85; 13 Cal. 353, 355; power of legislature to authorize local subscription to railroad stock, 13 Cal. 188; to authorize assessment for street improvement, 28 Cal. 358, 367, 372; and to apportion the assessment, 31 Cal. 677, 689; 32 Cal. 558; distinction in exercise of power of taxation and right of eminent domain, 28 Cal. 351; 2 Black, 513; Apportionment of assessment on condemnation of land, 31 Cal. 374.

People v. Mayor, etc., of Brooklyn, 6 Barb. 209. Cited, Street Improvements, apportionment of expense, 27 Cal. 620, 624.

People v. Mayor, etc., of N. Y., 10 Wend. 395. Cited, Mandamus, will not lie when there is a legal remedy, 3 Cal. 172, 173.

People v. Mayor, etc. of N. Y., 25 Wend. 680. Cited, Mandamus, will not lie where there is a legal remedy, 3 Cal. 173; Legislature, power over local taxation and appropriation, 13 Cal. 355. Denied, Supervisors, duty of, when not matter of discretion, 21 Cal. 699.

People v. Mayor, etc., of N. Y., 5 Barb. 45. Cited, Certiorari, lies to review judicial acts of municipal corporation, 16 Cal. 209.

People v. Mayor, etc., of N. Y., 10 Abb. Pr. 111. Cited, Receiver, appointment of, 26 Cal. 453.

People v. Mayor, etc., of N. Y., 2 Hill, 12. Approved, Certiorari, allowance of writ in judicial discretion, 42 Cal. 255.

People v. Mayor, etc., of N. Y., 3 Johns. Cas. 79. Approved, Office, remedy for intrusion into office, 3 Cal. 176.

People v. McCann, 16 N. Y. 58. Cited, Criminal Procedure, insanity, degree of proof required, 24 Cal. 237.

People v. McCauley, 1 Cal. 379. Cited, Instructions, to be given with reference to the facts proved, 1 Cal. 405; 30 Cal. 207; 39 Cal. 691; Juror and Jury, challenge for implied bias, 3 Nev. 460. Commented on, Judicial Districts, legislature may authorize judge of one district to hold court in another, 2 Cal. 207.

People v. McCreery, 34 Cal. 432. Approved, Taxation, statutes exempting private property from taxation are unconstitutional, 35 Cal. 678; so as to possessory claims to public lands, 37 Cal. 55; State property not taxable, 36 Cal. 222. Commented on, Double Taxation, 38 Cal. 464. Approved, Tax Deed, when void, 38 Cal. 682; 4 Nev. 335; Power of legislature over local taxation and appropriation, 41 Cal. 530.

People v. McCumber, 18 N. Y. 315. Cited, Pleading, sham answer, what constitutes, 18 Cal. 388; 32 Cal. 573; 34 Cal. 161; 35 Cal. 646.

People v. McEwen, 23 Cal. 54. Approved, Redemption, by part owner cannot be effected by payment of proportionate part of judgment, 23 Cal. 596.

People v. McGee, 1 Denio, 21. Cited, Evidence, admission of hearsay evidence erroneous, 21 Cal. 265.

People v. McHatton, 7 Ill. 638. Cited, Surety, in specialty, when discharged by extension of time, 10 Cal. 426.

People v. McLeod, 1 Hill, 377. Cited, Criminal Procedure, admission to bail, 19 Cal. 544.

People v. McMakin, 8 Cal. 547. Cited, Instructions, to accord with proof of facts, 10 Cal. 87.

People v. McNair, 21 Wend. 608. Commented on, Witness, competency of infant, practice, 10 Cal. 67.

People v. McNealy, 17 Cal. 332. Commented on, Indictment, when misnomer in, is fatal, 35 Cal. 114.

People v. Haws, 21 How. Pr. 178. Cited, County, services performed for benefit of, apportionment of expense, 41 Cal. 532.

People v. Mead, 24 N. Y. 114. Cited, Mandamus, cannot issue to control discretionary power of supervisors, 41 Cal. 77.

People v. Mellon, 40 Cal. 654. Approved, Criminal Procedure, offense committed partly in two counties may be tried in either, 8 Nev. 212.

People v. Mier, 24 Cal. 61. Approved, Jurisdiction, concurrent jurisdiction in action to collect taxes, 28 Cal. 328; 34 Cal. 580. Distinguished, 38 Cal. 394, 395; in actions to abate nuisance, 30 Cal. 581. Cited, Pleading, when prayer in complaint is significant, 37 Cal. 304; Judgment, of justice's court, in suit for taxes, 31 Cal. 221.

People v. Michigan S. R. R. Co., 3 Mich. 496. Cited, Constitutional Construction, compensation for condemnation of land, 31 Cal. 554, 559.

People v. Milgate, 5 Cal. 127. Approved, Criminal Procedure, instructions as to character of defendant properly refused, 6 Cal. 217; Evidence, degree of proof relatively necessary to establish a fact for or against defendant, 6 Cal. 410; 24 Cal. 236; 8 Nev. 301; Malice, implied from acts, 43 N. H. 233.

People v. Miller, 12 Cal. 292. Cited, Criminal Procedure, defense of statute of limitations, 19 Gratt. 818.

People v. Mizner, 7 Cal. 519. Commented on, Constitutional Construction, restriction on power of governor to fill vacancy in office, 8 Cal. 15. Approved, 10 Cal. 7; Id. 46; 28 Cal. 392. Commented on, 37 Cal. 618, 619, 621, 622, 625; Id. 642, 647, 649. Cited, 3 Or. 535; 13 Flor. 18.

People v. Moore, 8 Cal. 90. Cited, Criminal Procedure, when erroneous ruling not a sufficient ground for new trial, 8 Cal. 441; Murder in first degree, what constitutes, 17 Cal. 399.

People v. Moore, 29 Cal. 427. Cited, Jurisdiction, concurrent in actions to abate nuisance, 30 Cal. 577.

People v. Morrill, 26 Cal. 336. Cited, Parties, in equitable actions, 31 Cal. 427; State Lands, "tide lands" defined, 32 Cal. 363; swamp and overflowed lands, Id. 364; 40 Cal. 473; Injunction, lies to restrain injury to State lands, 32 Cal. 595; Pleading demurrer does not lie to prayer of complaint, 38 Cal. 234.

People v. Morris, 13 Wend. 325. Cited, Legislature, power of taxation, apportionment of assessment, 13 Cal. 355; power over property of municipal corporations, 15 Cal. 612. Commented on, Municipal Corporations, powers of, 16 Cal. 234; legislative discretion on apportionment of expense, on opening new streets, 41 Cal. 532.

People v. Morrison, 22 Cal. 74. Cited, Taxation, public domain not liable, 30 Cal. 655. Distinguished, Possessory claim to public lands liable to assessment, 30 Cal. 657. Commented on, 1 Nev. 107.

People v. Morrison, 1 Park. Cr. Rep. 625. Commented on, Criminal Procedure, former conviction or acquittal as a defense, 28 Cal. 464.

People v. Mott, 3 Cal. 502. Cited, Office, term of, appointment to fill vacancy, 7 Cal. 523; 13 Flor. 18. Cited in dissenting opinion of Field, J., Vacancy created by failure to qualify, 10 Cal. 49. Distinguished, 37 Cal. 620.

People v. Mullins, 10 Cal. 20. Cited, Indictment, entitling, sufficient, 14 Cal. 572.

People v. Murray, 8 Cal. 519. Statutes distinguished, Crimes and Punishments, burglary, 28 Cal. 218; 34 Cal. 245.

People v. Murray, 10 Cal. 309. Cited, Indictment, sufficiency of, 25 Cal. 533; 32 Cal. 38; 49 N. H. 405. Commented on, Criminal Procedure, reputation of deceased, evidence of, 41 Cal. 644; 46 Miss. 708; 2 Kan. 430.

People v. Murray, 15 Cal. 221. Approved, Powers, time prescribed for performance of public duty, not the essence of the authority, 30 Cal. 526.

People v. Murray, 41 Cal. 66. Cited, Criminal Procedure, evidence necessary to conviction for crime, 42 Cal. 540.

People v. Murray, 5 Hill, 468. Cited, Statutory Construction, effect of repeal, 4 Cal. 168.

People v. Myers, 20 Cal. 518. Commented on, Criminal Procedure, burden of proof of insanity, 24 Cal. 236. Cited, 32 Iowa, 52; 20 Gratt. 875.

People v. Myers, 20 Cal. 76. Approved, Indictment, allegation of ownership of property essential, 41 Cal. 237.

People v. Naglee, 1 Cal. 232. Approved, Taxation, constitutionality of State license laws, 4 Cal. 52; 20 Cal. 584; 28 Cal. 360; 34 Cal. 448, 450.

People v. Nearing, 27 N. Y. 306. Commented on, Legislature, powers of, in eminent domain and taxation, 31 Cal. 674.

People v. Nevada, 6 Cal. 144. Cited, Supervisors, judicial powers cannot be conferred on, 24 Cal. 127. Approved, 9 Cal. 599; 30 Id. 167.

People v. Nichol, 34 Cal. 211. Cited, Criminal Procedure, charge as to murder, degrees of, 39 Cal. 697; 25 Ark. 415.

People v. Niles, 35 Cal. 282. Approved, Taxation, money at interest, where taxable, 38 Cal. 467; personal property transiently in county, 39 Cal. 115.

People v. Norton, 16 Cal. 436. Cited, Mandamus, when it lies, 30 Cal. 579.

People v. Norton, 9 N. Y. 176. Cited, guardian, cannot dispute legality of his appointment, 32 Cal. 120.

People v. Nugent, 4 Cal. 341. Followed, same term, Indictment, in People v. Packer, and People v. Mayo (not reported.) Commented on, Negative qualification, as "want of provocation," not an essential averment, 6 Cal. 562. Cited, 30 Cal. 218; 8 Nev. 321.

People v. O'Connell, 23 Cal. 281. Cited, Appeal, orders setting aside judgment by default, in discretion, 29 Cal. 424; when order will be reversed, 41 Cal. 21.

People v. O'Hara, Cal. Sup. Ct. Jan. T. 1859 (not reported.) Approved, Criminal Procedure, charge of court to be in writing, 12 Cal. 347.

People v. Olcott, 2 Johns. Cas. 301. Cited, Criminal Procedure, discharge of jury when not an acquittal, 27 Cal. 399. Denied as to misdemeanors, 26 Ala. 141.

People v. Olds, 3 Cal. 167. Cited, Mandamus, what writ will direct, 7 Cal. 183; title to office cannot be t ed by, 23 Cal. 320.

People v. Olivera, 7 Cal. 403. Cited, Indictment, sufficiency of, 25 Cal. 533; 32 Cal. 38.

People v. Olwell, 28 Cal. 456. Cited, New Trial, on reversal on appeal in criminal case, 33 Iowa, 368.

People v. Oulton, 28 Cal. 44. Approved, Office, right of incumbent to hold over, 28 Cal. 387, 389, 390; 37 Cal. 623; Id. 643, 646. Cited, 8 Nev. 109. Commented on, 46 N. Y. 65; Salary of Office, an incident to the title, 37 Cal. 195; 5 Nev. 250.

People v. Pacheco, 27 Cal. 175. Cited, Constitutionality of Statute, funding acts, 28 Cal. 395. Denied, that act did not create a debt, Deady, 498; Legislature, power of taxation and appropriation, 28 Cal. 355; 30 Cal. 439.

People v. Pacheco, 29 Cal. 210. Commented on and limited, Mandamus, party to action, 36 Cal. 605, 606. Cited, When People not proper party in *certiorari*, 40 Cal. 480.

People v. Park, 23 Cal. 138. Commented on, Taxation, choses in action, where assessable, 25 Cal. 603. Cited, 29 Cal. 546; 38 Cal. 467; 2 Or. 330.

People v. Parker, 37 Cal. 639. Cited, Constitutional Construction, restriction of appointing power of governor, 37 Cal. 621. Approved, in dissenting opinion of Crockett, J., Id. 627, 630.

People v. Parsons, 6 Cal. 487. Disapproved, Indictment, sufficiency of, under statute, 7 Cal. 404. Cited, 9 Cal. 236; Id. 584; 25 Cal. 533; 32 Cal. 38.

People v. Payne, 8 Cal. 340. Cited, Trespass, owner of property may repel force by force, 10 Cal. 87. Approved, Criminal Procedure, oral instructions without consent erroneous, 10 Cal. 196; 14 Cal. 438; 26 Cal. 79; 37 Cal. 276; 1 Nev. 36.

People v. Peck, 11 Wend. 604. Commented on, Election, irregularities which will not invalidate, 11 Cal. 57. Cited, Powers, time of performance not of essence of authority to act under a power, 30 Cal. 527.

People v. Peterson, 9 Cal. 313. Cited, Indictment, sufficiency of, for larceny by bailee, 19 Cal. 601.

People v. Phœnix, 6 Cal. 92. Cited, Statutory Construction, statutes to be construed together, general provisions controlled by special, 11 Cal. 339.

People v. Pico, 20 Cal. 595. Approved, Taxation, insufficiency of description of real estate in assessment, 25 Cal. 302, 305; 31 Cal. 199. Cited, 39 Cal. 673.

People v. Pinckney, 32 N. Y. 377. Cited, Municipal Corporations, powers of, 41 Cal. 532.

People v. Placerville & S. V. R.R. Co., 34 Cal. 656. Cited, Taxation, assessment void for want of legal qualification of assessor, 39 Cal. 359.

People v. Plummer, 9 Cal. 298. Disapproved, Criminal Procedure, objections to competency of juror taken after verdict as ground for motion for new trial, 43 Cal. 146. Cited, Postponement of consideration of motion for change of venue, 3 Nev. 461. Review on appeal and granting new trial, jurisdiction, 6 Nev. 349.

People v. Poggi, 19 Cal. 600. Cited, Indictment against bailee for larceny, 23 Cal. 280; 25 Cal. 533.

People v. Porter, 6 Cal. 26. Approved, Election, proclamation and notice as to special elections, necessary to validity, 11 Cal. 63, 66; 12 Cal. 411; 14 Cal. 187. Criticised, right of resignation of office, 3 Nev. 573.

People v. Potter, 35 Cal. 110. Cited, Corporation, irregularities in formation of, not to invalidate, 39 Cal. 514.

People v. Pratt, 28 Cal. 166. Cited, Mandamus, what writ will direct, 28 Cal. 641; 35 Cal. 214; 37 Cal. 534; Judicial discretion not reviewable on mandamus, 39 Cal. 411. Commented on, Action, dismissal of, in judicial discretion, 29 Cal. 266.

People v. Provines, 34 Cal. 520. Cited, Officers, judicial officers may be empowered to perform ministerial duties, 40 Cal. 346.

People v. Purdy, 2 Hill, 31. Reversed, 4 Hill, 385. Commented on, Statute, passage of, evidence on impeachment of validity, 2 Cal. 169; 30 Cal. 259, 260, 261, 263, 268; 32 Miss. 688; 35 Ill. 137.

People v. Quesenberry, 3 Stewt. & P. 308. Cited, Juror and Jury, challenge of juror, 1 Cal. 385; Evidence, of character of deceased, 10 Cal. 310.

People v. Quincy, 8 Cal. 89. Cited, Trial, continuance, what showing required, 23 Cal. 158; 24 Cal. 38.

People v. Quinn, 18 Cal. 122. Cited, Statutory Construction, effect of repeal of criminal statute, 19 Cal. 550, note.

People v. Ramirez, 13 Cal. 172. Approved, Criminal Procedure, refusal of charge by court, practice, 17 Cal. 148.

People v. Ransom, 4 Denio, 145. Affirmed, 2 N. Y. 490. Cited, Mandamus, rules of pleading in, 27 Cal. 672, 684. Commented on, Redemption, execution of sheriff's deed to redemptioner, 37 Cal. 130.

People v. Ransom, 7 Wend. 417. Cited, New Trial, when granted on grounds of irregularity, 9 Cal. 537; 49 N. H. 497.

People v. Raymond, 34 Cal. 495. Statute distinguished, Constitutionality of statutes regulating commerce, 42 Cal. 585.

People v. Rector, 19 Wend. 579. Cited, Witness, impeachment of, rule of examination, 27 Cal. 635.

People v. Reed, 11 Wend. 157. Cited, Trespass, right to resist intrusion, 28 Cal. 192.

People v. Reid, 6 Cal. 289. Commented on, Office, constitutional construction, provision for holding over construed, 8 Cal. 11. Cited, 10 Cal. 49. Disapproved, 37 Cal. 616, 618, 619, 620, 621, 625, 627. Commented on, Vacancy in office, 37 Cal. 642. Distinguished, Power to fill, 28 Cal. 392. Cited, Rule of constitutional construction, 22 Cal. 312.

People v. Reinhart, 39 Cal. 449. Approved, Witness, oral evidence not competent to prove previous conviction to discredit witness, 39 Cal. 617; Id. 698.

People v. Renfrow, 41 Cal. 37. Cited, Criminal Procedure, practice, 6 Nev. 352.

People v. Rensselaer Ins. Co., 38 Barb. 323. Cited, Corporation, condition precedent to formation of railroad corporation, 42 Cal. 209.

People v. Reynolds, 16 Cal. 128. Approved, Juror and Jury, law and practice on challenge for bias in criminal cases, 17 Cal. 146; 22 Cal. 351; 27 Cal. 512; 37 Cal. 259; Id. 279; 41 Cal. 38; 3 Nev. 429; Id. 460; as to impanneling jury, 37 Cal. 690. Cited, 4 Nev. 275.

People v. Reynolds, 28 Cal. 111. Approved, Taxation, board of equalization, jurisdiction, 39 Cal. 673.

People v. Reynolds, 10 Ill. 1. Approved, Legislature, may delegate certain powers, 8 Cal. 383.

People v. Richardson, 4 Cow. 97. Cited, Office, testing right to, under common law, 1 Cal. 343; nature of proceeding by *quo warranto*, Id. 344.

People v. Roberts, 6 Cal. 214. Cited, Instructions to be framed with reference to the evidence, 6 Cal. 547. Approved, Indictment, sufficiency of presentment by grand jury, 8 Cal. 439. Cited, 20 Cal. 148; Juror and Jury, objections when to be taken to pannel, 24 Cal. 234; Instructions to be given with reference to the evidence, 39 Cal. 691.

People v. Robinson, 17 Cal. 363. Cited, County Courts, intendments in favor of their jurisdiction in criminal cases, 27 Cal. 67.

People v. Rodriguez, 10 Cal. 50. Cited, Grand Jury, insufficient objections to pannel, 15 Cal. 329. Distinguished, 3 Nev. 76.

People v. Romero, 18 Cal. 89. Approved, Mandamus, conditions precedent, what must be averred, 22 Cal. 75. Cited, 37 Cal. 363; 23 Wis. 429; Juror and Jury, objections to pannel when to be taken, 24 Cal. 234; 28 Cal. 469.

People v. Runkle, 8 John. 464; S. C. 9 John. 147. Cited, Statutory Construction, 11 Cal. 57; Forcible Entry and Detainer, what constitutes possession, 16 Cal. 109. Commented on, Office, right to hold over, 28 Cal. 53, 54.

People v. Sanchez, 24 Cal. 17. Cited, Murder, degrees of, defined, 25 Cal. 365; 1 Colorado, 446; Instructions to be given with reference to facts proved, 30 Cal. 207; 39 Cal. 691. Commented on, Matters of law as to degrees of murder, 36 Cal. 265; 1 Colorado, 446. Cited, 39 Cal. 697; adjournment of court for failure of judge to appear, 8 Nev. 241; 7 Kan. 386.

People v. Sanderson, 30 Cal. 160. Disapproved, Constitutional Construction, legislature may invest judicial officer with other than judicial functions, 34 Cal. 529, 532, 539.

People v. San Francisco, 4 Cal. 127. Commented on, Statutory Construction, statutes not to be construed retrospectively, McAll. 518. See People v. Hays.

People v. San Francisco, 11 Cal. 206. Cited, Legislature, power over affairs and property of municipal corporations, 17 Cal. 461; 41 Cal. 530.

People v. San Francisco, 21 Cal. 668. Cited, Mandamus, to supervisors to enforce performance of duty, 28 Cal. 431; 36 Cal. 605; 41 Cal. 77.

People v. San Francisco, 27 Cal. 655. Cited, Estoppel, former judgment as an estoppel, *res adjudicata,* 36 Cal. 38; Municipal Corporations, subscription to stock in railroads, 7 Kan. 506.

People v. San Francisco, 28 Cal. 429. Cited, Mandamus, when will issue to supervisors to enforce official duty, 41 Cal. 77.

People v. San Francisco, 36 Cal. 595. Cited, Legislature, power of, over affairs and property of municipal corporations, 42 Cal. 557, 558.

People v. San Francisco Savings Union, 31 Cal. 132. Commented on, Taxation, limitation of power of legislature to pass curative acts to validate assessments, 34 Cal. 437; assessment roll conclusive as to want of valuation, Id. 575; assessment void for want of valuation, 38 Cal. 224; 8 Nev. 25.

People v. San Joaquin Co., 28 Cal. 228. Cited, Mandamus, to supervisors to enforce performance of duty, 36 Cal. 604.

People v. Sassovich, 29 Cal. 480. Approved, Office, title to, cannot be questioned collaterally, 34 Cal. 523; 40 Cal. 656.

People v. Saviers, 14 Cal. 29. Cited, Indictment, sufficiency of, 25 Cal. 533; 32 Cal. 38.

People v. Scannel, 7 Cal. 432. Commented on, Official Bonds, approval of, 7 Cal. 394. Approved, Proceedings essential to discharge of sureties, 29 Cal. 433, 434.

People v. Schoharie C. P., 2 Wend. 260. Cited, Appeal, restitution on reversal, 14 Cal. 678.

People v. Schuyler, 4 N. Y. 173. Approved, Trespass, liability of sheriff on official bond, 14 Cal. 197.

People v. Schwartz, 32 Cal. 160. Cited, Indictment, company name in, 36 Cal. 248. Approved, Statement of acts in indictment against accessory, 40 Cal. 142.

People v. Seaman, 5 Denio, 409. Cited, Election, validity of, not affected by mere delinquency of inspector, 26 Cal. 214.

People v. Sears, 18 Cal. 635. Cited, Instruction to be submitted under rules of court, 29 Cal. 562; 32 Cal. 289.

People v. Senter, 28 Cal. 502. Affirmed on principle of *stare decisis*, Probate Act, not retroactive, 33 Cal. 424; jurisdiction over estates prior to passage of act, 37 Cal. 89, 91.

People v. Sexton, 24 Cal. 78. Approved, Mandamus to judicial tribunal, what writ will direct, 28 Cal. 169; Id. 641; when will not issue, 29 Cal. 309, 214.

People v. Seymour, 16 Cal. 331. Cited, Taxation, personal liability in action for delinquent tax, 18 Cal. 403; 39 Cal. 115. Commented on, 23 Cal. 116; sufficiency of complaint in action, 23 Cal. 184. Explained, Obligation and liability created by taxation, 20 Cal. 351; validity of statutes providing for joint assessments, 23 Cal. 58; legislative power on apportionment of assessments, 15 Wis. 463; 19 Wis. 516; Constitutionality of Statute, 29 Iowa, 415.

People v. Shall, 9 Cow. 778. Cited, Indictment for forgery, insufficiency of, 35 Cal. 507.

People v. Shear, 7 Cal. 139. Cited, Jurisdiction of Supreme Court, in criminal cases, 21 Cal. 169; 30 Cal. 101; 35 Cal. 390.

People v. Shearer, 30 Cal. 645 Approved, Taxation, preemption claim to public lands, liable to taxation, 31 Cal. 148; Id. 211; 37 Cal. 54. Cited, Description of lands held by Mexican grant sufficient in assessment, 33 Cal. 154; Public Lands, rights acquired by location of land warrant, 31 Cal. 268; 33 Cal. 262; 1 Saw. 621; 9 Wall. 105. Commented on, Rights of preëmptioner, lands reserved from sale, 37 Cal. 490, 491, 495, 502, 504; taxes payable in coin, 2 Or. 140.

People v. Sheriff of N. Y., 7 Abb. Pr. 96. Cited, Habeas Corpus, functions of writ, 35 Cal. 101.

People v. Shirley, 18 Cal. 121. Cited, Surety on Bond, justification, no part of contract, 37 Cal. 273. Commented on, 38 Cal. 603.

People v. Shoonmaker, 19 Barb. 657. Commented on, Special Cases, what are, 15 Cal. 92.

People v. Shotwell, 27 Cal. 394. Cited, Indictment, sufficiency of, for forgery, 28 Cal. 513; 31 Cal. 461. Approved, Objections, when waived by failure to demur, 29 Cal. 626; 32 Cal. 62; 35 Cal. 118.

People v. Shuler, 28 Cal. 490. Cited, Criminal Procedure, circumstantial evidence, 30 Cal. 154.

People v. Skidmore, 17 Cal. 261. Referred to, same case, 27 Cal. 291, 292.

People v. Smith, 1 Cal. 9. Cited, Judicial notice taken of geographical divisions, 39 Cal. 40.

People v. Smyth, 28 Cal. 21. Cited, Salary of Office, an incident to the title, 28 Cal. 51; 37 Cal. 195; 53 Ill. 432. Denied, 20 Mich. 183; but see opinion of Cooley, J., Id. 192. Cited as inapplicable, 28 Cal. 58.

People v. Sneath, 28 Cal. 615. Cited, Taxation, valid assessment necessary to create liability, 30 Cal. 538; 31 Cal. 482; 32 Cal. 332; sufficient description of personal property, 34 Cal. 441.

People v. Squires, 14 Cal. 12. Cited, Supervisors, power to fill vacancies in office, 14 Cal. 103; Legislature, power over legislative offices, 22 Cal. 319; 27 Cal. 475; over fees and salaries, 26 Cal. 118.

People v. Stevens, 5 Hill, 616. Commented on, Mandamus, will not lie to try right to office, 3 Cal. 171, 172, 176; Office, action contesting right to, 7 Cal. 394; right to office, Id. 439, 442.

People v. Steventon, 9 Cal. 273. Approved, Indictment, for murder, sufficiency of, 10 Cal. 311; Id. 314; 27 Cal. 510; 34 Cal. 200; 3 Nev. 465.

People v. Stewart, 7 Cal. 140. Cited, Juror and Jury, competency of juror, 8 Cal. 361.

People v. Stillman, 7 Cal. 117. Commented on, Criminal Procedure, review of non-appealable orders, 8 Cal. 57; 24 Cal. 84.

People v. Stone, 16 Cal. 369. Cited, Larceny, of property by bailor, 34 Cal. 672.

People v. Stonecifer, 6 Cal. 405. Cited, Appeal, affidavits not included in bill of exceptions no part of record, 10 Cal. 86; 32 Cal. 92; Criminal Procedure, preponderating proof establishes fact in defendant's favor, 24 Cal. 236; burden of proof as to provocation on defendant, 20 Iowa, 116; 42 N. Y. 7.

People v. Stout, 23 Barb. 339. Cited, Mandamus, to executive officer to compel issuance of warrants, 16 Cal. 45.

People v. Stratton, 25 Cal. 242. Approved, State Lands, who may attack State patent, 28 Cal. 101; Patent, when subject to collateral attack, 32 Cal. 362; 38 Cal. 83.

People v. Stratton, 28 Cal. 382. Cited, Office, vacancy in, when it ensues, 37 Cal. 643, 646; 13 Flor. 20.

People v. Strong, 30 Cal. 151. Cited, Instructions in Criminal Cases, reasonable doubt, 32 Cal. 435.

People v. Stuart, 4 Cal. 218. Approved, Juror and Jury, insufficient ground of challenge to pannel, 21 Cal. 403; Judgment in Criminal Case, validity of, 31 Cal. 627; 43 Ala. 56.

People v. Supervisors of Greene, 12 Barb. 217. Commented on, Elections, power of supervisors, 24 Cal. 453, 454; Mandamus, when writ will lie, 28 Cal. 432.

People v. Supervisors of New York, 10 Abb. Pr. 233. Affirmed, 21 How. Pr. 288. Commented on, Mandamus, relief by, 27 Cal. 683.

People v. Supervisors of New York, 21 How. Pr. 322. Cited, Mandamus, when it lies, 28 Cal. 432.

People v. Supervisors of Orange, 17 N. Y. 235. Cited, Statutory Constructions, intendments in favor of validity, 25 Cal. 569.

People v. Supervisors of Richmond Co., 20 N. Y. 253. Cited, Mandamus, province of writ, 41 Cal. 77.

People v. Swift, 31 Cal. 26. Distinguished, Contract, ratification of, by municipal corporation, 36 Cal. 245. Cited, 8 Nev. 188.

People v. Symonds, 22 Cal. 348. Approved, Criminal Procedure, new trial not granted for irregularities where no injury is shown, 23 Cal. 633; insufficient grounds for new trial, 29 Cal. 262; for surprise, Id. 564.

People v. Taylor, 36 Cal. 255. Cited, Evidence, on collateral issues, not admissible, 36 Cal. 580.

People v. Taylor, 3 Denio, 91. Cited, Indictment, matters of description in, 36 Cal. 247.

People v. Templeton, 12 Cal. 394. Commented on, Office, constitutional term of, 14 Cal. 187.

People v. Tetherow, 40 Cal. 286. Followed in People v. Parker, Nos. 2356 and 2366; People v. Poole, Nos. 2358 and 2359, same term. Approved, Appeal, report of evidence forms no part of bill of exceptions, 42 Cal. 539.

People v. Thompson, 4 Cal. 238. Approved, Indictment may be transferred to district court without indorsement by clerk of court of sessions, 4 Cal. 226; 13 Flor. 655. Cited, Trial, what showing required on application for continuance, 23 Cal. 158; 24 Cal. 38; 38 Cal. 188.

People v. Thompson, 28 Cal. 214. Cited, Indictment, containing several counts, 28 Cal. 513; 41 Cal. 649; 6 Nev. 325; Evidence, presumptions from identity of name, 29 Cal. 520; Appeal, in criminal case, record made up by bill of exceptions, 32 Cal. 92; 42 Cal. 538; settlement of bill of exceptions, 34 Cal. 310; 37 Cal. 275; assignment of errors, 40 Cal. 287.

People v. Thompson, 25 Barb. 73. Cited, Mandamus lies, where there is no legal remedy, 20 Cal. 75.

People v. Thurston, 5 Cal. 69. Cited, Indictment, when void, 18 Iowa, 442.

People v. Tibbets, 4 Cow. 384. Cited, Statutory Construction, statutes not to have retrospective effect, 4 Cal. 136; 28 Cal. 506.

People v. Tieman, 30 Barb. 193; S. C. 8 Abb. Pr. 359. Cited, Office, salary incident to title of office, 28 Cal. 25. Distinguished, Holding over on expiration of term, Id. 53–55.

People v. Tillinghast, 10 Cal. 585. Cited, San Francisco, duty of treasurer under provisions of funding act, 14 Cal. 11, 12; 19 Cal. 194. See Peopfe v. Bond.

People v. Tilton, 37 Cal. 614. Cited, Office, vacancy in, and appointment to fill the same, 3 Or. 535; 13 Flor. 18.

People v. Took Chew, 6 Cal. 636. Cited, Instructions, rules of practice, 32 Cal. 289.

People v. Todd, 23 Cal. 181. Cited, Taxation, enforcement of tax, 19 Wis. 517.

People v. Torres, 38 Cal. 141. Cited, Appeal in Criminal Cases, presumptions as to instructions where no bill of exceptions is filed, 29 Wis. 169.

People v. Town of Nevada, 6 Cal. 143. Cited, Municipal Corporation, incorporation act void, 9 Cal. 599; 24 Cal. 127; 30 Cal. 167.

People v. Townsley, 39 Cal. 405. Followed, Larceny, indictment for, 39 Cal. 407.

People v. Trim, 37 Cal. 274; S. C. 39 Cal. 75. Approved, Indictment of accessory, 40 Cal. 141; 41 Cal. 431. Cited, Appeal, report of evidence forms no part of bill of exceptions, 42 Cal. 539.

People v. Trinity Church, 22 N. Y. 44. Cited, Pleading, bar of statute of limitations waived by failure to plead, 31 Cal. 46.

People v. Troy House Co , 44 Barb. 634. Cited, Railroad, condition precedent in formation of corporation, 42 Cal. 209.

People v. Turner, 1 Cal. 143. Approved, Mandamus, jurisdiction of supreme court, 1 Cal. 153; Id. 348; 8 Nev. 250. Distinguished, Relief obtainable on, 1 Cal. 156; when writ will not issue, 14 Cal. 642. Commented on, Attorney and Counsel, mandamus to restore rights of, 20 Cal. 430; 12 Flor. 285; 7 Wall. 379. Cited, Contempt, order must show facts, 25 Ala. 88.

People v. Tyler, 35 Cal. 553; S. C. 36 Cal. 522. Cited, Witness, examination of party as, in criminal cases, 41 Cal. 431.

People v. Utica Ins. Co., 15 John. 358. Cited, Written Instruments, construction of, 29 Cal. 304.

People v. Vail, 20 Wend. 12. Cited, Election, not invalidated by mere official delinquency, 26 Cal. 214.

People v. Vanard, 6 Cal. 562. Approved, Verdict, assault with a deadly weapon not a felony, 9 Cal. 260; 40 Cal. 427. Cited, Verdict, conclusive as to grade of crime, 30 Cal. 218; Indictment, includes all lesser grades of offense charged, 8 Nev. 319, 321.

People v. Vance, 21 Cal. 400. Cited, Indictment, sufficiency of, 27 Cal. 501; 28 Cal. 208.

People v. Van Horne, 18 Wend. 518. Commented on, Office, when vacancy exists, 25 Cal. 99.

People v. Van Rensselaer, 9 N. Y. 291. Cited, Pleading, bar of statute waived by failure to plead, 31 Cal. 46.

People v. Van Santvoord, 9 Cow. 655. Disapproved, Criminal Procedure, lapse of time as a defense to action, 12 Cal. 295.

People v. Van Slyck, 4 Cow. 297. Cited, Election, not invalidated by mere official delinquency, 26 Cal. 214. Commented on, Canvassing votes, 30 Cal. 337.

People v. Vermilyea, 7 Cow. 108. Disapproved, Juror and Jury, disqualification of juror, 1 Cal. 384.

People v. Vice, 21 Cal. 344. Commented on, Indictment, allegation of ownership, 28 Cal. 494. Cited, 41 Cal. 237.

People v. Vick, 7 Cal. 165. Cited, Appeal, jurisdiction of supreme court in criminal cases, confined to felonies, 30 Cal. 101; 35 Cal. 390.

People v. Wallace, 9 Cal. 30. Followed, Indictment, for murder, requisites of, 9 Cal. 33. Approved and followed, 10 Cal. 335. Cited, 27 Cal. 509. Commented on, 3 Nev. 465.

People v. War, 20 Cal. 117. Cited, Appeal, jurisdiction of supreme court in criminal cases, 30 Cal. 101.

People v. Washington, 36 Cal. 658. Disapproved, Evidence, amendment to federal constitution not in conflict with power of State legislature, 40 Cal. 215. See Id. 221.

People v. Webb, 38 Cal. 467. Commented on, Discharge of jury as an acquittal, 41 Cal. 215.

People v. Weller, 11 Cal. 49. Followed, Office, appointment to fill vacancy, 11 Cal. 339. Approved, Election, proclamation by governor of special election essential, 14 Cal. 187; 12 Cal. 411; 1 Nev. 80. Cited, Statutory provisions directory, 26 Wis. 392.

People v. Weller, 11 Cal. 77. Approved, Constitutional Construction, term of office, 12 Cal. 391; 3 Or. 538; rule of judicial construction, 13 Cal. 182; 22 Cal. 322.

People v. Wells, 2 Cal. 198. Approved, Office, vacancy in, when it exists, 7 Cal. 523; 10 Cal. 48; 13 Flor. 21.

People v. Weston, 28 Cal. 639. Cited, Mandamus will not lie to compel a court to reinstate a case, 35 Cal. 214;

36 Cal. 287; or to control judicial discretion, 37 Cal. 534; what writ will direct, 4 Nev. 447.

People v. White, 34 Cal. 183. Distinguished, Counterfeiting, jurisdiction of State courts, 38 Cal. 150.

People v. White, 11 Ill. 341. Cited, Surety, on note, not discharged by mere delay, 10 Cal. 342.

People v. White, 11 Barb. 26. Cited, Railroad, takes only an easement in land condemned, 19 Cal. 596.

People v. White, 22 Wend. 167. Reversed, 24 Wend. 520. Commented on, Court of Sessions, composition of court, 5 Cal. 105. Cited, Office, title to, cannot be collaterally questioned, 29 Cal. 485.

People v. Whiteside, 23 Wend. 9. Cited, Election, notice of special election essential, 11 Cal. 66.

People v. Whitman, 10 Cal. 38. Cited, Statutory Construction, presumption as to effects intended, 10 Cal. 191. Commented on, Election, votes cast for ineligible candidate not counted for next highest candidate, 13 Cal. 153. Cited, Office, constitutional term of, 3 Or. 535. Doubted, vacancy in, and power of governor to fill the same, 15 Cal. 62. Commented on, 37 Cal. 618-623; Id. 643, 647, 650.

People v. Whitman, 6 Cal. 659. Criticised, Constitutional Construction, computation of time on return of bill by governor, 8 Cal. 415. Cited, Mandamus, to controller to draw warrant, 16 Cal. 47, 63; province of writ, 41 Cal. 77.

People v. Williams, 17 Cal. 142. Cited, Juror and Jury, bias, grounds of challenge, 27 Cal. 512; Evidence, confessions as, 30 Cal. 158; threats of deceased, 37 Cal. 687. Approved, Instructions, should not assume guilt, 6 Nev. 140. Distinguished, 1 Nev. 228.

People v. Williams, 24 Cal. 31. Approved, Criminal Procedure, insufficient grounds for change of venue, 28 Cal. 495. Cited, for continuance, what must be shown, 29 Cal. 563; 34 Cal. 663; 7 Nev. 156.

People v. Williams, 32 Cal. 280. Approved, Instructions, may be given twice to a given point, 32 Cal. 436; to be given in reference to evidence adduced, 39 Cal. 691.

People v. Williams, 35 Cal. 671. Cited, Indictment, for larceny, sufficiency of, 8 Nev. 269.

People v. Wolf, 16 Cal. 385. Cited, Recognizance, insufficient defense in action on, 18 Cal. 499; when responsibility of sureties attaches, 37 Cal. 273.

People v. Woods, 7 Cal. 579. Cited, Municipal Corporations, funding acts, construction of, 10 Cal. 570; 19 Wis. 472; power of municipal corporations, 21 Gratt. 617.

People v. Woppner, 14 Cal. 437. Approved, Appeal, in criminal cases, statute requiring statement directory, 14 Cal. 511; 1 Nev. 460. Cited, Criminal Procedure, oral charge without consent erroneous, 26 Cal. 79; 37 Cal. 276.

People v. Wright, 5 How. Pr. 23. Cited, Criminal Procedure, change of place of trial, 21 Cal. 265.

People v. Wyman, 15 Cal. 70. Commented on, Verdict, impeachment of, 25 Cal. 475; Evidence, declarations of defendant when part of *res gestæ*, 28 Cal. 470; confessions, 30 Cal. 158.

People v. Ybarra, 17 Cal. 166. Cited, Indictment, sufficiency of, 28 Cal. 211; 7 Nev. 384. Commented on, Instructions, in criminal cases, province of jury, 3 Nev. 447; Id. 482.

Peoria v. Kidder, 26 Ill. 351. Cited, Taxation, remedy by appeal to board in case of irregular assessment, 29 Cal. 87.

Pepper v. Dunlap, 9 Rob. 283. Commented on, Interest, legal interest under Mexican law, 2 Cal. 570. Cited, Appeal, effect of judgment of reversal, 20 Cal. 172.

Perine v. Dunn, 4 Johns. Ch. 140; S. C. 3 Johns. Ch. 508. Cited, Redemption from Mortgage, terms of decree in action, 34 Cal. 655. Commented on, 36 Cal. 56, 61.

Perkins v. Dyer, 6 Geo. 401. Cited, Guardian and Ward, appointment of guardian, 9 Cal. 592.

Perkins, Ex parte, 2 Cal. 424. Cited, Constitutional Construction, exclusion of slavery, 9 Cal. 169; validity of acts to enforce reclamation of slaves, 9 Ohio St. 187. Distinguished, Habeas Corpus, jurisdiction on, 28 Cal. 251. Cited, 27 Tex. 106; 32 Ill. 464; contra, review of order on, Id. 454.

Perkins, Ex parte, 18 Cal. 60. Cited, Contempt, proceedings on, 40 Ala. 168.

Perkins v. Gay, 3 Serg. & R. 331. Cited, Partition, division line, under parol agreement, 25 Cal. 631. Commented on, 4 Penn. St. 236.

Perkins v. Gilman, 8 Pick. 229. Cited, Covenant not to sue, no bar to action, 5 Cal. 502. Denied, 2 Mich. 415.

Perkins v. Hawkshaw, 2 Starkie, 239. Cited, Witness, privileged communications, 5 Cal. 451.

Perkins v. Lyman, 9 Mass. 522; S. C. 11 Mass. 76. Cited, Contract, in restraint of trade, when valid, 36 Cal. 358; damages on breach of, 6 Cal. 263.

Perkins v. N. Y. Central R. R. Co., 24 N. Y. 196. Commented on, Common Carriers, contract of, construed, 27 Cal. 44.

Perkins v. Portland, Saco and P. R. Co., 47 Me. 573. Approved, Common Carriers, liability of, on contract for transportation through, 31 Cal. 53. Cited, 48 N. H. 358.

Perkins v. Thornburgh, 10 Cal. 189. Cited, Claim and Delivery, verdict of sheriff's jury no defense, 28 Cal. 123.

Perkins v. Walker, 19 Vt. 147. Cited, Res Adjudicata, former judgment as an estoppel, 36 Cal. 37.

Perkins v. Wright, 3 Har. & McH. 324. Cited, Specific Performance, when lapse of time will defeat action, 10 Cal. 330.

Perlberg v. Gorham, 10 Cal. 120. Referred to, Trespass of Sheriff, in S. C. *sub nom.* Pelberg *v.* Gorham, 23 Cal. 350.

Perley v. Balch, 23 Pick. 285. Commented on, Contract, rescission of, for fraudulent representations, 29 Cal. 593.

Perre v. Castro, 14 Cal. 519. Commented on, Mortgage, tender after law day, 26 Cal. 544; 37 Cal. 226.

Perrin v. Blake, 4 Burr, 2579. Commented on, Will, construction of devise, 27 Cal. 443, 445; 2 How. 56; 26 Ind. 257; 29 Vt. 243; Stare Decisis, as a rule of property, 31 Cal. 402.

Perrine v. Cheeseman, 6 Halst. 174. Cited, Contract, time of performance may be waived by parol, 39 Cal. 175.

Perrine v. Chesapeake & Del. Can. Co., 9 How. 172. Cited, corporations, can exercise no powers other than those conferred by statute, 15 Cal. 624. Approved, 16 Cal. 236.

Perrine v. Striker, 7 Paige, 598. Cited, Witness, competency of, 9 Cal. 102.

Perry v. Ames, 26 Cal. 372. Approved, Jurisdiction, of district courts, 30 Cal. 246; Concurrent Jurisdiction, Id. 583, 584. Cited, Jurisdiction of supreme court in special cases, 31 Cal. 90; 3 Nev. 216.

Perry v. Gerbeau, 5 Mart. N. S. 18. Cited, Evidence, parol evidence of declarations and admissions, 26 Cal. 44.

Perry v. Hyde, 10 Conn. 329. Cited, Public officer not liable on official contracts, 1 Cal. 392. Distinguished, 12 Vt. 331.

Perry v. Langley, 7 Am. Law Reg. N. S. 435. Commented on, Statutory Construction, when act takes effect, 37 Cal. 214.

Perry v. McHenry, 13 Ill. 227. Cited, Resulting Trust, when it arises, 25 Cal. 326.

Perry v. O'Hanlon, 11 Mo. 585. Cited, Patent, when void, is subject to collateral attack, 23 Cal. 443.

Perry v. Washburn, 20 Cal. 318. Approved, Taxes not debts in contemplation of the legal tender act, but are payable only in coin, 32 Cal. 154; 34 Cal. 681; 7 Wall. 81. Doubted, 2 Nev. 61; but see contra, Id. 63. Denied, 1 Idaho, 210. Cited, Mandamus, lies to enforce official duty, 41 Cal. 77.

Peter v. State, 4 Smedes & M. 31. Cited, Criminal Procedure, confessions, presumptions as to, 41 Cal. 455.

Peterie v. Bugbey, 24 Cal. 419. Cited, Appeal, error on order for new trial must affirmatively appear, 33 Cal. 525.

Peters v. Foss, 16 Cal. 357. Approved, Appeal, matters in discretion not reviewable on appeal except in cases of abuse, 17 Cal. 289; as to allowance of amendment for variance, 39 Cal. 175; New Trial, motion for, addressed to discretion of court, 19 Cal. 36; 26 Cal. 581.

Peters v. Jamestown Bridge Co., 5 Cal. 334. Cited, Mortgage, a mere security, 8 Cal. 267; 9 Cal. 410; cannot pass without transfer of debt, Id. 429; 13 Mich. 396; when debt is barred, remedy on mortgage is barred, 24 Cal. 498.

Peterson v. Grover, 20 Me. 363. Cited, Equity, relief from mistake, 19 Cal. 673.

Peterson v. Hornblower, 33 Cal. 266.   Cited, Homestead, exemption from sale subordinate to mortgage lien for purchase price, 5 Nev. 238.

Peterson v. Lothrop, 34 Penn. St. 223.   Cited, Ejectment, defense by landlord, evidence admissible, 37 Cal. 396.

Peterson, Matter of, 3 Paige, 510.   Cited, Attorney and Counsel, striking name from roll, 22 Cal. 320.

Pettingill v. Rideout, 6 N. H. 454.   Cited, Felony, conviction of, as a suspension of civil rights, 1 Cal. 435.

Pettit v. Shepherd, 5 Paige, 493.   Cited, Cloud on Title, equity will interfere to remove, or, by injunction, stay a sale which would create a cloud on title, 2 Cal. 589; 9 Cal. 548; 10 Cal. 11; Id. 576; 15 Cal. 132; 28 Cal. 527; 37 Cal. 133; 2 Black, 445.   Distinguished, 36 Barb. 48.

Peyroux v. Howard, 7 Pet. 324.   Approved, Judicial Notice, taken of geographical subdivisions, 39 Cal. 40.

Peytavin v. Winter, 6 La. 559.   Cited, Real actions under civil law, 1 Cal. 287.

Phelan v. Olney, 6 Cal. 478.   Approved, Mortgage, a mere incident to debt, 9 Cal. 410; indorsement and delivery of note secured, carries *pro rata* share of security, 23 Cal. 30.

Phelan v. San Francisco, 6 Cal. 531; S. C. 9 Cal. 15; 20 Cal. 39.   Commented on, Municipal Corporation, construction of ordinances, 7 Cal. 380; but see dissenting opinion of Murray, C. J., Id. 388; powers of ratification, 16 Cal. 272.   Affirmed, Court of Sessions cannot be invested with other than judicial functions, 20 Cal. 43.   Disapproved, 34 Cal. 527.   Cited, Appeal, effect of reversal, 30 Cal. 462; 39 Cal. 646.   Distinguished, 27 Cal. 295.   Cited, Law of the case controls in all future stages, 20 Cal. 311; Id. 416, 417; 21 Cal. 488; 28 Cal. 594.

Phelps v. Kellogg, 15 Ill. 131.   Cited, Preëmptioner, right of, defined, 30 Cal. 650; estopped from deying existence of lien created by attempted mortgage of fee, 31 Cal. 457.

Phelps v. Owens, 11 Cal. 22.   Distinguished, Trespass, by sheriff, measure of damages, 14 Cal. 557.   Commented on, 18 Cal. 325.

Phelps v. Peabody, 7 Cal. 50.   Cited, Fraud, equity will relieve from, 51 N. H. 245.

Phelps v. Smith, 15 Ill. 572.   Cited, Estates of Deceased, representative, who is, 26 Cal. 37.

Philadelphia & Reading R.R. Co. v. Derby, 14 How. 468. Cited, Principal, when liable for unauthorized acts of agent, 34 Cal. 599.

Philadelphia and Trenton R.R. Co. v. Stimpson, 14 Pet. 448.   Approved, Witness, cross-examination, rule of, 5 Cal. 452; 1 Black, 226.   Denied, 9 Mich. 425.

Philadelphia, W. & B. R.R. Co. v. Howard, 13 How. 307. Cited, Contract, when action lies on breach of an entire contract, 35 Cal. 242.   Commented on, Measure of Damages, Id. 244.

Philadelphi, W. & B. R.R. Co. v. Quigley, 21 How. 202. Cited, Corporation, may compose and publish a libel, 34 Cal. 52; liability for acts of agents, in torts, 34 Cal. 57.

Philips v. Gray, 1 Ala. 226.   Cited, Statutory Construction, statute not to be construed retrospectively, 4 Cal. 136.

Phillips v. Berger, 2 Barb. 608; S. C. 8 Barb. 528.   Cited, Specific Performance, when contract will be enforced in equity, 25 Cal. 571; tender and demand, rights reciprocal, 25 Cal. 576.

Phillips v. Berick, 16 John. 136.   Cited, Assignment, cause of action cannot be assigned in parts bar of prior judgment, 23 Cal. 387.

Phillips v. Bistolli, 2 Barn. & C. 511.   Commented on, Contract of Sale, void from misunderstanding, 40 Cal. 463.

Phillips v. Cook, 24 Wend. 389.   Commented on, Partnership, mortgagee of interest of partner, rights of, 25 Cal. 104, 106.

Phillips v. Huth, 6 Mees. & W. 594.   Cited, Factor, cannot pledge, 11 Cal. 402.

Phillips v. Pearce, 5 Barn. & C. 433.   Cited, Estoppel, when tenant not estopped, 33 Cal. 245.

Phillips v. Phillips, 1 Mylne & K. 649.   Cited, Partnership, real property of, how held, 28 Cal. 582.

Phillips v. Rogers, 5 Mart. 700.   Commented on, Alien, inheritance under civil law, 5 Cal. 376.

Phillips v. Rounds, 33 Me. 357.   Cited, Surety on Note, when discharged by agreement for delay, 10 Cal. 426.

Phillips v. State ex rel. Saunders, 15 Geo. 518.   Commented on, Constitutional Construction, liability of stockholders of corporations, 24 Cal. 558.

Phillips v. Thompson, 1 Johns. Ch. 131.   Cited, Specific Performance, when action lies on parol contract to convey land, 24 Cal. 142; 2 Wheat. 305, note a.

Philpott v. Jones, 2 Adol. & E. 41.   Cited, Debtor and Creditor, application of payments, 14 Cal. 449; 7 How. 690.

Phippen v. Stickney, 3 Met. 384.   Commented on, Contract, agreements when void as against public policy, 30 Cal. 591; 20 Mo. 293.

Phipps v. State, 7 Blackf. 512.   Commented on, Dedication, to public use, what constitutes, 14 Cal. 648.

Phœnix v. Dey, 5 John. 413.   Cited, Deed, declarations of grantor made after sale, not admissible in evidence, as to title, 38 Cal. 282.

Phœnix Wat. Co. v. Fletcher, 23 Cal. 481.   Approved, Water Rights, damages for injuries recoverable by appropriator, 23 Cal. 492; 27 Cal. 483.

Platt v. St. Clair's Heirs, 6 Ohio, 227.   Cited, Tax Title, when party in possession acquires no title at tax sale, 25 Cal. 45.

Pickard v. Sears, 6 Adol. & E. 469.   Commented on, Estoppel, equitable, how created, 14 Cal. 369; 26 Cal. 40.

Pickering v. Busk, 15 East, 38.   Cited, Factor cannot pledge, 19 Cal. 72, 76.

Pickering v. Hanson, 2 Sim. 488.   Cited, Amendment, may be made without prejudice to injunction granted, 33 Cal. 502.

Picket v. Weaver, 5 John. 120.   Cited, Covenant, for quiet enjoyment, what constitutes breach of, 33 Cal. 306.

Pickett v. Chilton, 5 Munf. 467.   Cited, Pleading, verity of, in chancery practice, 1 Cal. 142.

Pickett v. Pearsons, 17 Vt. 478.   Cited, Mortgage, estoppel of mortgagor by acceptance of proceeds of sale, 22 Cal. 594.

Pickford v. G. J. Railway Co., 8 Mees. & W. 372.   Cited, Pleading, tender of fare need not be alleged in action for expulsion from car, 34 Cal. 622.

Pico v. Columbet, 12 Cal. 414. Explained, Tenant in Common, accounting for rents and profits, 16 Cal. 471. Distinguished, 17 Cal. 237. Cited, Entitled to possession and use of common property, 30 Md. 125, 127.

Pico v. De LaGuerra, 18 Cal. 422. Cited, Probate Procedure, effect of allowance of claim, 23 Cal. 363; presentation of debts secured by mortgage, 24 Cal. 498.

Pico v. Stevens, 18 Cal. 376. Cited, Instructions, as to questions of fact erroneous, 24 Cal. 505.

Pico v. Sunol, 6 Cal. 294. Referred to incidentally, Injunction, judgments and decrees of courts of concurrent jurisdiction not subject to, 8 Cal. 27.

Pico v. Webster, 14 Cal. 202. Cited, Sureties, on undertaking, liability of, 13 Cal. 306, note; on administrator's bond, 7 Nev. 173.

Picot v. Masterson, 12 Mo. 303. Cited, Landlord and Tenant, removal of tenant, 29 Cal. 171.

Pierce v. Fuller, 8 Mass. 223. Cited, Contract, in restraint of trade, when valid, 6 Cal. 261; 36 Cal. 358; penalty, liquidated damages in, 6 Cal. 263; 19 Cal. 682.

Pierce v. Jackson, 6 Mass. 242. Cited, Partnership, property liable for partnership debts, 9 Cal. 67; rights of partnership creditors, 25 Cal. 104; attachment issued before maturity of debt, void, 13 Cal. 441; 18 Cal. 381.

Pierce v. Kearney, 5 Hill, 86. Cited, Judgment on joint liability as a bar to subsequent action, 13 Cal. 33.

Pierce v. Kennedy, 5 Cal. 138. Approved, Guarantor on Note, liability of, 13 Cal. 580; 34 Cal. 675; entitled to notice of non-payment, 16 Cal. 153.

Pierce v. Minturn, 1 Cal. 470. Approved, Estoppel, party entering into possession of land under another is estopped to deny title, 7 Cal. 416; 8 Cal. 402. Cited, Appeal, objections to rulings not reviewable unless brought up by statement or bill of exceptions, 14 Cal. 39.

Pierce v. Parker, 4 Met. 80. Cited, Written Instruments may be explained by parol evidence, 13 Cal. 556.

Pearce v. Piper, 17 Ves. Jr. 15. Cited, Voluntary Associations, equity jurisdiction over, 14 Cal. 537.

Pierce v. Robinson, 13 Cal. 116. Cited, Assignment, order for money, 14 Cal. 407; of choses in action, 30 Cal. 86;

38 Cal. 545; of part of demand, Id. 521. Cited, Deed, as a mortgage, parol evidence admissible to prove, 15 Cal. 291. Approved, 24 Cal. 390; 27 Cal. 606; 33 Cal. 332; Id. 690; 36 Cal. 46, 48, 62; 37 Cal. 454; 3 Nev. 131.

Pierce v. State, 13 N. H. 536. Cited, Juror and Jury, disqualification of juror, 32 Cal. 47.

Pierce's Admr. v. Trigg's Heirs 10 Leigh, 406. Commented no, Partnership, real property of, 28 Cal. 580, 581.

Pierce v. Woodward, 6 Pick. 206. Cited, Contract, in restraint of trade, when valid, 36 Cal. 358.

Piercy v. Crandall, 34 Cal. 334. Cited, Deed, construction of calls in deed, 38 Cal. 487.

Piercy v. Sabin, 10 Cal. 22. Approved, Pleading, new matter must be expressly pleaded, 10 Cal. 304; 21 Cal. 50; 30 Cal. 472. Cited, 3 Nev. 565. Explained, 14 Cal. 415. Cited, Sham Answer, what is, 18 Cal. 388; Ejectment, on prior possession, insufficient denials, 23 Cal. 536.

Pierpont v. Crouch, 10 Cal. 315. Cited, Constitutional Construction, provision as to title of act directory, 19 Cal. 513; 6 Kan. 335. Distinguished, Amendment of Statutes, 41 Ala. 20.

Pierson v. Cooley, 1 Code Rep. 91. Cited, Pleading, sham answer, practice, 1 Cal. 196.

Pierson v. David, 1 Iowa, 23. Cited, Public Lands, possessory title to, 30 Cal. 657; mortgage of, estoppel of mortgagor, 31 Cal. 457.

Pierson v. Hooker, 3 John. 68. Cited, Release of one partner binding on all, 10 Cal. 125.

Pierson v. McCahill, 21 Cal. 122; S. C. 22 Cal. 127; 23 Cal. 249. Cited, Place of Trial, change of, 22 Cal. 538; mistake in written instrument, parol proof of, 23 Cal. 124.

Piggot v. Eastern Counties R. R. Co., 54 Eng. C. L. 233; 3 C. B. 333. Approved, Negligence, of railroad company, *prima facie* proof of, 14 Cal. 389.

Pigman v. State, 14 Ohio, 555. Commented on, Criminal Procedure, intoxication, proof of, when admissible, 29 Cal. 683.

Pike v. Collins, 33 Me. 45. Cited, Mortgage, sufficient description of debt, 19 Cal. 351.

Pilot Rock Creek Can. Co. v. Chapman, 11 Cal. 161. Cited, Trial granting continuance, in discretion, 20 Cal. 181; 28 Cal. 590; 3 Or. 43.

Pimental v. San Francisco, 21 Cal. 351. Cited, Municipal Corporation, validity of city ordinance, 23 Cal. 318. Approved, Liability of city, 33 Cal. 140, 141. Cited, Statute of Limitations, action when deemed commenced, 34 Cal. 166.

Pinkerton v. Railroad, 42 N. H. 424. Commented on, Replevin, measure of damages, 39 Cal. 424.

Pinkham v. McFarland, 5 Cal. 137. Cited, Evidence, waiver of objections to indorsement on note, 35 Cal. 121.

Pinney v. Wells, 10 Conn. 104. Commented on, Charter Party, construction of, lien for freight, 1 Cal. 425.

Ploche v. Paul, 22 Cal. 105. Cited, Ejectment, unconstitutional provision in statute limiting action by patentee, 36 Cal. 633.

Piper v. Elwood, 4 Denio, 165. Cited, Execution, relief of purchaser at execution sale, 23 Cal. 362.

Piper v. Manny, 21 Wend. 282. Cited, Inkeepers, liability of, 33 Cal. 600, 602. Commented on, 23 Vt. 184.

Piper's Appeal, 32 Cal. 530. Approved, Street Assessments, for widening street, 32 Cal. 560, 568. Cited, Appeal in special cases, 42 Cal. 68; Verdict or Decision, when not set aside on conflict of evidence, 4 Nev. 307; 5 Nev. 366; 8 Nev. 176.

Piqua Bank v. Knoup, Treasurer of Miami Co., 6 Ohio St. 342. Cited, Jurisdiction of United States supreme court, 11 Cal. 184.

Pirtle v. State, 9 Humph. 663. Commented on, Murder, in first degree, 21 Cal. 546. Cited, Criminal Procedure, intoxication as an excuse for crime, 29 Cal. 683.

Piscataqua Bank v. Turnley, 1 Miles, 312. Cited, Felony, conviction of, as a suspension of civil rights, 1 Cal. 435.

Pitkin v. Leavitt, 13 Vt. 379. Cited, Covenant, measure of damages on eviction under, 33 Cal. 308.

Pitney v. Leonard, 1 Paige, 461. Cited, Equity, what sufficient notice, 36 Cal. 437; 2 Black, 389.

Pitt v. Shew, 4 Barn. & Ald. 208. Cited, Trial, reasonable time for performance as a question of fact, 30 Cal. 559.

Pittman v. Gaty, 10 Ill. 186. Cited, Conveyance, possession as notice of, 21 Cal. 628.

Pitts v. Waugh, 4 Mass. 424. Cited, Partnership, dormant, in purchase and sale of real estate, 9 Cal. 639.

Pittsburg v. Scott, 1 Penn. St. 309. Cited, Constitutional Construction, condemnation of land, 31 Cal. 554.

Pixley v. Huggins, 15 Cal. 127. Approved, Cloud on Title, test as to what constitutes, 15 Cal. 264; 17 Cal. 461; 25 Cal. 357; 27 Cal. 653; 28 Cal. 42; 29 Cal. 190; equitable jurisdiction to enjoin sale, 20 Cal. 484; 28 Cal. 527; 13 Flor. 301, 302. Distinguished, 37 Cal. 270, 271. Cited, Action to quiet title, when it lies, 34 Cal. 389; Husband and Wife, presumption that property acquired is common property, 23 Cal. 398; control of common property, 26 Cal. 420; Homestead, enjoining sale of, under execution, 28 Cal. 527.

Pixley v. Western Pacific R. R. Co., 33 Cal. 183. Approved, Corporation, liability on implied contract, 42 Cal. 467.

Place v. Sweetzer, 16 Ohio, 142. Cited, Partnership, equitable action to enforce lien of firm creditors, 13 Cal. 634.

Planche v. Colburn, 8 Bing. 15. Cited, Contract, when action maintainable on breach of entire contract, 35 Cal. 242.

Planters' and Merchants' Bank v. Andrews, 8 Port. 404. Commented on, Attachment, substitution of new bond in, 15 Cal. 32.

Plasket v. Beeby, 4 East, 490. Commented on, Infancy, validity of judgment against infant, 31 Cal. 279.

Platner v. Sherwood, 6 Johns. Ch. 118. Cited, Felony, effect of conviction for, on civil rights, 35 Cal. 398.

Platt v. Drake, 1 Doug. Mich. 296. Commented on, Negotiable Instruments, notice of protest, 8 Cal. 637.

Playfair v. Musgrove, 14 Mees. & W. 239. Cited, Execution, possession under sheriff's deed, how obtained at common law, 2 Cal. 555.

Pleasants v. N. B. and M. R. R. Co., 34 Cal. 586. Distinguished, Damages, when verdict for excessive damages will be set aside, 36 Cal. 485. Cited, Liability of carrier for misconduct of servant, 57 Me. 250.

Pleasants v. Pendleton, 6 Rand. 473. Cited, Sale and Delivery, sale of property in mass, 11 Cal. 403.

Plevin v. Brown, 7 Adol. & E. 447. Cited, Estoppel, when tenant not estopped, 33 Cal. 254.

Plowman v. Riddle, 7 Ala. 775. Cited, Mortgage, securing note, payable in description of currency at election of mortgagor, 31 Cal. 80. Distinguished, 35 Ala. 52.

Plume v. Seward, 4 Cal. 94. Cited, Land, possession not necessarily confined to actual inclosure, 5 Cal. 42; constructive possession under grant, 6 Cal. 272; 23 Cal. 537. Approved, What insufficient to constitute legal possession, 7 Cal. 302, 310. Cited, Ejectment, on prior possession, 6 Cal. 649; Actual Possession, what constitutes, 19 Cal. 690; 39 Cal. 44; under Van Ness ordinance, 19 Cal. 314, 317; 4 Nev. 67. Commented on, General rule as to what constitutes adverse possession, 32 Cal. 20. Cited, Possession *prima facie* evidence of title, 7 Cal. 319; 9 Cal. 427; 1 Nev. 72.

Plummer v. Webb, Ware, 78. Cited, Felony, suspension of civil rights by conviction for, 1 Cal. 435.

Plummer v. Webb, 4 Mason, 380. Cited, Parent and Child, emancipation of minor, 25 Cal. 152.

Plymouth v. Painter, 17 Conn. 585. Cited, Municipal Officers, presumptions in favor of their authority, 3 Cal. 453.

Pocopson Road, 16 Penn. St. 15. Cited, Roads and Highways, constitutionality of acts opening roads, 32 Cal. 255.

Poett v. Stearns, 28 Cal. 226; S. C. 31 Cal. 78. Cited, Legal Tender, constitutionality of congressional act, 38 Cal. 254, 259. Commented on, Foreclosure, sufficiency of allegations in complaint, 39 Cal. 391.

Poignand v. Smith, 8 Pick. 277. Distinguished, Evidence, preliminary to admission of written instrument, 10 Cal. 148.

Poinsett v. Taylor, 6 Cal. 78. Cited, Trespass, officer liable for acts done by deputy, 39 Cal. 318.

31

Polack v. McGrath, 25 Cal. 54. Commented on, Forcibl
Entry, what constitutes, 31 Cal. 127; Nonsuit, when
properly granted, 38 Cal. 697.

Polack v. McGrath, 32 Cal. 15. Referred to on second appeal, 38 Cal. 667. Cited, Ejectment, title by prior
possession, 38 Cal. 674; 4 Nev. 68.

Polack v. Pioche, 35 Cal. 416. Cited, Covenants in Lease,
liability of tenant for repairs, 106 Mass. 461.

Polack v. Smith, Cal. Sup. Ct. (not reported.) Explained,
Reference by consent, 4 Cal. 7.

Polhemus v. Trainer, 30 Cal. 685. Commented on, Mortgage, when created by absolute assignment, 36 Cal. 43,
49.

Police Jury v. McDonogh, 7 Mart. 8. Commented on,
Legislature may authorize municipal subscription to
railroad stock, 5 Cal. 217.

Police Jury v. Michel, 4 La. An. 84. Commented on, Execution, municipal property not subject to levy and sale,
15 Cal. 595.

Polk's Lessee v. Wendal, 9 Cranch, 87; S. C. 5 Wheat. 293.
Cited, Patent, conclusiveness of, 14 Cal. 469; 11 Wheat.
382, 384. Commented on, Conflicting Patents, 16 Cal.
330; Municipal Lands, title in trust, 15 Cal. 612; validity of grant to lands, 15 Cal. 553; 2 Pet. 237; grants
made without authority void, 16 Cal. 229; Stare Decisis, local adjudications, 15 Cal. 603; 14 How. 504.

Pollard v. Commonwealth, 5 Rand. 659. Cited, Juror and
Jury, disqualification of juror, 1 Cal. 385.

Pollard v. Files, 2 How. 591. Commented on, Mexican
Grants, title under, 18 Cal. 29.

Pollard v. Hagan, 3 How. 212. Commented on, State Sovereignty, eminent domain, 3 Cal. 226; 18 Cal. 252;
lands belonging to State, 26 Cal. 353; 13 How. 26.
Cited, National Law, laws of ceded territory, 10 Cal.
620. Distinguished, Protection of rights under treaty,
18 Cal. 28; Public Lands, proceedings to annul patent,
25 Cal. 250.

Pollock v. Cummings, 38 Cal. 683. Approved, Trespass, on
real estate, jurisdiction of justice of peace, 39 Cal. 319.

Pomeroy v. Smith, 17 Pick. 85. Cited, Conversion, damages
in action brought by pledgee, 34 Cal. 606, 608.

Pond v. Negus, 3 Mass. 230. Cited, Street Assessments, performance of duty by street superintendent, 36 Cal. 413.

Pond v. Pond, 10 Cal. 495. Commented on, New Trial, of issues framed in probate court, appeal from, 34 Cal. 687.

Pontalba v. Copland, 3 La. An. 86. Commented on, Spanish Grants, disclaimer, 14 Cal. 605.

Poole's Case, 1 Salk. 368. Commented on, Fixtures, removal of, by tenant, 14 Cal. 65.

Poole v. Cox, 9 Ired. 69. Distinguished, Sureties, on official bonds, construction of contract of, 11 Cal. 221.

Poole v. Gerrard, 6 Cal. 71. Cited, Homestead, alienation of, validity of deed, 7 Cal. 346; 8 Cal. 74; when husband may convey, 14 Cal. 508. Commented on, Nature of the estate, 14 Cal. 477; on what property may be established, 22 Cal. 638.

Poor v. Carleton, 3 Sum. 70. Commented on, Injunction, dissolution, in discretion of court, 39 Cal. 167.

Poorman v. Mills, 35 Cal. 118. Cited, Pleading, allegation of legal conclusions, surplusage, 36 Cal. 302.

Pooser v. Tyler, 1 McCord Ch. 18. Cited, Deed, parol evidence of recitals in, 24 Cal. 417.

Pope v. Biggs, 9 Barn. & C. 254. Cited, Mortgage, relation of purchaser under decree and tenant of mortgagor, 16 Cal. 590.

Pope v. Harkins, 16 Ala. 321. Commented on, Tenant in Common, not liable for rents and profits, 12 Cal. 423.

Pope v. Huth, 14 Cal. 403. Cited, Assignment, equitable assignments, 30 Cal. 521; of policy of insurance, assent of insurer required, 38 Cal. 545.

Popplewell v. Pierce, 10 Cush. 509. Cited, Negligence, liability of owner of ferocious animal for injuries, 41 Cal. 141.

Pordage v. Cole, 1 Saund. 320. Cited, Contract of Sale, covenants when dependent, 35 Cal. 663.

Port v. Jackson, 17 John. 239. Cited, Covenants, recovery on express and absolute conditions, 13 Cal. 525.

Porter v. Beverly, 10 Pet. 532. Cited, Debtor and Creditor, payment by note, effect of, 12 Cal. 323.

Porter v. Cresson, 10 Serg. & R. 257.   Cited, Pleading, firm name in complaint, 22 Cal. 358.

Porter v. Hill, 9 Mass. 34.   Denied, Tenant in Common, conveyance by co-tenant, 35 Cal. 587, 594.

Porter v. Miller, 3 Wend. 329.   Cited, Insolvency, showing required on pleading discharge, 33 Cal. 536.

Porter v. Read, 19 Me. 365.   Cited, Written Instrument, construction of, 10 Cal. 368.

Porter v. Scott, 7 Cal. 312.   Approved, Arbitration, award vitiated by alteration without consent of parties, 23 Cal. 368.

Porter's Heirs v. Robinson, 3 A. K. Marsh. 253.   Cited, Infancy, judgment against infant when voidable, 31 Cal. 285.

Portis v. Cole, 11 Tex. 157.   Doubted, Jurisdiction, in probate proceedings, 38 Cal. 89.

Portland Bank v. Apthorp, 12 Mass. 252.   Commented on, Legislature, constitutional power of taxation, 4 Cal. 52.

Portland Bank v. Stacey, 4 Mass. 661.   Cited, Sale and Delivery, sufficiency of delivery, 37 Cal. 638.

Portman v. Mill, 2 Russ. 570.   Commented on, Presumption of knowledge of law, in confirmation of acts, 7 Cal. 387, 388.

Posson v. Brown, 11 John. 166.   Cited, Judgment of Justice's Court, when parol evidence of docket not admissible, 34 Cal. 327, 328.

Post v. Arnot.   See Arnot v. Post.

Post v. Leet, 8 Paige, 337.   Cited, Judicial Sales, equitable relief from, 16 Cal. 470; Id. 564.

Posten v. Rassette, 5 Cal. 467.   Approved, Exceptions, objections to admission of evidence to be taken at trial, 7 Cal. 423.   Cited, Principal and Agent, express powers, when irrevocable, 8 Cal. 536; Conveyance, sufficiency of, under civil law, 12 Cal. 166; Evidence, presumptions of existence of record, from lapse of time, 22 Cal. 68.

Poston v. Jones, 2 Dev. & B. 294.   Cited, Judgment, in ejectment, of what conclusive, 14 Cal. 468.

Potter v. Baker, 19 N. H. 166.   Commented on, Res Adjudicata, verdict or judgment, of what conclusive, 15 Cal. 148; 26 Cal. 494.

Potter v. Merchants' Bank, 28 N. Y. 641. Cited, Judgment, collateral attack, 34 Cal. 428.

Potter v. Seale, 5 Cal. 410; S. C. 8 Cal. 217. Cited, Malicious Prosecution, want of probable cause to be shown, 29 Cal. 648; burden of proof, 39 Cal. 488.

Potter v. Todd, 1 Day, 238. Cited, Judicial Decisions, reasons no part of, 13 Cal. 26.

Potts, Lessee of, v. Gilbert, 3 Wash. C. C. 475. Disapproved, Title, by adverse possession, continuity of successive possessions, 37 Cal. 354.

Poulton v. Lattimore, 9 Barn. & C. 259; S. C. 17 Eng. C. L. 259. Cited, Pleading defenses in action on contract, 4 Cal. 20, 21; remedy on breach of warranty, 4 Cal. 358.

Powel v. Milbank, 1 Cowp. 103. Cited, Mandamus, title to office cannot be tried on, 3 Cal. 176.

Powell v. Clark, 5 Mass. 355. Cited, Deed, construction of description in, 12 Cal. 164, 165.

Powell v. Cleaver, 2 Bro. Ch. 504. Cited, Will, proof of, attestation clause, 10 Cal. 479.

Powell v. Edmunds, 12 East, 6. Cited, Warranty, cannot be added by parol to written contract of sale, 24 Cal. 464.

Powell v. Lloyd, 2 Younge & I. 379. Cited, Judicial Decisions, *obiter dictum,* 9 Cal. 732.

Powell v. Monson, 3 Mason, 459. Cited, Fixtures, law of, 10 Cal. 264; 14 Cal. 68.

Powell v. Trustees of Newburgh, 19 John. 284. Commented on, Municipal Corporation, liability on implied contract, 9 Cal. 472.

Powell's Heirs v. Hendricks, 3 Cal. 427. Cited, Evidence, copy of deed as, 27 Cal. 244.

Powers v. Bears, 12 Wis. 220. Cited, Eminent Domain, compensation as a condition precedent to condemnation, 31 Cal. 559.

Powers v. Bergen, 6 N. Y. 358. Cited, Constitutional Construction, inherent rights, 22 Cal. 318.

Powers v. Hurst, 2 Humph. 24. Cited, Office, constitutional term of, 11 Cal. 88; 12 Cal. 390.

Powlter's Case, 11 Coke, 29. Cited, Statutory Construction, title of act, 9 Cal. 522; 20 Cal. 582.

Prader v. Grim, 13 Cal. 585. Referred to, Injunction Bond, damages on, 13 Cal. 591.

Prader v. Grimm, 28 Cal. 11. Distinguished, Undertaking, liability on, 32 Cal. 25. Cited, 33 Cal. 212.

Prader v. Purkett, 13 Cal. 588. Referred to, Injunction Bond, liability on, 15 Cal. 12, note.

Pralus v. Jefferson G. & S. M. Co., 34 Cal. 558. Cited, Pleading, requisites of complaint in action to quiet title, 37 Cal. 307. Commented on, When action to quiet title lies, 39 Cal. 22.

Prather v. Johnson, 3 Har. & J. 487. Commented on, Evidence, receipt of third party as evidence, 41 Cal. 306.

Prather v. Prather, 4 Desaus. 33. Cited, Alimony, without divorce, 38 Cal. 270.

Pratt v. Adams, 7 Paige, 615. Cited, Specific Performance, of unlawful contract, will not be enforced, 29 Cal. 271.

Pratt v. Archer, 1 Sim. & S. 433. Cited, Amendment, may be made without prejudice to injunction, 33 Cal. 502.

Pratt v. Hull, 13 John. 334. Approved, Nonsuit, compulsory, 1 Cal. 114.

Pratt v. Parkman, 24 Pick. 42. Cited, Sale and Delivery, of goods to arrive, 8 Cal. 614.

Pratt v. Stephenson, 16 Pick. 325. Cited, Witness, vendor not competent to impeach sale to vendee, 23 Cal. 446.

Pratt v. Town of Swanton, 15 Vt. 147. Cited, Corporation, ratification of contract by, 16 Cal. 624.

Pratt v. Vanwyck's Exrs., 6 Gill & J. 495. Cited, Vendor's Lien, enforcement of, 15 Cal. 193.

Prendergast v. Cassidy, 8 La. An. 96. Cited, Husband and Wife, presumption as to property acquired by purchase, 12 Cal. 253; 17 Cal. 582.

Prendergast v. Turton, 1 Younge & C. 98. Cited, Presumptions, from lapse of time and acquiescence, 22 Cal. 592.

Presbyterian Congregation v. Johnson, 1 Watts & S. 9. Cited, Ejectment, on equitable title, 22 Cal. 617.

Prescott v. Hull, 17 John. 290. Commented on, Garnishee, liability of, 11 Cal. 350.

Prescott v. Nevers, 4 Mason, 330. Cited, Land, constructive possession under color of title, 23 Cal. 437; 25

Cal. 135; Ejectment, ouster by tenant in common, what constitutes, 24 Cal. 377; 27 Cal. 558; 28 Cal. 487.

Prescott v. Trueman, 4 Mass. 627. Cited, Assignment, choses in action not technically assignable, 37 Cal. 189.

President, etc., of Croton T. Road v. Ryder, 1 Johns. Ch. 610. Commented on, Franchises, protection of grant of road franchise, 6 Cal. 595.

Preston v. Boston, 12 Pick. 7. Cited, Mistake, money paid, when may not be recovered back, 18 Cal. 271; Taxation, choses in action where assessable, 23 Cal. 139.

Preston v. Kehoe, 15 Cal. 315; affirming S. C. 10 Cal. 445. Approved, Forcible Entry and Detainer, possession necessary to maintain action, 20 Cal. 84; pleadings in action, 31 Cal. 126; evidence in action, what must be proved, 1 Lans. 232.

Preston v. Keys, 23 Cal. 193. Cited, Instructions, practice, 38 Cal. 370.

Preston v. Sonora Lodge, 39 Cal. 116. Commented on, Mechanic's Lien, construction of statute, 41 Cal. 586, 587.

Price v. Brown, 1 Bradf. 291. Cited, Will, proof of execution of, 10 Cal. 479.

Price v. Dunlap, 5 Cal. 483. Cited, Pleading, in action on lost note, 16 Cal. 380; Indemnity, a condition precedent, 28 Cal. 564.

Price v. Earl of Torrington, 1 Smith's Lead. Cas. 139. Cited, Evidence, entries in book as, 14 Cal. 576.

Price v. Edmonds, 10 Barn. & C. 578. Cited, Sureties, liability of, 29 Cal. 100.

Price v. Johnson County, 15 Mo. 433. Cited, Judicial Decisions, opinions how construed, 9 Cal. 615.

Price v. Lea, 8 Eng. C. L. 156; 1 Barn. & C. 156. Cited, Fraud, vitiates sale of goods, 8 Cal. 213.

Price v. Sacramento Co., 6 Cal. 254. Cited, Counties may sue, 8 Cal. 305; or be sued, 28 Cal. 431.

Price v. State, 36 Miss. 533. Cited, Constitutional Construction, jeopardy, when it attaches, 41 Cal. 216.

Price v. Whitman, 8 Cal. 412. Cited, Constitution, literal criticism, 9 Cal. 522. Distinguished, 31 Cal. 245. Affirmed on principle of *stare decisis*, computation of time for return of bill by governor, 39 Cal. 542.

Priest v. Cummings, 20 Wend. 338.   Cited, Alien, inheritance of, 12 Cal. 456.

Priest v. Union Canal Co., 6 Cal. 170.   Cited, Water Rights, action on conflicting claims to water, 11 Cal. 153; Evidence, discretion in admission of, 42 Cal. 442.

Prigg v. Adams, 2 Salk. 674.   Commented on, Jurisdiction of inferior courts, presumptions as to, 18 Cal. 506.

Prigg v. Commonwealth, 16 Pet. 539.   Cited, State Sovereignty, reserved powers of State, 1 Cal. 236, 243.   Reviewed, States may enforce but cannot impair constitutional rights, 2 Cal. 430.   Approved, National Law, State not bound to recognize state of slavery as to foreign slaves in its territory, 9 Cal. 163.   Cited as to relative powers of Federal and State government, 5 How. 229; Id. 625, 629.   Commented on, 7 How. 427; Id. 555, 560; 14 How. 20; as to national recognition of slavery, 19 How. 534, 547; Id. 616, 624.

Primm v. Barton, 18 Tex. 206.   Cited, Estates of Deceased, common property liable for debts, 17 Cal. 540.

Prince's Case, 8 Coke, 28.   Commented on, Statute, testing validity of, 30 Cal. 259, 264.

Pritchard v. Brown, 4 N. H. 397.   Cited, Equity, what sufficient notice in, 19 Cal. 676; possession as notice of title, 21 Cal. 628; 22 Cal. 335; 36 Cal. 272.

Pritchard v. Wallace, 4 Sneed, 405.   Cited, Trust and Trustee, parol evidence of trust, 22 Cal. 579.

Prize Cases, 2 Black, 635.   Cited, National Law, war may exist without formal declaration, 27 Cal. 222.

Proctor v. Proctor, 2 Hagg. Const. 292.   Cited, Divorce, adultery, 10 Cal. 255.

Propeller Monticello v. Mollison, 17 How. 152.   Approved, Common Carriers, liable to owner for loss of property insured, 6 Cal. 471.

Proprietors of Baintree v. Battles, 6 Vt. 399.   Cited, Evidence, secondary, of destroyed instrument, 10 Cal. 148.

Proprietors of Claremont v. Carlton, 2 N. H. 369.   Cited, Deed, parol evidence admissible to explain, 10 Cal. 625.

Proprietors of the Kennebec Purchase v. Laboree, 2 Greenl. 275.   Cited, Lands, entry under deed, 25 Cal. 135.

Proprietors of the Kennebec Purchase v. Tiffany, 1 Greenl. 219. Cited, Grant, description in, 10 Cal. 623; 15 Cal. 306; 24 Cal. 444.

Proprietors of Monumoi Great Beach v. Rogers, 1 Mass. 159. Cited, Pleading, evidence admissible under general denial, 8 Cal. 590.

Proprietors of Quincy Canal v. Newcomb, 7 Met. 276. Commented on, Nuisance, who may sue for obstructions to public road, 41 Cal. 451.

Prosser v. Secor, 5 Barb. 607. Cited, Jurisdiction, no intendments in favor of inferior courts, 25 Cal. 309; not acquired by mere assertion, 30 Cal. 607.

Providence & W. R. R. Co. v. Wright, 2 R. I. 459. Cited, Taxation, street railroads, assessable property, 32 Cal. 509.

Providence Bank v. Billings, 4 Pet. 514. Cited, State Sovereignty, power of taxation, 1 Cal. 236; 28 Cal. 354; 11 Pet. 566; 6 How. 331; Id. 542; 8 How. 81; legislature cannot pass law impairing obligation of contracts, 16 Cal. 30.

Providence Gas Co. v. Thurber, 2 R. I. 15. Commented on, Taxation, assessment of easement as real property, 32 Cal. 508, 509.

Providence Tool Co. v. Prader, 32 Cal. 634. Approved, Default, entry by clerk a ministerial act, 3 Or. 251.

Provost v. Delahoussaye, 5 La. An. 610. Cited, Husband and Wife, presumption that property acquired is community property, 12 Cal. 253.

Pryor's Appeal, 5 Abb. Pr. 275. Cited, Street Assessment, review on appeal, 32 Cal. 544.

Puckett v. Bates, 4 Ala. 390. Commented on, Statute of Frauds, collateral promise when within statute, 9 Cal. 334; 12 Cal. 553.

Puckford v. Maxwell, 6 Term Rep. 52. Cited, Debtor and Creditor, payment by note, effect of, 12 Cal. 322; 3 McLean, 557.

Pugh v. Duke of Leeds, Cowp. 714. Cited, Time, computation of, on return of bill by governor, 8 Cal. 415; Id. 417; in lease, 25 Cal. 390.

Pulliam v. Christian, 6 How. 209. Cited, Partnership, finality of decree in action for an accounting, 9 Cal. 635.

Purce v. Snaplin, 1 Atk. 508. Cited, Will, specific legacy defined, 31 Cal. 601.

Purcell v. Purcell, 4 Hen. & M. 507. Cited, Alimony, without divorce, 38 Cal. 270.

Purcell v. McKune, 14 Cal. 230. Distinguished, Mandamus, to inferior tribunal, 22 Cal. 38.

Purdy v. People, 4 Hill, 384. Commented on, Statute, testing correctness or existence of, 30 Cal. 262, 263. Criticised, 30 Ind. 521.

Purdy v. Vermilya, 8 N. Y. 348. Cited, Mandamus, pleadings in, 27 Cal. 672.

Purple v. Horton, 13 Wend. 10. Commented on, Juror and Jury, competency of juror, 5 Cal. 350.

Purvis v. Coleman, 21 N. Y. 112. Commented on, Innkeeper, liability of, for loss of property, 33 Cal. 602.

Putnam v. Lewis, 8 John. 389. Cited, Debtor and Creditor, payment by note, effect of, 10 Cal. 427.

Putnam v. Man, 3 Wend. 202. Cited, Summons, return of, conclusive, 33 Cal. 686.

Putnam v. Wise, 1 Hill, 234. Approved, Contract, cropping contract construed, 17 Cal. 545, 546; 23 Cal. 521; 25 Cal. 63, 64.

Putnam v. Wood, 3 Mass. 481. Cited, Common Carriers, liability for loss or damage, 33 Cal. 70.

Putnam v. Wyley, 8 John. 432. Cited, Trespass, on personal property, constructive possession sufficient to maintain action, 12 Cal. 463.

Pyle v. Maulding, 7 J. J. Marsh. 202. Cited, Statutory Construction, "month" defined, 31 Cal. 176.

Pyle v. Pennock, 2 Watts & S. 390. Cited, Fixtures, what constitute, 14 Cal. 68.

Quackenbush v. Danks, 1 Denio, 128. Commented on, Constitutionality of Statutes, remedial statutes, 2 Cal. 552. Approved, Statutes not to be construed retrospectively, 4 Cal. 132, 134. Cited, 10 Iowa, 486.

Quarman v. Burnett, 6 Mees. & W. 499. Denied, Respondeat Superior, distinction as to contractor building on his own premises or those of another person, 8 Cal. 496, 498.

Queen, The, v. Corporation of Dunham, 10 Mod. 146. Cited, Officer, right to hold over, 28 Cal. 52.

Queen, The, v. Earl of Northumberland, 1 Plowd. 310. Denied, Sovereignty, right, by prerogative, to mines of gold and silver, 14 Cal. 308; 17 Cal. 219. Commented on, 2 Black, 221.

Queen v. Johnson, 8 Q. B. 99. Cited, Dedication, must rest in assent of owner, 14 Cal. 649.

Queiroz v. Trueman, 3 Barn. & C. 349. Commented on, Factor, cannot pledge, 19 Cal. 73.

Quin v. Moore, 15 N. Y. 432. Cited, Action, civil action for damages for injuries causing death, exclusively statutory, 25 Cal. 435.

Quiner v. Marblehead S. Ins. Co., 10 Mass. 476. Cited, Corporation, transfer of stock of, 5 Cal. 189.

Quinn v. Kenyon, 22 Cal. 82. Cited, New Trial, granting or refusing motion, in legal discretion, 33 Cal. 525; 5 Kan. 238.

Quivey v. Gambert, 32 Cal. 304. Cited, Appeal, settlement of exceptions, practice, 33 Cal. 553. Disapproved, Jurisdiction on appeal from order after final judgment, 42 Cal. 113. Cited, Review on appeal, 5 Nev. 262; New Trial, notice of motion when to be given, 41 Cal. 404. Disapproved, Practice on settlement of statement, Id. 434. Approved, Striking out statement and notice, 42 Cal. 117, 121.

Quivey v. Hall, 19 Cal. 97. Distinguished, Statute of Limitations, assertion of, in action by and against administrators, 23 Cal. 28.

Quivey v. Porter, 37 Cal. 462. Affirmed, Judgment, by default, recitals as to service of process import absolute verity, 37 Cal. 470.

Rabe v. Hamilton, 15 Cal. 31. Commented on, Appeal, time within which to appeal, 15 Cal. 386.

Rabe v. Wells, 3 Cal. 148. Cited, Appeal, error must be affirmatively shown, 5 Cal. 410; 2 Nev. 55.

Racouillat v. Rene, 32 Cal. 450. Cited, Pleading, immaterial averments, matters of evidence, 33 Cal. 128; 36 Cal. 233; 7 Nev. 172; Equity, beneficiaries of covenant may maintain action, 1 Saw. 631.

Racouillat v. Sansevain, 32 Cal. 376. Cited, Specific Performance, executory contract of married woman, 32 Cal. 653; as a lien, 36 Cal. 653. Approved, Construction of written instrument, Id. 657. Cited, Enforcement of contract, 40 Cal. 562; Beneficiaries of covenant may sue, 1 Saw. 631; Judgment, against executor, 42 Cal. 133.

Radcliff v. Mayor, etc., of Brooklyn, 4 N. Y. 195. Approved, Trespass, lawful act properly done, not a trespass, 9 Cal. 257; 23 Cal. 467. Applied, To laying down street railroad, 35 Cal. 333; to grading streets, 42 Cal. 438.

Radde v. Buckgaber, 3 Duer, 685. Cited, Pleading, defense constituting new matter, 10 Cal. 27.

Ragland v. Green, 14 Smedes and M. 195. Cited, Judicial Sale, lien of purchaser under void sale by administrator, 10 Cal. 120.

Railroad Co. v. Commrs. of Clinton Co., 1 Ohio St. 89. Cited, Legislature, power of taxation and appropriation, 13 Cal. 355.

Railway v. Legarde, 10 La. An. 150. Cited, Eminent Domain, compensation on condemnation, 31 Cal. 373.

Raleigh and G. R. Co. v. Davis, 2 Dev. & B. 451. Cited, Eminent Domain, exercise of right through private corporations, 18 Cal. 251; compensation as a condition precedent, 31 Cal. 550.

Ralph v. Duncan, 3 Mo. 195. Affirmed, 4 Mo. 598. Approved, State Rights, transit through free State with slave property, 9 Cal. 164; emancipation by residence in free State, 19 How. 602.

Ralph v. Harvey, 1 Q. B. 845. Cited, Mining Partnership, rights of partners, 23 Cal. 205.

Ralston v. Hughes, 13 Ill. 469. Distinguished, Judicial Sale, rights of purchaser, 14 Cal. 34.

Ralston v. Lahee, 8 Iowa, 17. Cited, Infant, conclusiveness of decree, 31 Cal. 283.

Ramires v. Kent, 2 Cal. 558. Cited, Alien, may hold real estate till office found, 5 Cal. 378; denouncement under Mexican law, 26 Cal. 477; 32 Cal. 386; non-resident aliens, 18 Cal. 219.

Ramsay v. McDonald, 1 W. Black. 30; Fost. Crim. L. 61. Cited, Felony, effect of conviction for, on civil rights, 35 Cal. 398.

Ramsdell v. Fuller, 28 Cal. 37. Approved, Husband and Wife, presumption that property acquired is common property, 30 Cal. 36; evidence of consideration in deed to wife, Id. 42, 55, 60; 31 Cal. 448. Commented on, Constructive notice of unrecorded deed to wife, 36 Cal. 697, 699, 700.

Ramsey v. Chandler, 3 Cal. 90. Cited, Injunction, lies to prevent injury to right of way, 22 Cal. 491.

Rand v. Sargent, 23 Me. 326. Cited, Conspiracy, when action will not lie, 25 Cal. 559.

Randall v. Buffington, 10 Cal. 491. Distinguished, Assignment, when void as to creditors, 23 Cal. 518.

Randall v. Lunt, 51 Me. 246. Cited, Husband and Wife, conveyance to wife, 30 Cal. 56.

Randall v. Parker, 3 Sand. 73. Cited, Sale and Delivery, change of possession defined, 25 Cal. 201.

Randall v. Randall, 7 East, 81. Commented on, Arbitration and Award, omissions in award, 12 Cal. 339; 1 Pet. 227.

Randall v. Yuba Co., 14 Cal. 219. Distinguished, County, liability on contracts made by officers, 20 Cal. 595.

Randell v. Mallett, 14 Me. 51. Cited, Res Adjudicata, conclusiveness of judgment, 15 Cal. 603.

Ranelaugh v. Hayes, 1 Vern. 189. Cited, Specific Performance, of general covenant to indemnify, 13 Cal. 523.

Ranger v. Cary, 1 Met. 373. Cited, Negotiable Instrument, presumptive dishonor, 39 Cal. 352.

Rangely v. Webster, 11 N. H. 304. Cited, Foreign Judgment, when not enforceable *in personam*, 8 Cal. 457.

Rankin v. Lydia, 2 A. K. Marsh. 467. Cited, State Sovereignty, right of transit with slave property, 9 Cal. 170. Commented on, Judicial Decisions, principles of determination, 9 Cal. 162, 163; 19 How. 536. Cited, Status of slavery, 19 How. 592, 624.

Rankin v. Scott, 12 Wheat. 177. Commented on, Judgment, prior lien, title under, to prevail, 42 Cal. 374; 3 How. 332.

Rannie v. Irvine, 7 Man. & G. 976. Cited, Contract in partial restraint of trade, valid, 36 Cal. 358.

Ransom, Ex parte, 3 Code Rep. 148. Cited, Special Cases, what included in, 24 Cal. 433; when appeal will not lie, Id. 454.

Rapson v. Cubitt, 9 Mees. & W. 710. Commented on, Respondeat Superior, when doctrine does not apply, 8 Cal. 490.

Rathbon v. Budlong, 15 John. 1. Cited, Principal, when bound by contract of agent, 13 Cal. 48.

Rathbone v. Bradford, 1 Ala. 312. Cited as inapplicable, Statutory Construction, 4 Cal. 136.

Rathbone v. Stocking, 2 Barb. 135. Cited, Money had and received, when action lies, 16 Cal. 638.

Rathbone v. Warren, 10 John. 587. Cited, Surety, rights of, 11 Cal. 220.

Raun v. Reynolds, 11 Cal. 14; S. C. 15 Cal. 459; 18 Cal. 275. Referred to, 12 Cal. 99; 14 Cal. 676. Affirmed, Foreclosure, terms of sale in decree, 14 Cal. 679. Cited, Judgment by default, relief granted on, 27 Cal. 102; 29 Cal. 168; 1 Nev. 317; Probate Proceedings, remedy under act ratifying judicial sale, 33 Cal. 55.

Rawdon v. Corbin, 3 How. Pr. 416. Cited, Summons, service by publication, practice, 20 Cal. 82.

Rawley v. Commrs. of Vigo Co., 2 Blackf. 355. Commented on, County, liability limited by statutory provisions, 30 Cal. 238.

Rawls v. Kennedy, 23 Ala. 240. Commented on, Stare Decisis, construction of statutes, 15 Cal. 622.

Rawson v. Johnson, 1 East, 203. Cited, Conditions precedent, tender or offer to perform, sufficient, 34 Cal. 622.

Ray v. Armstrong, 4 Cal. 208. Distinguished, Landlord and Tenant, notice to quit, 6 Cal. 189.

Ray v. Law, 3 Cranch, 179. Cited, Foreclosure, finality of decree, 9 Cal. 635. Approved, 2 Black, 531; 19 How. 286. Distinguished, 10 Wheat. 504.

Raymond v. Bearnard, 12 John. 275. Cited, Contract, of sale, when time is of the essence, 30 Cal. 407.

Raymond v. Simonson, 4 Blackf. 85. Commented on, Statute of Limitations, when action is barred on money receipted for, 24 Cal. 328.

Raynor v. Clark, 3 Code Rep. 231. Commented on, Pleading, what defects not cured by default or verdict, 10 Cal. 560, 561.

Rea v. Smith, 19 Wend. 293. Cited, Witness, vendor not competent to impeach sale, 23 Cal. 446.

Reab v. Moore, 19 John. 337. Cited, Contract, when action lies on entire contract, 2 Cal. 312.

Read v. Goodyear, 17 Serg. & R. 350. Cited, Presumptions from lapse of time and acquiesence, 22 Cal. 591.

Read v. Leeds, 19 Conn. 186. Cited, Easement, grant of right of way, what it passes, 31 Cal. 590.

Reade v. Livingstone, 3 Johns. Ch. 481. Approved, Parent and Child, deed to child when void as to creditors, 8 Cal. 126, 127.

Reading R. R. Co. v. Johnson, 7 Watts & S. 317. Commented on, Release of joint interest to be specific, 6 Cal. 375.

Reamer v. Nesmith, 34 Cal. 624. Cited, Deed, construction of calls in, 36 Cal. 615; 38 Cal. 486.

Reay v. Cotter, 29 Cal. 168. Cited, Estoppel, when tenant not estopped, 33 Cal. 245.

Redding v. White, 27 Cal. 282. Cited, San Francisco, municipal power over pueblo lands, 42 Cal. 556.

Rede v. Farr, 6 Maule & S. 125. Cited, Lease, rights of parties after forfeiture, 38 Cal. 251.

Redman v. Gulnac, 5 Cal. 148. Practice distinguished, Instructions, after retirement of jury, 26 Wis. 307.

Reece v. Allen, 10 Ill. 239. Commented on, Deed, as a mortgage, 14 Cal. 264.

Reed, Appeal of, 34 Penn. St. 207. Cited, Notice to agent is notice to principal, 31 Cal. 165.

Reed v. Beazley, 1 Blackf. 97. Cited, Husband and Wife, validity of agreements for separation, 9 Cal. 494.

Reed v. Calderwood, 22 Cal. 463. Approved, Action, dismissal as to some defendants, 29 Cal. 436.

Reed, Estate of, 23 Cal. 410. Cited, Homestead, filing declaration, essential, 24 Cal. 639.

Reed, Ex parte, 4 Hill, 572. Disapproved, Trespass by Officer, liability on official bond, 14 Cal. 197; 17 Gratt. 131.

Reed v. Spicer, 27 Cal. 58. Cited, Deed, parol evidence to explain, 34 Cal. 627; Ejectment, limitation of action brought under Mexican grant, 1 Saw. 559, 560.

Reed's Heirs v. McCormick, 4 Cal. 342. Commented on, Jurisdiction, powers of judiciary, 5 Cal. 44. Followed, Trial of issues made up in probate court, 5 Cal. 433; district court jurisdiction not appellate, 7 Cal. 240; 9 Cal. 86.

Reed v. Northfield, 13 Pick. 94. Cited, Statutory Construction, penal statutes, 29 Cal. 512.

Reed v. Omnibus R. R. Co., 33 Cal. 212. Affirmed, Street Railroads, actions against, for forfeiture, 36 Cal. 282.

Reed v. Passer, 1 Esp. 213. Cited, Marriage, sufficient proof of, 26 Cal. 133.

Reed v. State of Ohio, 15 Ohio, 217. Cited, Evidence, when incorporation may be proved by reputation, 41 Cal. 654.

Reedie v. London & N. W. R. Co., 4 Exch. 244. Cited, Respondeat Superior, doctrine not to apply as between municipal corporations and contractors, 6 Cal. 531. Approved, 8 Cal. 496, 498.

Rees v. Emerick, 6 Serg. & R. 288. Cited, Pleading, treble damages must be specially set up in complaint, 5 Cal. 240.

Rees v. Marquis of Headfort, 2 Camp. 574. Cited, Negotiable Instruments, check for illegal consideration void, 10 Cal. 526.

Reese, Appeal of, 32 Cal. 567. Cited, Appeal, in special cases, 42 Cal. 68.

Reese v. Mahoney, 21 Cal. 305. Referred to, 36 Cal. 513–521.

Reese v. Parkins, 2 Jac. & W. 390. Cited, Voluntary associations as partnerships, 14 Cal. 537.

Reese v. Shearns, 29 Cal. 273. Cited, Legal Tender Notes, relative values of money, 31 Cal. 80; 6 Nev. 48; Constitutionality of legal tender act, 38 Cal. 254; judgment for currency valuation, 35 Cal. 357.

Reeves v. Treasurer of Wood Co., 8 Ohio St. 333, Cited, Street Assessments, legislative power to direct, 28 Cal. 352. Commented on, Id. 368; action for recovery of, 31 Cal. 684.

Regents of University of Md. v. Williams, 9 Gill & J. 365. Commented on, Constitutionality of Statute, principles of judicial determination, 26 Cal. 183.

Regina v. Clarke, 1 Car. & K. 422. Cited, Indictment, sufficiency of, 32 Cal. 38.

Regina v. Cruse, 8 Car. & P. 541. Cited, Criminal Procedure, intoxication as an excuse for crime, 29 Cal. 683; 29 Miss. 609.

Regina v. Dyke, 34 Eng. C. L. 381; 8 Car. & P. 261. Cited, Criminal Procedure, corroborate evidence, when required, 16 Cal. 112.

Regina v. Lawes, 1 Car. & K. 62. Cited, Indictment, sufficiency of, 32 Cal. 38.

Regina v. Marcus, 2 Car. & K. 356. Cited, Indictment for forgery, insufficient, 35 Cal. 507.

Regina v. Moore, 3 Car. & K. 319. Commented on, Criminal Procedure, intoxication as an excuse, 29 Cal. 683.

Regina v. Roberts, 2 M. C. C. 258. Distinguished, Forgery, of order of goods, 10 Cal. 336.

Regina v. Smith, 33 Eng. L. & E. 567. Cited, Assault with intent to murder, wounding wrong person by mistake, 38 Cal. 143.

Regla v. Martin, 19 Cal. 463. Cited, Infancy, decree against infant valid till reversed, 31 Cal. 285.

Reid v. Allen, 18 Tex. 242. Cited, Probate Procedure, validity of sale of estate, 20 Cal. 386.

Reid v. Gifford, 6 Johns. Ch. 19. Cited, Injunction, essential allegations, 13 Cal. 190.

Reigal v. Wood, 1 Johns. Ch. 401. Cited, City, equity, relief from decree obtained by fraud, 5 Cal. 298.

Reilly v. Lancaster, 39 Cal. 354. Cited, Judgment, validity of, collateral attack, 39 Cal. 440.

Reina v. Cross, 6 Cal. 29. Cited, Freight money may be recovered back, 6 Cal. 370.

Reiss v. Brady, 2 Cal. 182. Denied, Appeal, review of order dissolving attachment, 1 Nev. 537.

Remick v. O'Kyle, 12 Me. 340. Cited, Negotiable Instruments, demand at time and place not of essence of contract, 11 Cal. 321.

32

Remsen v. Hay, 2 Edw. Ch. 535. Approved, Mortgage, purchase of equity of redemption by mortgagee, 26 Cal. 601.

Renner v. Bank of Columbia, 9 Wheat. 581. Cited, Evidence, secondary, of destroyed instrument, when admissible, 10 Cal. 148.

Renwick v. Morris, 7 Hill, 576. Cited, Rights and Remedies, under statute, 16 Cal. 525.

Requa v. Rea, 2 Paige, 339. Cited, Equity, when will relieve from mistake, 16 Cal. 565.

Respublica v. Richards, 2 Dall. 225. Cited, State Sovereignty, right of transit through free State with slave property, 2 Cal. 445.

Reubens v. Joel, 13 N. Y. 488. Cited, Fraudulent Conveyance, rights of creditors, 27 Cal. 315, 316.

Revalk v. Kraemer, 8 Cal. 66. Approved, Homestead, decree void in actions concerning, unless both husband and wife be joined, 8 Cal. 75; Id. 76; 9 Cal. 97; 13 Iowa, 584; 16 Iowa, 158; 5 Kan. 246, 249; mortgage on homestead, when void, 8 Cal. 76; Id. 353; not validated by subsequent death of wife, 13 Iowa, 583; power of husband on death of wife, 23 Cal. 120. Cited, Character of homestead estate, 8 Cal. 509; 25 Cal. 114. Denied, 14 Cal. 477. Cited, Nature of wife's interest, 19 Iowa, 68; on what property may be established, 22 Cal. 638; 23 Cal. 74. Approved, who entitled to, 31 Cal. 535; 51 N. H. 267, 273. Distinguished, Enjoining judgment, 15 Cal. 134. Cited, 37 Cal. 269; 22 Wis. 486.

Rex v. Appleby, 3 Stark. 33. Cited, Evidence, party not bound by statements of witnesses, 22 Cal. 237.

Rex v. Ball, 1 Camp. 324. Cited, Evidence, on trial for forgery, 28 Cal. 518.

Rex v. Barker, 3 Burr. 1266. Cited, Mandamus, when it lies, 3 Cal. 171, 173.

Rex v. Barr, 4 Camp. 16. Cited, Dedication to public use, how proved, 14 Cal. 649.

Rex v. Bartlett, 7 Car. & P. 832. Commented on, Evidence, acquiescence in statements of others, 32 Cal. 100.

Rex v. Beechy, 1 British C. C. 318; Russ. & R. 319. Commented on, Embezzlement, what constitutes, 31 Cal. 112.

Rex v. Bishop of Chester, 1 Term Rep. 396. Cited, Mandamus, when it lies, 3 Cal. 173; title to office cannot be tried, 3 Cal. 176.

Rex v. Bonner, 6 Car. & P. 386. Cited, Evidence, proof of dying declarations, 35 Cal. 52.

Rex v. Cabbage, Russ. & R. 292. Commented on, Larceny, what constitutes, 28 Cal. 381.

Rex v. Cambridge, 4 Burr. 2011. Cited, Office, term of, interpretation of statutes, 3 Cal. 500.

Rex v. Chalking, Russ. & R. 334. Cited, Burglary, "house" in statute, what it includes, 34 Cal. 244.

Rex v. Churchwardens of Taunton, 1 Cowp. 413. Cited, Mandamus, when it lies, 3 Cal. 173.

Rex v. Clarke, 2 Starkie, 241. Cited, Evidence, on trial for rape, 6 Cal. 223.

Rex v. Clarke, 1 Term Rep. 679. Cited, Sheriff, may act by deputy, 35 Cal. 713.

Rex v. Croke, 1 Cowp. 26. Commented on, Condemnation of land, special authority to be strictly pursued, 35 Cal. 258.

Rex v. Davis, East, Pl. of Cr. 955. Cited, Forgery, may be committed on unstamped paper, 28 Cal. 514.

Rex v. Davis, 7 Car. & P. 785. Commented on, Criminal Procedure, arrest, when authority need not be seown, 27 Cal. 576.

Rex v. Dean, 2 Show. 402. Cited, Execution, sale of property at common law, 2 Cal. 555.

Rex v. Decan' et Capitul' Dublin, 1 Stra. 536. Cited, Voluntary Associations, jurisdiction in equity on exclusion of member, 14 Cal. 538.

Rex v. Delaval, 3 Burr. 1436. Cited, Divorce, custody of children, 14 Cal. 517.

Rex v. De Mierre, 5 Burr. 2788. Cited, Alien, ineligible to office, 30 Cal. 188.

Rex v. Harvey, 1 W. Black. 20. Cited, Officer, provisions in act relating to, when directory, 7 Cal. 437.

Rex v. Hawkeswood, 1 Leach, 292. Cited, Forgery, may be committed on unstamped paper, 28 Cal. 514.

Rex v. Hawtin, 7 Car. & P. 281. Cited, Embezzlement, what constitutes, 31 Cal. 112.

Rex v. Head, 4 Burr. 2521. Cited, Municipal Corporations, official acts, validity of, 33 Cal. 21, 23.

Rex v. Hodgson, Russ. & R. C. C. 211. Commented on, Evidence, in action for rape, 6 Cal. 223; 28 Vt. 520.

Rex v. Inhab. of Audly, 2 Salk. 526. Commented on, Jurisdiction, authority for exercise of special powers must affirmatively appear, 35 Cal. 258.

Rex v. Inhab. of Great Bentley, 10 Barn. & C. 520. Cited, Statutory Construction, 26 Cal. 181.

Rex v. Inhab. of Hipswell, 8 Barn. & C. 471. Cited, Judicial Sale, purchase by administrator at his own sale voidable, 29 Cal. 40.

Rex v. Inhab. of St. Nicholas, Caldecott, 262. Cited, Fixtures, what constitute, 14 Cal. 66.

Rex v. Jeffries, 1 Stra. 446. Cited, Statute, printed statutes as evidence, 30 Cal. 264.

Rex v. Knight, 1 Salk. 375; S. C. 1 Ld. Ray. 527. Cited, Indictment for forgery, sufficiency of, 35 Cal. 507.

Rex v. Lithgo, Russ. & R. 357. Cited, Burglary, "house," what it includes, 34 Cal. 244.

Rex v. Lloyd, 1 Camp. 259. Cited, Dedication, to public use, what constitutes, 14 Cal. 649.

Rex v. Loxdale, 1 Burr. 445. Commented on, Statutory Construction, time when discretionary, 11 Cal. 55.

Rex v. Luffe, 8 East, 193. Cited, Parent and Child, presumption as to legitimacy, 13 Cal. 99.

Rex v. Mayor of Abingdon, 2 Salk. 431. Commented on, Mandamus, return of writ, sufficiency of, 27 Cal. 672.

Rex v. Mayor of Colchester, 2 Term Rep. 259. Cited, Mandamus will not lie to try title to office, 3 Cal. 176.

Rex v. Mayor of Grampond, 6 Term Rep. 301. Cited, Office, term of, not to be extended beyond time clearly defined, 3 Cal. 500.

Rex v. Mayor of Norwich, 1 Barn. & Ad. 310. Cited, Office, statutory term of, not to be extended beyond time defined, 3 Cal. 500.

Rex v. Mayor, etc., of Thetford, 8 East, 270. Cited, Office, statutory term of, not to be extended beyond time defined, 3 Cal. 500.

Rex v. Meakin, 7 Car. & P. 297. Cited, Criminal Procedure, evidence of intoxication when to be considered, 29 Cal. 682.

Rex v. Mosley, 2 British C. C. 102, 1 Moody. Commented on, Indictment, sufficiency of, for murder, 9 Cal. 275.

Rex v. Morely, 2 Burr. 1040. Cited, Certiorari, when it lies, 1 Cal. 156.

Rex v. Morton, 1 East, Pl. of Cr. 955. Cited, Forgery, may be committed on unstamped paper, 28 Cal. 514.

Rex v. Payne, 1 Moody C. C. 378. Cited, Criminal Procedure, arrest, authority when need not be shown, 27 Cal. 577.

Rex v. Ramsgate, 6 Barn. & C. 712. Commented on, Statutory Construction, 26 Cal. 181.

Rex v. Reason, 1 Stra. 500. Cited, Evidence, admission of proof of dying declarations, 10 Cal. 36.

Rex v. Reoulist, 2 Leach, 703. Cited, Forgery, may be committed on unstamped paper, 28 Cal. 514.

Rex v. Robinson, 2 Burr. 803. Cited, Rights and Remedies, remedies by statutes, cumulative, 16 Cal. 525, 530.

Rex v. Robotham, 3 Burr. 1472. Cited, Statutes, printed volumes as evidence, 30 Cal. 264.

Rex v. Rogier, 2 Dowl. & R. 431. Cited, Nuisance, gaming house a public nuisance, 1 Cal. 442.

Rex v. Rosser, 7 Car. & P. 648. Cited, New Trial, verdict not set aside where there is a conflict of evidence, 32 Cal. 542.

Rex v. Smith, 4 Car. & P. 411. Cited, Evidence, in cases of forgery, 28 Cal. 518.

Rex v. Smith, 2 Stra. 982. Cited, Divorce, custody of child, 14 Cal. 517.

Rex v. Smithies, 5 Car. & P. 332. Commented on, Evidence, acquiescence in statements of others, 32 Cal. 100.

Rex v. Snowley, 4 Car. & P. 390. Commented on, Embezzlement, what constitutes, 31 Cal. 112, 113.

Rex v. Sparrow, 2 Stra. 1123. Commented on, Statutory Construction, time when directory, 11 Cal. 55.

Rex v. St. John's College, 4 Mod. 241. Cited, Mandamus, return of writ, 27 Cal. 672.

Rex v. Stocker, 1 Salk. 342. Cited, Indictment, disjunctive allegations, insufficient, 35 Cal. 509.

Rex v. Stoughton, 2 Stra. 900. Cited, Indictment, disjunctive allegations insufficient, 35 Cal. 509.

Rex v. Taylor, 3 Barn. & C. 502. Cited, Nuisance, gaming houses public nuisances, 1 Cal. 442.

Rex v. Thomas, 7 Car. & P. 817. Approved, Crimes and Punishments, intoxication no excuse for crime, 29 Cal. 682.

Rex v. Thorley, 1 Moody C. C. 343. Cited, Embezzlement, what constitutes, 31 Cal. 112.

Rex v. Tomlinson, 6 Car. & P. 370; 25 Eng. C. L. 442. Cited, Indictment for murder, sufficiency of, 9 Cal. 275.

Rex v. Twyning, 2 Barn. & Ald. 386. Commented on, Divorce for adultery, evidence necessary to prove marriage, 17 Cal. 601; 20 Vt. 590.

Rex v. Warminster, 3 Barn. & Ald. 121. Cited, Judicial Decisions, obiter opinions, 9 Cal. 732.

Rex v. Whithorne, 3 Car. & P. 394. Commented on, Criminal Procedure, arrest, validity of, 27 Cal. 577.

Rex v. Wilkes, 4 Burr. 2575. Cited, Judgment, of imprisonment to commence at expiration of another term, valid, 22 Cal. 137.

Rex v. Bishop of Ely, 1 Burr. 387. Cited, Jurisdiction, special powers to be strictly pursued, and authority to affirmatively appear, 19 Cal. 59.

Rex v. Williams, 1 W. Black. 85. Cited, Statutory Construction, title to act, 9 Cal. 522; 20 Cal. 582.

Rex v. Williams, 6 Car. & P. 626. Commented on, Embezzlement, what constitutes, 31 Cal. 112.

Rex v. Williams, 7 Car. & P. 320. Cited, Witness, competency of childrens' presumptions, 10 Cal. 67.

Rex v. Wilson, 8 Term Rep. 357. Cited, Forcible Entry, what constitutes, 25 Cal. 59.

Rex v. Windham, 1 Cowp. 378. Cited, Mandamus, when it lies, 3 Cal. 173.

Rex v. Woodcock, 1 Leach. 563. Cited, Evidence, proof of dying declarations, 24 Cal. 23; 35 Cal. 52.

Rex v. Wright, 1 Burr. 543. Cited, Rights and Remedies, remedies by statute, cumulative, 16 Cal. 530.

Rexford v. Knight, 15 Barb. 627.   Affirmed, 11 N. Y. 308. Cited, Eminent Domain, compensation on condemnation of land, 31 Cal. 374; compensation to be provided, 31 Cal. 559.

Reyes v. Sanford, 5 Cal. 117.   Approved, Place of Trial, right of motion for change, waived by appearance and answer, 9 Cal. 643.   Cited, 3 Nev. 406; 8 Nev. 186.

Reynolds, Ex parte, 1 Caines, 499.   Commented on, Ejectment, who bound by judgment in, 22 Cal. 209.

Reynolds v. Geary, 26 Conn. 179.   Cited, Constitutionality of Statutes, remedial statutes, 22 Cal. 327.

Reynolds v. Harris, 14 Cal. 667.   Cited, Judgment, conclusiveness of erroneous judgment till reversed, 25 Cal. 273; 38 Cal. 377; Appeal, objection cannot be taken for the first time on appeal, 27 Cal. 138; findings of referee reviewable as part of record, 28 Cal. 595; 27 Id. 138.   Denied, 5 Nev. 253.   Commented on, Execution, setting aside sale under, 34 Cal. 301.   Approved, 18 Cal. 289.

Reynolds v. Jourdan, 6 Cal. 108.   Approved, Contract, action on breach, of special contract, election of remedy, 7 Cal. 151; 26 Cal. 20.

Reynolds v. Lathrop, 7 Cal. 43.   Cited, Execution, purchaser at judicial sale entitled to rents pending redemption, 8 Cal. 597.

Reynolds v. Lawrence, 15 Cal. 359.   Referred to, Appeal, practice on, 15 Cal. 357; review on appeal, 24 Cal. 372; statement must contain grounds of appeal, 28 Cal. 165.

Reynolds v. Nelson, 6 Madd. 20.   Cited, Specific Performance, effect of clause of forfeiture in contract, 40 Cal. 13.

Reynolds v. Page, 35 Cal. 296.   Cited, Action, dismissal of, for want of prosecution, 39 Cal. 451.

Reynolds v. Pixley, 6 Cal. 165.   Approved, Homestead cannot be established on land held in joint tenancy, 23 Cal. 517; 27 Cal. 425; 32 Cal. 483; 14 Iowa, 54; filing declaration, 31 Cal. 530.

Reynolds v. Boston & M. Railroad, 43 N. H. 580.   Cited, Stoppage in transitu, liability of carriers, 37 Cal. 632.

Reynolds v. Shuler, 5 Cow. 323.   Cited, Fixtures, what constitute, 14 Cal. 68.

Reynolds v. Stansbury, 20 Ohio, 344.   Cited, Pleading defenses in ejectment, 10 Cal. 27.

Reynolds v. West, 1 Cal. 322.   Approved, Alcaldes' Grants, valid, 1 Cal. 420; presumption, as to authority of officers, 3 Cal. 451; 16 Cal. 227; as to validity of grant, 16 Cal. 241.   Commented on, Powers of Alcaldes to make grants, 15 Cal. 558; title to pueblo lands, Id. 598.

Rhame v. Rhame, 1 McCord Ch. 197.   Cited, Alimony without divorce, 38 Cal. 270.

Rhine v. Bogardus, 13 Cal. 73.   Approved, Appeal, where no motion for new trial has been made, findings are conclusive, 27 Cal. 69.

Rhine v. Ellen, 36 Cal. 362.   Approved, Estoppel, by recitals in deed, 40 Cal. 610.

Rhoades v. Selin, 4 Wash. C. C. 718.   Cited, Evidence, official certificates, 16 Cal. 554.

Rhoads v. Gordon, 38 Penn. St. 277.   Cited, Husband and Wife, presumption that property acquired belongs to the community, 30 Cal. 43.

Rhodes v. Cincinnati, 10 Ohio, 160.   Cited, Municipal Corporations, liabilities of, 16 Cal. 270.

Rhodes v. Smethurst, 4 Mees. & W. 42.   Cited, Statute of Limitations, construction of, 35 Cal. 638.

Ricard v. Williams, 7 Wheat. 59.   Cited, Title, by adverse possession of water, 25 Cal. 509; 11 Wheat. 318, note. Approved, Ejectment, ouster by tenant in common, 24 Cal. 376; disseisor cannot qualify his own wrong, 27 Cal. 562.

Rice v. Austin, 17 Mass. 197.   Cited, Contract, broker's contract construed, 14 Cal. 76.

Rice v. Cunningham, 29 Cal. 492.   Distinguished, Alcaldes' records as evidence, 31 Cal. 514, 522.   Cited, Appeal, verdict or finding not disturbed where evidence was conflicting, 32 Cal. 537.   Explained, 33 Cal. 68; 35 Cal. 37.

Rice v. Commonwealth, 18 B. Mon. 472.   Cited, Attorney and Counsel, striking from roll, 22 Cal. 320.

Rice v. Foster, 4 Harr. 479.   Cited, Constitutionality of Statute, rule of judicial determination, 41 Cal. 160.

Rice v. Gashire, 13 Cal. 53.   Cited, Appeal, errors reviewable on bill of exceptions or statement, 25 Cal. 61, 159.

Rice v. Inskeep, 34 Cal. 224. Cited, New Trial, motion for the exclusive remedy for defective findings, 38 Cal. 531; Id. 536; Judgment in action against administrator, effect of, 42 Cal. 133.

Rice v. Parkman, 16 Mass. 329. Cited, Constitutionality of Statute, principles of judicial determination, 17 Cal. 562.

Rice v. Railroad Co., 1 Black, 360. Cited as inapplicable, Grant of land to railroad, 37 Cal. 497.

Rice v. Rice, 4 Pick. 349. Commented on, Conveyance, when a mortgage, 10 Cal. 208.

Rice v. Shute, 2 W. Black. 696. Cited, Stare Decisis, as a rule of property, 15 Cal. 621.

Rice v. Turnpike Co., 7 Dana, 81. Cited, Eminent Domain, compensation on condemnation of land, 31 Cal. 373.

Rich v. Davis, 4 Cal. 22. Affirmed, Partnership note, liability of firm, 6 Cal. 142.

Rich v. Maples, 33 Cal. 102. Cited, Mexican Grant, survey and segregation of, 38 Cal. 66.

Rich v. Penfield, 1 Wend. 380. Cited, Parties, objection to non-joinder how taken, 8 Cal. 516.

Richards v. Dagget, 4 Mass. 534. Cited, Legislative Grant, construction of, 13 Cal. 456.

Richards v. Edick, 17 Barb. 262. Cited, Pleading, grounds for demurrer, 10 Cal. 558.

Richards v. Holmes, 18 How. 143. Approved, Conveyance, recitals as to debt in mortgage, conclusive, 19 Cal. 351.

Richards v. Levin, 16 Mo. 596. Cited, Insolvency, interest of assignee in trust, 10 Cal. 277.

Richards v. McMillan, 6 Cal. 419. Approved, Confession of Judgment, deficiency of statement in affidavit, *prima facie* evidence of fraud, 12 Cal. 146; 18 Cal. 580; 27 Cal. 235, 237. Commented on, not subject to collateral attack, 37 Cal. 336.

Richards v. Richards, Wright, 302. Cited, Divorce, for adultery, 10 Cal. 254.

Richards v. Schroder, 10 Cal. 431. Distinguished, Delivery, what constitutes change of possession, 14 Cal. 336.

Richards v. Skiff, 8 Ohio St. 588. Cited, Judgment, conclusiveness of, collateral attack, 34 Cal. 428.

Richardson, Matter of, 2 Story, 580. Commented on, Statute, when it takes effect, 1 Cal. 407.

Richardson v. Ainsworth, 20 How. Pr. 530. Cited, Assignment, rights of assignee of thing in action, 33 Cal. 528.

Richardson v. Baker, 5 J. J. Marsh. 323. Cited, Vendor's Lien, enforcement of, 15 Cal. 193.

Richardson v. Boright, 9 Vt. 370. Cited, Infant, avoidance of contract by, 24 Cal. 215.

Richardson v. Kier, 34 Cal. 63. Affirmed, 37 Cal. 263. Cited, Negligence, liability of ditch owners for injuries done by water, 35 Cal. 683.

Richardson v. Kuhn, 6 Watts, 299. Cited, Vendor and Vendee, right of possession in vendee, 22 Cal. 617; 40 Cal. 567.

Richardson v. McNulty, 24 Cal. 339. Cited, Corporation, insufficient evidence of existence of, 29 Cal. 129. Approved, Abandonment, a question of intention, 30 Cal. 636; evidence of, 36 Cal. 218; Id. 337; ejectment from mining claim, doctrine as to title inapplicable, 38 Cal. 370.

Richardson v. Mead, 27 Barb. 178. Commented on, Assignment, validity of, 34 Cal. 149.

Richardson v. Mellish, 2 Bing. 248. Commented on, Judicial Decisions, interpretation of, 15 Cal. 599.

Richardson v. Scott, 6 La. 56. Cited, Real Actions, under civil law, 1 Cal. 287.

Richardson v. Sharpe, 29 Barb. 222. Commented on, Will, power of sale in, 32 Cal. 444.

Richardson v. White, 18 Cal. 102. Cited, Lis Pendens, rule as to actual notice not changed by statute, 22 Cal. 211; 23 Cal. 38; 28 Cal. 204. Approved, Filing *lis pendens* as only way of charging purchaser with constructive notice, 18 Cal. 205.

Richardson v. Williamson, 24 Cal. 289. Cited, Statute of Limitations, when begins to run against confirmee of Mexican grant, 26 Cal. 46; 27 Cal. 65; 36 Cal. 632; as to trespass on real property, 29 Cal. 335; 1 Saw. 559. Approved, Ejectment, title by adverse possession as a defense, 31 Cal. 230; must be specially pleaded, 34 Cal. 390.

Richardson v. Wilton, 4 Sand. 708. Cited, Pleading, sham answer, 25 Cal. 196.

Richmond v. Sac. V. R. R. Co., 18 Cal. 351. Cited, Statutory Construction, repeal by implication, 38 Cal. 581; Negligence, liability of railroads for injury to cattle, 5 Kan. 187.

Richmond v. Smith, 8 Barn. & C. 9. Dictum approved, Innkeepers, liability, 1 Cal. 228.

Richmond v. Tayleur, 1 P. Wms. 737. Cited, Infant, bound by decree, 31 Cal. 283.

Richter v. Selin, 8 Serg. & R. 425. Cited, Vendor and Vendee, rights and liabilities of vendee, 22 Cal. 618.

Ricketson v. Richardson, 19 Cal. 330. Referred to on second appeal, 23 Cal. 636, 649.

Ricketson v. Richardson, 26 Cal. 149. Cited, Summons, statute as to service by publication to be strictly pursued, 27 Cal. 314; 30 Cal. 617. Approved, Affidavit, what must show, 31 Cal. 354; Appeal, judgment may be reversed in part, 7 Nev. 115.

Rickett v. Johnson, 8 Cal. 34. Approved, Injunction, court cannot restrain proceedings of another court of coördinate jurisdiction, 8 Cal. 71; Id. 271; Id. 521; 9 Cal. 77; Id. 614; 37 Cal. 269. Cited, 39 Cal. 162; 22 Wis. 486. Cited as inapplicable, 15 Cal. 134.

Ricketts v. Bennett, 4 Com. B. 686. Cited, Mining Partnership, powers of partner limited, 23 Cal. 206; 28 Cal. 579.

Ricks v. Reed, 19 Cal. 551. Cited, Conveyance, valid as between parties without acknowledgment or record, 26 Cal. 405. Approved, Jurisdiction, of county court, as to claims to town lots, 31 Cal. 15.

Rico v. Spence, 21 Cal. 504. Cited, Action to quiet title, possession essential, 25 Cal. 437; 37 Cal. 307; allegation of possession, material, 34 Cal. 559. Cited, Mexican Grant, patentee as trustee, 30 Cal. 307; title in confirmee, 39 Cal. 246.

Riddell v. Blake, 4 Cal. 264. Cited, Contract, conditions precedent on rescission of, 8 Cal. 403.

Riddell v. Shirley, 5 Cal. 488. Commented on, Insolvency, fraudulent conveyance by debtor, 10 Cal. 494; 23 Cal. 518.

Riddle v. Baker, 13 Cal. 295. Cited, Sureties, when bound by decree against principal, 14 Cal. 204; 38 Cal. 601. Approved, Equity, relief from fraud, 18 Cal. 149; 20 Cal. 449. Cited, Appeal, findings in equity, reviewable only on motion for new trial, 18 Cal. 396.

Riddle v. County of Bedford, 7 Serg. & R. 386. Cited, Office, eligibility to judicial office, 20 Cal. 146.

Riddle v. Proprietors of Locks, etc., 7 Mass. 185. Cited, Corporations, power of self-dissolution, 38 Cal. 172.

Riddle v. Varnum, 20 Pick. 280. Cited, Sale and Delivery, of goods in mass, delivery without segregation, 8 Cal. 609.

Rider v. Kidder, 10 Ves. Jr. 360. Cited, Husband and Wife, gift to wife, burden of proof, 12 Cal. 255.

Ridgeway v. Underwood, 4 Wash. C. C. 129. Cited, Execution, right of purchaser at sale under, 29 Cal. 57.

Riggs v. Tayloe, 9 Wheat. 483. Commented on, Evidence, secondary, of lost instrument, when admissible, 9 Cal. 447; 10 Cal. 148.

Riggs v. Waldo, 2 Cal. 485. Affirmed, Negotiable Instruments, guarantor liability is strictly that of indorser, 4 Cal. 277; 5 Cal. 139; 13 Cal. 32; Id. 580; 16 Cal. 153; 39 Cal. 494, 495. Cited, 2 Kan. 526. Distinguished, 9 Cal. 23. Affirmed, Who is guarantor, 34 Cal. 675; promise of guarantor not within statute of frauds, 34 Cal. 675; 38 Cal. 135.

Right v. Beard, 13 East, 210. Cited, Contract for Conveyance, vendee as tenant at will, 24 Cal. 145.

Rightor v. Phelps, 1 Rob. La. 330. Cited, Appeal, Rehearing, practice, 1 Cal. 197.

Riley v. Heisoh, 18 Cal. 198. Cited, Mexican Grant, title under, 19 Cal. 97; 24 Cal. 580; 33 Cal. 108. Commented on, 21 Cal. 582; Appeal, review of evidence where motion for new trial has been made, 21 Cal. 484.

Riley v. State, 9 Humph. 654. Cited, Verdict, separation of jury, 21 Cal. 341.

Rinohey v. Stryker, 28 N. Y. 52. Cited, Execution, justification of levy, 34 Cal. 351.

Ring, Matter of Edward, 28 Cal. 247. Approved, Judgment, in criminal cases, 31 Cal. 499; 32 Cal. 49; authority for detention at State prison, 31 Cal. 623. Cited, Appeal, bill of exceptions part of record, 37 Cal. 275.

Ring v. Franklin, 2 Hall. 1. Cited, Deed as a mortgage, parol evidence admissible, 36 Cal. 44.

Ring v. Gibbs, 26 Wend. 502. Cited, Official Bond, sufficiency of, 7 Cal. 441.

Ring v. Gray, 6 B. Mon. 373. Cited, Conveyance, construction of Registry Act, 6 Cal. 315.

Ringo v. Bivins, 10 Pet. 269. Cited, Agent, acquiring title as trustee of principal, 33 Cal. 377.

Ringgold v. Haven, 1 Cal. 108. Approved, Nonsuit, when court should order, 1 Cal. 127; Id. 221, 222. Cited, Objections to denial of motion for, how waived, 6 Cal. 26. Approved, Common Carrier, liable for non-delivery, 1 Cal. 214; Appeal, presumptions as to findings and judgment, 24 Cal. 378; 28 Cal. 312; evidence necessary in action, 11 La. An. 321.

Risden v. Inglet, 2 Croke Eliz. 838. Cited, Arbitration and Award, effect of omissions in award, 12 Cal. 341.

Rising v. Stannard, 17 Mass. 282. Cited, Tenant in Common, conveyance by, 35 Cal. 587.

Ritchie v. Dorland, 6 Cal. 33. Cited, Pleading, possession by plaintiff a material allegation in action to quiet title, 34 Cal. 559; Equity, when jurisdiction will be exercised over titles to real estate, 13 Mich. 370.

Ritchie v. Davis, 5 Cal. 453. Cited, Pleading, defects cured by verdict, 22 Cal. 235.

Ritchie v. United States, 5 Cranch C. C. 605. Denied, Mexican Grant, title under, 6 Cal. 269.

Ritter v. Patch, 12 Cal. 298. Approved, Injunction, will not issue to restrain collection of taxes without allegation of irreparable injury, 12 Cal. 300. Cited, 43 Miss. 759; 2 Neb. 438.

Ritter v. Ritter, 5 Blackf. 81. Commented on, Divorce, grounds for, 13 Cal. 104.

Ritter v. Scannell, 11 Cal. 238. Cited, Attachment, levy on second writ, 29 Cal. 315.

Ritter v. Stevenson, 7 Cal. 388; S. C. 11 Cal. 27. Doctrine not conceded, Mechanic's Lien, in the nature of a mortgage, 8 Nev. 231.

Ritter v. Stock, 12 Cal. 402. Cited, Appeal, verdict not disturbed where evidence was conflicting, 15 Cal. 382; 33 Cal. 68.

Rives v. Wilborne, 6 Ala. 45.   Cited, Replevin, nature of the possession acquired, 11 Cal. 275

Rix v. McHenry, 7 Cal. 89.   Cited, Judgment, lien of, not to be extended, 10 Cal. 83; Homestead, actual residence necessary, 45 Miss. 178.

Rix v. Robinson, 2 Burr. 803.   Cited, Forfeiture created by statute, enforcement of, 33 Cal. 217.

Roach v. Cosine, 9 Wend. 227.   Cited, Conveyance, when a mortgage, 36 Cal. 41; parol evidence admissible to prove, Id. 44, 65; 3 Mich. 223.

Robb v. Mann, 11 Penn. St. 305.   Cited, Administrator's Sales, judicial, 9 Cal. 196.

Robb v. Robb, 6 Cal. 21.   Cited, Jurisdiction, power of courts over their judgments, lost on adjournment of term, 8 Cal. 521; 25 Cal. 52; 28 Cal. 337, 338.   Commented on, 19 Cal. 707.

Robbins v. Bacon, 3 Greenl. 346.   Cited, Assignments, by order or draft, valid, 12 Cal. 98.

Robbins v. Milwaukee and H. R.R. Co., 6 Wis. 636.   Commented on, Public Lands, rights of settlers on, 21 Cal. 261; right of way over, 24 Cal. 258.

Robbins v. Oldham, 1 Duval, 28.   Cited, Sale and Delivery, of growing crops, 37 Cal. 638.

Robbins v. Rice, 7 Gray, 203.   Commented on, Judicial Sale, effect of filing duplicate certificate of sale, 31 Cal. 312.

Robbins v. Willard, 6 Pick. 464.   Cited, Evidence, admissions of partner not competent to charge other partner, 23 Cal. 103.

Roberts v. Anderson, 2 Johns. Ch. 202.   Cited, Injunction, practice on motion to dissolve, 35 Cal. 60.

Roberts v. Bean, 5 Smedes & M. 590.   Cited, Vendor and Vendee, remedy of vendor on breach of conditions, 14 Cal. 73.

Roberts v. Faillis, 1 Cow. 238.   Cited, Verdict, when irregularly found, 5 Cal. 46; validity of, 25 Cal. 400.

Roberts v. Higgins, 5 Ind. 542.   Cited, Exceptions to instructions, when to be taken, 26 Cal. 267.

Roberts v. Holsworth, 5 Halst. 57.   Cited, Mandamus, when it will not lie, 24 Cal. 84.

Roberts v. Landecker, 9 Cal. 262. Cited, Attachment, liability of garnishee, 38 Cal. 614.

Robertson v. Bullions, 9 Barb. 64. Cited, Trust and Trustee, equitable jurisdiction, 10 Cal. 588.

Robertson v. Jackson, 2 Com. B. 412. Cited, Evidence, parol evidence to explain written instrument, 34 Cal. 629.

Robertson v. Pope, 1 Rich. 501. Commented on, Principal and Agent, instrument signed by agent, 13 Cal. 235.

Robertson v. Smith, 18 John. 459. Commented on, Judgment, as a bar, 6 Cal. 180.

Robin v. Castille, 7 La. 292. Cited, Husband and Wife, presumptions as to common property, 30 Cal. 31.

Robinett, Appeal of, 36 Penn. St. 174. Cited, Executors and Administrators, duties as to surplus funds, 37 Cal. 430.

Robinett v. Preston, 2 Rob. Va. 278. Commented on, Tenant in Common, validity of deed by co-tenant, 15 Cal. 369. Cited, 35 Cal. 588.

Robins v. Maidstone, 4 Q. B. 811. Cited, Pleading, admissions in, 33 Cal. 97.

Robinson v. Bidwell, 22 Cal. 386. Approved, Constitutionality of Statute, in part unconstitutional, 24 Cal. 546; 8 Nev. 342. Denied, Scope and object of act authorizing county aid to railroads, 24 Cal. 552, 555. Cited, Legislature, may authorize county aid to railroads, 7 Kan. 506; 27 Iowa, 81; 30 Iowa, 30.

Robinson v. Bland, 1 W. Black. 264; S. C. 2 Burr. 1077. Commented on, Money won at gaming not recoverable, 1 Cal. 443. Cited, Stare Decisis, as a rule of property, 15 Cal. 621.

Robinson v. Campbell, 8 Mo. 366, 615. Cited, Chattel Mortgage, legal effect and operation, 27 Cal. 269.

Robinson v. Charleston, 2 Rich. 317. Cited, Mistake, money paid under mistake of law not recoverable, 18 Cal. 271.

Robinson v. Chesseldine, 5 Ill. 333. Cited, Notice of motion will not operate as a stay, 8 Cal. 134.

Robinson v. Cropsey, 2 Edw. Ch. 138; S. C. 6 Paige, 480. Cited, Contract, conditional sale, 9 Cal. 551. Commented on, when a mortgage, 10 Cal. 207; 14 Cal. 435. Cited, 33 Cal. 333.

Robinson v. Doolittle, 12 Vt. 246.   Dictum qualified, Debtor and Creditor, application of payments, 14 Cal. 450.

Robinson v. Dauchy, 3 Barb. 20.   Cited, Contract, made in foreign State, presumption as to law of, 21 Cal. 227.

Robinson v. Flint, 16 How. Pr. 240.   Commented on, Pleading, joinder of causes of action, 17 Cal. 498.

Robinson v. Forrest, 29 Cal. 317.   Approved, State Lands, approved plat of survey not conclusive evidence that lands are swamp and overflowed, 31 Cal. 464.   Cited, Preëmption, rights of, not to be questioned by party not in privity with government, 33 Cal. 458.

Robinson v. Gaar, 6 Cal. 273.   Commented on, Taxation, injunction will not lie to restrain collection of taxes, 8 Cal. 388; 10 Cal. 403; 36 Cal. 71; 43 Miss. 759; Injunction to Supervisors, when it will not lie, 25 Cal. 120.

Robinson v. Gleadow, 2 Bing. N. C. 156.   Cited, Corporation, ratification by adoption of act of officers, 4 Cal. 171.

Robinson v. Howard, 5 Cal. 428.   Cited, Judgment, on demurrer, when conclusive, 22 Cal. 222.

Robinson v. Justice, 2 Penn. 19.   Cited, Estoppel, what does not constitute, 10 Cal. 631.

Robinson v. Leavitt, 7 N. H. 73.   Commented on, Mortgage, discharge of, 16 Cal. 199.

Robinson v. Magee, 9 Cal. 83.   Cited, Statutory Construction, statute when equivalent to a contract, 10 Cal. 162; Id. 572.   Commented on, Legislature cannot impair obligation of, 16 Cal. 32.   Cited, 39 Cal. 274.

Robinson v. Myers, 3 Dana, 441.   Cited, Execution, election by debtor of property exempt, 22 Cal. 507.

Robinson v. Reynolds, 2 Q. B. 196.   Approved, Negotiable Instruments, liability of acceptor, 22 Cal. 666.

Robinson v. Rowan, 3 Ill. 499.   Cited, Conveyances, construction of recording act, 7 Cal. 497.

Robinson v. Sacramento Co., 16 Cal. 208.   Cited, Supervisors, a quasi-judicial body, 18 Cal. 149; 25 Cal. 97; 7 Nev. 397; Certiorari, to review acts of supervisors, when will issue, 23 Cal. 495; 45 Mo. 56.

Robinson v. Schly, 6 Geo. 515.   Cited, Will, construction of, 17 Cal. 640.

Robinson v. Smith, 3 Paige, 222. Cited, Corporation, action by stockholder for removal of officers, and for an accounting, 16 Cal. 151; 28 Cal. 484.

Robinson v. Smith, 14 Cal. 95. Cited, Negotiable Instruments, transferable before maturity, 14 Cal. 454; Mortgage for preëxisting debt, 6 Nev. 310.

Robinson v. Weeks, 6 How. Pr. 161. Cited, Assignment, cause of action for personal injury not assignable, 22 Cal. 177; 33 Cal. 528.

Robison v. Swett, 3 Greenl. 316. Cited, Land, constructive possession under deed, 25 Cal. 135.

Roby v. West, 4 N. H. 290. Cited, Contract, void in part is void *in toto,* 40 Cal. 348.

Rochester City Bank v. Suydam, 5 How. Pr. 254. Cited, Witness, privileged communications, 23 Cal. 334.

Rockefeller v. Hoysradt, 2 Hill, 617. Cited, Variance, *allegata* and *probata* should correspond, 36 Cal. 178.

Rockville & W. T. Co. v. Van Ness, 2 Cranch C. C. 449. Cited, Estoppel *in pais,* technical defect in corporate act not to constitute, 40 Cal. 625.

Rockwell v. Hubbell, 2 Doug. Mich. 197. Disapproved, Statutory Construction, statutes not to be construed retrospectively, 4 Cal. 137, 160.

Rodebaugh v. Sanks, 2 Watts, 9. Commented on, Statutory Construction, provisions directory, 11 Cal. 58.

Rodgers v. Jones, 1 McCord Ch. 221. Cited, Foreclosure of Mechanic's Lien, necessary parties, 10 Cal. 552.

Rodman v. Harcourt, 4 B. Mon. 225. Cited, Office, eligibility to, 13 Cal. 154.

Rodrigues v. United States, 1 Wall. 582. Cited, Survey, conclusiveness of, 28 Cal. 660; conflicting surveys, 32 Cal. 666, 668; confirmation of survey conclusive, 38 Cal. 61, 63.

Rodriguez v. Comstock, 24 Cal. 85. Cited, Mexican Grant, validity of, 26 Cal. 628; New Trial, surprise, sufficiency of, 39 Cal. 558.

Roe v. Bank of U. S., 3 Ohio, 26. Disapproved, Jurisdiction of United States Supreme Court, 9 Cal. 724.

Roe v. Doe, 2 Term Rep. 644. Cited, Arbitration and Award, selection of umpire, 23 Cal. 367.

33

Roe v. Street, 2 Adol. & E. 329. Cited, Contract for Conveyance, occupant as a tenant at will, 24 Cal. 145.

Roe v. Swart, 5 Cow. 294. Cited, Judgment, lien of, statutory construction, 10 Cal. 80; how preserved, 37 Cal. 133; application of proceeds to prior lien, Id. 136.

Roe v. Pierce, 2 Camp. 96. Commented on, Principal and Agent, adoption of act of agent, 4 Cal. 170.

Rogers v. Bradshaw, 20 John. 735. Cited, Eminent Domain, compensation for condemnation, 18 Cal. 260.

Rogers v. Darnaby, 4 B. Mon. 240. Commented on, Sheriff, ex-sheriff to complete execution of process, 8 Cal. 409.

Rogers v. De Forest, 7 Paige, 277. Cited, Contract, void in part is void *in toto,* 8 Cal. 129.

Rogers v. Goodwin, 2 Mass. 475. Cited, Statutory Construction, contemporaneous interpretation, 22 Cal. 71.

Rogers v. Hall, 4 Watts, 359. Cited, Deed, recitals in, conclusive on grantor, 26 Cal. 87; contra, 8 Wis. 482.

Rogers v. Hoberlin, 11 Cal. 120. Construed, Public Administrators, authority to act, 17 Cal. 238; 34 Cal. 468.

Rogers v. Huie, 1 Cal. 429; S. C. 2 Cal. 571. Cited, New Trial, newly discovered evidence, showing required, 38 Cal. 194. Commented on, Auctioneer, when liable in conversion, 44 Mo. 544. Cited, Conversion defined, 41 Ala. 539.

Rogers v. Hurd, 4 Day, 57. Cited, Infant, ratification of contract by, 24 Cal. 213.

Rogers v. Jennings, 3 Yerg. 308. Statute distinguished, Execution, validity of sale under, 38 Cal. 655.

Rogers v. Kneeland, 10 Wend. 219. Cited, Guaranty, when not within statute of frauds, 5 Cal. 287.

Rogers v. Parkham, 8 Geo. 190. Cited, Contract, action for breach of entire contract when maintainable, 35 Cal. 242, 246.

Rogers v. Pitcher, 6 Taunt. 207. Cited, Estoppel, tenant when not estopped, 33 Cal. 254. Commented on, 35 Cal. 572, 574.

Rogers v. Rogers, 14 Wend. 131. Cited, Juror and Jury, challenge for bias, 1 Cal. 384.

Rogers v. Saunders, 16 Me. 101. Commented on, Specific Performance, when contract will not be enforced, 10 Cal. 328, 329.

Rogers v. Watrous, 8 Tex. 62. Cited, Statutory Construction, repeal by implication, 10 Cal. 316.

Roget v. Merritt, 2 Caines, 117. Cited, Debtor and Creditor, payment by note, 12 Cal. 323.

Roland v. Kreyenhagen, 18 Cal. 455. Cited, Ejectment, setting aside judgment by default, 22 Cal. 465; order setting aside, in discretion, 29 Cal. 423; jurisdiction to set aside, lost on expiration of term, 28 Cal. 338.

Rollins v. Ames, 2 N. H. 349. Commented on, New Trial, for bias of juror, 9 Cal. 310.

Rollins v. Forbes, 10 Cal. 299. Approved, Foreclosure, personal judgment in, 10 Cal. 444; 14 Cal. 157; 16 Cal. 422; 22 Cal. 127; 23 Cal. 623; 25 Cal. 349; Pleading, demurrer does not lie to prayer in complaint, 15 Cal. 495; 38 Cal. 234.

Rollins v. Stevens, 31 Me. 454. Cited, Surety, individual partner as surety on note, 37 Cal. 117.

Romaine, Matter of, 23 Cal. 585. Cited, Fugitives from justice, surrender of, proceedings, 106 Mass. 225.

Romaine v. Van Allen, 26 N. Y. 309. Commented on, Conversion, damages where value fluctuates, 39 Cal. 423.

Roman v. Moody, Dallam, 512. Approved, Office, constitutional term of, 11 Cal. 88.

Romilly v. James, 6 Taunt. 263. Cited, Evidence, opinion of witnesses when not admissible as to title, 29 Cal. 412.

Rondell v. Fay, 32 Cal. 354. Approved, Corporation, right to act not subject to collateral inquiry, 37 Cal. 541; 24 Mich. 394.

Ronkendorff v. Taylor's Lessees, 4 Pet. 361. Cited, Notice, publication of, computation of time, 32 Cal. 352.

Rood v. N. Y. & Erie R. R. Co., 18 Barb. 80. Commented on, Negligence, in the exercise of a lawful right, 9 Cal. 257.

Roome v. Webb, 1 Code Rep. 114. Cited, Injunction, practice on motion to dissolve, 35 Cal. 59.

Roosevelt v. Gardinier, 2 Cow. 463. Cited, Name, middle name immaterial in law, 6 Cal. 206.

Roosevelt v. Kellogg, 20 John. 208. Cited, Pleading, discharge in insolvency, what must be shown, 33 Cal. 536.

Root v. Chandler, 10 Wend. 110. Cited, Pleading, justification in trespass to be specially pleaded, 10 Cal. 304; constructive possession sufficient to maintain action, 12 Cal. 463.

Root v. French, 13 Wend. 570. Cited, Fraud, avoids contract of sale, 12 Cal. 462; title of *bona fide* purchaser, 12 Cal. 498; 23 Cal. 361. Commented on, 32 Ill. 423.

Root v. Lowndes, 6 Hill, 518. Cited, Slander, proof of malice, 39 Cal. 74.

Ropps v. Barker, 4 Pick. 238. Cited, Verdict, polling jury in civil action, 20 Cal. 72.

Rosborough v. Shasta Riv. Canal Co., 22 Cal. 556. Cited, Corporation, ratification of contract by, 33 Cal. 199.

Rose v. Beatie, 2 Nott & McC. 538. Approved, 1 McCord. 514. Cited, Damages, on breach of contract, 17 Cal. 496.

Rose v. Davis, 11 Cal. 133. Cited, Land, constructive possession under deed, 23 Cal. 437; 38 Cal. 487. Commented on, 25 Cal. 138.

Rose v. Houston, 11 Tex. 326. Commented on, Husband and Wife, separate property, 30 Cal. 38.

Rose v. Munie, 4 Cal. 173. Cited, Mortgage, priority of lien, construction of recording act, 6·Cal. 673; 15 Cal. 132.

Rose v. Story, 1 Penn. St. 191. Cited, Damages, measure of, in trespass on personal property, 11 Cal. 25.

Ross v. Barland, 1 Pet. 655. Distinguished, Evidence, patent as, 33 Cal. 88. Cited, Patent, conflicting patents, equity, title by relation, 34 Cal. 512; 42 Cal. 615; 3 How. 673; 21 How. 240.

Ross v. City of Madison, 1 Carter, 281. Commented on, Municipal Corporations, liability on implied contracts, 9 Cal. 470; 16 Cal. 267.

Ross v. Duval, 13 Pet. 45. Denied, Limitation of Actions, computation of time, 7 Cal. 5; 7 How. 780.

Ross v. Gould, 5 Greenl. 204. Cited, Land, constructive possession under deed, 25 Cal. 135.

Ross v. Hicks, 11 Barb. 481. Cited, Set-off, judgments, practice, 11 Cal. 103.

Ross v. Irving, 14 Ill. 173. Cited, Ejectment, damages on eviction, measure of, 7 Cal. 25.

Ross v. Luther, 4 Cow. 158. Cited, Pleading, defense of sheriff for violation of duty, 28 Cal. 286.

Ross v. Reddick, 2 Ill. 73. Cited, Judicial Notice, of political subdivisions, 16 Cal. 231.

Ross v. Supervisors of Outagamie Co., 12 Wis. 38. Cited, Taxation, of claim to public lands, 30 Cal. 648; Public Land, title acquired by preemptioner on payment, 37 Cal. 495; interest acquired by location of warrant, 31 Cal. 268.

Ross v. Wilson, 7 Smedes & M. 753. Cited, Debtor and Creditor, rights of creditor to property in hands of surety, 35 Cal. 145.

Rossiter v. Rossiter, 8 Wend. 494. Cited, Principal and Agent, when acts of special agent bind principal, 8 Cal. 244; 13 Cal. 48; 24 Cal. 140. Commented on, General words in power how construed, 14 Cal. 399.

Rothmahler v. Myers, 4 Desaus. 215. Cited, Wills cannot be altered, varied, or added to by parol, 35 Cal. 340.

Rothwell v. Dewees, 2 Black, 618. Cited, Trust, when implied trust arises, 30 Cal. 594.

Rothschild v. Corney, 9 Barn. & C. 388. Cited, Negotiable Instruments, presumptive dishonor, reasonable time, 40 Cal. 115.

Rouquier's Heirs v. Roquier's Executors, 5 Mart. N. S. 98. Cited, Husband and Wife, wife's interest in common property, 14 Cal. 604.

Rouse v. Bardin, 1 H. Black. 352. Rule of common law distinguished, Pleading, defense of justification in trespass, 27 Cal. 367.

Roush v. Van Hagen, 18 Cal. 668; S. C. 17 Cal. 121. Approved, Undertaking, on appeal, sureties before whom to justify, 21 Cal. 512.

Rousse v. Wheeler, 4 Rob. 118. Cited, Husband and Wife, separate property of wife, 30 Cal. 35.

Roussin v. Stewart, 33 Cal. 208. Cited, Pleading, sufficiency of denial " on confirmation and belief," 36 Cal. 234; 38 Cal. 163.

Rovee v. Farmer, 4 Term Rep. 146. Cited, Pleading, averments on pleading estoppel by judgment, 26 Cal. 505.

Rowan v. Lyttle, 11 Wend. 616.   Approved, Landlord and Tenant, tenancy by sufferance, when it ensues, 28 Cal. 555.

Rowan v. Portland, 8 B. Mon. 232.   Cited, Dedication, to public use by sale of lots on plat, 22 Cal. 489; 35 Cal. 501.

Rowbotham v. Wilson, 8 Ellis & B. 157.   Cited, Easement, what constitutes, 32 Cal. 506.

Rowe v. Chandler, 1 Cal. 167.   Construed, Judgment, in action on joint and several contract, 6 Cal. 183.   Cited, 7 Minn. 224.

Rowe, Ex parte, 7 Cal. 175; Id. 181; Id. 184.   Approved, Contempt, order reviewable on appeal, 9 Cal. 111.

Rowe v. Granite Bridge Co., 21 Pick. 344.   Commented on, Nuisance, equitable jurisdiction, 30 Cal. 388.

Rowe v. Kohle, 4 Cal. 285.   Cited, Married Woman, not liable on contract, 10 Cal. 267; how may bind her separate property, 38 Cal. 256; wherein statute has changed common law rule, McAll. 99.

Rowe v. Table Mt. Wat. Co., 10 Cal. 441.   Distinguished, Corporation, return of summons on, 10 Cal. 445; bound on note and mortgage by president and secretary, 23 Cal. 347.   Cited, Foreclosure, personal judgment in, 22 Cal. 127; 23 Cal. 623.

Rowe v. Young, 2 Brod. & B. 165.   Rule distinguished, Negotiable Instruments, demand at place of payment, 7 Cal. 167.   Commented on, 11 Cal. 324, 325.   Followed, 13 Ired. 77.   Cited, 11 Wheat. 174.   Contra, 2 McLean, 125.

Rowe v. Yuba Co., 17 Cal. 61.   Cited, Costs, counsel fees for gratuitous services not chargeable to county, 43 Mo. 344.

Rowland v. Kreyenhagen, 24 Cal. 52.   Cited, Appeal, effect of dismissal as to sureties on appeal bond, 29 Cal. 139; recall of remittitur for fraudulent procurement of dismissal, 36 Cal. 328.

Rowland v. Leiby, 14 Cal. 156.   Cited, Foreclosure, personal judgment in, 16 Cal. 422; 22 Cal. 127; 23 Cal. 623; 25 Cal. 34.

Rowlandson, Ex parte, 3 P. Wms. 405.   Commented on, Judgment on joint and several contracts, 6 Cal. 182; 9 How. 99.

Rowley v. Bigelow, 12 Pick. 308. Cited, Fraudulent Conveyance, title of innocent purchaser, 12 Cal. 498.

Rowley v. Brown, 1 Bin. 61. Commented on, Execution, sale in mass, 6 Cal. 52.

Rowley v. Stoddard, 7 John. 207. Cited, Surety, right to contribution, 11 Cal. 220; release of one is a release of all, 38 Cal. 531, 537.

Royalton v. R. and W. T. Co., 14 Vt. 311. Cited, Contract, when action lies on breach of an entire contract, 35 Cal. 242. Commented on, Id. 243.

Royce v. Hurd, 24 Vt. 620. Cited, Statute of Limitations, construed, 6 Cal. 433.

Rubottom v. McClure, 4 Blackf. 505. Cited, Trespass, lies for taking property condemned without compensation, 31 Cal. 554, 559.

Rucher v. Conyngham, 2 Pet. Adm. 300. Cited, Pledge, of vessel by master, when authorized, 8 Cal. 534.

Rudd v. Davis, 3 Hill. 287. Cited, Appeal, from order granting new trial, 26 Cal. 525.

Rudd v. Schlatter, 1 Litt. 19. Commented on, Constitutionality of Statute, statutes suspending remedies, 4 Cal. 169.

Ruff's Admrs. v. Bull, 7 Harr. & J. 14. Cited, Statute of Limitations, on death of creditor, 35 Cal. 638.

Rugby Charity v. Merryweather, 11 East, 375. Cited, Dedication, to public use, cul de sac. 35 Cal. 498.

Ruggles v. Bucknor, 1 Paine's C. C. Rep. 358. Commented on, Officers, certificates of, as evidence of official character, 16 Cal. 554.

Ruggles v. Hall, 14 John. 112. Cited, New Trial, surprise, showing required, 1 Cal. 433.

Ruggles v. Lawson, 13 John. 285. Cited, Deed, an escrow, 30 Cal. 212.

Ruggles v. Patten, 8 Mass. 479. Commented on, Negotiable Instrument, place of payment not of essence of contract, 1 Cal. 321.

Ruiz v. Norton, 4 Cal. 355; S. C. Oct. T. 1853 (not reported.) Cited, Pleading, special defenses by vendee in action on contract, 4 Cal. 20; warranty on sale of chattels, when implied, 5 Cal. 474. Approved, Parties, undisclosed principal may sue on contract made by agent, 12 Cal. 88; Counter-claim, unliquidated damages, 26 Cal. 305.

Runnells v. Jackson, 1 How. Miss. 358. Cited, Specific Performance, of verbal contract, when will be decreed, 35 Cal. 487; time not of essence of contract, 40 Cal. 11.

Runyan v. Lessee of Coster, 14 Pet. 122. Cited. Corporations, corporate powers of, defined, 1 Cal. 356.

Runyan v. Mersereau, 11 John. 534. Commented on, Mortgage, mere incident to the debt, 9 Cal. 408; mortgagee has but a chattel interest, 36 Cal. 41.

Rupert v. Dantzler, 12 Smedes & M. 697. Cited, Judgment, lien of, not extended by levy of execution, 10 Cal. 80.

Rupp v. Orr, 31 Penn. St. 517. Cited, Trust, implied trust, when it arises, 30 Cal. 594.

Rush v. Barr, 1 Watts, 110. Cited, Statute of Limitations, fraudulent concealment to avoid, 8 Cal. 460.

Rush v. Casey, 39 Cal. 339; followed in Rush v. Casey, same term (not reported.) Commented on, Mexican Grants, effect of rejection of land claim, 39 Cal. 368.

Rushton v. Aspinall, 2 Doug. 679. Cited, Judgment, must be supported by allegations in complaint, 30 Cal. 489. Distinguished, 9 Wheat. 595.

Russ v. Mebuis, 16 Cal. 350. Cited, Trust, resulting trust may be defeated or established by parol, 22 Cal. 579; when parol evidence admissible, 7 Kan. 207; Equity, will not relieve from mistake of law, 28 Cal. 637.

Russell v. Amador, 3 Cal. 400. Approved, Instruction, modification of, 5 Cal. 492. Denied, As to limitation of power of court to modify, 25 Cal. 470.

Russell v. Armador, 2 Cal. 305; followed in Sullivan v. Saunders, Pixley v. Rowe, and Smith v. Stevens, Cal. Sup. Ct. July T. 1854 (not reported.) Cited, Findings, of court form the basis of the judgment, 2 Cal. 321; Id. 475; 3 Cal. 111; Id. 135. Construed, 4 Cal. 216; 28 Cal. 596. Followed, 2 Cal. 419.

Russell v. Byron, 2 Cal. 86. Cited, Appeal, dismissal of case for want of grounds of action in complaint, 37 Cal. 228; Partnership, action will not lie by partner without praying for an accounting, 39 N. H. 53.

Russell v. Clapp, 7 Barb. 482. Cited, Pleading, ownership how set forth, 11 Cal. 168; insufficient denial in answer, 32 Cal. 573.

Russell v. Commonwealth, 7 Serg. & R. 489. Cited, Judgment of imprisonment to commence at end of term, valid, 22 Cal. 137.

Russell v. Conway, 11 Cal. 93. Commented on, Set-off, judgment as a set-off, 19 Cal. 659; 23 Cal. 627; when will be decreed, Id. 629.

Russell v. Copp, 5 N. H. 154. Cited, New Promise, sufficiency of acknowledgment, 36 Cal. 185.

Russell v. Dudley, 3 Met. 147. Cited, Constitutionality of Statute, suspending remedies, 4 Cal. 169.

Russell v. Elliott, 2 Cal. 245. Commented on, Reference, when may be ordered, 2 Cal. 261. Cited, Contract, law part of, 6 Cal. 59; Mandamus, when it lies, 7 Cal. 133; Replevin Bond, conditions precedent in action on, 7 Cal. 570.

Russell v. Ford. See Russell v. Byron.

Russell v. Hogan, 2 Ill. 552. Approved, Judgment, several judgment by default, when erroneous, 6 Cal. 182; 7 Cal. 448.

Russell v. Irby, 13 Ala. 131. Cited, Statutory Construction, penal sections to be strictly construed, 15 Cal. 474.

Russell v. LaRoque, 13 Ala. 151. Cited, Appeal, law of case not revisable, 15 Cal. 83; 20 Cal. 417.

Russell v. Mann, 22 Cal. 131. Approved, Pleading, tax title how pleaded, 35 Cal. 449; Facts, the foundation of statutory right to be set forth, 7 Nev. 172.

Russell v. Mayor, etc., of N. Y., 2 Denio, 461. Cited, Municipal Corporations, not liable for destruction of building to stop conflagration, 1 Cal. 357; not a condemnation to public use, 1 Cal. 356.

Russell v. Men of Devon, 2 Term Rep. 667. Commented on, County, inhabitants of, not liable for debts or obligations of, 10 Cal. 409; 2 Black, 52.

Russell v. Mixer, 39 Cal. 504. Referred to, Mortgage, relief from mistake in decree of foreclosure, 42 Cal. 478.

Russell v. Nicoll, 3 Wend. 112. Cited, Sale and Delivery, of goods to arrive, conditions precedent, 1 Cal. 447.

Russell v. Richards, 10 Me. 429. Commented on, Conveyance, several ownership of land and structure, 15 Cal. 197:

Russell v. Southard, 12 How. 154. Cited, Mortgage, rights of mortgagee on forfeiture, 26 Cal. 602.

Russell v. Todd, 7 Blackf. 239. Commented on, Vendor's Lien, enforcement of, 15 Cal. 193.

Russell v. Whipple, 2 Cow. 536. Cited, Pleading, sufficient averment in complaint on note, 36 Cal. 302.

Rutherford v. Greene's Heirs, 2 Wheat. 196. Cited, State Lands, legislative grant, validity of, 13 Cal. 414. Approved, Title passes though wanting identity to make it perfect, 27 Cal. 327, 328; when title becomes perfect, 16 Cal. 320; 38 Cal. 67. Distinguished, 17 How. 575.

Rutherford v. McGowen, 1 Nott & McC. 17. Cited, Ferrymen, as common carriers, 5 Cal. 364.

Ryan v. Daly, 6 Cal. 238. Distinguished, Confession of Judgment, 13 Cal. 334. Commented on, when void, 27 Cal. 233.

Ryan v. Dougherty, 30 Cal. 218. Cited, Appeal, when statement no part of record, 32 Cal. 312; Arbitration and Award, practice on submission of award, 42 Cal. 129.

Ryan v. Marsh, 2 Nott & McC. 156. Cited, Use and Occupation, when action lies for, 3 Cal. 203; 35 Cal. 194. Commented on, 2 How. 159.

Ryan v. Ryan, 9 Mo. 539. Cited, Divorce, recrimination, 10 Cal. 257.

Ryan v. Tomlinson, 31 Cal. 11. Referred to on second appeal, Statute of Frauds, 39 Cal. 643.

Ryberg v. Snell, 2 Wash. C. C. 403. Commented on, Sale and Delivery, delivery by bill of lading, 1 Cal. 80.

Ryde v. Curtis, 16 Eng. Co n. L. 335; 8 Dowl. & R. 62. Cited, Guaranty, when not within the statute of frauds, 5 Cal. 287.

Ryerson v. Nicholson, 2 Yeates, 516. Cited, Jurisdiction, power of court over its process, 14 Cal. 678.

Ryerss v. Rippey, 25 Wend. 432. Statute distinguished, Ejectment, who bound by judgment, 22 Cal. 209.

Ryerss v. Wheeler, 25 Wend. 437; S. C. 4 Hill, 466. Commented on, Ejectment, who bound by judgment, 22 Cal. 210.

Rynerson v. Kelsey, 34 Cal. 470. Cited, Election, of tax collector, legislative powers, 36 Cal. 382; Taxation, when assessment invalid, 39 Cal. 359.

Sabin v. Harkness, 4 N. H. 415. Cited, Fixtures, what constitute, 14 Cal. 68.

Sacket v. Wheaton, 17 Pick. 105. Cited, Water Rights, right to running water, disseisin of appropriator, 5 Cal. 447.

Sackett's Harb. Bk. v. Lewis Co. Bk., 11 Barb. 213. Cited, Corporations, powers of, under charter, 22 Cal. 630; defense of *ultra vires,* not available in action on contract, 16 Cal. 265.

Sacramento v. Bird, 15 Cal. 294. Cited, Statutory Construction, repeal by implication, 19 Cal. 512.

Sacramento v. Cal. Stage Co., 12 Cal. 134. Cited, Municipal Corporations, city licenses to stage companies, 17 Gratt. 186.

Sacramento v. Dunlap, 14 Cal. 421. Distinguished, Sureties, on official bond, liability of, 17 Cal. 509. Approved, liability on joint bond, 21 Cal. 589. Commented on, 25 Cal. 530.

Sacramento P. and N. R. R. Co., v. Harlan, 24 Cal. 334. Approved, Appeal lies from judgment in proceedings to condemn land, 29 Cal. 115; 39 Cal. 584. Cited, 42 Cal. 68.

Sacramento V. R. R. Co. v. Moffatt, 6 Cal. 74. Cited, Condemnation of Land, compensation a condition precedent to right, 29 Cal. 117; appeal lies in cases for condemnation of land, 42 Cal. 68.

Saddler's Co. v. Badcock, 2 Atk. 554. Cited, Insurance, against fire, policy void for want of interest in insurer, 30 Cal. 89. Approved, Character of contract of insurance, 38 Cal. 542.

Safford v. Annis, 7 Me. 168. Cited, Statute of Frauds, sale of growing crops not within, 23 Cal. 69.

Safford v. Drew, 3 Duer, 627. Cited, Pleading, material allegations in complaint, 14 Cal. 456. Cited, Action, civil action for death of person exclusively statutory, 25 Cal. 435.

Safford v. People, 1 Park. Cr. Rep. 474. Cited, Judgment, validity of, in criminal action, 31 Cal. 627.

Sager v. P. S. and P. and E. R. R. Co., 31 Me. 238. Cited, Common Carriers, contract of, 27 Cal. 33; liability on, 27 Cal. 38.

Sainter v. Ferguson, 7 Com. B. 716. Cited, Contract, liquidated damages in, 19 Cal. 682.

Salem Iron Factory v. Danvers, 10 Mass. 514. Cited, Taxation, *situs* of personal property, 23 Cal. 139, 140.

Salinger v. Luck, 7 How. Pr. 430. Cited, Pleading, insufficient denials, 31 Cal. 195.

Salmon v. Clagett, 3 Bland. Ch. 162. Cited, Foreclosure, of instalment mortgage, 23 Cal. 31.

Salmon v. Davis, 4 Bin. 375. Cited, Release, by partner, effect of, 10 Cal. 125.

Salmon v. Hoffman, 2 Cal. 138. Approved, Vendor and Vendee, lien of vendor, 6 Cal. 226; 22 Cal. 617; 32 Cal. 59; vendee in possession cannot reclaim purchase money without an eviction, 8 Cal. 403; 22 Cal. 617.

Salmon v. Symonds, 30 Cal. 301. Approved, Trust and Trustee, equity jurisdiction to enforce resulting trust, 32 Cal. 462; patent to land held in trust, 33 Cal. 263; 1 Saw. 205.

Salter v. Kidgly, Carth. 76. Cited, Deed, grantor cannot covenant with stranger to deed, 17 Cal. 53.

Saltmarsh v. Tuthill, 12 How. 389. Cited, Writ of error to U. S. supreme court, authority to issue citation, 32 Cal. 240.

Saltpetre Case, 7 Coke, 13. Commented on, Mines and Mining, right to mine, 14 Cal. 310.

Saltus v. Everett, 20 Wend. 268. Cited, Lien, warehouseman's lien how waived, 23 Cal. 511; Sale and Delivery, possession of personal property indicates ownership, 42 Cal. 147.

Salvidge v. Hyde, 5 Madd. 138. Commented on, Parties, in equitable action, 31 Cal. 429.

Salyer v. State, 5 Ind. 202. Cited, Sureties, on official bond, liability of, 25 Cal. 223.

Sam v. State, 33 Miss. 352. Commented on, Evidence, in criminal cases, 31 Cal. 568.

Sampeyreac v. United States, 7 Pet. 222. Cited, Legislature, power to pass special acts, 17 Cal. 556; Id. 562; power over remedies, 33 Cal. 457.

Sampson v. Hammond, 4 Cal. 184. Cited, Conversion, trover may be maintained for timber cut from realty, 25 Wis. 660.

Sampson v. Henry, 11 Pick. 379. Cited, Landlord and Tenant, forcible ejectment of tenant illegal, 15 Cal. 225.

Sampson v. Pattison, 1 Hare, 536. Cited, Deed, in trust, not a mortgage, 14 Cal. 263.

Sampson v. White, 1 McCord, 74. Cited, Will, due execution of, when presumed, 10 Cal. 479.

Sampson v. Williamson, 6 Tex. 109. Commented on, Homestead, right of alienation, 14 Cal. 475.

Samuels v. Gorham, 5 Cal. 226. Approved, Statute of Frauds, what constitutes a valid sale and delivery, 2 Nev. 246.

Sanchez v. Carriaga, 31 Cal. 170. Cited, Injunction, when will not issue to restrain execution of judgment, 37 Cal. 228; Id. 529.

Sanchez v. McMahon, 35 Cal. 218. Cited, New Trial, requisites of statement on, 5 Nev. 261.

Sanchez v. Roach, 5 Cal. 248. Commented on, Parties, substitution of legal representatives on death of party, 35 Cal. 468, 470.

Sanders v. Betts, 7 Wend. 287. Cited, Written Instrument, conclusiveness of recitals, 9 Cal. 226.

Sanders v. Leavy, 16 How. Pr. 308. Approved, Ejectment, sufficiency of complaint, 16 Cal. 245.

Sanders v. Whitesides, 10 Cal. 88. Cited, Appeal, suspends operation of judgment, 28 Cal. 91.

Sanderson v. Bowes, 14 East, 500. Denied, Negotiable Instruments, demand at place of payment, 11 Cal. 325; 5 Leigh, 543.

Sanderson's Case. See People v. Sanderson.

Sanderson v. Collman, 4 Man. & G. 209. Rule of common law distinguished, Pleading, estoppel *in pais*, 26 Cal. 38.

Sandford, Estate of, 4 Cal. 12. Commented on, Descents and Distributions, acknowledgment of paternity of illegitimate child, 31 Cal. 361, 363.

Sandford v. Hayes, 19 Conn. 591. Cited, Statute of Limitations, part payment, 17 Cal. 577.

Sandford v. Mayor, etc., of N. Y., 33 Barb. 150. Cited, Street Assessment, remedy by appeal to board, exclusive, 29 Cal. 87.

Sandfoss v. Jones, 35 Cal. 481. Approved, Trust, resulting trust, when it arises, 38 Cal. 460.

Sandon v. Hooper, 6 Beav. 246. Commented on, Mortgage, burdens cannot be imposed by mortgage, 14 Cal. 633.

Sands v. Codwise, 4 John. 536. Cited, Fraud, avoids written instrument, 13 Cal. 170.

Sands v. Gelston, 15 John. 511. Cited, New Promise, sufficiency of acknowledgment, 36 Cal. 185; 11 Wheat. 318; 2 Tex. 573.

Sands v. Hildreth, 14 John. 498. Commented on, Fraudulent Conveyance, burden of proof of solvency, 29 Cal. 59.

Sands v. Pfeiffer, 10 Cal. 258. Cited, Mortgage, fixtures covered by, 22 Cal. 631; 23 Cal. 217; 28 Cal. 203; Fixtures, by wrongful severance become personal property, 23 Cal. 170; 34 Ill. 440.

Sanford v. Bennett, 24 N. Y. 20. Cited, Statutory Construction, to be prospective, 27 Cal. 159.

Sanford v. Boring, 12 Cal. 539. Cited, Sheriff, responsibilities of, for property in legal custody, 44 Penn. St. 514.

Sanford v. Head, 5 Cal. 298. Commented on, Equity, jurisdiction over estates of deceased, 12 Cal. 436.

Sanford v. Jackson, 10 Paige, 266. Cited, Will, effect of acceptance of devise by wife, 29 Cal. 348, 351.

Sanford v. McLean, 3 Paige, 122. Commented on, Surety, subrogation of, 24 Cal. 608.

Sanford v. Mickles, 4 John. 227. Cited, Negotiable Instruments, when presumptively dishonored, 39 Cal. 352.

San Francisco v. Beideman, 17 Cal. 443. Cited, San Francisco, effect of Van Ness ordinance, 18 Cal. 525; interest of city in pueblo lands, 42 Cal. 556. Commented on and affirmed on the principle of *stare decisis*, Van Ness Ordinance, possession under, 19 Cal. 318; title under, 28 Cal. 223; as to amount of land, 30 Cal. 637,

643. Cited, Injunction, on *ex parte* motion, 33 Cal. 393; Quieting Title, possession in plaintiff essential to right of action, 34 Cal. 559.

San Francisco v. Calderwood, 31 Cal. 585. Cited, Dedication, what necessary to validity of, 42 Cal. 554; Legislature, power over pueblo lands, Id. 557.

San Francisco v. Clark, 1 Cal. 386. Distinguished, Nuisance, street obstructions, 1 Cal. 454.

San Francisco v. Fulde, 37 Cal. 349. Cited, Title, by adverse possession, continuity of possession essential, 41 Cal. 543; 30 Wis. 594.

San Francisco v. Hazen, 5 Cal. 169. Approved, Municipal Corporations, passage of city ordinances, validity on what depends, 7 Cal. 375, 380; 16 Cal. 618; 23 Cal. 318.

San Francisco v. Heydenfeldt, Cal. Sup. Ct. Oct. T. 1857 (not reported.) Commented on, Judgment, when not a bar, 19 Cal. 26.

San Francisco v. Lawton, 18 Cal. 465. Commented on, Foreclosure, adverse titles by prior conveyance from mortgagor not in issue, 23 Cal. 39; 38 Cal. 681. Cited, such titles to be saved in decree, 27 Cal. 425.

San Francisco v. Pixley, 21 Cal. 56. Cited, Execution, validity of title of purchaser at sale, on what depends, 38 Cal. 654; 13 Wall. 514.

San Francisco v. Scott, 4 Cal. 116. Approved, Eminent Domain, compensation a condition precedent to condemnation of land, 12 Cal. 528, 530; 29 Cal. 117; 31 Cal. 545, 546; Dedication, how may be effected, 22 Cal. 490.

San Francisco A. and S. R.R. Co. v. Caldwell, 31 Cal. 367. Cited, Appeal, jurisdiction in special cases, 42 Cal. 68

S. F. and S. J. R.R. Co. v. Mahoney, 29 Cal. 112. Distinguished, Condemnation of Land, for railroad purposes, constitutionality of statute, 31 Cal. 548. Cited, Appeal, jurisdiction in special cases, 42 Cal. 68.

S. F. Gas Co. v. S. F. See Gas Co. v. San Francisco.

S. F. S. and L. Society v. Thompson, 31 Cal. 347. Referred to on second appeal, 34 Cal. 77.

Sanger v. Craigue, 10 Vt. 555. Cited, Conveyances, statute to be strictly construed, 7 Cal. 294; irregularities in record not to impart notice, per Shafter, J., dissenting, 31 Cal. 321; Taxation, railroads assessed as real property, 32 Cal. 509.

San Jose v. Younger. See Commissioners v. Younger.

Sannicksen v. Brown, 5 Cal. 57. Cited, New Trial, when motion granted for irregularities at trial, 23 Cal. 337. Approved, Statute of Limitations, when receipts on account constitute written instruments, 24 Cal. 328.

Sansom v. Ball, 4 Dall. 459. Cited, Freight money may be recovered back on failure of transportation, 6 Cal. 32.

Santa Maria, The, 10 Wheat. 442. Cited, Appeal, law of the case conclusive, 15 Cal. 83; 3 How. 424; 6 How. 40; 15 How. 466.

Santo v. State, 2 Iowa, 208. Cited, Constitutionality of Statute, in part unconstitutional, 22 Cal. 386, 392; rule of construction to be adopted, 26 Cal. 229. Approved, Power of judiciary to determine, 41 Cal. 159. Cited, Legislature, power over organization of municipal courts, 22 Cal. 478. Approved, Constitutional Construction, distribution of powers under Article Third, 34 Cal. 538.

Sarah v. State, 28 Geo. 576. Cited, Judgment, validity of, in criminal cases, 31 Cal. 627.

Sarch v. Blackburn, 4 Car. & P. 297. Approved, Negligence, liability for injuries from ferocious animal, 41 Cal. 141, 142.

Sargeant, Heirs of, v. State Bk. of Indiana, 12 How. 371. Cited, Administrator's Sale, judicial, 9 Cal. 196.

Sargent v. Ballard, 9 Pick. 252. Cited, Dedication, to public use, must rest on assent of owner, 14 Cal. 649; 9 How. 31.

Sargent v. Denison, 5 Cow. 106. Cited, Verdict, not to be impeached by affidavit of juror, 25 Cal. 400.

Sargent v. Essex Mar. R. R. Corp., 9 Pick. 204. Cited, Corporation, transfer of stock, validity of, 5 Cal. 189.

Sargent v. Parsons, 12 Mass. 149. Commented on, Tenants in Common, accounting for rents and profits, 12 Cal. 421; 16 Gratt. 51.

Sargent v. Sturm, 23 Cal. 359. Approved, Claim and Delivery, demand not necessary to action for property tortiously acquired, 38 Cal. 584.

Sargent v. Webster, 13 Met. 497. Commented on, Corporation, right to sell its property, 37 Cal. 593.

Sargent v. Wilson, 5 Cal. 504. Cited, Homestead, conveyance of, by husband alone, void, 7 Cal. 346; 8 Cal. 74; contra, 45 Miss. 274. Cited, Wife's interest in, 19 Iowa, 68; Foreclosure, necessary parties to action, 13 Cal. 70; wife a necessary party in action on homestead, 10 Cal. 297; 13 Iowa, 584.

Saser v. State of Ohio, 13 Ohio, 453. Cited, Indictment, existence and character of corporation how established, 41 Cal. 654.

Sasser v. Herring, 3 Dev. 340. Cited, Evidence, establishment of boundaries by reputation, 15 Cal. 279.

Sasser v. Walker's Exrs., 5 Gill & J. 102. Cited, Undertaking, on appeal, complaint in action on, 9 Cal. 285.

Satterlee v. Matthewson, 16 Serg. & R. 191. Affirmed, 2 Pet. 380. Commented on, Constitutionality of Statutes, when legislature may divest rights vested by statute, 2 Cal. 245; 16 Cal. 238; 22 Cal. 327; 8 Pet. 110; 1 How. 331; 10 How. 402; Id. 539; power of judiciary to determine, 17 Cal. 562; 3 Blackf. 287. Denied, 39 N. H. 387.

Satterlee v. San Francisco, 23 Cal. 314. Approved, Municipal Corporations, ordinance for sale of city property null, 33 Cal. 140.

Saunders v. Cadwell, 1 Cow. 622. Cited, Confession of Judgment, not subject to collateral attack, 12 Cal. 133.

Saunders v. Clark, 29 Cal. 304. Cited, Deed, evidence to explain latent ambiguities admissible, 36 Cal. 615.

Saunders v. Drew, 3 Barn. & Ad. 445. Commented on, Freight money, recovery back for failure of transportation, 6 Cal. 370.

Saunders v. Haynes, 13 Cal. 145. Cited, Jurisdiction, special cases, what are, 15 Cal. 92; 42 Cal. 62; proceedings in election contests, judicial, 24 Cal. 126; and summary, Id. 452; 34 Cal. 610; Appeal, in special cases, 42 Cal. 68; Election, votes cast for ineligible candidate, 50 N. Y. 465.

34

Saunders v. Mills, 6 Bing. 215; S. C. 19 Eng. C. L. 104. Cited, Libel and Slander, evidence of former libelous publication not admissible, 41 Cal. 384.

Saunders v. Wilson. 15 Wend. 338. Common law rule distinguished, Pleading, defense of justification in trespass, 27 Cal. 367.

Saunderson v. Piper, 5 Bing. N. C. 425. Cited, Negotiable Instruments, construction of, superscription in figures, 39 Cal. 350.

Saunderson v. Rowles, 4 Burr. 2068. Cited, Judicial Decisions, extra-judicial opinion defined, 9 Cal. 732.

Savage v. Brewer, 16 Pick. 453. Cited, Attachment, liability for wrongful issuance of, 6 Cal. 685.

Savage v. Carroll, 1 Ball & B. 265. Cited, Resuling Trust, when it arises, 25 Cal. 326.

Savage v. Gulliver, 4 Mass. 177. Approved, Appeal, statute remedy exclusive, 8 Cal. 300.

Savenat v. Le Breton, 1 La. 523. Cited, Husband and Wife, burden of proof as to separate property, 30 Cal. 31.

Saville v. Roberts, 1 Ld. Ray. 378. Commented on, Conspiracy, without damage, not actionable, 25 Cal. 560.

Savings & L. Society v. Thompson, 32 Cal. 347. Cited, Notice, publication of, computation of time, 5 Nev. 426.

Sawyer v. City of Alton, 4 Ill. 127. Cited, Taxation, constitutional construction, 4 Cal. 51.

Sawyer v. Patterson, 11 Ala. 523. Cited, Surety, when released by agreement for delay, 10 Cal. 426.

Sawyer v. Sawyer, 1 Walker Ch. 52. Commented on, Divorce, for adultery, confessions not competent evidence, 13 Cal. 94.

Sawyer v. Warner, 15 Barb. 282. Cited, Pleading, when affirmative allegation is not new matter, 21 Cal. 436.

Saxeby v. Wynn, 3 Stark. Ev. 1160, note. Commented on, Conversion, what constitutes, 2 Cal. 574.

Sayles v. Wooden, 6 How. Pr. 84. Cited, Pleading, demurrer to inconsistent defenses, 13 Cal. 625.

Sayre, Ex parte, 7 Cow. 368. Cited, Attorney and Counsel, legislative control of right to practice, 22 Cal. 321.

Sayre v. Nichols, 7 Cal. 535; S. C. 7 Cal. 535. Cited, Principal and Agent, contract signed by agent, when agent liable, 29 Cal. 571; effect of signature as "agent," 6 Cal. 104; 2 Nev. 223; 1 Colorado, 286. Overruled, that the word "agent" appended to signature is a mere *descriptio personæ*, 7 Cal. 537; powers of agent to bind principal, 8 Cal. 247.

Sayre v. Smith, 11 Cal. 129. Commented on, Appeal, assignment of errors on, 25 Cal. 483.

Sayre v. Townsends, 15 Wend. 650. Cited, Resulting Trust, when it arises, 25 Cal. 326.

Sayre v. Wisner, 8 Wend. 663. Cited, Statutory Construction to be prospective, 27 Cal. 159.

Scales v. Scott, 13 Cal. 76. Referred to, Confession of Judgment, proceedings to set aside, 13 Cal. 634; when fraudulent in part is fraudulent *in toto*, 23 Cal. 236; when void for fraud, 27 Cal. 235; 35 Cal. 308.

Scarborough v. Dugan, 10 Cal. 305. Cited, Statutory Construction, statutes not to be construed retrospectively, 22 Cal. 554.

Scarlett v. Hunter, 3 Jones' Eq. 84. Cited, Vendor and Vendee, equitable title in vendee, 40 Cal. 570.

Scarlett v. Lamarque, 5 Cal. 63. Cited, Forcible Entry and Detainer, sufficient evidence of force to maintain action, 6 Cal. 66. Distinguished as to unlawful entry and forcible detainer, 24 Cal. 319.

Schellhous v. Ball, 29 Cal. 605. Cited, New Trial, granting or refusing motion in discretion of court, 30 Cal. 227; for surprise, showing required, 32 Cal. 212. Approved, when will be denied, 38 Cal. 456; 39 Cal. 557.

Schemerhorn v. Loines, 7 John. 311. Cited, Debt, payment by note, effect of, 12 Cal. 323.

Schemerhorn v. Vanderheyden, 1 John. 139. Cited, Debtor and Creditor, right of action of creditor on agreement of third party to pay debt, 37 Cal. 537.

Schenck v. McKie, 4 How. Pr. 246. Cited, Service, other than personal, strict compliance with statute required, 30 Cal. 184; defective proof of service by mail, 35 Cal. 187.

Schenectady & S. P. R. Co. v. Thatcher, 6 How. Pr. 227. Cited, Record, of action includes nothing but judgment roll, 33 Cal. 513.

Schenk v. Evoy, 25 Cal. 104. Cited, Tenants in Common, implied trust created by agreement to purchase lands in common, 30 Cal. 594. Approved, Grantee of specific quantity a tenant in common, 37 Cal. 520.

Schenley v. City of Alleghany, 25 Penn. St. 130. Commented on, Taxation, legislative power of, not subject to judicial control, 41 Cal. 173.

Schermerhorn v. Buell, 4 Denio, 425. Cited, Replevin, lies for fixtures wrongfully severed, 10 Cal. 265.

Schermerhorn v. Talman, 14 N. Y. 93. Cited, Contract, fully executed, cannot be avoided, 37 Cal. 607.

Schieffelin v. Harvey, 6 John. 171. Commented on, Carrier's Contract, liability on, 27 Cal. 32, 33.

Schlencker v. Risley, 4 Ill. 483. Cited, Municipal Officers, presumptions as to their authority, 3 Cal. 453.

Schloss v. His Creditors, 31 Cal. 201. Cited, Insolvency, proceedings in, 32 Cal. 413; proof of publication of notice to creditors, 33 Cal. 535.

Schmidt v. Wieland, 35 Cal. 343. Approved, Guardian and Ward, sale of ward's property without order of court, void, 42 Cal. 293.

Schnaderbeck v. Worth, 8 Abb. Pr. 38. Cited, Counterclaim, what is, 35 Cal. 281.

Schneider v. McFarland, 2 N. Y. 459. Commented on, Probate Court, jurisdiction of, limited and special, 7 Cal. 235, 239; validity of sale, on what depends, 33 Cal. 52.

School Dist. No. 1 v. Blaisdell, 6 N. H. 197. Cited, Pleading, want of capacity to be specially pleaded, 8 Cal. 590.

School Dist. No. 4 v. Benson, 31 Me. 384. Commented on, Title by adverse possession, 34 Cal. 383.

Schooner Paulina's Cargo v. United States, 7 Cranch, 52. Cited, Statutory Construction, 26 Cal. 181.

Schoonmaker v. Reformed Dutch Church, 5 How. Pr. 267. Cited, Injunction, practice on motion to dissolve, 35 Cal. 59.

Schroder v. Johns, 27 Cal. 274. Cited, Pleading, statute of limitations, insufficient statement, 31 Cal. 393.

Schroeder v. Clark, 18 Mo. 185. Statute distinguished, Sheriff, sheriff not protected by verdict of trial jury, 10 Cal. 191.

Schroeder v. Hudson Riv. R. Co., 5 Duer, 61. Cited, Common Carriers, liability on contract for transportation through, 31 Cal. 53.

Schuhman v. Garratt, 16 Cal. 100. Approved, Title by purchase of adverse claim, 36 Cal. 539.

Schultz v. Schultz, 10 Gratt. 358. Cited, Probate Proceedings, not subject to collateral attack, 18 Cal. 505.

Schuylkill Nav. Co. v. Farr, 4 Watts & S. 374. Cited, Ejectment, equitable title sufficient to maintain, 22 Cal. 617.

Scituate v. Hanover, 16 Pick. 222. Cited, Deed as a mortgage, parol defeasance, 36 Cal. 60.

Scott v. Ambrose, 3 Maule & S. 326. Cited, Insolvency, discharge of debt is equally a discharge of judgment thereon, 14 Cal. 175.

Scott v. Buchanan, 11 Humph. 468. Commented on, Infant, ratification of voidable deed, 24 Cal. 215, 217.

Scott v. Calvit, 3 How. Miss. 148. Cited, Probate, jurisdiction over wills, 18 Cal. 481.

Scott v. Fields, 7 Watts, 362. Cited, Homestead, mortgage claim for purchase money, 10 Cal. 385.

Scott v. Freeland, 7 Smedes & M. 409. Cited, Mortgage, purchase by mortgagee under power of sale, voidable, 21 Cal. 330.

Scott v. Gallagher, 14 Serg. & R. 333. Cited, Conveyance, notice imparted by possession, 12 Cal. 376. Denied, 36 Cal. 276.

Scott v. Hickox, 7 Ohio St. 90. Cited, Probate Sales, limitation of actions, 33 Cal. 521.

Scott v. Lloyd, 12 Pet. 145. Cited, Witness, competency of, how restored, 14 Cal. 268; 4 How. 417; 5 How. 94.

Scott v. Maynard, Dallam, 548. Cited, Husband and Wife, property acquired pending marriage presumed to be common property, 30 Cal. 38.

Scott v. McFarland, 13 Mass. 309. Cited, Conveyance, when a mortgage, 33 Cal. 332.

Scott v. McLellan, 2 Greenl. 199.   Cited, Costs, liability of indorser on action by indorsee against maker, 22 Cal. 250.

Scott v. Newsom, 4 Sneed, 457.   Commented on, Forcible Entry and Detainer, who turned out under writ of restitution, 29 Cal. 218.

Scott v. Pilkington, 110 Eng. C. L; S. C. 2 Best & S. 11. Cited, Pleading insufficient defenses in action on foreign judgment, 39 Cal. 539.

Scott v. Rogers, 31 N. Y. 676.   Commented on, Conversion, measure of damages on, 39 Cal. 424, 426.

Scott v. Sandford, 19 How. 446.   Cited, State Sovereignty, defined, 40 Cal. 342.

Scott v. Scott's Admr., 2 A. K. Marsh. 217.   Cited, Statute of Limitations, on warranty, on sale of chattels, 41 Cal. 115.

Scott v. Surman, Willes, 400.   Cited, Trust and Trustees, agent when trustee of principal, 9 Cal. 660; 2 Black. 385; application of statute of limitations, 40 Cal. 567.

Scott v. Van Alstyne, 9 John. 216.   Cited, Attorney and Counsel, privileges of, 22 Cal. 320.

Scott v. Ward, 13 Cal. 459.   Commented on, Husband and Wife, presumptions that property acquired during marriage belongs to the community, 14 Cal. 596.   Approved, Mexican Grant, as separate estate, 14 Cal. 611; 26 Cal. 565; 31 Cal. 433; 33 Cal. 702.

Scott v. Whipple, 5 Greenl. 336.   Cited, Appeal Bond, construction of, 13 Cal. 508; Deed, validity of, executed by part of grantors, 22 Cal. 501.

Scotthorn v. South Staff. Railway, 18 Eng. L. & E. 553. Cited, Common Carrier, liability on contract for transportation through, 31 Cal. 53.

Scovill v. City of Cleveland, 1 Ohio St. 135.   Cited, Street Assessments, power of legislature to direct, 28 Cal. 352.   Commented on, Id. 364.

Scribner v. Hickok, 4 Johns. Ch. 532.   Cited, Judgment, right of co-defendant to contribution, on payment of, 17 Cal. 245.

Scribner v. Lockwood, 9 Ohio, 184.   Cited, Conveyances, construction of registration act, 12 Cal. 377.

Scroggins v. Scroggins, 3 Dev. 535. Commented on, Divorce, grounds of, 13 Cal. 104.

Scudder v. Voorhis, 1 Barb. 55. Cited, Pleading, supplemental complaint, 27 Cal. 313.

Seagraves v. City of Alton, 13 Ill. 366. Commented on, Municipal Corporations, liability on implied contracts, 16 Cal. 266.

Seale v. Doane, 17 Cal. 476. Cited, San Francisco, property of municipal corporation not subject to levy and sale on execution, 42 Cal. 557.

Seale v. Ford, 29 Cal. 104. Cited, Mexican Grant, title under confirmed survey, 32 Cal. 462; 38 Cal. 65; takes effect by relation, 34 Cal. 253; 35 Cal. 88; title not perfect till lands segregated, 36 Cal. 145.

Seale v. Mitchell, 5 Cal. 401. Commented on and construed, San Francisco City title to pueblo lands, 15 Cal. 587, 598, 618. Approved, Superior Court, jurisdiction and powers of, 36 Cal. 696, 697; Statutory Construction, rule of *stare decisis,* 8 Nev. 344.

Seale v. San Francisco, Cal. Sup. Ct. July T. 1858 (not reported.) Denied as authority, Municipal Corporations not estopped by matters *in pais,* 16 Cal. 272. Cited, 28 Cal. 594.

Seaman v. Browning, 1 Leon. 157. Cited, Covenant in lease, what constitutes a breach, 33 Cal. 307.

Seaman v. Hicks, 8 Paige, 655. Cited, Equity, relief of purchaser under void decree, 16 Cal. 470; Id. 564.

Seaman v. Luce, 23 Barb. 240. Cited, Execution, selection by debtor of property exempt, 22 Cal. 506.

Seaman v. Vawdrey, 16 Ves. Jr. 393. Cited, Mines and Mining, property in State, by virtue of sovereignty, 3 Cal. 225.

Searcy v. Grow, 15 Cal. 117. Commented on, Election Contest, eligibility to office, 23 Cal. 320. Cited, Political rights of aliens, 30 Cal. 189; purpose of action in election contest, party plaintiff, 28 Cal. 139; 30 Cal. 400; proceedings in action, 24 Cal. 452; burden of proof on contestant, 34 Cal. 640; proceedings, special and summary, 34 Cal. 640.

Searle v. Lackawanna & B. R. R. Co., 33 Penn. St. 57. Cited, Evidence, opinions of witnesses when competent, 35 Cal. 262.

Searle v. Lane, 2 Vern. 37. Cited, Lis Pendens, to what actions applicable, 23 Cal. 38.

Searles v. Scott, 14 Smedes & M. 94. Cited, Equitable jurisdiction over estates of deceased, 24 Cal. 93.

Sears v. Dixon, 33 Cal. 326. Cited, Findings, presumptions as to, 34 Cal. 252; 35 Cal. 87; to support judgment implied, 38 Cal. 421; 41 Cal. 99; Homestead, alienation of, what essential, 36 Cal. 21; Deed, as a mortgage, parol evidence admissible to prove, 36 Cal. 49. Distinguished, 41 Cal. 28.

Sears v. Hathaway, 12 Cal. 277. Distinguished, Malicious Prosecution, damages, 36 Cal. 485.

Seaton v. Second Municipality of N. O., 3 La. An. 45. Cited, Contract, when action lies on breach of entire contract, 35 Cal. 242.

Seaver v. Fitzgerald, 23 Cal. 86. Cited, Summons, when returnable, 34 Cal. 646.

Seaver v. Lincoln, 21 Pick. 268. Cited, Negotiable Instruments, when presumptively dishonored, 39 Cal. 352.

Sea Witch, The, 1 Cal. 162. Commented on, Attachment against boats and vessels, proceedings, 1 Cal. 166. Approved, What vessels amenable to writ, 1 Cal. 403; Id. 452.

Secombe v. Steele, 20 How. 104. Cited, Specific Performance, construction of clause of forfeiture in contract, 40 Cal. 13.

Secrest v. Turner, 2 J. J. Marsh. 471. Cited, Conveyance, when construed as a mortgage and not a conditional sale, 10 Cal. 207.

Sedam v. Williams, 4 McLean, 51. Cited, Partnership, priority of lien of firm creditors, 13 Cal. 633.

Seddon v. Tutop, 6 Term Rep. 607. Cited, Pleading, averments in pleading estoppel, 26 Cal. 505; 1 McLean, 451.

Sedgwick v. Hollenback, 7 John. 376. Cited, Contract of Sale, when action will not lie against vendor, 1 Cal. 130; Covenant, no breach till eviction or invasion, 33 Cal. 307; 2 Wheat. 63, note c.

Seekright v. Moore, 4 Leigh, 30. Cited, Title, transitory seizin conveys no title, 8 Cal. 275.

Seeley v. Engell, 17 Barb. 530. Cited, Pleading, insufficient denials, 32 Cal. 573.

Seeling v. Crawley, 2 Vern. 385. Cited, Husband and Wife, agreement for separation, valid, 9 Cal. 492.

Seixo v. Provezende, 1 Law R. Ch. App. 192. Cited, Trade Marks, law of, 35 Cal. 76.

Selden v. Meeks, 17 Cal. 128. Cited, Mechanic's Lien, sufficiency of statement in notice, 8 Nev. 237.

Selden v. Vermilya, 4 Sand. Ch. 573. Cited, Amendment, may be allowed to complaint without prejudice to the injunction, 33 Cal. 502.

Seligman v. Kalkman, 8 Cal. 207; S. C. 17 Cal. 152. Disapproved, Fraud, sale not avoided by failure of purchaser to declare his insolvency, 4 Nev. 300; actual fraud necessary, 33 Cal. 626, 630. Cited, Appeal does not lie from an interlocutory judgment, 30 Cal. 21.

Selkirk v. Sacramento Co., 3 Cal. 323. Cited, Pleading, demurrer as an admission of facts, 8 Cal. 397.

Selkrig v. Davies, 2 Dow, 231. Cited, Partnership, liability of property for partnership debts, 28 Cal. 582.

Selleck v. French, 1 Conn. 32; 1 Am. Lead. Cas. 522. Cited, Interest, on interest after it falls due, 29 Cal. 392.

Sellers v. People, 4 Ill. 412. Commented on, Juror and Jury, incompetency of juror, 9 Cal. 312.

Selover v. American R. C. Co., 7 Cal. 266. Cited, Homestead, removal of wife when not an abandonment, 8 Cal. 72; Husband and Wife, sufficiency of acknowledgment of conveyance by married woman, 9 Cal. 592; 25 Cal. 374, 376. Distinguished, 23 Cal. 566. Construed, 30 Cal. 518. Cited, Conveyance by attorney in fact, 30 Cal. 142. Commented on, Husband to join with wife in conveyance of separate estate, 31 Cal. 644, 645; power of wife over her separate property, 40 Cal. 559.

Seman v. Whitney, 4 Eng. Ch. Cited, Deed cannot be varied by parol, 6 Cal. 358.

Semple v. Burkey, 2 Cal. 321. Cited, Findings on trial by court, construed, 28 Cal. 596. Followed, in Buchanan v. Egery, Cal. Sup. Ct. Oct. T. 1854 (not reported.)

Semple v. Hagar, 27 Cal. 163. Approved, Mexican Grant, decree of confirmation not subject to collateral attack,

29 Cal. 311, 312; 36 Cal. 143; 40 Cal. 668. Cited,
• Pleading insufficient allegations of fraud, 30 Cal. 674.

Semple v. Wright, 32 Cal. 666. Cited, Mexican Grant, confirmation of survey not subject to collateral attack, 36
Cal. 144; 38 Cal. 61, 63; Crockett, J., dissenting, Id.
72. Approved, Rights under prior grant, 1 Saw. 583;
Estoppel, waiver of estoppel in pleading, 42 Cal. 621.

Sentney v. Overton, 4 Bibb. 445. Cited, Evidence, of handwriting of party, 26 Cal. 412.

Sergeant of Court of Appeals v. George, 5 Litt. 199. Denied, Injunction, when it lies, 14 Cal. 143.

Serle v. St. Eloy, 2 P. Wms. 386. Cited, Will, devise of
lands subject to encumbrance, 31 Cal. 608.

Serpentine v. State, 1 How. Miss. 260. Cited, Statute of
Limitations, exceptions in, to be specially pleaded, 12
Cal. 295.

Service v. Heermance, 1 John. 91. Cited, Pleading, discharge in insolvency, what must be shown, 33 Cal. 536.

Servoss v. Stannard, 2 Code Rep. 56. Cited, Injunction,
practice on motion to dissolve or modify, 35 Cal. 59.

Seton v. Slade, 7 Ves. 265. Cited, Specific Performance,
when will be decreed, 11 Cal. 238. Denied, 1 Watts
& S. 557.

Settembre v. Putnam, 30 Cal. 490. Cited, Mines and mining stockholders in ditch companies, as tenants in
common, 35 Cal. 370; Trust and Trustees, resulting
trust, when it arises, 35 Cal. 487.

Seventeenth Street, Matter of, 1 Wend. 271. Cited, Dedication by sale of lots on plat, 22 Cal. 490.

Sexton v. Wheaton, 8 Wheat. 229. Cited, Fraudulent Conveyance, what is, 13 Cal. 72; 11 Wheat. 211; 7 How.
228.

Seymour v. Beach, 4 Vt. 493. Cited, Witness, vendor not
competent to impeach his own sale, 23 Cal. 446.

Seymour v. Bennet, 14 Mass. 266. Cited, Money paid on
voidable contract may be recovered back, 33 Cal. 195.

Seymour v. Delancey, 6 John. Ch. 222. Cited, Specific
Performance, when will be decreed, 21 Cal. 411. Approved, 42 Cal. 354; 12 How. 207.

Seymour v. Ellison, 2 Cow. 13. Commented on, Attorney and Counsel, 22 Cal. 313.

Seymour v. Van Slyck, 8 Wend. 414. Cited, Alcalde's Grant, presumption as to regularity, 30 Cal. 72.

Seymour v. Wyckoff, 10 N. Y. 213. Commented on, Bailment, right of owner to recover specific property, 42 Cal. 103.

Shackelford v. Smith, 5 Dana, 237. Cited, Pleading, inconsistent defenses cannot be set up, 24 Cal. 146.

Shafer v. Bear Riv. and A. Wat. and M. Co , 4 Cal. 294. Cited, Foreclosure, personal judgment cannot be rendered on a mere recital of the debt in the mortgage, 22 Cal. 620.

Shaffer v. Lee, 8 Barb. 415. Cited, Contract, when action maintainable on breach of entire contract, 35 Cal. 242.

Shanley v. Harvey, 2 Eden, 126. Commented on, State Sovereignty, reclamation of fugitive slaves, 2 Cal. 448.

Shannon v. Comstock, 21 Wend. 457. Cited, Contract, when action lies for breach of entire contract, 35 Cal. 242; measure of damages on breach of, for services, 38 Cal. 666.

Shannon v. Shannon, 2 Gray, 285. Cited, Sprague, J., dissenting, Alimony inseparable from divorce, 38 Cal. 277.

Shannon v. Speers, 2 A. K. Marsh. 698. Cited, Redemption, judgment on default in action to redeem, 34 Cal. 655.

Shapard v. Bailleul, 3 Tex. 26. Cited, Judgment, lien of, 10 Cal. 81.

Sharp v. Contra Costa Co., 34 Cal. 284. Approved, State or local subordinate governments or property not liable to action except by consent, 36 Cal. 223; remedy of creditor of county, 39 Cal. 275. Cited, Legislature, control over affairs and property of municipal corporations, 41 Cal. 530.

Sharp v. Daugney, 33 Cal. 505. Cited, Judgment Roll, motions and orders to strike out pleadings no part of, 36 Cal. 114; 1 Saw. 321.

Sharp v. Johnson, 4 Hill, 92. Cited, Statutory Construction, statutes divesting titles to be strictly pursued, 24 Cal. 432. Approved, Street Assessment, not a tax, 27 Cal. 620. Cited, Assessment on lands benefited, 31 Cal. 674.

Sharp v. Lumley, 34 Cal. 614. Cited, Execution, issuance before docket lien acquired, 37 Cal. 146; 1 Saw. 323; Id. 336.

Sharp v. Maguire, 19 Cal. 577. Cited, Statute of Limitations, when action deemed commenced, 21 Cal. 368; 34 Cal. 166.

Sharp v. Sharp, 2 Barn. and Ald. 405. Cited, Trust and Trustees, when act by portion of board of trustees is illegal, 6 Cal. 125.

Sharp v. Speir, 4 Hill, 76. Cited, Statutory Construction, statutes in derogation of common law to be strictly construed, 19 Cal. 60. Approved, 27 Cal. 628; so as to proceedings for probate sales, 19 Cal. 208; as to proceedings for condemnation of land, 24 Cal. 432; Jurisdiction, no intendments in favor of courts or officers of special jurisdiction, 25 Cal. 309; Street Assessment, not a tax, 27 Cal. 620; enforcement of, 31 Cal. 675.

Sharp v. United States, 4 Watts, 21. Cited, Bonds, no recovery can be had on joint bond executed by part only of the obligors, 14 Cal. 423, 424; 21 Cal. 583.

Sharpless v. Mayor of Philadelphia, 21 Penn. St. 147. Commented on, Municipal Corporations, powers limited by charter, 5 Cal. 217. Cited, Legislature, may authorize municipal aid to railroads, 13 Cal. 188. Commented on, 22 Cal. 395; power of local taxation and appropriation, 13 Cal. 355; 27 Iowa, 44; 19 Wis. 666; Government, relative powers of Federal and State, 41 Cal. 161.

Shattuck v. Carson, 2 Cal. 588. Approved, Cloud on Title, right to prevent or remove equity jurisdiction, 5 Cal. 75; 15 Cal. 133; 25 Cal. 357; 29 Cal. 56; Id. 190; 47 N. H. 270; McAll. 117; title to wife's separate estate, 10 Cal. 11.

Shaver v. Bear Riv. and A. Wat. & M. Co., 10 Cal. 400. Cited, Corporations, power to contract, 33 Cal. 696.

Shaver v. Murdock, 36 Cal. 293. Approved, Mechanic's Lien, statutory rights of sub-contractors, 38 Cal. 361.

Shaver v. Ocean Min. Co., 21 Cal. 45. Cited, Principal and Agent, liability on contract made by agent, 29 Cal. 571.

Shaver v. White, 6 Munf. 110. Cited, Execution, provisions of statute as to levy and sale directory, 6 Cal. 50.

Shaw v. Berry, 31 Me. 478. Cited, Innkeeper liable for loss of property of guest, 33 Cal. 600.

Shaw v. Crawford, 10 John. 236. Cited, Title, to water, by adverse possession, 27 Cal. 366.

Shaw v. Davis, 5 Cal. 466. Distinguished, Witness, competency of, interest in action, 7 Cal. 42.

Shaw v. Dennis, 10 Ill. 405. Cited, Legislature, may authorize municipal aid to railroads, 13 Cal. 188; power of local taxation and appropriation, Id. 355.

Shaw, Ex parte, 7 Ohio St. 81. Cited, Criminal Procedure, judgment, when erroneous but not void, 31 Cal. 628.

Shaw v. Hoadley, 8 Blackf. 165. Cited, Foreclosure, decree on whom conclusive, 23 Cal. 35.

Shaw v. McGregor, 8 Cal. 521. Approved, Jurisdiction, lost on adjournment of term, 25 Cal. 52; 28 Cal. 337. Cited, 3 Nev. 384.

Shaw v. Peckett, 26 Vt. 485. Commented on, Taxation, action lies for duty imposed by statute, 16 Cal. 525. Cited, Tax distinguished from "debt," 20 Cal. 350.

Shawman v. Whalley, 6 Taunt. 185. Cited, Bail, waiver of irregularities in process, 6 Cal. 59.

Sheafe v. Sheafe, 24 N. H. 567. Cited, Sprague, J., dissenting, Alimony, inseparable from divorce, 38 Cal. 277.

Sheafe v. Wait, 30 Vt. 735. Cited, Tenant in Common, relation created by deed conveying specific quantity of land, 37 Cal. 520.

Shearman v. N. Y. Cent. Mills, 1 Abb. Pr. 187. Commented on, Pleading, denials for want of information insufficient, 9 Cal. 468. Cited, 25 Cal. 196; 31 Cal. 195.

Shearman v. New York Cent. Mills, 11 How. Pr. 269. Cited, Injunction Bond, when action lies on, 18 Cal. 628.

Shed v. Brett, 1 Pick. 401. Cited, Negotiable Instruments, demand notice, 8 Cal. 634.

Sheehy v. Mandeville, 6 Cranch, 253. Overruled, 6 Wall. 226. Denied, Judgment in several suit on joint obligation as a bar, 6 Cal. 180; 33 Story, 651. Commented on, 2 McLean, 173; 9 How. 93.

Sheets v. Culver, 14 La. 452. Cited, Negotiable Instruments, certificates of deposit, 9 Cal. 418; indebted-

• ness thereon, when not attachable, 9 Cal. 418; 10 Cal. 340.

Sheets v. Selden, 7 Wall. 423. Cited, Lease, covenant to build, construed, 39 Cal. 153.

Shelby v. Houston, 38 Cal. 410. Approved, Forcible Entry and Detainer, "occupant" defined, 41 Cal. 632.

Shelby v. Johnson, Dallam, 597. Commented on, Office, term of, vacancy created by death, 8 Cal. 13; constitutional term of, 11 Cal. 88.

Sheldon v. Atlantic F. & M. Ins. Co., 26 N. Y. 460. Cited, Insurance, cancellation of policy for non-payment of premium, 38 Cal. 546.

Sheldon v. Cox, 2 Eden. 224. Cited, Notice to agent is notice to principal, 31 Cal. 165.

Sheldon v. Sill, 8 How. 450. Approved, Mortgage, a mere incident to debt, 24 Cal. 497.

Sheldon v. Wright, 5 N. Y. 517; 7 Barb. 39. Affirmed, Notice, publication of, computation of time, 5 N. Y. 497. Cited, 32 Cal. 352. Commented on, 5 Nev. 427; Judgment, collateral attack for want of jurisdiction of person, 34 Cal. 428.

Shelley's Case, 1 Coke, 90. Commented on, Will, construction of devise, estate in fee, 27 Cal. 443, 445; 34 Ala. 386.

Shelley v. Wright, Willes, 9. Cited, Estoppel, by recitals in written instrument, 13 Cal. 557; 14 Cal. 639; 4 Pet. 84.

Shelton v. Alcox, 11 Conn. 249. Approved, Estoppel, judgment as a plea in bar, 26 Cal. 494, 506.

Shelton v. State, 1 Stewt. & P. 208. Cited, Statute of Limitations, exceptions in, to be specially set forth, 12 Cal. 295.

Shephard v. Little, 14 John. 210. Cited, Deed, parol proof of consideration admissible, 36 Cal. 370. Denied, 1 Greenl. 5.

Shepard v. Potter, 4 Hill, 204. Cited, Evidence, burden of proof of payment, 15 Cal. 200.

Shepard v. Spaulding, 4 Met. 416. Cited, Fixtures, when tenant cannot remove, 14 Cal. 68.

Shepardson v. M. and B. R. R. Co., 6 Wis. 613. Cited, Eminent Domain, compensation a condition precedent· to condemnation of land, 31 Cal. 559.

Shepherd v. Commonwealth, 1 Serg. & R. 1. Cited, Jurisdiction, remedy against illegal execution and process, 14 Cal. 678.

Shepherd v. Johnson, 2 East, 211. Cited, Conversion, measure of damages, 33 Cal. 120.

Shepherd v. Kain, 5 Barn. & Ald. 240. Cited, Warranty, on sale of chattels, 4 Cal. 21.

Shepherd v. Nabors, 6 Ala. 637. Cited, Evidence, judicial notice not taken of foreign laws, 15 Cal. 254.

Shepherd v. Temple, 3 N. H. 457. Cited, Contract, conditions precedent on rescission of, 29 Cal. 594.

Shepley v. Rangely, Davies C. C. 249. Cited, Quieting Titles, what essential to maintenance of action, 15 Cal. 262.

Sherbourne v. Yuba Co., 21 Cal. 113. Approved, County not liable in damages for acts of its officers under statute, 25 Cal. 315; 44 Mo. 481.

Sherman v. Buick, 32 Cal. 241. Approved, Legislature cannot condemn lands for other than public uses, 39 Cal. 189.

Sherman v. Crosby, 11 John. 70. Cited, Evidence, receipt as *prima facie* evidence of payment, 41 Cal. 307.

Sherman v. Dodge, 6 Johns. Ch. 107. Cited, Title under sale executed under a power, validity of, how shown, 22 Cal. 590.

Sherman v. Story, 30 Cal. 253. Cited, Judgment, collateral attack on, 34 Cal. 424; Statute, not liable to collateral attack for fraud in procurement of its passage, 37 Cal. 363; motives of legislators not subject to collateral inquiry, 39 Cal. 202.

Sherwood v. Dunbar, 6 Cal. 53. Cited, Mortgage, void mortgage does not affect debt secured, 10 Cal. 402; rights of holders of several notes may be fixed by agreement, 23 Cal. 30.

Sherwood v. Seaman, 2 Bosw. 130. Cited, Lease, guaranty not implied in, 30 Cal. 626. Commented on, Obligations of lessor, 33 Cal. 346.

Sherwood v. Sutton, 5 Mason, 143. Commented on, **Statute** of Limitations, fraudulent concealment as a bar, 8 Cal. 460. Denied, 28 Miss. 736.

Shethar, Ex parte, 4 Cow. 540. Cited, Appeal, bonds, sufficiency of, 13 Cal. 509.

Shilknecht v. Eastburn's Heirs, 2 Gill & J. 115. Cited, Trust and Trustee, presumptions as to regularity of acts of trustee, 22 Cal. 591.

Shindler v. Houston, 1 Denio, 148; S. C. 1 N. Y. 261. Approved, Statute of Frauds, delivery not effected by words alone, 1 Cal. 402; 22 Cal. 105.

Shipp v. Miller's Heirs, 2 Wheat. 316. Cited, Res Adjudicata, local decisions when conclusive, 15 Cal. 603.

Shirly v. Harris, 3 McLean, 330. Commented on, Interest, contract for payment of excessive interest, when void, 6 Cal. 130.

Shirras v. Caig, 7 Cranch, 34. Cited, Mortgage, to secure future advances, 35 Cal. 309. Commented on, 23 How. 26.

Shiveley's Admr. v. Jones, 6 B. Mon. 275. Cited, Equity, relief of purchaser at sale under void decree, 16 Cal. 564.

Shone v. Lucas, 3 Dowl. & R. 218. Cited, Insolvency, when it ensues, 33 Cal. 625.

Shore v. Wilson, 9 Clark & F. 556. Commented on, Written Instruments, parol evidence admissible to explain, 12 Cal. 162; 38 N. H. 555. Approved, 18 Cal. 140.

Shores v. Scott Riv. Co., 21 Cal. 139; S. C. 17 Cal. 626. Cited, Foreclosure, conclusiveness of decree, 23 Cal. 35; Officer, acts of officer *de facto* not subject to collateral inquiry, 23 Cal. 320.

Short v. McCarthy, 3 Barn. & Ald. 626. Commented on, Statute of Limitations, when not a bar to action, 8 Cal. 459; 4 Pet. 182.

Shorter v. Smith, 9 Geo. 517. Cited, Rights and Remedies, statutory remedies when cumulative, 7 Cal. 129.

Shover v. State, 5 Eng. Ark. 259. Commented on, Sunday Laws, validity of, 9 Cal. 526; 18 Cal. 681.

Shriver v. Lovejoy, 32 Cal. 574. Cited, Negotiable Instruments, joint makers of note all principals, 34 Cal. 281.

Shultz v. Elliott, 11 Humph. 186. Cited, Estoppel, when tenant not estopped, 33 Cal. 253; 35 Cal. 571.

Shute v. Grimes, 7 Blackf. 1. Commented on, Mortgage, right to possession under, 9 Cal. 407.

Sibbald v. United States, 12 Pet. 491. Cited, Appeal, law of the case conclusive, 15 Cal. 83; 20 Cal. 417; 3 How. 426; Id. 620; 6 How. 38; 15 How. 466.

Sibley v. Aldrich, 33 N. H. 553. Cited, Innkeeper, liability of, 33 Cal. 600. Denied, 10 Ind. 214.

Sibley v. Waffle, 16 N. Y. 190. Cited, Appeal, intendments as to regularity of proceedings, 25 Cal. 309; objections to irregularities when not considered, 20 Cal. 387.

Sickles v. Hogeboom, 10 Wend. 563. Cited, Judicial Sale, appointment by court of suitable person to make deed, 8 Cal. 411.

Sidmouth v. Sidmouth, 2 Beav. 447. Commented on, Trust and Trustee, purchase by parent in name of child, trust not implied, 16 Cal. 356.

Siemssen v. Bofer, 6 Cal. 250. Cited, Alien, rights of, under treaty stipulations, 13 Cal. 283. Qualified as to right to maintain ejectment, 18 Cal. 219.

Siglar v. Van Riper, 10 Wend. 414. Cited, Ejectment, proof of ouster, 41 Cal. 610.

Sigourney v. Drury, 14 Pick. 391. Cited, Statute of Limitations, part payment, effect of, 17 Cal. 577.

Sigourney v. Munn, 7 Conn. 11. Cited, Partnership, real estate how held, 28 Cal. 580. Distinguished, 13 Conn. 434.

Silver Lake Bk. v. North, 4 Johns. Ch. 370. Commented on, Mortgage, discharge and substitution, 16 Cal. 199; Corporations bound by acts of its agents, Id. 265. Cited, Powers, as to making contracts, 22 Cal. 629.

Simers v. Saltus, 3 Denio, 219. Cited, Foreclosure, relation of purchaser and tenant of mortgagor, 16 Cal. 590.

Simkins v. Cobb, 2 Bailey, 60. Cited, Probate Procedure, conclusiveness on sureties of decree against administrator, 25 Cal. 223.

Simmons' Divorce Bill, 12 Clark & F. 339. Commented on, Divorce, adultery when not granted, 10 Cal. 256.

Simons v. Johnson, 3 Barn. & Ad. 175. Cited, Powers, construction of powers of attorney, 6 Cal. 375.

35

Simonson v. Blake, 12 Abb. Pr. 331. Cited, Judgment, by default, for excess of relief, remedy on, 37 Cal. 528.

Simpers v. Sloan, 5 Cal. 457. Cited, Homestead, cannot be conveyed by separate deed of husband and wife, 6 Cal. 72.

Simpson v. Allain, 7 Rob. La. 500. Cited, Execution, promissory note liable to levy and sale, 34 Cal. 88.

Simpson v. Denison, 13 Eng. L. & Eq. 359; S. C. 10 Hare, 51. Cited, Corporations, equitable rights of stockholders, 37 Cal. 582, 583.

Simpson v. Hand, 6 Whart. 324. Commented on, Negligence, failure of vessel to show light while moored, is negligence *per se*, 1 Cal. 460.

Sims v. Glazener, 14 Ala. 695. Cited, Damages, measure of, in trespass on personal property, 14 Cal. 557.

Sims v. Marryat, 17 Q. B. 290. Disapproved, Warranty, implied on sale of chattels by vendor, 41 Cal. 113.

Sims v. Smith, 19 Geo. 124. Commented on, Judgment, in ejectment, conclusiveness of, 26 Cal. 507; 32 Cal. 200.

Simson v. Eckstein, 22 Cal. 580. Approved, Trust and Trustee, resulting trust, when it arises, 22 Cal. 578.

Simson v. Hart, 1 Johns. Ch. 97; S. C. 14 John. 77. Approved, Equity, may enforce an equitable set-off, 11 Cal. 101. Doubted, 2 Sum. 634. Cited, Res Adjudicata, judgment or decree, finality of, 38 Cal. 647.

Simson v. Ingham, 2 Barn. & C. 65. Cited, Debtor and Creditor, appropriation of payments, 14 Cal. 449. Commented on, 7 How. 690.

Sinclair v. Wood, 3 Cal. 98. Approved, Partnership, evidence necessary to prove, 6 Cal. 455.

Sisson v. Seabury, 1 Sum. 239. Cited, Will, construction of, intention of testator, 27 Cal. 445.

Siter v. Jewett, 33 Cal. 92. Approved, Pleading, admissions made in one defense not available as proof of issues raised in other defense, 34 Cal. 47.

Skillern's Exrs. v. May's Exrs., 6 Cranch, 267. Cited, Appeal, law of the case controls, 15 Cal. 83.

Skillman v. Lachman, 23 Cal. 198. Cited, Mining Partnerships, powers and authority of partners, 28 Cal. 578.

Approved, 35 Cal. 369, 370, 372. Construed, Exceptional rule as to such partnerships, 42 Cal. 642. Distinguished, as to ratification of acts, 42 Cal. 194.

Skillman v. Riley, 10 Cal. 300. Cited, Appeal, statement, engrossment of, as amended, 23 Cal. 462; 31 Cal. 662.

Skinker v. Flohr, 13 Cal. 638. Cited, Evidence, copy of deed when admissible, 25 Cal. 129; 26 Cal. 413. Approved, sufficiency of preliminary evidence, 27 Cal. 55.

Skinner v. Dodge, 4 Hen. & M. 432. Cited, Factor, cannot pledge, liability of pledgee, 19 Cal. 72.

Skinner v. Miller, 5 Litt. 84. Cited, Conveyance, when construed as a mortgage, 10 Cal. 207.

Skinner v. Phillips, 4 Mass. 69. Cited, Officer, liability on bond for malfeasance in office, 14 Cal. 198.

Skinnion v. Kelley, 18 N. Y. 356. Cited, Judgment, where order of publication of summons is erroneous, 31 Cal 350.

Skipp v. Eastern Co. R. Co., 9 Exch. 223. Commented on, Master and Servant, liability of master for injury to servant, 31 Cal. 382.

Slack v. Maysville and L. R.R. Co., 13 B. Mon. 1. Cited, Legislature, may authorize municipal aid to railroads, 13 Cal. 188; Statute, validity of statute to take effect contingently, 17 Cal. 34.

Slade v. His Creditors, 10 Cal. 483. Cited, San Francisco, county jurisdiction of fourth district court, extent of, 17 Cal. 371.

Slade v. VanVechten, 11 Paige, 22. Cited, Trust and Trustee, trustee can gain no advantage to detriment of *cestui que trust*, 36 Cal. 432.

Slaughter v. State, 6 Humph. 410. Cited, Criminal Procedure, when discharge of jury operates as an acquittal, 38 Cal. 478.

Slee v. Bloom, 19 John. 456. Commented on, Surety, when not bound by judgment against principal, 14 Cal. 206; Officers, right to hold over, 28 Cal. 53, 54; Corporation, power of self-dissolution, 38 Cal. 172.

Slee v. Manhattan Co., 1 Paige, 48. Cited, Mortgage, purchase by mortgagee under power of sale, voidable, 21 Cal. 330. Commented on, Right of redemption, 23 Cal. 34; 7 Mich. 60.

Sleeper v. Kelly, 22 Cal. 456. Approved, Appeal, judgments and orders by consent not renewable, 37 Cal. 158; 42 Cal. 518.

Sloan v. Johnson, 14 Smedes & M. 50. Cited, Sheriff, remedy against, for failure to pay over moneys, 10 Cal. 488.

Sloan v. Smith, 3 Cal. 410. Cited, Reference, motion to set aside report of referee, 9 Cal. 225; change of place of trial, granting in discretion, 22 Cal. 131; 23 Cal. 378.

Slocum v. Despard, 8 Wend. 615. Cited, Contract, dependent promises conditions, precedent to action, 1 Cal. 338. Commented on, 9 Gratt. 158.

Slocum v. Mayberry, 2 Wheat. 1. Commented on, Jurisdiction, in admiralty, 9 Cal. 731.

Slosson v. Beadle, 7 John. 71. Cited, Contract, liquidated damages in, 9 Cal. 587.

Sly v. Edgley, 6 Esp. 6. Commented on, Respondeat Superior, in cases of negligent use of property, 8 Cal. 495, 498. Denied, 5 N. Y. 63.

Small v. Gwinn, 6 Cal. 449. Distinguished, Jurisdiction of justices of the peace, limitation of, 1 Nev. 140.

Small v. Mott, 22 Wend. 403. Commented on, Maintenance, offense unknown under statute law, 22 Cal. 95.

Smalley v. Lawrence, 9 Rob. 210. Cited, Husband and Wife, conveyance to wife, presumption as to common property, 12 Cal. 224. Commented on, Id. 253. Cited, Conveyance to wife, 17 Cal. 581.

Smead v. Williamson, 16 B. Mon. 492. Cited, Witness, vendor of chattel not competent to impeach sale, 23 Cal. 446.

Smedberg v. More, 26 Wend. 238. Cited, Specific Performance, construction of clause of forfeiture in contract, 40 Cal. 13.

Smith v. Acker, 23 Wend. 653. Cited, Chattel Mortgage, legal effect and operation, 27 Cal. 269; distinction as to pledge, 35 Cal. 411.

Smith v. American Life Ins. & T. Co., 1 Clarke Ch. 307. Cited, Injunction will not lie to restrain proceedings of a court of coördinate jurisdiction, 8 Cal. 36.

Smith v. Andrews, 6 Cal. 652. Cited, Pleading, judgments of probate court how pleaded, 7 Cal. 240; 1 Nev. 198; Probate Courts, of limited jurisdiction, 19 Cal. 205.

Smith v. Arnold, 5 Mason, 414. Denied, Administrator's Sales, judicial, 9 Cal. 196.

Smith v. Athearn, 34 Cal. 506. Approved, Patents, prior equities enforced in case of conflicting patents, 38 Cal. 65; 42 Cal. 615.

Smith v. Beattie, 31 N. Y. 544. Cited, Deed as a Mortgage, parol evidence admissible to prove, 36 Cal. 46.

Smith v. Benson, 1 Hill, 176. Commented on, Conveyance, what passes by, 15 Cal. 197. Denied, Conveyance by tenant in common, Id. 370.

Smith v. Blckmore, 4 Taunt. 474. Approved, Wagers, actions in affirmance of illegal wagers not maintainable, 37 Cal. 673.

Smith v. Billett, 15 Cal. 23. Cited, Pleading, after-acquired title as a defense in ejectment, 23 Cal. 242.

Smith v. Black, 9 Serg. & R. 142. Cited, Judgment, several judgment on joint liability as a bar, 6 Cal. 181; 13 Cal. 33.

Smith v. Bowditch, 7 Pick. 137. Commented on, Record, of court, imparts verity, 8 Cal. 245.

Smith v. Bradstreet, 16 Pick. 265. Cited, Attachment, lien, of, 29 Cal. 375.

Smith v. Brady, 17 N. Y. 173. Cited, Municipal Corporations, when not liable on implied contract, 20 Cal. 108.

Smith v. Brannan, 13 Cal. 107. Cited, Exceptions, objections to trial by jury on equitable cause of action, when to be taken, 16 Cal. 177. Approved, Quieting Title, equitable title sufficient to maintain action by party in possession, 35 Cal. 34.

Smith v. Bryan, 5 Md. 141. Cited, Statute of Frauds, sales of growing crops not within, 23 Cal. 69.

Smith v. Cheetham, 3 Caines, 57. Cited, Verdict, validity of, chance verdict invalid, 25 Cal. 400; Id. 402; 13 Vt. 327.

Smith v. Chichester, 1 Cal. 409. Approved, Judgment, rendered in vacation is void, 5 Cal. 493; 7 Cal. 53; 9 Cal. 175; 34 Cal. 333. Commented on and distinguished as to rendition, and entry of judgment, 20 Cal. 55; jurisdiction cannot be conferred by stipulation, 40 Cal. 184.

Smith v. Clay, 2 Amb. 645; S. C. 3 Bro. Ch. 639, note. Cited, Bill of Review, within what time to be prosecuted, 41 Cal. 321. Commented on, 10 Wheat. 150; 1 How. 193.

Smith v. Cofran, 34 Cal. 316. Approved, Street Assessments, when to be made, "unknown" owners, 38 Cal. 180.

Smith v. Cohea, 3 How. Miss. 35. Cited, Process, presumptions as to regularity of, 11 Cal. 248.

Smith v. Collyer, 8 Ves. Jr. 89. Cited, Injunction, when will be dissolved, 7 Cal. 323.

Smith v. Colvin, 17 Barb. 157. Commented on, Judicial Sale, title of purchaser, 9 Cal. 415; 10 Cal. 531; 31 Cal. 300.

Smith v. Compton, 6 Cal. 24. Cited, Error, cured by introduction of evidence, 8 Cal. 293; 10 Cal. 191; 17 Wis. 45.

Smith v. Comptroller of State, 18 Wend. 659. Approved, Mandamus, to compel issuance of warrants, 16 Cal. 45.

Smith v. Dall, 13 Cal. 510. Commented on, Conveyance, possession as notice of, 18 Cal. 367. Disapproved, that possession by tenant is insufficient notice, 21 Cal. 628. Commented on, Mistake of Recorder, to vitiate record, 36 Cal. 203.

Smith v. Daniel's Exrs., 3 Murphy N. C. 128. Commented on, Amendment, of sheriff's returns, 23 Cal. 81.

Smith v. Davis, 30 Cal. 536. Approved, Street Assessments, to be made to owners if known, otherwise to "unknown owners," 31 Cal. 481, 482; 34 Cal. 314; 38 Cal. 180; statute to be strictly pursued, 32 Cal. 331, 332; 40 Cal. 524; remedy by appeal, 34 Cal. 320.

Smith v. Doe, 15 Cal. 100. Approved, Mines and Mining, public mineral lands, right of entry on, improvements entitled to protection, 16 Cal. 155; 22 Cal. 453.

Smith v. Drew, 5 Mass. 515. Cited, Mechanic's Lien, provisions of statute to be strictly complied with, 1 Cal. 185.

Smith v. Eureka Flour Mills Co., 6 Cal. 1. Cited, Corporations, incidental power to make promissory notes, 22 Cal. 627; exercise of powers of contract or appointment of agents, 33 Cal. 696.

Smith v. Galloway, 5 Barn. & Ad. 43. Cited, Deed, construction of, false in part, 25 Cal. 299; what passes by, 27 Cal. 63.

Smith v. Gettinger, 3 Kelly, 145. Cited, Attachment, when void, 13 Cal. 441; 18 Cal. 382.

Smith v. Greenlee, 2 Dev. 129. Commented on, Agreements, when void as opposed to public policy, 30 Cal. 592.

Smith v. Greer, 31 Cal. 477. Cited, Husband and Wife, when wife not liable on contracts, 38 Cal. 233, 256.

Smith v. Griffith, 3 Hill, 333. Commented on, Damages, measure of, in action against carrier for loss of goods, 39 Cal. 423.

Smith v. Gugerty, 4 Barb. 619. Cited, Conditions precedent, when party cannot take advantage of non-performance of conditions, 7 Cal. 442.

Smith v. Halfacre, 6 How. Miss. 582. Disapproved, Office, constitutional term of, 11 Cal. 87. Commented on, 12 Cal. 390.

Smith v. Hall, 19 Cal. 85. Distinguished, Statute of Limitations, on death of debtor, 19 Cal. 99; on death of creditor, 23 Cal. 28.

Smith v. Harkins, 3 Ired. Eq. 613. Commented on, Ferry, protection of franchise, 6 Cal. 595, 598.

Smith v. Helmer, 7 Barb. 416. Cited, Eminent Domain, compensation for condemnation, constitutional construction, 31 Cal. 554.

Smith v. Hicks, 5 Wend. 51. Cited, Bill of Particulars, practice, 32 Cal. 638.

Smith v. Hodson, 4 Term Rep. 211. Cited, Acquiescence, in acts of others shown by action commenced, 4 Cal. 170. Commented on, 1 Watts & S. 110.

Smith v. Honey, 3 Pet. 469. Commented on, Appeal, amount in controversy, 2 Cal. 157.

Smith v. Hudson, 1 Cow. 430. Commented on, Amendment, of sheriff's returns, 23 Cal. 81.

Smith v. Hurd, 12 Met. 385. Cited, Fraud, equitable relief from, 28 Cal. 484.

Smith v. Hutchinson, Cal. Sup. Ct. Jan. T. 1855 (not reported.) Approved, Attachment, proceedings against garnishee, 6 Cal. 17.

Smith v. Inhab. of Readfield, 27 Me. 145. Cited, **Money** Paid, by mistake of law, not recoverable back, 18 Cal. 271. Doubted, 25 Ill. 420. Distinguished, 48 Me. 447.

Smith v. Jackson, 2 Edw. Ch. 28. Commented on, Partnership, tenure of real estate, 28 Cal. 581. Doubted, 20 Mo. 182. Denied, 27 N. H. 66.

Smith v. Jones, 4 Beav. 503. Commented on, Partnership, dissolution, when will be decreed, 14 Cal. 539.

Smith v. Jeyes, 15 John. 229. Cited, Assignment, splitting demands, 38 Cal. 519.

Smith v. Keen, 26 Me. 420. Cited, Execution, amendment of, 38 Cal. 381.

Smith v. Knowlton, 11 N. H. 191. Cited, Presumption, of life, when it ceases, 8 Cal. 65.

Smith v. Lampton, 8 Dana, 70. Cited, Will, construction of devise, 31 Cal. 603.

Smith v. Little, 10 N. H. 526. Cited, Negotiable Instruments, notice of dishonor, 8 Cal. 634

Smith v. Lorillard, 10 John. 338. Commented on, Ejectment on prior possession, 1 Cal. 309.

Smith v. Lowell, 6 N. H. 67. Cited, Fraudulent Conveyances, *prima facie* evidence of fraud, 13 Cal. 72. Approved, 16 N. H. 172. Qualification denied, 11 N. H. 459.

Smith v. Lowry, 1 Johns. Ch. 320. Commented on, Verdict, when not set aside, 12 Cal. 446.

Smith v. Lynes, 5 N. Y. 41. Questioned, Sale and Delivery, conditional sale, rights of second vendee, 36 Cal. 158. Construed, 40 N. Y. 318. Cited, 15 N. Y. 411.

Smith v. Martin, 2 Wm. Saund. 401. Cited, Grant, what passes by, 15 Cal. 196.

Smith v. McConnell, 17 Ill. 135. Cited, Cloud on Title, when action lies to remove, 39 Cal. 21.

Smith v. McIver, 9 Wheat. 532. Cited, Equity, when will not restrain judgment of court of law, 21 Cal. 442.

Smith v. Moody, 26 Ind. 299. Approved, Constitutionality of civil rights bill, 36 Cal. 667. Commented on, Id. 686.

Smith v. Moore, 11 N. H. 59. Commented on, Mortgage, purposes of, 9 Cal. 408.

Smith v. Morse, 2 Cal. 524. Approved, San Francisco, transfer of city property to commissioners of sinking fund void, 4 Cal. 148; 15 Cal. 514; 19 Cal. 21; 31 Cal. 39; 32 Cal. 449. Commented on, 16 Cal. 125. Cited, Title to city property, 15 Cal. 617. Approved, City estopped from setting up title in State, 15 Cal. 586, 587; Id. 636; Cloud on Title, right of protection from, 5 Cal. 75. Cited, Execution, validity of sale under writ of *venditioni esponas*, 8 Cal. 186; Corporations, general powers how restricted, 22 Cal. 627; Contract, law as a part of, 1 Saw. 712.

Smith v. N. Y. Cent. R. R. Co., 24 N. Y. 222. Commented on, Common Carriers, liability for loss by negligence, 27 Cal. 44.

Smith v. Ogg Shaw, 16 Cal. 88. Followed, Landlord and Tenant, when notice to quit and demand not required, 16 Cal. 92. Cited, 22 Cal. 229; 27 Cal. 105. Approved and applied, Replevin, demand when not necessary, 38 Cal. 512.

Smith v. Owens, 21 Cal. 11. Approved, Pleading, omission to plead special defense not cured by introduction of evidence, 28 Cal. 284.

Smith v. Painter, 5 Serg. & R. 225. Cited, Execution, rule of *caveat emptor*, 16 Cal. 564.

Smith v. Pelah, 2 Stra. 1264. Cited, Negligence, liability for injury from ferocious animal, 41 Cal. 141.

Smith v. Pollock, 2 Cal. 92. Approved, Reference, order cannot be made without consent of adverse party, 2 Cal. 261. Construed as to distinction between law and equity, 4 Cal. 7.

Smith v. Randall, 6 Cal. 47. Cited, Execution, validity of sale on what depends, 8 Cal. 186; sale in mass when valid, 19 Ind. 235; 23 Ind. 618. Approved, Not affected by neglect of officer, 9 Cal. 94; 17 Cal. 628. Cited, 22 Cal. 590; 38 Cal. 654; inadequacy of price bid not sufficient to avoid sale, 23 Cal. 302; Judgment, not subject to collateral attack, 12 Cal. 133.

Smith v. Rice, 11 Mass. 512. Cited, Judgment, on insufficient service of summons, void, 31 Cal. 356.

Smith v. Richards, 13 Pet. 26. Cited, Fraudulent Representations, evidence, 29 Cal. 592.

Smith v. Richmond, 15 Cal. 501; S. C. 19 Cal. 476. Cited, Pleading, demurrer on ground of statute of limitations, 20 Cal. 217; statute must be specially pleaded, 20 Cal. 626; 23 Cal. 353; admissions by failure to deny, 38 Cal. 290; Witness, indorser of note competent for either party, 25 Cal. 189; New Trial, granting, on ground of surprise, in discretion of court, 30 Cal. 227. Disapproved, New Promise, judgment on, 39 Cal. 438.

Smith v. Rines, 2 Sum. 338. Approved, Action, transfer of cause to federal court, 20 Cal. 169.

Smith v. Robinson, 11 Ala. 840. Cited, Demand, in action on bond for deed essential, 17 Cal. 276; 25 Cal. 279.

Smith v. Rowe, 4 Cal. 6. Cited, Trial, special issues in equity cases may be submitted to jury, 8 Cal. 286.

Smith v. Sacramento, 13 Cal. 531. Approved, Municipal Corporations may employ attorneys to protect public interests, 35 Cal. 670; 7 Nev. 293.

Smith v. Saxton, 6 Pick. 486. Cited, Statutory Construction, term "void" construed, 14 Cal. 475.

Smith v. Shackleford, 5 Dana, 232. Cited, Ejectment, general verdict, when conclusive on joint action, 4 Cal. 80.

Smith v. Sherwood, 2 Tex. 460. Cited, Trespass, on personal property, measure of damages, 11 Cal. 25; 14 Cal. 557.

Smith v. Sherwood, 4 Conn. 280. Commented on, Estoppel, limitation of bar of judgment in ejectment, 26 Cal. 502.

Smith v. Smith, 21 Penn. St. 370. Cited, Fraud, what sufficient to annul sale of goods, 33 Cal. 630.

Smith v. Smith, 12 Cal. 216. Cited, Husband and Wife, presumptions as to community property, 13 Cal. 470; on conveyance to wife, 15 Cal. 131; 23 Cal. 398; power of husband over community property, 31 Cal. 447; right of wife to share of, 39 Cal. 164. Approved, Effect of erection of building on separate property, 31 Cal. 449. Referred to, 42 Cal. 486.

Smith v. Smith, 3 How. Miss. 216. Cited, Probate Procedure, effect of allowance of claim, 6 Cal. 669.

Smith v. Smith, 15 N. H. 55. Cited, Mortgage, transfer of possession by mortgagee, 21 Cal. 626.

Smith v. Smith, 10 Paige, 470. Cited, Water Rights, partition of water, 27 Cal. 96.

Smith v. Smith, 4 Wend. 468. Cited, Agreement, what constitutes liquidated damages, 9 Cal. 587.

Smith v. Starkweather, 5 Day, 210. Cited, Ejectment, action maintainable on right of possession, 20 Cal. 162.

Smith v. Stewart, 6 John. 46. Cited, Use and Occupation, when action will not lie, 3 Cal. 203; 35 Cal. 194; 1 How. 159; 8 How. 413.

Smith v. Stillman, 5 Cal. 357. Denied, Office, power of legislature over office created by legislature, 14 Cal. 17.

Smith v. Strahan, 16 Tex. 320. Commented on, Husband and Wife, presumptions as to separate estate of wife, by gift from husband, 30 Cal. 39, 54; how far husband and wife are distinct entities, Id. 46; settlement on wife may be made from common property, 31 Cal. 447.

Smith v. Tennessee, 1 Yerg. 228. Cited, Attorney and Counsel, name stricken from roll, 22 Cal. 321.

Smith v. Trenton Del. Falls Co., 3 Green Ch. 508. Cited, Parties, in equity, 31 Cal. 427.

Smith v. Turner, 7 How. 283. Commented on, State Sovereignty, restriction as to regulation of commerce, 1 Cal. 236; passenger tax, Id. 242; 20 Cal. 582; residence of aliens, 1 Cal. 246.

Smith v. United States, 10 Pet. 326. Cited, Survey, private survey, effect of, 14 Cal. 359; International Law, law of ceded territory, 1 Cal. 314; vested rights protected, Id. 326; powers and duties of government, 18 Cal. 23; 11 How. 88; Mexican Grants, validity of floating grants, 3 Cal. 42. Distinguished, 37 Cal. 497. Commented on, effect of private survey, 13 Cal. 416; 14 Cal. 359.

Smith v. Ware, 13 John. 257. Cited, Express Promise, when action lies on, 2 Cal. 581.

Smith v. Whiting, 11 Mass. 446. Commented on, Judgment, when not a bar, 26 Cal. 494.

Smith v. Wilson, 3 Barn. & Ad. 728. Cited, Written Instruments, parol evidence admissible to explain, 11 Cal. 198; 34 Cal. 628.

Smith v. Wilson, 1 Dev. & B. 41. Approved, Evidence, preliminary evidence of lost instrument, 10 Cal. 147.

Smith v. Woodruff, 48 Barb. 438. Cited, Trade Marks, law of, 35 Cal. 82.

Smith v. Yreka Wat. Co., 14 Cal. 201.   Cited, Amendments, to complaint after demurrer filed, 30 Cal. 78.

Smith v. Yale, 31 Cal. 180.   Commented on, Conveyance, notice imparted by possession, 25 Wis. 95.

Smith's Heirs v. Frost, 2 Dana, 149.   Commented on, Lands, constructive possession under color of title, 25 Cal. 134.

Smith's Lessee v. Trabue's Heirs, 1 McLean, 87.   Cited, Ejectment, who liable to be turned out under judgment, 22 Cal. 206.

Smoot v. Baldwin, 1 Mart. N. S. 528.   Commented on, Judicial Notice, presumptions as to law of foreign State, 15 Cal. 253.

Smoot v. Russell, 1 Mart. N. S. 522.   Cited, Judicial Notice, not taken of foreign laws, 15 Cal. 254.

Smout v. Ilbery, 10 Mees. &. W. 1.   Cited, Principal and Agent, power of agent ceases on death of principal, 15 Cal. 18.

Smull v. Jones, 1 Watts & S. 128.   Commented on, Agreement of combination for purchase at sheriff's sale, when not illegal, 30 Cal. 592.

Sneed v. Osborn, 25 Cal. 619.   Referred to in same case, Land, boundary lines of land sold, 30 Cal. 433.

Sneider v. Geiss, 1 Yeates, 34.   Cited, Innkeeper, liability for loss of property, 33 Cal. 602.

Snelling v. Utterback, 1 Bibb, 611.   Cited, Evidence, admissibility of parol evidence of declarations and admissions, 26 Cal. 44.

Snodgrass v. Ricketts, 13 Cal. 359.   Cited, Estoppel, by standing by and suffering land to be sold, 31 Ill. 151.

Snyder v. Stafford, 11 Paige, 76.   Criticised, Execution, title of purchaser at sale, 31 Cal. 300.

Snyder v. Warren, 2 Cow. 518.   Cited, Foreclosure, right of redemption from sale, 9 Cal. 412.

Snydor v. Hurd, 8 Tex. 98.   Commented on, Principal and Agent, when liability on contract attaches to agent, 7 Cal. 541.

Society for Prop. of Gosp. v. New Haven, 8 Wheat. 464.   Cited, Alien, rights of, under treaty, 5 Cal. 382.

Society for Prop. of Gosp. v. Town of Pawlet, 4 Pet. 506. Cited, Estoppel, grantee in fee not estopped, 18 Cal. 476.

Society for Prop. the Gosp. v. Wheeler, 2 Gall. 105. Cited, Stare Decisis, local adjudications, 15 Cal. 603; Statutory Construction, statutes not to be construed retrospectively, 4 Cal. 136; 25 Cal. 310; 27 Cal. 159; 6 How. 327. Commented on, 2 Pet. 414.

Society for Prop. the Gospel v. Young, 2 N. H. 310. Cited, Presumptions from lapse of time, 22 Cal. 591.

Soggins v. Heard, 31 Miss. 426. Cited, Trust, resulting trust may be proved by parol, 22 Cal. 579; Statute of Frauds, provisions as to real estate, 35 Cal. 488.

Solano Co. v. Neville, 27 Cal. 465. Cited, Fees of Office, salary as exclusive remuneration, 30 Cal. 176; power of legislature, 36 Cal. 622.

Solarte v. Palmer, 8 Bligh. N. S. 874. Cited, Negotiable Instruments, notice of dishonor, 8 Cal. 636.

Solomon v. Reese, 34 Cal. 28. Cited, Appeal, statement when not required, 36 Cal. 232; *ad damnum* clause as the test of jurisdiction, 6 Nev. 162.

Somerset v. Inhab. of Dightown, 12 Mass. 383. Cited, Statutory Construction, 13 Cal. 456.

Somes v. Brewer, 2 Pick. 184. Cited, Fraudulent Conveyance, title of innocent purchasers, 12 Cal. 498.

Somes v. Skinner, 3 Pick. 52. Cited, Conveyance, without warranty, what estate passes, 14 Cal. 628.

Sorrell v. Carpenter, 2 P. Wms. 482. Cited, Lis Pendens, to what statute applies, 23 Cal. 38.

Soto v. Kroder, 19 Cal. 87. Commented on, Probate Act, how far retroactive, 28 Cal. 505; 33 Cal. 423. Approved, 37 Cal. 89, 91.

Souch v. Strawbridge, 2 Com. B. 813. Cited, Services, action upon *quantum meruit,* when it lies, 33 Cal. 195.

Soulard v. United States, 4 Pet. 511. Cited, International Law, vested rights under treaty of cession, 1 Cal. 326; 18 Cal. 23, 24; 20 Cal. 421; 8 How. 304; 13 How. 257.

Soule v. Dawes, 6 Cal. 473; S. C. 7 Cal. 575; 14 Cal. 247. Approved, Mechanic's Lien attaches by relation to commencement of work, 13 Cal. 56; 23 Cal. 525; Appeal, judgment on, when conclusive, 17 Cal. 195; 22 Cal. 222; what may be adjudged, 30 Cal. 463. Cited, Mortgage, what it includes, 22 Cal. 631.

Soule v. Ritter, 20 Cal. 522. Cited, Appeal, judgment on, for what may provide, 30 Cal. 463.

South, Ex parte, 3 Swanst. 393. Commented on, Assignment, order as an equitable assignment, 13 Cal. 121.

South, Heirs of, v. Hoy, 3 Bibb, 523. Commented on, Appeal, who may, 8 Cal. 315.

Southcomb v. Bishop of Exeter, 6 Hare, 213. Commented on, Specific Performance, diligence in seeking remedy, 10 Cal. 327.

Southgate v. Montgomery, 1 Paige, 47. Cited, Judgment, how far conclusive, 38 Cal. 647.

South Sea Co. v. Wymondsell, 3 P. Wms. 143. Approved, Statute of Limitations, avoided by fraudulent concealment, 8 Cal. 458.

Spalding v. Spalding, 2 Root, 271. Cited, Summons, return gives jurisdiction, 33 Cal. 686.

Spanagel v. Dellinger, 38 Cal. 278. Cited, Appeal, injury presumed from error, 42 Cal. 407.

Spangler v. Jacoby, 14 Ill. 298. Constitutional provision distinguished, Statute testing validity of, 30 Cal. 270, 274. Cited, 23 Mo. 366.

Sparks v. De La Guerra, 14 Cal. 108. Affirmed, Will, construction of secret bequest, 18 Cal. 678.

Sparks v. Hess, 15 Cal. 186. Distinguished, Vendor's Lien, enforcement of, by assignee, 20 Cal. 620. Approved, Assignability of vendor's lien, 21 Cal. 177. Commented on, when lien attaches, 32 Cal. 58; nature of, 35 Cal. 206. Cited, Enforcement of, 26 Wis. 543; as against administrator of grantee, 28 Cal. 638. Commented on, Conveyance, what passes by, 24 Cal. 487; 2 Wall. 188.

Sparks v. Kohler, 3 Cal. 299. Cited, Witness, competency of, 22 Cal. 574. Distinguished, 1 Nev. 27.

Sparks v. State Bank, 7 Blackf. 469. Cited, Fixtures, what constitute, 14 Cal. 68.

Sparrow v. Chesley, 19 Me. 79. Cited, Fraud, remedy against fraudulent vendee, 23 Cal. 236.

Sparrow v. Kingman, 1 N. Y. 242. Commented on, Vendor and Vendee, vendee may deny title of vendor, 18 Cal. 476.

Spear v. Ditty, 8 Vt. 419. Cited, Tax Titles, sufficiency of tax deed, 25 Cal. 48.

Spear v. Ward, 20 Cal. 659. Cited, Guardian and Ward, parties to action, 32 Cal. 119.

Speer v. Coate, 3 McCord, 227. Commented on, Evidence, parol evidence as to boundaries, 15 Cal. 280.

Specht v. Commonwealth, 8 Penn. St. 312. Denied, Sunday Laws, validity of statutes, 9 Cal. 505. Approved, dissenting opinion of Field, J., 9 Cal. 525. Cited, 18 Cal. 681.

Speck v. Commonwealth, 3 Watts & S. 324. Cited, Official Bonds, sufficiency of, 7 Cal. 441.

Spect v. Hoyt, 3 Cal. 413. Cited, Appeal, review of order granting new trial, 10 Cal. 341.

Spence v. Duren, 3 Ala. 251. Cited, Fraudulent representations as to title, when action will lie, 17 Cal. 385.

Spencer v. Babcock, 22 Barb. 326. Cited, Set-off, as an equitable defense, 19 Cal. 658; Counter-claim, what constitutes, 26 Cal. 309.

Spencer v. Brockway, 1 Ohio, 259. Cited, Judgment, when foreign judgment not enforceable, 8 Cal. 457.

Spencer v. Champion, 9 Conn. 536. Commented on, Office, right to hold over, 28 Cal. 53.

Spencer v. Grimball, 6 Mart. N. S. 355. Commented on, Title, Indian titles, nullity of, 1 Cal. 281; distinction as to absolute and relative nullity, Id. 291.

Spencer v. Prindle, 28 Cal. 276. Approved, Damages, assessment of, may be on a valuation founded on legal tender notes, 30 Cal. 181; 35 Cal. 357; Judicial Notice, not taken of distinction in money values, 31 Cal. 80.

Spencer v. Tobey, 22 Barb. 260. Commented on, Contract of Sale, license to enter, not implied, 15 Cal. 211.

Sperling v. Trevor, 7 Ves. Jr. 498. Cited, Title, rule of judicial determination, 25 Cal. 80.

Speyer v. Ihmels, 21 Cal. 280. Approved, Attachment, intervention by subsequent attaching creditors, 28 Cal. 287.

Spieres v. Parker, 1 Term Rep. 141. Cited, Judgment, must be sustained by facts alleged in complaint, 30 Cal. 489. Distinguished, 1 Gall. 267.

Spies v. Newberry, 2 Doug. Mich. 428. Commented on, Negotiable Instruments, protest construed, 8 Cal. 637.

Spong v. Spong, 1 Dow & C. 377; S. C. 3 Bligh. N. S. 102. Cited, Will, construction of devise of land, 31 Cal. 610.

Spooner v. Davis, 7 Pick. 146. Approved, Verdict, not conclusive upon collateral issues, 15 Cal. 148.

Spottiswoode v. Clark, 2 Sand. Ch. 629. Cited, Trade Marks, measure of damages, 40 Cal. 599.

Sprague v. Baker, 17 Mass. 586. Cited, Covenant, what sufficient eviction under, 39 Cal. 367, 368; 23 Mo. 161.

Sprague v. Birdsall, 2 Cow. 419. Cited, Statutory Construction, remedial statutes, 1 Cal. 163.

Sprague v. Caldwell, 12 Barb. 516. Cited, Witness, impeachment of, practice, 16 Cal. 179.

Sprague v. Norway, 31 Cal. 173. Cited, Statutory Construction, "month" defined, 32 Cal. 350; Election, returns not to be rejected for irregularities without injury, 34 Cal. 640.

Sprague v. Shed, 9 John. 140. Cited, Justice of Peace, loss of jurisdiction on dismissal of action, 29 Cal. 316.

Spratt v. Spratt, 4 Pet. 406. Approved, Naturalization, power of judicial, 5 Cal. 301; State Court, congress cannot confer powers on, Id.

Spriggs, Estate of, 20 Cal. 121. Cited, Probate Proceedings, for sale of estate, a distinct action, 20 Cal. 312. Approved, Order for sale conclusive, 22 Cal. 276.

Spring v. Russell, 7 Greenl. 273. Cited, Eminent Domain, legislature exclusive judges of public necessity, 18 Cal. 252; 34 Ala. 327.

Springer v. Keyser, 6 Whart. 187. Cited, Mechanic's Lien, sufficiency of description in notice, 2 Cal. 63.

Spring Valley W. W., Ex parte, 17 Cal. 132. Cited, Corporations, omissions in organization not to invalidate charter, 22 Cal. 441; Mandamus, when will issue, 41 Cal. 77; Appeal, entertained in special cases, 42 Cal. 68.

Spring Valley W. W. v. San Francisco, 22 Cal. 434. Approved, Corporations, proceedings in organization of, not invalidated by slight defects or omissions, 28 Cal. 519; 37 Cal. 361; Condemnation of land for railroads, powers of commissioners, limitation of, 29 Cal. 118.

Sprouce v. Commonwealth, 2 Virg. Cas. 375. Cited, Juror and Jury, juror when disqualified, 1 Cal. 385.

Spurr v. Trimble, 1 A. K. Marsh. 278. Cited, Presumption of death, when it arises, 38 Cal. 229.

Spurrier v. Fitzgerald, 6 Ves. Jr. 548. Cited, Specific Performance of verbal contracts, when decreed, 10 Cal. 158; Pleading, under statute of frauds, 29 Cal. 599.

Squier v. Gould, 14 Wend. 159. Cited, Pleading, special damages must be particularly stated, 41 Cal. 565.

Squire v. Harder, 1 Paige, 494. Cited, Parent and Child, resulting trust not created by purchase in name of child, 16 Cal. 357.

Squires v. Foorman, 10 Cal. 298. Cited, Appeal, affirmance for want of assignment of errors, 25 Cal. 483.

St. Albans v. Bush, 4 Vt. 58. Cited, Judgment, validity of, how put in issue, 30 Cal. 446, 447.

St. Joseph v. Anthony, 30 Mo. 538. Commented on, Street Improvement, apportionment of assessment, 28 Cal. 371.

St. Louis v. Coons, 37 Mo. 45. Commented on, Street Assessments, power of legislature to provide for enforcement of, 31 Cal. 685. Cited, Enforcement of, 31 Cal. 685.

St. Louis v. Gurno, 12 Mo. 414. Cited, Street Improvement, right of city to raise grade of street, 42 Cal. 438.

Stackpole v. Arnold, 11 Mass. 27. Approved, Principal when not bound by contract made by agent, 7 Cal. 539; 13 Cal. 48; 5 Gray, 571, 572. Cited, 35 Conn. 152. Commented on, 5 Gray, 565; contra, 9 Allen, 421. Cited, Contracts, liability on implied contracts, 14 Cal. 136.

Stacy v. Miller, 14 Mo. 478. Commented on, Dedication of Highway, what constitutes, 14 Cal. 647, 648.

Stafford v. Ingersoll, 3 Hill. 41. Cited, Rights and Remedies, under statute, election, 16 Cal. 525.

36

Stafford v. Lick, 7 Cal. 479; S. C. 10 Cal. 16. Cited, Constitutionality of Statute, provisions in recording act construed, 9 Cal. 85. Approved, 20 Cal. 224. Commented on, Recording of deeds made prior to passage of act, 36 Cal. 634. Approved, Forfeiture on failure to record homestead claim, 24 Cal. 640. Cited, Conveyance, what sufficient to pass title, 26 Cal. 469; possession as evidence of notice of ·unrecorded deed, 29 Cal. 490.

Stafford v. Mott, 3 Paige, 100. Cited, Execution, supplementary proceedings, parties, 7 Cal. 204.

Stall v. Catskill Bank, 18 Wend. 478. Cited, Partnership, when partner not bound by indorsement of co-partner as, 37 Cal. 117. Approved, Notice to third persons of want of authority, Id. 119.

Standifer v. Davis, 13 Smedes & M. 48. Denied, Vendor and Vendee, demand and tender of deed by vendee, 25 Cal. 279.

Stanford v. Dana, 10 Cal. 269. Cited, Insolvency, giving preference to creditor not fraudulent, 12 Cal. 474.

Stanford v. Taylor, 18 How. 409. Commented on, Mexican Grant, title of confirmee, 13 Cal. 411.

Stanford v. Worn, 27 Cal. 171. Cited, Statutes divesting estates to be strictly pursued, 30 Cal. 537; Appeal, jurisdiction entertained in special cases, 42 Cal. 68.

Stanley v. Green, 12 Cal. 148. Approved, Deed, construction of description in, 15 Cal. 496; 26 Cal. 632. Cited, Rule of construction of deeds, 23 Iowa, 225; Conveyance, what sufficient to pass title, 26 Cal. 469; Evidence, estoppel of grantor by declarations and admissions, 25 Cal. 597.

Stanmire v. Powell, 13 Ired. 312. Cited, State Lands, grants to, when void, 23 Cal. 443.

Stansell v. Roberts, 13 Ohio, 148. Cited, Conveyance, construction of recording act, 6 Cal. 315; 14 Ohio, 431; 17 Ohio, 500; 1 Ohio St. 113.

Stanton v. Button, 2 Conn. 527. Cited, Acknowledgment of Deed, authority of notary, 11 Cal. 298.

Stanton v. Kirsch, 6 Wis. 338. Cited, Husband and Wife, burden of proof as to separate property of wife, 30 Cal. 43.

Stanton v. Leland, 4 E. D. Smith, 94. Cited, Innkeeper, liability for loss of property, 33 Cal. 599.

Stanton v. Small, 3 Sand. 240. Cited, Sale and Delivery, delivery by warehouse receipts, 8 Cal. 614.

Stanwood v. Peirce, 7 Mass. 458. Cited, Statutory Construction, presumptions as to intent of legislature, 13 Cal. 456.

Staples v. Fairchild, 3 N. Y. 44. Cited, Summons, service by publication, sufficiency of affidavit, 27 Cal. 299; 31 Cal. 349.

Staples v. Franklin Bank, 1 Met. 43. Approved, Negotiable Instrument, presentment and demand, when to be made, 8 Cal. 632.

Staples v. Parker, 41 Barb. 648. Cited, Trial, agreements between parties as to day set for trial, construed, 35 Cal. 606.

Stapp v. Phelps, 7 Dana, 300. Cited, Redemption, demand in action to redeem, 22 Cal. 335.

Starin v. Town of Geneva, 23 N. Y. 446. Cited, Statutory Construction, validity of statute contingent on popular vote, 25 Cal. 646.

Stark v. Barnes, 4 Cal. 412. Cited, Lands, possession and actual appropriation as the test of priority of claim to, 6 Cal. 108. Explained, Forcible Entry and Detainer, who liable to action, 19 Cal. 387.

Stark v. Barrett, 15 Cal. 361. Cited, Mexican Grants, patent takes effect by relation, 18 Cal. 26; Id. 571; 20 Cal. 160; 1 Wall. 373; 1 Saw. 567, 579; Ejectment, by tenant in common, 20 Cal. 162; 21 Cal. 348; Id. 583; title or right of possession to be shown, 22 Cal. 516; 24 Cal. 147; Tenant in Common, conveyance by, not to prejudice co-tenant, 27 Cal. 64. Commented on, 69 Penn. St. 238; grantee entitled to possession, 27 Cal. 560; subject to contingency of loss on partition, 35 Cal. 588, 594, 595; validity of, 1 Saw. 256.

Stark v. Raney, 18 Cal. 622. Cited, Indemnity, liabilty on bond of, 33 Cal. 212.

Starke v. Hill, 6 Ala. 785. Cited, Vendor and Vendee, payment of purchase money cannot be resisted by vendee in possession, 5 Cal. 265.

Starr v. Child, 20 Wend. 149. Reversed, 4 Hill, 369. Commented on, Riparian Rights, judicial decisions as to common law, how far regarded, 8 Cal. 142; 33 N. Y. 484.

Starr v. Pease, 8 Conn. 547. Cited, Statutory Construction, rule of judicial determination, 17 Cal. 562.

State v. Adams, 4 Blackf. 147. Cited, Jurisdiction, crimes not cognizable in State courts, 38 Cal. 150.

State v. Ainsworth, 11 Vt. 92. Cited, Criminal Procedure, what constitutes a good plea of former conviction or acquittal, 28 Cal. 463.

State v. Allen, 1 McCord, 525. Cited, Verdict, polling jury, practice, 20 Cal. 72.

State v. Ambs, 20 Mo. 214. Cited, Sunday Laws, of binding force, 18 Cal. 681.

State v. Ancker, 2 Rich. 245. Approved, Corporations, powers of, can only be exercised by trustees when assembled as a board, 33 Cal. 23.

State v. Anderson, 3 Smedes & M. 753. Cited, Criminal Procedure, discharge of jury when it operates as an acquittal, 38 Cal. 478.

State v. Arledge, 1 Bailey, 551. Commented on, Public Lands, removal of intruders from, 12 Cal. 525.

State v. Baker, 19 Mo. 683. Cited, Criminal Procedure, when discharge of jury operates as an acquittal, 38 Cal. 478.

State v. Ball, 27 Mo. 324. Cited, Criminal Procedure, validity of judgment, 31 Cal. 627.

State v. Baltimore & O. R.R. Co., 12 Gill & J. 436; S. C. 3 How. 534. Cited, Legislature, power over local taxation and appropriation, 13 Cal. 355. Commented on, 16 Cal. 235, 236; power to pass repealing and confirmatory acts, 15 Cal. 624.

State v. Bancroft, 10 N. H. 105. Cited, Burglary, crime defined, 19 Cal. 578.

State v. Barrett, 35 Ala. 406. Cited, Criminal Procedure, discharge of jury when not an acquittal, 41 Cal. 216.

State v. Beckwith, 1 Stewt. 318. Cited, Pleading, exceptions in statute of limitation to be specially pleaded, 12 Cal. 295.

State v. Benton, 2 Dev. & B. 212. Commented on, Juror and Jury, power of court to excuse juror, 32 Cal. 47; challenge for bias, 16 Cal. 135.

State v. Boswell, 2 Dev. 210. Cited, Witness, impeachment of, practice, 27 Cal. 636; 12 How. 555.

State v. Bouche, 5 Blackf. 154. Cited, Criminal Procedure, when discharge of jury operates as an acquittal, 38 Cal. 478.

State v. Briggs, 34 Vt. 501. Cited, Indictment, sufficiency of, in case of forgery, 35 Cal. 507.

State v. Broughton, 7 Ired. 101. Approved, Witness, grand juror, privilege of, 31 Cal. 564.

State v. Brown, 4 Port. 410. Cited, Indictment, sufficiency of, on statutory offense, 14 Cal. 31.

State v. Brown, 16 Conn. 54. Cited, Criminal Procedure, when discharge of jury operates as an acquittal, 38 Cal. 478.

State v. Burris, 3 Tex. 118. Cited, Criminal Procedure, when discharge of jury operates as an acquittal, 38 Cal. 478.

State v. Callendine, 8 Iowa, 290. Cited, Criminal Procedure, when discharge of jury operates as an acquittal, 38 Cal. 478.

State v. Catlin, 3 Vt. 533. Cited, dedication, what acts necessary to constitute, 22 Cal. 489.

State v. Chase, 5 Ohio St. 529. Approved, Mandamus may issue to governor, 39 Cal. 211.

State v. Click, 2 Ala. 27. Cited, Indictment, sufficiency of, on statutory offense, 14 Cal. 31.

State v. Coleman, 5 Port. 40. Cited, Indictment, distinct acts constituting one offense, 27 Cal. 401.

State v. Collins, 20 Iowa, 90. Cited, Instructions, court may modify instructions presented, 30 Cal. 450.

State v. Commissioners of Perry Co., 5 Ohio St. 497. Cited, Constitutionality of statute in part void, 22 Cal. 386.

State v. Copeland, 3 R. I. 33. Cited, Constitutionality of statutes in part invalid, 22 Cal. 392.

State v. County Court St. Louis Co., 34 Mo. 546. Cited, Street Improvement, apportionment of expense, 41 Cal. 532.

State v. Davis, 4 Blackf. 346. Cited, Criminal Procedure, when discharge of jury operates as an acquittal, 38 Cal. 478.

State v. Dawson, 3 Hill, S. C. 100. Distinguished, Eminent Domain, condemnation without compensation, 31 Cal. 549. Approved, dissenting opinion of Richardson, J., 25 Vt. 66.

State v. DeHart, 2 Halst. 172. Cited, Criminal Procedure, when discharge of jury operates as an acquittal, 38 Cal. 478.

State v. Denton, 6 Ark. 259. Cited, Criminal Procedure, when discharge of jury operates as an acquittal, 38 Cal. 478.

State v. Dews, R. M. Charlt. 397. Cited, Officers, power of legislature over rights and duties of, 22 Cal. 319.

State v. Duncan, 9 Port. 260. Cited, Indictment, sufficiency of, on statutory offense, 14 Cal. 31.

State v. Elden, 41 Me. 165. Cited, Criminal Procedure, plea of former conviction, 32 Cal. 433.

State v. Dunn, 18 Mo. 423. Commented on, Criminal Procedure, malice implied from unlawful killing, 17 Cal. 398.

State v. Elliot, 11 N. H. 542. Cited, Fixtures, what constitute, 14 Cal. 68.

State v. Ellis, 4 Mo. 474. Cited, Indictment, conjunctive and disjunctive averments, 35 Cal. 509.

State v. Ephraim, 2 Dev. & B. 162. Doubted, Criminal Procedure, discharge of jury, effect of, 41 Cal. 217; 63 N. C. 530.

State v. Findley, 10 Ohio, 51. Cited, Office, official oath a mere ministerial act, 7 Cal. 441.

State v. Fisher, 28 Vt. 714. Statute distinguished, Office, proceeding by *quo warranto,* 15 Cal. 121.

State v. Fley, 2 Brev. 339. Cited, Criminal Procedure, accessories as principals, 10 Cal. 69.

State v. Ford, 3 Strob. 517. Approved, Criminal Procedure, testimony of threats to prove malice, 34 Cal. 206.

State v. Freeman, 13 N. H. 488. Cited, Indictment, validity of, 21 Cal. 373.

State v. Gilbert, 2 Bay, 355. Cited, Forcible Entry and Detainer, who bound by judgment, 10 Cal. 214.

State v. Governor of Ohio, 5 Ohio St. 534. Commented on, Mandamus to governor, 16 Cal. 43; distinction as to ministerial and discretionary acts, 30 Cal. 602.

State v. Guild, 5 Halst. 163. Cited, Evidence, presumptions as to confessions in criminal cases, 41 Cal. 455.

State v. Hamilton, 1 Harrison, 155. Commented on, Sheriff, execution process to be completed by ex-sheriff, 8 Cal. 408.

State v. Hand, 6 Ark. 169. Cited, Criminal Procedure, when discharge of jury operates as an acquittal, 38 Cal. 478.

State v. Hawkins, 8 Port. 461. Disapproved, Larceny, what constitutes, 28 Cal. 382.

State v. Herman, 13 Ired. 502. Cited, Parent and Child, legitimacy when presumed, 13 Cal. 99.

State v. Hill, 1 Tr. Const. C. Rep. 242. Commented on, Criminal Procedure, evidence admissible on application for bail, 19 Cal. 547.

State v. Holt, 27 Mo. 340. Cited, Sureties on administrator's bond concluded by judgment against principal, 25 Cal. 223.

State v. Hopkins, 1 Bay, 373. Cited, Juror and Jury, incompetency of juror in criminal action, 9 Cal. 311.

State v. Houston, 1 Bailey, 300. Commented on, Forgery, verdict of acquittal in former action, how far an estoppel, 28 Cal. 515.

State v. Jennings, 18 Mo. 443. Cited, Murder in first degree, what constitutes, 17 Cal. 399.

State v. Johnson, 8 Blackf. 533. Cited, Criminal Procedure, when discharge of jury operates as an acquittal, 38 Cal. 478.

State v. Johnson, 3 Hill, S. C. 1. Cited, Indictment, distinct acts constituting one offense, 27 Cal. 401.

State v. Judge of Fifth District, 5 La. An. 758. Commented on, Constitutionality of Statute, principles of judicial determination, 2 Cal. 207, 228.

State v. Kanouse, 1 Spen. 115. Cited, Criminal Procedure, when discharge of jury operates as an acquittal, 38 Cal. 478.

State v. Kittle, 2 Tyler, 471.   Cited, Criminal Procedure, when discharge of jury operates as an acquittal, 38 Cal. 478.

State v. Lamb, 28 Mo. 219.   Cited, Evidence, confessions, as proof of crime, 31 Cal. 569.

State v. Lee, 5 Cal. 353.   Approved, Appeal, discretion of court on granting or refusing change of venue reviewable on appeal, 3 Nev. 434.

State v. Longbottoms, 11 Humph. 39.   Cited, Indictment, bad for want of description, 14 Cal. 102.

State v. Lusk, 18 Mo. 333.   Denied, Office, vacancy in, 6 Cal. 290; 37 Cal. 641.   Cited, Restriction to appointing power of governor, 37 Cal. 621.

State v. Main, 16 Wis. 398.   Commented on, Election, constitutional qualification of voter, 26 Cal. 201.

State v. Martin, 3 Hawks, 381.   Cited, Criminal Procedure, when discharge of jury operates as an acquittal, 38 Cal. 478.

State v. Matthews, 37 N. H. 453.   Cited, Legislature, powers of, 29 Cal. 405.

State v. McBride, Rice, 400.   Cited, Constitutional Construction, judicial power where vested, 5 Cal. 302.

State v. McCauley, 15 Cal. 429.   Approved, Constitutionality of Statute appointing State Prison Commissioners, 16 Cal. 25.   Cited, State Capitol Act, 16 Cal. 253; repealing act, when void, 16 Cal. 194.   Commented on, Constitutional Construction, appropriations not creating State debt, 27 Cal. 207, 208, 219; 5 Nev. 25. Cited, Public Officers, deed or contract made by, 2 Wall. 187.

State v. McDonnell, 32 Vt. 492.   Commented on, Instructions to be given with reference to facts proved, 30 Cal. 207.

State v. McKee, 1 Bailey, 653.   Cited, Criminal Procedure, discharge of jury when not an acquittal, 38 Cal. 478; 41 Cal. 216.

State v. Mead, 27 Vt. 722.   Cited, Criminal Procedure, averment and proof of incorporation, 32 Cal. 166.

State v. Medbery, 7 Ohio St. 526.   Approved, Constitutional Construction, contracts creating State debts, 27 Cal. 210, 217.

State v. Melogue, 9 Ind. 196. Cited, Execution, exemption a personal right which may be waived, 22 Cal. 507.

State v. Mertens, 14 Mo. 94. Cited, Indictment, validity of, 21 Cal. 373.

State v. Miller, 8 Ind. 326. Disapproved, 26 Ind. 366. Cited, Criminal Procedure, effect of discharge of jury, 41 Cal. 216.

State v. Miller, 3 Zab. 383. Cited, Condemnation of Land, measure of compensation, 31 Cal. 373.

State v. Mills, 2 Dev. 421. Commented on, Criminal Procedure, application for release on bail, 19 Cal. 543.

State v. Morgan, 7 Ired. 387. Cited, Criminal Procedure, when discharge of jury operates as an acquittal, 38 Cal. 378.

State v. Moore, 12 Cal. 56. Explained, Taxation, property attached to mining claim not exempt, 14 Cal. 154. Distinguished, as to taxation of public domain, 22 Cal. 80. Approved, as to taxation of possessory claims, 30 Cal. 657.

State v. Morris, 1 Blackf. 37. Denied, Indictment, acquittal of greater and conviction of lesser offense, 4 Cal. 379.

State v. Nelson, 26 Ind. 366. Cited, Criminal Procedure, effect of discharge of jury, 41 Cal. 216.

State v. Newark, 3 Dutch. 185. Cited, Street Assessments, power of legislature to impose burdens, 28 Cal. 352. Commented on, Id. 358. Distinguished, 32 Cal. 522, 525. Denied, 104 Mass. 485.

State v. Niebling, 6 Ohio St. 43. Approved, Office, term of, 11 Cal. 87.

State v. Owens, 10 Rich. 169. Cited, Indictment, partnership, how alleged in, 36 Cal. 248.

State v. Pike, 15 N. H. 83. Cited, Jurisdiction, offenses over which State courts have not jurisdiction, 38 Cal. 150.

State v. Polke, 7 Blackf. 27. Cited, Surety, rights of, under contract, 11 Cal. 220.

State v. Poulterer, 16 Cal. 514. Affirmed on rehearing, Cal. Sup. Ct. Jan. T. 1861 (not reported.) Cited, Revenue, duty imposed on auctioneers, 19 Cal. 509.

State v. Prescott, 7 N. H. 287. Commented on, Criminal Procedure, separation of jury, burden of proof as to injury, 21 Cal. 341. Cited, Presumption against purity of verdict, 39 Cal. 375. Denied, 26 Miss. 82.

State v. Price, 6 Halst. 143. Commented on, Indictment, for arson, sufficiency of, 20 Cal. 79.

State v. Reily, 2 Brev. 445. Cited, Criminal Procedure, when discharge of jury operates as an acquittal, 38 Cal. 478.

State v. Reynolds, 4 Hayw. 110. Cited, Criminal Procedure, when discharge of jury operates as an acquittal, 38 Cal. 478.

State v. Rives, 5 Ired. 297. Cited, Condemnation of Land, estimate of benefits, 31 Cal. 372.

State v. Roach, 2 Hayw. 352. Cited, Pleading, exceptions in statute of limitation to be specially pleaded, 12 Cal. 295.

State v. Roberts. 1 Dev. 259. Cited, Evidence, presumptions as to confessions in criminal cases, 41 Cal. 455.

State v. Rogers, 13 Cal. 159. Cited, Aliens, statutory rights of non-resident aliens, 18 Cal. 219; 21 Iowa, 544; Constitutional construction, restriction on power of legislature must appear, 22 Cal. 308; relative powers of Federal and State governments, 41 Cal. 162.

State v. Slaughter, 6 Humph. 410. Cited, Criminal Procedure, effect of acquittal, 4 Cal. 379; contra, 29 Mo. 56.

State v. Sloane, 20 Ohio, 327. Cited, Officers, duties as to issuance of writs, 36 Cal. 214.

State v. Smith, 5 Day, 175. Cited, Judgment, in criminal procedure, validity of, 22 Cal. 137.

State v. Smith, 5 Humph. 396. Cited, Statutory Construction, sense of words, 13 Cal. 518.

State v. Somerville, 21 Me. 14. Cited, Indictment, on larceny from bailee, 28 Cal. 493.

State v. Spear, 6 Mo. 644. Cited, Criminal Procedure, when discharge of jury operates as an acquittal, 38 Cal. 478.

State v. Springfield Township, etc., 6 Ind. 88. Cited, Constitutional Construction, restrictions in, as to rights of aliens, 13 Cal. 165.

State v. Stallings, 2 Hayw. 490. Cited, Witness, impeachment of, practice, 27 Cal. 636.

State v. Stringfellow, 26 Miss. 157. Cited, Evidence, confessions as evidence, 31 Cal. 568.

State v. Taylor, 1 Hawks, 462. Cited, Criminal Procedure, when discharge of jury operates as an acquittal, 38 Cal. 478.

State v. Towns, 8 Geo. 360. Cited, dissenting opinion of Temple, J., Mandamus will not issue to governor, 39 Cal. 223.

State v. Trask, 6 Vt. 355. Cited, Dedication by Deed, when ineffectual, 42 Cal. 553.

State v. Turner, 19 Iowa, 148. Cited, Instructions, court may modify instructions presented, 30 Cal. 450.

State v. Updike, 4 Harr. Del. 581. Cited, Criminal Procedure, when discharge of jury not an acquittal, 41 Cal. 216.

State v. Walker, 26 Ind. 346. Cited, Criminal Procedure, effect of discharge of jury, 41 Cal. 216.

State v. Waterhouse, 1 Mart. & Y. 278. Cited, Criminal Procedure, when discharge of jury operates as an acquittal, 38 Cal. 478; 3 Sneed, 478; contra, 10 Yerg. 532.

State v. Williams, 3 Stewt. 454. Commented on, Juror and Jury, grounds of challenge, 1 Cal. 385.

State v. Woodlief, 2 Cal. 241. Approved, Summons, judgment by default not sustained by a defective summons, 8 Cal. 625.

State v. Wright, 3 Brev. 421. Cited, Criminal Procedure, when discharge of jury operates as an acquittal, 38 Cal. 478.

State v. Yarbrough, 2 Tex. 523 Cited, Criminal Procedure, admission to bail, 19 Cal. 547.

State v. Yarbrough, 1 Hawks, 78. Cited, Criminal Procedure, justification for killing, when may be pleaded, 17 Cal. 324.

State v. Young, 5 Am. Law Reg. N. S. 679. Referred to, in nate, Statute, testing validity of, 30 Cal. 280.

State Bank v. Fearing, 16 Pick. 533. Cited, Negotiable Instruments, undertaking of indorser on certificate of deposit, 22 Cal. 249.

State Bank v. Tweedy, 8 Blackf. 447. Cited, Mortgage, securing several notes, priority of rights of assignee, 23 Cal. 30.

State of Georgia v. Braislford, 2 Dall. 405. Cited, Injunction, when allegation of irreparable injury insufficient, 13 Cal. 190; 9 How. 29.

State of Indiana v. Woram, 6 Hill, 37. Commented on, Municipal Corporations, liability on implied contracts, 16 Cal. 265, 271.

State of Iowa v. Walpello Co., 13 Iowa, 393. Commented on, Stututes, validity of statutes granting municipal aid to railroads, 41 Cal. 185.

State of Louisiana v. Smith, 13 La. An. 424. Cited, Parties, attorney-general when a proper party-plaintiff, 25 Cal. 247.

State of Maryland v. Butler, 12 Niles' Reg. 115. Cited, Judiciary, congress cannot confer judicial powers on a State court, 5 Cal. 301.

State of Minnesota v. Bachelder, 5 Minn. 234. Cited, State Sovereignty, relation of general government to public lands, 30 Cal. 658.

State of Mississippi v. Johnson, 4 Wall. 509. Approved, Street Assessments, legislative power to direct, 31 Cal. 688.

State of New Jersey v. Wilson, 7 Cranch, 164. Cited, Legislature cannot impair obligation of contract created by statute, 10 Cal. 572; 16 Cal. 194; 4 Pet. 563; 6 How. 332.

State of Ohio v. Bowman, 10 Ohio, 445. Distinguished, Action on joint bond, recovery on bond signed by sureties only, 14 Cal. 423.

State of Ohio v. Commrs. of Perry Co., 5 Ohio St. 497. Cited, Constitutionality of Statute, in part invalid, 22 Cal. 390.

State of Pennsylvania v. Wheeling & B. B. Co., 18 How. 430. Cited, Legislature, power to pass special acts, 17 Cal. 562.

State of Wisconsin v. Giles, 1 Chandler, 117. Cited, Office, eligibility to State office, 10 Cal. 47; Election, votes cast for ineligible candidate, 13 Cal. 153.

State Treasurer v. Collector of Sangamon Co., 28 Ill. 509. Cited, Revenue, wharfage and dockage charges not within specific contract act, 34 Cal. 682.

Stauffer v. Commissioners, 1 Watts, 300. Approved, Execution, lien of, 37 Cal. 144, 145.

Steamboat Co. v. Livingston, 3 Cow. 713. Commented on, Ports and Harbors, what vessels liable to harbor dues, 10 Cal. 507.

Steamboat Orleans v. Phœbus, 11 Pet. 175. Commented on, Jurisdiction, in admiralty, 1 Cal. 164.

Steam Nav. Co. v. Weed, 17 Barb. 378. Commented on, Pleading, defense of *ultra vires*, not available to corporation, 16 Cal. 265.

Steam Nav. Co. v. Wright, 6 Cal. 258; S. C. 8 Cal. 585. Cited, Contract, liquidated damages in, 9 Cal. 587; 10 Cal. 517.

Stearns v. Aguirre, 6 Cal. 176. Cited, Judgment, several judgment on joint and several obligation as a discharge, 8 Cal. 135. Disapproved, 18 Cal. 400.

Stearns v. Aguirre, 7 Cal. 443. Approved, Appeal, effect of reversal of judgment, 9 Cal. 16; 15 Cal. 84; 30 Cal. 462; 39 Cal. 646; Judgment, by default, entered by clerk without authority is void, 14 Cal. 158; 30 Cal. 205; strict conformity to provisions of statute required, 17 Cal. 566; 28 Cal. 652. Distinguished, 30 Cal. 534; entry of default a ministerial duty, 30 Cal. 198.

Stearns v. Marsh, 4 Denio, 227. Commented on, Pledge, legal effect and operation, 3 Cal. 162. Cited, Notice required on sale of, 34 Cal. 132.

Stedman v. Gooch, 1 Esp. 3. Cited, Debtor and Creditor, effect of payment by note, 12 Cal. 322; 3 McLean, 557.

Stedman v. Smith, 8 El. & B. 1. Commented on, Tenant in Common, ouster by, what constitutes, 27 Cal. 559.

Steel v. Steel, 12 Penn. St. 64. Commented on, Parent and Child, emancipation of minor, 8 Cal. 123.

Steele's Exrs. v. Moxley, 9 Dana, 137. Cited, Will, power of sale under, 32 Cal. 442.

Steele's Heirs v. Taylor, 3 A. K. Marsh. 226. Commented on, Patent, evidence admissible to explain mistakes in call, 10 Cal. 625.

Stegall v. Stegall, 2 Brock. 261. Cited, Parent and Child, legitimacy of child when presumed, 13 Cal. 99.

Stein v. Mayor of Mobile, 24 Ala. 591. Cited, Legislature, power of taxation to promote internal improvements, 41 Cal. 180. Distinguished, 36 Ala. 432.

Steinbach v. Leese, 27 Cal. 295. Cited, Summons, sufficiency of affidavit of publication, 33 Cal. 514. Approved, 34 Cal. 419. Distinguished, Id. 428. Cited, Judgment by default, entry of, when void, 28 Cal. 651. Dictum denied, Appearance, service of notice, 3 Nev. 213.

Steinbach v. Moore, 30 Cal. 498. Approved, Mexican Grant, confirmation essential, 31 Cal. 131; San Francisco, tenure of pueblo lands, 42 Cal. 556.

Stelle v. Carroll, 12 Pet. 204. Commented on, Mortgage, estate of mortgagor, 9 Cal. 408.

Stephens v. Chiles, 1 A. K. Marsh. 334. Distinguished, Forcible Entry and Detainer, does not lie by party ousted under legal process, 29 Cal. 216.

Stephens v. Mansfield, 11 Cal. 365. Denied, Abandonment of land, 24 Cal. 344.

Stephens v. Myers, 4 Car. & P. 349. Cited, Assault, what constitutes, 27 Cal. 634.

Stephens v. Sherrod, 6 Tex. 294. Cited, Title, transitory seizin conveys no title, 8 Cal. 275.

Stephenson v. Heathcote, 1 Eden, 43. Cited, Will, construction of devise, 31 Cal. 600.

Sterling v. Hanson, 1 Cal. 478. Cited, Judgment, several on joint obligation, 7 Minn. 234.

Sterne v. Bentley, 3 How. Pr. 331. Cited, Execution, joint property in statute construed, 39 Cal. 96.

Sterns v. Martin, 4 Cal. 229. Cited, Counter-claim, demand for unliquidated damages not available, 36 Cal. 301.

Stetson v. Patten, 2 Greenl. 359. Cited, Principal and Agent, ratification by principal, 14 Cal. 400.

Stevens v. Cooper, 1 Johns. Ch. 429. Commented on, Evidence, parol evidence not admissible to vary written instrument, 8 Cal. 432.

Stevens, Ex parte, 4 Cow. 133. Distinguished, Redemption, rights of purchasers at judicial sale, 9 Cal. 414.

Stevens v. Irwin, 15 Cal. 503. Approved, Statute of Frauds, what constitutes an actual and continued change of possession, 19 Cal. 329; 26 Cal. 323; 29 Cal. 472; Id. 560; 2 Nev. 247; testimony admissible to prove, 23 Cal. 334.

Stevens v. Ross, 1 Cal. 97. Cited, Appeal, lies from erroneous judgment by default, 3 Nev. 385.

Stevens v. Rowe, 3 Denio, 327. Cited, Res Adjudicata, issue on joint title, 14 Cal. 229.

Stevens v. Wilson, 3 Denio, 476. Cited, Factor cannot pledge, 19 Cal. 72.

Stevenson v. Bennett, 35 Cal. 431. Commented on, Mexican Grant, perfect title under, 36 Cal. 145; 39 Cal. 237.

Stevenson v. Castle, 1 Chitt. 349. Cited, Execution, amendment of, 38 Cal. 376, 380.

Stevenson v. Crease, 4 Man. & R. 561. Cited, Sureties, on official bond, liability of, 29 Cal. 100.

Stevenson v. Roche, 9 Barn. & C. 707. Cited, Sureties, on official bond, release of, 29 Cal. 100.

Stevenson v. Smith, 28 Cal. 102. Cited, Appeal, order on motion to retax costs reviewable only on appeal from judgment, 33 Cal. 678. Explained, 41 Cal. 441. Cited, Id. 443; Pleading, special damages to be specially averred, 34 Cal. 162. Approved, 41 Cal. 565.

Stever v. Sornberger, 24 Wend. 275. Cited, Bail, waives irregularities of process, 6 Cal. 59.

Steward v. Biddlecum, 2 N. Y. 104. Cited, Conveyances, estates which pass, 14 Cal. 631.

Stewart v. Donnelly, 4 Serg. & R. 177. Cited, Mortgage, change in note secured by, 31 Cal. 80.

Stewart v. Doughty, 9 John. 108. Commented on, Lease, cropping contract construed, 25 Cal. 64; 27 N. H. 559. Distinguished, 21 Vt. 181. Doubted, 38 N. Y. 137.

Stewart v. Drake, 4 Halst. 141. Cited, Covenant of Warranty, what constitutes a sufficient eviction, 39 Cal. 366, 367, 368.

Stewart v. Hutchins, 13 Wend. 485. Commented on, Mortgage, right of possession under, 36 Cal. 58.

Stewart v. Mackey, 16 Tex. 56. Commented on, Homestead, alienation of, 14 Cal. 476; effect of mortgage by husband, 16 Cal. 218.

Stewart v. Polk Co., 30 Iowa, 9.   Commented on, Legislature, power to authorize local subscription to internal improvements, 41 Cal. 183, 186.   Denied, 1 Dill. 563.

Stewart v. Scannell, 8 Cal. 80.   Approved, Statute of Frauds, sale of goods returned by vendor as warehouseman, void as to creditors, 8 Cal. 561; 9 Cal. 273.   Followed, 10 Cal. 9.   Disapproved, what constitutes sufficient delivery and change of possession, 26 Cal. 323.

Stewart v. State, 1 Ohio St. 68.   Cited, Juror and Jury, power of court to excuse juror, 32 Cal. 47.

Stewart v. Wells, 6 Barb. 81.   Cited, Trespass, liability of joint trespassers under legal process, 34 Cal. 635.

Stiles v. Comstock, 9 How. Pr. 48.   Cited, Pleading, several defenses, 22 Cal. 680.

Stiles v. Granville, 6 Cush. 458.   Cited, Parent and Child, emancipation of minor, 25 Cal. 152.

Stiles v. Jackson, 1 Wend. 316.   Cited, Ejectment, defense by landlord, 22 Cal. 205.

Stiles v. Laird, 5 Cal. 120.   Cited, Rights and Remedies, statutory remedies when cumulative, 43 N. H. 417.

Still v. Saunders, 8 Cal. 281.   Disapproved, Appeal, review of facts in chancery case, 15 Cal. 381.

Stillman v. Squire, 1 Denio, 328.   Cited, Officer, liability of, for acts of deputy, 39 Cal. 318.

Stinchfield v. Little, 1 Greenl. 231.   Commented on, Public Officers, not liable on official contracts, 15 Cal. 457.

Stiver v. Stiver, 3 Ohio, 19.   Cited, Appeal, law of the case conclusive, 15 Cal. 83.

St. John v. Croel, 5 Hill, 573.   Commented on, Acknowledgment, certificates of, as evidence, 16 Cal. 553.

St. John v. Diggs, Hob. 130, a.   Cited, Attachment Bond, mistake in recital of, not to invalidate, 13 Cal. 558.

St. John v. Kidd, 26 Cal. 263.   Cited, Land, abandonment a question of intent, 30 Cal. 636.   Approved, 36 Cal. 218; Id. 338.

St. John v. Palmer, 5 Hill, 601.   Cited, Covenant, for quiet enjoyment no breach till eviction, 33 Cal. 306.

Stoakes v. Barrett, 5 Cal. 36. Approved, Mines and Mining, right of entry on mine limited to public domain, 5 Cal. 398; 6 Cal. 46; 14 Cal. 376, 379; 22 Cal. 454; 23 Cal. 456; State sovereignty over right of entry on mine, 7 Cal. 324; right of appropriation of land in mineral district, 11 Cal. 14.

Stockdale v. Treasurer of Webster Co., 12 Iowa, 538. Cited, Public Lands, relation of U. S. Government to lands within State, 30 Cal. 658.

Stockham v. Jones, 10 John. 21. Disapproved, Witness, competency of, 6 Cal. 194.

Stookley v. Hornidge, 8 Car. & P. 18. Cited, Malicious Prosecution, want of probable cause, 29 Cal. 648.

Stockton v. Stanbrough, 3 La. An. 390. Contra, Execution, right in promissory note subject to levy and sale, 34 Cal. 88.

Stockton v. Turner, 7 J. J. Marsh. 192. Commented on, Appeal Bond, how construed, 8 Cal. 551; estoppel by recitals in bond, 13 Cal. 557.

Stockton & V. R. R. Co. v. Stockton, 41 Cal. 147. Cited, Legislature may authorize municipal aid to railroads, 7 Kan. 541.

Stockwell v. Hunter, 11 Met. 448. Cited, Landlord and Tenant, construction of lease, 38 Cal. 90.

Stockwell v. Phelps, 34 N. Y. 363. Approved, Replevin, owner of land not the owner of crops actually harvested by party in possession, 39 Cal. 416, 417.

Stoddard v. Chambers, 2 How. 284. Distinguished, Patent, validity of State patent, 16 Cal. 330. Commented on, when void, 23 Cal. 443; 3 How. 53; 8 How. 362; 15 How. 538; 19 How. 332; 21 How. 431.

Stoddard v. Hart, 23 N. Y. 560. Cited, Mortgage, tender after law day, 37 Cal. 226.

Stoddard v. Onondaga Annual Conference, 12 Barb. 573. Cited, Pleading, affirmative averments in answer, when not new matter, 21 Cal. 436.

Stoddard v. Treadwell, 26 Cal. 294. Approved, Pleading, contract may be set out as to legal effect, or in *hæc verba*, 32 Cal. 649; 34 Cal. 175; 37 Cal. 253; 38 Cal. 603; Appeal, judgments or orders entered by consent not reviewable, 42 Cal. 518.

37

Stokes v. Berry, 2 Salk. 421. Cited, Title by adverse possession, 34 Cal. 383; 36 Cal. 541.

Stokes v. Hagar, 1 Code Rep. 84. Cited, Pleading, insufficient denials, 1 Cal. 196.

Stokes v. Landgraff, 17 Barb. 608. Cited, Trade Marks, 35 Cal. 64, 75, 76.

Stokes v. Saltonstall, 13 Pet. 181. Cited, Common Carriers, liabilities of, 13 Cal. 603; for negligence, 28 Cal. 628. Commented on, 21 Md. 298.

Stokes v. Shackleford, 12 La. 170. Cited, Title, subsequently acquired, inures to benefit of vendee, 8 Cal. 197.

Stokes v. Stokes, 1 Mo. 322. Cited, Divorce, adultery, evidence of, 10 Cal. 254.

Stone v. Commercial R.R. Co., 18 Eng. Ch. 122; 4 Mylne & C. 123. Cited, Injunction lies to restrain trespass on land, 13 Cal. 313.

Stone v. Elkins, 24 Cal. 127. Cited, Constitutional Construction, distribution of powers of government, 34 Cal. 541; Street Improvements, acceptance of work conclusive, 29 Cal. 85.

Stone v. Hansbrough, 5 Leigh, 422. Cited, Written Instruments, rule of construction, 12 Cal. 577.

Stone v. Marsh, 6 Barn. & C. 564. Commented on, Felony, as a suspension of civil rights, 1 Cal. 435.

Stone v. State, 20 N. J. Spencer, 401. Cited, Evidence, proof of corporate existence, 41 Cal. 653.

Stone v. Swift, 4 Pick. 389. Commented on, Malicious Prosecution, when liability to action attaches, 8 Cal. 225.

Storm v. Waddell, 2 Sand. Ch. 494. Cited, Attachment, priority of lien of, 29 Cal. 383.

Storrs v. Barker, 6 Johns. Ch. 166. Commented on, Estoppel, equitable estoppel *in pais*, 26 Cal. 42, 45; 27 Barb. 602; 40 Me. 353. Distinguished as to infants, 38 Ill. 157.

Story v. Elliot, 8 Cow. 27. Cited, Sunday Laws, binding force of, 18 Cal. 681.

Story v. N. Y. & H. R. R. Co., 6 N. Y. 85. Cited, Appeal, power of appellate court, 26 Cal. 155.

Story v. Windsor, 2 Atk. 630. Cited, Deed, recitals in deed conclusive on grantor, 26 Cal. 87.

Stoughton v. Lynch, 2 Johns. Ch. 209. Cited, Interest, when cannot be compounded, 35 Cal. 694.

Stoughton v. Pasco, 5 Conn. 442. Cited, Mortgage, securing future advances, valid, 19 Cal. 351.

Stout v. Coffin, 28 Cal. 65. Cited, Variance, *allegata* and *probata* must correspond, 36 Cal. 175.

Stoutenburgh v. Vandenburgh, 7 How. Pr. 229. Cited, Execution, priority of lien of, 37 Cal. 137.

Stover v. Herrington, 7 Ala. 143. Cited, Mortgage, to secure future advances, 35 Cal. 309.

Stow v. Tifft, 15 John. 458. Cited, Conveyance, transitory seizin conveys no estate, 8 Cal. 275. Doubted, 20 N. Y. 417.

Stow v. Wyse, 7 Conn. 214. Cited, Principal when not bound by act of agent, 24 Cal. 140.

Stowell v. Zouch, Plowd. 369. Cited, Statute of Limitations, construction of, exceptions in, 35 Cal. 640; 9 How. 380, 520; 19 How. 452, 462, 491, 560.

Strader v. Graham, 5 B. Mon. 173; S. C. 10 How. 93. Commented on, State Sovereignty, residence of slave in free State, 9 Cal. 166.

Stratman, Matter of, 39 Cal. 517. Approved, Municipal Court, act creating, is constitutional, 41 Cal. 131.

Strawbridge v. Curtis, 3 Cranch, 267. Cited, Trial, removal of cause to federal court, 28 Cal. 99.

Street v. Co. Com. of Gallatin, Breese, Ill. 25. Cited, Mandamus, to restore attorney and counsel, 1 Cal. 191.

Striker v. Kelly, 7 Hill, 9. Reversed, 2 Denio, 323. Cited, Statutory Construction, statutes in derogation of common law to be strictly pursued, 19 Cal. 60. Doubted, Statutory provisions in special act directory, 11 Cal. 57. Disapproved, 24 N. Y. 583. Cited, opinion of Bronson, J., Estates of Deceased, jurisdictional facts to appear in petition for sale of, 19 Cal. 208; 25 Cal. 309.

Stringer v. Davis, 30 Cal. 318. Cited, Variance, amendment allowed to pleading in case of, 36 Cal. 176.

Stringer v. Young's Lessee, 3 Pet. 320. Cited, Mexican Grants, presumptions as to official acts, 3 Cal. 448; patent not subject to collateral attack, 29 Cal. 311.

Strong v. Birchard, 5 Conn. 357. Cited, Statutory Construction, "month" defined, 21 Cal. 396; 31 Cal. 176.

Strong v. Blake, 46 Barb. 227. Cited, Tender, what constitutes a valid tender, 41 Cal. 423.

Strong, Petitioner, 20 Pick. 484. Cited, Mandamus, when it will not lie, 1 Cal. 191. Commented on, 3 Cal. 171, 173.

Strong v. Stewart, 4 John, Ch. 167. Cited, Deed as a Mortgage, parol evidence to prove, 13 Cal. 129. Commented on, Id. 130.

Strother v. Lucas, 12 Pet. 410. Cited, Mexican Grant, presumptions as to official authority, 1 Cal. 420; 15 Cal. 553; 16 Cal. 230; power of congress to require claim to be presented for confirmation, 3 How. 55; what claims required to be presented, 19 Cal. 269, 271; 9 How. 469; claim barred by failure to present it, 24 Cal. 666; consequences of non-presentment, 24 Cal. 671; survey and segregation essential, 30 Cal. 508; Law of Nations, of ceded territory, 1 Cal. 286, 314; customs and usage of conquered province equivalent to law, Id. 326; 16 Cal. 227; rights in private property under treaty of cession, 3 Cal. 38; 18 Cal. 23; 20 Cal. 421; 24 Cal. 659, 660; 9 How. 445.

Strout v. Curran, 7 How. Pr. 36. Cited, Pleading, unverified answer to verified complaint, stricken out, 9 Cal. 423.

Strout v. Natoma Wat. & M. Co., 9 Cal. 78. Cited, Corporation, assignment of certificates of stock when invalid, 20 Cal. 533.

Struver v. Ocean Ins. Co., 9 Abb. Pr. 23. Cited, Appeal, admission of service of notice, what it waives, 22 Cal. 657.

Stuart v. Allen, 16 Cal. 473. Cited, Probate Procedure, for sale of real estate, jurisdiction on what depends, 19 Cal. 206; Id. 409; 20 Cal. 383; 36 Cal. 689.

Stuart v. Haight, 39 Cal. 87. Cited, Mandamus may be issued to governor, 39 Cal. 210.

Stuart v. Hawley, 22 Barb. 619. Commented on, Negligence, what constitutes, 9 Cal. 257.

Stuart v. Laird, 1 Cranch, 95. Cited, Stare Decisis, contemporaneous interpretation of statutes, 22 Cal. 71; 19 How. 616.

Stuart v. Simpson, 1 Wend. 376. Cited, Nonsuit, power of compulsory nonsuit, 1 Cal. 114; Id. 222; when authorized, 26 Cal. 525.

Sturges v. Crowninshield, 4 Wheat. 122. Cited, Constitutional Construction, Federal Constitution, 11 Cal. 86; 7 How. 555; grant of powers of legislation to Congress, when not exclusive, 1 Cal. 235; Id. 241; 2 Cal. 432; 5 Pet. 47; 5 How. 585; Id. 625; 7 How. 556; 12 How. 319. Approved as to State legislation on insolvency, 37 Cal. 209, 210. Commented on, Unconstitutionality of acts impairing obligation of contracts, 4 Cal. 140; 9 Cal. 85; 37 Geo. 148. Approved, 6 Wheat. 134. Distinguished, 12 Wheat. 255. Cited, 1 How. 279; Id. 328; 5 How. 316; 6 How. 328, 330.

Sturges v. Sherwood, 15 Conn. 149. Cited, Statute of Limitations, construction of, 35 Cal. 638.

Sturtevant v. Ballard, 9 John. 337. Qualified, Statute o_ Frauds, actual and continued change of possession construed, 15 Cal. 506. Commented on, 29 Cal. 477.

Stuyvesant v. Davis, 9 Paige, 427. Cited, Lease, construction of clause of forfeiture, 38 Cal. 251.

Stuyvesant v. Mayor, etc., of N. Y., 11 Paige, 414. Commented on, Lease, construction of covenant to improve, 25 Cal. 395. Cited, Specific Performance, of contract for chattels, 25 Cal. 571.

Sublette v. Tinney, 9 Cal. 423. Cited, Pleading, exception in statute of limitation must be specially set up, 19 Cal. 481; 23 Cal. 353; 29 Cal. 44; 30 Cal. 444; 34 Cal. 258.

Suffolk Bank v. Worcester Bank, 5 Pick. 106. Cited, Statutory Construction, penal statute defined, 29 Cal. 512.

Sullivan v. Cary, 17 Cal. 85. Cited, Pleading, sufficiency of denial in justices' courts, 20 Cal. 49.

Sullivan v. Davis, 4 Cal. 291. Cited, Power of Attorney, construction of, 16 Cal. 512. Approved, Ejectment, may be maintained on ordinary quit-claim deed, 24 Cal. 123; 25 Cal. 168; 37 Cal. 521; Execution Sale, showing required on claim of title under, 31 Cal. 221; 6 Kan. 455; 4 Nev. 152.

Sullivan v. People, 15 Ill. 233. Cited, Statutory Construction, repeal by implication, 10 Cal. 316.

Sullivan v. Triunfo G. & S. M. Co., 29 Cal. 585. Cited in same case, Res Adjudicata, former judgment as a bar, 39 Cal. 464.

Sullivan v. Tuck, 1 Md. Ch. Dec. 59. Cited, Specific Performance, when will be decreed on contract for chattels, 25 Cal. 571.

Summers v. Dickinson, 9 Cal. 554. Approved, State Lands, office of State patent, 9 Cal. 324. Qualified as to who may impeach patent, 16 Cal. 330. Approved, Patent for swamp lands when void, 23 Cal. 441; title of State to swamp lands, 27 Cal. 89; validity of legislative grant, 27 Cal. 327. Qualified, 29 Cal. 322.

Summers v. Farish, 10 Cal. 347. Cited, Injunction Bond, allowance of counsel fees in judgment on bond, 12 Cal. 111. Approved, who may bring action on, 13 Cal. 591; 15 Cal. 11; 28 Cal. 543.

Sumner v. State, 5 Blackf. 580. Cited, Instructions, based on circumstantial evidence, 28 Cal. 426; 39 Cal. 333.

Sun Mut. Ins. Co. v. New York, 5 Sand. 10. Commented on, Constitutionality of Statute, judicial power of determination, 26 Cal. 227.

Sunol v. Hepburn, 1 Cal. 254. Cited, Alcaldes' Grants, when invalid, 1 Cal. 308. Approved, when insufficient to maintain ejectment, 1 Cal. 421. Distinguished, Constructive possession under grant, 6 Cal. 272; 25 Cal. 131.

Supervisors of Onondaga v. Briggs, 3 Denio, 173. Cited, Costs, when allowed, 6 Cal. 286.

Supervisors, etc., v. Briggs, 2 Denio, 26. Cited, Supervisors, judicial powers of, 16 Cal. 209; 18 Cal. 149.

Surget v. Little, 5 Smedes & M. 330. Cited, Evidence, map of U. S. surveyor not evidence as to boundaries without proof of authority, 11 Cal. 142.

Surtees v. Ellison, 4 Man. & R. 586; S. C. 9 Barn. & C. 750. Cited, Statutory Construction, not to be retrospective, law a part of the contract, 4 Cal. 135.

Susquehanna Canal Co. v. Bonham, 9 Watts & S. 28. Commented on, Franchises, grants of, not subject to sale on execution, 15 Cal. 590.

Sutter v. Cox, 6 Cal. 415. Cited, Pleading, defects waived by failure to demur, 22 Cal. 235; Writ of Possession, will not issue to strangers to the record, 37 Cal. 348.

Sutter v. San Francisco, 36 Cal. 112. Cited, Tenant in Common, grantee of, subject to contingency of partition, 69 Penn. St. 238.

Sutton v. Estate of Sutton, 13 Vt. 71. Cited, Probate Proceedings, conclusiveness of, 18 Cal. 505.

Suydam v. Hoyt, 1 Dutch. 231. Cited, Pleading, what constitutes a valid defense to action on foreign judgment, 39 Cal. 539.

Suydam v. Jenkins, 3 Sand. 614. Distinguished, Sale and Delivery, change of possession of goods sold in mass, 8 Cal. 609. Cited, Conversion, measure of damages, 14 Cal. 557; 39 Cal. 421; 40 Miss. 364.

Suydam v. Moore, 8 Barb. 358. Cited, Railroads, liability for injury to cattle, 18 Cal. 354.

Suydam v. Pitcher, 4 Cal. 280. Cited, Jurisdiction, lost on adjournment of term, 5 Cal. 407; 8 Cal. 521; 25 Cal. 52; 28 Cal. 338; Attorney and Counsel, appearance by, presumption as to authority, 13 Cal. 201; 22 Cal. 210.

Swain v. Chase, 12 Cal. 283. Cited, Jurisdiction, no intendments in favor of proceedings of inferior courts, 23 Cal. 403; 31 Cal. 169.

Swain v. Graves, 8 Cal. 549. Cited, Appeal Bonds, interpretation of, 13 Cal. 509.

Swain v. Naglee, 19 Cal. 127. Cited, Amendment of clerical errors in court records, 25 Cal. 53; 27 Cal. 495. Distinguished, 28 Cal. 338.

Swaine v. Perine, 5 Johns. Ch. 482. Cited, Husband and Wife, claim of wife to common property, 12 Cal. 226. Denied, 4 Leigh, 517.

Swan v. Bull, Cal. Sup. Ct. (not reported.) Cited, Fraud, when sale may be attacked for, 7 Cal. 566.

Swan v. Piquet, 3 Pick. 443. Commented on, Appeal, who entitled to appeal, 8 Cal. 315.

Swan v. State, 4 Humph. 136. Commented on, Criminal Procedure, evidence of intoxication when admissible, 29 Cal. 683.

Swan v. Williams, 2 Mich. 427.   Cited, Eminent Domain, exercise through medium of corporations, 18 Cal. 251; 31 Cal. 372.

Swart v. Service, 21 Wend. 36.   Cited, Mortgage and Conditional Sale, parol evidence when admissible, 8 Cal. 433; Deed as a Mortgage, parol proof of, 36 Cal. 44; Id. 65.   Commented on, 15 Conn. 586; 3 Mich. 223.

Swartwout v. Burr, 1 Barb. 495.   Cited, Vendor's Lien, rights of assignee of vendee, 2 Cal. 287.

Swartz v. Swartz, 4 Penn. St. 353.   Cited, Conveyance, what passes by, 15 Cal. 197.

Sweet v. Tuttle, 14 N. Y. 465.   Approved, Pleading, when inconsistent defenses may be set up in answer, 22 Cal. 679, 681.

Sweetland v. Froe, 6 Cal. 144.   Cited, Ejectment, on prior possession, 6 Cal. 649.   Approved, Strict compliance with provisions of possessory act essential, 7 Cal. 311; 15 Cal. 48; 23 Cal. 408; 42 Cal. 656.

Sweetser v. French, 2 Cush. 311.   Cited, Partnership, partner as surety on note, burden of proof as to authority, 37 Cal. 117.

Sweitzer v. Hummel, 3 Serg. & R. 228.   Cited, Vendor and Vendee, demand and tender of deed, 25 Cal. 279.

Swenson v. Walker's Adm., 3 Tex. 96.   Cited, Probate Procedure, effect of approval of claim, 26 Cal. 430.

Sweringen v. Eberius, 7 Mo. 421.   Statute distinguished, Attachment, lien of, dies with the debtor, 29 Cal. 367, 379.

Swett v. Patrick, 12 Me. 9.   Cited, Covenant, measure of damages on breach of, 33 Cal. 308.

Swift v. Cobb, 10 Vt. 282.   Cited, Judicial Sale, recitals in sheriff's deed as evidence, 30 Cal. 288.

Swift v. Crocker, 21 Pick. 241.   Approved, Attachment on debt not due is void, 18 Cal. 381.

Swift v. Dean, 11 Vt. 323.   Cited, Landlord and Tenant, when tenant not estopped in action for rent, 8 Cal. 596; 33 Cal. 253; 35 Cal. 571.

Swift v. Edson, 5 Conn. 532.   Cited, Foreclosure, decree on whom conclusive, 23 Cal. 35.

Swift v. Kingsley, 24 Barb. 541. Cited, Pleading, several distinct defenses in answer, 22 Cal. 680; admissions, effect of, 33 Cal. 97.

Swift v. Kraemer, 13 Cal. 526. Construed, Mortgage, substitution of new note and mortgage as an equitable assignment, 36 Cal. 23. Distinguished, 16 Iowa, 154.

Swift v. Muygridge, 8 Cal. 445. Cited, Findings of court as a basis for judgment, 28 Cal. 596.

Swift v. Tyson, 16 Pet. 1. Cited, Assignment of negotiable instrument not due, not subject to defenses existing between original parties, 8 Cal. 266; 14 Cal. 98; 40 Cal. 114; 8 How. 489; 22 How. 108. Distinguished, 2 How. 454.

Swift v. Williamsburgh, 24 Barb. 427. Cited, Municipal Corporation, power to bind city by contract, 29 Cal. 188.

Swires v. Parsons, 5 Watts & S. 357. Commented on, Contract, promise implied from performance of labor, 7 Cal. 513; when not implied, 22 Cal. 510.

Switzer v. Knapps, 10 Iowa, 72. Cited, Conveyance, effect of mistake in recording seal, 36 Cal. 203.

Switzer v. Skiles, 8 Ill. 529. Approved, Agreement, among several to combine in purchase at sheriff's sale not *prima facie* fraudulent, 30 Cal. 592, 594.

Sylvester v. Crapo, 15 Pick. 92. Cited, Negotiable Instrument, when presumptively dishonored, 39 Cal. 352.

Symmes v. Frazier, 6 Mass. 344. Cited, Reward, when action lies for, 14 Cal. 137.

Symonds v. Cincinnati, 14 Ohio, 147. Cited, Condemnation of Land, estimate of benefits, 31 Cal. 374.

Syracuse City Bank v. Davis, 16 Barb. 188. Cited, Corporations, irregularities in organization not to invalidate charter, 22 Cal. 428.

Taaffe v. Josephson, 7 Cal. 352. Cited, Contract void in part is void in toto, 8 Cal. 128; 10 Cal. 228; Fraud, concealment of insolvency to avoid sale of goods, 8 Cal. 215; so as to note, 10 Cal. 228; as to judgment, 13 Cal. 334; 1 Saw. 83. Disapproved, 13 Cal. 442; 15 Cal. 510. Cited, as to mortgage, 35 Cal. 308.

Taaffe v. Rosenthal, 7 Cal. 514. Denied, Appeal, does not lie from an order refusing to dissolve an attachment, 24 Cal. 448; 1 Nev. 537. Cited, Undertakings, in actions, form of, 29 Cal. 200.

Taber v. Omnibus R.R. Co., Cal. Sup. Ct. Oct. T. 1867 (not reported.) Followed, Jurisdiction, in actions for forfeiture against street railroads, 36 Cal. 282.

Table Mt. Tun. Co. v. Stranahan, 20 Cal. 198. Referred to, on second appeal, Law of the case to govern, 21 Cal. 551; S. C. 31 Cal. 387. Cited, Mining Claim, sale by parol accompanied by delivery of possession transfers title, 23 Cal. 179; Id. 222; Id. 576. Qualified, 25 Cal. 24. Commented on, 30 Cal. 363. Disapproved, 30 Cal. 481; 33 Cal. 318; 35 Cal. 652. Doctrine denied where interest is considered as real estate, 33 Cal. 381. Cited, Possession sufficient to maintain action for trespass, 7 Nev. 220.

Taft v. Brewster, 9 John. 334. Denied, Negotiable Instrument, indorser signing as agent not liable, 7 Cal. 541.

Taggard v. Curtenius, 15 Wend. 155. Cited, Pleading, defense on note, 36 Cal. 301.

Taggart v. Western Md. R. R. Co., 24 Md. 563. Cited, Railroad Corporation, conditions precedent in organization of, 42 Cal. 209.

Tait v. Lord Northwick, 4 Ves. Jr. 823. Cited, Will, construction of, 31 Cal. 600.

Talbert v. Hopper, 42 Cal. 397. Cited, Term of Court, presumption as to legality of sessions, 42 Cal. 397.

Talbot v. Bk. of Rochester, 1 Hill, 295. Cited, Negotiable Instruments, subsequent indorser's contract construed, 22 Cal. 249.

Talbot v. Dent, 9 B. Mon. 526. Cited, Legislature, power to authorize county aid to railroads, 13 Cal. 188. Distinguished, 13 B. Mon. 103.

Talliaferro v. King, 9 Dana, 331. Cited, Interest, on interest due, 29 Cal. 392.

Tallmadge v. Richmond, 9 John. 85. Cited, Mistake, in recital of bond, when will not vitiate, 13 Cal. 558.

Tallman v. Ely, 6 Wis. 244. Cited, Judgment, collateral attack on, 34 Cal. 427.

Tallman v. White, 2 N. Y. 70. Cited, Tax Titles, character of proceedings, 21 Cal. 303. Approved, Assessment of land, when void, 25 Cal. 299.

Talmadge v. Rensselaer & S. R. R. Co., 13 Barb. 493. Cited, Negligence of railroads, and injury to cattle, 18 Cal. 356.

Talman v. Barnes, 12 Wend. 227. Cited, Notice, admission of service, what it waives, 22 Cal. 657.

Tamplin v. Addy, 8 Cow. 239. Cited, Fraud, vitiates contract, and effects no change in title to property, 12 Cal. 462.

Tannahill v. Tuttle, 3 Mich. 104. Approved, Chattel Mortgage, distinguished from pledge, 35 Cal. 410.

Tappan v. Wilson, 7 Ohio, 190. Cited, Libel and Slander, pleading, 41 Cal. 481.

Tarbell v. C. P. R. R. Co., 34 Cal. 616. Distinguished, Verdict, excessive damages, 36 Cal. 485.

Tarbell v. Gray, 4 Gray, 445. Cited, Recognizance, essential averment in action on, 30 Cal. 630.

Tarpey v. Shallenberger, 10 Cal. 390. Cited, Appeal, damages on frivolous appeal, 33 Cal. 169.

Tarpley v Hamer, 9 Smedes & M. 310. Cited, Legislature, may impose additional duties in exercise of statutory right, 22 Cal. 328.

Tarpy v. Shepherd, 30 Cal. 180. Cited, Legal Tender, relative values of kinds of money, 31 Cal. 80.

Tartar v. Hall, 3 Cal. 263. Approved, Estoppel, of mortgagor, after sale on foreclosure, 4 Cal. 250; 14 Cal. 634; 31 Cal. 457.

Tartar v. Spring Creek Wat. Co., 5 Cal. 395. Approved, Public Lands, occupation of, policy of State, 6 Cal. 46; 12 Cal. 70; 14 Cal. 376; 22 Cal. 453. Commented on, Water Rights, diversion of water, 7 Cal. 325. Cited, Right of entry of miner, 23 Cal. 456.

Tate v. Parrish, 7 Mon. 325. Cited, Water Rights, liability for injuries to, 23 Cal. 488.

Tate v. Stooltzfoos, 16 Serg. & R. 35. Cited, Constitutionality of Statute, remedial statutes, 30 Cal. 144; 39 N. H. 387.

Tate v. Wymond, 7 Blackf. 240. Cited, Surety, on specialty, not discharged by parol agreement for delay, 10 Cal. 420; 34 Md. 516.

Tatlock v. Harris, 3 Term Rep. 174. Cited, Debtor, mutual agreement between third parties to pay debt of, not within statute of frauds, 22 Cal. 190.

Tatum v. Young, 1 Port. 298. Commented on, Juror and Jury, exclusion of, by court, not available on error, 32 Cal. 46.

Tayloe, Ex parte, 5 Cow. 39. Cited, Criminal Procedure, application for bail, 19 Cal. 547.

Tayloe v. Riggs, 9 Wheat. 483. Cited, Evidence, secondary, of destroyed instrument, preliminary evidence, 10 Cal. 147.

Tayloe v. Sandiford, 7 Wheat. 13. Cited, Contract, penalty in, 9 Cal. 587.

Taylor v. Auditor, 2 Ark. 174. Cited, Official Bonds, failure of approval, does not discharge sureties, 7 Cal. 441.

Taylor v. Baker, Daniels, 80. Cited, Title, notice imparted by adverse possession, 36 Cal. 272.

Taylor v. Benham, 5 How. 233 Cited, Trust and Trustee, when liable for negligence, 9 Cal. 695.

Taylor v. Brewer, 1 Maule & S. 290. Cited, Services, no action lies where remuneration is discretionary, 22 Cal. 510.

Taylor v. Brooks, 5 Cal. 332. Approved, County Warrants, priority in payment of, 6 Cal. 283.

Taylor v. Brown, 5 Cranch, 234. Cited, Mexican Grants, presumptions as to official regularity, 3 Cal. 448. Commented on, surplus lands in, Id. 43.

Taylor v. Brown. 4 Cal. 188. Cited, Officers, constables may act by deputy, 35 Cal. 713.

Taylor v. California Stage Co., 6 Cal. 230. Cited, New Trial, surprise insufficient grounds for, 22 Cal. 163; 23 Cal. 420; 24 Cal. 89; 38 Cal. 194; showing required on motion, 32 Cal. 212.

Taylor v. Carpenter, 2 Sand. Ch. 603. Cited, Trade Marks, law of, 35 Cal. 75.

Taylor v. Carpenter, 3 Story, 458. Cited, Trade Marks, protection of alien, 29 Cal. 296.

Taylor v. Claypool, 5 Blackf. 557. Cited, Judgment, as on joint demand as a bar, 6 Cal. 181; 13 Cal. 33.

Taylor v. Cole, 3 Term Rep. 292. Cited, Trespass, on lands, gist of action, 32 Cal. 580.

Taylor v. Commrs. of Newberne, 2 Jones' Eq. 141. Cited, Legislature may authorize county aid to railroads, 13 Cal. 188.

Taylor v. Craig, 2 J. J. Marsh. 454. Cited, Principal and Agent, agent when personally liable, 13 Cal. 48.

Taylor v. Croker, 4 Esp. 187. Cited, Infant, contract of, not void but voidable, 24 Cal. 209.

Taylor v. Donner, 31 Cal. 482. Cited, Street Assessment, to be made to owner if known, 32 Cal. 332. Approved, When title to land is in dispute, 38 Cal. 179.

Taylor, Estate of, 10 Cal. 482. Affirmed, Executors and Administrators, presentation of claims, 16 Cal. 434.

Taylor v. Forster, 2 Car. & P. 195. Cited, Witness, privileged communications, 5 Cal. 452.

Taylor v. Hargous, 4 Cal. 268. Approved, Homestead, joint estate with right of survivorship, 6 Cal. 73. Qualified, 8 Cal. 73. Cited, 8 Cal. 509; 12 Cal. 125; 31 Cal. 530. Disapproved, 14 Cal. 477. Cited, Construction of homestead law, 6 Cal. 235; removal of husband not an abandonment, 7 Cal. 345; 8 Cal. 71; 10 Cal. 297; abandonment a question of fact, 25 Cal. 114; on what property may be established, 22 Cal. 638.

Taylor v. Horde, 1 Burr. 119. Cited, Title, by adverse possession, 34 Cal. 383; 36 Cal. 541; 2 Black, 605.

Taylor v. Longworth, 14 Pet. 172. Cited, Specific Performance, when time is essence of contract, 6 Cal. 571; 10 Cal. 324. Commented on, 19 Cal. 459. Cited, Construction of clause of forfeiture in contract, 40 Cal. 13.

Taylor v. Luther, 2 Sum. 233. Cited, Deed as a Mortgage, parol evidence admissible to prove, 8 Cal. 429; 13 Cal. 128; Pleading, denials when evasive, 9 Cal. 465.

Taylor, Matter of, 9 Paige, 611. Cited, Marriage, proof of, what sufficient, 26 Cal. 133.

Taylor v. McKinney, 20 Cal. 618. Cited, Vendor's Lien, not assignable, 21 Cal. 178; attaches equally on conveyance, or on contract to convey, 32 Cal. 59.

Taylor v. McLean, 1 McMullan, 352. Disapproved, 1 Rich. 503. Cited, Principal and Agent, agent when bound by contract, 13 Cal. 235.

Taylor v. Miller, 13 How. 287. Distinguished, Judgment, lien of, not extended by levy of execution, 10 Cal. 82.

Taylor v. Mixter, 11 Pick. 348. Commented on, Attachment, lien of, not dependent on return of sheriff, 11 Cal. 248.

Taylor v. Neville, MS., cited in 3 Atk. 384. Cited, Specific Performance, on sale of chattels, 27 Cal. 463.

Taylor v. Palmer, 31 Cal. 240; dissenting opinion of Sawyer, J., Id. 666. Approved, Street Assessments, publication of resolution, computation of time, 31 Cal. 272; 34 Cal. 283. Cited, Constitutional Construction, 38 Cal. 477. Approved, 40 Cal. 514; proceedings need not be approved by mayor, 31 Cal. 473; 32 Cal. 275; Id. 487; to whom assessments to be made, 31 Cal. 481; 38 Cal. 179; assessments for benefits, 32 Cal. 526, 528; as a lien, Id. 529; irregularities waived by failure to appeal, Id. 278; remedy by appeal exclusive, 38 Cal. 75; personal judgment erroneous, 32 Cal. 279; 33 Cal. 296; 36 Cal. 105; Id. 292, 293. Cited, Statutory Construction, 35 Cal. 708; 6 Nev. 222.

Taylor v. Pettibone, 16 John. 66. Denied, Judgment, enforcement of, against party not served, 39 Cal. 97.

Taylor v. Porter, 4 Hill, 140. Approved, Legislature, cannot condemn property to private use, 7 Cal. 13; 22 Cal. 318. Cited, exclusive power to judge of public necessity or advantage, 18 Cal. 252. Denied, Statutory Construction, as to "private" roads, 32 Cal. 254.

Taylor v. Randall, 5 Cal. 79. Cited, Judgment, entered by consent of attorney, when conclusive, 22 Cal. 210.

Taylor v. Robinson, 14 Cal. 396. Distinguished, Principal and Agent, authority of agent, 18 Cal. 692.

Taylor v. Salmon, 4 Mylne & C. 13. Approved, Supreme Court, practice in, 1 Cal. 67; Equity, practice in courts of, 30 Cal. 297; relief from fraudulent acts of agent, 21 Cal. 100; 35 Cal. 488.

Taylor v. Savage, 1 How. 284; S. C. 2 How. 396. Cited, Executors and Administrators, effect of discharge of administrator, 24 Cal. 502.

Taylor v. Seymour, 6 Cal. 512. Cited, Sheriff not liable in damages for wrongful seizure, unless notified of party's claim, 8 Minn. 79. Denied, that demand is necessary before action commenced, 30 Cal. 191; 3 Nev. 563.

Taylor v. Steamer Columbia, 5 Cal. 268. Commented on, Jurisdiction, in admiralty, 9 Cal. 710, 733.

Taylor v. Stibbert, 2 Ves. Jr. 437. Cited, Conveyance, possession as notice of, 36 Cal. 272.

Taylor v. Stone, 2 La. An. 910. Contra, Execution, right in promissory note subject to levy and sale, 34 Cal. 88.

Taylor v. Weld, 5 Mass. 109. Cited, Mortgage, instrument construed as, 33 Cal. 333.

Taylor v. Welton, Cal. Sup. Ct. Oct. T. 1870 (not reported.) Followed, Deed by Trustee, 40 Cal. 350.

Teal v. Russell, 3 Ill. 319. Cited, Judgment, on joint and several obligation as a bar, 6 Cal. 181.

Tegarden v. McBean, 33 Miss. 283. Commented on, Dedication of Highway, how effected, 14 Cal. 650. Distinguished, 39 Miss. 387.

Tempest v. Fitzgerald, 3 Barn. & Ald. 680. Cited, Statute of Frauds, what change of possession sufficient, 1 Cal. 402; how must be shown, 22 Cal. 105.

Ten Eyck v. Holmes, 3 Sand. Ch. 428. Cited, Debtor and Creditor, rights of creditor to property in hands of surety, 35 Cal. 145.

Terrell v. Cutrer, 1 Rob. 367. Commented on, Husband and Wife, presumptions as to common property may be rebutted, 30 Cal. 33.

Terrett v. Taylor, 9 Cranch, 43. Cited, Statutory Construction, statutes impairing contract rights, void, 16 Cal. 194; 26 Cal. 48; statutes to be construed retrospectively, 27 Cal. 159.

Terrill v. Auchauer, 14 Ohio St. 80. Cited, Judicial Sale, purchase by administrator at his own sale voidable, 29 Cal. 35, 39.

Terrill v. Groves, 18 Cal. 149. Denied, Taxation, joint assessment of town lots, 3 Nev. 348.

Territory, The, v. Benoit, 1 Mart. 142. Cited, Criminal Procedure, bail in murder cases, 19 Cal. 544.

Terry v. Foster, 1 Mass. 146. Cited, Will, construction of codicil, 18 Cal. 302.

Terry v. Megerle, 24 Cal. 609. Cited, State Patent, as evidence, who may impeach, 25 Cal. 251; 3 Or. 113; 28 Cal. 101; Id. 403; 29 Cal. 312; when subject to collateral attack, 32 Cal. 362; Preëmption rights of preëmptioner, 25 Cal. 633; 29 Cal. 321; public lands not liable to preëmption till surveyed, 34 Cal. 512; State Lands, title of State under congressional act, 27 Cal. 328; 38 Cal. 33. Approved, selection of, 27 Cal. 520. Cited, Lands when not subject to selection, 33 Cal. 89; 40 Cal. 363; location of school land warrants, when void, 34 Cal. 512; 40 Cal. 370.

Terry v. Robins, 5 Smedes & M. 291. Cited, Vendor and Vendee, remedies of vendor, 14 Cal. 73.

Terry v. Sickles, 13 Cal. 427. Referred to, Account Stated, action on, 13 Cal. 643; proof adducible, 14 Cal. 415. Cited, effect of acquiescence in, 22 Cal. 239; Instructions, errors in, without prejudice to appellant, not considered, 17 Cal. 573; 18 Cal. 378; 32 Cal. 235.

Teresy v. Gory, MS., cited in 1 Ves. Sr. 344. Approved, Lost Note, indemnity in action on, 28 Cal. 566.

Teschemacher v. Thompson, 18 Cal. 11. Cited, Mexican Grant, survey and segregation the exercise of a political right, 19 Cal. 270. Commented on, Validity of grant within external boundaries, 1 Saw. 578. Cited, Conclusiveness of patent, 18 Cal. 572; not subject to collateral attack, 22 Cal. 111; third persons not concluded, who are, 1 Saw. 569; title under conflicting patents, prior equities, Id. 565; patent takes effect by relation, 19 Cal. 458; 34 Cal. 253; 35 Cal. 88; 1 Saw. 579. Commented on, Construction of Patent, 37 Cal. 435. Cited, Law of Nations, duty of government on acquisition of territory, 19 Cal. 270; 20 Cal. 422; rights of property under treaty of cession, 20 Cal. 421; 24 Cal. 669; 32 Cal. 370; State Lands, swamp and overflowed, what are, 26 Cal. 354.

Tevis v. Ellis, 25 Cal. 515. Approved, Ejectment, who cannot be dispossessed by writ of restitution, 26 Cal. 127; 30 Cal. 234; 36 Cal. 459; 37 Cal. 348. Cited, Injunction, when will not issue to restrain execution of writ, 37 Cal. 307.

Tevis v. O'Connell, 21 Cal. 512. Approved, Trial, practice on motions for new trial and on appeal, 23 Cal. 336.

Tevis v. Pitcher, 10 Cal. 465. Approved, Probate Courts have no jurisdiction where person died before adoption of constitution, 24 Cal. 123; 33 Cal. 423; 37 Cal.

89, 91; 23 How. 365; 1 Saw. 199. Distinguished, 28 Cal. 505. Cited, Mexican Law of Descents, 37 Cal. 89; customs as law, 31 Cal. 522.

Tevis v. Randall, 6 Cal. 632. Approved, State, designation of, 19 Cal. 681.

Tewkesbury v. Magraff, 33 Cal. 237. Approved, Estoppel, when tenant not estopped, 35 Cal. 566–571; Id. 576. Distinguished, 40 Cal. 250. Cited, Findings, practice on submission of, 36 Cal. 202; 38 Cal. 531.

Thacher v. Dinsmore, 5 Mass. 299. Cited, Principal and Agent, when agent liable on contract, 13 Cal. 48.

Thallhimer v. Brinckerhoff, 3 Cow. 647. Cited, Evidence, declarations when part of *res gestœ*, 1 Cal. 461. Approved, Maintenance, offense unknown to statutes, 22 Cal. 95.

Thames Manf. Co. v. Lathrop, 7 Conn. 550. Commented on, Statutory Construction, provisions when peremptory, 11 Cal. 55. Cited as to time for levy of taxes, 34 Cal. 442.

Thatcher, Ex parte, 7 Ill. 167. Commented on, Contempt, order when void, 1 Cal. 154.

Thatcher v. Miller, 11 Mass. 413. Cited, Amendment of officers' returns, 23 Cal. 81.

Thatcher v. Powell, 6 Wheat. 119. Cited, Jurisdiction, no intendments in favor of special or inferior jurisdiction, 25 Cal. 309.

Thayer v. Clemence, 22 Pick. 493. Cited, Covenant, not technically assignable, 37 Cal. 189.

Thayer v. Deen, 2 Hill, S. C. 677. Cited, Evidence, books of account as, 17 Cal. 466.

Thayer v. Mann, 19 Pick. 535. Distinguished, Mortgage, no remedy when debt is barred by statute, 18 Cal. 489, 490; 42 Cal. 502.

Thayer v. White, 3 Cal. 228. Cited, Specific Performance, enforcement of verbal contract of sale, 10 Cal. 160; 19 Cal. 457. Approved, Insufficient averments in answer, 4 Cal. 267. Cited, Defense of want of title may be imposed, 22 Cal. 598.

Theall v. Theall, 7 La. 226. Cited, Will, effect of wife's acceptance of devise, 29 Cal. 350.

38

Theriat v. Hart, 2 Hill, 380. Commented on, Statutory Construction, statutes not to be construed retrospectively, 4 Cal. 138.

Thickstun v. Howard, 8 Blackf. 535. Cited, Innkeeper, liability for loss of guest's property, 33 Cal. 600.

Thirty-Second Street, Matter of, 19 Wend. 128. Cited, Dedication, must rest in assent of owner, 14 Cal. 649; by sale of lots on street, 22 Cal. 489.

Thirty-Ninth Street, Matter of, 1 Hill, 192. Cited, Dedication, by sale of lots on street, 22 Cal. 489.

Thomas v. Allen, 1 Hill, 145. Cited, Indemnity, measure of liability on, 13 Cal. 525.

Thomas v. Armstrong, 7 Cal. 286. Cited, Supervisors, judgments and orders of, not subject to collateral attack, 23 Cal. 303; not subject to control under writ of mandate, 41 Cal. 77; Franchises, corporate franchises not subject to assignment or forced sale without consent of granting party, 24 Cal. 487; 2 Or. 238. Approved, 41 Cal. 511.

Thomas v. Baillo, 7 La. 415. Cited, Real action under civil law, 1 Cal. 287.

Thomas v. Desmond, 12 How. Pr. 321. Cited, Pleading, facts constituting right must be set forth, 11 Cal. 168.

Thomas v. Dow, 33 Me. 390. Cited, Surety, when discharge by agreement for delay, 10 Cal. 426.

Thomas v. Fogarty, 19 Cal. 644. Approved, Term of Court, adjournment on failure of judge to appear, 24 Cal. 21; 7 Kan. 386.

Thomas v. Geiger, 2 Nott & McC. 528. Commented on, Estoppel by Judgment, in real actions, 26 Cal. 506.

Thomas v. Harvie, 10 Wheat. 146. Cited, Bill of Review, time allowed for prosecution of, 41 Cal. 321.

Thomas v. Harrow, 4 Bibb, 563. Cited, Land, constructive possession by entry under deed, 25 Cal. 133. Commented on, 38 Cal. 488.

Thomas v. Hatch, 3 Sum. 170. Cited, Grant, description in, by reference to map, 10 Cal. 623; 15 Cal. 306.

Thomas v. Isett, 1 Greene, Iowa, 470. Cited, Trespass, measure of damages in, 1 Cal. 25.

Thomas v. Leland, 24 Wend. 66. Cited, Legislature, power of, over taxation for municipal purposes, 13 Cal. 188; Id. 355; 41 Cal. 532.

Thomas v. Oakley, 18 Ves. Jr. 184. Commented on, Injunction lies for trespass on mining claim, 7 Cal. 320.

Thomas v. Owens, 4 Md. 189. Distinguished, Office, salary of, legislative appropriation for, 9 Cal. 348.

Thomas v. Patten, 13 Me. 329. Cited, Deed, description in, by reference to map, 24 Cal. 446.

Thomas v. State, 27 Geo. 287. Cited, Juror and Jury, court may excuse qualified juror, 32 Cal. 47.

Thomas v. State, 5 How. Miss. 20. Cited, Superior Court, validity of act organizing municipal courts, 10 Cal. 295; 36 Cal. 697.

Thomas v. Williams, 10 Barn. & C. 671. Cited, Contract, void in part is void in toto, 40 Cal. 348.

Thomas v. Wright, 9 Serg. & R. 87. Cited, Ejectment, on equitable title, 22 Cal. 617.

Thomas Jefferson, The, 10 Wheat. 428. Cited, Jurisdiction, in admiralty, in cases of contract, 34 Cal. 679; 46 Ill. 511; Newb. Adm. 204. Disapproved, 12 How. 455.

Thompson v. Bostick, 1 McMull. Eq. 75. Denied, Tenants in Common, liability of one to another, 12 Cal. 423.

Thompson v. Brown, 4 Johns. Ch. 619. Cited, Trust, trustee, liability of, 9 Cal. 695. Commented on, 33 Md. 395.

Thompson v. Commonwealth, 8 Gratt. 637. Approved, Verdict, when not a chance verdict, 25 Cal. 401.

Thompson v. Dominy, 14 Mees. & W. 403. Denied, Bills of Lading, as negotiable instruments, 1 Cal. 79.

Thompson v. Dupuy, 3 La. 432. Cited, Warranty, eviction necessary to breach of, 2 Cal. 570.

Thompson v. Ellsworth, 1 Barb. Ch. 627. Cited, Appeal, adverse party, 38 Cal. 641.

Thompson v. Grand Gulf R. R. & Bk'g. Co., 3 How. Miss. 240. Cited, Condemnation of Land, compensation a condition precedent, 13 Cal. 318; 31 Cal. 559.

Thompson v. Green, 4 Ohio St. 216. Cited, Title, by adverse possession, 34 Cal. 383; 36 Cal. 541; 2 Black, 605.

Thompson v. Lack, 54 Eng. C. L. 540; 3 M. G. & S. 540. Cited, Statutory Construction, to be prospective, 27 Cal. 159.

Thompson v. Lacy, 3 Barn. & Ald. 286. Cited, Inn, what definition includes, 33 Cal. 596.

Thompson v. Lockwood, 15 John. 256. Cited, Bond, taken by an officer without authority, is void, 2 Cal. 255. Denied, 5 Leigh, 288.

Thompson v. Lyon, 14 Cal. 39. Cited, Pleading, answers in abatement to be strictly construed, 36 Cal. 134.

Thompson v. Manrow, 1 Cal. 428. Cited, Evidence, records of foreign judgments how certified, 7 Cal. 249; identity of name is *prima facie* evidence of identity of person, 28 Cal. 218; Id. 221.

Thompson v. Monrow, 2 Cal. 99. Cited, Judicial notice not taken of foreign laws, 4 Cal. 253.

Thompson v. People, 3 Park. Cr. Rep. 208. Cited, Indictment, sufficiency of, in murder cases, 21 Cal. 403.

Thompson v. Perkins, 3 Mason, 232. Cited, Money had and received, liability of factor to principal, 22 Cal. 518; 2 Black, 385. Doubted, 33 Md. 429.

Thompson v. Rowe, 2 Cal. 68. Commented on, Supervisors, power over revenues, 6 Cal. 285.

Thompson v. Smith, 28 Cal. 527. Cited, Forcible Entry and Detainer, averments construed, 31 Cal. 126. Distinguished, 32 Cal. 346; what constitutes an unlawful entry, 38 Cal. 422.

Thompson v. Tolmie, 2 Pet. 157. Cited, Probate Proceedings, conclusive, 22 Cal. 64; 22 How. 14.

Thompson v. Williams, 6 Cal. 88. Cited, Injunction, power of county judge, 23 Cal. 468. Commented on and overruled so far as it affirms previous rule as to distribution of official powers, 34 Cal. 526, 531. Cited, State Sovereignty, 41 Cal. 162.

Thompson's Appeal, 22 Penn. St. 17. Commented on, Conversion of trust funds, rights of *cestui que trust*, 31 Cal. 22.

Thomson v. Davenport, 9 Barn. & C. 78; 2 Smith Lead. Cas. 222. Cited, Principal and Agent, contract by agent of undiscovered principal, 1 Cal. 482. Doubted, 6 Cold. 19.

Thorn v. New York Central Mills, 10 How. Pr. 19. Commented on, Pleading, denials, from want of knowledge, insufficient, 9 Cal. 465, 467.

Thornburgh v. Hand, 7 Cal. 554. Cited, Pleading, justification for seizure must be specially pleaded, 10 Cal. 304; 3 Nev. 550; Fraudulent Sale, who may not attack, 19 Cal. 112; Id. 622; 23 Cal. 93; 34 Cal. 350; sufficiency of complaint in action to set aside, 23 Cal. 78; Witness, cross-examination, practice, 25 Cal. 213.

Thorne v. Cramer, 15 Barb. 112. Commented on, Constitutionality of statute transferring legislative power to people, 17 Cal. 32. Denied, 13 Gratt. 97.

Thorne v. San Francisco, 4 Cal. 127. Approved, Corporation, restrictions on powers of, 7 Cal. 375. Approved, dissenting opinion of Heydenfeldt, J., Judicial Sales, redemption from, 38 Cal. 439. Cited, State Sovereignty, power of legislature, 41 Cal. 162. Contra, Constitutionality of Statute suspending remedies, 15 Iowa, 137. See People v. Hays.

Thornhill v. Gilmer, 4 Smedes & M. 153. Cited, Chattel Mortgage, legal operation and effect of, 27 Cal. 269.

Thornton v. Borland, 12 Cal. 438. Cited, Amendment, after demurrer sustained, 14 Cal. 202; 30 Cal. 78; Injunction, when will lie, 51 N. H. 245.

Thornton v. Dixon, 3 Bro. C. C. 199. Commented on, Partnership, tenure of real estate by, 28 Cal. 582; 1 Sum. 183. Doubted, 20 Mo. 182.

Thornton v. Fitzhugh, 4 Leigh, 209. Cited, Interest, statute changing rate of, prospective in its view, 42 Cal. 285.

Thornton v. Hooper, 14 Cal. 9. Approved, San Francisco, constitutionality of funding act, 20 Cal. 658. Cited, Legislature, power over municipal affairs and finances, 21 Gratt. 617.

Thornton v. Mahoney, 24 Cal. 569. Approved, Appeal, stay of proceedings pending, 26 Cal. 139; 28 Cal. 91; Id. 658; 33 Cal. 479. Cited, Mexican Grant, title under, 27 Cal. 564; 31 Cal. 494; 36 Cal. 145.

Thorp v. Burling, 11 John. 285. Cited, Trespass, constructive possession sufficient to maintain, 12 Cal. 463.

Thredgill v. Pintard, 12 How. 36. Cited, Ejectment, maintainable by claimant to public lands, 30 Cal. 657; Estoppel, mortgagor estopped to deny existence of lien, 31 Cal. 457.

Threllfall v. Lunt, 7 Sim. 627. Cited, Equity, will not entertain jurisdiction where there is a remedy at law, 10 Cal. 576.

Thresher v. East Lond. Wat. Works Co., 2 Barn. & C. 608. Cited, Lease, construction of, right to remove fixtures, 14 Cal. 70, 72.

Throckmorton v. Burr, 5 Cal. 400. Approved, Parties, tenant in common may maintain several action in ejectment, 7 Cal. 40; 8 Cal. 79.

Thurber v. Blackbourne, 1 N. H. 242. Cited, Foreign Judgment, when not binding *in personam,* 8 Cal. 458; 14 How. 340.

Thurman v. Cameron, 24 Wend. 87. Commented on, Evidence, certificate of acknowledgment to deed, 16 Cal. 553.

Thursby v. Plant, 1 Wms. Saund. 237. Cited, Lease, construction of, when rent becomes due, 25 Cal. 391.

Thurston v. Blanchard, 22 Pick. 18. Cited, Conversion, demand not necessary in case of tortious possession, 12 Cal. 462.

Thurston v. Hancock, 12 Mass. 220. Cited, Negligence, in grading streets, not presumed, 42 Cal. 438; 15 Conn. 131. Doubted, 5 Wis. 46.

Thurston v. Hooper, 7 Cal. 579. Cited, Legislature, power over municipal taxation and appropriation, 21 Gratt. 617.

Thurston v. Percival, 1 Pick. 415. Cited, Evidence, judicial notice not taken of foreign laws, 15 Cal. 254.

Tibeau v. Tibeau, 19 Mo. 78. Cited, Trial, legal and equitable defenses, 10 Cal. 160; 19 Cal. 457.

Tillman v. Cowand, 12 Smedes & M. 262. Cited, Conveyance, when record of, imparts no notice, 6 Cal. 315.

Tilton v. Tilton, 9 N. H. 385. Cited, Mistake, equity will relieve from, 19 Cal. 673.

Tinkler v. Walpole, 14 East, 226. Commented on, Vessels, registration of, as evidence of ownership, 1 Cal. 483.

Tinney v. Ashley, 15 Pick. 546. Commented on, Covenant in contract of sale, "good and sufficient deed" construed, 6 Cal. 573; 10 Cal. 322. Cited, Preparation of deed, on whom devolves, 25 Cal. 279.

Tinney v. Endicott, 5 Cal. 102. Cited, Instructions, court may modify, 32 Cal. 289.

Tipping v. Tipping, 1 P. Wms. 730. Cited, Will, construction of bequest, 31 Cal. 603.

Tipton v. Triplett, 1 Met. Ky. 570. Cited, Warranty, when statute of limitations begins to run, 41 Cal. 115.

Tissot v. Darling, 9 Cal. 278. Cited, Undertaking on Appeal, in action on nonpayment of judgment may be shown without issuing execution, 38 Cal. 604; pleading in action on replevin bond, 3 Nev. 565.

Tissot v. Throckmorton, 6 Cal. 471. Referred to, Appeal Bond, validity of, 9 Cal. 285.

Titus v. Scantling, 4 Blackf. 90. Cited, Evidence, judicial notice not taken of foreign laws, 15 Cal. 254; 29 Ind. 161.

Tobey v. Barber, 5 John. 68. Approved, Debtor and Creditor, payment by note, 8 Cal. 506; 12 Cal. 322, 324; 25 Cal. 542.

Todd v. Cochell, 17 Cal. 97. Cited, Negligence, degree of care necessary in lawful use of property, 15 Wall. 538.

Tohler v. Folsom, 1 Cal. 210. Commented on, Conveyance, sufficiency of, parol sale of real estate under Mexican law, 7 Cal. 490. Distinguished, Specific performance of verbal contract of sale of land, 4 Cal. 93.

Toland v. Mandell, 38 Cal. 30. Commented on, State Lands, purchasers in good faith of State selections, 40 Cal. 71, 73.

Toller v. Carteret, 2 Vern. 494. Cited, Specific Performance, jurisdiction, when it attaches, 38 Cal. 201.

Tolman v. Spaulding, 4 Ill. 13. Approved, Judgment, entry of, on joint obligation, 6 Cal. 182; 7 Cal. 448.

Tolson v. Elwes, 1 Leigh, 436. Cited, Sheriff, remedy against, for failure to pay over moneys, 10 Cal. 488. Construed, 25 Miss. 35.

Tombs v. Rochester & S. R. R. Co., 18 Barb. 583. Cited, Waiver, rights created by statute may be waived, 22 Cal. 571; as to fencing required on railroad tracks, 33 Cal. 236.

Tomlinson v. Hoyt, 1 Smedes & M. 520. Cited, Summons, statute providing for service other than personal, to be strictly pursued, 11 Cal. 379.

Tomlinson v. Rubio, 16 Cal. 202. Commented on, Injunction, when will not issue to restrain sheriff, 25 Cal. 519. Disapproved, Id. 520.

Tompkins' Estate, 12 Cal. 114. Cited, Homestead, nature of the estate, 22 Cal. 638. Denied, 25 Cal. 114; Jurisdiction as to title in case of dissolution of community by death, 23 Cal. 418.

Tompkins v. Tompkins, 1 Story C. C. 547. Commented on, Probate Proceedings, conclusive, jurisdiction of court exclusive, 18 Cal. 481; 20 Cal. 268.

Tonawanda R.R. Co. v. Munger, 5 Denio, 255; S. C. 4 N. Y. 349. Commented on, Negligence, liability of railroad company for injury to cattle, 37 Cal. 417, 418. Denied, 9 Wis. 214.

Tooms v. Randall, 3 Cal. 438. Cited, Verification, objection to want of, how waived, 6 Cal. 68; Place of Trial, objections to, how waived, 9 Cal. 643; 3 Nev. 406.

Toothaker v. Cornwall, 4 Cal. 28. Disapproved, Negotiable Instruments, premature notice to indorser, 8 Cal. 630.

Topping v. Root, 5 Cow. 404. Cited, Pleading, conditions precedent in action on, dependent promises, 1 Cal. 338.

Torrey v. Jordan, 4 How. Miss. 401. Cited, Appearance, recital of, in judgment, not conclusive, 13 Cal. 561.

Touchard v. Crow, 20 Cal. 150. Cited, Ejectment, title of confirmee of Mexican Grant, 21 Cal. 221. Approved, Tenant in common may maintain action, 21 Cal. 348; Id. 583; 1 Wall. 373; Officers, powers of deputy, 25 Cal. 186; 36 Cal. 203.

Touchard v. Keyes, 21 Cal. 202. Approved, Alcalde's records as evidence, 26 Cal. 45; 38 Cal. 219, 226, 227. Cited, Tenants in Common, may sue jointly in ejectment, 30 Cal. 484.

Touchard v. Touchard, 5 Cal. 306. Commented on, Municipal Grants, forfeiture, 6 Cal. 525. Disapproved, 15 Cal. 699, 618. Approved, Contracts, construction of contracts of municipal corporations, 16 Cal. 270.

Toulmin v. Copland, 3 Younge & C. 625. Cited, Evidence, declarations and admissions, acquiescence by silence, 22 Cal. 238.

Towdy v. Ellis, 22 Cal. 650. Approved, New Trial, statements and bills of exceptions, practice, 23 Cal. 549; Appeal, from judgment and from order on new trial, remedies concurrent, 25 Cal. 168.

Towle v. Forney, 14 N. Y. 423. Commented on, Stare Decisis, judicial decisions, 15 Cal. 621.

Town of East Hartford v. Hartford Bridge Co., 10 How. 511. Commented on, Municipal Corporations, power of legislature over, 16 Cal. 236; grant of bridge or ferry franchise not exclusive, 21 Cal. 252.

Townsend v. Blewett, 5 How. Miss. 503. Cited, Ferry Franchises, protection of, 6 Cal. 597.

Townsend v. Bogart, 11 Abb. Pr. 355. Disapproved, Fraud, liability of partners for, acquiescence not presumed, 36 Cal. 166.

Townsend v. Burbank, 5 Wall. 337, note. Cited, San Francisco, tenure of pueblo lands, 42 Cal. 557.

Townsend v. Corning, 23 Wend. 435. Cited, Principal and Agent, instrument signed by agent, 13 Cal. 235; when principal bound, 29 Cal. 353. Commented on, 21 Cal. 69.

Townsend v. Gordon, 19 Cal. 188. Cited, Probate Proceedings, authority for sale of estate limited by statute, 20 Cal. 312; strict compliance with statute essential, 20 Cal. 314.

Townsend v. Greeley, 5 Wall. 326. Cited, San Francisco, tenure of pueblo lands, 42 Cal. 557.

Townsend v. Griggs, 3 Ill. 365. Cited, Summons, return by deputy, when insufficient, 11 Cal. 379.

Townsend v. Hubbard, 4 Hill, 351. Cited, Principal and Agent, who bound on contract signed by agent, 13 Cal. 235.

Townsend v. Jemison, 9 How. 413. Cited, New Promise, effect of statute of limitations, 42 Cal. 499; 13 How. 215.

Townsend v. Munger, 9 Tex. 300. Cited, Probate Procedure, appeal from, 7 Cal. 240.

Townsend v. Riddle, 2 N. H. 448. Cited, Surety on note, not released by mere delay, 10 Cal. 425.

Townsend v. Susquehanna T. Road, 6 John. 90. Cited, Negligence, liability does not attach for reasonable exercise of a right, 7 Cal. 340.

Townsend v. Tallant, 33 Cal. 45. Cited, Probate Sale, jurisdiction of person essential, 3 Or. 507.

Townsend v. Wells, 3 Day, 327. Cited, Demand under agreement to pay fixed sum in grain, not necessary, 23 Cal. 69.

Townsend v. Wilson, 1 Barn. & Ald. 608. Cited, Trust and Trustee, execution of powers of, 6 Cal. 125; 6 Rich. Eq. 23.

Townshend v. Stangroom, 6 Ves. Jr. 328. Cited, Mistake, equity will relieve from, 19 Cal. 673.

Towsey v. Shook, 3 Blackf. 268. Cited, Evidence, burden of proof of want of authority to contract, 1 Cal. 340.

Towsley v. McDonald, 32 Barb. 604. Cited, Jurisdiction, of person, by substituted service of process, 31 Cal. 349.

Towson v. Havre de Grace Bank, 6 Har. & J. 47. Cited, Innkeeper, liable for loss of guest's property, 33 Cal. 602.

Tracy v. Swartwout, 10 Pet. 80. Cited, Public Officers, liability for misfeasance in office, 36 Cal. 214; 3 How. 263; Id. 796; 4 How. 149; 10 How. 234; 12 How. 292.

Tracy v. Talmage, 14 N. Y. 162. Distinguished, Contract, against public policy, void, 37 Cal. 175; 44 N. Y. 91.

Trafford v. Boehm, 3 Atk. 440. Cited, Trust and Trustees, effect of acquiescence in acts of, 9 Cal. 696.

Trafton v. United States, 3 Story C. C. 646. Cited, Judgment, several judgment on joint action as a bar, 6 Cal. 182.

Train v. Gold, 5 Pick. 480. Cited, Surety, when judgment against principal conclusive on surety, 14 Cal. 204; consideration on contract of, 22 Cal. 93.

Trapnall v. Richardson, 13 Ark. 543. Cited, Judgment, lien of, not extended by levy of execution, 10 Cal. 81.

Travers v. Crane, 15 Cal. 12. Approved, Principal and Agent, agency revoked by death, 28 Cal. 648.

Travis v. Waters, 12 John. 500. Cited, Foreclosure, finality of decree, 9 Cal. 635.

Treadway v. Semple, 28 Cal. 652. Cited, Mexican Grants, conflicting surveys, conclusiveness of proceedings, on confirmation and survey, 32 Cal. 666, 667, 668; 36 Cal. 144. Commented on, 38 Cal. 61, 63, 72; 1 Saw. 565, 583.

Treadwell v. Davis, 34 Cal. 601. Disapproved, Appeal, review of facts to sustain judgment, 40 Cal. 630.

Treadwell v. Salisbury Manf. Co., 7 Gray, 393. Commented on, Corporation may sell property, 37 Cal. 591, 592; construction of statute as to distribution of capital stock in dividends, 38 Cal. 318.

Treasurer v. Commercial C. M. Co., 22 Cal. 390. Cited, Specific Performance, when will be decreed, 38 Cal. 453.

Treat v. Browning, 4 Conn. 408. Cited, Libel and Slander, evidence inadmissible, 41 Cal. 384.

Treat v. McCall, 10 Cal. 511. Cited, Appeal, when judgment by default will be reversed, 16 Cal. 68.

Treat v. Orono, 26 Me. 217. Cited, Taxation, assessment of city lots in gross, 18 Cal. 152.

Treat v. Strickland, 23 Me. 234. Commented on, Mortgage, when written instruments constitute, 9 Cal. 549.

Treat v. Stuart, 5 Cal. 113. Commented on, Forcible Entry and Detainer, what plaintiff must show, 28 Cal. 191.

Trecothick v. Austin, 4 Mason, 16. Cited, Executors and Administrators, liability for trust funds of estate, 31 Cal. 25; 5 How. 271, 276.

Tredwen v. Bourne, 6 Mees. & W. 461. Cited, Mining Partnerships, liability of shareholders, 23 Cal. 205.

Trimble v. Thorne, 16 John. 152. Cited, Appeal, reversal of judgment founded in part on incompetent evidence, 1 Cal. 232.

Tripler v. Olcott, 3 John. Ch. 474. Cited, Jurisdiction, power of court over its process, 14 Cal. 678.

Tripner v. Abrahams, 47 Penn. St. 220. Cited, Husband and Wife, property acquired during marriage, 30 Cal. 43.

Trott v. McGavock, 1 Yerg. 469. Statute distinguished, Execution, title of purchaser on what depends, 38 Cal. 655.

Trott v. Warren, 11 Me. 227. Cited, Statute of Frauds, title of innocent purchaser, 12 Cal. 498.

Troup v. Smith, 20 John. 33. Affirmed, 5 Wend. 30. Approved, Statute of Limitations, fraudulent concealment, effect of, 8 Cal. 459; 2 Black, 605; 9 How. 529.

Trout v. Gardiner, 39 Cal. 386. Approved, Statutory Construction, effect of repeal, 41 Cal. 438.

Trow v. Vermont Cent. R. R. Co., 24 Vt. 494. Commented on, Negligence, mutual negligence, rule releasing defendant, 37 Cal. 422.

Troy & B. R. R. Co. v. North. Turnpike Co., 16 Barb. 100. Cited, Eminent Domain, compensation for condemnation, 32 Cal. 510.

Troy & Rutland R. R. Co. v. Kerr, 17 Barb. 581. Cited, Corporation, formation of, minor omissions not to invalidate charter, 22 Cal. 440.

Truchelut v. Charleston, 1 Nott & McC. 227. Cited, Legislature, power of taxation and appropriation, 13 Cal. 355.

Truebody v. Jacobson, 2 Cal. 269. Approved, Vendor's Lien, for unpaid purchase money, 6 Cal. 226; 32 Cal. 59; not affected by notes given, 8 Cal. 403.

Trueheart v. Addicks, 2 Tex. 217. Cited, Election, irregularities not to invalidate, 12 Cal. 361.

Trull v. Moulton, 12 Allen, 396. Cited, Revenue Stamp, no part of note, 34 Cal. 175.

Trull v. Skinner, 17 Pick. 216. Commented on, Conveyance, when a mortgage, 26 Cal. 605.

Truly v. Wanger, 5 How. 141. Cited, Jurisdiction, concurrent, when equity will not set aside judgment at law, 21 Cal. 442.

Trustees, etc., v. Chamberlain, 14 Ill. 495. Cited, Constitutionality of Statute, affecting remedies, 7 Cal. 5.

Trustees, etc., v. Lawrence, 11 Paige, 80. Cited, Probate Proceedings, order of payment of debts, 26 Cal. 67.

Trustees v. Zanesville C. & M. Co., 9 Ohio, 203. Cited, Corporations, power of self-dissolution, 38 Cal. 172.

Tryon v. Sutton, 13 Cal. 490. Referred to, Mortgage, indefiniteness of description in, 13 Cal. 539. Cited,

Equity, when will relieve from judgments at law, 14 Cal. 143; Husband and Wife, conveyance to wife constitutes common property, 22 Cal. 288.

Tubb v. Madding, 1 Minor, Ala. 129. Cited, Instructions, as to facts erroneous, 17 Cal. 170.

Tucker v. Aiken, 7 N. H. 113. Cited, Election, notice of special election essential, 11 Cal. 66.

Tucker v. Boston, 18 Pick. 162. Cited, Will, intention necessary to deprive child of distributive share, 35 Cal. 343.

Tucker v. Harris, 13 Geo. 1. Denied, Jurisdiction, of probate courts, 19 Cal. 206.

Tucker v. Moreland, 10 Pet. 75. Cited, Infant, confirmation of deed by, 24 Cal. 212.

Tucker v. Tower, 9 Pick. 108. Cited, Corporations, what property may acquire, 24 Cal. 489.

Tucker v. Tucker, 11 Jur. 893. Cited, Divorce, proof of adultery, 13 Cal. 98.

Tucker v. Welsh, 17 Mass. 160. Doubted, Evidence, when parol evidence of written instrument admissible, 9 Cal. 594.

Tuckerman v. Newhall, 17 Mass. 581. Cited, Release of one co-surety is a release of all, 11 Cal. 220; 38 Cal. 532, 537.

Tufts v. Tufts, 18 Wend. 621. Cited, Judgment, lien of, not extended by levy of execution, 10 Cal. 80; 37 Cal. 133.

Tuite v. Wakelee, Cal. Sup. Ct. (not reported.) Affirmed, in same case, Principal and Agent, when agent personally liable for money had and received, 19 Cal. 705.

Tullett v. Armstrong, 1 Bev. 21; S. C. 4 Mylne & C. 393. Cited, Husband and Wife, separate property of wife, power of alienation, 32 Cal. 385.

Tuolumne Co. v. Stanislaus Co., 6 Cal. 440. Disapproved, Legislature may impose other than judicial duties on judicial officers, 34 Cal. 527, 531.

Tuolumne Redemption Co. v. Sedgwick, 15 Cal. 515. Cited, Redemption, statutes providing for redemption from judicial sales, constitutional, 38 Cal. 439.

Tuolumne Wat. Co. v. Chapman, 8 Cal. 392. Cited, Injunction, to stay threatened injury to right of way, 22 Cal. 491.

Turley v. County of Logan, 17 Ill. 152. Commented on, Statutes, test of validity of, 30 Cal. 274.

Turner v. Billagram, 2 Cal. 520. Cited, Official Bonds, subsequent acts not essential to binding force of, 2 Or. 319.

Turner v. Caruthers, 17 Cal. 431. Approved, Attorney and Counsel, power of court over its officers, 35 Cal. 540.

Turner v. Fendall, 1 Cranch, 117. Cited, Execution, identity of money lost when in hands of officer, 21 Cal. 172. Denied, as to loss of title, 3 Humph. 438.

Turner v. Goodrich, 26 Vt. 707. Cited, Covenant, what constitutes eviction under, 39 Cal. 367.

Turner v. Melony, 13 Cal. 621. Cited, Election, eligibility to office cannot be collaterally inquired into, 23 Cal. 320.

Turner v. McIlhany, 6 Cal. 287. Cited, Appeal, no reversal for error without injury, 8 Cal. 534.

Turner v. Moore, 1 Brev. 236. Cited, Conveyance, passing an equitable title, 10 Cal. 368.

Turner v. Morgan, 8 Ves. Jr. 143. Commented on, Partition, when action lies, 12 Cal. 423.

Turner v. Morrison, 11 Cal. 21. Cited, New Trial, on ground of surprise, when granted, 29 Cal. 609.

Turner v. N. B. & M. R. R. Co., 34 Cal. 594. Followed, Damages, measure of, for violation of personal rights, 34 Cal. 590. Cited, liability for removing person from railroad car, 37 Cal. 409. Distinguished, Excessive Damages, in actions for malicious prosecution, 36 Cal. 485. Commented on, 57 Me. 250. Approved, Principal, liable for damage caused by agent or servant, 40 Cal. 586; Id. 662.

Turner v. Tuolumne Wat. & M. Co., 25 Cal. 397. Approved, Verdict, when not a chance verdict, 25 Cal. 473; affidavits of jurors not admissible to impeach verdict, 25 Cal. 474, 476; 29 Cal. 262. Cited, Exceptions to rulings must be taken in court below, 34 Cal. 586; "acts of God," what constitute, 35 Cal. 423.

Turner v. Turner, 1 Litt. 101. Cited, Will, attestation to, presumption as to due execution, 10 Cal. 479.

Turney v. Saunders, 5 Ill. 531. Commented on, Ejectment, maintainable on possessory right to public land, 30 Cal. 656.

Turnipseed v. Hawkins, 1 McCord, 272. Cited, Administrator's Sale, presumptions as to regularity, 22 Cal. 591.

Turnpike Co. v. Commonwealth, 2 Watts, 433. Cited, Contract, rescission of conditions precedent, 15 Cal. 458.

Turrill v. Boynton, 23 Vt. 142. Cited, Surety on note, when discharged by agreement for delay, 10 Cal. 426.

Tustin v. Faught, 23 Cal. 237. Cited, Husband and Wife, common property, control of, 26 Cal. 420. Construed and distinguished, Conveyance to married woman construed, 30 Cal. 56, 63. Disapproved, 41 Cal. 608. Construed, Ejectment, title acquired pending action, 30 Cal. 474.

Tuthill v. Tracy, 31 N. Y. 157. Cited, Foreclosure, necessary parties to, 40 Cal. 238.

Tuttle v. Jackson, 6 Wend. 213. Commented on, Sheriff, completion of execution of process by ex-sheriff, 8 Cal. 410. Cited, Conveyance, possession as notice of, 29 Cal. 488; 36 Cal. 272; what sufficient notice in equity, 36 Cal. 437.

Tuttle v. Montford, 7 Cal. 358. Cited, Mechanic's Lien, when it attaches, doctrine of relation, 23 Cal. 525; construction of statute, 25 Ark. 494.

Tuttle v. Walton, 1 Kelly, Geo. 43. Commented on, Corporation, lien on unpaid stock, 9 Cal. 115.

Twenty-Ninth Street, Matter of, 1 Hill, 189. Cited, Dedication, must rest in assent of owner, 14 Cal. 649.

Twogood, Ex parte, 11 Ves. Jr. 517. Distinguished, Set-off, when justified in equity, 7 Cal. 548.

Twyne's Case, 3 Coke, 80. Cited, Statute of Frauds, sale of chattels, 15 Cal. 505.

Tyler v. Houghton, 25 Cal. 26. Cited, Certiorari, jurisdiction of supreme court, 25 Cal. 96; State Patent, who may contest right to, Id. 259. Commented on, Power and jurisdiction of register of State lands, 30 Cal. 608; Mandamus, proceedings by, as an action, 27 Cal. 684. Approved, Jurisdiction of supreme court by mandamus, 28 Cal. 71.

Tyler v. Taylor, 8 Barb. 585. Cited, Chattel Mortgage, securing separate debts, 27 Cal. 273.

Tyler v. Wilkinson, 4 Mason, 401. Cited, Water Rights, prior appropriator, rights of, 23 Cal. 486; relative rights as to subsequent appropriator, 28 Cal. 314.

Tyson v. Watts, 1 Md. Ch. Dec. 13. Commented on. Specific Performance, mutuality in contract required, 21 Cal. 411.

Tyson v. Wells, 2 Cal. 122. Approved, Reference, report of referee has legal effect of an award, 2 Cal. 325; on what grounds may be set aside, 4 Cal. 125. Cited. Exceptions to rulings of referee, when taken, 7 Cal. 53. Denied, power of court to grant new trial, 19 Cal. 608.

Udell v. Kenney, 3 Cow. 590. Cited, dissenting opinion of Sprague, J., Alimony, inseparable from divorce, 38 Cal. 278.

Uhlfelder v. Levy, 9 Cal. 607. Approved, Injunction, court cannot restrain judgment of another court of coördinate jurisdiction, exception stated, 11 Cal. 76. Cited, 37 Cal. 269; 22 Wis. 486. Distinguished, 15 Cal. 134; 39 Cal. 162.

Underwood v. Campbell, 14 N. H. 393. Cited, Conveyances, purpose and design of recording act, 6 Cal. 314.

Underwood v. Newport Lyceum, 5 B. Mon. 129. Commented on, Corporation, liability for torts, 16 Cal. 269.

Underwood v. Stuyvesant, 19 John. 186. Cited. Dedication, by laying out lots on streets, 35 Cal. 500.

Union Bank v. Emerson, 15 Mass. 159. Cited, Fixtures, what pass by conveyance, 10 Cal. 264; 14 Cal. 68; 4 Met. 311.

Union Ins. Co. v. Van Rensselaer, 4 Paige, 85. Cited, Foreclosure of mortgage securing several notes, 23 Cal. 32.

Union Water Co. v. Crary, 25 Cal. 509. Cited, Water Rights, title by adverse possession, 27 Cal. 366; 32 Cal. 35.

Union Wat. Co. v. Murphy's F. F. Co., 22 Cal. 620. Cited, Corporations, power to make contracts, 22 Cal. 427. Approved, Mortgage covers fixture subsequently attached to premises, 23 Cal. 217.

United Ins. Co. v. Scott, 1 John. 111. Cited, Vessel, master of, when authorized to pledge, 8 Cal. 534.

United States v. Amedy, 11 Wheat. 392. Cited, Crimes, commission of crime not presumed, 28 Cal. 133; Criminal Procedure, existence *de facto* of corporations need only be shown, 28 Cal. 519; 41 Cal. 652. Approved, 29 Cal. 260, 263.

United States v. Appleton, 1 Sum. 492. Cited, Mexican Grants, construction of, 26 Cal. 109, 110.

United States v. The Armistad, 15 Pet. 590. Cited, State Sovereignty, effect of temporary residence of slaves, 2 Cal. 446.

United States v. Arredondo, 6 Pet. 691; S. P. 13 Pet. 133. Cited, International Law, law of ceded territory, 1 Cal. 286; Id. 314; Mexican Grant, construction of, 13 Cal. 455; 9 Pet. 236. Approved, Presumption as to official authority, 1 Cal. 420; Id. 326; 3 Cal. 39; 16 Cal. 227, 229; 9 Pet. 134; 2 Black, 340; 9 How. 444; 20 How. 63; 22 How. 459. Cited, Records of grant as evidence, 13 Cal. 573; rights of property under perfect titles protected by treaty, 24 Cal. 660; 2 Black, 366; 9 How. 445; 19 How. 372; want of survey when not to affect title of grantee, 3 Cal. 42; 10 How. 556; title under conflicting patents, 33 Cal. 88.

United States v. Bailey, 9 Pet. 272. Cited, Jurisdiction, when exclusive in Federal courts, 38 Cal. 151; 5 How. 209.

United States v. Barker, 2 Wheat. 395. Cited, Costs, county not liable for, 30 Cal. 239.

United States v. Bassett, 21 How. 412. Referred to, Mexican title, 16 Cal. 550; 1 Black, 37.

United States v. Bevans, 3 Wheat. 336. Cited, Constitutional Construction, powers of Federal Government, 1 Cal. 235; 5 Wheat. 115.

United States v. Boisdore, 11 How. 63; S. P. 8 How. 113. Cited, Mexican Grant, test of validity of, 3 Cal. 42; conditional grant, 6 Cal. 270. Commented on, 12 How. 434; execution trust under treaty the exercise of a political power, 3 Cal. 26.

United States v. Booth, 21 How. 506. Cited, Jurisdiction, concurrent, conclusiveness of proceedings, when jurisdiction attaches, 27 Cal. 170.

39

United States v. Boyd, 15 Pet. 187. Cited, Sureties, rights under contract, 17 Cal. 508; 1 How. 114; 21 How. 76.

United States v. Burgevin, 13 Pet. 85. Cited, Mexican Grants, conditions in, 3 Cal. 40.

United States v. Burr, 2 Wheel. Cr. Cas. 573; 1 Burr's Trial, 312. Commented on, Criminal Procedure, application for bail, evidence admissible, 19 Cal. 546.

United States v. Cambuston, 20 How. 59. Construed, Mexican Grants, presumptions as to validity of, 16 Cal. 459; 19 Cal. 96.

United States v. Chicago, 7 How. 190. Cited, Dedication, by sale of lots on plat, 35 Cal. 501; 2 How. 31.

United States v. Clarke, 8 Pet. 436. Cited, Alcalde Grants, validity of, 15 Cal. 553; presumptions as to official authority, 16 Cal. 230; 9 Pet. 134. Commented on, Mexican Grants, when titles are perfect under, 24 Cal. 667.

United States v. Cornell, 2 Mason, 91. Commented on, Juror and Jury, court may excuse qualified juror, 32 Cal. 45. Cited, Jurisdiction, when exclusive, 38 Cal. 151.

United States v. Curry, 6 How. 113. Cited, Writ of Error to U. S. Supreme Court, who may approve security and issue citations, 32 Cal. 240; 12 How. 389. Approved, Practice, 19 How. 183.

United States v. Cutts, 1 Sum. 133. Approved, Corporations, transfer of stock when effective, 5 Cal. 187.

United States v. Daniel, 6 Wheat. 542. Cited, Judicial Decisions, rule of, on equal division of justices, 32 Cal.. 633; 5 How. 224.

United States v. Delespine, 15 Pet. 319. Cited, Mexican Grants, validity of floating grants, 3 Cal. 42; 3 How. 787; 10 How. 557.

United States v. Drummond, 13 Pet. 84. Cited, Spanish Grants, conditions annexed to, 3 Cal. 40.

United States v. Ferreira, 13 How. 40. Cited, Judiciary, powers of, exclusively judicial, 5 Cal. 22; 14 How. 120; power to determine constitutionality of statute, 17 Cal. 562.

United States v. Fisher, 2 Cranch, 358. Cited, Constitutional Construction, powers of Federal government, 1 Cal. 235. Commented on, 25 Cal. 422. Cited, Statutory Construction, not to be retrospective, 4 Cal. 136; intention of legislature to govern, 11 Cal. 225.

United States v. Fitzgerald, 15 Pet. 407. Cited, Preemption, rights of preemptioner, 37 Cal. 495.

United States v. Forbes, 15 Pet. 173. Cited, Conveyance, void from insufficient description, 6 Cal. 312; 3 How. 787.

United States v. Fossatt, 21 How. 447. Cited, Mexican Grants, conditions requisite to perfect title, 13 Cal. 418. Commented on, Confirmation of inchoate titles essential, 16 Cal. 548; 18 Cal. 571; 19 Cal. 269. Distinguished, 24 Cal. 670. Cited, Title not perfect till survey and segregation, 24 Cal. 579; 36 Cal. 145.

United States v. Gibert, 2 Sum. 19. Cited, New Trial, when irregularities insufficient grounds for, 9 Cal. 537. Commented on, Appeal, effect of reversal in criminal action, 28 Cal. 463. Cited, Criminal Procedure, when discharge of jury operates as an acquittal, 38 Cal. 478.

United States v. Gomez, 23 How. 326. Referred to, Appeal, effect of, on injunction, 28 Cal. 88, 89.

United States v. Guthrie, 17 How. 284. Cited, Office, term of, 6 Cal. 292; Parties, State as a party, how entitled, 7 Cal. 71. Commented on, Mandamus, title to office, cannot be tried on, 7 Cal. 80; 16 Cal. 42, 61.

United States v. Hamilton, 3 Dall. 17. Commented on, Supreme Court, jurisdiction on issuance of writs, 1 Cal. 147; 5 How. 189; 14 How. 132.

United States v. Hanson, 16 Pet. 196. Cited, Mexican Grant, private survey ineffectual to perfect title, 13 Cal. 416; 14 Cal. 359.

United States v. Harding, 1 Wall. Jr. 127. Cited, Criminal Procedure, reversed judgment when not a bar to a new trial, 28 Cal. 465.

United States v. Hartnell's Exrs., 22 How. 286. Cited, Mexican Grant, decree of confirmation not subject to collateral attack, 27 Cal. 168.

United States v. Haskell, 4 Wash. C. C. 402. Cited, Criminal Procedure, retrial on discharge of jury, 27 Cal. 399. Doubted, 2 Sum. 57.

United States v. Henry, 4 Wash. C. C. 228. Cited, Witness, accomplice, competent in criminal case, 5 Cal. 185.

United States v. Hooe, 3 Cranch, 73. Approved, Mortgage to secure future advances, valid, 35 Cal. 309; 4 Wheat. 120; 23 How. 27.

United States v. Howard, 3 Sum. 12.   Cited, Indictment, surplusage in, 20 Cal. 80.

United States v. Howell, 4 Wash. 620; S. C. 2 Am. Lead. Cas. 432.   Cited, Surety, discharge of, by delay, 24 Cal. 165; 34 Md. 516; Assignment, equitable assignment, 38 Cal. 545.

United States v. Inhab. of Waterborough, Davies, 154. Cited, Trust and Trustee, enforcement of trust on specific property, 31 Cal. 24.

United States v. Jones, 2 Wheel. Cr. Cas. 461.   Commented on, Criminal Procedure, instructions as to circumstantial evidence, 34 Cal. 203.

United States v. Jones, 3 Wash. C. C. 224.   Commented on, Criminal Procedure, application for bail, evidence admissible, 19 Cal. 546.

United States v. Keen, 1 McLean, 429.   Cited, Criminal Procedure, retrial on reversal of judgment, 28 Cal. 465.

United States v. King, 3 How. 773; S. C. 7 How. 833. Cited, Mexican Grant, survey to be made under official authority, 13 Cal. 416; 9 How. 469; 11 How. 127.

United States v. Kingsley, 12 Pet. 476.   Cited, Spanish Grants, conditions annexed, 3 Cal. 40; what essential to perfection of title, 6 Cal. 270.

United States v. Kirkpatrick, 9 Wheat. 720.   Commented on, Debtor and Creditor, application of payments, 14 Cal. 450.   Cited, Office, appointment to fill vacancy, 7 Cal. 526; 20 Cal. 508.

United States v. Larkin, 18 How. 559.   Cited, Mexican Grants, construction of conditions in, 13 Cal. 410.

United States v. Lathrop, 17 John. 4.   Cited, Constitutional Construction, judicial powers where vested, 5 Cal. 302; 5 Wheat. 69.

United States v. LaVengeance, 3 Dall. 297.   Cited, Judicial notice taken of geographical divisions, 39 Cal. 40.

United States v. Lawrence, 3 Dall. 42.   Cited, Mandamus, what writ to judicial officer to direct, 28 Cal. 641; 5 Pet. 207.

United States v. Lawton, 5 How. 10.   Cited, Mexican Grant, validity of floating grant, 3 Cal. 42.

United States v. LeBaron, 19 How. 73. Cited, Office, conditions precedent to right to, 10 Cal. 44, 47.

United States v. Lyman, 1 Mason, 482. Commented on, Taxation, when action of debt lies for duties imposed by statute, 16 Cal. 527; 5 Mason, 396.

United States v. Magill, 1 Wash. C. C. 463. Cited, Statutory Construction, meaning of words and phrases, 13 Cal. 518.

United States v. Maurice, 2 Brock. 96. Commented on, Office, definition of, 13 Cal. 155.

United States v. Mill's Heirs, 12 Pet. 215. Cited, Spanish Grant, conditions annexed, 3 Cal. 40.

United States v. Miranda, 16 Pet. 153. Cited, Mexican Grants, validity of floating grant, 3 Cal. 42; 10 How. 557.

United States v. More, 3 Cranch, 159. Cited, Appeal to U. S. Supreme Court in admiralty cases, 9 Cal. 736; 11 Wheat. 474, note; 9 How. 572; 14 How. 120.

United States v. Nye, 21 How. 410. Referred to, Mexican Title, when invalid, 16 Cal. 549; 1 Black, 37; 21 How. 414.

United States v. Pacheco, 20 How. 261. Commented on, Appeal, suspension of proceedings pending, 24 Cal. 584; 28 Cal. 91. Cited, Finality of judgment, 33 Cal. 478.

United States v. Peralta, 19 How. 343. Referred to, Evidence, documentary, of title, 24 Cal. 657. Commented on, Mexican Grant, title to confirmed grant, 39 Cal. 237, 246. Dictum disapproved, 13 Wall. 488.

United States v. Percheman, 7 Pet. 86. Cited, International Law, law of ceded territory, 1 Cal. 286; Id. 314; Id. 326. Approved, Title to, and rights of property protected under stipulations of treaty of session, 1 Cal. 326; 2 Cal. 46; 3 Cal. 38; 10 Cal. 619; 18 Cal. 22; 20 Cal. 421; 24 Cal. 660, 662; 9 How. 445; 11 How. 102. Cited, Mexican Grants, validity of pueblo grants, 15 Cal. 549, 553; 16 Cal. 459; presumptions as to official authority, 16 Cal. 227; 15 How. 7.

United States v. Perez, 9 Wheat. 579. Cited, Criminal Procedure, retrial on discharge of jury, 27 Cal. 399.

United States v. Peters, 5 Cranch, 115. Cited, Jurisdiction, concurrent, conclusiveness of proceedings, when jurisdiction attaches, 27 Cal. 170.

United States v. Potter, 6 McLean, 186. Cited, Indictment, disjunctive averments bad for uncertainty, 35 Cal. 509.

United States v. Railroad Bridge Co., 6 McLean, 517. Cited, State Sovereignty, right of eminent domain, 18 Cal. 252.

United States v. Reading, 18 How. 1. Cited, Mexican Grants, right of possession under, 13 Cal. 410. Commented on, what necessary to perfect title, 10 Cal. 617; 26 Cal. 628; confirmation of grant, 27 Cal. 168.

United States v. Reynes, 9 How. 127. Cited, Mexican Grant, validity of, 18 Cal. 29; 12 How. 51; 13 How. 9.

United States v. Rhodes, 7 Am. Law Reg. N. S. 233. Approved, Constitutionality of Statute, Civil Rights bill, 36 Cal. 667. Denied, dissenting opinion of Crockett, J., Id. 686.

United States v. Ritchie, 17 How. 533. Doubted, Mexican Grant, title under inchoate grant, 6 Cal. 269. Commented on, segregation and location of, 13 Cal. 418; proceedings in district court on confirmation of grant, 19 Cal. 573.

United States v. Robertson, 5 Pet. 650. Cited, Legal Tender, discharge of promise to pay money generally, 27 Cal. 161; 6 How. 120; Id. 329.

United States v. Roudenbush, 1 Bald. 517. Cited, Criminal Procedure, evidence of intoxication when admissible, 29 Cal. 683.

United States v. Schooner Peggy, 1 Cranch, 103. Cited, Decree, finality of, 33 Cal. 478; appeal from, effect of, Id. 479.

United States v. Sepulveda, 1 Wall. 104. Commented on, Mexican Grants, segregation and survey of, 25 Cal. 453; 43 Cal. 292.

United States v. Shoemaker, 2 McLean, 114. Cited, Criminal Procedure, retrial on discharge of jury, 27 Cal. 399; when discharge of jury equivalent to an acquittal, 38 Cal. 478.

United States v. Skiddy, 11 Pet. 75. Commented on, State Sovereignty, effect of temporary residence of slave, 2 Cal. 446.

United States Bank v. Smith, 11 Wheat. 172. Cited, Appeal, verdict can be reviewed only on appeal from order on new trial, 8 Cal. 109.

United States v. Sutherland, 19 How. 364. Approved, Mexican Grant, construction of, 10 Cal. 629.

United States v. Sutter, 21 How. 171. Referred to, Mexican Title, 16 Cal. 427; 21 How. 411.

United States v. Thompson, Gilpin, 614. Cited, Sureties, rights of, under contract, 11 Cal. 220.

United States v. Todd, 13 How. 52, note. Cited, Officers, judicial, excluded from other than judicial functions, 5 Cal. 22.

United States v. Vallejo, 1 Black, 555. Cited, Mexican Grant, right of preëmption on rejected grant, 37 Cal. 484.

United States v. Vaughn, 3 Bin. 394. Cited, Estoppel, binds only parties and privies, 11 Cal. 349.

United States v. Wiggins, 14 Pet. 334. Cited, Spanish Grant, performance of conditions essential, 3 Cal. 40; 6 Cal. 270. Commented on, Perfect titles not necessary to be submitted for confirmation, 24 Cal. 662.

United States v. Wood, 2 Gall. 361. Cited, Office, Federal officers, 13 Cal. 154.

United States v. Worrall, 2 Dall. 384. Cited, Judicial Decisions, rule of, on equal division of justices, 32 Cal. 633. Commented on, 1 Davies, 386.

United States v. Wright, 1 McLean, 512. Cited, Office, right of resignation, 6 Cal. 28. Commented on, 3 Nev. 571.

United States Bank v. Bank of Georgia, 10 Wheat. 347. Cited, Execution Sale, redemption by payment in Treasury notes, 26 Cal. 663.

United States Bank v. Dandridge, 12 Wheat. 70. Cited, Corporation, ratification of contract *ultra vires*, 33 Cal. 191, 192.

United States Bank v. Halstead, 10 Wheat. 51. Commented on, Judicial Decision, as to construction of local statutes, 4 Cal. 156; 1 How. 324; 2 How. 615; 6 How. 330.

United States Bank v. Schultz, 2 Ohio, 471. Commented on, Cloud on Title, equity, jurisdiction to enjoin sale, 15 Cal. 133.

Unwin v. Wolseley, 1 Term Rep. 678. Cited, Public Officers, not personally bound on official contracts, 15 Cal. 457.

Updegraff v. Trask, 18 Cal. 458. Cited, Estates of Deceased, title vests in heirs, 31 Cal. 604; when heir may maintain ejectment, 42 Cal. 464.

Upton v. Else, 12 Moore, 303. Cited, New Promise, pleadings in action on, 19 Cal. 482.

Upton v. S. R. B. Railway Co., 8 Cush. 600. Cited, Eminent Domain, compensation on condemnation, estimate of benefits, 31 Cal. 374.

Uridias v. Morrill, 22 Cal. 473. Disapproved, Constitutional Construction, distribution of powers of government, 34 Cal. 529, 531, 538.

Uridias v. Morrill, 25 Cal. 31. Cited, Landlord and Tenant, tenancy by sufferance how created, 28 Cal. 554; Pleading, inconsistent defenses, practice, 43 Cal. 269.

Utica Ins. Co. v. Lynch, 11 Paige, 520. Cited, Administrator, when chargeable with interest on estate funds, 42 Cal. 289.

Vaise v. Delaval, 1 Term Rep. 11. Cited, Verdict, affidavits of jurors not admissible to impeach, 25 Cal. 400.

Valencia v. Couch, 32 Cal. 339. Commented on, Forcible Entry and Detainer, complaint in action, 38 Cal. 419.

Valentine v. City of Boston, 22 Pick. 75. Cited, Dedication, what necessary to, 14 Cal. 649.

Valentine v. Foster, 1 Met. 522. Cited, New Promise, effect of, 19 Cal. 484.

Valentine v. Mahoney, 37 Cal. 389. Approved, Estoppel, when landlord bound by judgment against tenant, 38 Cal. 263.

Valentine v. Piper, 22 Pick. 89. Cited, Evidence, secondary, of execution of written instrument, 26 Cal. 409; proof of handwriting, Id. 412; 27 Cal. 310; Powers, authority of ex-sheriff to complete execution of process, 8 Cal. 407. Commented on, Authority to sell, what it includes, 17 Cal. 591.

Valentine v. Stewart, 15 Cal. 387. Approved, New Trial, amendment to statement allowed, 18 Cal. 204; grounds of motion to be set forth in statement, 25 Cal. 489.

Cited, Fraud, no remedy by action or defense can be based on fraud, 34 Cal. 90; agreement void in part is void in toto, 13 Flor. 568.

Valentine v. Teller, 1 Hop. Ch. 422. Cited, Writ of Assistance, when purchaser entitled to, 11 Cal. 193.

Vallejo v. Clark. See Leese v. Clark.

Vallejo v. Fay, 10 Cal. 377. Cited, Ejectment, joint judgment in, 18 Cal. 224.

Vallejo v. Green, 16 Cal. 160. Cited, Motion, service of notice of, essential, 41 Cal. 313.

Vallejo v. Randall, 5 Cal. 461. Disapproved, Place of Trial, change of, should be made by court of its own motion, 13 Cal. 324.

Vallett v. Parker, 6 Wend. 515. Cited, Negotiable Instruments, illegality of consideration does not render void, in hands of *bona fide* holder, 2 Cal. 67.

Van Alstine v. Wimple, 5 Cow. 164. Cited, Contract void in part is void in toto, 38 Cal. 110.

Van Alstyne v. Erwine, 11 N. Y. 331. Cited, Jurisdiction of Person, sufficiency of evidence of publication of summons, 31 Cal. 350.

Van Arsdale v. Krum, 9 Mo. 393. Cited, Attachment, equities in favor of most diligent creditor, 8 Cal. 573; irregularities which do not invalidate, 18 Cal. 155.

Van Buren v. Olmstead, 5 Paige, 10. Commented on, Deed as a Mortgage, parol proof of, 8 Cal. 429; 13 Cal. 129. Cited, 19 How. 300.

Van Buskirk v. Roy, 8 How. Pr. 425. Cited, Assignment by order drawn for money, rights of drawee, 12 Cal. 99.

Van Campen v. Snyder, 3 How. Miss. 66. Cited, Execution, directing levy in excess of judgment voidable, not void, 38 Cal. 380.

Vance v. Boynton, 8 Cal. 554. Cited, Sale and Delivery, sale when void as to creditors, 8 Cal. 517. Approved, 9 Cal. 273.

Vance v. Fore, 24 Cal. 435. Cited, Deed, description in, by reference to map, 30 Cal. 543; 38 Cal. 448. Approved, Construction of doubtful calls, 34 Cal. 341; 36 Cal. 125; Id. 617. Referred to, 41 Cal. 693.

Vance v. Olinger, 27 Cal. 358. Approved, Pleading, abatement, what must be shown on plea of another action pending, 32 Cal. 195; 36 Cal. 134.

Van Cleef v. Fleet, 15 John. 147. Cited, Fraud, vitiates sale of goods, title does not pass, 12 Cal. 462.

Van Cortlandt v. Kip, 1 Hill, 591. Reversed, 7 Hill, 346. Cited, Will, construction of codicil, 18 Cal. 302.

Van Cortland v. Underhill, 17 John. 405. Cited, Arbitration and Award, selection of umpire, 23 Cal. 367.

Vanderbilt v. Adams, 7 Cow. 349. Commented on, Legislature, power to delegate its authority, 33 Cal. 285.

Vanderbilt v. Mathis, 5 Duer, 307. Cited, Malicious Prosecution, what must be shown in action for, 29 Cal. 657.

Vanderhein v. Mallory, 22 Wend. 526. Cited, Married Woman, rights as to her separate estate, 7 Cal. 270.

Vanderheyden v. Mallory, 1 N. Y. 472. Cited, Married Woman, separate property of, for what debts liable, 15 Cal. 312.

Vanderheyden v. Young, 11 John. 157. Cited, State Sovereignty, creation of State debts, 27 Cal. 223.

Vanderslice v. Hanks. See Clarkson *v.* Hanks.

Van Deusen v. Hayward, 17 Wend. 67. Commented on, Official Bond, when void, 7 Cal. 441; sufficiency of appeal bonds, 13 Cal. 509.

Van Doren v. Mayor of N. Y., 9 Paige, 388. Cited, Cloud on Title, injunction will not lie to restrain enforcement of tax, 2 Cal. 469; when equity will entertain jurisdiction, 10 Cal. 576; 15 Cal. 134.

Vandyke v. Herman, 3 Cal. 295. Approved, Judicial Sale, 9 Cal. 413; priority of lien of purchaser, Id. 118.

Van Eps v. City of Schenectady, 12 John. 436. Cited, Covenant, "good and sufficient deed" construed, 10 Cal. 322.

Van Eps v. Dillaye, 6 Barb. 244. Cited, Debt, payment by note, effect of, 12 Cal. 323.

Van Epps v. Van Deusen, 4 Paige, 74. Cited, in dissenting opinion of Sprague, J., Alimony inseparable from divorce, 38 Cal. 278.

Van Etten v. Hurst, 6 Hill, 311. Cited, Pleading, justification for seizure must be specially pleaded, 10 Cal. 304.

Van Etten v. Jilson, 6 Cal. 19. Cited, Jurisdiction of justice's court as to mining claims, 6 Cal. 414; Id. 449; 7 Cal. 105; test of jurisdiction, 22 Cal. 468; 1 Nev. 141; no presumptions in favor of, 12 Cal. 286.

Van Gorden v. Jackson, 5 John. 441. Cited, Boundaries, river as boundary line, 25 Cal. 144.

Vanhook v. Barnett, 4 Dev. 268. Cited, Deed, delivery a question of fact, 5 Cal. 318.

Van Horne v. Crain, 1 Paige, 455. Cited, Covenant, in lease, what assignable, 9 Cal. 677.

Van Horne v. Everson, 13 Barb. 532. Cited, Parties, defendants, construction of statute, 9 Cal. 270.

Van Horne v. Fonda, 5 Johns. Ch. 388. Cited, Trust and Trustee, implied trust, when it arises, 30 Cal. 594; trustee can gain no advantage to prejudice of *cestui que trust,* 36 Cal. 432. Approved, Tenant in Common, purchase of outstanding title by, 33 Cal. 43; 2 Black, 618.

Van Horne v. Petrie, 2 Caines, 213. Cited, Costs, when allowed in action, 6 Cal. 286.

Vanhorne's Lessee v. Dorrance, 2 Dall. 309. Cited, Conveyance, on conditions precedent, construction of, 10 Cal. 108. Approved, Constitution of State, how construed, 26 Cal. 182.

Van Husan v. Kanouse, 13 Mich. 313. Questioned, Mortgage, payment or tender after law day as a discharge, 37 Cal. 226.

Van Keuren v. Parmelee, 2 N. Y. 530. Cited, Evidence, admissions of partner after dissolution not sufficient to charge co-partner, 23 Cal. 103.

Van Maren v. Johnson, 15 Cal. 308. Cited, Husband and Wife, common property liable for ante-nuptial debts, 17 Cal. 537; 35 Cal. 215; interest of wife in community property, 39 Cal. 164. Approved, Parties, when wife may sue alone, 19 Cal. 129; husband may be joined, 32 Cal. 90. Cited, Pleading, supplemental answer, 27 Cal. 247; 30 Cal. 474.

Van Ostrand v. Reed, 1 Wend. 424. Commented on, Warranty, in contract of sale, 24 Cal. 464.

Van Pelt v. Littler, 14 Cal. 194. Cited, Appeal, objections to verdict which cannot be made on appeal, 41 Cal. 519; New Trial, insufficient certificate of settlement of statement, 7 Nev. 323; Trespass, of officer, liability on official bond, 17 Gratt. 131.

Van Pelt v. McGraw, 4 N. Y. 110. Cited, Mortgage, right of action in mortgagee for injuries impairing security, 24 Cal. 473.

Van Rensselaer v. Clark, 17 Wend. 25. Cited, Conveyance, notice to agent as notice to principal, 41 Cal. 50.

Van Rensselaer v. Jewett, 2 N. Y. 147. Cited, Lease, demand of rent necessary to create forfeiture, 25 Cal. 392.

Van Rensselaer v. Kearney, 11 How. 297. Commented on, Conveyance, what estate passes by, 14 Cal. 629.

Van Rensselaer v. Kidd, 4 Barb. 17. Cited, Injunction, will not lie to restrain collection of tax, 2 Cal. 469.

Van Rensselaer v. Sheriff of Albany, 1 Cow. 501. Cited, Judicial Sale, lien of purchaser, 9 Cal. 412; Statutory Construction, remedial statutes to be liberally construed, 4 Cal. 137; effect of repeal, 15 Cal. 523.

Van Rensselaer v. Sheriff of Onondago Co., 1 Cow. 443. Cited, Judicial Sale, lien of purchaser, 9 Cal. 412. Explained, 31 Cal. 300.

Van Rensselaer v. Smith, 27 Barb. 140. Cited, Common Carriers, construction of contract of, 27 Cal. 38.

Van Valkenburg v. McCloud, 21 Cal. 330. Cited, State Lands, vested interest in school lands, 25 Cal. 255.

Van Waggoner v. McEwen, 1 Green Ch. 412. Cited, Conveyance, after-acquired title inures to benefit of mortgagee, 14 Cal. 634.

Vanwinkle v. Curtiss, 2 Green Ch. 422. Cited, Injunction, when will issue to restrain trespass, 27 Cal. 646.

Van Winkle v. Hinckle, 21 Cal. 342. Commented on, Quieting Title, possession essential to maintenance of action, 25 Cal. 438; averment of possession material, 34 Cal. 559.

Van Wormer v. Mayor, etc., of Albany, 15 Wend. 263. Commented on, Legislature, power to delegate its authority, 33 Cal. 286.

Van Wyok v. Alliger, 6 Barb. 511. Cited, Mortgage, rights of mortgagor in possession, 27 Cal. 436.

Van Wyck v. Seward, 18 Wend. 375. Commented on, Parent and Child, settlement on child when void, 8 Cal. 127, 128.

Van Wyck v. Wright, 18 Wend. 157. Cited, Boundaries, acquiescence in division line, 25 Cal. 627; Conveyances, construction of, facts to be considered, 36 Cal. 618.

Vanzant v. Jones, 3 Dana, 464. Cited, New Trial, when granted for excessive damages, 24 Cal. 517.

Vardeman v. Lawson, 17 Tex. 10. Cited, Vendor and Vendee, statute does not run against vendee in possession, 40 Cal. 572.

Varick v. Briggs, 6 Paige, 330; S. C. 22 Wend. 543. Cited, Statutory Construction, principles of judicial determination, 9 Cal. 512. Commented on, Legislature, power of, in passage of recording acts, 7 Cal. 488, 496.

Varick v. Edwards, 11 Paige, 290. Reversed, 5 Denio, 664. Cited, Conveyance without Warranty, what estate passes by, 14 Cal. 628; Vendor and Vendee, vendee in possession under contract to convey, 40 Cal. 570.

Varick v. Smith, 5 Paige, 137. Cited, Eminent Domain, exercise of power through corporations, 18 Cal. 251; supremacy of legislative power, 41 Cal. 169; 3 C. E. Green, 67.

Varick v. Tallman, 3 Barb. 113. Cited, Statutes, divesting rights, to be strictly pursued, 21 Cal. 300.

Varnum v. Abbot, 12 Mass. 474. Cited, Tenant in Common, grantee of, takes subject to contingency of partition, 15 Cal. 369; 35 Cal. 595; sale cannot be made to prejudice of co-tenant, Id. 588.

Vassault v. Austin, 32 Cal. 597. Approved, Pleading, denials on information and belief, when insufficient, 33 Cal. 211; 36 Cal. 234; 38 Cal. 163; 43 Cal. 397. Referred to, 40 Cal. 75.

Vassault v. Seitz, 31 Cal. 225. Cited, Pleading, replication on plea of statute of limitations, 34 Cal. 390; manner of pleading statute, 36 Cal. 632.

Vattier v. Hinde, 7 Pet. 252. Cited, Conveyance, insufficient to pass legal title, 10 Cal. 368.

Vaughn v. Barret, 5 Vt. 333. Cited, Probate Procedure, limitation of jurisdiction, 12 Cal. 190. Commented on, 32 Conn. 321.

Vaughn v. Ely, 4 Barb. 159. Cited, Execution, right of redemption from sale, 9 Cal. 415; right of purchaser pending redemption, 26 Cal. 661.

Vaughn v. English, 8 Cal. 39. Cited, Office, clerks of departments as public officers, 6 Wall. 393.

Veazie v. Parker, 23 Me. 171. Cited, Conveyance, possession of tenant as notice, 21 Cal. 628.

Vedder v. Alkenbrack, 6 Barb. 327. Cited, Statutory Construction, statutes affecting remedies, 4 Cal. 160.

Veeder v. Guppy, 3 Wis. 522. Cited, State Lands, title under State patent, 16 Cal. 320.

Venable v. Beauchamp, 3 Dana, 321. Cited, Trust and Trustee, implied trust, when it arises, 30 Cal. 594.

Venable v. McDonald, 4 Dana, 337. Cited, Tenant at Will, who is, 24 Cal. 145.

Vermilyea, Ex parte, 6 Cow. 555. Disapproved, Juror and Jury, disqualification for bias, 1 Cal. 384; Edm. Sel. Cas. 91.

Vermule v. Bigler, 5 Cal. 23. Cited, Constitutional Construction, powers of legislature, 22 Cal. 308. See People v. Bigler.

Vermule v. Shaw, 4 Cal. 214. Cited, Reference, report of referee when to be filed, 22 Cal. 473.

Vernon v. Alsop, T. Raym. 68. Cited, Appeal Bond, validity of, 8 Cal. 551.

Vernon v. Bethell, 2 Eden, 113. Cited, Redemption, right of, cannot be waived, 13 Cal. 125.

Vernon v. Smith, 5 Barn. & Ald. 1. Commented on, Covenants, in lease, construed, 9 Cal. 676.

Vernon Society v. Hills, 6 Cow. 23. Cited, Elections, notice of special election essential, 11 Cal. 57.

Verplanck v. Mercantile Ins. Co., 1 Edw. Ch. 84. Cited, Corporations, equity cannot restrain operations of, 16 Cal. 150.

Verplank v. Sterry, 12 John. 536. Cited, Deed, parol evidence of consideration clause, 6 Cal. 137.

Vestal v. Burditt, 6 Blackf. 555. Cited, Appeal, does not lie from orders entered on consent, 6 Cal. 666.

Vibbard v. Johnson, 19 John. 77. Commented on, Warranty, on sale of chattels, 41 Cal. 116.

Vice v. Lady Anson, 7 Barn. & C. 409. Doubted, Mining Partnership, powers and liabilities of partners, 23 Cal. 203.

Vick v. Vicksburg, 1 How. Miss. 420. Commented on, Stare Decisis, effect of local adjudications, 15 Cal. 604; 3 How. 476; Id. 480. Cited, Dedication to Public Use, how may be effected, 22 Cal. 489.

Vidal v. Girard's Exrs., 2 How. 191. Cited, Corporation, authority of, under charter, not subject to collateral inquiry, 22 Cal. 630; 6 How. 322. Commented on, 7 Wall. 14.

Viele v. Hoag, 24 Vt. 46. Cited, Sureties, when not discharged by contract giving extension, 10 Cal. 426.

Vilhac v. Biven, 28 Cal. 409. Cited, New Trial, striking out statement on, 32 Cal. 326; specifications in statement essential, 5 Nev. 26; Appeal, from order on new trial, when findings not reviewable, 38 Cal. 280.

Villars' Heirs v. Kennedy, 5 La. An. 725. Commented on, Cities and Towns, lands of, 15 Cal. 594.

Vincent, Ex parte, 26 Ala. 145. Cited, Statutory Construction, of words and phrases, 13 Cal. 518.

Vincent v. Huff's Lessee, 4 Serg. & R. 297. Cited, Witness, competency of, practice, 26 Cal. 132.

Vines v. Whitten, 4 Cal. 230. Disapproved, Evidence, construction of surveyor's act, 31 Cal. 145.

Vinton v. Crowe, 4 Cal. 309. Affirmed on principle of *stare decisis*, Assignment, of note overdue, to what equities not subject, 39 Cal. 60.

Vischer v. Yates, 11 John. 29. Approved, Wagers, on elections, void, 37 Cal. 672; on disaffirmance, money staked may be recovered, 11 Cal. 348, 350; 37 Cal. 673, 675; 6 Yerg. 292; 23 Ark. 224.

Viser v. Bertrand, 14 Ark. 267. Cited, Contract, contravening public policy, no remedy on, 15 Cal. 405.

Visher v. Webster, 8 Cal. 109. Commented on, Negotiable Instruments, holder may fill blank with rate of interest, 22 Mich. 430.

Visher v. Webster, 13 Cal. 58. Approved, Statute of Frauds, what sufficient change of possession under, 17 Cal. 545; sale of growing crops not within, 37 Cal. 638; Evidence, declarations of vendor when not admissible to impeach sale, 36 Cal. 207. Cited, Costs, follow the judgment as a matter of right, 29 Cal. 282.

Visscher v. Hudson Riv. R. R. Co., 15 Barb. 37. Cited, Special cases, proceedings on condemnation of land, 24 Cal. 433; review of, on appeal, Id. 454.

Von Schmidt v. Huntington, 1 Cal. 55. Approved, Equity, verity of pleadings, 1 Cal. 142; Mexican Law, customs and proof of, 6 Cal. 160; 10 Cal. 477; 31 Cal. 522; Mining Claims, customs to be strictly construed against claim of forfeiture, 23 Cal. 248; what must be shown to establish a forfeiture, 25 Cal. 237.

Vooght v. Winch, 2 Barn. & Ald. 662. Cited, Judgment, as a bar in subsequent action, 15 Cal. 182; 15 Ill. 460.

Voorhees v. Bank of U. S., 10 Pet. 449. Cited, Constitutionality of Statute, power of judiciary to determine, 9 Cal. 512; Probate Proceedings, not subject to collateral attack, 22 Cal. 63. Approved, judgment, collateral attack on, 34 Cal. 428; 2 How. 343; 6 How. 40; 8 How. 412; 12 How. 386; 14 How. 588; 24 How. 203.

Voorhees v. De Meyer, 2 Barb. 37. Cited, Contracts, construction of clause of forfeiture, 40 Cal. 13.

Voorhis v. Childs' Exr., 17 N. Y. 354. Cited, Probate Procedure, order of payment of debt, 26 Cal. 67.

Voorhis v. Freeman, 2 Watts & S. 116. Commented on, Fixtures, what constitute, 14 Cal. 67, 68; 1 Ohio St. 537.

Votan v. Reese, 20 Cal. 89. Cited, Appeal, jurisdiction as governed by "amount in dispute," 23 Cal. 202; costs no part of "amount in dispute," 27 Cal. 107. Explained and distinguished, 23 Cal. 286. Construed, 41 Cal. 442. Dictum disapproved as to measurement of amount, on appeal by plaintiff, 34 Cal. 33. Cited, Orders on motion to retax costs reviewable only on appeal from judgment, 33 Cal. 678. Qualified, if made after entry of judgment, order appealable, 41 Cal. 442.

Vreeland v. Blunt, 6 Barb. 182. Cited, Assignment, by order drawn on special fund, 8 Cal. 105.

Vreeland v. Bruen, 1 Zab. 222. Cited, Attachment, lien acquired by, 29 Cal. 372, 375.

Vreeland v. Loubat, 1 Green Ch. 104. Cited, Decree void for want of jurisdiction, 16 Cal. 564.

Vrooman v. Phelps, 2 John. 177. Cited, Seal imports consideration, 10 Cal. 463.

Waddington's Case, 2 East's P. C. 513. Denied, Indictment, for burglary, statement of hour, 35 Cal. 117.

Wade v. American C. Society, 7 Smedes & M. 663. Cited, Corporations, authority under charter not subject to collateral inquiry, 22 Cal. 630.

Wade v. Killough, 3 Stewt. & P. 431. Cited, Vendor and Vendee, vendee in possession cannot resist payment, 5 Cal. 265.

Wade v. Lindsey, 6 Met. 407. Cited, Title, by adverse possession, continuity of possession required, 37 Cal. 354.

Wade v. Thayer, 40 Cal. 578. Approved, Principal and Agent, measure of liability of principal for acts of agent, 40 Cal. 662.

Wade v. Thurman, 2 Bibb, 583. Commented on, Fraudulent representations as to title, action by vendee, 9 Cal. 227. Doubted, 1 N. Y. 314.

Wadleigh v. Veazie, 3 Sum. 165. Cited, Pleading, when another action pending may be pleaded, 29 Cal. 314; 32 Cal. 630.

Wadlington v. Gary, 7 Smedes & M. 522. Cited, Surety on specialty, when discharged by agreement for extension, 10 Cal. 426.

Wadsworth v. Havens, 3 Wend. 411. Cited, Fraudulent Conveyance, what constitutes proof of fraud, 13 Cal. 72.

Wadsworth v. Thomas, 7 Barb. 445. Cited, Statutory Construction, not to be retrospective, 4 Cal. 138.

Wagenblast v. Washburn, 12 Cal. 208. Cited, Mistake, in contract, power of court of equity to correct, 23 Cal. 124.

Wager v. Troy Union R. R., 25 N. Y. 526. Cited, Condemnation of Land, for railroads, conditions precedent, 32 Cal. 510.

Wagstaff v. Wagstaff, 2 P. Wms. 258. Commented on, Stare Decisis, as a rule of property, 15 Cal. 621.

Wagy v. Lane, 4 Ill. 237. Cited, Evidence, burden of proof as to authority to contract, 1 Cal. 340.

Wagman v. Hoag, 14 Barb. 232. Cited, Surety, on note, when discharged by delay of creditor, 10 Cal. 425; when not discharged, Id. 426.

40

Waite v. Barry, 12 Wend. 377. Cited, Arbitration and Award, what essential to validity of award, 37 Cal. 201.

Waite, Case of, 1 Leach Cr. Cas. 36. Cited, Criminal Procedure, rights of prisoner, 42 Cal. 167.

Wakefield v. Martin, 3 Mass. 558. Cited, Insurance, assignment of policy, 38 Cal. 545.

Wakely v. Hart, 6 Bin. 316. Denied, Witness, competency of, 6 Cal. 194.

Wakeman v. Lyon, 9 Wend. 241. Commented on, Exceptions, to instructions, when to be taken, 26 Cal. 266.

Wakker, Matter of, 3 Barb. 162. Approved, Constitutional Construction, title of act, what to embrace, 2 Cal. 299.

Walden v. Murdock, 23 Cal. 540. Distinguished, Appeal, dismissal of, if taken too late, 42 Cal. 31.

Waldman v. Broder, 10 Cal. 378. Cited, Execution, property held jointly may be levied on and interest of debtor be sold, 17 Cal. 547.

Waldo v. Chicago St. P. & F. Du L. R. R. Co., 14 Wis. 580. Cited, Corporations, authority of railroad how restricted, 40, Cal. 88.

Waldron v. Marsh, 5 Cal. 119. Cited, Injunction, question of insolvency when important, 23 Cal. 85; 13 Flor. 384.

Waldron v. McCarty, 3 John. 471. Cited, Covenant, no breach of, till eviction, 2 Cal. 44; 33 Cal. 306; 2 Wheat. 62. Qualified, 39 Cal. 364, 365. Commented on, 4 Geo. 607. Denied, 11 N. H. 83; 12 Penn. St. 374.

Waldron v. Rensselaer & S. R. R. Co., 8 Barb. 390. Cited, Negligence, of railroad, resulting in injury to cattle, 18 Cal. 355.

Walker v. Blackwell, 1 Wend. 557. Cited, Commerce, vessels in coasting trade, 10 Cal. 507.

Walker, Estate of, 3 Rawle, 230. Cited, Probate Procedure, claim of wages by son of decedent, 8 Cal. 125. Commented on, Will, construction of special bequest, 31 Cal. 602.

Walker v. Fort, 3 La. O. S. 538. Cited, Conveyance, construction of, 26 Cal. 469.

Walker v. Hauss-Hijo, 1 Cal. 183. Cited, Mechanic's Lien, statute to be strictly complied with, 29 Cal. 286.

Walker v. Jeffreys, 1 Hare, 341; S. C. 23 Eng. Ch. 348. Cited, Contract of Conveyance, time when of essence of, 10 Cal. 327; acquiescence presumed from lapse of time, 22 Cal. 592.

Walker v. Kendall, Hardin, 404. Cited, Executors, under power of sale in will, 32 Cal. 440.

Walker v. Roberts, 4 Rich. 591. Cited, Attachment, when void, 13 Cal. 441.

Walker v. Sedgwick, 5 Cal. 192. Approved, Trial, party not entitled to jury in equity case, 8 Cal. 286. Distinguished, 15 Cal. 380, 383. Approved, Findings not necessary in equity cases, 18 Cal. 448; but practice changed by statute, Id. Doubted, 15 Cal. 382.

Walker v. Sedgwick, 8 Cal. 398. Cited, Set-off, when will not be enforced in equity, 23 Cal. 627.

Walker v. Sherman, 20 Wend. 636. Commented on, Fixtures, what constitute, 14 Cal. 65, 72; 4 Met. Ky. 361; 2 Watts & S. 118.

Walker v. Swartwout, 12 John. 444. Cited, Officers, public officers not personally liable on official contracts, 1 Cal. 392.

Walker v. Turner, 9 Wheat. 541. Cited, Jurisdiction, of person, sufficiency of evidence of publication of summons, 31 Cal. 349.

Walker v. Walker, 3 Kelly, Geo. 302. Cited, Injunction, amendment may be made without prejudice to injunction, 33 Cal. 502.

Walker v. Woods, 15 Cal. 66. Disapproved, Attachment, what necessary to justify levy, 34 Cal. 351.

Wall v. Langlands, 14 East, 370. Cited, Statutory Construction, property defined, 9 Cal. 142.

Wall Street, Matter of, 17 Barb. 617. Cited, Statutory Construction, finality of judgment in proceedings for street improvements, 42 Cal. 56.

Wallace Admr. v. Cook, 5 Esp. 117. Cited, Principal and Agent, termination of authority on death of principal, 15 Cal. 18.

Wallace v. Eldridge, 27 Cal. 498. Approved, Judgment, entry by clerk merely ministerial, 28 Cal. 214; Id. 652; 32 Cal. 636; 3 Or. 252; when judgment erroneous and when void, 30 Cal. 535.

Wallace v. McConnell, 13 Pet. 136.   Cited, Negotiable Instruments, demand at place of payment not of essence of contract, 11 Cal. 324.   Commented on, 13 Ired. 77.

Wallace v. Moody, 26 Cal. 387. ` Cited, Evidence, certified copies of deeds, 27 Cal. 245.

Wallace v. San Jose, 29 Cal. 180.   Commented on, Municipal Corporation, not liable on contract *ultra vires*, 33 Cal. 198.   Distinguished, Id. 201.

Wallen v. Huff, 3 Sneed, 82.   Cited, Ejectment, who bound by judgment in, 22 Cal. 207.

Waller v. Harris, 20 Wend. 561.   Cited, Redemption, statutory right to be strictly pursued, 14 Cal. 57.

Walling v. Miller, 15 Cal. 38.   Cited, Attachment, when garnishment does not give preference over assignees, 22 Ohio St. 404.

Wallingsford v. Wallingsford, 6 Har. & J. 485.   Cited, in dissenting opinion of Sprague, J., Alimony, inseparable from divorce, 38 Cal. 278.

Wallis v. Loubat, 2 Denio, 607.   Cited, Attorney and Counsel, official character, 22 Cal. 315.

Walls v. Preston, 25 Cal. 59.   Cited, Appeal, review confined to specification of grounds for new trial, 26 Cal. 524; order affirmed on failure to specify grounds, 5 Nev. 262.

Wallworth v. Holt, 4 Mylne & C. 635.   Cited, Equity, Jurisdiction, when it attaches, 30 Cal. 297.

Walmsley v. Booth, 3 Barnardiston Ch. 478.   Cited, Attorney and Counsel, official character of, 22 Cal. 315.

Walmsley v. Child, 1 Ves. Sr. 345.   Cited, Lost Note, indemnity in action, 28 Cal. 566.

Waln's Assignee v. Bank of N. A., 8 Serg. & R. 73.   Cited, Corporation, lien on unpaid stock, 9 Cal. 115.

Walsh v. Hill, 38 Cal. 481; S. C. 41 Cal. 571.   Approved, Lands, constructive possession under deed, modification of sale, 38 Cal. 674.   Commented on, 39 Cal. 280.

Walsh v. Matthews, 29 Cal. 123.   Approved, Street Assessment, objections to acceptance of work waived by failure to appeal to board, 29 Cal. 131; assessment for street work not taxation, 40 Cal. 514.

Walsh v. Rutgers F. Ins. Co., 13 Abb. Pr. 39.   Cited, Foreclosure, rights of subsequent mortgagee, 40 Cal. 237.

Walsh v. Whitcomb, 2 Esp. 565. Cited, Trust and Trustee, trust created by transfer of property for benefit of creditors, 39 Cal. 287.

Walter v. Lockwood, 23 Barb. 228. Cited, Ejectment, sufficiency of complaint, 16 Cal. 245.

Walter v. Ross, 2 Wash. C. C. 283. Commented on, Factor, lien of, 1 Cal. 80.

Walters v. Junkins, 16 Serg. & R. 414. Cited, Verdict, polling jury in civil cases, 20 Cal. 71.

Waltham v. Carson, 10 Cal. 178. Cited, Trial, jury waived by failure to appear, 16 Cal. 433.

Walton v. Cronly's Admr., 14 Wend. 63. Cited, Mortgage, mortgagee out of possession not liable for rents, 15 Cal. 293; parol evidence admissible to prove deed as a mortgage, 36 Cal. 44, 65; 19 How. 300. Denied, 4 Zab. 496; 3 Mich. 223.

Walton v. Maguire, 17 Cal. 92. Cited, Appeal, error or abuse of discretion must affirmatively appear, 33 Cal. 525.

Walton v. Minturn, 2 Cal. 362. Cited, Pleading, new matter must be specially set up in answer, 10 Cal. 30.

Walton v. Walton, 7 Johns. Ch. 258. Cited, Will, construction of, 31 Cal. 603, 608; 14 How. 396.

Warburton v. London & B. R. R. Co., 2 Beav. 254. Cited, Injunction, amendment to complaint without prejudice to injunction, 33 Cal. 502.

Warburton v. Mattox, Morris, Iowa, 369. Cited, Estoppel, of mortgagor, 31 Cal. 457.

Ward v. Arredondo, 1 Paine, 410. Cited, Action, removal of cause to Federal court, 28 Cal. 99. Commented on, Specific Performance, jurisdiction, when it attaches, 38 Cal. 200.

Ward v. Barber, 1 E. D. Smith, 423. Cited, Attorney and Counsel, unauthorized appearance of, remedy of client, 30 Cal. 447.

Ward v. Bartholomew, 6 Pick. 410. Cited, Title, by adverse possession, continuity of possession requisite, 37 Cal. 354.

Ward v. Evans, 2 Ld. Ray. 928. Cited, Debtor and Creditor, payment by note, 12 Cal. 322.

Ward v. Henry, 5 Conn. 596. Cited, Sureties, enforcement of contribution between co-sureties, 20 Cal. 136.

Ward v. Johnson, 13 Mass. 148. Cited, Judgment, several on joint demand as a bar, 6 Cal. 181; 13 Cal. 33; Sureties, right to contribution, 11 Cal. 220. Commented on, 2 Greenl. 193; 2 Sum. 438.

Ward v. Mulford, 32 Cal. 365. Referred to, Patent, lands embraced in, 37 Cal. 435.

Ward v. People, 6 Hill, 144. Cited, Witness, privilege of, practice, 35 Cal. 96.

Ward v. State, 8 Blackf. 101. Cited, Evidence, dying declarations, 35 Cal. 52.

Ward v. Turner, 1 Lead. Cas. in Equity, 666; 2 Ves. Sr. 431. Cited, Mortgage, equitable mortgage how created, 32 Cal. 652.

Ward v. Whitney, 3 Sand. 399. Affirmed, 8 N. Y. 442. Cited, Contract, to give note, demand not necessary to action on, 26 Cal. 22; Sureties, justification no part of contract, 38 Cal. 603.

Wardell v. Fosdick, 13 John. 325. Commented on, Fraudulent representations as to title, when action lies, 9 Cal. 226.

Wardell v. Howell, 9 Wend. 170. Commented on, Negotiable Instruments, pledged as collateral security, 3 Cal. 164.

Warden v. Mendocino Co., 32 Cal. 655. Disapproved, Practice, exceptions, to be presented in a statement, 33 Cal. 556.

Wardrobe v. California Stage Co., 7 Cal. 118. Cited, Negligence, exemplary damages when allowed, 48 N. H. 320. Commented on, 57 Me. 256.

Ware v. Barker, 49 Me. 358. Statute distinguished, Execution, validity of purchaser's title on what depends, 38 Cal. 655.

Ware v. Gay, 11 Pick. 106. Cited, Common Carrier, liability for negligence resulting in injury, 28 Cal. 628.

Warfield, Matter of, 22 Cal. 51. Cited, Probate, judgments not subject to collateral attack, 22 Cal. 73. Distinguished, 33 Cal. 53.

Waring v. Clarke, 5 How. 461. Construed, Jurisdiction, in admiralty, 9 Cal. 732.

Waring v. Crow, 11 Cal. 366. Approved, Mining Claims, customs to be strictly construed against claim of for- feiture, 23 Cal. 248; what insufficient to establish a forfeiture, 25 Cal. 239; Abandonment, intention alone to govern, 36 Cal. 338; mining partners as tenants in common, 1 Nev. 206.

Waring v. Robinson, 1 Hoff. Ch. 524. Commented on, Insolvency, rights of creditors, 7 Cal. 198. Distinguished, Priority of claims of firm creditors, 8 Cal. 157. Commented on, Proceedings by creditors to obtain a preference, 9 Cal. 28.

Waring v. Smyth, 2 Barb. Ch. 135. Commented on, Mortgage, estate of mortgagor, 9 Cal. 409; 35 Cal. 414.

Warmstrey v. Lady Tanfield, 2 Lead. Cas. in Eq. 532; 1 Ch. 29. Cited, Assignment, equitable, of choses in action, 13 Cal. 123.

Warner v. Barker, 3 Wend. 400. Cited, Set-off, when demands may be, 19 Cal. 658; 41 Cal. 59.

Warner v. Beers, 23 Wend. 132. Commented on, Statute, impeachment of, 30 Cal. 259, 263. Doubted, 1 Denio, 18; 2 Denio, 392.

Warner v. Carlton, 22 Ill. 424. Commented on, Statute of Frauds, actual and continued change of possession, 26 Cal. 326.

Warner v. Hall, 1 Cal. 90. Approved, Appeal, jurisdiction by certiorari, 1 Cal. 92.

Warner v. Holman, 24 Cal. 228. Commented on, Appeal, dismissal for premature service of notice, 24 Cal. 96. Cited, Service, when to be made, 26 Cal. 263; Judgment, when reversed for defective findings, 29 Cal. 142; objections which cannot be raised on appeal, 4 Nev. 336.

Warner v. People, 2 Denio, 272. Cited, Office, legislative power over fees of, 22 Cal. 319.

Warner v. Martin, 11 How. 228. Cited, Factor, cannot pledge, 11 Cal. 402; liability of pledgee, 19 Cal. 72.

Warner v. Robinson, 1 Root, 194. Cited, Verdict, validity of, 25 Cal. 400.

Warner v. The Uncle Sam, 9 Cal. 697. Approved, Jurisdiction, in admiralty cases, 13 Cal. 372.

Warner v. Wilson, 4 Cal. 310. Cited, Pleading, objection to defect of parties waived by failure to demur, 10 Cal. 170; Probate Proceedings, not subject to collateral attack, 18 Cal. 505. Dictum disapproved, Evidence, admission of records of probate court, 6 Cal. 654.

Warren v. Allnutt, 12 La. 454. Cited, Negotiable Instruments, demand at place of payment not of essence of contract, 11 Cal. 324.

Warren v. Charlestown, 2 Gray, 84. Cited, Statute, when unconstitutional, 22 Cal. 386. Commented on, Provisions unconstitutional make act void, 19 Cal. 530; 22 Cal. 390; 24 Cal. 547. Distinguished, 7 Cal. 104.

Warren v. Eddy, 13 Abb. Pr. 30. Cited, Judgment, entry of, on decease of party, 35 Cal. 467.

Warren v. Jacksonville, 15 Ill. 241. Commented on, Dedication of Highway, assent of owner necessary, 14 Cal. 648.

Warwick v. Richardson, 10 Mees. & W. 284. Commented on, Indemnity, to sheriff, conditions precedent to action on bond, 32 Cal. 25.

Washburn v. Alden, 5 Cal. 463. Approved, Witness, incompetency from interest of defaulting defendant, 22 Cal. 574.

Washburn v. Bank of Bellows Falls, 19 Vt. 278. Cited, Partnership, leviable interest of debtor partner, 25 Cal. 104; Equity, jurisdiction on conflict between individual and firm creditors, 13 Cal. 634.

Washburn v. Dewy, 17 Vt. 92. Cited, Specific Performance, when will be decreed, 25 Cal. 281.

Washburn v. Washburn, 9 Cal. 475. Cited, Divorce, for failure to support, when action will fail, 42 Cal. 446.

Washington v. Page, 4 Cal. 388. Commented on, Constitutional Construction, provision directory, 6 Cal. 504. Cited, 40 Miss. 295; 6 Kan. 335. Approved, 9 Cal. 523; 10 Cal. 316. Disapproved as to rule of construction, 6 Cal. 504.

Washington v. Planters' Bank, 1 How. Miss. 230. Cited, Negotiable Instruments, demand at place of payment not of essence of contract, 11 Cal. 324.

Washington Bank v. Lewis, 22 Pick. 24. Construed, Negotiable Instruments, pledged as collateral, 3 Cal. 164.

Washington B. Co. v. Stewart, 3 How. 413. Approved, Law of the case, 2 Cal. 377; 6 Cal. 688; 15 Cal. 82, 83; 20 Cal. 417; 6 How. 38.

Waterloo v. Aub. & R. R. Co., 3 Hill, 569. Cited, Railroad, street railroad as real property, 32 Cal. 510.

Waterman v. Smith, 13 Cal. 373. Cited, Mexican Grants, survey of, by government, essential to perfect title, 13 Cal. 486; 19 Cal. 270; 20 Cal. 228; Survey, a political right, 38 Cal. 66, 67. Construed, 18 Cal. 202. Disapproved, as to supervision and control of surveys, 20 Cal. 229. Cited, Title under grant before survey and segregation, 24 Cal. 580; 38 Cal. 67; 1 Saw. 572; confirmed survey takes effect by relation, 28 Cal. 657; 29 Cal. 107; 34 Cal. 253; 35 Cal. 88; 1 Saw. 580; confirmation of grant conclusive, 14 Cal. 362; 16 Cal. 124; 24 Cal. 669; 1 Saw. 565; Patent conclusive, 15 Cal. 366; 18 Cal. 572; 22 Cal. 111; 26 Cal. 626, 627; of what conclusive, 33 Cal. 456; "third parties," who are, 1 Saw. 569.

Waters v. Gilbert, 2 Cush. 27. Cited, Exception to rulings, to be specific, 10 Cal. 268; 12 Cal. 245. Commented on, 18 Cal. 324.

Waters v. Howard, 1 Md. Ch. Dec. 112. Cited, Specific Performance, of contract, for chattel, 25 Cal. 571.

Waters v. Moss, 12 Cal. 535. Cited, Common Law, how far adopted, 38 Cal. 581; Negligence, liability of railroad company for injury to cattle, 5 Kan. 187.

Waters v. Simpson, 7 Ill. 570. Cited, Sureties on specialty, when discharged by agreement for extension, 10 Cal. 426.

Waters v. Travis, 9 John. 465. Cited, Specific Performance, limitation of action, 40 Cal. 13.

Waters v. Whittemore, 22 Barb. 595. Cited, Attorney and Counsel, official character, 22 Cal. 315.

Watertown v. Cowen, 4 Paige, 510. Cited, Dedication, assent how proved, 14 Cal. 649.

Watervliet Bank v. Clark, 1 How. Pr. 144. Cited, Reference, when report of referee will be set aside, 5 Cal. 92.

Watkins v. Ashwicke, 1 Cro. Eliz. 132. Cited, Mortgage, tender of debt when invalid, 32 Cal. 170.

Watkins v. Crouch, 5 Leigh, 522. Cited, Negotiable Instruments, place of payment in note, 11 Cal. 324.

Watkins, Ex parte, 3 Pet. 193. Commented on, Criminal Procedure, validity of judgment, 31 Cal. 627; presumptions in favor of validity of judgments, 34 Cal. 413.

Watkins v. Holman, 16 Pet. 25. Cited, Land, actual possession, what constitutes, 1 Cal. 322; Statute, validity of confirmatory acts, 2 Cal. 546. Commented on, 39 Cal. 186; construction of, power of judiciary, 17 Cal. 562; Vendor and Vendee, vendee not estopped, 18 Cal. 476; the relation of landlord and tenant does not exist between, 24 Cal. 145.

Watkins v. Stevens, 4 Barb. 174. Cited, Land, actual possession, what constitutes, 19 Cal. 483, 484.

Watkinson v. Laughton, 8 John. 217. Cited, Common Carrier, liability of, for injuries, presumptions, 27 Cal. 430.

Watkyns v. Watkyns, 2 Atk. 97. Cited, Alimony, without divorce, 38 Cal. 269.

Watlington v. Howley, 1 Desaus. 170. Cited, Lis Pendens, to what actions applicable, 23 Cal. 38.

Watmough v. Francis, 7 Penn. St. 206. Explained, Sheriff, duty of, in execution of process, 8 Cal. 256. Cited, 15 Cal. 82.

Watson v. Ambergate, N. & B. Railway, 2 Eng. L. & E. 497; 15 Jur. 448. Cited, Commom Carrier, construction of contract for transportation through, 31 Cal. 53; 1 Gray, 505; 23 Conn. 475.

Watson v. Bailey, 1 Bin. 470. Cited, Acknowledgment of Deed, powers of notary, 11 Cal. 298; 8 Pet. 109.

Watson v. Duykinck, 3 John. 335. Approved, Freight, may be recovered back on failure of transportation, 6 Cal. 31; Id. 370.

Watson v. Husson, 1 Duer, 252. Doubted, Appeal, dismissal as an affirmance, 15 Cal. 326.

Watson v. King, 4 Camp. 272. Cited, Principal and Agent, authority terminates at death of principal, 15 Cal. 18.

Watson v. McClay, 4 Cal. 288. Cited, New Trial, granting or refusing for insufficient evidence, in discretion of court, 5 Kan. 133.

Watson v. Mercer, 8 Pet. 88. Commented on, Legislature, power to enact laws how restricted, 2 Cal. 545; power to pass retrospective laws, 30 Cal. 144; 39 Cal. 186; 6 How. 331; 10 How. 401; 17 How. 463. Denied, 39 N. H. 387.

Watson v. Spence, 20 Wend. 260. Cited, Foreclosure, incumbrancers necessary parties, 10 Cal. 552; decree void for want of jurisdiction, 16 Cal. 564. Commented on, Statute, validity of confirmatory acts, 16 Cal. 238.

Watts v. Van Ness, 1 Hill, 76. Cited, Sunday Laws, of binding force, 18 Cal. 681.

Watts v. White, 13 Cal. 321. Cited, Place of Trial, mining claims, regarded as real estate, 23 Cal. 506; 8 Nev. 186.

Wattson v. Dowling, 26 Cal. 124. Referred to, 26 Cal. 127. Cited, Ejectment, who bound by judgment, 32 Cal. 195; 35 Cal. 129. Commented on, who to go out on writ of possession, 29 Cal. 671. Approved, 30 Cal. 234; 35 Cal. 129; 36 Cal. 460; 37 Cal. 348; restoration to possession, 31 Cal. 337. Distinguished, 34 Cal. 487.

Waugh v. Chauncy, 13 Cal. 11. Cited, Supervisors, duties of, 7 Nev. 397; judgments and orders of, not subject to collateral attack, 23 Cal. 303; Certiorari, lies to review order granting ferry franchise, 23 Cal. 495.

Way v. Sperry, 6 Cush. 241. Approved, Pleading in action barred by statute or discharge in insolvency, 19 Cal. 483, 484.

Wayland v. Tucker, 4 Gratt. 268. Cited, Jurisdiction, in equity, to enforce contribution between co-sureties, 20 Cal. 135.

Weatherwax v. Cosumnes V. Mill Co., 17 Cal. 344. Approved, Statute of Limitations, on accounts, 30 Cal. 131, 134; 4 Nev. 103.

Weaver v. Conger, 10 Cal. 233. Cited, Abatement, another action pending, what must be shown, 10 Cal. 523; Pleading, when demurrer will be overruled, Deady, 407.

Weaver v. Eureka Lake Wat. Co., 15 Cal. 271. Approved, Water Rights, diligence required, in perfecting claim to, by diversion, 37 Cal. 314.

Weaver v. Page, 6 Cal. 681. Cited, Verdict, when will be set aside for excessive damages, 36 Cal. 484; Action, lies for malicious suing out of attachment, 57 Ill. 294.

Weaver v. Wible, 25 Penn. St. 270. Cited, Tenant in Common, purchase of outstanding adverse title, 39 Cal. 133.

Webb v. Peet, 7 La. An. 92. Cited, Husband and Wife, community property, 12 Cal. 224; burden of proof as to separate property of wife, Id. 253.

Webb v. Rice, 6 Hill, 219, reversing 1 Hill, 606. Denied, Deed as a Mortgage, parol evidence of, 8 Cal. 429, 433; 36 Cal. 43, 44, 45, 46; Id. 62, 65.

Webber v. Cox, 6 Mon. 110. Cited, Purchaser at sheriff's sale, 38 Cal. 654.

Webber v. Mallett, 16 Me. 88. Cited, Stare Decisis, local adjudications, 15 Cal. 603.

Weber v. Marshall, 19 Cal. 447. Cited, Trial, legal and equitable defenses, 19 Cal. 273; Id. 671; Pleading, defense of equitable title in ejectment, 24 Cal. 141; 4 Nev. 460; averments essential, 13 Wall. 103.

Weber v. San Francisco, 1 Cal. 455. Cited, Injunction, when will not issue to restrain tax sale, 36 Cal. 71.

Webster v. Commonwealth, 5 Cush. 386. Commented on, Criminal Procedure, instructions as to reasonable doubt of guilt, 32 Cal. 284.

Webster v. Byrnes, 34 Cal. 273. Cited, Elections, rejected votes to appear on poll list, 3 Or. 241.

Wedderspoon v. Rogers, 32 Cal. 569. Cited, Pleading, allegation of owner and holder a legal conclusion, 35 Cal. 121; 36 Cal. 302.

Weddle v. Stark, 10 Cal. 301. Cited, Appeal, error or abuse of discretion must affirmatively appear, 33 Cal. 525.

Weed v. McQuilkin, 8 Blackf. 335. Cited, Taxation, validity of assessment on what depends, 10 Cal. 404; tax sale when invalid, 36 Cal. 73.

Weed v. Saratoga & S. R. R. Co., 19 Wend. 534. Cited, Common Carriers, construction of contract for transportation through, 31 Cal. 53.

Weed v. Van Houten, 4 Halst. 189. Commented on, Negotiable Instruments, demand at place of payment not of essence of contract, 11 Cal. 323.

Weeks v. Milwaukee, 10 Wis. 256. Cited, Street Assessments, power of legislature to impose burdens, 28 Cal. 352; 2 Black, 515. Commented on, 28 Cal. 369; 34 Ill. 273, 281.

Weeks v. Pryor, 27 Barb. 80. Cited, Negotiable Instruments, presumptive dishonor, 39 Cal. 352.

Weems's Lessee v. Disney, 4 Har. & McH. 157. Commented on, Evidence, depositions as evidence of boundaries, 15 Cal. 281.

Weeton v. Woodcock, 7 Mees. & W. 14. Commented on, Fixtures, right of removal by tenant, 14 Cal. 69.

Weiberg v. The St. Oloff, 2 Pet. Adm. 428. Cited, Jurisdiction, of State courts, as to seaman's wages, 1 Cal. 487.

Weil v. Paul, 22 Cal. 492. Approved, Appeal, effect of stipulation as a waiver of objections to transcript, 26 Cal. 320.

Weimer v. Lowery, 11 Cal. 104. Cited, Mines and Mining, rights of miner to use of water, 22 Cal. 453.

Weinzorpflin v. State, 7 Blackf. 186. Cited, Criminal Procedure, when discharge of jury operates as an acquittal, 38 Cal. 478.

Weissinger and Crook, Ex parte, 7 Ala. 710. Cited, Mistake, in recital of written instrument, not to vitiate, 13 Cal. 558.

Welby v. Duke of Rutland, 2 Bro. Par. Cas. 395. Cited, Quieting title, remedy by action, 15 Cal. 263.

Welch v. Sullivan, 8 Cal. 165. Cited, Acknowledgment of Deed, sufficiency of form, 8 Cal. 584; Ejectment, on prior possession, insufficient defense, 10 Cal. 30. Commented on, San Francisco, tenure of pueblo lands, 15 Cal. 588; validity of alcalde grants, 21 Cal. 41.

Welch v. Tennent, 4 Cal. 203. Cited, Action, when may be removed to Federal court, 7 Ohio St. 453.

Welland Canal Co. v. Hathaway, 8 Wend, 480. Commented on, Estoppel, when to be specially pleaded, 3 Cal. 308; Estoppel, *in pais*, what necessary to constitute, 14 Cal. 370; 26 Cal. 40.

Wellborn v. Williams, 9 Geo. 86. Cited, Vendor's Lien, rights of assignee of, 21 Cal. 176, 177.

Wells v. Banister, 4 Mass. 513. Commented on, Conveyance, what passes by, 15 Cal. 197; 17 Vt. 411.

Wells v. Brander, 10 Smedes & M. 348. Cited, Attachment, lien of, 29 Cal. 372.

Wells v. Cockrum, 13 Tex. 127. Cited, Husband and Wife, community property, 12 Cal. 253.

Wells v. Cruger, 5 Paige, 164. Cited, Default, practice on opening, 29 Cal. 426.

Wells v. Martin, 1 Ohio St. 389. Cited, Evidence, preliminary, of lost instrument, 10 Cal. 147.

Wells v. N. Y. Central R. R. Co., 24 N. Y. 183. Cited, Common Carriers, receipt construed as a contract, 27 Cal. 38. Denied, Id. 43, 44.

Wells v. Robinson, 13 Cal. 133. Cited, Married Woman, separate property, husband as trustee, 14 Cal. 660; Trust, resulting trust, when it arises, 22 Cal. 578, 593; right of election of *cestui que trust*, 31 Cal. 23.

Wells v. Smith, 2 Edw. Ch. 78. Cited, Demand, essential in action on bond for deed, 17 Cal. 276; Specific Performance, insufficient defense in action, 40 Cal. 13.

Wells v. Steam Navigation Co., 8 N. Y. 375. Commented on, Common Carriers, liability of, for injuries or loss, 27 Cal. 32.

Wells v. Stout, 9 Cal. 479. Cited, Husband and Wife, agreements of separation valid, 9 Wall. 751.

Wells v. Wells, 3 Ired. Eq. 596. Cited, Specific Performance, time not of essence of contract, 40 Cal. 11.

Welton v. Adams, 4 Cal. 37. Approved, Lost Instrument, indemnity a condition precedent to action on, 5 Cal. 484; 28 Cal. 564; Negotiable Instruments, certificates of deposit, 9 Cal. 418; 22 Cal. 248; 29 Cal. 505; 35 Cal. 120.

Welton v. Palmer, 39 Cal. 456. Cited, Deed by Trustee, when void, 40 Cal. 350.

Wenborn v. Boston, 23 Cal. 321. Referred to, Lis Pendens, effect of, 23 Cal. 410; New Trial, insufficient grounds for, 33 Cal. 36.

Wendell v. People, 8 Wend. 190. Commented on, Grants of Land, construction of, 34 Cal. 345.

Wendell v. Van Rensselaer, 1 Johns. Ch. 354. Approved, Estoppel, by passively permitting purchase and improvement of land, 8 Cal. 467.

Wenman v. Mohawk Ins. Co., 13 Wend. 267. Common Law rule distinguished, Statute of Limitations, on death of party, 19 Cal. 100. Cited, on death of creditor, 35 Cal. 638.

Wentworth v. Day, 3 Met. 352. Cited, Reward, action lies to recover, 14 Cal. 137.

Wentworth v. Whittemore, 1 Mass. 471. Cited, Debts, contingent liabilities not debts, 37 Cal. 525.

West v. Blakeway, 2 Man. & G. 729. Commented on, Fixtures, construction of lease, 14 Cal. 71.

West v. Cochran, 17 How. 403. Approved, Mexican Grant, segregation and survey by government essential, 13 Cal. 412, 413; 1 Black, 199; 19 How. 82; Id. 336.

West v. State, 2 Zab. 212. Cited, Criminal Procedure, validity of judgment, 31 Cal. 627.

West v. Walker, 2 Green Ch. 279. Cited, Injunction, when will issue to restrain trespass, 27 Cal. 646.

West v. Wentworth, 3 Cow. 82. Approved, Conversion, measure of damages where value fluctuates, 33 Cal. 120. Qualified, 39 Cal. 422, 423; 42 N. H. 458. Cited, 40 Miss. 364.

West v. West, 10 Serg. & R. 445. Cited, Conveyance, by married woman, when invalid, 13 Cal. 498.

Westbrook v. Douglass, 21 Barb. 603. Cited, Jurisdiction of inferior courts, evidence *aliunde* the record, 34 Cal. 327.

Westbrook v. Rosborough, 14 Cal. 180. Cited, Office, term of, power of governor to fill vacancy, 13 Flor. 18.

Western Ins. Co. of Buffalo v. Eagle F. Ins. Co. of N. Y., 1 Paige, 284. Cited, Foreclosure, necessary parties, 40 Cal. 238.

Western Trans. Co. v. Marshall, 37 Barb. 509. Cited, Mining Stock is personal property, 42 Cal. 147.

Westervelt v. Gregg, 12 N. Y. 202. Cited, Constitutional Construction, restrictions on power of legislature, 22 Cal. 318.

Westmeath v. Marchioness of Westmeath, 1 Dow & Clarke, 519. Cited, Husband and Wife, validity of agreement of separation, 9 Cal. 492.

Weston v. Barker, 12 John. 276.   Cited, Assignment, order as an equitable assignment, 14 Cal. 407; 1 Wheat. 237, note.   Commented on, 5 Pet. 580; 12 Leigh, 225; 12 Rich. 530.

Weston v. Bear Riv. & A. Wat. & M. Co., 5 Cal. 185; S. C. 6 Cal. 425.   Distinguished, Execution, purchase of pledged corporation stock at sale on, 6 Cal. 429.   Cited, Corporations, transfer of stock, 9 Cal. 80; 20 Cal. 533. Affirmed, on principle of *stare decisis*, 35 Cal. 655. Cited, Validity of transfer, 40 Cal. 625.

Weston v. City Council of Charleston, 2 Pet. 449.   Commented on, Appeal, final judgment, what is, 1 Cal. 138; 14 Pet. 611; 1 Black, 273.   Cited, State Sovereignty, restriction of powers of taxation, 21 Cal. 571; 2 Black, 629; 7 How. 534, 538.   Distinguished, 43 Cal. 427.

Wetherbee v. Carroll, 33 Cal. 549.   Cited, Appeal, nonappealable orders reviewable only by means of statement, 35 Cal. 290; effect of failure to make statement on case presented on other evidence than affidavits, 35 Cal. 128.

Wetherbee v. Dunn, 32 Cal. 106.   Referred to in same case, 36 Cal. 149.

Wethey v. Andrews, 3 Hill, 582.   Cited, Negotiable Instruments, when presumptively dishonored, 39 Cal. 352.   Commented on, 41 N. Y. 585.

Wetmore v. Campbell, 2 Sand. 341.   Distinguished, Street Improvements, liability for expense of, 7 Cal. 474. Cited, Liability for street assessment, 31 Cal. 674.

Wetmore v. Click, 5 Jones, 155.   Cited, Witness, vendor not competent to impeach his own sale, 23 Cal. 446.

Wetmore v. Tracy, 14 Wend. 250.   Cited, Nuisance, abatement of public nuisance, 1 Cal. 466.

Whaley v. Dawson, 2 Sch. & L. 370.   Commented on, Parties, may be joined in equity, 31 Cal. 429; 5 How. 132.

Wharton v. Fitzgerald, 3 Dall. 503.   Cited, Use and Occupation, when action lies, 3 Cal. 203.

Wheatley v. Lane, 1 Wms. Saund. 216 a.   Cited, Executors and Administrators, not liable in actions for torts, 38 Cal. 23.

Wheatley v. Strobe, 12 Cal. 92.   Approved, Assignment, order for money as an equitable assignment, 14 Cal. 408.

Wheaton v. Sexton, 4 Wheat. 503. Commented on, Execution, validity of title of purchaser on what depends, 11 Cal. 248.

Wheeler v. Brewer, 20 Vt. 113. Cited, Statute of Limitations, construction of, 6 Cal. 433.

Wheeler's Estate, 1 Md. Ch. Dec. 80. Cited, Subrogation, of joint judgment debtor to rights of plaintiff, 17 Cal. 245.

Wheeler v. Hampson, Cal. Sup. Ct. 1860 (not reported.) Referred to, Van Ness Ordinance, validity of, 15 Cal. 623.

Wheeler v. Hays, 3 Cal. 284. Cited, Appeal, findings in equity case not disregarded, 18 Cal. 449.

Wheeler v. Horne, Willes, 209. Commented on, Tenant in Common, competency in action for an accounting, 12 Cal. 420.

Wheeler v. Newbould, 16 N. Y. 392, affirming 5 Duer, 29. Cited, Pledge, sale by pledgee, 34 Cal. 132; 36 Cal. 429. Doubted, Sale of commercial paper pledged as security, 38 Cal. 351, 352, 356. Commented on, 27 N. Y. 375; 31 N. Y. 84; 32 N. Y. 559.

Wheeler v. Raymond, 5 Cow. 231. Cited, Set-off, of judgments, 19 Cal. 658.

Wheeler v. Russell, 17 Mass. 257. Cited, Corporations, equity will not enforce acts prohibited by law, 38 Cal. 310; 2 Black, 507.

Wheeler v. Ryerss, 25 Wend. 437; S. C. 4 Hill, 466. Cited, Ejectment, who bound by judgment in, 22 Cal. 209.

Wheeler v. S. F. & A. R.R. Co., 31 Cal. 46. Cited, Common Carrier, power to contract for transportation through, 40 N. Y. 179, note.

Wheeler v. Van Houten, 12 John. 311. Cited, Estoppel, former recovery as a bar, 38 Cal. 647. Commented on, 2 N. H. 30.

Wheeler v. Washburn, 24 Vt. 293. Cited, Surety, on note, when discharged by agreement for delay, 10 Cal. 425.

Wheeler v. Wheeler, 9 Cow. 34. Cited, Assignment, order for money as an assignment, 12 Cal. 98.

Wheelock v. Moulton, 15 Vt. 521. Commented on, Corporations, corporate powers how exercised, 33 Cal. 19; 19 Vt. 258.

41

Wheelock v. Warschauer, 21 Cal. 309; S. C. 34 Cal. 265. Cited, Forcible Entry and Detainer, against tenant, landlord estopped by eviction of tenant, 36 Cal. 310; 37 Cal. 395.

Whelan v. Whelan, 3 Cow. 537. Cited, Attorney and Client, rule as to transactions between, 33 Cal. 440.

Wherry v. United States, 10 Pet. 338. Cited, Spanish Grants, validity of floating grant, 3 Cal. 42.

Whipley v. McKune, 12 Cal. 352. Referred to, Election, contest of, 13 Cal. 150. Cited, Provisions in statute directory, 16 Mich. 324.

Whipley v. Mills, 9 Cal. 641. Cited, Appeal, what necessary to constitute, 10 Cal. 31.

Whipple, Ex parte, Cal. Sup. Ct. Jan. T. 1866 (not reported.) Commented on, Official Bond, judgment on, how payable, 32 Cal. 155, 156.

Whipple v. Foot, 2 John. 418. Cited, Statute of Frauds, sale of growing crops not within, 37 Cal. 639.

Whipple v. Stevens, 22 N. H. 227. Cited, Statute of Limitations, part payment, effect of, 17 Cal. 577.

Whistler's Case, 10 Coke, 63. Cited, Grant, construction of government grant, 13 Cal. 454.

Whitaker v. Williams, 20 Conn. 104. Commented on, Estoppel, *in pais,* 14 Cal. 369. Cited, Equitable Estoppel, when it arises, 26 Cal. 41.

Whitbeck v. Cook, 15 John. 485. Cited, Covenant, in lease, no breach until eviction, 33 Cal. 306. Doubted, 27 Vt. 745; 10 Conn. 431.

White v. Abernethy, 3 Cal. 426. Cited, Appeal, intendments in favor of judgment, 10 Cal. 50; errors as to instructions when not considered, 10 Cal. 93.

White v. Arndt, 1 Whart. 91. Cited, Fixtures, what constitute, 14 Cal. 68.

White v. Bailey, 3 Mass. 270. Commented on, Statute of Limitations, construction of "return" to State, 16 Cal. 96.

White v. Carpenter, 2 Paige, 238. Cited, Trust, resulting trust when it arises, 25 Cal. 326. Commented on and dictum disapproved, 5 Denio, 231.

White v. C. & S. C. R. R. Co., 6 Rich. 47. Cited, Eminent Domain, compensation, estimate of benefits, 31 Cal. 374.

White v. Clark, 8 Cal. 512. Cited, Execution on Justice's Judgment, within what time to issue, 26 Cal. 157.

White v. Cole, 24 Wend. 141. Reversed, 26 Wend. 511; Judicial Sale, validity of sale of mortgaged property, 23 Cal. 302. Explained, 7 Hill, 59.

White v. Cuyler, 6 Term Rep. 176. Cited, Principal and Agent, contract made by agent, 13 Cal. 48.

White v. Eagan, 1 Bay, 247. Commented on, Deed, parol evidence to explain, 10 Cal. 625.

White v. Franklin Bank, 22 Pick. 184. Cited, Municipal Corporations, restrictions in charter to what liabilities to apply, 16 Cal. 632; Contracts, no remedy on contracts against public policy, 37 Cal. 175. Commented on, 15 Rich. 304.

White v. Fratt, 13 Cal. 521. Cited, Equity, when relief not obtainable in, 37 Cal. 228.

White v. Frye, 7 Ill. 65. Cited, Appeal, statute remedy exclusive, 8 Cal. 300.

White v. Johnson, 1 Wash. Va. 159. Cited, Sheriff, liable for wrongful acts of deputy, 14 Cal. 199.

White v. Levy, 10 Ark. 411. Cited, Equity, subrogation to rights of creditor, 24 Cal. 608.

White v. Molyneux, 2 Geo. 126. Cited, Landlord and Tenant, liability for rent after destruction of building, 39 Cal. 153.

White v. Moses, 21 Cal. 34, 43. Approved, Alcalde's Grant, validity of, 25 Cal. 491. Cited, Power to grant pueblo lands in whom vested, 27 Cal. 285; 42 Cal. 556; validity of alcalde's grant, 9 Wall. 602.

White v. Phelps, 12 N. H. 385. Cited, Chattel Mortgage, distinguished from a pledge, 35 Cal. 411.

White v. Spettigue, 13 Mees. & W. 602. Commented on, Conversion, lies for goods stolen, 1 Cal. 435.

White v. Syracuse & U. R. R. Co., 14 Barb. 559. Cited. Legislature, may authorize county subscription to railroad stock, 13 Cal. 188.

White v. The Mary Ann, 6 Cal. 462. Cited, Statutory Construction, remedial statute to be liberally construed, 22 Cal. 98; Id. 125.

White v. Todd's V. Wat. Co., 8 Cal. 443. Cited, Water Rights, conflicting claims to water judicially adjusted, 11 Cal. 153; diligence required in perfecting right, 37 Cal. 314.

White v. Trumbull, 3 Green, 314. Cited, Debtor and Creditor, appropriation of payments, 14 Cal. 449.

White v. Wakefield, 7 Sim. 401. Distinguished, Vendor's Lien, against whom enforceable, 36 Cal. 275.

White v. White, 5 Rawle, 61. Cited, Verdict, cannot be impeached by testimony of juror, 1 Cal. 405.

White v. Williams, 1 Paige, 506. Cited, Vendor's Lien, assignee of note given by vendee, 21 Cal. 176.

White, Lessee of, v. Sayre, 2 Ohio, 110. Commented on, Tenant in Common, validity of conveyance by, 15 Cal. 370.

Whitecomb v. Jacob, 1 Salk. 161. Commented on, Estates of Deceased, property of decedent as factor, part of assets, 9 Cal. 660.

Whiteford v. Commonwealth, 6 Rand. 721. Cited, Murder, degrees of, defined, 17 Cal. 398.

Whitehead v. Anderson, 9 Mees. & W. 518. Cited, Common Carrier, sufficiency of notice of stoppage *in transitu*, 7 Cal. 632.

Whitehead v. Walker, 10 Mees. & W. 695. Cited, Assignment of note overdue, to what equities subject, 41 Cal. 59.

Whiteside v. Jackson, 1 Wend. 418. Cited, Exceptions, point of objection to be stated, 10 Cal. 268; 12 Cal. 245.

Whitfield v. Longest, 6 Ired. 268. Cited, Municipal Corporations, validity of police ordinances, 23 Cal. 372.

Whitfield v. Southeastern Railway Co., 96 Eng. C. L. 115; El. B. & El. 115. Cited, Libel and Slander, corporation liable to action for, 34 Cal. 52.

Whiting v. Bank of U. S., 13 Pet. 6. Cited, Foreclosure, decree of sale, finality of, 9 Cal. 635; 23 Cal. 33; 2 Black, 531; 6 How. 203.

Whiting v. Clark, 17 Cal. 410. Cited, Surety, right to pay debt and proceed against principal, 26 Cal. 543; 42 Cal. 500, 507.

Whitlock's Case, 8 Coke, 69. Cited, Deed, reservations in deed void, 17 Cal. 53.

Whitney v. Allaire, 1 N. Y. 313. Commented on, Fraudulent Representations, when action by vendee will not lie, 9 Cal. 227.

Whitney v. Allen, 21 Cal. 233. Cited, Appeal, undertaking on, in foreclosure, requisites of, 25 Cal. 354.

Whitney v. Board of Delegates, 14 Cal. 479. Approved, Certiorari, power of court to compel return of writ, 32 Cal. 53. Cited, what reviewable on, 19 Cal. 156; 5 Nev. 318; 6 Nev. 103; 7 Nev. 92; Special Cases, powers of court, 24 Cal. 452; proceedings in election contests, special, 34 Cal. 640. See People v. Board of Delegates.

Whitney v. Buckman, 13 Cal. 536. Cited, Estoppel, of mortgagor, 31 Cal. 457.

Whitney v. Butterfield, 13 Cal. 335. Cited, Officer, liable for trespass by deputy, 39 Cal. 318.

Whitney v. Dutch, 14 Mass. 457. Commented on, Infant, may contract through agent, 24 Cal. 208; 10 Pet. 70.

Whitney v. Higgins, 10 Cal. 547. Cited, Parties, necessary, in equity, 11 Cal. 314. Commented on, in action to foreclose Mechanic's Lien, 23 Cal. 459. Cited, in action to foreclose mortgage, 28 Cal. 204; 40 Cal. 238; Mortgage, estate of mortgagor, 16 Cal. 468; Redemption, rights of subsequent mortgagees, 15 Cal. 510. Construed, Equitable right of redemption, when to apply, Id. 25, 26.

Whitney v. Olney, 3 Mason, 280. Commented on, Conveyance, what passes by, 15 Cal. 196.

Whitney v. Whitney, 14 Mass. 88. Cited, Statutory Construction, presumption as to intent of legislature, 13 Cal. 456; Written Instruments, construction of, 29 Cal. 304.

Whitsett v. Womack, 8 Ala. 466. Cited, Bond, for release of attachment, validity of, 13 Cal. 556.

Whittick v. Kane, 1 Paige, 202. Cited, Deed as a Mortgage, parol proof of, 8 Cal. 429; 13 Cal. 129; 12 How. 147.

Whittier v. Cocheco Manf. Co., 9 N. H. 454. Commented on, Water Rights, change in use by prior appropriator, 15 Cal. 181.

Whittington v. Christian, 2 Rand. 353. Common law rule distinguished, Ejectment, conclusiveness of judgment as to title, 14 Cal. 468.

Whitwell v. Barbier, 7 Cal. 54. Cited, Appearance, when not a waiver of defective summons, 8 Cal. 340; Appeal, when judgment by default will be reversed, 16 Cal. 68; Judgment by Default, remedy on defective service of summons, 33 Cal. 685; Judgment, what jurisdiction necessary to sustain, 8 Cal. 568; no presumptions in favor of judgment of justice's court, 12 Cal. 286; 23 Cal. 403; Foreclosure, judgment not subject to collateral attack, 9 Cal. 321; Injunction, when will issue to enjoin judgment, 14 Cal. 143. Commented on, Jurisdiction, no intendments in favor of special jurisdiction, 31 Cal. 169. Cited, Presumptions in favor of courts of general jurisdiction, 33 Cal. 512.

Wickens v. Evans, 3 Younge & J. 318. Cited, Contract in partial restraint of trade, valid, 36 Cal. 358.

Wickliffe v. Ensor, 9 B. Mon. 253. Cited, Land, possession under deed by entry of tenant, 38 Cal. 492.

Wicks v. Ludwig, 9 Cal. 173. Construed, Judgment, entry of, in vacation, 20 Cal. 56. Cited, rendition of, in vacation, void, 24 Cal. 127; what essential in rendition of judgment, 34 Cal. 333.

Wier v. Bush, 4 Litt. 434. Commented on, Office, term of, 28 Cal. 53.

Wiggin v. Bush, 12 John. 306. Approved, Negotiable Instruments, illegality of consideration when not to affect rights of *bona fide* indorsee, 2 Cal. 67.

Wiggin v. Mayor, etc., of N. Y., 9 Paige, 16. Cited, Cloud on Title, jurisdiction in equity to prevent or set aside, 15 Cal. 134; when jurisdiction will be exercised, 2 Cal. 469.

Wiggin v. Tudor, 23 Pick. 434. Cited, Sureties, rights of, under contract, 11 Cal. 220.

Wiggins v. Tallmadge, 11 Barb. 461. Cited, Dedication, of street, *cul de sac*, 35 Cal. 498.

Wiggins v. Wiggins, 1 Cranch, C. C. 299. Cited, Office, constitutional term of, 2 Cal. 230.

Wight v. Meredith, 5 Ill. 360. Approved, Judgment, entry of several judgment on joint demand, when erroneous, 6 Cal. 182; 7 Cal. 448.

Wike v. Lightner, 11 Serg. & R. 198. Cited, Witness, impeachment of, practice, 27 Cal. 636.

Wilbraham v. Snow, 2 Saund. 47. Cited, Sheriff, completion of execution of process by ex-sheriff, 8 Cal. 407.

Wilby v. West Cornwall R. Co., 2 H. & N. 703; S. C. 30 Law Times, 261. Commented on, Common Carriers, liability on contract for transportation through, 31 Cal. 60.

Wilcombe v. Dodge, 3 Cal. 260. Explained, Negotiable Instruments, action on note when premature, 8 Cal. 634. Cited, 18 Cal. 381.

Wilcox v. Jackson, 13 Pet. 498. Cited, State Lands, title of State to swamp lands, 27 Cal. 89. Commented on, 16 Cal. 330; 16 Ark. 21; 7 Minn. 299.

Wilcox v. Roath, 12 Conn. 550. Cited, Infant, ratification of contract of, 24 Cal. 213.

Wilcox v. Smith, 5 Wend. 231. Cited, Election, validity of, not subject to collateral inquiry, 23 Cal. 320.

Wilcoxson v. Burton, 27 Cal. 228. Commented on, Fraudulent Conveyance, what constitues, 35 Cal. 308. Distinguished, Confession of judgment, not subject to collateral attack for fraud, 37 Cal. 336.

Wild v. Brewer, 2 Mass. 570. Cited, Will, construction of, omission to provide for child, 18 Cal. 302.

Wild v. Holt, 9 Mees. & W. 672. Cited, Trespass on Mining Claim, measure of damages, 23 Cal. 310.

Wild v. Rennards, 1 Camp. 425, n. Commented on, Negotiable Instruments, demand at place of payment in note, 11 Cal. 325.

Wild v. Van Valkenburgh, 7 Cal. 166. Disapproved, Negotiable Instruments, demand at place of payment, 11 Cal. 326.

Wilde v. Jenkins, 4 Paige, 495. Cited, Accounts, when stated, accounts may be opened up, 9 Cal. 361.

Wilde v. Joel, 15 How. Pr. 320. Commented on, Injunction Bond, liability on what depends, 25 Cal. 172.

Wilder v. Fondey, 4 Wend. 100. Cited, Judgment, void in part is void in toto, 7 Cal. 355.

Wilder v. Goss, 14 Mass. 357. Cited, Will, construction of, omission of child from distributive share, 18 Cal. 302; 35 Cal. 343. Commented on, 29 N. H. 542; contra, 18 Pick. 167.

Wilder v. Keeler, 3 Paige, 169. Cited, Partnership, priority of lien of joint creditors, 13 Cal. 632.

Wildman v. Rademaker, 20 Cal. 615. Cited, Chattel Mortgage, rights of parties how determined, 27 Cal. 268.

Wilds v. Hudson Riv. R. R. Co., 24 N. Y. 430; S. C. 23 How. Pr. 492. Denied, Negligence, liability of railroad for injury to cattle, 37 Cal. 418.

Wildy v. Washburn, 16 John. 49. Commented on, Certiorari, what reviewable on, 16 Cal. 210.

Wiley v. White, 3 Stewt. & P. 355. Cited, Estates of Deceased, authority for probate sales restricted by statute, 20 Cal. 312.

Wiley v. Yale, 1 Met. 553. Approved, Rights and Remedies, statutory remedies to be strictly pursued, 16 Cal. 525; 33 Cal. 217.

Wilkes v. Ferris, 5 John. 335. Cited, Sale and Delivery, of property in mass, delivery by accepted orders when sufficient, 8. Cal. 607, 614; 30 Cal. 376.

Wilkin v. Wilkin, 1 Johns. Ch. 116. Cited, Judgment, relief obtainable on trial, 2 Cal. 285.

Wilkins v. Despard, 5 Term Rep. 112. Cited, Statutory Construction, forfeitures and penalties, 25 Cal. 241.

Wilkins v. Earle, 19 Abb. Pr. 190; S. C. 3 Rob. 352; 4 Am. Law Reg. N. S. 742. Denied, Innkeepers, liability of, 33 Cal. 605.

Wilkins v. Jadis, 2 Barn. & Ad. 188. Commented on, Negotiable Instruments, presentment and demand, reasonable hours, 8 Cal. 633.

Wilkins v. Stidger, 22 Cal. 235. Cited, Pleading, common counts sufficient, 32 Cal. 175.

Wilkins's Exrs. v. Sears, 4 Mon. 344. Cited, Chattel Mortgage, bill in equity to redeem, 35 Cal. 416.

Wilkinson v. Leland, 2 Pet. 627. Approved, Legislature, power to change remedies without affecting rights, 2 Cal. 542, 547; 17 Cal. 562; power of local taxation and appropriation, 13 Cal. 355. Commented on, restrictions on power of, 7 Cal. 14; validity of confirmatory acts, 16 Cal. 238; 39 Cal. 186. Denied, 39 N. H. 387. Cited, Statutory Construction, intention to govern, 28 Cal. 150.

Wilkinson v. Parrott, 32 Cal. 102. Cited, Master, when liable for acts of servant, 38 Cal. 634.

Wilkinson v. Payne, 4 Term Rep. 468. Cited, Marriage, evidence of, where marriage not the foundation of the claim, 26 Cal. 133.

Wilkinson v. Scott, 17 Mass. 257. Cited, Deed, consideration, parol proof of, 30 Cal. 24. Approved, 36 Cal. 370.

Wilkinson v. Sterne, 9 Mod. 427. Cited, Debtor and Creditor, appropriation of payments, 14 Cal. 449; 7 How. 689.

Wilkinson's Admr. v. Oliver's Representatives, 4 Hen. & M. 450. Commented on, Probate Procedure, infant when bound by decree, 31 Cal. 280.

Wilks v. Back, 2 East, 142. Cited, Principal and Agent, contract made by agent, 13 Cal. 48.

Willard v. Longstreet, 2 Doug. Mich. 172. Cited, Constitutionality of Statute, waiver of right to question, 4 Cal. 168.

Willard v. People, 5 Ill. 461. Cited, State Sovereignty, power of legislature as to fugitives from labor, 2 Cal. 436; right of transit with slave property, 9 Cal. 163; rule of comity, Id. 167.

Willard v. Sperry, 16 John. 121. Cited, Assignment, splitting demands, recovery on part as a bar, 38 Cal. 519. Distinguished, 21 Iowa, 91.

Willard v. Warren, 17 Wend. 257. Approved, Forcible Entry and Detainer, forcible entry defined, 5 Cal. 157, 159.

Willendson v. Forsoket, 1 Pet. Adm. 197. Cited, Jurisdiction of State courts in actions for seaman's wages, 1 Cal. 487.

Willett v. Pringle, 2 Bos. & P. New. Rep. 193. Cited, Insolvency, effect of discharge, 14 Cal. 175.

Willey v. Scoville's Lessee, 9 Ohio, 43. Cited, Taxation, city lots cannot be assessed in gross, 18 Cal. 152.

William v. Gwyn, 2 Saund. 46. Commented on, Appeal, who may appeal, 8 Cal. 314.

William and Anthony St., Matter of, 19 Wend. 694. Cited, Street Improvements, estimate of benefits, 27 Cal. 624. Commented on, Powers of commissioners, 32 Cal. 542.

Williams v. Amory, 14 Mass. 20. Statutes distinguished, Execution, insufficient return to vitiate levy, 11 Cal. 248; 38 Cal. 655.

Williams v. Bartholomew, 1 Bos. & P. 326, 475. Cited, Landlord and Tenant, when tenant not estopped, 33 Cal. 254; 1 McLean, 311.

Williams v. Benton, 24 Cal. 424. Cited, Reference, in action of partition, 35 Cal. 552.

Williams v. Bosanquet, 1 Brod. & B. 238. Cited, Assignment, assignee held to performance of covenants, 15 Cal. 292. Denied, 16 Mo. 292; 5 Wend. 616.

Williams v. Callow, 2 Vern. 752. Cited, Alimony, without divorce, 38 Cal. 269.

Williams v. Cammack, 27 Miss. 222. Cited, Street Assessments, power of legislature to direct, 28 Cal. 352.

Williams v. Carwardine, 4 Barn. & Ad. 621. Cited, Reward, action lies for recovery of, 14 Cal. 137.

Williams' Case, cited in 2 Russ. on Cr. 870. Cited, Evidence, confessions in criminal case must be voluntary, 10 Cal. 60.

Williams v. Clough, 3 Hurl. & N. 258. Commented on, Master when not liable for injury to servant, 31 Cal. 380.

Williams v. Commonwealth, 2 Gratt. 567. Denied, Criminal Procedure, effect of discharge of jury, 41 Cal. 216.

Williams v. Craig, 1 Dall, 338. Cited, Arbitration and Award, presumptions as to award, 2 Cal. 78.

Williams v. Dakin, 22 Wend. 201. Cited, Contract in restraint of trade, liquidated damages in, 9 Cal. 587. Commented on, 6 Cal. 262; 25 Cal. 71, 73.

Williams v. Davies, 2 Sim. 461. Cited, Set-off, when enforced in equity, 7 Cal. 547.

Williams v. Gill, 6 J. J. Marsh. 487. Cited, Execution, when irregular but not void, 38 Cal. 379.

Williams v. Gregory, 9 Cal. 76. Cited, New Trial, sufficiency of statement on, 9 Cal. 210. Doubted, Waiver of service of notice, 2 Nev. 43.

Williams v. Gridley, 9 Met. 482. Commented on, Statute of Limitations, effect of part payment, 21 Cal. 150.

Williams v. Healey, 3 Denio, 367. Cited, Contracts to convey real estate, covenants dependent, 35 Cal. 663.

Williams v. Henshaw, 11 Pick. 79. Cited, Partnership, priority of partnership over individual debts, 9 Cal. 67.

Williams v. Holden, 4 Wend. 227. Cited, Street Assessments, remedy by appeal to board, 29 Cal. 87.

Williams v. Holland, 6 Car. & P. 23. Cited, Negligence, contributory, when will defeat right of action, 37 Cal. 422.

Williams v. Houghtaling, 3 Cow. 86. Cited, Interest, not to be compounded except by stipulation in contract, 35 Cal. 694.

Williams v. Hutchinson, 5 Barb. 122. Commented on, Parent and Child, promise of pay for services of child not implied, 7 Cal. 513.

Williams v. Jackson, 5 John. 506. Cited, Boundaries, river as boundary line, 25 Cal. 144; construction of boundary lines in deed, 32 Cal. 230.

Williams v. Johnson, 2 Bosw. 1. Cited, Trade Marks, law applicable to, 35 Cal. 75, 76.

Williams v. Little, 11 N. H. 71. Cited, Negotiable Instrument, pledged as collateral security, 3 Cal. 164.

Williams v. Michigan Cent. R. Co., 2 Mich. 259. Cited, Negligence, railroads when liable for damage done to cattle, 18 Cal. 358.

Williams v. Mayor of Detroit, 2 Mich. 560. Commented on, Street Assessments, power of legislature to impose burdens, 28 Cal. 352, 369.

Williams v. Nelson, 23 Pick. 141. Cited, Water Rights, title by adverse possession, 25 Cal. 509.

Williams v. N. Y. Cent. R. R. Co., 16 N. Y. 100. Cited, Railroad, estate in easement as real property, 32 Cal. 510, 511; right of street railroad to lay track, 35 Cal. 331, 332; Eminent Domain, legislative discretion as to right and mode of its exercise, 31 Cal. 372.

Williams v. Peyton's Lessee, 4 Wheat. 78. Cited, Tax Title, purchaser at tax sale, what he must show, 21 Cal. 299; Jurisdiction, no intendments in favor of courts of inferior jurisdiction, 25 Cal. 309.

Williams v. Pritchard, 4 Term Rep. 2. Cited, Statutory Construction, repeal by implication, 18 Cal. 443.

Williams v. Roberts, 5 Ohio, 35. Cited, Vendor's Lien, waived by acceptance of personal security, 17 Cal. 74.

Williams v. Rogers, 5 John. 163. Cited, Amendment, to official returns, 23 Cal. 81.

Williams v. Rorer, 7 Mo. 556. Cited, Chattel Mortgage, legal effect and operation, 27 Cal. 269.

Williams v. Russell, 19 Pick. 165. Cited, Parties, in equity, 31 Cal. 427.

Williams v. Sheldon, 10 Wend. 658. Cited, Evidence, certified copy of recorded instruments, 13 Cal. 574.

Williams v. Smith, 6 Cal. 91. Approved, Judicial Sale, insufficient defense in action against purchaser, 9 Cal. 94.

Williams v. Talbot, 16 Tex. 1. Cited, Lease, construction of forfeiture clause, 38 Cal. 251.

Williams v. Walbridge, 3 Wend. 417. Cited, Partnership, partner as surety, burden of proof of partnership liability, 37 Cal. 117.

Williams v. Young, 17 Cal. 403. Cited, Homestead, judgment no lien on, 23 Cal. 400; not subject to sale under execution on judgment at law for purchase money, 36 Cal. 319.

Williams v. Young, 21 Cal. 227. Cited, Vendor's Lien, not assignable, 36 Cal. 321.

Williams College v. Mallett, 12 Me. 398. Cited, Stare Decisis, local adjudications how far conclusive, 15 Cal. 603.

Williamson v. Brown, 15 N. Y. 354. Cited, Conveyance, possession as notice of, 29 Cal. 488, 490. Approved, Sufficiency of notice in equity, 36 Cal. 272, 277; Id. 437; 2 Black, 390; 30 Ind. 476.

Williamson v. Farrow, 1 Bailey, 611. Cited, Statutory Construction, "month" defined, 31 Cal. 176.

Williamson v. Field's Exrs., etc., 2 Sand. Ch. 533. Cited, Foreclosure, subsequent incumbrancers, necessary parties, 10 Cal. 552.

Williamson v. Logan, 1 B. Mon. 241. Commented on, Execution, sale in gross when legal, 6 Cal. 52.

Williamson v. Wilson, 1 Bland Ch. 418. Commented on, Insolvency, operates as a dissolution of partnership, 7 Cal. 198; rights of creditors, 8 Cal. 157.

Williford v. State, 23 Geo. 1. Cited, Criminal Procedure, when discharge of jury does not operate as an acquittal, 41 Cal. 216.

Willing v. Brown, 7 Serg. & R. 467. Cited, Ejectment, on equitable title, 22 Cal. 617.

Willink's Lessee v. Miles, Pet. C. C. 429. Cited, Evidence, official certificates as *prima facie* evidence of official authority, 16 Cal. 554.

Willis v. Farley, 24 Cal. 490. Cited, Homestead, valid liens to be enforced in district court, 29 Cal. 104; enforcement of, against heirs, 29 Cal. 122. Distinguished, 42 Cal. 505.

Willis v. Green, 5 Hill, 232. Cited, Tenants in Common, not bound by acts of co-tenant, 6 Cal. 621.

Willis v. Newham, 3 Younge & J. 518. Commented on, Statute of Limitations, evidence of new promise, 21 Cal. 150.

Willis v. People, 2 Ill. 401. Cited, Indictment, essentials of, for murder, 6 Cal. 209.

Willis v. Wozencraft, 22 Cal. 607. Cited, Vendor's Lien, attaches equally on conveyance or contract to convey, 32 Cal. 59. Approved, Rights of vendee to possession, 40 Cal. 567.

Willot v. Sandford, 19 How. 81. Disapproved, Mexican Grant, conclusiveness of survey and patent, 13 Cal. 413.

Willoughby v. Comstock, 3 Hill, 389. Cited, Chattel Mortgage, notice of sale of property pledged, 27 Cal. 273.

Willson v. Blackbird Creek M. Co., 2 Pet. 245. Commented on, Constitutional Construction, powers of Federal government not exclusive, 1 Cal. 235; 1 Nev. 308; regulations of commerce, 1 Cal. 241; 8 Cal. 371; 20 Cal. 567; 7 How. 397; 12 How. 319; 13 How. 585; Id. 599; 3 Wall. 743; 16 B. Mon. 797; reserved powers of State, 41 Cal. 189; 7 How. 555.

Willson v. Broder, 10 Cal. 486. Referred to in same case, 24 Cal. 191.

Willson v. Cleaveland, 30 Cal. 192. Cited, Pleading, irrelevant matter of evidence and description in complaint, 30 Cal. 565; 32 Cal. 456; 36 Cal. 233; separate defenses, when may be inconsistent, 43 Cal. 269; Default, entry by clerk a ministerial act, 32 Cal. 635; Estoppel, when tenant released from, 33 Cal. 244; Abandonment, when may be proved without pleading, 36 Cal. 218; rule as to admission of evidence of, 36 Cal. 340; 3 Or. 251.

Willson v. McElvoy, 25 Cal. 169. Approved, Injunction Bond, counsel fees when not allowed in action on, 28 Cal. 12; what must be shown in complaint, 32 Cal. 25; 33 Cal. 212; Jurisdiction, power of court to set aside orders, 30 Cal. 198.

Willyard v. Hamilton, 7 Ohio, 453. Cited, Trial, constitutional right of trial by jury defined, 16 Cal. 255.

Wilson v. Allen, 3 How. Pr. 369. Statute distinguished, Appeal, time within which to file undertaking, 15 Cal. 386.

Wilson v. Berryman, 5 Cal. 44. Cited, Verdict, chance verdict will be set aside, 23 Cal. 48; 25 Cal. 400, 402; juror when not allowed to impeach, Id. 475.

Wilson v. Brandon, 8 Geo. 136. Commented on, New Trial, on ground of surprise, 24 Cal. 88; 30 Mo. 599.

Wilson v. Brannan, 27 Cal. 258. Cited, Chattel mortgage and pledge distinguished, 35 Cal. 411; sale of pledge by pledgee, 36 Cal. 429; 3 Nev. 318.

Wilson v. Castro, 31 Cal. 420. Cited, Mexican Grant, passes title sufficient to maintain ejectment, 42 Cal. 603; patentee when trustee of beneficiary, 33 Cal. 263. Commented on, 42 Cal. 622; 1 Saw. 205; 13 Wall. 496. Affirmed on principle of *stare decisis*, Estates of decedents, dying prior to probate act, governed by Mexican law of descents, 33 Cal. 424; 37 Cal. 91; land granted to husband became his separate estate, 33 Cal. 703. Cited, Jurisdiction under Mexican law, 37 Cal. 89.

Wilson v. Clements. 3 Mass. 1. Cited, Negotiable Instruments, liability of drawee on promise to accept, 29 Cal. 601. Commented on, 2 Wheat. 76.

Wilson v. Commrs. of Huntington, 7 Watts & S. 199. Cited, County, duty of supervisors as to payment of judgments, 10 Cal. 410.

Wilson v. Coupland, 5 Barn. & Ald. 228. Cited, Statute of Frauds, agreement to pay liability of third party, when not within statute, 22 Cal. 190.

Wilson v. Daniel, 3 Dall. 401. Commented on, Appeal, jurisdiction, amount in controversy, 2 Cal. 157; 11 How. 526. Disapproved, 3 Pet. 34; Id. 469; 1 Met. Ky. 568.

Wilson v. Fitch, 41 Cal. 363. Cited, Libel and Slander, what must be shown in complaint, 41 Cal. 480.

Wilson v. Forsyth, 24 Barb. 105. Cited, Conveyance, who may maintain action to set aside for fraud, 27 Cal. 315, 316.

Wilson v. Fosket, 6 Met. 402. Cited, Will, construction of, omission to provide for child, 18 Cal. 302. Commented on, 35 Cal. 342, 343.

Wilson v. Graham's Exrs., 5 Munf. 297. Cited, Vendor's Lien, waived by acceptance of personal security, 17 Cal. 74.

Wilson v. Hill, 3 Met. 66. Approved, Insurance, assignment of policy, 38 Cal. 542, 343, 545.

Wilson v. His Creditors, 32 Cal. 406. Cited, Insolvency, statement of facts in petition, 33 Cal. 541.

Wilson v. Lassen, 5 Cal. 114. Cited, Partition, necessary parties in, 36 Cal. 116.

Wilson v. Little, 2 N. Y. 445. Cited, Pledge, delivery essential, 30 Cal. 376; assignment and delivery of chose in action, 34 Cal. 132; of negotiable instruments, 36 Cal. 429; Id. 442; of shares of corporate stock, 37 Cal. 25. Commented on, 3 Cal. 161, 163. Cited, General property in stock pledged, 37 Cal. 26; sale of pledged or mortgaged chattel, 27 Cal. 271. Commented on, 27 N. Y. 375; rights of pledgor to recover identical stock pledged, 42 Cal. 101; 41 N. Y. 244.

Wilson v. Martin, 1 Denio, 602. Cited, Contract, measure of damages for breach of contract for services, 38 Cal. 666. Commented on, 2 Hilt. 299.

Wilson v. Mathews, 24 Barb. 295. Cited, Conversion, measure of damages where value fluctuates, 33 Cal. 120; 39 Cal. 423.

Wilson v. Mayor, etc., of N. Y., 1 Abb. Pr. 4. Cited, Injunction will not lie to restrain collection of taxes, 12

Cal. 299; Street Improvements, right of city to grade streets, 42 Cal. 438.

Wilson v. Mayor of N. Y., 4 E. D. Smith, 675. Disapproved, Taxation, of foreign insurance companies, 29 Cal. 544; 23 N. Y. 236.

Wilson v. Melvin, 4 Mo. 592. Cited, Constitutional Construction, right of transit with slave property, 9 Cal. 164. Commented on, 19 How. 552, 602.

Wilson v. Munday, 5 La. O. S. 483. Cited, Execution, right in promissory note liable to levy and sale, 34 Cal. 88; contra, 18 La. An. 57.

Wilson v. Roach, 4 Cal. 362. Cited, District Court, equity jurisdiction over estates of minors, 8 Cal. 411; 9 Cal. 129; 23 Cal. 429.

Wilson v. Sacramento, 3 Cal. 386. Cited, Certiorari, purpose of issuance of writ, 40 Cal. 480.

Wilson v. Supervisors of Albany, 12 John. 414. Cited, Mandamus, will not lie to control official discretion, 4 Cal. 179.

Wilson v. Troup, 2 Cow. 195. Cited, Mortgage, cannot be assigned without assignment of debt, 30 Cal. 688; estate of mortgagor and of mortgagee, 36 Cal. 41.

Wilson v. Williams, 14 Wend. 146. Cited, Appeal, effect of affirmance of order granting new trial for insufficiency of evidence, 26 Cal. 525.

Wilson v. Wilmington and M. R.R. Co., 10 Rich. 52. Cited, Negligence, liability of railroads for injury to cattle, 18 Cal. 355.

Wilson v. Wilson, 14 Sim. 405. Cited, Husband and Wife, agreements of separation valid, 9 Cal. 492.

Wilson v. York, N. & B. R. Co., 18 Eng. L. and Eq. 557. Cited, Common Carriers, construction of contract for transportation through, 31 Cal. 53; 100 Mass. 28.

Winans v. Christy, 4 Cal. 70. Commented on, Ejectment, right of defendants to sever, 7 Cal. 417. Approved, Ejectment, maintainable on prior possession, 7 Cal. 319; 9 Cal. 427; McAll. 232; plaintiff may bring joint action, 15 Cal. 264; right of defendants to sever, 7 Cal. 417; on failure to sever, general verdict conclusive, 6 Cal. 200; 7 Cal. 417; general findings conclusive, 26 Cal. 276; where defendants sever, joint judgment is erroneous, 28 Cal. 35.

Winans v. Huston, 6 Wend. 471. Cited, Covenant not to sue, no bar to action, 5 Cal. 502. Denied, 2 Mich. 415.

Windsor v. Field, 1 Conn. 284. Cited, Street Assessments, review of, by appeal to board, 29 Cal. 87.

Winfield v. Bacon, 24 Barb. 160. Cited, Injunction will not lie to restrain proceedings of court of coördinate jurisdiction, 9 Cal. 614.

Wing v. Owen, 9 Cal. 247. Approved, New Trial, grounds of, essential in statement, 25 Cal. 488; 5 Nev. 262.

Wingate v. Republic of Texas, Alexander's Dig. 254, sec. 54. Commented on, Criminal Procedure, application for bail, 19 Cal. 546.

Wingate v. Smith, 20 Me. 287. Cited, Timber, cut from realty, election of remedy, 16 Cal. 578.

Winne v. Reynolds, 6 Paige, 407. Commented on, Vendor and Vendee, rights of vendee, 7 Cal. 509.

Winne v. Sickles, 9 How. Pr. 217. Cited, Pleading, sham answer, what is, 10 Cal. 29.

Winship v. Connor, 42 N. H. 344. Cited, Evidence, presumption of death from lapse of time, 38 Cal. 223.

Winn's Heirs v. Jackson, 12 Wheat. 135. Cited, Writ of Review, when it lies to U. S. Supreme Court, 20 Cal. 172; 5 Pet. 206.

Winslow v. Gilbreth, 50 Me. 93. Cited, Husband and Wife, burden of proof as to separate property of wife, 30 Cal. 44.

Winslow v. Merchants' Ins. Co., 4 Met. 306. Commented on, Fixtures, as between mortgagor and mortgagee, 10 Cal. 265; 14 Cal. 72; 23 Cal. 217; 28 Vt. 437.

Winter v. Fitzpatrick, 35 Cal. 269. Cited, Appeal, lies in cases of certiorari, 37 Cal. 456.

Winter v. Jones, 10 Geo. 190. Cited, Legislature cannot impair obligation of contract created by statute, 10 Cal. 572; State Grants, when may be impeached collaterally, 23 Cal. 443.

Winter v. Walter, 37 Penn. St. 155. Cited, Husband and Wife, presumption that property is common property, 30 Cal. 43.

Wintermute v. Clarke, 5 Sand. 247. Cited, Inn, definition of, 33 Cal. 596.

42

Winthrop v. Curtis, 3 Greenl. 110. Cited, Deed, construction of description in, 32 Cal. 230.

Wintle v. Freeman, 11 Adol. & E. 539. Commented on, Execution, relative rights of senior and junior attaching creditors, 8 Cal. 252.

Winton v. Cornish, 5 Ohio, 477. Cited, Lease, destruction of building when a termination of tenancy, 38 Cal. 95.

Wiscart v. Dauchy, 3 Dall. 321. Affirmed, 3 Dall. 337. Commented on, Jurisdiction, appellate jurisdiction of Supreme Court of United States, 9 Cal. 735; 7 Cranch, 110; 7 How. 865.

Wise v. Hilton, 4 Greenl. 435. Cited, Attachment, rights and liabilities of garnishee, 11 Cal. 350.

Wise v. Wheeler, 6 Ired. 196. Commented on, Conveyance, what passes by, 15 Cal. 196.

Wiser v. Blachly, 1 Johns. Ch. 437. Cited, Parties, in equity, 31 Cal. 427; 9 How. 106.

Wiseman v. Bernard, 2 Coke, 15. Cited, Covenant, to stand seized to uses, consideration essential, 6 Cal. 313.

Witchcot v. Nine, Brownl. & G. 81. Cited, Covenant, in lease, what insufficient to create a breach, 33 Cal. 307.

Withy v. Cottle, 1 Sim. & S. 174. Cited, Contract, legal tender and demand, 25 Cal. 576.

Wixon v. Bear Riv. & Aub. Wat. & M. Co., 24 Cal. 367. Cited, New Trial, grounds for motion must be specified, 26 Cal. 524; 27 Cal. 410.

Woart v. Winnick, 3 N. H. 473. Cited, Statutory Construction, not retrospective, 4 Cal. 136. Denied, 39 N. H. 387.

Wodcoke's Case, Year Book, 33 Hen. 6; 14 P. 6. Commented on, Fraudulent Conveyance, title of innocent purchaser, 12 Cal. 498.

Woglam v. Cowperthwaite, 2 Dall. 68. Commented on, Replevin, effect of, on prior lien, 11 Cal. 272; 1 N. Y. 167.

Wolcott v. Meech, 22 Barb. 321. Cited, Variance, immaterial, to be disregarded, 32 Cal. 14.

Wolcott v. Van Santvoord, 17 John. 248. Approved, Negotiable Instrument, demand at place of payment not of essence of the contract, 11 Cal. 318, 322.

Wolf v. Baldwin, 19 Cal. 306. Affirmed, on principle of *stare decisis*, Title, under Van Ness Ordinance, 28 Cal. 223; 30 Cal. 638, 643; by actual possession, 40 Cal. 309; what constitutes actual possession, 32 Cal. 18, 22; 39 Cal. 44, 46, 47; 41 Cal. 582.

Wolf v. Beales, 6 Serg. & R. 242. Cited, Set-off, judgments when set-off in equity, 23 Cal. 629.

Wolf v. Fink, 1 Penn. St. 435. Cited, Witness, incompetency of party to record, 6 Cal. 195; 3 Penn. St. 300; Id. 361.

Wolf v. Fleischacker, 5 Cal. 244. Approved, Homestead, lands held in joint tenancy not subject to dedication, 6 Cal. 167; Id. 417; Id. 565; 23 Cal. 517; 27 Cal. 425; 32 Cal. 483; 26 Wis. 581. Statute distinguished, 14 Iowa, 54; 27 Ark. 660.

Wolf v. Fogarty, 6 Cal. 224. Cited, Acknowledgment, of deed, when insufficient, 7 Cal. 162; 10 Cal. 244.

Wolf v. St. Louis Independent Wat. Co., 10 Cal. 541. Cited, Negligence, liability for injuries by breakage of reservoir, 17 Cal. 98. Approved, no liability on reasonable care in construction, 23 Cal. 225; 35 Cal. 683; 15 Wall. 538.

Wolfe v. Frost, 4 Sand. Ch. 72. Cited, Easement, estate conveyed by grant of, 27 Cal. 366; 32 Cal. 506; 38 Cal. 116.

Wolfe v. Goulard, 18 How. Pr. 64. Cited, Trade Marks, law applicable to, 35 Cal. 75, 76.

Wolf v. St. Louis Independent W. Co., 15 Cal. 319. Cited, Witness, stockholder of corporation when incompetent, 23 Cal. 329.

Wolfskill v. Malajowich, 39 Cal. 276. Cited, Possessory Act, constructive possession under, how established 42 Cal. 152.

Wollaston v. Hakewill, 3 Man. & G. 315. Cited, Negligence, liability does not attach, on reasonable exercise of a right, 7 Cal. 340.

Womack v. Womack, 8 Tex. 397. Commented on, Conveyance, by married woman, of her separate property, 7 Cal. 273. Cited, 31 Cal. 646.

Wood v. Auburn & R. R. Co., 8 N. Y. 167. Cited, Contract for mortgage by corporation, sufficiency of, 32 Cal. 654.

Wood v. Benson, 2 Cromp. & J. 94.   Cited, Contract, entire contract, what is, 15 Cal. 257.

Wood v. Bullens, 6 Allen, 516.   Cited, Money, relative values of, cannot be judicially determined, 25 Cal. 576.

Wood v. Colvin, 5 Hill, 229.   Approved, Execution, levy on real property, 37 Cal. 132, 142, 144.

Wood v. Derrickson, 1 Hilt. 410.   Cited, Appeal Bond, when liability attaches, 38 Cal. 604.

Wood v. Dudley, 8 Vt. 435.   Commented on, Chattel Mortgage, pledge distinguished, 35 Cal. 410.

Wood v. Dummer, 3 Mason, 322.   Cited, Principal and Agent, when agent held as trustee of principal, 13 Cal. 141; 15 How. 308.

Wood v. Dwight, 7 Johns. Ch. 295.   Approved, Appeal, from order dissolving injunction, effect of, 15 Cal. 110. Commented on, 15 Gratt. 198.

Wood v. Fitz, 10 Mart. O. S. 196.   Cited, Judicial notice taken of official signatures, 32 Cal. 108.

Wood v. Harrison, 2 Sand. 665.   Cited, Trial, special issues framed in equity cases, 4 Cal. 8.

Wood v. Jackson, 8 Wend. 9.   Cited, Estoppel, judgment, as a bar, 26 Cal. 494; by verdict, 15 Cal. 148; 28 Cal. 516.   Denied, 12 Conn. 370.

Wood v. Mann, 3 Sum. 326.   Cited, Contempt, refusal of bidder at judicial sale to pay amount bid, 9 Cal. 196; 23 How. 12.

Wood, Matter of, Hop. Ch. 6.   Commented on, Attorney and Counsel, official character, 22 Cal. 313, 315.

Wood v. McCain, 7 Ala. 800.   Cited, Principal and Agent, effect of ratification by principal, 14 Cal. 399.

Wood v. Morewood, cited in 3 Q. B. 440.   Commented on, Trespass on Mining Claim, measure of damages, 23 Cal. 310.

Wood v. Oakley, 11 Paige, 403.   Cited, Statutory Construction, to be prospective, 27 Cal. 159.

Wood v. Partridge, 11 Mass. 488.   Cited, Conveyance, creating only an equity in grantee, 10 Cal. 368; Covenants, in lease, construed, 37 Cal. 526.

Wood v. San Francisco, 4 Cal. 190.   Approved and followed, San Francisco, corporation has no power to convert public easements to private use, 9 Cal. 45. Distinguished, San Francisco, title to city property, 15 Cal. 587, 615.

Wood v. Truckee T. Co., 24 Cal. 474. Cited, Easement, not an estate in land, 31 Cal. 589. Approved, 3 Nev. 373; right of entry on land by owner of easement, 32 Cal. 581; not subject to assignment or forced sale on execution, except with consent of granting party, 32 Cal. 529; 41 Cal. 510.

Wood v. Veal, 5 Barn. & Ald. 456. Denied, Dedication, of *cul de sac*, 35 Cal. 498.

Wood v. Washburn, 2 Pick. 24. Cited, Bond, no recovery on joint bond signed by sureties only, 14 Cal. 423; 21 Cal. 589.

Wood v. Wheeler, 7 Tex. 13. Cited, Homestead, who entitled to declare, 8 Cal. 73.

Wood v. Williams, 4 Madd. 186. Cited, Mortgage, with power of sale, construed, 22 Cal. 125.

Wood v. Wood, 5 Paige, 596. Cited, Parent and Child, rights of parent, 8 Cal. 123.

Wood v. Wood, 2 Paige, 113. Cited, Divorce, adultery, sufficient proof of, 10 Cal. 254.

Woodbridge v. City of Detroit, 8 Mich. 276. Commented on, Street Assessment, apportionment per front foot, 28 Cal. 369; 18 Mich. 522; 19 Mich. 43; validity of assessment on what depends, 31 Cal. 685. Constitution distinguished, 34 Ill. 281.

Woodbury v. Bowman, 13 Cal. 634. Cited, Appeal, effect of, 28 Cal. 91.

Woodcock v. Bennett, 1 Cow. 711. Cited, Variance, *allegata* and *probata* must agree, 10 Cal. 331; Execution, sale under void execution, effect of, 38 Cal. 376; 4 How. 77; when irregular, Id. 378.

Wooden v. Waffle, 6 How. Pr. 145; Code Rep. N. S. 392. Cited, Trial, in equity cases, 4 Cal. 8.

Woodfolk v. Nashville & C. R.R. Co., 2 Swan, 422. Cited, Condemnation of Land, compensation, measure of, 31 Cal. 373.

Woodman v. Segar, 25 Me. 90. Cited, Evidence, proof of handwriting of subscribing witness, 26 Cal. 410, 412.

Woodruff v. Taylor, 20 Vt. 65. Commented on, Probate Procedure, judgments conclusive, 20 Cal. 270.

Woodruff v. Trapnall, 10 How. 190. Cited, Legislature, cannot impair obligation of contract created by statute, 10 Cal. 572. Commented on, 19 Gratt. 752.

Woods v. Farmere, 7 Watts, 386. Cited, Conveyance, possession as notice of, 36 Cal. 272. Distinguished, 4 Penn. St. 177.

Woods v. Freeman, 1 Wall. 398. Cited, Taxation, assessment when void, 30 Cal. 619.

Woods v. Kimbal, 5 Mart. N. S. 247. Cited, Vendor and Vendee, subsequently acquired title vests in vendee, 8 Cal. 197.

Woods v. Lane, 2 Serg. & R. 53. Cited, Ejectment, when possession, coupled with color of title, to prevail, 4 Cal. 79.

Woods v. McGee, 7 Ohio, 467. Criticised, Sale and delivery of property in mass, 11 Cal. 403; 27 Cal. 463.

Woods v. Monell, 1 Johns. Ch. 502. Commented on, Execution, sale in gross when legal, 6 Cal. 52.

Woodson v. Skinner, 22 Mo. 23. Commented on, Forfeiture of estates at common law, 25 Cal. 240.

Woodward v. Backus, 20 Cal. 137. Cited, Default, what necessary to show on motion to set aside, 23 Cal. 129; 33 Cal. 325; Orders, setting aside, in discretion of court, 29 Cal. 424.

Woodward v. Harbin, 4 Ala. 534. Cited, Amendment of official returns, 23 Cal. 81.

Woodward v. Newhall, 1 Pick. 500. Cited, Judgment, several judgment on joint obligation, 1 Cal. 169.

Woodworth, Estate of, 31 Cal. 595. Cited, Estates of Deceased, marshalling assets, 33 Cal. 667; title to real estate on death of ancestor, 42 Cal. 463.

Woodworth v. Fulton, 1 Cal. 295. Cited, Ejectment, possessory actions under civil law, 1 Cal. 286; what sufficient evidence of possession, 1 Cal. 289; possession under color of title, 1 Cal. 421. Approved, Alcalde's Grants, validity of, 1 Cal. 325; Id. 375; Id. 387; Id. 414. Disapproved, 3 Cal. 451. Commented on, as overruled, 8 Cal. 187; Id. 198; 15 Cal. 498; Id. 558; Id. 598; Id. 619; 9 Wall. 602; legal presumptions in favor of official authority, 3 Cal. 453.

Woodworth v. Knowlton, 22 Cal. 164. Cited, Pleading, admission by failure to deny, 26 Cal. 418; 38 Cal. 290.

Woodyer v. Hadden, 5 Taunt. 142. Denied, Dedication, of *cul de sac*, 35 Cal. 498. Cited, 15 Watts & S. 142.

Woolever v. Knapp, 18 Barb. 265. Approved, Tenant in Common, when not liable for rents and profits, 12 Cal. 422.

Woolnoth v. Meadows, 5 East, 463. Cited, Libel. and Slander, requisites of complaint, 34 Cal. 59.

Worcester v. Eaton, 11 Mass. 368. Commented on, Contract, though illegal, if fully executed, passes the title, 37 Cal. 607.

Word v. Cavin, 1 Head, 507. Cited, Warranty, when statute of limitations begins to run on breach of, 41 Cal. 116.

Worford v. Isbel, 1 Bibb, 247. Commented on, New Trial, when granted for excessive damages, 24 Cal. 517.

Worland v. Kimberlin, 6 B. Mon. 608. Cited, Insolvency, preference of creditor not illegal, 10 Cal. 277; Id. 494; 19 Cal. 46.

Wormley v. Wormley, 8 Wheat. 421. Cited, Action, removal of cause to Federal court, 28 Cal. 99; 10 Wheat. 188.

Worrall v. Munn, 5 N. Y. 229. Cited, Common Carrier, construction of contract, 27 Cal. 38; Agreement, for mortgage, construed as a contract, 32 Cal. 654.

Worster v. Proprietors of Canal Bridge, 16 Pick. 547. Approved, Damages, for personal injuries, a question for the jury, 25 Cal. 473.

Worthington v. Hylyer, 4 Mass. 205. Cited, Deed, void from uncertainty in description, 6 Cal. 312. Distinguished, 29 Mo. 115.

Worthington v. McRoberts, 9 Ala. 299. Cited, Probate Sales, judicial, 9 Cal. 196; *caveat emptor* applies, Id. 197.

Wortman v. Wortman, 17 Abb. Pr. 70. Cited, Jurisdiction of Person, evidence of publication of summons, 31 Cal. 350.

Wren's Admr. v. Span's Admr., 1 How. Miss. 115. Cited, Probate Procedure, effect of allowance of claim, 6 Cal. 669.

Wright v. Atkyns, 1 Ves. & B. 314. Cited, Mortgage, rights of mortgagor in possession, 27 Cal. 436.

Wright v. Bates, 13 Vt. 348. Commented on, Deed as a Mortgage, parol proof of, 13 Cal. 130. Cited, 8 Cal. 430; 12 How. 147.

Wright v. Denn, 10 Wheat. 239. Cited, Will, construction of, 36 Cal. 81.

Wright v. Douglass, 2 N. Y. 373. Cited, Judicial Sale, estate of purchaser pending time for redemption, 9 Cal. 415; 31 Cal. 302; Id. 315.

Wright v. Hicks, 15 Geo. 160. Commented on, Parent and Child, presumptions as to paternity, 13 Cal. 99, 100.

Wright v. Hunter, 5 Ves. Jr. 792. Cited, Jurisdiction, concurrent in law and equity as to contribution between co-sureties, 20 Cal. 135.

Wright v. Jesson, 5 Maule & S. 95. Reversed, 2 Bligh. 1. Commented on, Will, construction of devise, 27 Cal. 448; 1 Sum. 249; 3 Mason, 398.

Wright v. Levy, 12 Cal. 257. Cited, Assignment, rights of assignee of judgment, 23 Cal. 255; Id. 626.

Wright v. Mattison, 18 How. 56. Approved, Color of Title, definition of, 33 Cal. 676.

Wright v. Miller, 1 Sand. Ch. 120. Cited, Fraud, equity jurisdiction to set aside decrees, 5 Cal. 298.

Wright v. Moore, 21 Wend. 230. Distinguished, Vendor and Vendee, right of possession in vendee, 22 Cal. 619; 24 Cal. 145.

Wright v. Parker, 2 Aiken, 212. Cited, Mortgage, securing several notes, rights of mortgagees, 23 Cal. 30.

Wright v. Proud, 13 Ves. Jr. 137. Cited, Attorney and Client, rule as to transactions between, 33 Cal. 440.

Wright v. Reed, 3 Term Rep. 554. Cited, Redemption, what money sheriff may receive, 26 Cal. 663.

Wright v. Ross, 36 Cal. 414. Distinguished, Trust and Trustee, purchase of trust property, 38 Cal. 460.

Wright v. Rutgers, 14 Mo. 585. Cited, Patent to lands reserved from sale, void, 23 Cal. 443.

Wright v. Ryder, 36 Cal. 357. Approved, Contract, in restraint of trade, when void, 40 Cal. 254.

Wright v. Solomon, 19 Cal. 64. Cited, Sale and Delivery, title under conditional sale, 36 Cal. 158.

Wright v. State, 5 Ind. 290. Cited, Habeas Corpus, what cannot be tried on, 41 Cal. 220; Criminal Procedure, discharge of jury when it operates as an acquittal, 38 Cal. 478.

Wright v. Swan, 6 Port. 84. Cited, Preëmption, who cannot question validity of claim, 33 Cal. 458.

Wright v. Whitesides, 15 Cal. 46. Cited, Ejectment, under possessory act, showing required, 16 Cal. 573; 23 Cal. 408; 42 Cal. 656.

Wright v. Wilcox, 19 Wend. 343. Cited, Principal and Agent, when principal not liable for acts of agent, 34 Cal. 599.

Wright v. Wright, 1 Ves. Sr. 409. Cited, Assignment of policy of insurance, 30 Cal. 90.

Wright v. Wright, 3 Tex. 168. Cited, Divorce, adultery, sufficient evidence of, 10 Cal. 254.

Wright v. Wright, 5 Cow. 197. Cited, Arbitration and Award, validity of award, 12 Cal. 340.

Wright's Lessee v. Deklyne, 1 Pet. C. C. 199. Cited, Decree, how far conclusive, 20 Cal. 483; 7 How. 217.

Wrinkle v. Tyler, 3 Mart. N. S. 111. Cited, Covenant, no breach till eviction, 2 Cal. 570.

Wyatt v. Barwell, 19 Ves. Jr. 435. Cited, Conveyance, possession as notice of, 12 Cal. 376.

Wyatt's Admr. v. Rambo, 29 Ala. 510. Cited, Probate Courts, jurisdiction of, 19 Cal. 209. Denied, 32 Ala. 199.

Wyke v. Allan, 2 Hagg. Adm. 95. Commented on, State Sovereignty, effect of temporary residence of slave in free State, 2 Cal. 449.

Wyke v. Rogers, 12 Eng. L. & Eq. 163. Cited, Sureties, when not discharged by time given to principal, 10 Cal. 426.

Wykoff v. Wykoff, 3 Watts & S. 481. Cited, Vendor and Vendee, right of possession in vendee, 22 Cal. 617.

Wyld v. Pickford, 8 Mees. & W. 443. Cited, Common Carriers, liability for loss or damage, 27 Cal. 38.

Wyman v. Farnsworth, 3 Barb. 370. Cited, Mistake of law, money paid under, not recoverable back, 18 Cal. 272.

Wyman v. Fowler, 3 McLean, 467. Cited, Demand, in action on written instruments, not necessary, 22 Cal. 278.

Wyman v. Mayor, etc., of N. Y., 11 Wend. 486. Cited, Dedication, by sale of lots on map, 22 Cal. 489. Approved, 35 Cal. 500; title of purchasers, 22 Cal. 490. Distinguished, 11 Abb. Pr. 199.

Wyman v. Mitchell, 1 Cow. 316. Cited, Pleading, discharge in insolvency, what must be shown, 33 Cal. 536.

Wynehamer v. People, 13 N. Y. 433. Commented on, Constitutional Construction, rights of property, 22 Cal. 318, 320, 322; 20 How. Pr. 83.

Wynn v. Alden, 4 Denio, 163. Construed, Negotiable Instruments, sufficiency of notice to fix liability on indorser, 14 Cal. 163; 9 Abb. Pr. 425.

Wynn v. Lee, 5 Geo. 217. Cited, Title, by adverse possession, 34 Cal. 383.

Wynne v. Raikes, 5 East, 514. Cited, Negotiable Instruments, what constitutes an acceptance, 29 Cal. 600; 98 Mass. 291.

Yale v. Dederer, 22 N. Y. 452. Reversed, 18 N. Y. 265. Approved, Married Woman, separate estate, control over, 25 Cal. 379, 380; power of alienation, 32 Cal. 385.

Yankee Jim's U. W. Co. v. Crary. See Union Water Co. *v.* Crary.

Yarbrough v. State, 2 Tex. 523. Cited, Criminal Procedure, admission to bail in capital cases, 19 Cal. 547.

Yarborough v. Palmer, 10 La. 140. Cited, Real Actions, under civil law, 1 Cal. 287.

Yarborough v. Thompson, 3 Smedes & M. 291. Cited, Attachment, liability of garnishee, 11 Cal. 350.

Yates, Case of, 4 John. 369. Cited, Contempt, power of courts over, 7 Cal. 178.

Yates v. Foot, 12 John. 1. Cited, Bailment, title to property in hands of bailee, 11 Cal. 350. Commented on, 4 Zab. 772. Approved, Wager, disaffirmance and recovery of money staked, 37 Cal. 674, 676; 23 Ark. 224. Doubted, 15 Conn. 31; 4 Mich. 332.

Yates v. Houston, 3 Tex. 433. Commented on, Husband and Wife, property acquired pending marriage, 14 Cal. 599.

Yates v. Joyce, 11 John. 136. Cited, Mortgage, action by mortgagee, lies for injuries to premises, 24 Cal. 473.

Yates v. Lansing, 5 John. 297. Commented on, Habeas Corpus, allowance in term time, in discretion, 11 Cal. 226.

Yates v. People, 6 John. 337. Commented on, Jurisdiction, of appellate court, 1 Cal. 137.

Yates v. Smith, 38 Cal. 60. Affirmed, S. C. 40 Cal. 662. Followed, Survey, of Mexican grant, 42 Cal. 620.

Yeates v. Groves, 1 Ves. Jr. 280. Approved, Debtor and Creditor, order to creditor an equitable assignment, 13 Cal. 121; 14 Cal. 407.

Yeomans v. Bradshaw, Carth. 373. Cited, Probate, power of administrator over assets of estate, 12 Cal. 190.

Yocum v. Barnes, 8 B. Mon. 496. Cited, Appeal Bond, construction of, 8 Cal. 551; Evidence, proof of handwriting of written instrument, 26 Cal. 412.

Yoder's Heirs v. Easley, 2 Dana, 245. Cited, Forcible Entry and Detainer, fact of possession alone to be tried, 20 Cal. 47.

Yonge v. P. M. S. S. Co., 1 Cal. 353. Cited, Damages, contemplated and contingent profits not allowed, 2 Cal. 78; Appeal, new trial granted on erroneous instructions, 39 Cal. 577.

Young v. Adams, 6 Mass. 182. Cited, Money Paid, recovery back, on failure of consideration, 22 Cal. 463; 10 Wheat. 342; 11 How. 159; contra, 11 Vt. 582; 11 Wend. 9; 13 Wend. 101.

Young v. Black, 7 Cranch, 565. Cited, Judgment, as a bar, limitation may be shown, 26 Cal. 505.

Young v. Frost, 1 Md. 394. Cited, Appeal, law of the case on new trial, 20 Cal. 417.

Young v. Grundy, 6 Cranch, 51. Cited, Injunction, effect of appeal from order granting or dissolving, 15 Cal. 111.

Young v. Raincock, 7 Com. B. 310.   Cited, Pleading, estoppel by deed or matter of record must be specially pleaded, 26 Cal. 38.

Young v. Remer, 4 Barb. 442.   Cited, Judgment, of justice's court, lien not extended by docketing, 26 Cal. 157.

Young v. Rummell, 2 Hill, 478.   Rule distinguished, Pleading, evidence admissible under general issue, 10 Cal. 27; conclusiveness of judgment as a bar, 26 Cal. 494; Id. 505; 36 Cal. 38.

Young v. State, 7 Gill & J. 253.   Cited, Official Bond, validity of, 7 Cal. 441.

Young v. Triplett, 5 Litt. 247.   Cited, Vendor and Vendee, payment of purchase money cannot be resisted by vendee in possession, 5 Cal. 264.

Younge v. Harris' Admr., 2 Ala. 108.   Cited, Vendor and Vendee, setting aside contract for fraudulent representations as to title, 17 Cal. 385.

Youngs v. Bell, 4 Cal. 201.   Approved, Pleadings, denial of indorsement, under oath, not required, 18 Cal. 391; several defenses may be pleaded, 22 Cal. 680.

Youngs v. Freeman, 3 Green N. J. 30.   Cited, Landlord and Tenant, right of assignee of landlord to remove tenant, 29 Cal. 171.

Yount v. Howell, 14 Cal. 465.   Cited, Ejectment from Mexican Grants, action maintainable on right of entry and possession, 38 Cal. 43; what plaintiff must show, 22 Cal. 516; 37 Cal. 389; sufficiency of complaint in, 15 Cal. 151, 366.   Approved, sufficiency of description of land, 23 Cal. 163; issues raised by denials, 1 Wall. 374; conclusiveness of patent as evidence, 15 Cal. 366; 18 Cal. 26, 571; 20 Cal. 160; patent not subject to collateral attack, 22 Cal. 111; judgment in, what it determines, 32 Cal. 194; rents and profits anterior to ouster recoverable only in independent action, 14 Cal. 637.   Referred to, Mexican Grant, survey of, a political and not a judicial right, 13 Cal. 489.

Youse v. McCreary, 2 Blackf. 243.   Cited, Negotiable Instruments, measure of recovery by indorsee against indorser, 16 Cal. 160.

Yuba Co. v. Adams, 7 Cal. 35.   Cited, Intervention, by judgment creditors, 18 Cal. 381; Taxation, lien created by levy of tax, 30 Cal. 244.

Yule v. Yule, 2 Stockt. 138. Cited, in dissenting opinion of Sprague, J., Alimony, inseparable from divorce, 38 Cal. 277.

Zander v. Coe, 5 Cal. 230. Approved, Justice's Court, jurisdiction of, 5 Cal. 331. Cited, 22 Cal. 172; 25 Cal. 196; Constitutional Construction, judiciary system, 9 Cal. 86, 87; that constitutional limit cannot be enlarged by legislation, 6 Cal. 449; 7 Cal. 105. Construed, Limitation not to apply to forcible entry cases, 6 Cal. 162; 7 Cal. 105. Disapproved, that legislature cannot confer concurrent jurisdiction, 30 Cal. 577, 579. Cited, Appeal, from void judgment, 2 Nev. 97.

Zanesville v. Richards, 5 Ohio St. 589. Commented on, Taxation, uniformity in, 28 Cal. 365; 2 Black, 516.

Zebach v. Smith, 3 Bin. 69. Cited, Will, power of sale under, 32 Cal. 440; 4 Wheat. 699; 5 How. 267, 273.

Zeller's Lessee v. Eckert, 4 How. 296. Cited, Mortgage, possession by mortgagee does not extend lien, 24 Cal. 411; 5 How. 276; Vendor and Vendee, vendor retains possession as tenant of vendee, 37 Cal. 374.

Ziegler v. Commonwealth, 12 Penn. St. 227. Cited, Officers, duties and liabilities of public officers, 36 Cal. 214.

Ziel v. Dukes, 12 Cal. 479. Approved, Demand in suit on promissory note not a condition precedent, 22 Cal. 278; 38 Cal. 409. Approved, Judgment will not be set aside for clerical errors, 30 Cal. 534.

Zottman v. San Francisco, 20 Cal. 96. Cited, Municipal Corporations, power to contract restricted by statute, 20 Cal. 503. Approved, Mode as directed by statute to be strictly followed, 24 Cal. 550, 552; 33 Cal. 145; 35 Cal. 705. Qualified, 33 Cal. 197; ratification equivalent to previous authority, 31 Cal. 28; 8 Nev. 188. Approved and quoted, liability on implied contract, 31 Iowa, 392. Cited, 22 Ind. 95.

Zouch v. Parsons, 3 Burr. 1794. Cited, Infant, deed of infant not void but voidable, 24 Cal. 211; 10 Pet. 67, 68. Approved, 10 Pet. 67. Commented on, 26 N. H. 291.

ADDENDA.

Beale Street, Matter of, 39 Cal. 495. Cited, Judgment, on appeal, effect of, 43 Cal. 99.

Beans v. Emanuelli, 36 Cal. 117. Cited, New Trial, grounds of motion must be specified, 43 Cal. 424.

Bear Riv. and Aub. W. & M. Co. v. New York Min. Co., 8 Cal. 327. Commented on, Water Rights, rights of first appropriator, 1 Mont. 568.

Beard v. Knox, 5 Cal. 252. Cited, Husband and Wife, community property, wife's interest in, 8 Cal. 510.

Bell v. Bed Rock T. & M. Co., 36 Cal. 214. Doubted, Mining Customs, construction of, 1 Mont. 241.

Bell v. Brown, 22 Cal. 672. Cited, Pleading, inconsistent defenses, practice, 43 Cal. 269.

Belloc v. Davis, 38 Cal. 242. Commented on, Mortgage, rights of junior incumbrancers, 43 Cal. 188.

Benedict v. Bray, 2 Cal. 251. Approved, Replevin Bond, when action will not lie on bond taken by justice of peace, 38 Ind. 516.

Bishop of Winchester v. Paine, 11 Ves. Jr. 197. Cited, Lis Pendens, effect of notice, 43 Cal. 262.

Boggs v. Merced Min. Co., 14 Cal. 279. Distinguished, Estoppel, owner of lands when estopped, 43 Cal. 602.

Bolton v. Lawrence, 9 Wend. 435. Cited, Execution, fees of sheriff on sale under, 43 Cal. 380.

Boston & M. R. R. Co. v. Bartlett, 3 Cush. 224. Cited, Consideration, in contract for sale of lands, 43 Cal. 464.

Bowen v. Morris, 2 Taunt. 374. Cited, Specific Performance, contract signed only by vendor, 43 Cal. 465.

Brennan v. Swasey, 16 Cal. 141. Cited, Mechanic's Lien, sufficiency of statement, 43 Cal. 522.

Brooks v. Hyde, 37 Cal. 374. Commented on, Van Ness Ordinance, possession by assignee of tenant, 43 Cal. 476.

Brown v. Orr, 29 Cal. 120. Cited, Pleading, general denial in action on note, 43 Cal. 397.

Brown v. Scott, 25 Cal. 195. Cited, Pleading, insufficient denials, 43 Cal. 397.

Brummagim v. Spencer, 29 Cal. 661. Approved, County Court, jurisdiction in actions for unlawful detainer, 43 Cal. 304.

Bryant v. Williams, 21 Iowa, 329. Cited, Judicial Sale, title of purchaser, 43 Cal. 651.

Butterfield v. Central P. R. R. Co., 37 Cal. 381. Cited, New Trial, grounds of motion must be specified, 43 Cal. 424.

Calderwood v. Pyser, 31 Cal. 333. Approved, Parties, joinder of husband and wife, 32 Cal. 90.

Calk v. Stribling, 1 Bibb. 123. Cited, Deed, construction of calls in, 25 Cal. 143.

Campbell v. Morris, 3 Har. & McH. 554. Cited, Citizenship, privileges and immunities, 43 Cal. 50.

Carpentier v. Oakland, 30 Cal. 439. Cited, Judgment, not subject to collateral attack, 43 Cal. 490.

Carpentier v. Williamson, 25 Cal. 161. Cited, Foreclosure, legal title not divested by sale under, 43 Cal. 601.

Casgrave v. Howland, 24 Cal. 457. Cited, Appeal, when statement on new trial not considered, 43 Cal. 638.

Castro v. Hendricks, 23 How. 438. Commented on, Mexican Grant, supervision over survey of, 43 Cal. 291.

Caulfield v. Stevens, 28 Cal. 118. Approved, County Court, jurisdiction in actions for unlawful detainer, 43 Cal. 304.

Cincinnati W. & Z. R.R. Co. v. Commrs. of Clinton Co., 1 Ohio St. 89. Cited, Legislative power of taxation and appropriation for local improvements, 13 Cal. 355.

Clark v. Lockwood, 21 Cal. 222. Commented on, Mexican Grant, effect of confirmation, 43 Cal. 622.

Clark v. Troy, 20 Cal. 219. Cited, Conveyance, what to be recorded, 43 Cal. 343.

Clary v. Rolland, 24 Cal. 147. Doubted, Sureties, on replevin bond, liabilities of, 1 Mont. 592.

Clary's Admrs. v. Clary, 2 Ired. 78. Cited, Evidence, opinions of witnesses as to sanity, 43 Cal. 33.

Clason v. Bailey, 14 John. 484. Commented on, Specific Performance, when decreed on executory contract, 43 Cal. 465.

Cohen v. Barrett, 5 Cal. 195, Cited, Statutory Construction, title to act, how considered, 39 Ind. 71.

Colman v. Clements, 23 Cal. 245. Approved, Mines and Mining, customs to be strictly construed against forfeiture, 1 Mont. 241.

43

Commonwealth v. Hardy, 2 Mass. 317. Cited, Criminal Procedure, proof of general character of defendant when admissible, 43 Cal. 149.

Commonwealth v. Slate, 11 Gray, 60. Cited, Indictment, for receiving stolen goods sufficient, 43 Cal. 200.

Cooper v. Pena, 21 Cal. 403. Cited, Specific Performance, of contract signed by vendor alone, 43 Cal. 465. Disapproved, that contract must be mutual, Id. 466.

Cravens v. Dewey, 13 Cal. 40. Cited, Nonsuit, rule of determination on appeal, 1 Mont. 479.

Crandall v. Woods, 8 Cal. 136. Commented on, Water Rights, riparian rights on public lands, 1 Mont. 685.

Cullerton v. Mead. 22 Cal. 95. Cited, Statutory Construction, statutes to be construed together and made to harmonize, 6 Nev. 222.

Darst v. Rush, 14 Cal. 81. Cited, Nonsuit, principles of determination on review of order, presumptions, 1 Mont. 479.

Davis v. Davis, 26 Cal. 23. Cited, Mexican Grant, final confirmation, when statute of limitations begins to run, 43 Cal. 291, 294; Estoppel in pais, who not subject to, 43 Cal. 530.

Davis v. Gale, 32 Cal. 26. Approved, Water Rights, change in use of water appropriated, 1 Mont. 543.

Davis v. Livingston, 29 Cal. 283. Cited, Mechanic's Lien, sufficiency of statement, 43 Cal. 522. Commented on, Id. 523.

De Ro v. Cordes, 4 Cal. 117. Cited, Nonsuit, rule of determination on review of order, presumptions, 1 Mont. 480.

Dimick v. Campbell, 31 Cal. 238. Cited, Appeal, rulings forming no part of judgment roll not reviewable, 43 Cal. 370.

Dimick v. Deringer, 32 Cal. 488. Cited, Judgment, by default, who may move to set aside, 43 Cal. 262.

Dorsey v. Manlove, 14 Cal. 553. Distinguished, Replevin, measure of damages, 1 Mont. 166.

Dougherty v. Creary, 30 Cal. 290. Cited, Mining Partnership, liability of partners, 1 Mont. 227.

Dow v. Gould & Currey Min. Co., 31 Cal. 629. Cited, Nonsuit, principles of determination on review of order, presumptions as to evidence, 1 Mont. 480.

Dowling v. Polack, 18 Cal. 625. Cited, Action, effect of dismissal of, 1 Mont. 208.

Dred Scott v. Sandford, 19 How. 393. Cited, Citizenship, as affected by constitutional amendments, 43 Cal. 47.

Duryea v. Burt, 28 Cal. 569. Cited, Mining Partnership, copartners as tenants in common, 1 Mont. 227.

English v. Johnson, 17 Cal. 107. Cited, Mining Claims, boundaries of, to be marked according to regulations, 1 Mont. 223.

Esmond v. Chew, 15 Cal. 137. Approved, Negligence, when action will not lie for injuries to property, 1 Mont. 221.

Estrada v. Murphy, 19 Cal. 272. Commented on, Mexican Grant, effect of confirmation, 43 Cal. 622.

Everett v. Hydraulic F. T. Co., 23 Cal. 225. Cited, Negligence, no liability for injury without proof of negligent use of property, 51 N. Y. 487.

Evoy v. Tewksbury, 5 Cal. 285. Approved, Guaranty, sufficiency of, 7 Cal. 34.

Ewald v. Corbett, 32 Cal. 493. Approved, Conveyance, by married woman, void from defective acknowledgment, 43 Cal. 472, 473.

Farmer v. Grose, 42 Cal. 169. Commented on, Deed and agreement to reconvey, when not a mortgage, 42 Cal. 83.

Farmers' F. Ins. & L. Co. v. Edwards, 26 Wend. 541. Denied, Mortgage, tender and refusal after law day as a discharge, 14 Cal. 529.

Fish v. Redington, 31 Cal. 185. Cited, Conveyance, possession as notice of, 25 Wis. 81.

Fitch v. Bunch, 30 Cal. 208. Cited, New Trial, assignment of errors, too general not considered, 1 Mont. 663.

Fitler v. Beckley, 2 Watts & S. 458. Cited, Negotiable Instruments, place of payment in note, 11 Cal. 323.

Flight v. Bolland, 4 Russ. 298. Cited, Specific Performance, of contract signed by vendor alone, 43 Cal. 465.

Fowler v. Harbin, 23 Cal. 630. Cited, Judgment, when not an estoppel, 37 Cal. 238. See Boggs v. Hargrave, 16 Cal. 563.

Fowler v. Peirce, 2 Cal. 165. Commented on, Statute, testing validity of, power of court, 5 W. Va. 91.

Fowler v. Smith, 2 Cal. 39; S. C. Id. 568. Commented on, Interest under Spanish law, 14 Cal. 179.

Fox v. Fox, 25 Cal. 587. Cited, Evidence, depositions, sufficiency of, 1 Mont. 162.

Frary v. Dakin, 7 John. 75. Cited, Pleading, discharge in insolvency, how pleaded, 33 Cal. 536.

Fratt v. Clark, 12 Cal. 89. Approved, Election of remedy waiver of tort, on conversion, 43 Cal. 382.

Frisch v. Caler, 21 Cal. 71. Commented on, Pleading, general denial in action on note, 43 Cal. 397.

Fuller v. Fuller, 17 Cal. 605. Cited, Witness, competency not dependent on religious belief, 43 Cal. 34.

Funes y Carillo v. Bank of U. S., 10 Rob. La. 533. Cited, Negotiable Instruments, presentment and demand at place specified, 11 Cal. 324.

Gates v. Salmon, 28 Cal. 320. Approved, Appeal, from interlocutory decree in partition, 43 Cal. 627.

Gee v. Moore, 14 Cal. 472. Cited, Deed, covenants in, how far an estoppel, 1 Mont. 708.

Gernet v. Lynn, 31 Penn. St. 94. Cited, Will, construction of devise, 43 Cal. 204.

Gray v. Eaton, 5 Cal. 448. Referred to, 9 Cal. 637.

Green v. Wells, 2 Cal. 584. Approved, Contract, parol agreement varying terms of, when enforceable, 4 Cal. 330.

Greening v. Wilkinson, 1 Car. & P. 625. Approved, Conversion, measure of damages where value is fluctuating, 9 Cal. 563.

Haden v. Garden, 7 Leigh, 157. Cited, Jurisdiction, when equity will not relieve from judgment at law, 21 Cal. 442.

Hager v. Shindler, 29 Cal. 55. Approved, Cloud on Title, when equity will relieve from, 43 Cal. 88.

Hahn v. Kelly, 34 Cal. 391. Cited, County Court, jurisdiction of, 43 Cal. 314. Approved, Judgment, conclusiveness of recitals in, 43 Cal. 652.

Hall v. Crandall, 29 Cal. 568. Approved, Principal, when liable for note made by agent, 43 Cal. 501.

Hardy v. Harbin, 1 Saw. 194. Cited, Mexican Grant, patentee as trustee of beneficiary, 30 Cal. 307.

Harper v. Minor, 27 Cal. 113. Cited, New Trial, construction of order extending time, 43 Cal. 321; construction of statutory provisions, Id. 322.

Harrison v. Jackson, 7 Term Rep. 209. Cited, Principal and Agent, liability of principal for acts of agent, 14 Cal. 400.

Harshey v. Blackmarr, 20 Iowa, 187.   Cited, Judicial Sales, title of purchaser, 43 Cal. 651.

Hastings v. Halleck, 13 Cal. 203.   Cited, Appeal, effect of stipulation, 43 Cal. 588.

Hatchet v. Marshal, Peake's Cas. 172.   Cited, Items of Account, practice, 32 Cal. 638.

Havens v. Dale, 18 Cal. 366.   Cited, Conveyance, sufficiency of, 43 Cal. 624.

Hawley v. Delmas, 4 Cal. 195.   Distinguished, Attachment, sufficiency of affidavit, 1 Mont. 56.

Haynes v. Waite, 14 Cal. 446.   Cited, Debtor and Creditor, appropriation of payments, 1 Mont. 48.

Herman v. Sprigg, 3 Cons. La. Rep. 58; 3 Mart. N. S. 190. Cited, Interest, what not allowable, 2 Cal. 570.

Heston v. Martin, 11 Cal. 41.   Cited, Mechanic's Lien, sufficiency of statement, 43 Cal. 522.

Hewes v. Doddridge, 1 Rob. Va. 143.   Cited, Factor, cannot pledge, pledgee held to knowledge of powers of factor, 19 Cal. 72.

Hicks v. Coleman, 25 Cal. 122.   Cited, Land, constructive possession under deed, 43 Cal. 575; Exceptions, to charge of court, when to be taken, 1 Mont. 554.

Hidden v. Jordan, 28 Cal. 301.   Cited, Findings, opinion of court not a finding, 1 Mont. 664.

Hill v. Smith, 27 Cal. 476.   Distinguished, Water Rights, liability for injury to water, 1 Mont. 567.

Hobbs v. Duff, 23 Cal. 596.   Referred to, and law of case announced, 43 Cal. 488.

Hook v. White, 36 Cal. 300.   Commented on, Pleading, insufficient denial in action on note, 43 Cal. 397.

Hooper v. Wells, 27 Cal. 11.   Distinguished, Judgment in action on contract may include interest, 28 Cal. 631.

Horton v. Morgan, 6 Duer, 56.   Affirmed, 19 N. Y. 172. Approved, Conversion of corporate stock by bailee, rights of owner, 42 Cal. 105.

Hughes v. Davis, 40 Cal. 117.   Approved, Deed, as a mortgage, conveys legal title, 43 Cal. 604.

Humphreys v. McCall, 9 Cal. 62.   Cited, Pleading, insufficient denial in action on note, 43 Cal. 397.

Hunsaker v. Borden, 5 Cal. 288.   Cited, State Warrants, vested rights in, 1 Mont. 39.

Hunt v. Loucks, 38 Cal. 372. Cited, Jurisdiction, power of court to amend judgment, 51 Mo. 186; proceedings which are amendable are not void, Id. 245; not subject to collateral attack, Id. 190.

Hunt v. Robinson, 11 Cal. 262. Cited, Replevin, lien obtained by, 1 Mont. 578. Approved, Id. 579, 580.

Hutchinson v. Wetmore, 2 Cal. 310. Cited, Contract, when recovery cannot be had on entire contract for services, 1 Mont. 451.

Hutton v. Reed, 25 Cal. 478. Cited, Appeal, assignment of errors, too general, will not be considered, 1 Mont. 663.

Irwin v. Phillips, 5 Cal. 140. Commented on, Water Rights, water on public domain, 1 Mont. 685.

Irwin v. Scriber, 18 Cal. 498. Cited, Jurisdiction, special proceedings when not subject to collateral attack, 19 Cal. 171.

Jackson v. Garnsey, 16 John. 189. Cited, Abandonment, party holding legal title cannot divest himself by parol disclaimer, 43 Cal. 602.

Jackson v. Norton, 6 Cal. 187. Cited, Contract, conditions precedent to rescission of, 17 Cal. 385.

Jackson v. Shawl, 29 Cal. 267. Cited, Municipal Corporation, validity of city ordinance, 43 Cal. 249.

Johnson v. Russell, 37 Cal. 670. Construed, Contract, no remedy on illegal contract, 43 Cal. 616.

Johnson v. Van Dyke, 20 Cal. 225. Commented on, Mexican Grant, what constitutes final confirmation, 43 Cal. 291; when statute of limitations begins to run, Id. 294.

Kimball v. Semple, 25 Cal. 440. Cited, Deed, warranty, to what it attaches, 1 Mont. 708.

Klink v. Cohen, 13 Cal. 623. Cited, Pleading, inconsistent defenses, practice, 43 Cal. 269.

Lane v. Vick, 3 How. 464. Commented on, Stare Decisis, local adjudications, 15 Cal. 604.

Lawrenson v. Butler, 1 Sch. & L. 13. Cited, Specific Performance, mutuality in contract, 43 Cal. 465.

Leese v. Sherwood, 21 Cal. 151. Cited, Action, effect of dismissal, 1 Mont. 209.

Lent v. Morrill, 25 Cal. 500. Approved, Mortgage, burdens cannot be increased as against junior mortgagees, 43 Cal. 188.

Lent v. Shear, 26 Cal. 361. Approved, Mortgage, burdens cannot be increased as against junior mortgagees, 43 Cal. 188.

Leviston v. Swan, 33 Cal. 480. Cited, Jurisdiction, power of court to amend judgment, 1 Mont. 205.

Lignot v. Redding, 4 E. D. Smith, 285. Cited, Counterclaim, test as to what constitutes, 26 Cal. 309.

Livett v. Wilson, 3 Bing. 116. Cited, Dedication, to public use, what constitutes, 14 Cal. 649.

Longridge v. Dorville, 5 Barn. & Ald. 117. Distinguished, Forfeiture, what constitutes, 25 Cal. 241.

Lord v. Allen, 26 Cal. 141. Approved, Mortgage, burdens cannot be increased as against junior mortgagees. 43 Cal. 188.

Lord v. Morris, 18 Cal. 482. Approved, Mortgage, burdens cannot be increased as against junior mortgagees, 43 Cal. 188.

Lyddal v. Weston, 2 Atk. 20. Doubted, Public Lands, ownership of mining lands, 3 Cal. 225.

Mahoney v. Van Winkle, 33 Cal. 448. Commented on, Mexican Grant, when statute of limitations begins to run, 43 Cal. 292.

Main v. Tappaner, 43 Cal. 206. Approved, Attachment, lien of, how created, 43 Cal. 580.

Maeris v. Bicknell, 7 Cal. 261. Approved, Water Rights, purpose of appropriation may be changed, 1 Mont. 543.

Manrow v. Durham, 3 Hill, 584. Cited, Guaranty, on note, what constitutes, 16 Cal. 153.

Martin v. Mitchell, 2 Jac. & W. 413. Cited, Specific Performance, of contract signed by vendor alone, 43 Cal. 465.

Martin v. Travers, 12 Cal. 243. Cited, Exceptions, objections to admission of testimony must be specific, 23 Cal. 264; 25 Cal. 627.

Martin v. Wade, 37 Cal. 168. Approved, Contract, no remedy on illegal contract, 43 Cal. 616.

Martinez v. Gallardo, 5 Cal. 155. Cited, Appeal, transcript when may be filed, 5 Kan. 279.

Maye v. Yappen, *sub nom* Maye v. Tappan. See *ante.*

McCarthy v. White, 21 Cal. 495. Approved, Mortgage, burdens cannot be increased as against junior mortgagees, 43 Cal. 188.

McCarty v. Roots, 21 How. 432. Cited, Railroads, restrictions under charter, 40 Cal. 88.

McClory v. McClory, 38 Cal. 575. Cited, Findings, opinion of court not a finding, presumptions, 1 Mont. 664.

McCourtney v. Fortune, 42 Cal. 387. Approved, Appeal, orders not reviewable on appeal from final judgment, 43 Cal. 627.

McCulloch v. State of Maryland, 4 Wheat. 316. Distinguished, State Sovereignty, power of State to tax corporate property, 43 Cal. 426–429. Commented on, Id. 428, 429.

McDonald v. Bear Riv. & Aub. W. & M. Co., 13 Cal. 220. Cited, Water Rights, no distinction as to purposes of appropriation, 1 Mont. 658.

McGarrity v. Byington, 12 Cal. 426. Doubted, Mines and Mining, forfeiture, construction of mining customs, 1 Mont. 241.

McKee v. Greene, 31 Cal. 418. Cited, Nonsuit, presumptions as to evidence on review of order, 1 Mont. 480.

Mecham v. McKay, 37 Cal. 154. Approved, County Courts, jurisdiction in actions for unlawful detainer, 43 Cal. 304.

Merle v. Mathews, 26 Cal. 455. Cited, Conveyance, sufficiency of, 43 Cal. 624.

Miles v. Thorne, 38 Cal. 335. Commented on, and rule restricted, Trust, enforcement of agreement on procurement of franchise, 43 Cal. 20, 21.

Miliken v. Huber, 21 Cal. 166. Approved, Certiorari, when it lies, 43 Cal. 27.

Minter v. Crommelin, 18 How. 87. Cited, Patent, impeachment of, 16 Cal. 328.

Minturn v. Brower, 24 Cal. 644. Commented on, Mexican Grant, perfect titles under, 43 Cal. 622.

More v. Del Valle, 28 Cal. 174. Cited, Appeal, rulings forming no part of judgment roll not reviewable, 43 Cal. 370.

More v. Massini, 37 Cal. 432. Referred to, on second appeal, 43 Cal. 390.

Morrison v. Wilson, 13 Cal. 494; S. C. 30 Cal. 344. Cited, Estoppel, not to apply to married women, 1 Mont. 561; Deed, construction of, Id. 708.

Morris v. DeCelis, 41 Cal. 331. Distinguished, New Trial, vacating order granting, 43 Cal. 454.

Muldrow v. Norris, 2 Cal. 74. Cited, Arbitration and Award, effect of void award, 12 Cal. 345.

Mulford v. Le Franc, 26 Cal. 108. Approved, Conveyance, construction of "cedo" in Mexican conveyance, 43 Cal. 624.

Murdock v. DeVries, 37 Cal. 527. Cited, Judgment, though erroneous, not void, 43 Cal. 653.

Myers v. English, 9 Cal. 341. Cited, State Warrants, vested rights of holders of, 1 Mont. 39.

Natoma Wat. & Min. Co. v. Clarkin, 14 Cal. 544. Cited, Nonsuit, consent to, when not a waiver of exceptions, 1 Mont. 78.

Nevada Co. & S. C. Co. v. Kidd, 37 Cal. 282. Approved, Pleading, causes of action which cannot be united, 43 Cal. 184.

New Orleans, O. & G. W. R. R. Co. v. Lagarde, 10 La. An. 150. Cited, Eminent Domain, compensation without estimate of benefits, 31 Cal. 373.

Nickerson v. Chatterton, 7 Cal. 568. Doubted, Sureties on Replevin Bond, liabilities of, 1 Mont. 592, 595.

Newman, Ex parte, 9 Cal. 502. Denied, Sunday Laws, constitutionality of, 20 How. Pr. 84.

Oates v. Jackson, 2 Stra. 1172. Cited, Will, construction of devise, 43 Cal. 204.

Ormond v. Anderson, 2 Ball. & B. 363. Cited, Specific Performance, of contract signed by vendor alone, 43 Cal. 465.

Ortman v. Dixon, 13 Cal. 34. Commented on, Water Rights, limitation of right by appropriation, 43 Cal. 375, 376. Cited, no distinction as to purposes of appropriation, 1 Mont. 658.

Osborn v. Bank of U. S., 9 Wheat. 738. Distinguished, State Sovereignty, power of State to tax corporate property, 43 Cal. 427.

Palmer v. Scott, 1 Russ. & M. 391. Cited, Specific Performance, of contract signed by vendor alone, 43 Cal. 465.

Partridge v. San Francisco, 27 Cal. 415. Cited, New Trial, assignment of errors, too general, not considered, 1 Mont. 663.

Parks v. Jackson, 11 Wend. 442. Cited, Lis Pendens, effect of notice, 43 Cal. 262.

Parsons v. Bowdoin, 17 Wend. 14. Cited, Execution, fees of sheriff, on sale under, 43 Cal. 380.

Patapsco Ins. Co. v. Southgate, 5 Pet. 622. Cited, Insurance, effect of abandonment, 6 Cal. 471.

Patterson v. Ely, 19 Cal. 28. Distinguished, Damages, profits when not recoverable, 1 Mont. 156.

Payne v. Bensley, 8 Cal. 260. Cited, Fraud, title of *bona fide* purchaser from fraudulent vendee, 16 Wis. 661; Negotiable Instrument, assignment of, as security for precedent debt, 36 Ill. 495.

Patty v. Mansfield, 8 Ohio, 370. Statutes distinguished, Sheriff, proceedings on trial of right of property not judicial, 10 Cal. 192.

Pearce v. Piper, 17 Ves. Jr. 15. Cited, Partnership, equity jurisdiction over voluntary associations, 14 Cal. 537.

Peck v. Brummagim, 31 Cal. 446. Cited, Husband and Wife, validity of deed of gift to wife, 43 Cal. 585.

Peirce v. Partridge, 3 Met. 44. Cited, Judgments, like contracts, void in part are void in toto, 7 Cal. 355. Commented on, 13 Cal. 441.

People v. Ah Fong, 12 Cal. 345. Approved, Criminal Procedure, charge to jury to be in writing, 43 Cal. 35.

People v. Beeler, 6 Cal. 246. Approved, Criminal Procedure, charge to jury must be in writing, 43 Cal. 35.

People v. Belencia, 21 Cal. 544. Approved, Instruction, as to effect of intoxication in criminal actions, 43 Cal. 352.

People v. Black Diamond C. M. Co., 37 Cal. 54. Approved, Taxation, solvent debts cannot be exempted, 43 Cal. 336.

People v. Bodine, 1 Denio, 314. Cited, Criminal Procedure, evidence of reputation of defendant, 43 Cal. 150.

People v. Campbell, 40 Cal. 129. Cited, Indictment, for murder, sufficiency of, 43 Cal. 555.

People v. Caswell, 21 Wend. 86. Cited, Indictment, for receiving stolen goods, sufficiency of, 43 Cal. 200.

People v. Chares, 26 Cal. 78. Commented on, Criminal Procedure, charge to jury must be in writing, 43 Cal. 36.

People v. Cottle, 6 Cal. 227. Approved, Juror and Jury, ground of challenge, 43 Cal. 531, 532.

People v. Cronin, 34 Cal. 191. Cited, Indictment, for murder, sufficiency of, 43 Cal. 31.

People v. Demint, 8 Cal. 423. Approved, Criminal Procedure, charge to jury must be in writing, 43 Cal. 35.

People v. Edwards, 41 Cal. 640. Approved, Juror and Jury, grounds of challenge, 43 Cal. 531.

People v. Fair, 43 Cal. 137. Cited, New Trial, in criminal case, insufficient ground, 43 Cal. 167.

People v. Gerke, 35 Cal. 677. Approved, Taxation, solvent debts cannot be exempted, 43 Cal. 336.

People v. Hays, 4 Cal. 127. Commented on, Constitutionality of Statute, affecting remedies, McAll. 518.

People v. Hays, 5 Cal. 66. Approved, Judicial Sale, rights of purchaser dependent on payment of purchase money, 6 Cal. 92; 9 Cal. 94.

People v. King, 27 Cal. 507. Approved, Instruction as to effect of intoxication in criminal action, 43 Cal. 352.

People v. Kohl, 40 Cal. 127. Distinguished, Taxation, of choses in action, 43 Cal. 596.

People v. Lewis, 36 Cal. 531. Approved, Instruction as to insanity in criminal action, 43 Cal. 352.

People v. McAuslan, 43 Cal. 55. Approved, Appeal, when order for new trial will not be disturbed, 43 Cal. 177.

People v. McCreery, 34 Cal. 432. Approved, Taxation, solvent debts liable to, 43 Cal. 594; cannot be exempted, 43 Cal. 336.

People v. Mier, 24 Cal. 61. Cited, District Court, jurisdiction in action for delinquent taxes, 43 Cal. 494.

People v. Nichol, 34 Cal. 211. Cited, Instruction as to deliberation, in criminal action, 43 Cal. 352.

People v. Payne, 8 Cal. 341. Approved, Criminal Procedure, charge to jury must be in writing, 43 Cal. 35.

People v. Pease, 3 Johns. Cas. 333. Cited, Pardon, disabilities removed by, 43 Cal. 443.

People v. Plummer, 9 Cal. 298. Disapproved, Juror and Jury, objections to competency when to be made, 43 Cal. 146, 147.

People v. Roberts, 6 Cal. 217. Approved, Instructions to be drawn with reference to the evidence, 43 Cal. 351.

People v. Reynolds, 16 Cal. 130. Cited, Juror and Jury, insufficiency of challenge for implied bias, 43 Cal. 448.

People v. Renfrow, 41 Cal. 37. Cited, Juror and Jury, insufficient challenge for implied bias, 43 Cal. 448.

People v. Sanford, 43 Cal. 29. Approved, Instructions, oral instructions in criminal action when erroneous, 43 Cal. 384.

People v. Schwartz, 32 Cal. 160. Cited, Indictment, for murder, as principal and as accessory, 43 Cal. 555. Approved, 6 Nev. 331.

People v. Stonecifer, 6 Cal. 405. Approved, Trial, acceptance of juror, an estoppel to objections to qualification, 43 Cal. 32.

People v. Stuart, 4 Cal. 225. Approved, Juror and Jury, validity of order to summon jurors during term, 43 Cal. 349.

People v. Trim, 39 Cal. 75. Cited, Indictment, for murder, as principal and as accessory, 43 Cal. 555.

People v. Vance, 21 Cal. 400. Approved, Juror and Jury, validity of order to summon jurors during term, 43 Cal. 349.

People v. Whartenby, 38 Cal. 461. Approved, Taxation, solvent debts cannot be exempted, 43 Cal. 336.

Phœnix Wat. Co. v. Fletcher, 23 Cal. 481. Commented on, Water Rights, liability for injury to rights of first appropriator, 1 Mont. 268.

Pierpont v. Crouch, 10 Cal. 315. Cited, Statutory Construction, repeal by implication, 43 Cal. 564.

Quinn v. Kenyon, 38 Cal. 502. Cited, Preëmption, transfer of right of, 43 Cal. 514.

Quivey v. Gambert, 32 Cal. 309. Commented on, New Trial, amendment to statement, practice, 43 Cal. 322.

Racouillat v. Rene, 32 Cal. 456. Cited, Pleading, evidence should not be set forth, 43 Cal. 236.

Rankin v. Scott, 12 Wheat. 177. Cited, Cloud on Title, what does not constitute, 43 Cal. 90.

Reamer v. Nesmith, 34 Cal. 624. Commented on, Deed, of mining claim, description in, 1 Mont. 695.

Rex v. Bush, Russ. & R. Cr. Cas. 372. Cited, Indictment, for receiving stolen goods, sufficiency of, 43 Cal. 200.

Rex v. Jervis, 6 Car. & P. 156. Cited, Indictment, for receiving stolen goods, sufficiency of, 43 Cal. 200.

Richardson v. McNulty, 24 Cal. 343. Cited, Lands, abandonment, what constitutes, 43 Cal. 476.

Roberts v. Anderson, 2 Johns. Ch. 202. Cited, Injunction, practice on motion to dissolve, 9 Cal. 554; 35 Cal. 60.

Richardson v. White, 18 Cal. 102. Cited, Lis Pendens, effect of filing, 43 Cal. 263.

Rose v. Estudillo, 39 Cal. 270. Commented on, County, funding acts, power of legislature, 43 Cal. 538. Approved, Id. 540.

Rowley v. Howard, 23 Cal. 401. Cited, Judgment, though erroneous, not subject to collateral attack, 1 Mont. 591.

Rust v. Gott, 9 Cow. 169. Cited, Contract, no remedy on illegal contract, 43 Cal. 617.

Ryan v. Dougherty, 30 Cal. 218. Cited, Arbitration and Award, jurisdiction, on what depends, 43 Cal. 395.

Ryan v. Johnson, 5 Cal. 86. Cited, Constitutionality of special statutes, 43 Cal. 434.

Sanders v. Rains, 10 Mo. 770. Distinguished, Judgment, not subject to collateral attack, 7 Cal. 64.

San Francisco v. Calderwood, 31 Cal. 585. Cited, Easement, dedication to public use of right of way, 1 Mont. 417.

San Jose v. Trumble, 41 Cal. 536. Cited, Alcalde Grants, limitation of actions to recover under, 43 Cal. 253.

Sayre v. Nichols, 7 Cal. 535. Cited, Principal and Agent, liability on contract signed by agent, 1 Mont. 177.

Sears v. Hyer, 1 Paige, 483. Cited, Lis Pendens, effect of notice of, 43 Cal. 262.

Seeley v. Bishop, 19 Conn. 128. Cited, Nuisance, when individual action will not lie to abate, 41 Cal. 451.

Selden v. Meeks, 17 Cal. 128. Cited, Mechanic's Lien, sufficiency of statement, 43 Cal. 522.

Seton v. Slade, 7 Ves. Jr. 265. Cited, Specific Performance, of contract signed by vendor alone, 43 Cal. 465.

Sheets v. Andrews, 2 Blackf. 274. Cited, Vendor and Vendee, demand for deed by vendee a condition precedent to action, 25 Cal. 279.

Shelley's Case, 1 Coke, 90. Construed, Will, construction of devise, 43 Cal. 204.

Sherman v. Story, 30 Cal. 253. Cited, Statute, when conclusive evidence of legislative will, 43 Cal. 564.

Shirley v. Shirley, 7 Blackf. 452. Cited, Specific Performance, of contract signed by vendor alone, 43 Cal. 465.

Shrader, Ex parte, 33 Cal. 279. Cited, Legislature, may authorize municipal regulations for preservation of health, 43 Cal. 249.

Sichell v. Carillo, 42 Cal. 493. Approved, Mortgage, burdens cannot be increased as against junior mortgagees, 43 Cal. 188.

Sinnot v. Davenport, 22 How. 227. Cited, Constitutional Construction, power to regulate commerce, 34 Cal. 498.

Smith v. Fowler, Cal. Sup. Ct. July T. 1854 (not reported.) Cited, Pleading, insufficient averments in answer to action for purchase money of land, 4 Cal. 267.

Smith & Keating, Ex parte, 38 Cal. 709. Cited, Appeal, decision of supervisors as to construction of ordinance not reviewable, 43 Cal. 480.

Smith v. Smith, 12 Cal. 225. Cited, Husband and Wife, deed of gift to wife, not *per se* void, 43 Cal. 585.

Spangel v. Dellinger, 42 Cal. 148. Cited, Appeal, effect of assignment of interest in judgment, 43 Cal. 492.

Stafford v. Lick, 7 Cal. 479. Cited, Conveyances, what to be recorded, 43 Cal. 343.

Stalker v. McDonald, 6 Hill, 93. Commented on, Negotiable Instrument, pledged as security, sale of, 3 Cal. 166; 36 Ill. 494. Cited, Title of *bona fide* purchaser, 16 Wis. 661.

State v. Murphy, 6 Ala. 845. Cited, Indictment, for receiving stolen goods, sufficiency of, 43 Cal. 200.

Steamboat P. H. White v. Levy, 10 Ark. 411. Cited, Equity, subrogation to rights of creditor, 24 Cal. 608.

Steinbach v. Stewart, 11 Wall. 566. Commented on, Mexican Grant, sufficiency of conveyance of, 43 Cal. 624; construction of decree of confirmation, Id. 625.

Stephens v. Mansfield, 11 Cal. 365. Cited, Lands, abandonment, what constitutes, 43 Cal. 476.

Steuart v. Mayor, etc., of Baltimore, 7 Md. 500. Cited, Eminent Domain, compensation a condition precedent to condemnation, 31 Cal. 559.

St. John v. Kidd, 26 Cal. 263. Commented on, Mining Claims, forfeiture, construction of mining customs, 1 Mont. 241.

Stuyvesant v. Hall, 2 Barb. Ch. 151. Cited, Lis Pendens, effect of notice, 43 Cal. 262.

Swain v. Chase, 12 Cal. 283. Cited, Jurisdiction of Person, process of inferior court void for insufficiency of affidavit, 1 Nev. 98; facts necessary to jurisdiction must be shown, 1 Nev. 198.

Swain v. Naglee, 19 Cal. 127. Cited, Jurisdiction, power of court to amend judgment, 1 Mont. 205.

Taaffe v. Rosenthal, 7 Cal. 514. Cited, Parties, real party in interest, 1 Mont. 590.

Tarpey v. Shillenberger, 10 Cal. 390. Commented on, Injunction Bond, complaint in action on, 1 Mont. 370.

Taylor v. Hargous, 4 Cal. 268. Cited, Homestead, selection of, by occupancy, 7 Mich. 504.

Thomson v. Pacific Railroad, 9 Wall. 579. Approved, State Sovereignty, power of State to tax railroads and telegraph lines, 43 Cal. 429, 430.

Teall v. Felton, 1 N. Y. 537. Cited, Jurisdiction, of Federal courts, not exclusive, 9 Cal. 728.

Todd v. Cochell, 17 Cal. 97. Cited, Negligence, no liability for breakage of dam without proof of negligence, 51 N. Y. 487.

Torrey v. Jordan, 4 How. Miss. 401. Cited, Judgment, recital of appearance not conclusive, 13 Cal. 561.

Turner v. N. B. & M. Railroad Co., 34 Cal. 594. Commented on, Damages, principal when liable for exemplary damages for misconduct of agent, 3 S. C. N. S. 598.

Union Water Co. v. Crary, 25 Cal. 504. Approved, Water Rights, may be lost by limitation, 1 Mont. 544.

United States v. Jones, 2 Wheel. Cr. Cas. 451. Cited, Executive, pardoning power of, 43 Cal. 443.

United States v. Sepulveda, 1 Wall. 104. Commented on, Mexican Grant, finality of approved survey, 43 Cal. 292.

United States v. Wilson, 7 Pet. 159. Cited, Executive, pardoning power of, 43 Cal. 442.

Uridias v. Morrell, 25 Cal. 31. Cited, Pleading, inconsistent defenses, practice, 43 Cal. 269.

Vassault v. Austin, 32 Cal. 606. Cited, Pleading, insufficient denials, 43 Cal. 397.

Wakefield v. Greenhood, 29 Cal. 599. Cited, Pleading, sufficient averment of agreement to sell lands, 43 Cal. 463.

Waring v. Robinson, 1 Hoff. Ch. 524. Commented on, Judgment, priority of lien of, 7 Cal. 198.

Wells, Ex parte, 18 How. 310. Commented on, Executive, pardoning power of, 43 Cal. 442.

Weston v. City Council of Charleston, 2 Pet. 449. Distinguished, State Sovereignty, power of State to tax corporate property, 43 Cal. 427.

Wheaton v. Neville, 19 Cal. 44. Cited, Attachment, lien how created, 43 Cal. 209.

Wheeler v. Sage, 1 Wall. 518. Approved, Partnership, obligations of partners how restricted, 43 Cal. 134.

Williams v. Suffolk Ins. Co., 3 Sum. 277. Cited, Stare Decisis, effect of local adjudications, 15 Cal. 604.

Willson v. Cleveland, 30 Cal. 192. Cited, Pleading, inconsistent defenses, practice, 43 Cal. 269.

Wilson v. Castro, 31 Cal. 438. Commented on, Mexican Grant, effect of confirmation, 43 Cal. 622.

Yrisarri v. Clement, 3 Bing. 440. Cited, Libel and Slander, sufficient defense, 43 Cal. 250.